PAN-ASIAN SPORTS
AND THE EMERGENCE
OF MODERN ASIA
1913–1974

PAN-ASIAN SPORTS

AND THE EMERGENCE OF MODERN ASIA 1913–1974

STEFAN HUEBNER

NUS PRESS
SINGAPORE

Published by:

NUS Press
National University of Singapore
AS3-01-02, 3 Arts Link
Singapore 117569

Fax: (65) 6774-0652
E-mail: nusbooks@nus.edu.sg
Website: http://nuspress.nus.edu.sg

ISBN: 978-981-4722-03-2 (Paper)

First edition 2016
Reprint 2017

National Library Board, Singapore Cataloguing-in-Publication Data

Names: Huebner, Stefan.
Title: Pan-Asian sports and the emergence of modern Asia, 1913-1974 / by Stefan Huebner.
Description: Singapore : NUS Press, [2016] | Includes bibliographic references.
Identifiers: OCN 933369043 | ISBN 978-981-4722-03-2 (paperback)
Subjects: LCSH: Sports--Social aspects--Asia--History. | Nationalism and sports--Asia--History. | Asia --Civilization--20th century.
Classification: LCC GV706.34 | DDC 306.483095--dc23

Designed by: Nelani Jinadasa
Printed by: Markono Print Media Pte Ltd

Contents

List of Figures vii
List of Tables ix
Acknowledgements x
Abbreviations xiii
Conventions xiv
Introduction 1

CHAPTER 1
Muscular Christianity and the 'Western Civilizing Mission': Elwood S. Brown, the YMCA, and the Founding of the Far Eastern Championship Games 17

CHAPTER 2
The Far Eastern Championship Games and the Western Asiatic Games in the 1920s and 1930s: 'Games of the Asians, by the Asians, for the Asians' 55

CHAPTER 3
Building Nehru's Asia through Sport: The First Asian Games, Decolonization, International Peace, Modernization, and Development (4–11 March 1951) 102

CHAPTER 4
A 'Free Country' Belonging to the 'free world': Philippine Independence, Dubious Democracy, and the Second Asian Games (1–9 May 1954) 125

CHAPTER 5
'Give Us the Olympic Games': Peaceful Internationalism, 'Reborn' Japan, Olympic-Scale Perfection, and the Third Asian Games (24 May–1 June 1958) 147

CHAPTER 6
Turning Indonesia into the Beacon of a Non-Aligned Asia: The Sukarno Administration, the Fourth Asian Games, and the Struggle against Imperialism and Neocolonialism (24 August–4 September 1962) 174

CHAPTER 7
The King, the Military, and Thai Development: Hosting the Fifth and the Sixth Asian Games Consecutively (9–20 December 1966 and 1970) 202

CHAPTER 8
Iran and the Indian Ocean Region Project: The Great Persian Empire, Oil Wealth, and the Seventh Asian Games (1–16 September 1974) 230

Conclusion 261
Notes 278
Bibliography 350
Index 387

List of Figures

Fig. 1.1	The evolution of a constabulary sergeant from an Igorot headhunter	21
Fig. 1.2	The New Olympian	36
Fig. 1.3	Uncle Sam teaching the Asian children sports values	36
Fig. 1.4	Marquis Ōkuma addressing the Filipino, Japanese, and Chinese athletes at the Third FECG (Tokyo 1917)	47
Fig. 1.5	Ten Widows' Arches trophy	49
Fig. 1.6	Temple of Heaven trophy	49
Fig. 1.7	Silver cup donated by Antonio R. Roxas	51
Fig. 1.8	Medal, Second FECG (1915)	51
Fig. 1.9	Emblem, Second FECG (1915)	51
Fig. 1.10	Medal, Third FECG (1917)	51
Fig 2.1	Feminine bayonet drill	84
Fig 2.2	The Meiji Jingu Gaien sports complex (1930)	87
Fig 2.3	The tribune of honour	87
Fig 2.4	The Emperor trophy	93
Fig 2.5	Porcelain Tower of Nanjing trophy	93
Fig 2.6	Statue of an Asura	94
Fig 2.7	Medal, Ninth FECG	94
Fig 2.8	Monogram of the FEAA	95
Fig 2.9	Flag of the Western Asiatic Games (1934)	95
Fig 2.10	Japanese female tennis players, Seventh FECG (1925)	98
Fig 2.11	Chinese female swimmers, Tenth FECG (1934)	98

Fig 3.1	National stadium and surroundings (1951)	116
Fig 3.2	National stadium, panoramic view (1951)	116
Fig 3.3	Emblem used at the First Asian Games (1951)	118
Fig 3.4	Medal, Ashoka Chakra (1951)	118
Fig 3.5	Medal, India Gate (1951)	119
Fig 3.6	Trophy, Lion Capital of Ashoka (1951)	119
Fig 4.1	Cariñosa dance at the opening ceremony's entertainment program	135
Fig 4.2	Victory medal, Second Asian Games	137
Fig 4.3	Commemorative medal, Second Asian Games	138
Fig 4.4	Victory medal, 1948 Olympics	138
Fig 4.5	George XVI, King of the PAAF	142
Fig 5.1	Main stadium (1958)	158
Fig 5.2	Meiji Shrine Outer Garden sports complex (1958)	158
Fig 5.3	Chakkiri bushi ('Tea-cutting song')	167
Fig 5.4	Yagi bushi ('Yagi-song')	167
Fig 5.5	Victory medal, Third Asian Games, front	169
Fig 6.1	The main Stadium	189
Fig 6.2	Hotel Indonesia (from the back)	189
Fig 6.3	Cloverleaf interchange	190
Fig 6.4	National bank building	190
Fig 6.5	Mass calisthenics by children	195
Fig 6.6	Female high school students	195
Fig 6.7	Seudati war dance	197
Fig 6.8	Pendet welcome dance	197
Fig 7.1	The main stadium	213
Fig 7.2	Kittikachorn indoor stadium	215
Fig 7.3	Kittikachorn indoor stadium (aerial view)	216
Fig 7.4	The king lighting the Games' lamp in 1970	219
Fig 7.5	Male cadets engaging in a precision drill	223
Fig 7.6	Female students forming the AGF symbol	223
Fig 7.7	Commemorative medal, Sixth Asian Games, back	225
Fig 7.8	Commemorative coin, Fifth Asian Games, back	225

Fig 8.1	Aryamehr Stadium (serving as a dam)	247
Fig 8.2	Main sports hall	247
Fig 8.3	Cadets with colored placards depicting doves	249
Fig 8.4	The Iranian flag formed by the choir	250
Fig 8.5	Zurkhaneh demonstration	251
Fig 8.6	Iranian folk dances	251
Fig 8.7	Flag display of the police cadets	253
Fig 8.8	The scoreboard, depicting the Royal Family	253

List of Tables

Table A	The Far Eastern Championship Games and the Western Asiatic Games: Dates, Host Countries, and Overall Champions	15
Table 2.1	Estimated Numbers of Individual Athletes at the FECG	78
Table 2.2	Estimated Numbers of Individual Athletes at the WAG	79

Acknowledgements

Many people and institutions have given me indispensable help in writing this book. First and foremost, I wish to express my deepest gratitude to Marc Frey, whose encouragement, support, and interest in my research have been a great motivation to finish this project. I also want to thank Corinna Unger and Harald Fischer-Tiné for their helpful criticism and guidance. Moreover, for their feedback I am grateful to Nicola Spakowski, who together with Marc Frey supervised the research project "Asianisms in the 20th Century" (funded by the German Research Foundation) in which I was involved as a research associate at Jacobs University Bremen, and my former project colleagues, Stefani Jürries and Torsten Weber. Other colleagues and graduate students made further valuable remarks at retreats. I also want to thank everybody else who was so kind as to provide helpful comments on parts of my manuscript and related articles, in particular (in alphabetical order) Walter Demel, Ulrich Hofmeister, Rotem Kowner, Sönke Kunkel, Sven Saaler, Dominic Sachsenmaier, Agus Setiawan, Amanda Shuman, Martyn Smith, Carolien Stolte, and Takashima Kō, who also kept me informed about his own publications and those of some of his Japanese colleagues, and a variety of anonymous reviewers.

Over the last few years, I presented parts of this book project at about 40 conferences, workshops, summer institutes, and research seminars, and I am grateful to all the organizers, discussants, and participants who showed interest in my research. I am especially indebted in this regard to Jürgen Osterhammel and Harry Liebersohn, the conveners of a SIAS Summer Institute on "Cultural Encounters" (Wissenschaftskolleg Berlin 2013; National Humanities Center, NC, 2014), and the other fellows, with whom I spent four very productive weeks in Berlin and North Carolina. I want to thank all of them for their feedback on my paper and my presentation related to this book, especially those whose work was relatively close to mine (in almost alphabetical order, leaving out already mentioned persons): Yurou Zhong (who also had the nerves for some lengthy discussions and email correspondence on the Social Gospel, the YMCA's 'moral empire', and global circulations), Erica Heinsen-Roach, Emma Martin, Fiona McDonald, Jesse

Murray, Steffen Rimner, J. Barton Scott (organizing the weekend trip), Teresa Segura-Garcia, Kira Thurman, Nurfadzilah Yahaya, and meLê yamomo. One of the SIAS Summer Institute's outcomes is a special issue of the *Journal of World History* on "Civilizing Missions" and I am very grateful to senior editor Fabio López Lázaro for offering us this opportunity.

Furthermore, I owe a great debt of gratitude to Paul Kratoska of NUS Press, who not only does a great job as publishing editor, but also brought me in contact with Merce Planta, whom I want to thank for her much appreciated help and her advice during my stay in Manila. Lena Qua and Christine Chong of NUS Press, too, were very helpful. In Singapore, S. S. Dhillon, former secretary-general of Singapore's National Olympic Council, was kind enough to agree to an interview and provided me with some personal material. In Washington, DC, Uta Balbier aided me. Many others—who hopefully forgive me that this acknowledgement is not the length of a chapter—gave me hints on archives, publications, and sources, a generosity I appreciate very much. Since readability is an important point, I moreover want to mention the wonderful assistance in copy-editing I received from three former colleagues in Bremen, Peng Shiyan, Craig P. Taylor, and especially Christopher G. Shaw.

Quite obviously, this book could not have been written without support from the "good souls" in Bremen, Bianca Bergmann and Rena Dickel; in Munich, Michaela Prohaska; from several student assistants, as well as from a large group of librarians, archivists, and administrators in Europe, the US, and Asia. I am particularly grateful to Lara Christianson of Jacobs University Bremen's library, Horikoshi Yoko of the German Institute for Japanese Studies Tokyo, Ryan Bean of the Kautz Family YMCA Archives, Maricel Raynera and Patrick D. Flores of the Jorge B. Vargas Museum and Filipiniana Research Center, Jeffrey Monseau of Springfield College's archives and Brian McGuinness of its International Center, Claude-Alain Danthe of the YMCA International's archives in Geneva, and the staff of the IOC's Olympic Studies Centre in Lausanne, the Library of Congress, the British Library, Harvard Yenching, Widener, and Houghton Library, the National Library of Singapore, the National Archives of Singapore, Waseda University's library and its archives, the library of the School of Oriental and African Studies of the University of London, Tokyo Metropolitan Library, Sophia University's library, the newspaper collection of the South Asia Institute of Ruprecht-Karls-University Heidelberg, the library and archives of the University of the Philippines Diliman, the library of the University of Hong Kong, the Bundesarchiv Berlin-Lichterfelde, Bentley Historical Library, the L.A. '84 Foundation Library, the Nationaal Archief in Den Haag, the National Archives and Records Administration (National Archives II) in College Park, MD, the National Archives of Japan, the National Library of the Philippines, the Prince Chichibu Memorial Sports Museum, Regenstein Library of the University of Chicago, the Diplomatic Archives of the Ministry of Foreign Affairs of Japan, the UK's National Archives, and Bundeswehr University Munich's library.

For their funding, which allowed me to do a lot of research abroad, I owe a great deal to the German Research Foundation (DFG), the German Historical Institute Washington, the German Institute for Japanese Studies Tokyo, Jacobs University Bremen, the University Libraries of the University of Minnesota, Minneapolis, and Bundeswehr University Munich.

Finally, this book would not have come about without the love and patience of my family, in particular my late grandmother, Gisela Reumschüssel, who did not see its publication, my sister, and my parents, Rita and Hans Hübner.

Minor parts of this book have been earlier published by *Diplomatic History*, Brill, and NUS Press. I am grateful to these publishers for permission to use heavily revised and updated versions of these articles and book chapters in this book.[1]

Abbreviations

For abbreviations of archives in the notes, see the bibliography.

AGF	Asian Games Federation
ASEAN	Association of Southeast Asian Nations
CENTO	Central Treaty Organization
CIA	Central Intelligence Agency
FEAA	Far Eastern Athletic Association
FECG	Far Eastern Championship Games
FIFA	Fédération Internationale de Football Association/ International Federation of Association Football
GANEFO	Games of the New Emerging Forces
GANEFOA	Games of the New Emerging Forces of Asia
IAAF	International Amateur Athletic Federation (now: International Association of Athletic Federations)
IOC	International Olympic Committee
JAAA	(Great-) Japan Amateur Athletic Association/(Dai-) Nihon Taiiku Kyōkai
NGO	Non-governmental Organization
NHK	Japan Broadcasting Company/Nippon Hōsō Kyōkai
NOC	National Olympic Committee
PAAF	Philippine Amateur Athletic Federation
SEAP Games	Southeast Asian Peninsular Games
SEATO	Southeast Asia Treaty Organization
USD	US Dollar
WAG	Western Asiatic Games
YMCA	Young Men's Christian Association
YWCA	Young Women's Christian Association

Conventions

In the main body of this study, Japanese, Chinese, and Korean names are rendered in their usual order, the family name preceding the given name. In the bibliography, the family name comes last. Independent of that, in the main body text all persons are addressed by their family name, with the exception of Thais, who are addressed by their given name. Moreover, noble titles such as Count, Prince, Raden, Sultan, Luang, and so on have been added to names, while academic and other titles have not been added.

Introduction

"'East is East, West is West, and never the twain shall meet'
it is said,[1] but they do meet on the same terms,
under the same rules, in friendly competition
on the athletic field, with great advantage to both.
(...) Undoubtedly the East has gained from its association
with the West in the Olympic Movement and its adoption
of Western methods of physical training, in [shaping] a stronger
and healthier people. (...) Well, if the East gains
in a physical sense, perhaps the West will gain
intellectually and spiritually. The wisdom of the East
is proverbial, and Asia, after all, was the birthplace
of all the great religions. Fair play and good sportsmanship
are a part of all religions as well as of the Olympic Code."[2]

*—Avery Brundage, president of the International Olympic Committee,
in his address opening the 54th session of the IOC
that took place during the Third Asian Games (Tokyo 1958)*

This book is about Asian sports events. However, it is also about the relations—or power asymmetry—between the East, meaning Asian actors, and the West, here meaning primarily US-American actors, but sometimes others as well.[3] This power asymmetry, the result of the 'Great Divergence' and the rise of the West,[4] manifested itself during the nineteenth century in the form of a large-scale expansion of Western civilization. It also had a tremendous impact on physical education in Asia. Western amateur sport, in particular, was perceived as an important element of Western civilization due to its impact on public health and its educational value. One result of the large-scale expansion of Western civilization into Asia was the desire of benevolent and paternalistic Western physical educators, many of them members of the American[5] branch of the Young Men's Christian Association (YMCA), to 'civilize' Asians by teaching them amateur sport. In the American YMCA's view 'Asia was one': it was a region united by its backwardness and in need of Western tutelage to become more like the West. Regional sports events, or "regional development games" as they were called in some YMCA letters, should serve as platforms to promote sportive citizenship training and scientific approaches to fitness among Asians as a means to remedy their problems.[6] President of the International Olympic Committee (IOC) Avery Brundage, an American, hinted at this purpose when he talked about the impact of Western amateur sport on Asia. Among many outcomes he mentioned in passing, sport had led to the shaping of a 'stronger and healthier people'. To a certain degree, the choice of a quote from an American as the epigraph of this study thus serves to represent that, at least initially, Asian elites did not have much say in intra-Asian sport.

Brundage's above remarks can, in connection to the transfer of Western sport to Asia, be understood as a 'civilizing mission'.[7] In the beginning, the strong influence of the American YMCA gave this transfer of an element of Western civilization, rooted in Christianity and the Enlightenment, a religious dimension. The YMCA's intention was to encourage Christian ideals in Asia through sport. In this study the religious aspect of the term 'mission' therefore is highly important. The accompanying term 'civilization' is comparatively imprecise. Initially the term described the means—tools, skills, media—used by human groups to socially and economically organize themselves, while 'culture' described the aims and goals of these groups. However, Western elites in the nineteenth and early twentieth century increasingly *equated* the cultures of Western countries with 'Civilization'. The capital 'C' indicated that after the rise of the West, 'Civilization' became the *standard* under which 'inferior' non-Western civilizations were ordered in a vertical hierarchy. In a horizontal sense, a 'civilizing mission' can have different targets. Brundage talked about Western elites affecting Asia through sport, including both its international system and individual Asian societies. However, engaging in a 'civilizing mission' was an affair not limited to foreigners, and Asian elites, too, could attempt to 'uplift' their home countries and Asia as a whole.

The latter is exactly what happened after growing anti-colonial nationalism beginning in the late 1910s resulted in Asian elites gaining control over Asian sport. Many of them continued to support the American YMCA's Christian-Protestant ideals—internationalism, egalitarianism, and economic progress—as elements that should contribute to creating a modern Asia. However, the Asian elites integrated these ideals into their local cultural contexts, a process that often involved a certain degree of secularization and the adoption of elements of the Olympic movement. The sportive 'civilizing mission' thus was not abandoned, but now carried on by Asians under the more distant patronage of the IOC. As a result, the perception of Asian 'unity in backwardness' that was inherent in the sportive 'civilizing mission' was still acknowledged by its Asian promoters. Only during the 1970s did increasing resistance to the sportive 'civilizing mission' and its supporters within Asian sports organizations and the IOC lead to its end. Before that, and helping drive this change, regional Asian sports events since the late 1950s had increasingly served as platforms to showcase the host countries' rapid *modernization and development processes*. The emergence of this second aim corresponded with a decrease in the importance of the initial purpose of hosting low-cost events for *educating* and 'uplifting' Asians by encouraging them to take up amateur sport.

Brundage also talked about another possible 'civilizing mission' in the second part of the quoted remarks. This time the 'civilizing mission' emerged from Asia to 'cure' some of the perceived ills of the West. The idea of a 'spiritual Asia'—materially poor but rich in harmony—and of a 'materialist West'—materially rich but ethically bankrupt and on the road to self-destruction—complementing each other was not a genuinely Asian one. It originated in the West, though it was embraced by various Asian elites and used to further pan-Asian goals of creating a more positive image of Asia.[8] At least in the spiritual dimension they could claim to be superior to the West, which could lead to a more equal exchange. Admittedly, this claim represented only one of many Asian reactions to the power asymmetry between the West and Asia, but serves to further underline that the pan-Asian rejection of Western colonialism did not automatically mean rejecting Western civilization per se. Instead, it involved interacting with Western civilization by appropriating some of its elements, challenging others, and sending messages back to the West. The 'Western civilizing mission' and Asian resistance therefore are the foundations of all the developments in the realm of early Asian sports events. As a consequence, these factors need to be covered in some greater detail to emphasize their importance in shaping a modern Asia.

A variety of scholars have shown that the idea of a universal Western modernity—meaning that it was perceived as *the* standard to be reached by *all* of humanity in a linear process of Enlightenment-inspired progress, with all countries or peoples not yet having reached it being considered backward—had gained momentum during the nineteenth century.[9] However, the brutal behavior of the Western powers, particularly during the era of imperialism, and a more racist and exclusionary view regarding non-Whites contradicted the self-ascriptions of the 'civilized' nations. The 'Western civilizing mission' rhetoric—which primarily served to legitimize Western imperialism and colonialism—was recognized as hypocritical and came under particularly heavy attack. The calamity of the First World War (1914–18) and its aftermath at the Paris Peace Conference (1919), where American President Woodrow Wilson's principle of self-determination was denied to almost all non-Europeans, were seen as further illustrations of the hypocrisy of the 'civilizing mission'. Nevertheless, the idea of an 'American civilizing mission' in particular was even more strongly fueled by victory in the First World War, which was presented as having resulted from the 'superiority' of American democratic culture, norms, and values. Therefore, not even the First World War caused a breakdown of the rhetoric of the 'civilizing mission', nor did Americans and Europeans necessarily give up their struggle to 'uplift' humanity. To a certain degree, the 'Western civilizing mission' continued in a modified form even during the period of large-scale decolonization[10] that followed the Second World War. Teleological ideas of modernization[11] and development[12]—particularly modernization theory[13]—still centered on the West (or, in the case of Marxism, on the USSR-led countries). The model of a liberal democratic market economy (or of communism) was still promoted as the model to be followed by the decolonizing countries and as the *universal destiny of humanity*—the oft proclaimed 'End of History'. As my study shows, Asian elites regularly had to deal with these claims, particularly during colonialism. However, during decolonization they increasingly rejected the idea that Western civilization represented the only possible way to modernity as a claim made by people who focused only on a few decades or centuries of human history. According to their view, in the long run, the supremacy of Western civilization would be nothing but a temporary aberration of history. In the sense of multiple modernities,[14] modernization processes would be rooted in reemerging Asian civilizations and finally result in their parity with Western civilization.

According to Michael Adas, the norms and values the 'Western civilizing mission' propagated were Western middle class ones such as rationality, empiricism, progressivism, systematic inquiry, industriousness, discipline, punctuality, and honest dealing. Asians (and many others), on the other hand, were described as superstitious, indolent, reactionary, oblivious to a sense of time, passive, and excessively emotional. Supporters of imperialism and colonialism therefore argued that the West, because it was active, energetic, and committed to efficiency and progress, would have to change the conditions within those regions it gained control of. Internal pacification and political order were to be enforced by ending despotic rule and permanent warfare, while education and religious conversion should accompany and support this process. Corrupt local regimes were to be replaced with honest and efficient bureaucracies and societies reorganized to encourage a capitalist industrial order.[15]

Modern sports are completely based on norms. Moreover, their spread to Asia since the nineteenth century as a result of Western imperialism and colonialism was seen by Westerners as useful for encouraging many of the norms and values listed by Adas. Numerous Asian sports officials later agreed with this assessment. This agreement meant that Western cultural hegemony was, as already mentioned in connection to the 'civilizing mission', at least partially accepted.[16] *Modern* sports can thereby be characterized by equality, bureaucratization, specialization, rationalization, quantification, an obsession with records, and secularism (although this last point will, to a certain degree, be questioned here).[17] In this study, the spread of sport will be covered primarily as an outcome of the spread of 'mega events' to Asia. 'Mega events' can be defined as "large-scale cultural (including commercial and sporting) events which have a dramatic character, mass popular appeal and international significance. They are typically organized by variable combinations of national governmental and international non-governmental organizations and thus can be said to be important elements in 'official' versions of public culture."[18]

One of the most important impacts of the confrontation with the West in the form of colonialism was the emergence of anti-colonial nationalism and the sense of belonging to a distinct civic or ethnic entity.[19] A second result, which was partially in conflict with nationalism, was Asian deliberations regarding a supra-national connectedness of Asian countries and peoples. This provided a possible means to forge alliances, or at least to produce a counter-discourse against claims of Western political, economic, and cultural superiority. The result, pan-Asianism or Asianism, can be defined as "perceptions and processes that focus on similarities or common interests between Asian regions, draw on common historical roots and traditions or consider integration as a politico-cultural vision".[20] The term 'Asia' was now no longer just a concept imported from the West, but began to be filled by transnational Asian actors with ideas of Asian commonalities such as common ethnicity, common culture, common history, and a common opponent or enemy in the form of the West.

As has been shown in a variety of important studies,[21] the outcome was very often, but not always, a political or cultural anti-Westernism and a strong rejection of the 'Western civilizing mission'. In the view of many Asian politicians and revolutionaries, Japan's victory over Russia in 1905 already contradicted the claim that non-Western countries could not undergo a successful modernization process without Western 'assistance' in the form of colonialism. Japan had done exactly that and through its victory had, to a certain degree, become an equal to the West. As mentioned above, the events at the Paris Peace Conference of 1919 further increased Asianist rhetoric, although not necessarily in a militant sense. Attacks on Western civilization gained in intensity, and ancient Asian civilization(s) were promoted as equal alternatives to it, though in the process these increasingly became remodeled after Western civilization. In the 1930s and especially during the Pacific War (1941–45), Japanese-led pan-Asianism—its most well-known expression being the 'Greater East Asia Co-Prosperity Sphere'—gained a strongly militant dimension and was instrumentalized by the Japanese government and military to justify expansion. Even though the term 'pan-Asianism' became tainted due to the brutal behavior of the Japanese forces in occupied areas, the idea itself experienced a revival after the war. Decolonizing Asian countries in particular, such as India and Indonesia, aimed at Asian integration as a means to defend their newly gained independence. Some important results were, for example, the hosting of the Asian Relations Conference (New Delhi, 1947) and the Asia-Africa Conference (Bandung, 1955).

The main topics of this study are three successive series of Asian sports events: the Far Eastern Championship Games (FECG; 1913–34) organized by the Far Eastern Athletic Association (FEAA), the Western Asiatic Games (WAG; 1934), and the early Asian Games (1951–74) organized by the Asian Games Federation (AGF; in 1982 it was replaced by the Olympic Council of Asia). My focus is on analyzing transfers of norms, values, and images both between Asia and the West and within Asia, based on the example of these three sports events. I thereby intend to provide new insights into Western and Asian perspectives on what defines modern Asia, including topics such as civilization, modernization, development, regional and national identity, and the public staging of shifting power relations in Asia and between Asia and the West. Covering a period of about six decades (1913–74) will show continuities and discontinuities during that most turbulent period of the twentieth century. Personal continuities and discontinuities are of central importance therein. I therefore use an actor-centered approach and the main interest of this study is the goals and activities of Western and Asian *elites*[22]—mostly YMCA physical education directors, sports officials, civil servants, and politicians—who were involved in organizing the sports events. This includes an analysis both of the political discourses[23] they produced in connection with the Games and of the staging of the events. I thus do not talk about a passive diffusion but the active *spread* of sports. Moreover, I follow the argument that *Protestant missionaries*—here the YMCA—*had a decisive impact on encouraging mass education*—here physical education—in the colonial world.[24] This focus on the activities of elites relegates certain topics, such as the actual impact on individual Asians or the victories and defeats of athletes, to a position of less importance.[25] The same is true for the 'Orientalist'[26] coverage of some of the Games in Western media published outside of Asia, which I have covered elsewhere.[27]

When discussing the sports-related modernization aims and the visions of Asia held by the respective elites, I regularly focus on three ideals that defined how sport should shape a 'new Asian man' and later also a 'new Asian woman'[28]: *internationalism, egalitarianism,* and *economic progress.* As ideals they had a universal claim, which corresponds to the concept of the 'civilizing mission'. They also were by no means relevant only in the context of regional Asian sports events, but I will limit myself to an analysis of their interpretation or rejection by actors involved in these games. Moreover, in the context of this study the three ideals' origin was Protestant-Evangelical America, represented by the YMCA and its concept of Christian masculinity. Before they became more secular or were integrated into local cultural contexts, it is therefore appropriate to talk about Christian internationalism, Christian egalitarianism, and a 'Protestant work ethic'.

(Christian) *internationalism* here refers to an ideal that became prominent in the West in the nineteenth century as a counter-model to (extreme) nationalism caused by the rise of the nation-state. Internationalism promoted international exchange, peaceful cooperation, and regional integration. During the twentieth century, particularly after each of the world wars, internationalism led to the creation of increasing numbers of international organizations (both governmental and non-governmental), although the idea of the nation-state was not necessarily intended to be cast aside in the process.[29] In the context of sport, the founding of the IOC in 1894 can be seen as a secular example of this trend.[30] *Christian* internationalism had strongly intensified during the nineteenth century when growing numbers of European and American missionaries moved to Asia and Africa. For example, the educational, disaster relief, and missionary activities of American overseas missionaries contributed much to what Ian Tyrrell called America's 'moral empire'. Inspired by the revival of the 1880s, the Protestant-Evangelical 'moral empire' lasted until the Great Depression, when philanthropic donations became scarce. Though still understudied, the 'moral empire' saw a large-scale circulation of American and non-American YMCA missionaries and experts contributing to a global spread of scientific knowledge in transforming societies. Moreover, Christian organizations such as the YMCA, the Young Women's Christian Association (YWCA), the World Student Christian Federation, and others encouraged cooperation between national branches by establishing international headquarters.[31] A central figure in Christian internationalism was John R. Mott, a Nobel Peace Prize winner (1946) and longtime leader of the American YMCA and the World Student Christian Federation, who was also involved in the Student Volunteer Movement. In 1900, he took up earlier missionary ambitions and propagated the aim of evangelizing the world within one generation.[32] His activities in expanding the 'Kingdom of God' in the late nineteenth and early twentieth centuries contributed much to the growth of the YMCA network in Asia, the continent where most non-Christians lived. This expansion will be very relevant for the first chapter.

A second ideal is (Christian) *egalitarianism*. This ideal had a strong impact on Western political thinking following the Enlightenment, including the emergence of civil societies, and was a pillar of the American and French revolutions. The claim in the US Declaration of Independence, for example, that 'all men are *created* equal' and that they are 'endowed, by their *creator*, with certain unalienable rights' makes obvious the ideal's compatibility with many interpretations of Christianity. The central aim was to reduce violence caused by the 'arbitrary' rule, for example, of monarchs and by the victims' resistance against their unequal treatment. In the case of sport, Norbert Elias and Eric Dunning considered modern sport to be one expression of a 'civilizing process' characterized by self-pacification and declining inter-human violence. A mutual acceptance of rules binding for *everybody*, hence not granting special permissions to one certain person (or side) to use more force than others were allowed or to rearrange rules during an event, made it possible to limit or forbid violence.[33] Horizontally organized mass sport thus primarily encourages the autonomy of all participants. This is different than, for example, gymnastics, which promotes conformity among participants and hierarchical relations between them and the organizers.[34] In a Christian context, team games such as basketball or volleyball, both invented by YMCA physical educators, should encourage cooperation between players of different ethnicities or social strata and teach them to respect each other.[35] Moreover, the (initial) equality of all participants and non-discrimination are intrinsic conditions for the creation of a new, non-permanent hierarchy achieved by determining the best athlete/s.[36] On an international level the ideal of egalitarianism means that all relevant countries must have the possibility of sending athletes to an event and that all delegations have the same rights.

The third ideal is *economic progress* (or the 'Protestant work ethic'), which can be seen as a form of bio-politics related to regulating and optimizing public health.[37] Economic progress was another highly important topic, at least in the West, even before the Enlightenment. Max Weber in his seminal (though sometimes vague) study on the 'Protestant work ethic' viewed modern capitalism as having come into existence due not to 'materialistic' but religious reasons: the notion of the 'calling'.[38] However, Weber's thesis has been heavily criticized and alternative explanations are available. For example, the requirement that Protestants be able to read the Bible encouraged universal schooling, thus increasing the human capital of Protestants.[39] In a nutshell, *education* was the decisive factor for economic success, but was inspired by Protestantism. This explanation corresponds to the topic of this study, which focuses on the implementation of the ideal of economic progress, not its origin. As noted by Weber, a capitalism-driven perceived necessity for employers to make employees more productive already existed in the early twentieth century. Their main targets were people accustomed to living a relatively 'unproductive' life that was sufficient to sustain them and who therefore saw no reason to work more, since doing so would reduce their leisure time.[40] (This state of affairs obviously does not preclude individual willingness for self-improvement on the part of employees and others.) In the context of sport, the human capital of Protestants (and others) could be increased if Protestant organizations such as the YMCA encouraged participation. In a bio-political sense, sport shapes fitter people, who are more productive because they are less often sick. A longer life also means that investments in education pay off better. Moreover, sport encourages a belief in personal effort as the way to success: hard training is necessary to (legally) win an event, while a belief in fate or luck (as in the case of many forms of gambling) will lead to an almost certain defeat.[41] By teaching discipline, sport could also serve to fight 'vices' such as drinking, drugs, or promiscuity. In this context, it is important to mention that for a long time Western academia considered religious-cultural systems such as Hinduism, Buddhism, and Confucianism to be hostile to economic progress.[42] Therefore, it is not that surprising that Asian countries influenced by these systems became targets of the sportive 'civilizing mission'.

It needs to be stated that almost all actors covered in this study thought that this combination of (initially Christian) ideals and of modern sport only worked as long as putting winning above everything else did not become the dominant ethos. Professionalism, including the payment of money and the selection of small groups of elite athletes, was therefore undesirable. Only a strict enforcement of mass-based amateurism would ensure that amateur ideals could regulate interaction and spread respectful behavior between as many people as possible. This difference between the aims of amateur sport—'civilization' or education—and of professional sport—commercial entertainment—will be of great importance for this study.

The three ideals are important in terms of Western and Asian elites' discourses concerning the shaping of a modern Asia and the role of *sportive pan-Asianism*. Asian elites only partially accepted the Western model, which during the period of proto-decolonization that began in the 1920s led to increased calls for modernization without Westernization. More precisely, the result was an *acceptance* of the ideals but a *rejection* of the claim that these were the product of Western civilization and, particularly, of Christianity. The ideal of internationalism is also important when discussing the respective Games' impact on strengthening Asian nationalisms, whose existence was directly linked to that of inter-*nationalism*. While international Games thus first supported the emergence of nationalism in the 1910s, anti-colonial and later state nationalism quite quickly became—for the remaining decades covered in this study—more important than internationalism.[43] Moreover, internationalism and, to a certain degree egalitarianism, were preconditions for various forms of sportive pan-Asianism. As will be shown, the opinions of the respective organizers of the Games strongly differed concerning Asianist *contents* such as cultural elements, but the *conception* of Asia was less debated. Most actors agreed on a conception one today would call a *regionalist* pan-movement, thus based on egalitarianism between individual nations. This does not exclude that some of the organizers envisioned a more *hegemonic* or *imperialist* pan-movement centered on their own nation. Independent of that, one can talk about an *anti-colonial* pan-movement already during the 1920s.[44] The Asianist claims thus became more 'Asian' after Asians started organizing the Games in the 1920s, although they sometimes 'only' served to promote individual national goals by threatening Western institutions with seemingly 'united' Asian action against them. However, the egalitarian internationalism promoted by the Games also served as a counter-model to the many violent conflicts that arose in Asia between the 1910s and 1970s. It should nevertheless be obvious that the Games were only one of many events that had an impact on the regional order in Asia and on regional integration (or its absence) and that this impact was strongly dependent on the decisions—and the freedom of action—of the organizing elites.[45] One can also argue that the encouragement of masses of 'common people' to take up sport and to live according to the related ideals was a more immediate and important goal.

The staging of the Games, too, was heavily affected by the three ideals.[46] Particularly in the 1910s and 1920s, hosting the Games (similar to hosting world expositions) served a communicative purpose. Even though the aim of the Games—promoting amateur sports as citizenship training based on the three ideals—did not change much until the early 1970s, the limited media access of many Asians in the 1910s and 1920s made it particularly important to provide examples to masses of people in the stadium. Developing infrastructure to develop sport was thus also relevant from the beginning. However, beginning in the late 1950s and particularly during the 1960s—the so-called 'decade of development'[47]—and early 1970s, when the Games were held in (semi-)authoritarian countries, developing infrastructure greatly increased in importance. The motives included nation-branding, fulfilling large-scale social engineering aims, and legitimizing the government by demonstrating its intention to improve the living conditions of the people. The staging of the Games thereby became directly affected by the discourse of modernization without Westernization. As a consequence, the staging visually and acoustically underlined both that aim and the implicit one of reducing the power asymmetry vis-à-vis the West.

In a nutshell, this study is a history of ideas about the nation and the meaning of 'Asia' in the twentieth century, based on sports events. Its *main question* is this: Why and how did the early Asian Games and their predecessors turn into sites of contestation of the nation and of visions of a modern Asia? This main question is accompanied by several side questions: Why were the respective Games founded? How did Asian elites react to the transfer of modern Western sports and the accompanying Christian ideals, norms, and values to Asia? How did decolonization influence the Games? How were the various Games used to showcase Asian modernization and development processes? How was this meant to influence the power relations between the West, Asia, and the respective participating countries? Why and how did the 'civilizing mission' end?

Such questions are rather new to research on sport and sports events in Asia and their impact on the modernization of Asian countries. Moreover, such topics are comparatively understudied, although the 2008 Beijing Olympics (and, to a lesser degree, the Soccer World Championship of 2002 in Japan and South Korea) led to an increased academic interest in these events.[48] Research on the FECG is quite limited, although, for example, Takashima Kō has recently (writing in Japanese) contributed much to the topic.[49] In the case of the WAG research is almost non-existent.[50] Even more problematic is that several of the few studies written on the early Asian Games are plagued by academic problems such as a neglect of the relevant historical background, an undue political bias, or a lack of sources.[51] This publication is based on archival material obtained in eight countries and further sources such as cartoons, photos, official reports, and newspapers from five additional ones.

My book is a contribution to international history, especially its politico-cultural dimension. Due to its strong focus on Western and especially Asian transnational elites, it includes an element of global history. The attention paid to Asian elites also means that the study fits into New Imperial History and New Cold War History. These relatively recent approaches to history writing have opened up a large variety of research fields. They link, for example, international organizations and the foreign policy of nation-states with issues such as modernization, development, nation-branding, and the relations of nations, empires, and regions to each other. Theoretical approaches for studying sports events nevertheless are still very much in their infancy.[52] Three concepts can be productively applied to the study of modernization and development, as well as of nationalism and Asianism.

The first is James Scott's 'authoritarian high modernism',[53] which explains the modernization and development aims of the organizers of the Games, and why so many Asian sports officials were senior politicians and bureaucrats, not civil society actors.[54] While Scott's case studies were heavily criticized,[55] and are in any case not important here, his description of 'authoritarian high modernism' is of interest since different levels of feasibility become evident when discussing the large-scale plans of many organizers. Particularly when the Games took place in (semi-)authoritarian countries during the 1960s and 1970s, large parts of the population were to be—and, in contrast to more democratic systems, could be—affected. The regimes in Indonesia, Thailand, and Iran all claimed to have a 'revolutionary' mandate and sought to use it to change society; all were overthrown within five years of their Games by groups of people rejecting the respective modernization processes the government was enforcing. I do not propose to draw a direct connection between these events, but suggest that they underline that the hosting of large-scale regional sports events was part of a broader 'high modernist' agenda. Colonies—sometimes called 'laboratories of modernity'—also gave modernizers comparatively great freedom of action.[56] After all, as will be shown, the sportive 'civilizing mission' started in the 1910s in the Philippines under American colonial rule. The American YMCA certainly was not an authoritarian organization. However, its intention to use its newly created contacts with colonial administrations and Asian governments to affect the lives of millions of Asians had a strong 'high modernist' touch and indirectly paved the way for more authoritarian approaches. After all, the population became more 'legible', since bio-political information to administer public health and fitness was gained. 'Authoritarian high modernism' can in this context be understood as "[i]ndustrial-strength social engineering" that takes place in systems where the aspiration of elites to administratively order nature and society can rely on the power of a modern state, while a weak or almost non-existent civil society cannot prevent these plans. When discussing 'authoritarian high modernism's' origin in the West, Scott also says that "it is best conceived as a strong (one might even say muscle-bound) version of the beliefs in scientific and technical progress that were associated with industrialization in Western Europe and in North America from roughly 1830 until World War I."[57]

The second concept this study is based on is Anthony D. Smith's ethno-symbolism. It helps to explain nationalism and Asianism and can be used to analyze the staging of the Games. Ethno-symbolism strongly focuses on the traditional cultural elements of certain ethnic communities that constitute a nation. 'Traditional' here refers to what contemporary elites considered a traditional cultural element. In this setting, the term thus does *not* have a meaning similar to "backward". Among these traditional cultural elements are, for example, languages, religions, values, myths of ancestry or election, memories of 'golden ages', heroes and saints, dances, music, dresses, and architecture. Such cultural elements are deemed especially important because they play a vital role in shaping social structures and cultures. These distinctive symbolic repertoires also serve to differentiate a certain community from other analogous communities. Finally, such cultural elements help to ensure a sense of continuity with past generations of a community. The choice of cultural elements by elites therefore shows their perception of which *parts of the past of a nation* were (or are) relevant for the *present* and to the *future*. Hence, shifts in power relations and the emergence of new elites due to colonialism or decolonization often led to changes in the officially prescribed pool of cultural elements.[58] The staging of the Games thus was one of the most important ways of communicating power relations between the host nation,[59] Asia, and the West. Before decolonization, the staging also mirrored the power asymmetry between Western colonizers and Asian elites.

Although Smith's focus is on nationalism, the approach can be modified to be made useful for explaining the staging of supra-national sportive pan-Asianisms. For example, cultural elements common to several Asian nations could be used in the staging, cultural elements of a host nation could be modified to be more compatible with those of other nations, and cultural elements of different nations could be shown together to imply Asian unity in diversity. Moreover, cultural elements could be completely 'invented' with a claim to be binding for all Asian nations, and cultural elements foreign to all Asian nations could be appropriated for an Asian context.

The third concept is nation-branding. In addition to national or regional integration goals, the use of certain cultural elements such as architecture, dances, and music, especially if integrated into the modern context of a sports event, can serve nation-branding purposes. Nation-branding here is understood as a deliberate attempt to create a certain representation of a country or colony through a theatrical display of growing power as an alternative to applying economic or military power. Such attempts were not only targeted at the local population, but also at foreigners. Even early nation-branding 'experts' already thought that influencing the reputation and credibility of a country or colony could produce some political capital (which the YMCA, for example, could use in the 1910s and 1920s to collect donations for its activities). Limited nation-branding thus began in 1913, when the First FECG was held. Since the late 1950s, one can speak of well-planned nation-branding in connection with the Games. Nation-branding then reflected a desire for power, either by staging already existing national power or power to be gained in the future. For example, the staging of the early Asian Games was regularly used to communicate successful modernization and development processes. Such staging often served to legitimize the respective elites' 'high modernist' agendas, but was also meant to reduce the power asymmetry vis-à-vis the West by visually and acoustically challenging claims of Asian backwardness. This included featuring non-Western cultural elements prominently, thereby creating connections between the postcolonial present and the precolonial past as a demonstration that colonialism was a temporary disturbance that had been overcome. In terms of power not yet gained, the staging of the Games produced teleological narratives by projecting cultural elements connected to times of perceived national greatness into the future. In this way, it constructed a vision of national greatness to be regained. These cultural elements could be Asian ones, such as heroes or architectural styles. However, during colonialism the elements often were those of the colonizers and their 'civilizing mission'. During decolonization, the mix of Western and Asian elements showed an appropriation process. In the sense of ethno-symbolism, nation-branding thus can show us, over the course of 60 years, the organizers' changing visions of the future. Quite obviously, nation-branding was not limited to defining and redefining a country's or colony's position in the international system, but also served more 'profane' purposes, such as attracting tourists or impressing the IOC.[60]

My analysis follows a chronological structure, beginning with the founding of the FECG by the American YMCA and ending with the inclusion of the People's Republic of China and many West Asian countries into the AGF in the context of the Seventh Asian Games (Tehran 1974), the first Asian Games event to take place in West Asia. While the first two chapters on the FECG and the WAG each cover several events due to the still relatively limited size of the Games, from the third chapter onward every chapter deals with one Asian Games event. This structure means that readers interested, for example, in certain countries or time periods can easily find what they need. It also prevents the confusion a thematic structure would cause since a broad range of Asian countries are covered and not every reader might be familiar with every single country.

The first chapter begins by showing why American YMCA physical (education) directors in the Philippines, thus leading sports experts who had followed the American expansion into the Pacific, decided to found Asia's first international sports event in Manila in 1913. I also explain how they used the Far Eastern Championship Games to promote their vision of a Christian Asia. Asian civilizations were perceived as backward compared to Western civilization. Spreading Western-Christian amateur sports ideals such as Christian internationalism, Christian egalitarianism, and a 'Protestant work ethic' through a completely new platform—a regional sports event attracting strong media attention—thus served to 'uplift' Asian societies to white American Protestant civilizational standards. The YMCA's vision of a Christian Asia hence focused on curing perceived Asian social deficits and on overcoming ethnic and political tensions in the region by creating a common sports ideology that united Chinese, Japanese, and Filipinos.

The second chapter deals with the question of why and how the Far Eastern Championship Games and the Western Asiatic Games turned into sites mirroring anti-colonial nationalisms and why mutually exclusive visions of Asia led to the breakdown of the former event in the 1930s. The expulsion or withdrawal of American YMCA officials from organizing both Games visibly communicated the emancipation of Asians from Western colonialism. The ensuing appropriation of only selected elements of Western civilization then transformed Western amateur ideals into an Asian commonality that served as the central component of sportive Asian integration. The anti-colonial nationalisms that affected the Games nevertheless also contributed, in East Asia, to a clash of mutually exclusive Chinese and Japanese visions of 'Asia', particularly concerning the status of Manchukuo and its right to join the FECG.

The third chapter questions why and how Indian visions of Asian integration led to the founding of the Asian Games. I conclude that Nehruvian Asianism encouraged the hosting of the First Asian Games (New Delhi 1951) as a symbol of peaceful internationalism and of Asian modernization, repudiating discredited Western ideas of civilization.

Notions of Asian integration are taken up again in the fourth chapter, which covers the Second Asian Games (Manila 1954) and addresses the questions of why and how communist-ruled countries were excluded from the Games. I show that Filipino 'Cold Warriors' created a discourse of amateur sports being an offspring of democracy and based on internationalism, thus incompatible with communism. The chapter furthermore asks why and how the event served Philippine postcolonial nation building. I demonstrate that by displaying the Philippines' manifold cultural heritage, former claims of American civilizational superiority were rejected, paving the way for Philippine-controlled modernization.

The fifth chapter questions why and how the Third Asian Games (Tokyo 1958) served to locate post-war Japan in Asia and why expensive nation-branding now became of critical importance for the organizers. Here I explain that the organizers intended to overcome negative wartime images by spreading the image of post-war Japan embracing peaceful internationalism, and to bring the 1964 Olympic Games to Tokyo by demonstrating that Japan was still Asia's most developed and competent country.

The sixth chapter asks why the Indonesian government's vision of Asia led to serious tensions within the Asian Games Federation and why nation-branding was again so important during the Fourth Asian Games (Jakarta 1962). I explain that the Indonesian vision of a non-aligned (pro-socialist) Asia clashed with the ideals of (universal) internationalism and egalitarianism that included political entities such as Israel and Taiwan. I also show that a large-scale infrastructure construction program in Jakarta defied the image of former colonial backwardness, served to unite different Indonesian ethnicities, and supported President Sukarno's rule.

The seventh chapter analyzes why and how the authoritarian organizers of the Fifth and Sixth Asian Games (Bangkok 1966 and 1970) used the events to promote their vision of anti-communist Asian cooperation. Moreover, I explain that due to the collaboration between the military and the monarchists, the Games contributed to the personality cult of the king as the semi-sacral figurehead of the Thai nation. I also focus on the exhibition of Thailand as a rapidly developing country that nevertheless embraced its Buddhist cultural heritage.

The last chapter covers the Seventh Asian Games (Tehran 1974), questioning why and how this event was utilized for nation-branding and Iranian-led Asian integration. I conclude that branding Iran as a rich and developed country willing to assist Asian countries suffering from the Oil Crisis in 1973 encouraged Iranian-led anti-Soviet regional cooperation, communicated the rebirth of an Iranian great power, and legitimized the government's modernization plan by portraying it as being based on the Great Persian Empire's cultural heritage.

Table A The Far Eastern Championship Games and the Western Asiatic Games: Dates, Host Countries, and Overall Champions[61]

Far Eastern Championship Games/ Western Asiatic Games	Host Country	Overall Champion[62]
First FECG (January–February 1913)	Philippines (Manila)	Philippines
Second FECG (May 1915)	China (Shanghai)	China
Third FECG (May 1917)	Japan (Tokyo)	Japan
Fourth FECG (May 1919)	Philippines (Manila)	Philippines
Fifth FECG (May–June 1921)	China (Shanghai)	Philippines
Sixth FECG (May 1923)	Japan (Osaka)	Japan
Seventh FECG (May 1925)	Philippines (Manila)	Philippines
Eighth FECG (August–September 1927)	China (Shanghai)	Japan
Ninth FECG (May 1930)	Japan (Tokyo)	Japan
Tenth FECG (May 1934)	Philippines (Manila)	None (de facto Japan)
First WAG (February–March 1934)	India (Patiala and New Delhi)	None (de facto India)

CHAPTER 1

Muscular Christianity and the 'Western Civilizing Mission': Elwood S. Brown, the YMCA, and the Founding of the Far Eastern Championship Games

"That is, athletics was the least common denominator."[1]

—Elwood Stanley Brown, a leading physical educator of the YMCA, answering a question about why he had founded the Far Eastern Championship Games

The most important person in the founding of the Far Eastern Championship Games (FECG) was Elwood Stanley Brown of the American branch of the YMCA. His move to Manila in 1910 resulted in a transfer of white American Protestant norms and values first to the Philippines, and later to other Asian countries. It thus was the beginning of a 'high modernist' scheme of sport-related large-scale social engineering that will be a main topic of this study. While the scheme had a strong paternalistic touch, it cannot be called authoritarian. After all, the American YMCA as a non-governmental organization was limited by the support it received (or did not receive) from the American and other colonial administrations and from Asian governments. It neither had the manpower, nor the financial means to bring about these changes on its own. One of the aims of the sportive 'civilizing mission' even included supporting the creation of a civil society. Nevertheless, it began in a colony of the United States, where organized resistance against large-scale changes was all in all minimal. Within years, the scheme was also applied to other East Asian (meaning Northeast and Southeast Asian) countries considered inferior to white American Protestant civilization.

Christian egalitarianism, Christian internationalism, and a 'Protestant work ethic' were the ideals upon which the remodeling of East Asian societies was to be based. The sportive 'civilizing mission' therefore was a means to promote internationalism and create a more egalitarian and economically progressive civil society. The American YMCA's intention was to educate and 'uplift' East Asians through amateur sports, not to entertain them and produce spectators.

Sports events certainly needed to create interest, which was necessary to draw spectators to the meeting grounds, but sport was neither to become a means in itself (as money making is in the case of professional sport) nor become entangled with politics. Strictly speaking, this discourse of 'apolitical sport' ignored the fact that the sportive 'civilizing mission' itself was political, being based on a Western vision of modernization grounded in the values of Christianity and the Enlightenment. This rejection of 'politics' included foreign policy-based boycotts or violations of amateur norms and values for purposes of systemic competition, which would be a demonstration that certain nationalistic and 'backward' officials, organizations, or governments were trying to prevent a more cooperative and 'civilized' regional order. Seen from the perspective of the YMCA, all people trying to become modern would necessarily support its aims, and therefore any 'political attack' on amateur sport was deemed unacceptable, even morally wrong.

This chapter covers the American YMCA's vision of a modern East Asia based on muscular Christian ideals. I show how Elwood Brown's and his colleagues' social engineering activities in the Philippines led to the founding of the FECG in 1913 and to the idea of setting up further regional games in the 1920s. I also highlight the process of him finding American, Filipino, and Chinese supporters and of overcoming Japanese resistance. The American YMCA thus steadily increased its profile until it gained significant influence on national physical education programs and Asian transnational relations, allowing it to affect millions of people.

Muscular Christianity, the YMCA, and Mutual Perceptions of Americans and Asians

Even though its roots go back to the Middle Ages and even to ancient times, muscular Christianity, as Clifford Putney and others have shown, came into existence in Britain during the middle of the nineteenth century as a reaction to urbanization and industrialization. Promoters of muscular Christianity perceived the 'civilizing' effects of modern sport—social control and self-improvement—as the implementation of Protestantism into the realm of physical education. Through amateur sport, people were to live according to the three ideals that defined the YMCA's vision of Christian-Protestant masculinity.[2] Amateur sport therefore was one of the answers to the question 'What would Jesus do?': it served to train people for Christian citizenship.

From the 1880s onwards, industrialization and urbanization led to a boom in muscular Christian ideas in the United States. Office work instead of hard physical work on farms, 'over-civilization' (of which nervousness and neurasthenia were considered symptomatic) and growing numbers of more physically fit Catholic lower class immigrants beginning to struggle for a place in society provided fertile ground for warnings of a 'degeneration of the white Protestant Anglo-Saxon race'.

Social Darwinist assumptions and bio-political concerns thus also played a role. Moreover, many Protestants considered a more 'masculine' religion necessary to make it more appealing to boys and young men than 'female' Victorian Protestantism was, although this did not necessarily mean the exclusion of women.[3] Following a similar aim, 'body as temple' theologians like Bishop Charles H. Brent considered the body to be a mirror of the soul. Jesus was turned into a 'manly' man, strong in faith, but also equipped with a muscular body hardened by his nomadic life as a missionary in the Holy Land. Being reminiscent of (idealized) medieval images of knights as champions of Christianity, imitating Jesus thus included being physically able to actively improve the world. To build a strong and healthy body was therefore deemed as necessary as training the mind and spirit (this trinity being symbolized by the YMCA's triangle), giving muscular Christianity a strongly progressive and educative dimension that was meant to have a positive impact on the willingness—and ability—of people to lead an economically productive and 'civilized' life.[4]

The American branch of the YMCA as a religious mass organization therefore started to build physical (education) departments in many of its offices to provide young men with a place for sportive recreation. Moreover, its physical directors at the International YMCA College in Springfield, Massachusetts, where volleyball and basketball were invented, and at other places engaged in sports medical and sport pedagogical research, contributing to the scientificity of physical education. The YMCA had been founded in Britain in 1844 as a Protestant lay organization to encourage young men to engage in religious studies instead of enjoying 'vices' comparatively anonymous city life made more accessible. Within several years, the YMCA spread to the United States, and offices were set up in big cities and at universities, numbering more than 200 by 1860 and rapidly increasing afterwards to 693 city YMCAs in 1916. During the Progressive Era, growing wealth and philanthropic donations meant that YMCA leaders such as John Mott decided to actively tackle the roots of social ills such as poverty, inadequate healthcare, and social violence, and to encourage Christian character-building both in the United States and overseas.[5]

Modern amateur sport was a part of the 'Western civilizing mission', which produced hierarchies of races and civilizations, placing the West on top. In the case of the United States, the defeat of Spain in the Spanish-American War (1898) led to deliberations on how to proceed with the remnants of the Spanish colonial empire in Asia and the Caribbean. For example, the main reason (or justification) for the American decision to conquer the Philippines and fight President Emilio Aguinaldo's forces had been the perceived backwardness of the Filipinos. In congressional debates and in the public discourse in newspapers, racial images of Filipinos as child-like, 'uncivilized' savages, Native Americans, or 'Negroes' were mixed up with Christian rhetoric. Uncle Sam was often displayed as a fatherly figure or as a teacher having somehow to deal with the small Filipinos. The pro-imperialists argued for a duty to 'uplift' the Filipinos to superior white

American Protestant standards and to save them from Spanish oppression or from the outbreak of chaos due to their incapacity for self-government. Based on ideas like American Exceptionalism, Manifest Destiny, and the *frontier*, the United States would have to accept the 'White Man's Burden'[6] of 'benevolent' imperialism. Even the American anti-imperialists, who rejected the idea of annexing the Philippines as contrary to the principles that the US was founded upon, had an image of the Filipinos that did not significantly differ from that of the pro-imperialists.[7]

As Paul Kramer concludes, early American colonial administrations used keywords such as 'progress', 'development', 'capacity', and 'possibility' to create a discourse of racial inclusiveness of Filipinos. The 'nigger theory', which was popular especially in the American South and combined the 'inferiority' of non-white races vis-à-vis the white race with the impossibility of 'uplifting' non-whites, was impracticable for encouraging Filipino elites to collaborate. Therefore, they were instead described as *being able* to learn self-government, but still far away from doing so. Hereby, a justification for long-term colonialism was created. The images which had come up during the American debate on annexation were later supplemented by further ones. The centuries old Black Legend of corrupt Spanish colonial practices promoting exploitation and feudalism saw a revival and was presented together with Filipino 'racial deficits' as having had a disastrous influence on Christian Filipino elites. The broad masses, on the other hand, were ignorant, passive, superstitious, and lazy. Most of the non-Christians were said to be savages needing American guidance.[8]

These discourses contributed significantly to the 'Western civilizing mission' rhetoric, here in its American form. One of the most exemplary images (fig. 1.1) was that of an Igorot headhunter, who, according to Dean C. Worcester, an American zoologist and Secretary of the Interior in the Philippine Commission until 1913, had within two years been turned into a 'civilized'-looking constabulary sergeant.

Filipino politicians, too, came rather quickly to the conclusion that there was no realistic alternative to collaboration with the Americans and that they would have to use the discourse of 'civilization' as effectively as possible against them. Self-government and independence, regularly requested by the Philippine Assembly through declarations that Filipinos were capable of managing the country, nonetheless was not considered until the election of a Democrat, Woodrow Wilson, as US President in late 1912.[9]

The 'American civilizing mission', which had gained momentum through the conquest of the Philippines, did not remain limited to it. The American image of China was also negative. China was perceived as an ancient civilization, but at the same time as worn out, sick, physically decadent, weak, and unable to learn new ideas. The Chinese Revolution and the end of the monarchy in 1911/12 added another image: that of the Chinese as ignorant, but educable. China thus became another country in need of American tutelage. Americans concerned with China also considered it promising that many of the new political leaders, including

FIGURE 1.1.
'The evolution of a constabulary sergeant from an Igorot headhunter': Dean Worcester used such images to show that American colonialism would turn even 'savages' into 'civilized' citizens.

Dean C. Worcester, "Head-Hunters of the Philippines Are Fast Becoming Good Citizens." *Washington Post* (25 October 1908), p. S3. (Courtesy of the *Washington Post*)

Chinese (Provisional) President Yuan Shikai, had been or were in contact with missionaries or had even received a Christian education in the United States.[10]

This new generation of Chinese politicians, on the other hand, now had to deal with the problem of how to ensure their country's survival in an imperialist world order characterized by Social Darwinist competition. The Chinese notion of a cosmic order with China at its center as the leading civilization had already been shattered in the nineteenth century by Western great powers and Japan. One of their many problems was that the idea of a modern nation-state was unknown to most Chinese except for some educated individuals familiar with the West. Another problem directly linked with this one was the deterioration of central power in China and the split between the north and the south. One illustration was President Yuan, whose power base lay in northern China, eagerly establishing autocratic military rule, dissolving national and provincial assemblies and forcing the southern China (especially Nanjing) based revolutionary leader Sun Yat-sen and his Kuomintang (Chinese Nationalist Party) out of power. After Yuan attempted to become a new Chinese emperor in 1915, tensions between different regional factions further increased, and following his death in 1916 China completely fragmented into separate areas controlled by warlords. The following humiliation of China at the Paris Peace Conference (1919) ending the First World War, where Japan received the German concessions in Shandong province, then led to the May Fourth Movement, which marked the beginning of nationalism as a mass phenomenon and was characterized by anti-imperialist demonstrations and rioting.[11]

Finally, the American image of Japan was relatively positive. The successful modernization process following the Meiji Restoration (1868) and the military victory of an 'enlightened' government (Meiji meaning 'enlightened rule') over 'tyrannical' tsarist Russia in 1905 had impressed many Americans. Tokyo thus was perceived as the most successful Asian 'pupil' when it came to Western style reforms. Nonetheless, the monarchical system was seen as a sign of 'backwardness', and the idea of a 'yellow peril', which also included the Chinese, expressed itself in the fear of white America being 'overrun' by Asian immigrants. For example, anti-Japanese immigration laws in California in 1913 demonstrated that racial equality was hardly accepted there.[12]

In the view of Japanese and other Asian politicians and revolutionaries, however, Japan's victory over Russia had illustrated that Asian countries were able to modernize themselves without the proclaimed need for Western colonialism, underlining the hypocrisy of the imperialist 'Western civilizing mission' and the racial hierarchies linked with it. Nevertheless, the Japanese government continued its policy of non-cooperation with the independence movements in the Western colonies. Japanese elites even established their own colonial empire by taking over Taiwan (1895) and Korea (1910), where they started their own 'civilizing mission' while continuing to 'civilize' their own population at home. Japanese elites also looked down more and more on the Chinese and, especially, the Filipinos.[13]

The Origin of the Games: Elwood Brown's Activities and Experiences as YMCA Physical Director in Manila

One of the most important promoters of muscular Christianity in Asia was Elwood Brown. To illustrate his aims and his initial experiences in the Philippines, which led to the founding of the FECG, I begin with his background and social engineering projects in the American colony between 1910 and 1913.

Brown was born in Cherokee, Iowa, in 1883 to a Baptist minister.[14] In 1892, he became a member of the YMCA. After completing high school, Brown joined the Chicago central YMCA where he received training in physical education (1898–1903). He also coached several teams at Wheaton College, a Christian liberal arts college in Illinois, and attended lectures there. Following a season as a coach at the University of Illinois at Urbana-Champaign (1904/05), he took up association work at the Salt Lake City YMCA in March 1906. Here, he served most of his time as physical director until he was offered the position of YMCA physical director in Manila by the YMCA's foreign department. On 25 January 1910, he left the United States.[15] Before leaving, he had been briefed by Charles H. Robertson of the Tientsin (Tianjin) YMCA regarding the YMCA's sports activities in other parts of Asia.[16]

At that time, Filipinos had engaged in various types of traditional physical education practices. However, modern sports were unknown to them, with the exception of some members of the *ilustrado* elite educated during Spanish colonialism, before they were spread during the American colonial era (1898–1946). During the initial years, American teachers and soldiers started to teach sports to the local population or provided them an opportunity to imitate them. Prior to 1909, when the colonial government became involved in physical education programs, such endeavors nevertheless were still in the process of institutionalization.[17] One important reason for the colonial administration's growing interest in the bio-politics of physical education was that it could present itself as the guarantor of public health and fitness. Calls for independence could be discredited by claiming that the Philippine oligarchs' neglect of the common people would result in a massive health threat should the Americans leave. Social control purposes also mattered, meaning that the American YMCA's professional physical education knowledge was very welcome.

Shortly after his arrival in early 1910, Brown was asked by the American Governor-General, W. Cameron Forbes, if he could go to Baguio to set up a sports program for approximately 400 to 500 Filipino clerks. The American-controlled Philippine Commission intended to stay for three months at Baguio, a newly built town in northern Luzon, to escape the heat of Manila, taking the Filipino assemblymen and clerks with them. The Filipinos, having to leave family and friends back in Manila, expressed their dissatisfaction and boredom through minor acts of sabotage, such as ripping open mosquito nets around beds, clogging toilets, or disconnecting telephones. The newly devised sports program was designed to appeal to them and provide them an opportunity for recreation. Brown later stated that the acts of sabotage were not only significantly reduced, but also most of the Filipinos actually took up sports like baseball and volleyball at Baguio. It seems that he had been highly successful, because he was invited to do the same thing again during the next hot season.[18] Therefore, I assume that the percentage Brown gave (98 per cent) is more or less right, since everybody was to be affected. Even if he exaggerated the rate by 10 or 20 per cent, since the YMCA's overseas activities depended on success stories to receive funding from American philanthropists (a problem I address elsewhere), it would still be very high.[19]

In addition to improving the YMCA's relations with the governor-general, Brown also approached the Bureau of Education, responsible for, among other business, physical education programs in public schools. The Director of Education, Frank R. White, was already a member of the YMCA's board of directors and the Assistant Director (later Director), Frank L. Crone, was a member of the YMCA's physical department committee. Brown got the chance to develop a physical education program for the new public school system, focusing on games with many participants that did not require much equipment, such as volleyball, baseball, and relay races. The idea was to affect as many pupils as possible: masses of boys and girls (who now had to change their traditional dress code) were to be addressed, instead of supporting only a few, talented children. Although the implementation took some time, more than 400,000 Filipino pupils eventually took up modern sports and games.[20]

Obviously, both the sports program for Baguio and the physical education program for public schools were based on the YMCA's ideas of the 'civilizing' effects of sports and their (bio-political) value as a clean and healthy form of recreation. As Brown's subsequent activities in 1910 will show, he thoroughly believed that

> [p]lay and recreation affect citizenship in the sense of developing those qualities that are desirable in a good citizen of any country—in other words, those qualities that contribute to sturdy character, initiative, physical energy, right thinking, sportsmanship, respect for the rights and ability of the other fellow, shame at showing a 'yellow streak', courage, good health, and normal outlets for physical energy.[21]

Probably the most important event during his busy first year in the Philippines was the discussion in November 1910 about the founding of the Philippine Amateur Athletic Federation (PAAF). In January 1911, the PAAF was officially set up with Brown as its secretary, while Governor-General Forbes, later followed by Bishop Charles H. Brent, became its president. Other prominent officials who supported Brown in his further plans were Crone, as well as an officer and lawyer named William Tutherly. If not already in existence, clubs and associations (Interbureau Athletic Association, United States Army, Filipino Constabulary, clubs for Filipinos, etc.) were set up in the process of establishing the PAAF, uniting all of them under its leadership.[22]

Brown was one of the most important advocates for the elimination of all professionalism, which he campaigned for every year during the election of the PAAF officials.[23] He saw the enforcement of strict amateurism as necessary. The earlier lack of an organization controlling the national championships held during the annual Manila Carnival[24] would have meant that professionalism had started to "creep in", leading to "more hotly contested" matches and rivalries between clubs.[25] Therefore, the championships were put under the control of the PAAF, with Brown becoming the Carnival's Director of Athletics in early 1911. These championships, one between schools and another open to everybody independent of race or skin color, were strictly limited to amateurs. Although elite sport had already been dampened, 'play for everybody' was now strengthened even more by holding "educational demonstrations of group games for everybody" during the Carnival championships.[26] Under such conditions, championships were considered a useful instrument for encouraging people (both men and women) through 'contagion' to take up sport—media access was, after all, still very limited.[27]

Due to Brown's activities, the YMCA gained de facto control of more or less all physical education programs and amateur sports championships in the Philippines and was able to shape them according to its 'civilizing' aims. Moreover, by ignoring racial segregation, for example during the 1911 Carnival, and letting Americans and Filipinos compete against each other,

Elwood Brown stated that he had gained important experience concerning the value of sport:

> The American soldier was more inclined to take a swift kick at the Filipino than anything else, but athletics brought them together on what was a common basis and on more than one occasion a speedy Filipino runner would beat out a white man and that made an impression on the soldier and he acquired a little bit of a changed attitude, so it occurred to me we might bring the Chinese and Japanese and Filipinos together on the same basis.[28]

In contrast to the anxiety in other colonial empires that games between colonizers and colonized could promote resistance and nationalism in the event that the 'subjects' defeated their 'masters', Brown apparently had no doubts regarding the dominance of the Americans.[29] On the contrary, he started to perceive amateur sports as a way to improve the negative image which various peoples, including Americans, Japanese, and Chinese, had of Filipinos (and which he shared) by acquainting them with one another and creating respect.

The idea of using the equalizing effects of amateur sport to reduce the tensions between different peoples, the potential of which Brown had personally experienced, can be considered as having been the next step in his 'civilizing scheme'. He now supported the creation of a more egalitarian regional order in East Asia. In 1911, the PAAF invited foreign athletes to compete during the Manila Carnival of 1912. Brown reported proudly to his YMCA superiors in the United States that "Olympic games for the Far East are not beyond the grounds of possibility."[30] In addition to two Japanese tennis players, Waseda University's baseball team also competed in the Carnival, resulting in the first-ever official baseball game between the Japanese and Filipinos. Athletes from the United States, Hong Kong, Singapore, and other places participated in the championship as well. John H. Crocker, YMCA national physical director for China, also traveled to Manila for several days.[31] Now, with this demonstration of the willingness of Asian (and Western) athletes to compete against each other, the basic condition for holding a 'Far Eastern Olympiad' was fulfilled.

In the summer of 1912, Brown traveled as secretary of the PAAF to Japan and China to officially invite these countries to send athletes to the next Carnival and to join a multinational sports organization. In the case of China, the YMCA—in particular John Crocker—became the most important institution for convincing Chinese authorities and for preparing a delegation. In pre-modern China, physical activity had, in contrast to studying, not been regarded as appropriate for members of the educated class. Therefore, physical education programs and sport, which had been introduced in the second half of the nineteenth century, were more or less limited to big, coastal cities with foreign enclaves and Western-style universities.

The YMCA had gained an influential position since the turn of the century, having helped in hosting the first national sports meeting in Nanjing in 1910.[32]

In Japan, the YMCA had to contact Kanō Jigorō. Kanō was the founder of modern judo. He also served as the president of Tokyo Higher Normal School (*Tōkyō Kōtō Shihan Gakkō*) and thus was strongly involved in Japan's teacher education. In 1909, he had been elected the first (and only) Asian member of the International Olympic Committee (IOC) and set up the (Great-)Japan Amateur Athletic Association (JAAA/*Dai-Nippon Taiiku Kyōkai*), whose president he became. As in China, modern sport had come to Japan in the second half of the nineteenth century. During the Meiji Era (ending 1912), the diffusion rate was still very limited. Physical education had been made a part of school curricula, but focused mainly on military and 'normal' gymnastics, encouraging hierarchical relations between teachers and pupils and conformity among the latter.[33] More problematic was that when Brown arrived in Tokyo in September 1912 to talk with the JAAA, Kanō was still in Europe after observing the Stockholm Olympic Games and was unwilling to support him. After some negotiations, a Japanese newspaper (Ōsaka Mainichi Shinbun) agreed to bear the cost of sending two athletes to Manila, while Meiji University's baseball team decided to participate as well.[34] During the last days of September, an agreement was made public for setting up a 'Far Eastern Olympic Association', which planned to include all Asian-Pacific countries and islands except Russia. Between 31 January and 8 February 1913, the first Far Eastern Olympic Games—a short time later renamed as the FECG—were finally held between Filipino, Japanese, and Chinese athletes. Brown became the Far Eastern Athletic Association's (FEAA) secretary, holding this position until he left the Philippines in 1918. He was supported by Tutherly and Crone, who served as members of the contest committee, and by Forbes, who became the FEAA's president.[35]

Taken all together, Americans' negative perceptions of Filipinos, which Brown shared, had resulted in an institution-building project to spread amateur sports norms and values in the Philippines and to reduce social and 'racial' tensions. Brown at first collaborated with the colonial administration and later, still receiving support from the network he had created, engaged in setting up new institutions on his own. One of his main motives was to guarantee amateur standards as the core of the 'civilizing' project and to reduce professionalism, which was considered a threat.

Promoting Amateur Sport in the Whole Orient: The Far Eastern Championship Games as an Instrument for Christian Internationalism

The FECG have to be seen as a project to encourage a more 'civilized' and interdependent regional order, but also—on a more local level—more 'civilized' and interdependent national orders in the three participating countries. Regional integration especially is a topic that would be relevant not only for the FECG, but also for many of the Asian Games events held after the disastrous Second World War. Some of the results described below seem to have been contingencies, but Brown was aware that the First Games in 1913 were "a strange spectacle" with "three types of oriental peoples competing in purely American contests and using the English language".[36] 'Purely American' may be considered an exaggeration: 'Western' would be a more appropriate term. One can also assume that not all of the athletes could speak English well, even though the limited need of communication during a contest (compared, for example, to a school lesson) certainly facilitated interaction between American organizers and Asian athletes. However, the American control over the internationalist project, strictly speaking that of Brown and the American YMCA, was obvious.

As had been the case with the PAAF championships held during the Carnival, the FECG were a means to teach and popularize sport.[37] The difference was that this time not only Filipinos were the target group, but rather the whole 'Far East' was to become a region more closely united through American Protestant values. More precisely, the region Brown initially focused upon consisted of the Philippines, Japan, China, Siam, and the Malay Peninsula.[38] In his view, potential host cities would be Shanghai, Hong Kong, Singapore, and Manila.[39] All of them were international cities strongly influenced by Western culture. After the First Games had been successfully concluded, Brown traveled to Siam and Malaya in 1914 as the FEAA's secretary. In Bangkok, he talked with the King of Siam and received a promise that a soccer team and some other athletes would attend the next Games. In Malaya, he apparently discussed the Games with the Sultan of Johor and with sports organizations in Singapore.[40] Second Lieutenant (later Captain) Noor Mohamed Hashim, the president of the Malaya Football Association who would later become a member of the Legislative Council of the Straits Settlements, and Joseph Caulfield James, who had been the principal tutor to Prince Vajiravudh of Siam (the later Rama VI) and was a leading figure in the Royal Bangkok Sports Club, were chosen as delegates. Malaya and Siam thus both became new members in 1915, but since they never sent any delegations to the Games, they disappeared from the member list some years later.[41] In contrast, despite Kanō's initial lack of interest and doubts regarding the JAAA's competence to manage the Third FECG, Japan was always represented, even if only by rather small delegations during the First, Second, and Fourth Games.[42]

Although Brown left the Philippines in January 1918 to join the YMCA's detachment to the American Expeditionary Forces that were sent to the European battlefields, he maintained a strong interest in the further development of the Games. In September 1919, he became secretary of physical education in the American YMCA's foreign department in New York, gaining a strong influence over its physical education programs abroad.[43] Despite initial problems in successfully enlarging the FEAA, he expected that in the Fifth FECG (Shanghai

1921) "Siam will be represented" and that the YMCA, now also becoming active in the Dutch East Indies, would see to it "that we will have Java in and very soon the whole Far East will be engaged".[44] Prince Yugala of Siam had visited the Fourth FECG; despite this, the country did not send any athletes in the future. In contrast, the Dutch East Indies, which Brown had visited in 1920, eventually sent a delegation in 1934.[45] As Tutherly stated, the constitution of the FEAA had been changed already in 1919 to include "all Asiatic countries". Despite this, both he and Brown thought that for administrative reasons (i.e., to keep travel costs low) another sports organization, including India and West Asia, would be preferable.[46] This project will be covered in the next chapter.

The FECG were not only meant to attract interest in modern sports in as many *countries* of the 'Far East' as possible. Like the PAAF championships, it was also hoped they would affect as many *people* as possible, especially within the respective host countries. Thus, at the First Games it was decided the games would be an annual event held in a different country every year. Due to the outbreak of the First World War, and certainly also due to a lack of experience in hosting international events, this could not be realized. In any case, following Brown, the (until 1927) biennial championships were no more than a means to an end: "We kept in these games group sports like volleyball, for example, always keeping to the fore the general idea, the mass idea, play for everybody, and continued it at every series of games to give demonstrations of these other sports."[47] For example, in the case of the Second FECG, Brown brought a group of Filipino girls to Shanghai to play exhibition matches of indoor baseball. Afterwards, further exhibition matches took place in Beijing before Chinese school girls and finally Brown's group and some other athletes were received by President Yuan.[48]

Amateur sports values were also supposed to actively keep political and ethnic tensions out of the realm of sport, serving to encourage egalitarian internationalism. Under such conditions, it was considered easy to change the spirit of rivalry to one of respect after initial contacts had been established: "The question of who won was of secondary importance, however, when it was realized that at last an activity had been discovered in which a Chinese, a Japanese, and a Filipino could meet in friendly, social intercourse without arousing the racial antagonisms that constantly appeared in business, religious, and social affairs."[49] It is therefore no wonder that Brown was proud of the 'civilizing' effects the Third FECG in Tokyo in 1917 had on the three 'Oriental' nations, while Western civilization was at the same time slaughtering itself on the European battlefields.[50] For him, it was an illustration of the superiority of his vision of an egalitarian, interdependent, and more Protestant-American world order (here still a regional order), compared to a 'realist' world order characterized by anarchy, which had driven the European great powers into war.

Following the idea of the open championship at the Carnival, so-called Open International Games were regularly held after the FECG. Here, amateur athletes of all nationalities would compete against each other and against those participants of the FECG willing to take part. Although these Games gained less fame than the FECG, their mere existence, which overcame racial segregation, illustrated that tensions were to be reduced not only between Asians, but also between Asians and Westerners.[51]

Despite such international understanding, it was obvious that the Games had at least some patriotic appeal, as President Yuan had acknowledged in 1915: "He expressed his delight that the youth of the three Oriental races had engaged in friendly competition, and particularly that, despite bitter political differences, representatives of North and South China had all gladly competed for 'China'." It seems that Brown and his colleagues, too, had initially under-estimated the 'unifying power' of the Games for China, since before the First FECG they had planned to have both a 'North Chinese' (Shanghai) and a 'South Chinese' (Hong Kong) team in them.[52] Later on, the question of the contribution of international sports competitions to the growing anti-colonial nationalism in China even raised concerns among some members of a still very Western IOC. After being asked his opinion by IOC president Henri de Baillet-Latour in 1926, Franklin Brown, the YMCA's national physical director in Japan, subtly hinted at the IOC members' fears (which stood in obvious contrast to the ideal of egalitarian internationalism) that international sports events, such as the planned African Games in Egypt, might endanger their African colonial empires by creating nationalism: "I gather from what you said that some of your European colleagues feared that athletics had more or less to do with it [growing nationalism in China] and perhaps doubted the advisability of spreading the doctrine of International sport in Africa, for that reason." Franklin Brown explained that in China international sport was only one of many factors responsible for the rising anti-colonial nationalism. Nonetheless, the leading colonial powers in Africa—Britain and France—prevented the hosting of the African Games in Alexandria in 1929.[53]

Promoting aggressive nationalism was, however, not Elwood Brown's intention, as he feared that doing so would be as disastrous as professionalism if it resulted in anti-foreign sentiments or an excessive competitiveness. As Crone had said regarding the inter-school competition during the Carnival, some initial rivalry between groups had to be provoked to promote sport, but as fast as possible had to be changed and channeled into a positive outcome: "By working up town rivalry, teams were organized and equipped and received the support of their towns. As soon as this town rivalry was thoro[ugh]ly worked up for the benefit of athletics it began to be modified until now in most places in the Philippines it has become a healthy and sportsmanlike rivalry."[54]

In the case of the FECG, it was not town rivalries, but national rivalries, that were to be utilized and then modified to create 'sportsmanlike rivalry'. Instead of village teams receiving the support of their hometowns, national teams were to receive the support of the members of their respective nations. Therefore, international championships were also useful for building nation-states by making athletes and officials of the same national team accept a common national identity. The reduction of tensions between people from northern and southern China mentioned by Yuan thus was more the outcome of the general Christian-egalitarian aim of assisting in the creation of a new regional order in East Asia by bringing different people together through sport, and less about the question of whether this took place on the *inter*-national or the national level (which could still mean an *inter*-ethnic or *inter*-town level).

After the end of the First World War and after Brown became secretary of physical education in the American YMCA's foreign department in New York in September 1919, he attempted to reproduce the idea of the FECG in cooperation with the IOC. Official patronage and recognition were granted after Brown attended the post-war IOC meeting in Antwerp in August 1920.[55] There it was decided that new, YMCA-initiated national and regional games were to be set up in India, Latin America, the Near East, and the Balkans. Brown thus hoped that American ideals of "fair play, good sportsmanship, amateur standards, and the importance of clean bodies and clear minds", which he had successfully tested in East Asia, would "attract the attention of millions" and thus become accepted all around the globe.[56] The wave of liberal internationalism that American propaganda, the Allied victory in the First World War, and the founding of the League of Nations had created had certainly been an inspiration. Most likely, the disastrous results of the medical examinations of American recruits following the United States' entry into the war in 1917 had also contributed to a perception that an even stronger support of amateur sports as a scientific approach to public health and fitness would be necessary both in the US and globally. Almost half of all American recruits had been diagnosed as having some sort of physical defect and about one-fifth were therefore rejected.[57]

Taken all together, the FECG were set up to spread Western amateur sports norms and values as the foundation of Christian internationalism in as many East Asian nations as possible. This was to serve in 'civilizing' the *region*, but also improving relations between people of different places within each *country*. After initial successes with the Philippines, Japan, and China, Brown at first tried to enlarge the region the Games covered. Later on, he used the model of the FECG in an attempt to instead encourage Christian internationalism in other non-Western parts of the world by setting up further regional games in cooperation with the IOC.

Modernizing Customs and Value Systems: The Far Eastern Championship Games, Christian Egalitarianism, and the 'Protestant Work Ethic'

In addition to the 'civilizing' effects of amateur sport on the interaction between different peoples and ethnicities, the relationship between the individual and society—Christian egalitarianism and the 'Protestant work ethic'—was also of importance. To learn self-control, to play fair and in a team, to value personal effort instead of luck, to engage in capitalist wage labor, and to refrain from vices dangerous to both body and mind were considered as highly useful for overcoming the perceived social deficits of East Asian concepts of masculinity and for establishing egalitarian and economically progressive civil societies. Moreover, delegitimizing local knowledge by criticizing Asian physical education practices as unscientific and unhealthy also served to convince American donors of the necessity of the YMCA's sports program abroad.

With this goal in mind, YMCA reformers claimed that the spreading of modern amateur sport in China served to combat the traditional 'loss of face' after a defeat. Amateur sports norms and values such as self-control appeared capable of effecting this change.[58] The aggressive behavior of Filipinos after losing or the humiliation of an opponent after winning was also to be changed. According to Crone, a perfect example of the progressing 'American civilizing mission' was the case of 'primitive' peoples in Northern Luzon and Mindanao. Their feuds were now solved through sport instead of more brutal traditional means such as headhunting, and public humiliations were no longer automatically answered with violence: "One old chief declared that it was a wonderful thing that such a meeting [athletic meeting in 1911] could be held without serious trouble. 'And just look at that', he said, 'the umpire has just called our batter out. A few years ago no umpire could have called our batter out.'"[59] Independent of that, Brown reported that a certain Dr. J. B. Rogers of the Presbyterian Mission in the Philippines had confirmed that the Filipinos' "tendency to tell untruths" was gradually being overcome by fair play.[60] Also of importance is Brown's later idea of using amateur sport to tackle the caste system in India, according to him another "unnatural barrier" to a more egalitarian civil society. Here, he again saw play as the "least common denominator" for overcoming such social barriers.[61]

Modern sport was also considered to be a 'clean', scientific, and healthy substitute for other types of recreation that could serve to regulate and optimize public health.[62] For instance, Brown's decision to bring two Filipina indoor baseball teams to China was meant to encourage female sports participation and to discourage foot-binding and porcelain shoes. In the Philippines, Brown thought that "foolish" (meaning unscientific) activities like cock-fighting (a blood sport) or *Sipa* (a pre-Spanish ball game) should be eliminated. Other people, like Crone and Bishop Brent, also saw cock-fighting and, more generally, all gambling elements in sportive recreation as a problem, supporting the idea of personal effort and training instead of belief in fate or luck.[63]

The development of a spirit of competition, however, and the value of sport as a preparation for becoming a successful businessman and for setting up an economic system based on waged labor hardly came up in Brown's writings. This idea, acceptable as long as amateur values were guaranteed, was apparently more important for representatives of the American colonial administration than for religious actors like Brown, who had a slightly different focus. Governor-General

Forbes, a former investment banker, can serve as an example. Forbes's address to the young Asian athletes, the majority of whom were students or school boys, during the opening ceremony of the First FECG thus also fits within the 'civilizing mission' aim of establishing an economically progressive civil society: "We hope that all the contest[s] will be carried on in the spirit of fair play and sportsmanship, which goes to make up success in the walks of young people and success late[r] in the world of business, and I hope that in the contests that are to come the best athlete may bear off the prizes and the best team may always win." He also encouraged Filipinos, Chinese, and Japanese to develop stronger business relations. More generally, Forbes stated in a letter to William M. Sloane, an American IOC member, that he expected that physical education would help Filipinos to "improve themselves in moral, social and mental development along healthy lines".[64]

In 1914, Ossie Garfield Jones, a member of the Bureau of Education during Forbes' tenure as governor-general, published an article explaining how sport had been used as a tool to train Filipinos for self-government. About one year later, Jones also became involved in the debate between Democrats and Republicans regarding the Filipinization process initiated by Francis B. Harrison, whom Woodrow Wilson had appointed in 1913 as the new governor-general.[65] Afterwards, Jones decided on an academic career, wrote his PhD thesis (1919) at Berkeley about 'The Development of Self-Government in the Philippine Islands since the American Occupation', and became a professor of political science and the athletic director at the University of Toledo in Ohio.[66]

In his 1914 article, Jones focused mainly on four fundamental aspects of how sport could 'uplift' the Filipinos, thus providing a systematic overview of Brown's and the Bureau of Education's physical education activities in the Philippines aimed at American-style modernization: individual self-control, fair play, respect for duly-constituted authority, and a society based upon a municipal (or community) as opposed to a relationship (or kinship) basis.[67] In modern terms, he was talking about a state monopoly on violence, good governance, duty and civic virtue, and the emergence of a civil society in the Aristotelian sense of self-government by free equals. Jones' role model was the United States and its republican form of government, whose superiority and exceptionalism were inherent in his writing, even though Britain, too, was given some credit. The contrast Jones used was revolutionary Mexico, which was plagued by civil war during most of the 1910s. Like the more problematic Philippines, Mexico suffered from its Spanish cultural and political heritage. In contrast, however, the Philippines was undergoing a peaceful modernization process leading to an egalitarian and economically progressive civil society similar to that of the United States. This would happen in a relatively short time due to American tutelage. Jones also made it plain that a mass approach had been necessary and that the youth were the main target. Although he did not say so explicitly, underlining the importance of the public schools for which the Bureau of Education was responsible as the place where new concepts of femininity and masculinity could be taught also legitimized the Bureau's work and American colonialism in general.

To illustrate the first aspect of sportive citizenship training, individual self-control (the 'state monopoly on violence'), Jones provided several examples of inter-municipal games that had descended out of control and ended in—sometimes massive—violence. This nonetheless was not meant to illustrate that sport was a problem. In contrast, he observed that the same thing happened at other events and was the result of many Filipinos not being able—or willing—to control their emotions. Though not using the term, Jones de facto declared this to be a major deficit in Philippine concepts of masculinity. According to Jones, the main reason for this lack of control from a sociological point of view was that the Filipinos' family- and clan-based social system limited competition and responsibility to a small elite of family heads. The dependent masses had therefore never been forced to develop out of the mental state of children by becoming responsible for themselves, and thus could hardly be individuals. Applying parts of Woodrow Wilson's essay 'Character of Democracy in the United States' (1889) to the Philippine case, Jones came to the conclusion that "the future of democracy in the Philippine Islands does not depend upon the cleverness of the aristocratic class of Filipinos so much as upon the kind of every-day training in individual self-control that the mass of the people receive."[68] An American-style democracy (in the sense of an egalitarian civil society) would necessarily need Filipino citizens who could control their emotions and refrain from violent outbursts. It would, however, not be possible to learn that control from books. Rather it would have to be practiced under stressful conditions. Sports contests would provide a platform for this, providing maximum strain while limiting the potential for disaster. In contrast to older Filipinos, younger ones practicing sports therefore would be able to better accept a defeat in a game, but also in other situations, including political contests.[69]

According to Jones, the direct political outcome of the second aspect, fair play ('good governance'), was more difficult to judge. Fair play was seen as incompatible with favoritism, perceived as the source of inefficiency and graft. Jones declared that Filipinos of both sexes would now be taught fair play at school. This meant that women, too, would become better citizens and pass the idea of fair play on to their children, accelerating the effect. Therefore, corrupt Spanish-Mexican practices like 'Ley de Fuga' would not be accepted by a people having grown up with the fair play ideal. The 'Law of Fugitives' or 'Law of Flight' was the permission of guards to shoot escaping prisoners, and was often misused for execution purposes. For example during the coup d'état in February 1913, Mexican President Francisco I. Madero and Vice President José Maria Pino Suárez had been murdered in this way while being transported from the National Palace to the prison.[70] Jones certainly had read about this event. Even more, the spirit of fair play would solve the problem the Puritans in England had in 1653 when trying to set up a republic: the lack of an "educated and trained self-conscious body politic".[71] The pioneer,

England, took until the nineteenth century to produce such a body politic, but the Filipinos would need significantly less time. Jones hereby remarked that this would happen partially due to the modern American pedagogical approaches, describing British ones as conservative.[72]

The third of Jones' aspects, respect for duly-constituted authority ('duty and civic virtue'), was rather self-explanatory for him: "Dictatorship in a country is an open confession that the people of that country respect nothing but military force."[73] The negative example again was Mexico. Jones nevertheless confessed that in the United States, too, a decade before he wrote the article an umpire would have needed certain fighting skills, thereby asserting that the American 'civilizational margin' in this respect was not that large, though it was still superior. Simultaneously he criticized American boys for having become 'over-individualistic', which according to Jones was caused by 'laissez-faire' and declining parental authority. One answer to such problems would be umpires and coaches teaching discipline to young athletes, a solution which could also be implemented in the Philippines.[74]

Jones' final aspect focused on a society based upon a municipal as opposed to a kinship basis (a 'civil society of free equals ready for self-government'). This meant dealing with the perceived shortcomings of Filipino social organization already touched upon when he discussed individual self-control:

> Aristotle said, 'The state is prior to the individual.' That is, society is originally made up of clans, or families, and the self-conscious, self-willing individual does not emerge until political and economic interests arise that split up these compact groups and cause new alignments in the form of political parties, craft guilds, and religious sects that cut across the original blood relationships and emancipate the individual.[75]

According to Jones, sport would be a useful means of changing the form of social control. Practical efficiency, which he perceived as an important element of Western civilization, and a merit system would be encouraged. Competitions between towns would make it necessary to recruit the most competent local players, instead of relatives and friends, into the team. 'Familiarism' would be reduced and the individual emancipated, but the lack of control immediately substituted with community ties of shared interest to prevent the outbreak of anarchy. For example, in the United States, baseball would be the shared interest of immigrants from various countries, bringing them together and thus serving to overcome social barriers and to integrate them into civil society. In the Philippines, different 'races' like Spaniards, Chinese, Malays, and 'Negritos' as well as 'factions' like *ilustrados* (Jones called them 'aristocrats') and *taos* ('commoners') would be made to cooperate with each other. Again quoting from Wilson's essay on democracy, he described the necessity of a strong municipal self-consciousness as the foundation for the next step in the Philippines, successful American-style nation-building: "Long and slowly widening experience in local self-direction must have prepared them for national self-direction."[76] The FECG and the earlier matches against teams from other countries were the example for reaching this next level. The egalitarian communities, created by increasing the sportive rivalry between them, would be integrated into the *nation-state* (which Jones perceived as the normal form of social organization) by repeating the same procedure on an international level.[77]

All in all, the American aim was to set a sportive modernization process in motion, which initially would shape Filipinos into 'civilized' citizens, which included changing their concepts of masculinity and femininity. White American Protestant norms and values were to replace local ones to encourage egalitarianism and economically progressive thinking through mass amateur sport, meant to support the implementation of a democratic political order and a capitalist economic system.

Collaboration and Partial Resistance: Initial Chinese, Filipino, and Japanese Responses to the Games

During the First FECG, Asians hardly exercised any control over the Games. Americans affiliated with the YMCA organized the Games and were in charge of both the Chinese and the Filipino teams. The ideals of the sportive 'Western civilizing mission' were also not debated by those Chinese and Filipinos, most of them politicians, who gained some influence from the time of the Second Games. Even more important is that for more than a decade, they would not even question the role Americans played in the Games, accepting de facto American leadership as a necessity, since local physical educators were perceived as not yet ready to take over the 'civilizing mission'. Only the very small Japanese delegation remained under its own control, but lacked, as already mentioned, official backing from the JAAA, which was at first unwilling to collaborate with the American YMCA.

On the day after the First FECG began, the *Philippines Free Press*, authored both in English and Spanish and thus addressing both the Americans and the Filipino elite, published an image of 'The New Olympian' (fig. 1.2).[78] With an appearance similar to a white American athlete except for the shape of the eyes, he symbolized the celebrated American ideal of strong, proud, and completely 'Americanized' (or assimilated) Filipinos, Japanese, and Chinese. Another cartoon published by the *Philippines Free Press* on the opening of the Fourth FECG in 1919, held in Manila, depicted the means to realize the ideal (fig. 1.3). A large, grown-up Uncle Sam (supported by *Filipinas*, the national allegory of the Philippines) taught sports values to a Filipino, a Japanese, and a Chinese athlete, all of them depicted as still being children. Even though many athletes really were school boys or young students, the 'civilizational' and power asymmetry displayed in the cartoon is

FIGURE. 1.2

'The new Olympian': The cartoon, published when the First FECG took place during the Manila Carnival, shows the aim of assimilating Asians through sports.

"The New Olympian. Los Nuevos Juegos Olímpicos." *Philippines Free Press* (1 February 1913): 1. (Courtesy of the Library of Congress)

FIGURE 1.3

'Uncle Sam teaching the Asian children sports values': The cartoon, published while Westerners decided Asia's future at the Paris Peace Conference, shows the benevolent but paternalistic treatment of Asians (depicted as children) by Americans at the Fourth FECG.

"The 'Olympiad'. La 'Olimpiada'." *Philippines Free Press* (10 May 1919): 1. (Courtesy of the Library of Congress) obvious, underlining the fact that Asians initially had to accept the dominant role of the American YMCA in the Games.

Chinese Christian politician and diplomat Wu Tingfang attended the First FECG, but limited himself to representative functions. His role did not change much after he was chosen as the FEAA's as well as the contest committee's president for the Second FECG in Shanghai, since the most important positions —the respective secretaries—were awarded to Elwood Brown and John Crocker.[79] Nevertheless, Wu had studied in Hong Kong and England and later held several positions, including that of Chinese minister to the United States, which meant that he had gained a basic idea of Western amateur sport. In his book *America through the Spectacles of an Oriental Diplomat*, published in 1914, one year after the First FECG, he still expressed some doubts regarding modern sport and the success sportive nation-building could have with the Chinese masses. First, he had certain restraints regarding sportive competition. Competition should be a means to an end, but not the end itself. If it was only about competition (which the YMCA rejected), in his opinion the aim should be the exhibition of health and a perfect body, not total exhaustion. Second, he did not think that modern sport would fit into Chinese culture, which valued scholarship much more than physical activity: "They [sports] are too violent, and, from the oriental standpoint, lack in dignity."[80] Third, he did not expect much Chinese interest and could not imagine Chinese people watching other people playing games or buying a newspaper to read the sports section. Fourth, by discussing only male athletes, it becomes obvious that he did not expect Chinese women to engage in sport. Despite these reservations, he was ready to assist in a transfer of modern sports from the United States to China: "They [sports] certainly increase the physical and mental faculties, and for this reason, if for no other, deserve to be warmly supported".[81] Even more, he perceived certain values which modern sports could teach to Chinese boys and young men as very important:

> China suffers because her youths have never been trained to team-work. We should be a more united people if as boys and young men we learned to take part in games which took the form of a contest, in which, while each contestant does his best for his own side, the winning or losing of the game is not considered so important as the pleasure of the exercise.[82]

In Jones's terms, this would be a change in social control, moving from family and clan ties to community and nation. Moreover, Wu conceded a need for fair play as well as the ability to publicly accept defeats, which can be subsumed under individual self-control.[83]

As a result of the Second FECG, hosted in Shanghai in May 1915, Wu's opinion of modern sports seems to have further improved. Japan's Twenty-One Demands, which President Yuan had (partially) accepted only days before the Games began, had made it obvious to many Chinese that China's international decline had hardly been stopped. To Wu, critical of Yuan despite not openly attacking him before 1916, it must have made the impression of the Chinese Revolution's deterioration even worse. For him the hosting of the FECG therefore became a starting point for remedying the situation by accepting Protestant American cultural superiority and by trying to modernize Chinese society through American methods. According to Brown, Wu described the apparently very successful Games as "a great moral force destined to awaken the Orient" and as "the greatest practical contribution that have [sic] yet been made to the modernization and civilization of the Orient, with all the possibilities for the future". He even (unsuccessfully) challenged his generation of people of 70 years or older to run a half mile race.[84] Wu's statements gain even more importance if one considers that in his book he still had, in a typical reaction to the 'Western civilizing mission' and despite being a Christian, perceived 'Asian morality' (here meaning *Confucianism*) as necessary to accompany 'Western materialism', which would destroy feelings of community and shared values.[85] In 1915, he seems to have noticed that the American YMCA's approach to sport had arisen as a reaction to similar perceived deficits such as a loss of morality and of Christian community feelings, which, among other factors, industrialization and urbanization had brought about in the United States.

Another early Chinese supporter of the YMCA was Wang Zhengting (C. T. Thomas Wang), who would later serve as another representative of China in the FEAA. Wang was the son of a Chinese pastor, becoming a charter member of the Tianjin YMCA already during his studies at the newly founded Peiyang University (now Tianjin University). Before he began his studies in the United States, he worked for several years as a YMCA secretary in Japan while studying there. After his return to China in 1911 he served as the associate general secretary and the first Chinese general secretary of the national committee of the YMCA in China, interrupted by about two years spent as a Kuomintang leader during the Chinese Revolution and its aftermath. Later on, the rising politician became one of China's delegates at the Paris Peace Conference, foreign minister, China's first member of the IOC, and an important advocate of governmental bio-politics. In his memoirs, Wang explained that his education by Americans at Peiyang University had had a strong impact on his opinion on modern sport as a scientific approach to health and fitness. The over-emphasis of scholarly activity to pass imperial exams to become a scholar-official and the negative perception of physical strength in China had, he stated, led to a situation in which muscular people were looked down upon.[86] Wang hereby accepted the Western discourse of China's upper class being physically decadent and its military led by undereducated people. Moreover, he considered the education he had received, which included physical education and military training, as decisive for himself and for the 'regeneration' of China:

> This innovation of an age-long ideal of 'a sound mind in a sound body' has brought about revolutionary changes in the life of our students. Those who have been benefited by open-air exercises found themselves in the best of

> health. I was one of these. Being sickly in my life up to the time I went to Tientsin [Tianjin], I was a frail boy, short in stature and poor in health. On my second visit home, that is, two years after I was in the 'new' school [Peiyang University], I grew so much and so strong as to astonish my mother, who had to make new clothes for me not only longer but broader. As I look back in my life I consider that to have good health is the greatest blessing of a mortal being. Because of this conviction I have thrown myself whole-heartedly to the promotion of athletics.[87]

The Second FECG also seems to have had a strong impact on Wang. In an article published after the Games had ended, he explained his observations and provided his own summary of how sport could support Chinese modernization and help China become ready for successful self-government in a Social Darwinist world order. Like Wu he was less systematic than Jones, but his ideas nevertheless came very close to the American ones. The social, cultural, and political benefits of amateur sport were embraced to increase China's power.

First, Wang considered competition the foundation of progress. Moreover, he said the Games had made the whole nation join forces, uniting China's north and south into one team. The Games, and especially the Chinese victory, had also captured the attention of the 'world', making people aware of China regaining its strength. Furthermore, Wang perceived teamwork as a way to overcome the lack of willingness of individual Chinese to cooperate. In addition, sport would teach persistence, necessary to achieve great things, and the physical strength of the Chinese 'race' would be enhanced, showing a eugenic dimension. Without such a recovery, a weak country like China would be conquered and vanish. Wang thus perceived physical education for all Chinese, both men and women, as important. Finally, sport promised a bright future, while a lack of sport would lead to decay. China's aim therefore would have to be to rise to a level where its athletes would be able to defeat Westerners living in the East.[88] The internationalist dimension in Wang's thinking therefore existed, but was relatively weak compared to American YMCA officials, and was regularly tested during the FECG. Internationalism was, however, what constituted the difference between Wang's—representing the pro-YMCA reformers—and, for example, Mao Zedong's thinking. Mao's writings in 1917 (not linked to the FECG) completely lacked this dimension: "The principal aim of physical education is military heroism."[89]

Wu, and even more strongly Wang, saw the spreading of modern sport in China as one of the ways to stop China's international decline and to prevent its elimination. Christian educator and founder of Nankai University Zhang Boling, Chinese President Yuan, Vice President Li Yuanhong, and others both from northern and southern China held similar views. Lacking Chinese experts in physical education, they had to welcome the activities of the American YMCA physical directors.[90] Nevertheless, in contrast to the Philippines in 1913, complete American dominance, meaning the lack of local representatives in the Games, was unacceptable to them. It would mean visually acknowledging a colonial situation comparable to that of the Philippines, a scenario the Chinese actually wanted to prevent through the spreading of sport. The American YMCA, being aware that it could gain influence over China's national physical education system more easily through its Chinese sympathizers and members, also accepted the pro forma Chinese leadership of Wu, Wang, and Zhang as presidents of the FEAA and the contest committee or as representatives of the Chinese government, while de facto being in control for the first six Games events.[91]

As mentioned, no Filipino representative of the Philippines had been chosen for the First FECG. Nevertheless, many Filipinos accepted American education and at least partial assimilation both at public schools and at the newly built American universities as a means to achieve a higher living standard. For example, Macario Bernardo, a law student at the American-founded University of the Philippines who probably had participated as a student athlete in the FECG or had watched them in Manila, had by 1915 publically accepted the YMCA's ideal of egalitarian internationalism. In a semi-academic paper on the Games, he dealt mostly with self-control and the creation of a "social man", thus a new concept of masculinity, in East Asia: "In conclusion, I might say, that the 'Eastern Olympic Games' will be one of the most important means of socializing the people of the Orient in the future. It will make them know the character of the other Orientals, which will mean harmony between them."[92]

Certainly linked with the Filipinization process initiated by Wilson and Harrison in late 1913, national representation became a matter of importance beginning with the Second FECG. For many of the leading Filipino politicians, it was the first step in the direction of sportive self-government, being one of many ways to convince American authorities that Filipinos were ready for independence. The Filipinos' starting point thus was different from that of the Chinese, who tried to rely on Americans to prevent sinking down to the level of a colony and therefore held more Social Darwinist fears. Deliberately advocating the taking up of Western sport and peacefully collaborating with the American YMCA and the colonial administration was a way in which Filipino politicians sought to finally force the US government into conceding that the 'Western civilizing mission' was fulfilled and that colonialism was no longer justifiable.

Jaime de Veyra, a former governor of Leyte, assemblyman, and member of the Philippine Commission, served as the first official representative of the Philippines in 1915.[93] In 1917, Manuel L. Quezon, probably the most important *Nacionalista Party* politician, who would later secure the official promise of independence and serve as the President of the Commonwealth of the Philippines from 1935 onwards, was chosen for the office. The implementation of the Jones Law in 1916 had led to the formation of the Philippine Senate as an upper house, meaning that Quezon as its president was the highest ranking non-American representative of the Philippines.[94] In 1920, Assistant Director of Education Camilo Osías, a leading education politician of the *Nacionalista Party* who had close relations with the Manila YMCA, was elected secretary of the PAAF and served until 1922. Afterwards, he was a vice president until 1929, when he gave up his office upon becoming a resident commissioner in the US. Osías would represent the Philippines abroad at the FECG between 1921 and 1927, the latter being the year when almost complete sportive self-government was reached and a Filipino, Regino R. Ylanan, finally managed the delegation.[95] Ylanan had participated in the early FECG and had been trained by the YMCA at the International YMCA College in Springfield, MA (the future Springfield College). In 1927, he became the second national physical director of the Philippines, an administrative office created mainly through Osías' influence.[96] His American predecessor, Frederick O. England, had initially gone to Manila after Elwood Brown had asked the government for a playground supervisor. In 1922 England had been promoted to national physical director, the highest-ranking civil servant responsible for physical education. Thus, the Filipino delegation first had been under the control of Elwood Brown, working for the American YMCA, and between 1919 and 1925 under the control of American government officials such as Director of Education Walter W. Marquardt, and afterwards England.[97] Despite the success in 1927, when all important positions in the delegation were occupied by Filipinos, complete Filipino self-government in sport could, in contrast to Japan and China, never be realized in the context of the FECG. Until the Games' breakdown in 1934 the Filipinos would have to share responsibility for national representation with the American governor-general when the Games were held in Manila.[98]

In the case of Japan, Brown was eager to challenge the martial arts-based idea of individual training and non-dependence on other players (or warriors), which he perceived as 'backward' and a remnant of former feudalism. Some of the most important amateur norms and values were team spirit and non-violent competition, based on the ideal of egalitarianism and promoted through team sports. It should be mentioned, for example, that participants do not even touch each other in YMCA-invented team sports such as volleyball and basketball. Kanō Jigorō, on the other hand, was especially interested in physical education as a way to shape stronger and healthier soldiers and workers loyal to the emperor and the Japanese Empire. During his lifetime, Japan had experienced a civil war as well as the Sino-Japanese War, the Boxer Uprising, and the Russo-Japanese War. Thus, in the heyday of nationalism and imperialism—the First World War began only one year after the First FECG were held—he considered the defense and support of the empire of utmost importance. Physical training had to be independent of space (such as playgrounds), equipment, and the presence of other people. Moreover, training had to strengthen individuals as effectively as possible. With the exception of judo, which was seen as the best possible training, the first condition allowed for gymnastics, fencing (*kendō*), long-distance running, and swimming, but excluded most team sports. Baseball was still acceptable, since dependence on other team members was limited. Regarding the second condition, however, all team sports would only help in training certain muscles, and athletes would remain idle for parts of the game. Another reason to reject the YMCA's Christian version of team sports and its tutelage, which would put Japan on a level with the Philippines and China, was directly linked to this. Kanō's physical education ideology was deeply rooted in the Bushidō (Way of the Warrior) philosophy of individual honor and the duty of samurai.[99] Elwood Brown, on the other hand, perceived these as 'backward' and 'militarist' ideas linked with 'pre-modern' duals.[100] All in all, Kanō saw team sports as an inefficient and ridiculous way of training imperial subjects, which he did not want to see spreading in Japan. Volleyball, basketball, and soccer, however, were *regularly held disciplines* of the FECG, the others being track and field, swimming, baseball, and tennis. Kanō also had not been chosen by the IOC because he had been particularly interested in the Olympic Games. The Japanese government had suggested him. He even stated that he had had no knowledge at all about Western sports ideologies, including 'Olympism', when he first went to the Olympics in 1912, accompanied by his team of two distance runners. During the following years, his contact with the IOC remained limited due to the First World War, since no meetings or Olympic Games took place.[101]

It was the preparations for and hosting of the Third FECG (1915–17) which marked a turning point in Kanō's thinking. Japanese interest in physical education and fears of 'physical degeneration' seem to have increased at about that time. For example, Franklin Brown of the Tokyo YMCA in 1915 mentioned that many Japanese perceived young people as physically decadent and that amateur sports could help to overcome this. This fear certainly was linked with Japan's involvement in the First World War and, possibly, with the translation of Max Nordau's well-known book '*Entartung*' ('Degeneration'; initially published in 1892), dealing with the 'degeneration' of the body in modern art, into Japanese in 1914.[102] After the Second FECG in spring 1915, public pressure extending from Tokyo to the *Kansai* region (Osaka-Kobe) forced Kanō to finally promise to host the next Games in 1917 in Japan. One of his conditions had been to renegotiate the disciplines after the Games. However, Elwood Brown later stated that he and his YMCA colleague Franklin Brown in Tokyo had personally converted Kanō to team sports through the broad public interest the new sports attracted during the Games.[103] Although Franklin Brown talked only about a partial change of mind, Kanō finally started to accept team sports at Tokyo Higher Normal School and no longer inhibited their spread around Japan. Kanō's own physical education ideology thus had suffered a serious defeat, as Elwood Brown later said, having "crumble[d] before the oncoming recreative element which the young men of Japan simply had to have".[104] Kanō, too, conceded that the YMCA's team sports (and competitive sports in general) evoked more public attention, which would be important for making people take them up, than many other methods of training. He also said that seen from a national standpoint, he would have to accept them, so that Japan would not fall behind in this modern approach to physical education based on the idea of play. The result was an appropriation process. Kanō focused more strongly on internationalism and at the same time deliberated on how judo, which would not be included in the Olympic Games until 1964, and modern sport could be brought together. Encouraging judo in the West as a *scientific* physical education practice and leaving out its *cultural* background eventually helped. One might even say that the preparations for the Third FECG from 1915, their hosting in 1917, and the IOC officially recognizing the FECG in 1920 marked the beginning of Kanō's, until then very limited, career as a promoter of 'Olympism' in Japan, even if it was still a Bushidō-based 'Olympism'.[105]

As a compromise with the YMCA, Kanō had become president of the FEAA for the Third FECG, while Elwood Brown remained the secretary. Franklin Brown, who until then had had only very limited influence in Japanese physical education, became the secretary of the contest committee, the other nine members being Japanese. Elwood Brown had already confided to IOC president Pierre de Coubertin that in contrast to the Olympic movement the officials in East Asia would always be those of the host country (not a mixed group), with the possible exception of the secretary of the FEAA and the contest secretary, since Asians would lack the necessary competence for these offices: "We find in the Orient that these men must be of the white race if things are to move."[106] Since the Japanese were cautious to appear like they did not need American tutelage as the Filipinos and the Chinese did, Franklin Brown had to approach things very subtly: "F. H. Brown's great work in guiding the Games, added to the tactful way he made the Japanese think they were doing it all, has put him in a commanding place in physical education in Japan."[107] Franklin Brown thus also became the contest secretary for the Sixth FECG in Osaka in 1923 and remained a senior advisor until 1930, when he returned to the United States after the Ninth FECG in Tokyo.[108]

All in all, the American YMCA's networking was at its peak from 1917 until 1923, when the Chinese started to struggle for sportive self-government. The hosting of the Second FECG in Shanghai in 1915 and the Third FECG in Tokyo in 1917 strongly increased the YMCA's prestige and, more importantly, gave it access to important Chinese and Japanese politicians and educators willing to collaborate, even though not all of them entirely agreed with the YMCA's sports ideology. This is a very good illustration of the YMCA's attempt to utilize, through 'extension' (advisory policy), the resources of (semi)-authoritarian governmental authorities in East Asia to speed up its 'high modernist' plan, instead of only trying to slowly increase its own local membership and spread its aims via its members. The second chapter will show how this approach started to create problems after government policy changed in the early 1930s. Nonetheless, in 1917, Elwood Brown could still state quite optimistically that the door was now open to spread the Social Gospel via public institutions, as it had already been done in the Philippines: "Association leadership is everywhere accepted. It is our great day of opportunity in the Far East, our chance to establish the best ideals in physical training with these eager people just awakening to an appreciation of the splendor of the human body." In 1904, Bishop Brent had published *The Splendor of the Human Body,*[109] a 'body as temple' theology-based book. The reference illustrates even more strongly that Elwood Brown was not only interested in citizenship training, but also really intended to engage in a regional sportive conversion scheme, which was to begin with accepting the YMCA's Protestant American ideals.[110] After all, John Mott had set the goal to evangelize the world in one generation.

Kanō's decision to make the JAAA leave the FEAA before the Fourth Games in 1919 was only a temporary setback. The Chinese failure at the Paris Peace Conference to force Japan to return the German concessions in Shandong province it had won during the war, as well as the nationalist awakening of the May Fourth Movement and boycotts of Japanese goods, which were direct results of the humiliation at the Peace Conference, had worsened relations between Japan and China. The Japanese Foreign Ministry therefore rejected Japan's participation, while the Ministry of Education complained about the organizers' unwillingness to reschedule the Games so that Japanese student athletes would not miss exams. Since the JAAA still lacked money and obviously got none from the government, Kanō apparently was compelled to take this decision, which in the long run would force him to step down as the JAAA's president. His compliance with governmental pressure provoked resistance from Japanese civil society. Sports officials from the *Kansai* region seceded from the JAAA and set up their own organization, the Japan Athletic Youth Club (*Nihon Seinen Undō Kurabu*), to participate in the Games under the command of the same people who had been in charge during the Second FECG.[111] After this event and after the IOC asked Kanō in 1920 to attend the FECG as an IOC observer, he did not question Japan's participation again.

In conclusion, Filipino and Chinese elites were willing to collaborate with the American YMCA in spreading amateur sport in East Asia. The Filipinos gained limited influence in representing their nation and received the chance to appear willing to support the 'Western civilizing mission', which—in theory—would result in independence after being accomplished. The Chinese, on the other hand, perceived the Games as a tool to modernize their society and to turn China into a unified and efficient country, thus better able to resist imperialism and colonialism. Finally, some Japanese civil society actors were willing to support the YMCA. The JAAA under Kanō Jigorō, however, three times rejected participation. For several years, Kanō was unwilling to accept the American YMCA's Christian-internationalist sports ideology as superior to his own Bushidō-based and more nationalist physical education ideology. The foreign policy tensions between Japan and China also inhibited internationalist endeavors. The successful hosting of the

Third FECG in Japan in 1917 and the IOC's recognition of the Games in 1920 finally made Kanō at least partially accept the aims of the YMCA and its leading role in the Games.

Initial Meeting Grounds and Ceremonies

The American YMCA's aim to educate, not entertain, spectators characterized the staging of the early FECG. It meant that, together with anti-professionalism (and, to a lesser degree, anti-commercialism), the staging was meant to encourage the taking up of amateur sport at home and to teach simple and low-cost approaches to mass sport to support modernization. The Games were also neither to be instrumentalized by politicians for electoral, domestic, or foreign policy purposes except 'civilized' egalitarian internationalism, nor was the program to become too spectacular, for example excessively illustrating 'political' visions of national glory. Furthermore, money in general (necessary for a spectacular staging or to pay professional athletes) was not to become an important issue. All this could draw attention away from the amateur sports themselves. Strictly speaking, this approach would remain the official guidelines until the Third Asian Games (Tokyo 1958).

The meeting grounds and the ceremonies of the early FECG illustrate the main aim of low-cost games: to popularize sport and amateur values. Initially, none of the three participating countries possessed a permanent sports complex. The First FECG were held at the Carnival Grounds at Wallace Field, which is now a part of Rizal Park, the same place where those events had been held that had led to the founding of the Games. The simple opening ceremony was vaguely inspired by the opening program of the Stockholm Olympic Games in 1912. Led by Elwood Brown, Tutherly, and Crone, the three athletic delegations, equipped with flags and emblems of their countries, and about 700 school children marched across the field to the tribune of honor. After Governor-General Forbes had given his speech, some of the children sang a welcome song, the musical accompaniment being provided by the constabulary band. Afterwards, the other children, who had been trained by Elwood Brown, engaged in a callisthenic drill.[112]

On the one hand, the message of a new generation of healthier, more disciplined, and physically stronger Filipinos was communicated, while the spectators learned physical education practices they could take up at home. On the other hand, the three groups of Asian athletes were obvious personifications of their respective nations and therefore actively served in giving their otherwise only imagined national communities a face.[113] Moreover, all three nations were treated as formally equal in the ceremony and were willing to accept each other's presence. It symbolized a more 'civilized' and egalitarian behavior between Asians, which was one of the American YMCA's main goals. At the same time, however, the

American YMCA—not Asians—organizing the Games for Asians and guiding the children visibly underlined the power asymmetry between 'Western teachers' and 'Far Eastern pupils'.

The YMCA also provided part of the infrastructure that the Games needed, such as housing (the idea of an Olympic village did not come up until the 1932 Olympic Games), entertainment, and sometimes the venue where the final trophy award ceremony took place. As one might expect, the YMCA used its influence to spread the gospel to the athletes. During the early Games, teams were often housed in YMCA facilities, where they were encouraged to attend services, listen to sermons, go to church, join Christian associations; they also received Christian publications at Christian events.[114] The first six Games thus seem to not have featured any competitions on Sundays.[115] Simultaneously, entertainment, and sometimes housing, strengthened contacts between the nations participating in the Games and their respective diasporas, in the case of the First FECG Chinese and Japanese overseas communities. The overseas communities normally welcomed the delegations, entertained them at their clubs, and supported them during the Games. Moreover, representatives of the Chinese diaspora, for example in Hong Kong, the Straits Settlements, Hawaii, and the Dutch East Indies, were often part of the Chinese team or at least attended the Games.[116]

During the Second and Fifth FECG in Shanghai, the YMCA received permission to use the sports infrastructure at the Hongkou Recreation Ground (now Lu Xun Park). For the events, the ban on Chinese citizens, who otherwise were not allowed to enter such facilities controlled by Westerners, was temporarily lifted. Moreover, ash trays and grandstands were built. The opening ceremony in 1915 was similar to the one in 1913, the only difference being about 700 Chinese boys, who, in pouring rain, performed a callisthenic drill, which was repeated during the other days of the Games. On one of these days, although not part of the official program, a boy scout competition was scheduled to take place. The scouts were expected to engage in various competitions displaying their wilderness survival skills.[117] One has to agree with Andrew Morris' conclusion that the activities of the Chinese Scouts certainly "highlighted the youthful strength and modern creativity of the young men of China and provided useful reminders of what could be accomplished by properly unified Chinese".[118]

The Third FECG in Tokyo took place at an open space in Shibaura next to Tokyo Bay. Again, a temporary sports complex including a cinder track encircling a volleyball court and a basketball field, a baseball-football field including its own grandstands, tennis courts, and other facilities were set up. The swimming course was formed by damming up part of the bay between an island and the mainland. Apparently the quality of the temporary sports complex was limited, since the wind affected the events, especially on rainy days. A special pavilion was constructed for the imperial princes, Hirohito, Chichibu, and Takamatsu, who attended the Games. Foreign Minister Viscount Motono Ichirō also watched them, while

FIGURE 1.4
'Marquis Ōkuma addressing the Filipino, Japanese, and Chinese athletes at the Third FECG' (Tokyo 1917): For the first time all three countries sent large teams to the Games.
Source: Gregory, "Modern Athletics", p. 199. (Courtesy of archive.org)

former Premier and educator Marquis Ōkuma Shigenobu, by then almost 80 and apparently showing signs of senility,[119] gave a speech during the opening ceremony (fig. 1.4). Some influential members of his cabinet had issued the Twenty-One Demands to China in 1915, meaning that one has to assume that Ōkuma generally was disliked by the Chinese athletes. With these exceptions, the attendance and feedback of Japanese elites was quite limited as compared to the Sixth FECG in Osaka, which will be covered in the next chapter. Franklin Brown later described governmental recognition in 1917 as "scarcely whole hearted", particularly due to an unwillingness to provide *funding*, meaning that the Games were financed by donors and philanthropists.[120] Nevertheless, the Games were the first international games held in Japan and, like the Second FECG in China, opened the country to the region and to a more cooperative and interdependent regional order.

All in all, sports infrastructure was quite limited during the early FECG. In the Philippines, public facilities such as the Carnival Ground could be used. In China, the Hongkou Recreation Ground, which otherwise was closed to Chinese, served as the venue. In Japan, a temporary sports complex was erected, since no facility large enough for the Games existed. More important than the venues were the ceremonies and the educative events, which were used to communicate the message of social improvement through modern sport and amateur norms and values.

Trophies, Medals, and Visions of Asian Modernization

Even more so than the ceremonies and educational events, the design of trophies and medals illustrated the initially dominant role of Americans and their ideals in the Games. However, trophy donation was also important since Asians could articulate their agreement with or doubts about this state of affairs. Due to the initial lack of trophies, until 1923, all of them were the permanent property of the FEAA and had to be returned before the next Games.

All the trophies donated for the First FECG came from the Philippines and had a Western shape. Both the American and the Filipino elite publicly communicated their approval of Elwood Brown's activities of 'uplifting' Asians to Western or American standards. For example, Governor-General Forbes ordered a cup as used in the public school athletic leagues in the United States.[121] Other cups were donated by Filipinos such as Sergio Osmeña, one of the most important *Nacionalista Party* politicians, and businessmen such as Antonio R. Roxas (fig. 1.7), Juan Teus, and Teodoro R. Yangco, a leading YMCA member who would later serve as resident commissioner. More generally, one can even say that such donations were a sign of a comparatively quick acceptance of American colonialism, since, for example, former president Emilio Aguinaldo, retiring from politics for a long time, did not donate a trophy before 1934. Several clubs based in Manila, as well as A. G. Spalding, a sporting goods company that certainly perceived this as good advertising, also donated two cups.[122]

Seen from the perspective of trophies, the Second FECG, hosted in May 1915 in Shanghai, received strong approval from leading Chinese politicians (and their artists). They did, however, decide against Western-style cups or symbols, in favor of their personal view of Chinese authenticity. President Yuan donated a replica of the 'Ten Widows' Arches' (fig. 1.5), a *pailou* (a memorial archway gate), for the decathlon. According to Elwood Brown, the building was located in Beijing, but he might have named China's capital only since it was Yuan's place of residence—there is no evidence that the building is situated there, but many imperial tomb complexes could also have inspired Yuan (or, more likely, an artist close to Yuan and knowing his taste). Brown also stated that the idea had been that each of the ten arches stood for one discipline of the decathlon. On the other hand, he explained that the ten widows were the widows of a former Chinese emperor.[123] What he did not mention, since it did not fit well into American-style sportive modernization, though it must certainly have come to his mind, was that the trophy therefore also stood for the Chinese Empire, not for the new Chinese Republic founded in 1912. After all, President Yuan invested much energy into becoming a new Chinese emperor, which he finally achieved in late 1915, even if only for a short period of time. Vice President Li, dependent on Yuan's support and protection, seems to have supported this mixing of sportive modernization and Chinese imperial tradition. Li donated a trophy for the pentathlon modeled after the Temple of Heaven (fig. 1.6), another symbol of the Chinese monarchy, where emperors (and President

FIGURE 1.5
'Ten Widows' Arches': Chinese President Yuan Shikai donated this trophy in 1915.
Source: Gregory, "Modern Athletics", p. 197. (Courtesy of archive.org)

FIGURE 1.6
'Temple of Heaven': Chinese Vice President Li Yuanhong donated this trophy in 1915.
Source: Brown, F., The Sixth, p. 173. (Courtesy of The Olympic Studies Centre)

Yuan) had for centuries prayed to the gods for a good harvest. Simultaneously, the trophy also stood for the new emerging sports movement in China, since the Second National Meeting, organized by the YMCA as a preparation for the FECG, had taken place on the grounds of the Temple of Heaven.[124]

In strong contrast to the Chinese trophies was the one American IOC members William M. Sloane, Allison V. Armour, and Evert J. Wendell sent the FEAA after the Second Games were successfully hosted. It was a golden laurel wreath, an obviously Olympic-Grecian symbol. The silver cup donated by the Commercial Press, a publishing company interested in sports-related publishing, also followed the idea of using Western shapes.[125]

Trophy donation for the Third FECG in Tokyo was symptomatic of Kanō's and the JAAA's initial rejection of the Games – not a single Japanese (indeed, nobody from any country) donated one. In 1919, President of the Senate Quezon, who had been chosen as the president of the FEAA, apparently felt obliged to show his support and also donated a Western-style trophy, another silver cup similar to the ones used since the First FECG.[126] Finally, after the IOC had recognized the FECG in 1920, Kanō and Kishi Seiichi, his successor as president of the JAAA, who will be introduced in the next chapter, presented two identical silver cups.[127] One has to assume that they considered cups the appropriate shape for trophies for an event now under the patronage of the IOC. It meant that they were willing to accept an element of Western civilization if it was supported by the IOC, but not if it was supported only by the American YMCA and its collaborators. In contrast to the Philippines and China, who still had no IOC members, the asymmetry of not being treated as an equal in the IOC, at least in theory, was not present for the Japanese. Moreover, the events the trophies were used for were the five mile run and swimming. Even though I found no further documents to base this interpretation upon, the two disciplines fitted, in contrast to team sports, very well into Kanō's physical education ideology. The donation was an icebreaker, even though not a single Japanese politician presented a trophy before the Sixth Games in 1923 in Osaka, as will be shown in the next chapter. Japanese behavior, illustrating their doubts regarding the American YMCA's activities, stood in strong contrast to that of American, Filipino, and Chinese elites, who demonstrated their approval through trophy donation.

Medals and emblems (supplementing trophies in some disciplines), on the other hand, were not donated by supporters, but ordered by the respective organizing committees. All of these (until 1927) were under the control of Americans, either YMCA physical directors or officials of the colonial administration in the Philippines. For example, a medal awarded at the First and Second FECG came close to the image of the 'New Olympian' depicted in the *Philippines Free Press* in 1913, mentioned above. It showed an Asian athlete, dressed in Western sports clothes and with short hair (not the traditional Chinese queue, a former symbol of submission to the Qing dynasty) engaging in modern sports (fig. 1.8). An emblem used at the same Games, inspired by R. Tait McKenzie's bas-relief *The*

FIGURE 1.7

'Silver cup donated by Antonio R. Roxas': Roxas donated this trophy in 1913, supporting the founding of the FECG.

Source: Brown, F., *The Sixth*, p. 183. (Courtesy of The Olympic Studies Centre)

FIGURE 1.8 (*LEFT*)

'Medal, Second FECG' (1915): The athlete was also depicted on the medal used in 1913.[128]

Preliminary Announcement. Far Eastern Championship Games, p. 12. (Courtesy of the Bavarian State Library)

FIGURE 1.9 (*CENTRE*)

'Emblem, Second FECG' (1915).

Preliminary Announcement. Far Eastern Championship Games, p. 17. (Courtesy of the Bavarian State Library)

FIGURE 1.10 (*RIGHT*)

'Medal, Third FECG' (1917).

Photo taken by Stefan Huebner, Prince Chichibu Memorial Sports Museum.

Joy of Effort that was entered in the 1912 Olympic art competition, depicted three athletes jumping over a hurdle (fig. 1.9). While again practicing modern sports, the three athletes in the Asian context symbolized the three East Asian peoples meeting on equal terms for the Games. Below them, the slogan 'The Joy of Effort' was inscribed. The emblem therefore incorporated the idea of an egalitarian and economically progressive modernity in East Asia supported by modern sport. The gold medals awarded at the Third FECG in Tokyo were even more characteristic of the YMCA's vision of a modern East Asia. Perhaps due to the strong influence of Franklin Brown, or to a certain lack of interest by the Japanese members of the contest committee, the medal depicted a winged humanoid creature awarding a prize. Looking like a Christian angel, but simultaneously also vaguely reminiscent of the Greek goddess *Nike* (the 'Winged Goddess of Victory'), it had a strong touch of muscular Christianity (fig. 1.10). The motif thus went further than the mere transfer of American Protestant norms and values, and included religious conversion as well.

All in all, the mentioned medals and emblems, even more so than the trophies, communicated the message of muscular Christianity and a Western-style modernization process incorporating formal equality and economically progressive thinking.

Assessment

The FECG, initially the result of a transnational cultural transfer, developed out of Elwood Brown's experiences as YMCA physical director in Manila. Eager to assist in establishing an egalitarian civil society via promoting muscular Christianity based on amateur sports ideals and their 'civilizing' effects, he forged alliances with various organizations. Brown also knew that national championships could serve as an effective way to attract East Asian interest in modern sports and to spread them via 'contagion', since other forms of visual transmission were still very limited. Furthermore, he started to consider sport to be the 'least common denominator' between different peoples, such as Americans, Filipinos, and others, who would otherwise not meet for recreational reasons. The FECG therefore can be seen as one link in the developing chain of Brown's ideas, which would finally make him try to globalize muscular Christianity via national and regional sports events modeled after the FECG and to be held in other 'backward' regions. 'Play for all' implied that as many people as possible in as many East Asian countries as possible should be encouraged to take up amateur sport. Females therefore were included, even if they did not participate as athletes in the early FECG. This proclaimed universal dimension was typical both for the 'civilizing mission' and for Christian missionary activities, trying to make certain Christian ideals binding for everybody and to 'evangelize the world in one generation', as John Mott had intended. As part of its 'civilizing' aim, amateur sports would overcome 'unnatural barriers' and reduce social and political tensions, within societies and between peoples. Christian citizenship training, a form of cultural transnationalism promoted by the YMCA as a non-governmental organization, thus was to serve both in individual nation-building and in establishing a regional community of nations based on shared values. However, in Japan, in contrast to China, the Games met partial resistance. JAAA president Kanō Jigorō, who considered team sports an inefficient training method for shaping better soldiers and workers, had already developed his own Bushidō-based physical education ideology and did not want to have Americans put Japan on the same level with China and the Philippines. Nonetheless, Elwood Brown and Franklin Brown, as well as public pressure, convinced Kanō to host the Third FECG in Tokyo in 1917, which became an important turning point and spurred a process of internationalization and appropriation in Kanō's thinking. Simultaneously, the American YMCA's regional integration scheme was not only a counter-model to 'realist' views of an anarchic world 'order', which drove the European great powers into war in 1914. It was also a counter-model to a community of mere mass consumers of sports mega events, who do not necessarily live according to certain values, but only share entertainment interests, and of small groups of professional elite athletes, whose main aim is to win, as encouraged by commercialism and professionalism.

Modern scientific sport was also considered a substitute for certain traditional recreational activities in the 'Far East' such as cock-fighting and gambling, demonstrating the goal of spreading the 'Protestant work ethic'. The promotion of amateur sports values and Christian concepts of masculinity and femininity, especially through team sports, was a means to alter traditional customs and behavioral patterns such as lying, 'loss of face', aggressiveness, strong hierarchical thinking, and clan orientation. The ideal of economic progress, however, was less important (although not totally unimportant) for Elwood Brown, than for the American colonial administration.

This does not mean that collaboration with the Forbes administration, which was also interested in more 'civilized' Filipinos, could not be fruitful. Obviously, Brown hoped to extend the influence of the YMCA on the national physical education program in this way. His initial successes in the Philippines were definitely one of the reasons for the creation of the FECG. In Japan and China, the Games opened many doors for the YMCA, if only for a limited period of time, as will be shown in the next chapter.

Finally, the staging of the early FECG was relatively inexpensive and simple. One of the reasons was the educative message of the Games. At all FECG calisthenics, simple games, and sometimes wilderness survival techniques were performed, in line with the idea of popularizing mass sport and physical education, and appealing to those people who would never become highly skilled athletes. The staging therefore was the visual implementation of the YMCA's ideal of a Christian modernity—meaning internationalist, egalitarian, and economically progressive –through amateur sports. Traditional elements of Asian culture were relatively rare, but not nonexistent, as illustrated by President Yuan's and Vice President Li's trophies. The staging was a manifest demonstration that—at least for the time being—Filipino, Chinese and eventually Japanese elites were willing to accept, or at least to not openly question, the leading role of both benevolent and paternalistic Americans and their ideals in the organizing of a sports event primarily held for Asians. Muscular Christianity thus has to be seen as the root of most of the early international sports activities in East Asia.

CHAPTER 2

The Far Eastern Championship Games and the Western Asiatic Games in the 1920s and 1930s: 'Games of the Asians, by the Asians, for the Asians'

"In the Physical work nationally there has been no difficulty with the local associations but in the country as a whole there has appeared considerable disapproval of Foreign leadership in National Athletic Organizations. I feel that American leadership has about passed out of the Far Eastern Athletic Association, to be taken over by the people of each country in turn."[1]

—John H. Gray, the YMCA's National Physical Director in China, informing his superiors in late 1923 about Asian struggles for sportive self-government

In the early 1920s, it was obvious to American Young Men's Christian Association (YMCA) officials such as Elwood Brown and Franklin Brown that, should they hand over responsibility to Asians, the existence of the Far Eastern Championship Games (FECG) and their ideals would be jeopardized by the seemingly neverending political animosities between China and Japan. Even though the American YMCA's activities were intimately entangled with other forms of Western colonialism via the 'civilizing mission' rhetoric, their aim was not to create discourses of Asian inferiority to justify prolonged colonial rule over a certain territory. Instead, the American YMCA's objection reflected a cultural-religious fear that Asians had insufficiently embraced norms and values it considered Protestant and were, as a result, not yet able to 'save' themselves on their own. The American YMCA therefore was, if possible, to make its control over the Games permanent. Power should only be transferred when the education and assimilation of their Asian 'pupils' had reached *such a degree* that sportive self-government, meaning allowing Asians to bear the sportive 'civilizing mission' and to spread common amateur ideals on their own, would not jeopardize the American YMCA defined aims.

The core problem was the reduced credibility of the 'civilizing mission' rhetoric after the horrors of the First World War and, more importantly, US President Woodrow Wilson's supposed betrayal at the Paris Peace Conference. The result was a strong growth of anti-colonial nationalism in Asia, which included claims of national and Asian *'awakenings'*, since increasing numbers of Asians now considered it necessary to overcome *'oppression'* on their own—two topoi that will regularly come up in this chapter.[2] The growth of anti-colonial nationalism led not only to the above mentioned foreign policy problems between China and Japan, but also reduced the Asian, especially the Chinese, willingness to accept an 'unequal' partnership wherein American YMCA officials acted as paternalistic superiors rather than advisors to Asians. The result was an Asiatization process of the Games, which led to them eventually being almost completely organized by Asians.

The Asiatization process also had a significant impact on power relations between the Asian delegates, especially between Japan and China. Moreover, the process affected the symbolic staging of the Games, which continually grew in size. Similar things are true for India, which since the 1920s had attempted to host a regional sports event in West Asia. These efforts resulted in the Western Asiatic Games (WAG) of 1934. In India, the Asiatization process also affected the staging, but the organization of the WAG encountered so many problems and failures that the image of Indian backwardness was hardly challenged. In this regard, one can thus draw a direct line between the problems of the WAG and those of the First Asian Games, which will be covered in the third chapter.

This chapter deals with the Asiatization process the FECG experienced in the 1920s and 1930s. One element of this process was a leadership transfer from Americans to Asians, meaning that Asians took over responsibility for Asian affairs. Another element of the process was the integration of the Games and of amateur sports ideals into local cultural backgrounds to give them more authenticity and reduce the Christian dimension. The chapter also focuses on similar events in India and on the breakdown of the FECG, when Chinese and Japanese visions of East Asian integration became incompatible.

The Changing Political Situation in East and South Asia in the 1920s and 1930s

The 1920s in East and South Asia were strongly influenced by Woodrow Wilson's call for a 'new diplomacy' of multilateralism and international cooperation. In Japan, Wilson's ideas were not entirely rejected by realistic civilian leaders, even though their implementation meant giving up most of the gains made in China during the First World War and even potentially endangering Japan's concessions in Manchuria. Non-cooperation was, however, not a realistic option for Japan, since allies were not available. The Japanese government thus deemed it necessary to integrate their country into the new Anglo-Saxon world order. In the 1920s, Japanese foreign policy was therefore characterized by multilateral internationalism. Relations with China remained problematic, but did not escalate into a full-scale war, which can be considered a result of 'Shidehara Diplomacy', named after Foreign Minister Shidehara Kijūrō, who served in several cabinets between 1924 and 1931.[3] Japanese domestic affairs responded to the boom of democratic thinking following the First World War, created in parts of the world by the founding of the League of Nations and the breakdown of monarchies in Germany, Austria-Hungary, the Ottoman Empire, and Russia. However, political dissent and particularly its left-wing manifestations in Japan remained suppressed.[4]

In 1920s China, civil society developed and anti-colonial nationalism grew, fueled primarily by foreign policy events. At the Paris Peace Conference in 1919, the Japanese had been allowed to keep the German concessions in China's Shandong province, which they had gained during the war. The May Fourth Movement, the 'beginning' of Chinese nationalism as a mass movement, emerged immediately after as an anti-imperialist protest against the great powers' disregard of Chinese territorial rights. Only through a bilateral treaty, concluded as a part of the Washington Treaty System established in 1921/22, did Japan eventually return sovereignty of Shandong province to China.[5]

However, the growing popular anti-imperialist nationalism meant that the Chinese warlords, too, had to pay lip service to the protection of China's territorial unity and integrity. In March 1923, the Beijing government repudiated all treaties based on the Twenty-One Demands and demanded the return of the Kwantung Leased Territory that Japan had gained after the Russo-Japanese War. After Japan refused, another wave of popular boycotts and demonstrations erupted. Between 1926 and 1928, Kuomintang forces led by Chiang Kai-shek—Sun Yat-sen had died in 1925—commenced the Northern Expedition to defeat the warlords in northern China. Compromising with the Japanese, who wanted to keep them out of Manchuria, the Kuomintang eventually agreed not to invade, but gained formal control over the region as a part of China. China thus became reunited under a single government, though it was at best a formal unity.[6]

In Chinese domestic affairs, nationalism and a 'democratic-socialistic' society were of importance. Sun Yat-sen's 'Three Principles of the People'—nationalism (*minzu*), democracy (*minquan*) and livelihood (*minsheng*)—provided his highly interpretable legacy and the theoretical basis for constructing a modern state. Sun described the 'Principles' as being inspired by Abraham Lincoln's principles from the 'Gettysburg Address': government *of* the people, *by* the people, and *for* the people. Chiang would follow Sun's 'Principles' and justified his autocratic rule as a necessary transition period of Chinese elites—not foreigners—'civilizing' the Chinese masses. Chiang also had close contact with Christian organizations; his wife Soong May-ling, whom he married in 1927, was a Young Women's Christian Association (YWCA) leader. By 1928, five of eight ministers in the Kuomintang cabinet were Christians.[7] The idea of Western amateur sport as egalitarian, internationalist, and economically progressive citizenship training thus all in all was compatible with the Kuomintang's modernization aims.

As a result of the Great Depression, which began in 1929, Japanese geopolitical interests finally clashed with strongly increasing Chinese anti-imperialist nationalism. In September 1931, Japanese officers began eliminating local military resistance in Manchuria. In early spring 1932, steps were taken to completely cut the territory off from China by making local collaborators declare the region an independent country—Manchukuo. In 1934, a foreign ministry spokesman also declared that other powers should not intervene into Sino-Japanese relations, a stance that contradicted the Washington Treaty System. These actions reflected a foreign policy now explicitly based on Japanese-led, not egalitarian, pan-Asianism, serving to support its expansion in East Asia.[8]

In the Philippines, the *Nacionalista Party* politicians began to demand complete independence after Tokyo had accepted the Washington treaties and thereby the territorial status quo in East Asia. Nonetheless, the Republican administrations in office between 1921 and 1933 had no intention of complying with these demands. On the contrary, the Filipinization process, which had gained momentum during the presidency of Woodrow Wilson, was slowed, although not completely stopped. Its results were claimed to have demonstrated that Filipinos were not yet ready for self-government, and it was impossible to say when they would be. In late 1932, during the Great Depression and amidst domestic agitation against the Philippines as an economic burden, things finally started to move. The Tydings-McDuffie Act of 1934 promised the Philippines independence after a transition period of ten years of self-government.[9]

In terms of the 'Western civilizing mission', many politico-cultural similarities between British-dominated India and the 'Far East' can be found. British colonial rule had produced various images of Indians as degenerated inheritors of a once great civilization and India as a country of superstition, corruption, sexual perversion, and despotism. British colonialism therefore would be the way to 'uplift' and 'civilize' India. As a reaction to Western colonialism and images of Indian civilizational inferiority, but also as a means to inspire fellow Indians to take on more social responsibility, intellectuals such as religious reformer Swami Vivekananda in the late nineteenth century and Literature Nobel Prize winner (1913) Rabindranath Tagore in the early twentieth century, especially after the catastrophic First World War, attempted to 'reinvent' India and Asia. Drawing on Western discourses about Asia as a spiritual continent, they reduced Western modernity to its 'materialist' dimension of science and technology, while a 'rediscovered' ancient Indo-Asian civilization was declared the source of the 'spiritual' energy necessary to complement it. Their writings had immense impact on the educated classes in India and led to the emergence of a nationalistic image of Asia as a 'Greater India', which served to depict India as a 'civilized country'. Moderate nationalists such as Indian National Congress politician Jawaharlal Nehru limited themselves to mentioning pre-colonial cultural-religious contact between India and many other Asian counties. Hindu nationalists went further, declaring Hinduism and Buddhism the same religion and declaring in an 'out of India-theory' that large parts of Asia—especially East (including Southeast) Asia—had been 'civilized' through Indian culture and religion.[10]

Similar to the East Asian countries, interwar India was characterized by a growing anti-colonial nationalism. Since the Paris Peace Conference had brought no important change in the status of colonial peoples, demands for *Swaraj* (self-rule within the British Empire) became more intense, while Indian resistance became better organized and less violent. Mohandas Gandhi, leader of the Indian National Congress since 1920, also desired a stronger unity between the different castes and religious faiths. In contrast to Gandhi, modernizers such as Nehru imagined a democratic-socialist modernization and an industrialization process to create an India able to hold its own with the Western great powers. Meanwhile, the semi-independent rulers in the Princely States, whom Britain tried to bind to itself through education and culture, were often sceptical of the Congress' message of liberation. Some of them supported a modernization process, but had little intention of giving up their power.[11]

Sportive Pan-Asian Aspirations I: Chinese Anti-Colonial Nationalism, Japanese Internationalism, and the American YMCA's Retreat (1921–25)

Boycotts of the FECG by Chinese civil society actors and government officials illustrate how East Asian foreign policy issues and anti-colonial nationalism jeopardized the Games' message of egalitarian internationalism. After (Great-) Japan Amateur Athletic Association (JAAA) president Kanō Jigorō's boycotts of the FECG in the 1910s, now Chinese boycotters began denying this ideal, which they perceived as collaboration with Japan. The boycotts of 1921 and 1923 thus perpetuated the American YMCA's belief that the Chinese in particular were not yet ready for sportive self-government and were unable to continue the 'civilizing mission' without American supervision. The boycotts even resulted in a crisis within the American YMCA over the question of whether to give up the Christian internationalist project or to enforce it by further increasing control over it. The Japanese government and civil society actors, in contrast, increasingly supported the Games, a stance which was symptomatic of Japan's internationalist foreign policy in the 1920s. Moreover, one of the results of the secession of the *Kansai* region in 1919, covered in the previous chapter, had been Kanō's stepping down as JAAA president. The role was taken up by Kishi Seiichi, a leading lawyer who had practiced Western amateur sports during his studies at Tokyo Imperial University and was less critical of them than Kanō.[12]

During the Fifth FECG, hosted in Shanghai in May 1921, the tensions between Japan and China were overcome only through the intervention of the American

YMCA. This point in time was still characterized by strong anti-Japanese outbursts in China, since the Japanese withdrawal from Shandong was not officially agreed upon before winter 1921/22. For the first time, Chinese sports officials, even those who were leading YMCA members, intended to show their anti-Japanese sentiments by boycotting Japanese participation. Wang Zhengting, now an important diplomat and businessman, had been elected president of the Far Eastern Athletic Association (FEAA) and of the contest committee. Elwood Brown, since 1919 secretary of physical education in the YMCA's foreign department in New York, had to convince him to support egalitarian internationalism instead of giving in to nationalistic reactions against Japanese imperialism:

> It devolved upon him to sign the invitations or notices to Japan and the Philippines. At that particular time he was the leading spirit in the group of Chinese business men in Shanghai who were urging a boycott of all things Japanese. He felt that it would not be consistent for him to be the active backer of the Japanese boycott plan and at the same time to have an active part in a plan to bring Japanese to China on a friendly basis.[13]

Wang finally informed (not invited) the Japanese delegation to participate, but limited contact with them as much as possible. As one might expect, Elwood and Franklin Brown thereafter tried to further increase the YMCA's control over the Games to prevent their breakdown as a result of the international tensions in East Asia. In Franklin Brown's view, a major problem was that the main organizer in 1921, their YMCA colleague John H. Gray, hardly tried to suppress the anti-Japanese behavior at the Games, because he saw Elwood Brown's project of the FECG and other regional games as a waste of the YMCA's time and money. In contrast to the Philippines and Japan, hosting international games in a politically fragmented and 'backward' country such as China would be a futile endeavor, since no efficient central government existed that could be utilized to finance the YMCA's modernization plans or to implement them in public schools. Gray later also stated that, in his opinion, training more local YMCA leaders and physical educators would have been the better option.[14] This attitude of a fellow YMCA national physical director of letting the Games be affected by international tensions instead of using the former to serve in overcoming the latter was summarily rejected by Franklin Brown.[15]

Even worse in his view was that Gray's stance sabotaged his and Elwood Brown's attempt to increase control over the Games. After Elwood Brown had convinced the relevant people in the Philippines, the Japanese delegates declared that they were willing to support Franklin Brown becoming the permanent secretary—or at least serving for a period of six years (i.e., three Games)—of the FEAA. This attempt to further strengthen the American YMCA's control over the Games nevertheless had to be dropped because the strong anti-Japanese stance of the Chinese made it unrealistic that they would accept permanent headquarters in Tokyo.[16] Even more problematic for Franklin Brown was Gray's apparent inability to retreat to the position of a gray eminence, as he himself had done, who would de facto have more influence than the official Japanese delegates. Gray would thereby, in not giving the Chinese more self-government, endanger his position in China by attracting some of the anger created by Western and Japanese colonialism. The makeup of the delegates at the meeting of the FEAA had visibly demonstrated Gray's deficit in encouraging official Chinese representation: "China—*two Americans* and one *Chinese*; Philippines—*two Filipinos* and *one American*; Japan—*three Japanese*. The only Chinese to open his mouth at the meeting was the President." According to Franklin Brown, choosing at least two Chinese delegates would also have made a much better impression on the Japanese, who accepted Americans speaking for Filipinos, but would be skeptical regarding American dominance of Chinese issues.[17]

The Japanese delegation consisted of JAAA leaders who were for the first time attending a FECG event hosted abroad by the American YMCA and its supporters. They indeed got the impression of an immense American influence over the Games. This influence was further illustrated by the fact that almost all referees were Americans (or British), which resulted in claims that the Asians were mere puppets in an American puppet theatre.[18] For the time being these anti-colonial feelings did not affect their further participation. However, they certainly fueled aspirations regarding an Asiatization of the Games in the long run, which—as an unintended outcome—later resulted in regular complaints about nationalistic or biased decisions by *Asian* referees.

The anti-colonial reaction came soon afterwards as a result of the Sixth FECG in May 1923 in Osaka.[19] Anti-Christian movements had further fueled nationalism in China and Chinese boycotts of Japanese products had erupted again in March 1923 after the Japanese government proved unwilling to retrocede the Kwantung Leased Territory. The problem in May was not that Japanese athletes were to be invited to China despite anti-Japanese boycotts. Instead, it was that the Chinese team would have to attend Games held under Japanese control, which many Chinese—Franklin Brown called them "earnest but misguided patriots"—strongly opposed.[20] The fact that Gray—instead of a Chinese official—led the comparatively small delegation defying the boycott and gave the speech for the Chinese team during the opening ceremony, combined with the rather poor performance of the Chinese athletes, caused a wave of anti-colonial criticism that eventually drove him out of office. One can thus argue that Gray's expectations of sooner or later losing control over Chinese sports resulted in a self-fulfilling prophecy. Nonetheless, Franklin Brown still wielded a lot of *informal* authority even in 1930, when the American YMCA was already in the process of aborting its foreign work due to insufficient donations from American philanthropists suffering from the Great Depression. Gray's decision to give the opening speech for the Chinese demonstrated that he had no intention of being so subtle. The following quarrel between the YMCA-controlled and a newly founded amateur sports association caused Gray to make the statement quoted at the beginning of the chapter on the American YMCA losing its influence. In July 1924, the two organizations merged into the China National Amateur Athletic Federation (*Zhonghua quanguo tiyu xiejinhui*), which limited Gray's role to that of an advisor. China had gained sportive self-government and from then on, the Chinese would try to handle the sportive 'civilizing mission' themselves.[21]

In Japan, no boycotts of China or the Philippines took place in 1921 or 1923. While Chinese civil society actors increasingly rejected egalitarian internationalism if Japan was involved, large sections of Japan's political elite began to show open support for the Games after the partial boycotts of 1913, 1915 and 1919. This support was an outcome of international and domestic factors. The speeches given at the Games in 1923 reflected Japan's adjustment to the new international system based on the Washington treaties that advocated cooperation, interdependence, and demilitarization. Prince Chichibu, who served as the patron of the Sixth Games, declared in his address, "[it] is my fervent desire that you, the participants in the present Far Eastern Games, who I believe fully understand the aims of such events, will do your utmost and contribute to the further development of the true spirit of sportsmanship."[22] Kanō, as the representative of the International Olympic Committee (IOC), followed this line, linking the FECG with the Olympic movement and thereby giving the internationalist project a more global dimension. Minister of Education Kamada Eikichi's congratulatory message after the Games and Mayor of Osaka Ikegami Shirō's closing address also dealt with East Asian sportsmanship and cooperation.[23]

This newly emerging broad support for the Games from leading Japanese politicians and members of the royal family also reflects domestic changes during the early part of the interwar period. It illustrates that the American-style modernization process now received official governmental support, which the American YMCA had tried to gain from the beginning. The socio-cultural implications included, for example, a growing number of Japanese citizens taking up modern sport recreationally and the founding of clubs and national associations for various sports. Another consequence was a stronger focus on sport at certain schools, even though Swedish gymnastics were dominant, showing that conformity and hierarchical thinking still played an important role.[24] Similar events also happened in other countries undergoing a democratization process after the First World War. For example, Weimar Germany experienced a comparable boom in competitive sport, which challenged traditional norms, values, and behavioral patterns of both male and female majority culture.[25] The same, though on a much smaller level, is true for India and for *many* other countries affected by Elwood Brown's *global attempt* to set up further regional games, as discussed in the first chapter, and by the YMCA's own transnational sports program.[26]

To sum up, the growing anti-colonial nationalism in China had manifested itself in two serious challenges to the FECG's aim of egalitarian East Asian regional integration. These were overcome by the American YMCA, though it lost its influence on (or control over) the Chinese in the process. In contrast, in Japan the new foreign policy in the 1920s as well as the increased, though still limited, democratization within the country had ended the period of boycotts that had characterized the 1910s. Japanese elites started to show approval of the FECG and the American YMCA's ideas of egalitarianism and internationalism.

Sportive Pan-Asian Aspirations II: Visions of a 'Chinese National Awakening' and of Asian Cooperation at the Eighth FECG (1927)

Rhetoric of 'civilized' interaction and of East Asian regional integration based on egalitarian internationalism always had a certain paternalistic and colonialist touch when it came from American YMCA members such as Elwood Brown, Franklin Brown, or John Gray. The Asiatization process meant that now Asians took over. As a result, not only the athletes but also the officials managing the Games personified Asian kinship instead of a 'teacher-pupil' relationship between Americans and Asians.

Shen Siliang (William Z. L. Sung) organized the Eighth Games in Shanghai as contest secretary. Shen had been trained in the United States at Oberlin College and Columbia University and had returned to China in 1923, where he became head of the physical education department at St John's University in Shanghai. There, he aspired to improve the still problematic situation of amateur sport in China.[27] Before the Eight FECG commenced, Regino R. Ylanan, a trainee of the American YMCA and now a government official, had taken over as the national physical director of the Philippines. He headed the Philippine delegation. JAAA vice president Hiranuma Ryōzō represented the JAAA at the Games, since Kishi could not leave Japan. Hiranuma was a businessman and Japanese Upper House member who was purged from his public offices after the Second World War, but some years later was elected mayor of Yokohama. Moreover, he had taken up Western sports during his studies at Keiō University and later became involved in the physical department of the Yokohama YMCA. He also had been the head of the 'secessionist' Japan Association of Athletic Federations that had split from the JAAA and seems to have been less willing to listen to Franklin Brown.[28] Brown's lack of influence in 1927 therefore can be interpreted in the light of a growing anti-colonial nationalism, at least among younger Japanese officials, who intended to finally bring the Games into the hands of Asians. Many of the Asian officials thus were affiliated with local YMCAs or had been trained by the American YMCA, even though their willingness to be patronized by Americans significantly decreased. This closeness to the YMCA network meant that the promotion of amateur sports norms and values as a means for regional integration, either as muscular Christianity or, in a secularized form, as egalitarian and internationalist citizenship training, continued. Strong tensions between Japan and China in 1927, due to the Kuomintang's Northern Expedition, thus did *not* end in a boycott of the Games by the Chinese or Japanese.

To have the Eighth Games organized by Chinese officials was a chance to illustrate—and *propagate*—their capability for successful sportive self-government and for taking over the 'civilizing mission' from the Americans. Vice-Foreign Minister Guo Taiqi (Quo Tai-chi), who had been educated in the United States and had attended the Paris Peace Conference, represented the Kuomintang government, which had by then already gained control over large parts of southern China.[29] His speech at the opening ceremony integrated the Games into the nationalist movement in China and the Kuomintang's struggle to unite and reform China into a modern state able to survive on its own in a Social Darwinist world order. His speech illustrates the newly gained hope, fueled by anti-imperialist movements and especially the Northern Expedition, that the Chinese people in a 'national awakening' would finally be willing and able to overcome China's semi-colonial status not only in sport, but in general. Chinese achievement of self-awareness as a nation was also declared a precondition for a more serious sportive pan-Asianism to be promoted by the Games. This pan-Asian dimension of the Games, which now combined the above mentioned Asian 'kinship' of athletes and officials with the internationalist element of Western amateur ideals, was then suggested as an example for a possible change in East Asian foreign policies:

> This is the first meet managed entirely by Chinese. This is symbolical of New China, it is in keeping with the Nationalist movement. We are in our way adjusting ourselves to meet the demands of a modern world! We in our way are working for our own national salvation to be attained only by our strenuous efforts. You represent the flower of young manhood of the renascent Orient, alert, physically fit, and under keen self-discipline. You, together with our own young men, represent the hope of the Pacific. You will, I trust, learn from each other, and try to understand and appreciate each other's national aspirations and problems. You have a golden opportunity to learn from each other during this congenial gathering. You will carry the spirit of fairplay that characterizes clean amateur sportsmanship and friendly rivalry into your future life work; fair play that is essential in international dealings, and in everything concerning human intercourse. It does not matter much whether games are lost or won, if they are fairly and well played. A game can be honorably lost the same as it ought to be justly won. To you collectively and individually this meet means much, but to the future of friendly international relations among the three nations represented, perhaps it means more.[30]

It does not matter here whether Guo truly believed in *egalitarian*—certainly what he was hinting at with 'fair play'—sportive pan-Asianism, or just used it for political purposes such as to prevent the Japanese from attempting to further disturb the Northern Expedition. His contemplation about turning Japan into an ally to 'regenerate' the 'Orient', meaning to potentially get rid of both Japanese and Western imperialism, either expressed pan-Asian idealism or the idea of using one 'barbarian' to check another. In any case, his pan-Asian discourse certainly was not without earlier foundations. Sun Yat-sen had been a strong advocate of political pan-Asianism, and in his well-known 1924 speech in Kobe, Japan, had argued for a united front of Asian nationalist movements against European oppression. In his speech Sun had urged the Japanese to decide if they intended to support the despotic Occidental 'Rule of Might' or the Asian 'Rule of Right', based on equality and the emancipation of Asia from colonialism and unequal treaties.[31] One year later, in 1925, Kuomintang Foreign Minister Wu Chaoshu (Wu Tingfang's son) had attended the Seventh FECG and there argued for a Chinese national uprising against the warlord government in Beijing as a means to unify China, certainly as a first step toward fighting Western imperialism.[32] Moreover, the FECG had been fostering regional integration through common amateur norms and values for more than fourteen years, thus making the Games a reasonable platform for Guo's linking of anti-colonial nationalism and Asianism. Foreign policy issues between China and Japan also failed to create obstacles similar to those that had spawned the boycott attempts of 1921 and 1923.[33] However, Guo explicitly did not exclude the possibility that sportive pan-Asianism might completely fail in the long run ('perhaps it means more'). The Games, then, still served to popularize mass sport in China and to show Chinese competence. This was still useful for China's own 'national regeneration' plan and, ultimately linked to it, national defense purposes. In any case, the rising Kuomintang had more to gain than lose through the FECG.

Camilo Osías, meanwhile, had been elected as a senator for the *Nacionalista Party*. He, too, saw no problem of authenticity in using Western amateur sports values as a tool for a more concrete pan-Asian project of regional integration. After all, the important officials were now all Asians: "The Olympiad is an opportunity to establish friendship which may serve as capital in the future for an effective pan-Orientalism. The program of the association's activities should contribute to the development of a pan-Orientalism of intellect and spirit based on broad sympathies."[34]

After the Games, Yamamoto Tadaoki came to similar conclusions as Guo and Osías. Yamamoto was a professor at Waseda University and a leading YMCA member who served as a JAAA delegate to the Games.[35] He focused on Asian control over the event, cooperative behavior by the delegates, and successful people's diplomacy via the athletes showing sportsmanship. Since all these factors came together for the first time, the Games were perceived as a breakthrough. He nevertheless also valued the Games and sports in general as a tool for 'national regeneration' through overcoming the perceived slackening in spirit (*ki*) of the Japanese, which he certainly saw as an outcome of the country's modernization process.[36]

The activities of the leader of the Japanese delegation, JAAA vice president Hiranuma, are also noteworthy in the context of regional integration based on the ideal of egalitarian internationalism. At the same time they provide further evidence for the Japanese appropriation of Western sport mentioned in connection with Kanō Jigorō. The Christian dimension of amateur sports norms and values was substituted with Japanese cultural elements to give them authenticity. After their ship had left Japan, Hiranuma explained to the team that everybody must behave according to *Bushidō*-based sportsmanship and fairness, thus linking his demand to interpretations of national honor and to Zen-Buddhism. In his speech at the opening ceremony, he furthermore declared that international goodwill would be the aim of the Japanese delegation.[37]

In conclusion, the Eighth FECG were strongly affected by the Kuomintang's Northern Expedition and by Chinese feelings of a 'national awakening'. That Chinese, instead of Americans, organized the Games and thereby showed their capability in sportive self-government further contributed to these feelings. This 'awakening' as a nation, which meant taking China's future into their own hands and finally overcoming colonialism and 'national weakness', was simultaneously described as the precondition for a serious project of pan-Asian regional integration. Japanese and Filipino delegates agreed that the Eighth Games had been a breakthrough.[38]

Sportive Pan-Asian Aspirations III: Indian Participation, Further Visions of Regional Integration, and their Cultural and Geographical Limits at the Ninth FECG (1930)

The Ninth FECG, taking place in May 1930 in Tokyo, were still strongly influenced by the ideal of egalitarian internationalism, which in the pan-Asian context of the Games included reducing the power asymmetry vis-à-vis the West. It was not only Japanese, Chinese, and Filipino officials who supported that goal—so did a newly arrived Indian delegation. Nonetheless, despite pan-Asian claims based on common amateur norms and values and on Asian 'kinship', financial issues showed the geographical limits of Asian integration. Moreover, the still strong influence of Franklin Brown reminded the Asian officials of the Protestant American origins of the Games, which they could not shed so easily.

In the official Japanese rhetoric no major changes had taken place since 1927. Japanese elites such as Prince Chichibu, who again served as the official patron of the Games, Minister of Education Tanaka Ryūzō, Prime Minister Hamaguchi Osachi, who had sent an address, and JAAA president Kishi continued to bring up common amateur norms and values as the means to egalitarian and peaceful regional integration. Moreover, the JAAA's official report described the Games as a symbol of the "rising Orient".[39] While Kishi had demonstrated his belief in amateur ideals many times before, the discourses of the politicians are more interesting. They, too, seem fitting, since the Hamaguchi administration, based on 'Shidehara Diplomacy', was still trying to continue a policy of international cooperation and disarmament. In 1930, the year the Ninth Games took place, Japan even recognized the Kuomintang government.[40]

Jorge B. Vargas had been chosen as the new representative of the Philippines after Camilo Osías became a resident commissioner in 1929. Vargas is another example of the first generation of American-educated Filipinos eager to take over the sportive 'civilizing mission' from the Americans, spreading its rhetoric, and trying to integrate it into their local cultural background. Vargas had been trained at the newly established University of the Philippines, after which he began climbing the ranks of the government bureaucracy, becoming under secretary of agriculture and commerce in 1928 and a minister, the Secretary to the President of the Philippines, in 1935. During the Second World War, he advanced to chairman of the Executive Committee, the civil administration set up by the Japanese invasion forces, and ambassador to Japan (1943–45).[41]

Since his youth, Vargas had shown a strong interest in modern sports, especially tennis. He had watched the First FECG in Manila and had accompanied Philippine representative Jaime de Veyra as his secretary to the Second Games in China in 1915. From 1918 until 1935, Vargas served as a member of the executive committee of the Philippine Amateur Athletic Federation (PAAF), becoming its president in 1935 and the Philippines' first IOC member in 1936.[42] In terms of amateur sports norms and values, Vargas strongly advocated sportive citizenship training.[43] He did not explicitly identify the norms and values as Protestant ones, though he hinted that he considered living according to them to be the result of an appropriation process that brought him much closer to American Protestantism, especially Baptism.[44] However, Vargas did not change his Catholic denomination, meaning that he represented those very liberal Philippine Catholics influenced by American Protestantism who were uneager to attract, through conversion, the wrath of conservative Catholics. Vargas also described Elwood Brown as a "liberal-minded American", whose efforts to modernize East Asian societies he valued highly.[45] On the other hand, some of Vargas's activities can serve as an example, similar to the Japanese and Chinese boycotters in the 1910s and 1920s, that in the view of the American YMCA, he was very likely another Asian who had insufficiently embraced amateur ideals. In some cases, Vargas seems to have been quite willing to give these up in favor of foreign and domestic policy gains or for personal reasons.[46] However, in his speech at the opening ceremony Vargas promoted common amateur norms and values as a means of advancing egalitarian internationalism, serving both regional integration and overcoming the power asymmetry between the 'Orient' and the West, at least in terms of sport. His rhetoric thus fitted well into the general rhetoric at the Games and hinted at the need to eliminate the 'inferiority' of Asians compared to Westerners:

"We will naturally try to win in all of the games if we can, but whether we win or we lose, we shall consider our efforts and sacrifices well rewarded only if after the conclusion of these games we will have known another better, understand each other more fully, our friendship stronger than ever, and the standing of the oriental athlete demonstrated to be the equal of any other."[47]

The participation of an Indian team in the FECG was completely new, since its participation had been canceled in 1927.[48] The head of the three athletes, Sharajit Kumar Mukerjee (sometimes Mukerjie), was the YMCA's physical director in Calcutta (Kolkata), secretary of the provincial Bengal Olympic Association, and had been trained at the International YMCA College in the United States (the future Springfield College). In 1931, he accepted a professorship at the University of Bombay (Mumbai) and, after India's independence, went into business.[49] The participation of this small Indian delegation, representing Asian 'kinship' since it was, as all the other delegations, led by an Asian, did not challenge but rather strengthened the pan-Asian atmosphere of the Ninth FECG. Moreover, Mukerjee's speech at the opening ceremony especially emphasized this Asian 'kinship'. His speech therefore is strongly reminiscent of the speeches given at the 1927 Games, but now connected India to this East Asian discourse. In another similarity, Mukerjee also supported common Western amateur ideals as the means for egalitarian regional integration in Asia:

> First, India is claiming her rightful place among the oriental nations. India is realizing that she has just as much to learn from as to contribute to the Japanese, Chinese and Filipinos—her own kith and kin. Secondly, India has not only come to compete in the Championship Games, but has also sent her chosen Champions as ambassadors to convey to their brother and sister Champions of Japan, China and the Philippine Islands the spirit of peace, good-will and friendship.[50]

Earlier on, after he had arrived in Japan, Mukerjee had already dealt with the pan-Asian dimension of the Games in another way: "It [coming to Japan to participate] was one of the signs of India progressing in nationality among other Asiatic nations, and it was a renewal, on the basis of sport, of the intimacy of intercourse that existed long ago in the domain of religion and literature."[51] Mukerjee thus described the FECG as a modern addition to ancient forms of pan-Asianism and of Indo-Asian civilization. In doing so he was certainly influenced by the religious and literary discourses Swami Vivekananda and Rabindranath Tagore, among others, had spread in India and which had been the foundation on which Indian nationalists had based their ideas of Asia as a 'greater India'.[52] Mukerjee nonetheless has to be considered a moderate nationalist, since his pan-Asian discourse did not explicitly mention India as the country dominant in what he called an ancient 'intimacy of intercourse'. In comparison, his discourse is much closer to Jawaharlal Nehru's at the First Asian Games in 1951, covered in the next chapter, than to those of the organizers of the WAG in 1934, discussed below.

Rash Behari Bose can serve as a representative of a stronger Indian anti-colonial nationalism. Bose was a revolutionary who, after failing to assassinate the British viceroy in 1912 and instigate a military uprising in 1915 during the First World War, had fled to Japan. In Tokyo, he had joined pan-Asian circles and during the Second World War, would become strongly involved in the founding of the anti-British Indian National Army. During the Ninth FECG, he and some supporters lowered the flag of the British viceroy at the Indian delegation's accommodation, leading to a dispute concerning national representation. In the end, both the viceroy's flag and the Indian National Congress flag were flown, even though only the viceroy's flag was permitted in the stadium.[53]

India was not made a member of the FEAA, which underlined the geographical—and financial—limits of sportive pan-Asianism. The explanation Mukerjee received was that the Indian delegation was too small to be taken seriously as a member; India should send a bigger one next time.[54] However, a significantly larger delegation—China and the Philippines had both sent more than 100 athletes and the Dutch East Indies would send 27 in 1934—was, as *everybody* knew, very unrealistic, since transportation costs were too high. Indian teams to the Olympic Games had regularly lacked money.[55] The financial problems the Indian organizers of the WAG and First Asian Games would encounter later will further illustrate this problem. One certainly has to assume that Kishi also did not trust the general quality of games hosted in colonies such as India or the Dutch East Indies, if they could be financed at all, and did not consider the former a 'Far Eastern' country.[56] The amateur character of the FECG meant that money was relatively scarce and that foreign delegations needed to find donors or receive funding from their governments to pay for their trips. Large-scale sportive pan-Asianism, at least in a geographical sense of regional integration, thus was not possible for another two decades since the necessary funding was simply not available. Elwood Brown's plan to establish *two* regional events in Asia thus still served as a guideline.

One last, influential person to be mentioned in connection with the pan-Asian rhetoric of the Ninth FECG and its Protestant origin is no Asian, but Franklin Brown. The JAAA had not asked him to become the contest secretary, but he was still involved in several committees.[57] During a meeting he convinced the Asian FEAA officials that changing the Games' title from 'Far Eastern' to 'Oriental', which Camilo Osías already had suggested in 1927 to emphasize the Asian instead of the American influence in the Games, would not be helpful.[58] Brown's arguments highlight that he tried to discourage what he might have seen as the anti-Western activism of a group of Asians trying to overcome an inferiority complex driven identity crisis, but unwilling to give up the blessings that Protestant American civilization had brought them, which nonetheless were the root of that identity crisis. One also has to assume that he had personal reasons not to support this blunt, though only half-hearted, attempt by the Asian officials to reduce connections to the American origin of the Games. His first argument was that 'Orient' would, like 'Far East', still be in the English language. This was certainly true and it reminded the audience that the use of English as the language of the Games had, for practical reasons, never been an issue during the FECG even after Asians gained control over them. This was a noteworthy difference to the Asian Games, as will be discussed in the next chapter. One nonetheless has to assume that 'Orient', though having connotations of 'backwardness', sounded somewhat better in the ears of the Asians than 'Far East'. The 'Orient' could also be interpreted as the complement to the 'Occident' and could, as mentioned in the introduction to this chapter, be filled with various claims of a spiritual superiority to challenge 'Western materialism'. 'Far East', in contrast, was a term signifying a region 'far east' of *Europe*, which then served as the center of the world. Also very interesting is Brown's second argument that a renaming would result in unnecessary confusion and the FEAA giving up a branding it had created via nine events. In the end, the Asians accepted his advice, though the topic arose again in 1934 and the founding of the Amateur Athletic Association of the *Orient*, covered below, was certainly an outcome of this anti-colonial pan-Asian mood.

All in all, the second Games primarily hosted by Asians passed without major problems. Officials from Japan, China, the Philippines, and India had represented Asian 'kinship', while they and the Japanese elites had advocated the ideal of egalitarian internationalism. The integration of India, nonetheless, had been incomplete, since the regional focus remained limited by insufficient funding and still high transportation costs for traveling between East and South Asia. The Games had also shown that, despite some anti-Western claims, the Asian officials did not really attempt to extinguish the American Protestant influence in the Games. The main aim thus had been the transfer of power from Americans to Asians.

Sportive Pan-Asian Aspirations IV: The End of the 'Far Eastern' Championship Games (1934)

After the Japanese army's conquest of Manchuria in 1931/32, the Kuomintang government was unwilling to officially recognize the loss of territory. Japan's new foreign policy and Chinese resistance against it ended the vision of egalitarian pan-Asian integration through peaceful mutual cooperation, at least on the level of the FEAA's officials. Several studies have already been written about the history of the events leading to the breakdown, which need not be repeated here in detail.[59] The Japanese are normally considered the culprits in the breakdown, having dissolved the FEAA together with the Filipino delegates. In terms of events this is certainly correct, but it basically sees the events from an ex-post perspective, situating them in a sequence leading to the violence and destruction caused by the Second Sino-Japanese War and the Pacific War, and finally Japan's defeat. It does not fully take contemporary perspectives into consideration. The following re-evaluation is, however, meant to determine neither a moral responsibility for the breakdown (the criteria are too vague) nor the status of Manchukuo, which despite not being officially recognized by some Western great powers and Kuomintang-China, de facto existed for more than a decade outside the reach of the Chinese administration.

First, all Japanese actors intended to make Manchukuo a member of the FEAA, be it as a colony, similar to the Philippines, or as an 'independent' country. There was, however, great disagreement as to whether this should take place by upholding the ideal of egalitarian internationalism or not. The Imperial Japanese Army demanded that the JAAA boycott the Games if Manchukuo was not admitted.[60] Its supporters, such as physical educator Okabe Heita, who had gone to Manchuria before the conquest to improve relations between the local Chinese and Japanese via sport, advocated a strong, pro-Manchukuo stance.[61] Okabe had been trained at several American universities and after his return to Japan, had left Kanō's judo headquarters, eventually getting involved in the power struggle between the JAAA and other Japanese sports organizations in the 1920s.[62] Okabe also considered amateurism a contradictory ideology unable to solve the political question of participation or boycott.[63] He certainly had a point when declaring that sport and politics could not be separated, at least if one considered egalitarian internationalism, which included taking China seriously as a formally equal partner, to be a *political aim* and not a *moral duty*. So boycotting the Games, as he suggested, would be no more political than if his opponents took travel funding from the Ministry of Education. His stance, after all, served to enforce a different version of egalitarian internationalism, which included giving Manchukuo the right to participate as a *formally equal partner*. One has to see his view as the outcome of a more general paradigm shift in Japan, which was marked by Japanese dominated pan-Asianism now becoming an officially accepted and even supported alternative to Western civilization and the Washington Treaty System.[64] Sympathizers of the army and of Okabe also assaulted the Japanese team during its training for the Games and threatened JAAA officials.[65] However, JAAA vice president Hiranuma, de facto the most influential person in light of Kishi's death in 1933 and the ongoing vacancy of the office of JAAA president in 1934, and others were against a boycott. They feared that it would prevent further negotiations about Manchukuo. Shortly before the Japanese team, reduced in size due to athletes deciding against participation, had boarded their ship under tight security, Prince Chichibu reminded Hiranuma to act according to amateur ideals and not to boycott or leave the Games. Hiranuma thus, according to his memoirs, decided to delay the discussion about the inclusion of Manchukuo until the Games were over to prevent such a possible negative outcome.[66]

Second, the Chinese side generally disagreed with Manchukuo becoming a member. In contrast, for example, American diplomats declared that the question of Manchukuo taking part in the Games or not was irrelevant for them and only a matter for the FEAA: "The Far Eastern games are simply an athletic event and the question of Filipino athletes competing against the nationals of a nation not recognized by the United States is considered to have no diplomatic importance".[67] IOC president Baillet-Latour also was curious as to why China would agree to French Indochina, which had once been under Chinese control, becoming a new member of the FEAA in 1934, but would block Manchukuo.[68] This difference highlights that the Chinese anti-colonial nationalism that had grown continuously throughout the 1920s, too, was an obvious obstacle to continuing the internationalist project in its current form (which, arguably, had benefitted from China's weakness). The Chinese side was unwilling to officially recognize Manchukuo in any form, while the question of Indochina had already been officially settled about 50 years ago. Moreover, Jorge Vargas, the Philippines' main delegate, later stated that, as in the post-war case of mainland China denying the de facto independence of Taiwan, the new Chinese nationalism had been unwilling to accept the reality of power relations in 1934.[69] After the Filipinos had offered a compromise in the form of not making Manchukuo a member of the FEAA, but allowing a team to participate as India had participated in 1930, the Chinese delegation refused to accept this and left the meeting. Japanese journalists simultaneously cabled home the news that their delegates had agreed to the Philippine compromise, which meant that the next host country—China—could conceivably choose to not invite Manchukuo. This seems to have led to an uproar among ultranationalists, about which the delegation was immediately informed, increasing their fear of violent consequences at home.[70] What is important is that at the end of the meeting on 20 May, the Filipinos were not willing to dissolve the FEAA or to continue discussions.

Apparently, during the following night and morning hours, the Japanese devised a 'good cop, bad cop' scheme to make them give up their compromise idea and to cooperate in dissolving the FEAA.[71] Abe Kitarō of the Japanese delegation (a 'good cop') in his memoirs stated that he, with tears in his eyes, had visited Vargas during the night and had begged him to continue discussing the issue the next day.[72] This must have been an important (and very annoying) event, since Vargas eventually agreed to open another meeting. The Filipinos thus were definitely not helpless victims and must have been quite aware that the important Chinese minority in the Philippines would react negatively.[73] Since I think that a senior civil servant like Vargas was not impressed but rather bored by the 'good cop, bad cop' scheme, the main reason for the Filipinos' cooperation probably was that the Chinese delegates decided not to show up, even after several hours spent waiting for them, and that the Japanese seem to have offered *concessions*.[74] For example, after dissolving the FEAA, the delegates immediately founded a new organization, the Amateur Athletic Association of the Orient, its name now implementing Camilo Osías' earlier demand regarding Asian authenticity ('Orient' instead of 'Far East'). With the exception of the absence of China (which was asked to join the new Games), the inclusion of Manchukuo, a modification of the admission rule, and the different title, nothing changed.[75] At bottom, the situation in 1934 was not that different from earlier situations such as those in 1915, 1919, 1921 and 1923, when strong international tensions had arisen between Japan and China due to Tokyo demanding concessions or not retroceding territory. The ideal of egalitarian regional integration had been almost constantly attacked by nationalistic groups and governments, but this time, in contrast to former events under the control of American YMCA officials, neither the Japanese nor the Chinese were willing to openly oppose these groups.[76]

Third, except for the major Philippine newspapers, almost nobody cared that the Filipino and Japanese delegates dissolved the FEAA. In 1936, the IOC, for instance, perceived the FECG to be no longer relevant since Japan (1912), the Philippines (1924), and China (1932) had all begun to participate in the Olympic Games. Independent of that, the Asians would have until 1938 to solve the issue and could, as the IOC concluded, join the newly created WAG.[77] Other signs that the dissolution was deemed unimportant were that Vargas had no problems in becoming an IOC member in 1936 and that Japan was awarded the 1940 Olympic Games that same year. One has to come to the conclusion that the real reason for the end of the FECG—if one does not consider the games hosted in the late 1930s and early 1940s or the Asian Games as their continuation under another name—was not the sleight of hand in 1934, but full-scale war between Japan and China since 1937.

All in all, the core problem in 1934 was that the ideal of egalitarian internationalism, which was supported through amateur sport, only worked as long as political borders did not change violently. The creation of Manchukuo could be seen either as aggression against China or as the (aggressive) liberation of the territory from an opium- and gambling-addicted warlord aligned with the 'incompetent' and anti-Japanese Kuomintang government. Egalitarian internationalism would reject both forms of aggression against a formally equal partner, which already brings up a moral problem. The real contradiction came into focus when the question of how to proceed with a now de facto existent Manchukuo emerged. If one accepted the act of aggression as a given and focused on the status quo, which was likely if one considered it justified, egalitarian internationalism made it necessary to treat Manchukuo as formally equal and give it the right to participate in the Games. If one did not, and focused on the status quo ante, it would be necessary to reject participation and to return Manchuria to China. It was, and here Okabe Heita was right, not possible to come to a definite solution within the framework of amateur ideals, since the two strings of argumentation are based on the same core ideals, though the (temporal) conditions are different. The Asian officials were unable to solve the contradiction and thus had to rely on power relations. After the Chinese had rejected what the Filipinos considered a compromise offer, the Filipinos cooperated with the Japanese to solve the issue by dissolving the FEAA and setting up another sports organization excluding China and including Manchukuo.

Sportive Pan-Asian Aspirations V: Sports in India and the Idea of Western Asiatic Games (1934)

During the 1920s and 1930s, India experienced events in the development of amateur sport quite similar to those in East Asia. In India, too, American YMCA officials had had a prominent role in establishing national structures, organizing competitions, and sending teams abroad.[78] The promotion of sport and amateur norms and values nevertheless was limited by many political, cultural, religious, and economic factors such as limited funding, malnutrition, and tensions between different religious groups and castes. Moreover, in another similarity to East Asia, Indian officials had taken over the most important offices in the late 1920s, though the American YMCA remained an advisory organization and was still very influential on the provincial level. Inspired by plans of the American YMCA, in 1930, an Indian team had participated in the Ninth FECG in Tokyo and in 1934, the First WAG were held in New Delhi and Patiala.[79]

John Gray, who served in South Asia before and after he came to China, had become active in India in 1908, and in 1913, a physical education department had been founded within the colonial administration. Britain's and India's involvement in the First World War, however, prevented the hosting of any major events. In 1920, the IOC had accepted Elwood Brown's suggestion of the Indian Empire Games or Indian Olympic Games (now called the National Games). Afterwards, American YMCA physical directors Harry C. Buck, Arthur G. Noehren, and John Gray gained control of Indian sport on the national level. The approach was similar to that followed in East Asia. The YMCA lacked the financial means and manpower to spread amateur sports completely on its own; thus hosting the Indian Olympic Games served promotion and networking purposes. Contact partners for its networking were, like in East Asia, the public administration and Western-educated elites. In the case of India this meant the colonial administration, provincial parliaments, and especially the industrialist Dorab Tata, who in 1920 became India's IOC member. Using these connections, the YMCA College of Physical Education, which trained generations of physical educators, was, also in 1920, set up in Madras (Chennai). When the Indian Olympic Games were finally established in 1924, they drew to Delhi athletes of different ethnicities and religions including Hindus, Muslims, Anglo-Indians, and Sinhalese, illustrating the YMCA's egalitarian ideal.[80] India at that time nonetheless lagged behind by almost one and a half decades, compared to the American YMCA's activities in China (First National Meeting in 1910) and the Philippines (Carnival of 1911).

Despite this late start, an Asiatization or Indianization process regarding officials had taken place in the late 1920s. The Indian delegation to the Ninth FECG in 1930 was led, as already mentioned, by a YMCA-trained Indian, S. K. Mukerjee. Another important official was Guru Dutt Sondhi, who in 1927 took over the office of secretary of the Indian Olympic Association after Arthur

Noehren left India. Sondhi, a professor of economics and political science at Punjab University in Lahore and later the principal of the Government College (now Government College University), had been a hockey player and runner during his studies in India and at the University of Cambridge. Previously, in 1924, he had become secretary of the provincial Punjab Olympic Association. Sondhi also had close contact with Bhupinder Singh, the maharaja of Patiala, who in 1928 had succeeded an already very old Dorab Tata as the president of the Indian Olympic Association.[81]

Sondhi's case serves to illustrate the secularization process of amateur sport in India. Like the YMCA, he perceived sport as a tool for Western-style citizenship training and valued team games and low-cost events very highly. Sondhi nevertheless did not envision, or at least did not advocate, an explicitly Christian or any religious form of amateur sport. One has to assume that the linking of amateur norms and values with a particular religion in a heterogeneous and non-Christian country like India seemed to him both not useful and likely to attract resistance. Vaguer terms such as 'Indian spirituality', however, could provide Western sport some authenticity and facilitate its spreading by integrating it into the local Indian context. This would also explain why Sondhi was more sympathetic to 'Olympism'—he succeeded Tata as India's IOC member and attended his first meeting in 1932—than to the YMCA's muscular Christianity. However, this did not inhibit him from working with the YMCA and using some of its and the IOC's main concepts. He later, for instance, said that the development of the *trinity* of body, mind, and spirit was most important in sports. The opposite of this ideal were "new-time gladiators" determined to win by any means, who would, not guided by egalitarian and internationalist ideals, be "made to fight for National Glory".[82]

Sondhi and the maharaja of Patiala had at first been heavily criticized, for one, by John Gray. They were in his view "a semi-interested small group of people" not capable of being accepted by most of the other provinces. Dorab Tata, too, had uttered doubts regarding the maharajas in general, feeling they would primarily be interested in prestigious upper-class sports such as hunting and polo, but not in 'simple' and low-cost mass sports such as track and field. Moreover, as Boria Majumdar and Nalin Mehta have shown, the rivalries between different Indian sports officials and between the maharajas, who were their patrons, were quite strong, since the latter especially perceived sport as a tool to gain prestige.[83]

Only in 1931, did Sondhi become active and resurrect the American YMCA's plan for regional games in what he considered 'West Asia'. One might assume that he was both encouraged and shocked by the poor performance of the Indian team at the Ninth FECG in 1930.[84] Regional games in West Asia would keep travel costs low and provide India with less experienced opponents than those at the Olympic Games—hockey being the only discipline in which India had excelled since 1928—and the FECG. Since the African Games had been prevented by Britain and France in 1929, as was briefly mentioned in the first chapter in connection with rising Chinese anti-colonial nationalism, the expectations of the IOC were low.[85] Sondhi nonetheless sent letters to at least Afghanistan, Burma, Ceylon, Malaya, the Hejaz, Iraq, Nepal, Palestine, Persia, Siam, the Straits Settlements, Syria, Turkey, and apparently also to French Indochina. He thereby employed a broad definition of 'West Asia', covering everywhere between Singapore and the Suez. He did not receive a single answer. After Sondhi came back from the 1932 Olympic Games, the plan became more concrete and he began sending invitations to the same countries for the First WAG to be held in New Delhi and Patiala in 1934. Reactions were again poor, though very small teams from Ceylon and Afghanistan were eventually attracted. Moreover, the YMCA network, which had also served in establishing the FECG, was utilized. The Jerusalem YMCA sent a small group of athletes, while similar attempts by the YMCA in Burma and Iraq failed. The Persian government was unable to put a team together, but nominated its diplomatic representatives in India as delegates.[86] The rest of West Asia, due to financial problems, lack of interest, and possibly pressure from the colonial regimes (including travel restrictions) remained absent.

Similar to S. K. Mukerjee at the Ninth FECG, the Indian organizers in 1934 integrated the WAG into discourses about the relationship between the West and the East:

> A clarion call to the youth of Western Asia, it [the WAG] was a movement, advocating a sporting fraternity. Some historians have expressed an opinion that the ancient Greek [Olympic] Games were practically of Asiatic origin. Be that as it may, the Western Asiatic Games are an attempt at a synthesis of the ideals of physical and mental fitness of Ancient Greece and of the ideals of Brotherhood and unity of the East. Thus the Scheme not only looked back to ancient Greece, but actually revived the Eastern ideals of sportsmanship, which formed an integral part of the cultural education of the ideal state of ancient India. Our sacred books and mythologies abound in anecdotes emphasizing the foremost place which athletic-training occupied amongst our Aryan ancestors who participated in horse-races and chariot races, not only for the sake of keeping their horses and themselves fit and strong but also for the thrill that they offered.[87]

This time the dualism of a 'spiritual East', or Asia, based on ideals of 'unity' and 'brotherhood', and a more 'materialist West', characterized by 'fitness', was created. Like in similar discourses produced, for example, by Tagore or Vivekananda, claims of the superiority of Western civilization were thereby denied. More precisely, authenticity for India's sportive modernization process was 'invented' by using the traditional physical education practices of Aryan (Indo-European) peoples. Chariot racing itself was obviously not to be revived, but its spiritual dimension and modern amateur sports norms and values were declared to be the same. A Western spiritual contribution from, for example, ancient Greek religion or American Protestantism was outright denied. In terms of spirituality, India therefore was presented not as becoming more Western, but as going back to its roots. In racial terms, Indians were declared to belong to the white race. Moreover, a minor blow was also aimed at the authenticity of the ancient Olympic Games as an early product of Western civilization. Based on still vague research on the expansion of the Indo-Europeans, and certainly influenced by the nationalist 'out of India-theory', the Olympics were said to be potentially of Asian origin.[88] If true, it would further upvalue the image of Indo-Asia, implying that not only the 'spiritual', but also the 'materialist' ('fitness') dimension of the WAG were offspring of the 'ancient Indo-Asian civilization', which would, in consequence, turn the WAG into an entirely Indo-Asian event. All in all, these dramatic-sounding claims contained a strong element of Hindu nationalism.

A second staging of the WAG never took place. Sondhi had decided on a rotation scheme to determine the host country (a system the FEAA de facto also used), but Afghanistan in 1937 declared that it would be unable to host the Games in 1938. Palestine, experiencing the Arab Revolt (1936–39), gave up in May 1938. By then Sondhi had lost his position as secretary of the Indian Olympic Association to the principal of Bihar National College in Patna, S. E. Moin-ul-Haq. As secretary of the provincial Punjab Olympic Association, Sondhi suggested to the Indian Olympic Association that Lahore might be able to host the second WAG in spring 1939, but this was not realized. The Indian Olympic Association rejected his resolution in October 1938, claiming that few countries would participate anyway.[89] The staging of the First WAG, which will be covered below, had been very poorly done, not presenting Sondhi's organizing skills in the best light. This, possibly in combination with an anti-Sondhi mood in the Indian Olympic Association and perhaps a lack of foreign feedback due to financial issues, indifference, or British interventions, has to be assumed as the reason for the rejection. From autumn of 1939 until 1945, Britain's—and India's—involvement in the Second World War made a second WAG even more unrealistic.

All in all, the WAG, like the FECG, aimed at spreading amateur sport as egalitarian, internationalist, and economically progressive citizenship training in West Asia. Similar to events in East Asia, Indians assumed control of the Indian Olympic Association in the late 1920s. The WAG were therefore an attempt by Indians to take over the American YMCA's 'civilizing mission'. This attempt included substituting muscular Christianity with more secular 'Olympism' and hints at a 'spiritual East' as a necessary complement to an allegedly only 'materialist West', but otherwise they accepted the aims. The WAG nonetheless hardly had the impact that the FECG developed in East Asia. Not even a second event could be organized.

Modernization, Media, and Masses of Spectators

It is impossible to definitively determine the number of people who came into contact with the FECG or WAG via watching them in the stadium, viewing films and newsreels about them in the cinema, or being informed by newspapers or the radio. In the case of Japan and the Philippines, one can assume that large parts of the population were reached. In China, knowledge of the Games might have been significantly more widespread in urban areas, where Westerners lived, than in the many still relatively remote villages. John Gray after the 1921 FECG thought that of 400 million Chinese, about one quarter (100 million) knew about modern sport and less than five per cent (20 million), almost all living in big cities strongly influenced by Western civilization such as Hong Kong and Shanghai, had accepted them.[90] The same is probably true for India and West Asia, though since the WAG took place only once, even in cities knowledge of them might have been limited to Western-educated Indians. However, it is possible to provide at least some basic information on the numbers of participants, the number of spectators drawn to the athletic grounds or stadia, and on media coverage.

As the following table shows, from 1921, when the JAAA began regularly sending athletes to the Games after the boycotts of 1913, 1915 and 1919, the number of *individual* athletes (which sometimes was lower than the overall number of entries, since athletes participated in several events) from the Philippines, Japan, and China remained relatively high. The turbulent situation in China in 1923, when the American YMCA had to deal with a protest against the team going to Japan, had an impact, but the number of athletes remained comparatively high. The same is true for 1930, when the Great Depression certainly had a financial impact, and 1934, when some Japanese athletes left the team to protest the exclusion of Manchukuo from the Games or due to threats from ultranationalists. In comparison, the size of the team from the Dutch East Indies, and even more so the one from India, looked slightly pathetic. The difference hints at not only less developed athletic standards in these colonies, but also at the financial difficulties (i.e., transport costs) involved.

Table 2.1 Estimated Numbers of Individual Athletes at the FECG (excluding officials and coaches)[91]

FECG	Philippines	Japan	China	India	Dutch East Indies	Total
1913 (Manila)	~80	13	36			~129
1915 (Shanghai)	67	14	154			235
1917 (Tokyo)	103	154	91			348
1919 (Manila)	102	14	92			208
1921 (Shanghai)	142	96	110			348
1923 (Osaka)	143	183	103			429

Table 2.1 ***(cont'd)***

FECG	Philippines	Japan	China	India	Dutch East Indies	Total
1925 (Manila)	175	140	120			435
1927 (Shanghai)	149	174	170			493
1930 (Tokyo)	150	191	115	3		459
1934 (Manila)	186	132	134		27	479

A comparison of the number of athletes at the FECG to those at the WAG makes the latter's organizational problems obvious. The numbers were, even compared to the First FECG, marginal.

Table 2.2 Estimated Numbers of Individual Athletes at the WAG[92]

WAG	India	Ceylon	Afghanistan	Palestine	Total
Patiala and New Delhi (1934)	≥42	8	25	≥5	≥80

The number of spectators entering the stadia and athletic grounds during the FECG is significantly more difficult to determine. The American YMCA published numbers and later official reports also provided vague information, but it is impossible to judge whether these are correct or not. Many people certainly attended more than one match, which means that the number of *individual* visitors was most likely below the *total* numbers provided below. Different types of tickets (single, family, season) add to the problem of comparing tickets and estimated numbers of spectators. If one considers the FECG a 'civilizing project' for Asians, one also cannot distinguish how many Asians and how many Westerners attended (nor how many men and how many women), though the Asians were certainly in the majority. Another problem is that it is not always clear whether the Open International Games were included or not. Finally, the relatively small population of the Philippines (~10 million; Manila: 300,000) compared to Japan (~65 million) and China (~400 million),[93] the different capacities of the respective sports venues, and the impact of bad weather on attendance should be considered when comparing the numbers. Despite all these methodological problems, one can definitely say that over time the number of spectators rose strongly in each country, alongside a growing interest in sport and an increasing number of events.

Table 2.3 Alleged Total Number of Spectators or of Tickets Sold[94]

FECG	Alleged Total Number of Spectators or of Tickets Sold	Claimed by
1913 (Manila)	~150,000 (Carnival tickets) ~75,000 (FECG tickets)	Elwood Brown, YMCA
1915 (Shanghai)	90,000–100,000 (spectators)	L. C. Wilson, YMCA
1917 (Tokyo)	~60,000 (spectators)	Franklin Brown, YMCA
1919 (Manila)	significantly fewer than 60,000 spectators	*Philippines Herald*
1921 (Shanghai)	~155,000 (spectators)	Official Report, FEAA
1923 (Osaka)	~250,000 (spectators)	Official Report, FEAA
1925 (Manila)	57,000–60,000 (spectators)	*Philippines Herald*
1927 (Shanghai)	~330,000 (spectators)	*Graphic*
1930 (Tokyo)	~547,600 (tickets)/400,000–450,000 (spectators)	Official Report, JAAA/ *Graphic* + *New York Times*
1934 (Manila)	~200,000 (spectators)	*Manila Daily Bulletin*

Providing information on the WAG is more problematic. The second day of the swimming events in Patiala was said to have lured 2,000 spectators to the grounds, which might mean that a total of 4,000 spectators (the number of individual spectators therefore ranging between 2,000 and 4,000) saw the two days of events. These events however also included the third All-India Aquatic Championships.[95] In New Delhi, head organizer Sondhi had asked the chief commissioner to declare a half-holiday, but was informed that this could not be done. Based on the resulting very low gate fees (no other information could be obtained), one can vaguely guess that a total number of about 5,000–10,000 spectators (about 10,000 tickets) might have watched the two days of events in New Delhi.[96]

Growing media attention is highly important, since it served to communicate the FECG's contribution to East Asian modernization and development processes to a broad audience. Strictly speaking, this included the development of East Asian media infrastructures, which reflects the increasing public interest in and consumption of sport and the FECG, especially since the 1920s.[97] While increasing numbers of East Asians profited from improvements in the media infrastructure, the different media's reporting about the Games could be directly turned into money: newspapers (I here include news magazines) sold more copies, films and newsreels produced entrance fees, and radio broadcasters could justify fees or inspire more people to buy a radio. Moreover, the American YMCA used lantern slide presentations within the United States that showed images of its educational activities abroad. Some of the slides also featured images of ongoing Asian backwardness, implying the message that the successful YMCA, if properly funded by donations, would be able to overcome this remaining benightedness too.[98]

The emergence of newspaper companies as 'big business' between the 1910s and 1930s was of great importance for popularizing the Games. An increasing number of people not only became interested in sports and other news, but also had become literate due to public school systems.[99] Starting with the First FECG, many newspapers reported on the Games, some of them even publishing special gravure sections or supplements on them.[100] Due to the close connection of the Philippines to the United States, several big American newspapers also provided basic information on the Games, which they obtained via their branch offices or through news agencies such as the *Associated Press*.[101] The same is true for China, and here especially for Shanghai, where newspaper coverage of the Games, which included both Chinese-language newspapers and others, strongly increased.[102] As mentioned in the first chapter, a newspaper in Japan, the *Ōsaka Mainichi Shinbun*, had initially supported the American YMCA by sponsoring Japanese athletes who desired to participate in the FECG. In doing so, it had assisted in producing news it could report.[103] Many other newspapers also increasingly focused on the Games. The fact that practically every important Japanese newspaper and news agency sent its own reporters, 13 in total, to the 1934 FECG in Manila illustrates that public interest in the Games (and possibly in foreign policy) in Japan had overtaken that in China by far. Differences in the media systems between the two countries certainly also played a role, since in China the news system was almost completely concentrated in Shanghai and news agency reports more important. In the end, only the Chinese *Central News Agency* (*Zhongyang Tongxunshe*) sent a reporter, who supplied information to Chinese newspapers via Shanghai to Nanjing, the new capital.[104] The influx of Japanese reporters in 1934 also prompted the decision to install special rapid-speed telegraphs—the first of their kind in the Philippines—in the press box. In 1925, Japanese reporters had still had to pay out of their own pocket to have private telephones connecting the field to the telegraph office set up.[105] The 1934 WAG, in contrast, seems to have found no noteworthy echo in the international press, although within India some leading newspapers such as the *Times of India* published several articles on them.[106]

Data on documentary films, lantern slides, and radio programming are quite difficult to obtain: More than 60 lantern slides on the Second FECG were used by the YMCA during the following months to promote modern sport in China.[107] Even earlier, in 1913, Meiji University's baseball team had received a film as a souvenir. In 1917, again some of the events had been recorded and shown to the athletes, although it is unknown if the material was turned into a film. In the case of the Fifth FECG in 1921, John Gray had managed to have a film on the Games produced. Like the slides, it was intended to help popularize physical education in more 'remote' regions of China and served to circumvent the problem of illiteracy. Nonetheless, it is difficult to say anything regarding the impact of the film, except that according to Franklin Brown the Chinese, the Japanese, and the Philippine delegation each bought copies of it. Another film confirmed to have been produced covered the 1925 Seventh FECG in Manila.[108] It can nevertheless be safely assumed that these were not the only films made, and that some of the material from such recordings found its way into newsreels.

Since the 1920s and especially in the 1930s, radio gained significantly in importance. While films provided visual information on the Games, a different form of technical progress now allowed almost immediate communication of events and results over long distances, thus better serving to share the spontaneous excitement sports events created. In 1925 in Manila the necessary equipment was installed at the athletic field to enable one or two American radio companies to broadcast parts of the Games live to the Philippines, Japan, and China.[109] However, one must assume that the coverage was entirely in English, meaning that most Chinese and Japanese did not understand and therefore did not listen to it. More details are available for 1934, by which time the radio had become more widespread. In Japan, for example, about two million radios (in a country of about 14 million households) were registered by that point.[110] Sufficient technical equipment was set up in all the stadia to allow the American radio stations KZRM (Radio Manila) and KZEG (Erlanger and Galinger) to provide live coverage and summaries of events. To increase public attention, in the weeks before the Games, they also broadcasted interviews with Filipino athletes and, after their arrival, with the leaders of the foreign teams. The broadcasts nonetheless again seem to have been exclusively in English.[111] In China, the radio station XQHA (Radio Shanghai) used KZRM reports.[112] One has to assume that it relayed KZRM's news live, but in English, though it is not impossible that it translated them or at least provided summaries in Chinese (and certain local languages).

In contrast, Japanese radio stations JOAK and JOGK (Nippon Hōsō Kyōkai/NHK, branch offices in Tokyo and Kumamoto) went to the root of the language problem. In 1932, at the Los Angeles Olympics, Japanese reporters had not gotten access to facilities allowing live broadcasting and therefore had, after important events, recorded a 'reenacted' live broadcast in a studio. In 1934, real live broadcasting became possible, since a microphone connected to a radio station was set up for them. Their Japanese reports on the events were wired to Japan, where they were relayed to 26 radio stations that also covered Korea, Taiwan, and Manchukuo.[113] At least in theory, several million people in Japan and its colonial empire, if radios were shared, might have listened to this first live broadcasting of a major international sports event held outside of Japan in a language they understood. Especially if compared to China, this, like the relatively high number of newspaper reporters, demonstrated Japanese ability to provide efficient and comprehensible mass communication to a growing, mostly urbanized, consumer society.[114] The difference between Japan and India was even greater. The WAG were not broadcasted on the radio. The only microphone set up served to facilitate addressing the spectators.[115]

All in all, between the 1910s and 1930s, both the number of athletes and of spectators significantly increased. This was true for all three East Asian countries. Compared to these high numbers, the WAG appears as a rather unimportant event that not many people took notice of. In the three East Asian countries, newspaper coverage and media interest corresponded to this increasing interest of the population. In Japan, journalists had initially been the most prominent supporters of the FECG in order to produce news when the JAAA was still boycotting them. By 1934, interest, especially in Japan, had risen to such a degree that many newspapers sent special reporters to the Games. However, not only newspapers (and news magazines), including some big American ones, heavily covered the FECG. The Games were also broadcasted over the radio and at least some films on them were produced. This further illustrates the growing importance of the Games, since technical progress was directly utilized to cover them live, hence much faster than a newspaper, or visually, through moving pictures. Finally, the growing media coverage is also symptomatic of the problems the ideal of mass-based amateurism was to encounter. Increasing numbers of Asians became aware of Western sports, thus achieving one of the basic aims of the American YMCA's 'civilizing mission'. The possibility, however, that the initial aim of education and citizenship training would slowly turn into entertainment, which could be more lucrative for many media, was inherent. In contrast, such concerns were not relevant for the WAG, which received some attention from big Indian newspapers, but were neither the subject of a film nor of radio broadcasting.

Advanced Meeting Grounds and Ceremonies

The staging of the FECG corresponded to the growing public interest and the 'high modernist' plans of the organizers. Mass exhibitions very often still served to teach spectators physical education practices, thus continuing the American YMCA's aims. The growing numbers of people, often children, mobilized for these exhibitions also reflected a bureaucratization and standardization process in the field of physical education and sports. This was at least partially a result of the YMCA's networking, which included affecting governmental education institutions. Simultaneously, since the 1920s, infrastructure development and the construction of permanent stadia gained in importance. Concrete stadia became a new 'standard' in the three East Asian countries and showed a growing public willingness to spend money on further promoting the sportive modernization process, though it is not yet appropriate to talk of large-scale nation-branding. In contrast, the problem-ridden WAG lacked all these features.

The staging of the Fifth FECG in May 1921 in Shanghai was special in several ways. For the first time, Chinese women were represented during the daily educative mass demonstrations of different forms of physical education. About 1,000 school-girls, guided by Vera V. Barger, director of the Normal School of Hygiene and Physical Education of the Shanghai YWCA, played 35 different games and performed in a mass drill.[116] This can be interpreted as a strong call for more gender equality and female health and education. As will be shown below,

FIGURE 2.1
'Feminine bayonet drill': The photo shows a part of the mass demonstrations at the Fifth FECG (1921).[118]
"Feminine Bayonet Drill." *China Press* (5 June 1921): 5 (Olympic Games Special). (Courtesy of the of Library of Congress)

female physical educators remembered this well when in 1927 the next FECG took place in China. On other days, young Chinese men engaged in calisthenics, group games, pyramid building, and cage ball. Martial arts inspired 'Chinese new calisthenics' were also shown. They provided some Chinese authenticity, but were nonetheless modernized in such ways that they fitted into the category of modern sport. Chinese boy scouts, too, again presented their skills. This time, however, they were accompanied by a group of Chinese girl guides. The latter, among other performances, gave a demonstration of combat with wands, which at least one newspaper, the *China Press*, described as looking like a bayonet drill (fig. 2.1).[117]

Considering that the May Fourth Movement had caused growing sentiments of a 'national awakening' and had intensified Chinese-Japanese tensions, the militaristic touch created by the 'bayonet drill' or the martial arts performance was certainly meant to communicate a concrete message to the world, especially to Japan. China would support egalitarian and internationalist citizenship training through the FECG, but at the same time its youth would become more able to defend China against foreign aggression in case others did not accept a more cooperative regional order. Wang Zhengting had, after all, already made similar statements linked with the Second FECG, as discussed in the first chapter.

The Sixth FECG in May 1923 was the first event to be held in a concrete stadium (the Osaka City Ground), which had a grandstand and bleachers that could hold about 27,000 people. The construction had been one of the conditions in the compromise made between *Kantō* region and *Kansai* region officials to reunite and to award Osaka the right to host the Games. Even though the stadium outdid all former meeting places, it still had one big deficit: no shelter was provided except for the 'royal box', meaning that spectators got wet on the many rainy days.[119]

Accommodation for the athletes also proved problematic in Osaka. The YMCA/YWCA transnational network and Chinese diaspora contacts again became important, as they already had been (and would be) for those FECG held in more 'international' cities such as Manila, Shanghai, and Tokyo. The Chinese athletes found shelter in the China Chamber of Commerce and the female athletes were taken care of by the YWCA, which was temporarily granted a villa by a rich sponsor. The Filipino team, which had brought tents, was eventually offered a better alternative in the form of a newly erected, not yet opened primary school.[120] The housing issue is interesting since it illustrates the still moderate ideas concerning the hosting of international sports events. Education of modern citizens was still much more important than issues of large-scale infrastructure development and nation-branding. A concrete stadium was certainly a prestigious project for Osaka's rivalry with Tokyo and for (to a certain degree) equaling stadia in the West. The main aim was, however, to support the spreading of sport within the city and the region around it. Using the FECG for a large-scale building program as a challenge to the capitals of the Western great powers, or at least Tokyo, was not important.

While the opening ceremony was simple and had apparently lost all its appeal due to the heavy rain, the educative daily mass game demonstrations were even more ambitious than those at the Fifth Games. Close to 30,000 boys and girls from 123 schools and 47 associations were scheduled to engage in games, folk dances, and gymnastic drills, though several of the events were canceled because of rain. These different physical education practices, which were reminiscent of those practiced in Japanese schools, highlight the change from military gymnastics to Swedish gymnastics and sports during the interwar period before the conquest of Manchuria. The American YMCA's aim of influencing school curricula thus once more becomes obvious, since schools willing to participate in the Games sometimes needed to modify their curricula to prepare their students in advance. Franklin Brown said he would have preferred even more sports demonstrations, which would have better communicated the YMCA's message of egalitarian amateur sports, instead of gymnastic drills (which encouraged conformity and hierarchical thinking), but had to content himself with the opinion of his Japanese co-organizers.[121]

For the Filipinos, the concrete stadium in Osaka became both the model and the incentive for improving the sports infrastructure for the Seventh FECG in May 1925, which they had already had in mind since 1921. The attempt to erect a 'José Rizal Stadium'—the name was suggested by Camilo Osías—within less than two years nevertheless failed due to legal issues and a lack of money and time. The Games thus again took place at the Carnival Grounds. The sports complex needed several more years, until in 1934, most of the venues were ready for the Tenth FECG.[122] This construction project taking place in a colonial setting has to be seen as even more closely linked with the 'Western civilizing mission' than the one in Osaka. A stadium would visually illustrate progress in supporting sport as a 'blessing' of Protestant American modernity. Moreover, the stadium visually underlined the transformation of the Philippines from a 'backward' country into a modern one. Filipino politicians rejecting colonialism but not Western civilization itself therefore could argue, using the 'civilizing mission' rhetoric, that this was another demonstration that American colonialism was no longer justifiable, since its premise—Filipino backwardness—had been overcome. This anti-colonialist *and* progressive dimension is further highlighted by carrying Osías' motion to christen the main stadium and the complex after the national hero José Rizal, who had been executed in 1896 for his criticism of Spanish colonialism and his revolutionary activities. Rizal had been a strong advocate of modernization and Western education, meaning that the American colonial administration had been able to use his legacy to justify its colonialism as one different from Spanish colonialism. However, despite all rhetoric of American benevolence, Rizal's name primarily stood for Filipino self-government.

The Eighth FECG, held in August and September 1927, again took place in the International Settlement in Shanghai, which was protected by barbed wire and machine guns against possible Chinese military intrusions as a result of the Kuomintang's campaign against the warlord regimes.[123] John Gray had planned, after the Fifth Games, to construct a stadium for the Eighth Games and leased a portion of land from the Rockefeller Foundation, an important donor to the YMCA. His idea was similar to those linked with the development projects in Japan and the Philippines. In contrast to the otherwise restricted Hongkou Recreation Ground, the new grounds would be under full Chinese control and permanently accessible. It therefore allowed for the training of the athletes for the Eighth Games, the hosting of minor events to increase interest in sport, and could serve as an example for recreation grounds to be built in other provinces or cities.[124] Shen Siliang, who organized the Games in 1927 instead of Gray, was not entirely happy with the situation. Since 1925, he had wished to have the Games hosted in Beijing. Shen's aim was to demonstrate the impact of physical education on China to the warlord government there, which had contributed insufficient funding for the team traveling to the Seventh Games. Moreover, no permanent structures could be erected on the leased land, which according to Shen lowered the overall quality of the facilities.[125] Another problem was Shanghai being occupied by Kuomintang forces in spring 1927, which certainly delayed preparations. For instance, Kanaguri Shisō, head of the Japanese track and field team, commented that the infrastructure looked as if it had been set up in a hurry. The educative mass demonstrations, too, were not as large this time as at former events, taking place on only two days.[126] Despite these overall minor issues, the Chinese organizers were, as Guo Taiqi had mentioned in his opening speech, extremely proud of having organized the meeting on their own without serious problems. Large parts of China being affected by civil war made the endeavor look even more impressive.

FIGURE 2.2
'The Meiji Jingu Gaien sports complex' (1930).
Dainihon Taiiku Kyōkai, *Dai-9kai*, p. 284. (Courtesy of the of Nihon Taiiku Daigaku library)

The successful organizing of the Ninth FECG in May 1930 in Tokyo seems to have had the most important impact of all the FECG. The main venue was the Meiji Jingu Gaien Stadium, built in 1924 in the Meiji Shrine Outer Gardens, after which it was named (fig. 2.2 and 2.3). In symbolic terms, it linked sportive modernization and infrastructure development with the heritage of the Meiji emperor (r. 1868–1912), under whom Japan's modernization process had begun. The shrine and the gardens nonetheless provided an environment that used many traditional elements of Japanese religion and culture, thus linking the stadium and the modernization process to Japanese authenticity.[127]

FIGURE 2.3
'The tribune of honor': The flags represent the countries (the American-colonized Philippines, Japan, China, and British-colonized India) participating in 1930.[128]
Dainihon Taiiku Kyōkai, *Dai-9kai*, p. 290. (Courtesy of the of Nihon Taiiku Daigaku library)

Without doubt inspired by the Games, Nagata Hidejirō, who shortly before they took place had become Tokyo's new mayor, asked JAAA official Yamamoto Tadaoki in June 1930 if it would be possible to attract the Olympic Games to Tokyo. Yamamoto was to travel to Europe at the end of June for the Third Student Track and Field World Competition and therefore was in a position to find out how Europeans would react to an application.[129] In the end, after some Western and Japanese IOC members had initially shown doubts regarding Tokyo's capability, it was, in 1936, awarded the 1940 Olympic Games. Being the first non-Western country allowed to host the Olympics was an immense success for Japan in terms of recognition as a modern nation and an equal to the West. Long debates took place regarding how a Japanese-Asian civilization could be effectively communicated to the 'world' via the Games, which were scheduled to take place during the celebrations for the 2600th anniversary of the Imperial Era. However, due to the protracted Second Sino-Japanese War, all these plans were not realized and the games abandoned.[130] It would take until 1959 for the Japanese to again be awarded the Olympic Games (Tokyo 1964) as the first non-Western country, this time having used the Third Asian Games to support their application. This topic will be covered in the fifth chapter.

The mass demonstrations during the Ninth Games were similar to those at the Sixth Games, but were a bit more limited in scale. About 10,000 male and female participants from primary, middle, and normal schools as well as from social welfare organizations such as the YMCA took part. Compared to 1923, when Franklin Brown had still been the central person in organizing the Games, sports demonstrations had diminished in importance and almost all of the demonstrations were Swedish gymnastics, mass games, or Japanese folk dances, showing that the Japanese increasingly modified the staging of the Games according to their own desires. Brown's Tokyo YMCA engaged in human pyramid building and, certainly due to his awareness that Japanese physical education authorities still were more interested in gymnastics than in sport, together with school teachers introduced Niels Bukh's Danish gymnastics. Bukh's very intensive gymnastics, synchronizing the movements of masses of people and heavily focusing on muscular development, brought about a revolution in physical education in the 1930s not only in Japan, but also in other countries such as Nazi Germany. It further contributed to an ideal of masculine and feminine beauty based on health, discipline, and physical efficiency, and can be seen as encouraging conformity between participants and a hierarchical relationship between them and the organizers. After the exhibition, Japanese educational institutions became so interested that they decided to invite Bukh to Japan; he visited in the autumn of 1931.[131]

In addition to Bukh's gymnastics, the Games featured further new elements. For the first time during the ceremonies, an official song of the Games dealing with the Asian athletes coming together had been prepared. The Olympic element of releasing some doves as a symbol of peace was also adopted. During the ancient Olympic Games the doves, flying back to their respective homes, had informed the people there that the Games had begun. The birds were equipped with the flags of the four participating countries.[132] Such new trappings served to visually and acoustically underline the message of internationalism and egalitarianism.

The staging of the Tenth FECG was directly influenced by the above mentioned debate about Manchukuo and Filipino fears that the Games might be canceled or take place without Japan. For Vargas, Quezon, Osías, and Ylanan the Tenth Games were important as the first event organized by Filipinos, which therefore could be used to demonstrate Filipino capability in sportive self-government via the display of organizational skills and the successful completion of the Rizal Memorial Sports Complex. On the one hand, this newly gained opportunity backfired when the press heavily criticized Vargas as being involved in corrupt practices and in destroying the FEAA.[133] On the other hand, the organizing, which was done mostly by Ylanan as the contest secretary, was accomplished without many serious incidents. The Rizal Memorial Stadium offered 12,000–15,000 seats and was equipped with up-to-date technology such as loudspeakers (instead of officials manually using megaphones). This main stadium, the baseball stadium, and the swimming stadium of the Rizal Memorial Sports Complex altogether offered about 35,500 seats and were connected to each other via telephone lines for easier communication between officials. A fourth stadium was not yet finished and was not expected to be ready for the Games, but the available facilities apparently looked very impressive.[134] Some problems that only surfaced after using them nonetheless existed.[135]

The Eleventh FECG in 1938 never took place, meaning that comparing the Chinese sports complex to that of the Filipinos is difficult. In terms of size, the sports complex (now part of the Nanjing Institute of Physical Education) the Kuomintang started to build in the new capital Nanjing, which would have been the most likely place to host the Eleventh Games, outclassed the one in Manila. Its Central Stadium alone seated 40,000 spectators. It should nevertheless be mentioned that the Chinese plan generally differed from that of the Filipinos. Osías, Vargas, Ylanan, Quezon, and their colleagues aimed at a certain prestigious but limited development project useful for further supporting the sportive modernization process and hosting various public events. The Chinese, in contrast, intended to rebuild their new capital, Nanjing, into an impressive city symbolic of the 'new' China the Kuomintang intended to create, based on Chiang Kai-shek's interpretation of Sun Yat-sen's legacy. Large parts of Nanjing, had been destroyed during the Taiping Rebellion (1850–64) and thus provided a lot of open space.[136] Since the Eleventh FECG in 1938 were never held in Nanjing, the construction program is not considered here, but otherwise this would have been the first large-scale nation-branding project notable for its connection with the FECG. It was, however, not very successful, due to the Great Depression, the fighting against the communists, and later the Second Sino-Japanese War. Despite this, it fits in well with the endeavors of later organizers of the Asian Games such as Indonesia, which will be covered in the sixth chapter.

In contrast, the WAG held several months earlier in India can at best be described as unimpressive, among other reasons because overall interest was apparently small and Sondhi failed to rouse it. In 1931, when Sondhi started to enquire about who would be interested in having games in West Asia, India had no venue providing even an acceptable cinder track. Despite his attempts, no stadium was built. When the main events took place in New Delhi on 2–3 March, 1934, the Irwin Amphitheater, which had been completed about one year before the Games began and had been paid for by the maharaja of Bhavnagar, was used as a substitute for a stadium. After the very small foreign delegations arrived, both days saw several athletic events held between Afghanistan, Ceylon, India, and Palestine, and on the first day a hockey match between India and Afghanistan was played.[137] The swimming events had already been hosted more than 200 km away on 25–26 February in Patiala at the maharaja's private pool in the Moti Bagh Palace Grounds (now part of the National Institute of Sports), since in New Delhi no pool was made available. One swimmer from Palestine, Guth Efraim Alfred, competed against several Punjabi and Bengali swimmers, who also decided the Third Indian Aquatic Championship among themselves.[138] Both official ceremonies were very simple, following Olympic guidelines. In Patiala, the maharaja declared the Games open, while the viceroy did so in New Delhi. Some doves, as a symbol of peace, were set free, but educative elements, such as the mass exhibitions that characterized the FECG, did not take place. Accommodation, too, was rather basic and failed to live up even to the accommodations at the FECG held about one decade earlier. In New Delhi, the foreign athletes had to sleep in big tents (which at least had electrical lights) during their stay lasting two weeks, during which they also engaged in some sightseeing. In Patiala, the situation seems to have been better, since the maharaja had more control over the infrastructure and treated the athletes as state guests, who nonetheless also were quartered in tents, certainly to keep costs low.[139] Since initial donations had been significantly smaller than Sondhi had expected and an apparently quite limited attendance in New Delhi meant that tickets did not produce much income, the Games made a huge loss, which in the end was covered by several maharajas.[140]

The failure of the first donation campaign shows that one cannot simply blame all the problems on India's colonial situation or the admittedly only mildly interested colonial administration, which was less eager than those in East Asia to provide support for international sport and therefore left civil society actors more or less on their own. The First WAG showed that Sondhi certainly was a very enthusiastic sports official and strong supporter of amateur sports values. However, the rather poor shape of the WAG illustrated that he did not at all possess the organizational skills of the American YMCA officials active in East Asia and India or of the often YMCA-trained East Asian organizers responsible for the later FECG. This was an important reason why his authority would later several times be heavily questioned or attacked, as will be shown in the third and sixth chapters.

All in all, the FECG in the 1920s and 1930s experienced a growth both in terms of educative mass exhibitions and stadia construction. The 'high modernist' scheme initiated by the American YMCA thus was further intensified, even though its results differed between Japan, China, and the Philippines. The mass exhibitions, in which tens of thousands of people participated, highlighted the spread of sport and physical education in the three countries. Stadia, on the other hand, were visual illustrations of the progress of sportive modernization and of reducing the power asymmetry between East Asia and the West. The successful hosting of the Ninth FECG even became the inspiration for the attempt to bring the 1940 Olympic Games to Japan as the first non-Western host country. The WAG stood in strong contrast to all that, being plagued by financial and other problems and not providing any mass exhibitions.

Trophies and Medals: Asiatization and Olympization of the Games

Like during the early FECG in the 1910s, trophy donation communicated support of the ideals the FECG represented. Moreover, the shapes of these trophies, medals, and other items used at the FECG and the WAG reflected the transfer of leadership from American YMCA physical directors to Asians. Western amateur sports ideals now were increasingly integrated into Asian cultural-religious value systems. This included appropriation processes mixing Western and Asian cultural elements, but also a certain secularization process based on the usage of Olympic elements after the IOC became the patron of the FECG in 1920 and later on also of the WAG.

The Sixth FECG (Osaka 1923) brought a change, compared to the Japanese elite's lack of interest in 1917. About 20 trophies were presented to the FEAA by Japanese politicians, businessmen, companies, and the emperor. The donations were, like the discursive recognition of the FECG in the speeches quoted above, another sign of cooperation from the Japanese elite. This was further highlighted by the fact that most of the trophies were either silver cups or strongly inspired by 'Olympic' elements as promoted by Pierre de Coubertin and the IOC. Ikegami Shirō, who was both Osaka's mayor and leading sports official, for example, presented a replica of a nude Grecian-looking athlete.[141] Osaka-based newspapers such as the *Ōsaka Mainichi Shinbun* and the *Asahi Shinbun* decided on a bronze plate with a Latin inscription (*victoribus [pretium] palmae*—'The Reward of Victory to the Winners') and an image of another nude Grecian athlete, as well as two Grecian style bronze vases depicting athletic scenes.[142] One exception, coming closer to Asian authenticity, was a silver bust of an Asian athlete donated by Baron Sumitomo Kichizaemon, a businessman and collector of Asian art.[143] All this was broad evidence that the IOC's 'reinvented' ideals of Grecian 'Olympism'—which had a Christian dimension but used ancient pagan symbols—became increasingly accepted in Japan. The usage of these symbols can be regarded as a compromise between obviously Christian symbols such as angels, which were closely entangled with Western missionary activities and claims of Japanese cultural inferiority, and more authentic Japanese elements, which lacked some of the internationalist message the Olympic symbols possessed.

The emperor trophy, between 1923 and 1930 awarded to the country that won the most individual championships, can be regarded as such an element of Japanese authenticity (fig. 2.4). It was very significant for certain Japanese, but was not particularly important to, for example, the Filipinos. Despite being shaped like a Western cup, the fact that the emperor as the embodiment of Japanese sovereignty had awarded it and that the imperial seal was depicted on it turned it into a minor holy relic for some of the Japanese athletes and delegates. For example, JAAA vice president Hiranuma in his memoirs complained about the Filipinos, who won the trophy in 1925, displaying it in a shop window in Manila. Filipinos, in Hiranuma's view, had a different national character than the Japanese, for whom this would have been sacrilege and who therefore would have had to show their heroic determination to retake the cup during the next Games. Hiranuma also described winning it after an extremely hard fight in 1927 as having brought great joy and relief. Sports competitions could thus serve not only to encourage physical education, but also create national prestige and patriotism.[144] This was certainly not a new finding, considering that Chinese President Yuan had noticed it already in the early 1910s, and it was acceptable to the YMCA and others as long as the internationalist ideal was not challenged. Hiranuma's stirring and somewhat martial description, as well as the Filipinos' more secular treatment of the trophy, nonetheless highlight how entirely different meanings could be attributed to a single item.

After the political and other elites of all three participating countries had shown their acceptance of the Games, the topic of trophy donation lost much of its importance and became a standard procedure. The FEAA began to award many of them permanently after the same nation or athlete had won it three times, since replenishing the supply was no longer a problem. One last trophy worthy of special mention, however, is the one donated by Chiang Kai-shek in 1930. It underlined the Kuomintang's further support of the Games. More important was that it was, following President Yuan's and Vice President Li's trophies for the 1915 FECG, a third symbol of Chinese identity and authenticity. In contrast to Yuan's and Li's replicas of buildings associated with the Chinese Empire, Chiang presented a trophy communicating an entirely different message, that of 'national revolution'. It was modeled on the Porcelain Tower of Nanjing, an impressive and famous building destroyed in 1856 during the Taiping Rebellion against the Qing dynasty (fig. 2.5). It therefore stood for the Kuomintang's new capital of China, Nanjing, which was to experience a large-scale building program, instead of the Qing dynasty's and the warlords' capital, Beijing. Moreover, in contrast to Sun Yat-sen, Chiang seems to not have liked the Taiping rebels very much. One has to assume that the fact that the revolutionary Taiping destroyed the pagoda therefore caused him no ideological problems. Instead, the shape of the trophy was also certainly a

FIGURE 2.4 (*LEFT*)
'The Emperor trophy': The Japanese emperor donated this trophy in 1923.
Dainihon Taiiku Kyōkai, *Dai-8kai*, picture page. (Courtesy of the Nihon Taiiku Daigaku library)

FIGURE 2.5 (*RIGHT*)
'Porcelain Tower of Nanjing': Chinese President Chiang Kai-shek donated this trophy in 1930.
"For Winning Country." *Japan Advertiser* (22 May 1930): 3. (Courtesy of the Library of Congress)

promise that Chiang would end social unrest and rebuild a once powerful China, whose ancient might and glory was symbolized by the pagoda.[145]

The images on the medals awarded since the Sixth FECG, too, highlight experiments in adopting Western Olympic (not Christian) elements, 'inventing' more authentic Asian ones, or combining both of them to create a modern sports identity for the three East Asian countries. Not all of them can be covered here.[146] However, particularly noteworthy is a medal awarded at the Ninth Games (Tokyo 1930) that featured an entity with six arms, riding on a cloud (fig. 2.7). JAAA president Kishi sent copies of the medal to other IOC members, which can be understood as systematic nation-branding. He also explained to the IOC that the figure was a 'God of Sports', "created by modernizing the heroic figures of pure Oriental Gods". This 'God of Sports' was obviously 'invented' by using traditional Japanese images of Buddhist deities, such as *Asura* (*Ashura*) (fig. 2.6). Its many limbs, holding different items or making certain movements, symbolized omnipotence in sport and physical education. Kishi also mentioned that such deities normally possessed three heads in addition to their many limbs, so one has to assume that the engraver could not realize this detail.[147] Despite this, the

FIGURE 2.6 (*LEFT*)
'Statue of an Asura'. The statue is exhibited in the Kōfuku-ji (a Buddhist temple) in Nara, Japan.
https://upload.wikimedia.org/wikipedia/commons/6/67/ASURA_Kohfukuji.jpg [accessed: 18 July 2013].

FIGURE 2.7 (*ABOVE*)
'Medal, Ninth FECG': The medal depicts an Asura doing sports.
Dainihon Taiiku Kyōkai, *Dai-9kai*, picture part. (Courtesy of the Nihon Taiiku Daigaku library)

motif had certainly also been chosen since it appeared as if the three member countries had been incorporated into one being, symbolizing their unity. Even though there is no written evidence for it, one might go so far as to perceive the *Asura* as retaliation in terms of religion and authenticity for the Third FECG's gold medal displaying an angel. Moreover, Japanese sports officials must have liked the motif very much, since it was also used at the 1930 National High School Baseball Championship that took place some months later.[148]

The motif of the medals, the badges, and the flag of the First WAG was basically the same. Medals featured the sun, which can be interpreted as the symbol of the 'Orient' or the 'Continent of the Rising Sun'. The FEAA had set an example by creating a flag, which did, however, simply depict a Western style monogram (fig. 2.8). Sondhi thus also designed a flag for the WAG (fig. 2.9), which seems to have later served as an inspiration for the flag of the Asian Games (fig. 3.3; p. 118). Here the 'Oriental' element of the sun was combined with a seemingly Olympic one. A red sun was placed on a white background and was accompanied by five colored rings, each standing for one of the five member countries. The Olympic flag, developed in 1914, had definitely been a model, also featuring five rings, though of different colors, on a white background. This Olympic motif was, however, not decisive, since Sondhi had planned to increase the number of rings had further countries joined the WAG. His design thus must have been a compromise, protecting the Olympic 'trademark', showing the WAG's belonging to the Olympic movement, and adding an Asian touch to it.[149]

In conclusion, the Asiatization process of the FECG in the 1920s, recognition by the IOC, and acceptance by Japanese elites all had a strong impact on the

FIGURE 2.8 (*LEFT*)
'Monogram of the FEAA'.
Brown, F., *Official Report of the Ninth*, front cover. (Courtesy of The Olympic Studies Centre)

FIGURE 2.9 (*RIGHT*)
'Flag of the Western Asiatic Games' (1934).
Programme. First Western Asiatic Games and VI Indian Olympic Games, front page. (Courtesy of The Olympic Studies Centre)

religious-cultural elements used in their staging. Certain trophies such as the emperor trophy strongly focused on Asian—here Japanese—cultural elements, but lacked an internationalist message. In contrast, Olympic elements became more common, but were also appropriated by sometimes being combined with Asian elements. The integration of Olympic elements can thus be considered a compromise between creating authenticity for only individual Asian countries, and creating unity, but lacking authenticity, by using only Western elements. This appropriation process at the same time can be interpreted as a secularization process, since 'Olympism', in contrast to muscular Christianity, had no direct connection to a still existent religion and therefore had a *higher integration potential.* Sondhi at the WAG decided for a similar approach, combining a more general Asian element—the sun—and Olympic elements.

Creating Women's Events

From the beginning, the message Elwood Brown and the YMCA had intended to spread via the Games had been that of everybody—men and women, adults and children—taking up amateur sports to modernize Asian societies based on the ideals of Christian internationalism, Christian egalitarianism, and of a 'Protestant work ethic'. Brown's development of a physical education system for public schools in the Philippines that included both boys and girls was an early demonstration of this purpose, as was shown in the first chapter. The FECG, too, had an influence on the emancipation of female Asians.

Although there had been no contests between female Asians from different countries in the early FECG, they had participated in mass games and drills during opening ceremonies, had been given room to demonstrate sports or scouting activities to spectators, and had been received by leading politicians such as Chinese President Yuan Shikai. In Japan, the first athletic meeting for women featuring multiple events had been held in Tokyo in 1922, organized by the YWCA. The Sixth FECG in Osaka in 1923 for the first time allowed female athletes to compete against each other in several official invitation contests. These contests did not count toward the general championship, meaning that women still did not contribute to it. Instead, the declared aim was to further educate and encourage women in the three participating countries to take up sport by now featuring more institutionalized female competitions. This seems to have had an impact. For example, in Japan, strongly backed by a newspaper (again the *Ōsaka Mainichi Shinbun*), the Japanese Women's Olympic Games (*Nihon Joshi Orimupikku Taikai*) were held annually between 1924 and 1936.[150]

The initial driving force for including female events had been Camilo Osías, who during discussions concerning the Sixth Games had suggested indoor baseball, which had already been used for exhibition matches between Filipinas in 1915 in China, and tennis. He had also proposed holding these new international competitions either as exhibitions or as championships. The latter had been rejected, illustrating that perceptions of gender relations (and equality) in the Philippines, at least in terms of physical education, had become more liberal than in China or Japan. Different school curricula and YWCA training practices also created problems. Tennis was accepted by the FEAA delegates, but indoor baseball was played in neither China nor Japan. Vera Barger of the Shanghai YWCA later suggested bringing together a volleyball team and the Japanese also set up two teams (*Kansai* and *Kantō* region), but volleyball was not played by schoolgirls in the Philippines, so no sufficiently prepared team could be sent. The same year saw schoolgirls in Manila starting to take up volleyball. [151] One has to expect Osías' or Frederick England's direct involvement in that development.

The Seventh Games, too, included tennis and volleyball matches, as did the Eighth, but again without a Filipina volleyball team.[152] This lack of progress in increasing female participation evoked criticism from several sides. Zhang Huilan (Chang Hwei Lan), the 'mother of women's modern physical education'[153] in China, had been sent by the YWCA to the University of Wisconsin at Madison to study physical education. In 1927, she became chair of physical education at Jinling Women's College in Nanjing. Shortly beforehand, she de facto accused the Kuomintang organizers of not giving women enough involvement in the Games and of not living up to the Fifth FECG, during which many girls had participated in exhibitions. Female participation would be necessary to promote citizenship training of the masses and to get rid of the image of China as the 'sick (hu-)man of East Asia'.[154] The activities of the women's division of the National Amateur Athletic Federation of America, which Elwood Brown and the YMCA/YWCA had helped establish, should serve as a model.[155] Zhang's criticism apparently produced some results. During the Ninth FECG in 1930, a new place for women in Chinese society was symbolically hinted at by two female athletes walking next to the two male flag bearers, together leading the delegation during the opening ceremony.[156] Osías in his speech at the final banquet in 1927 also deemed more women's events necessary to spread the message of amateur sport. Even though they would never count toward the general championship, from 1930 onwards further events, including track and field and swimming, were added to the program.[157]

The FECG certainly promoted the emergence of modern (at least middle- and upper-class) women in East Asia, who wanted to be considered relevant to society, be more equally treated, and whose bodies were shaped by a new ideal of beauty at least partially based on physical efficiency. They thereby accompanied other 'progressive' women's movements such as that for voting rights, which were expressions of the so-called 'Taishō Democracy' in Japan, the 'nationalist awakening' in China, and the social transformation in the Philippines.[158] As Garfield Jones had stated regarding the American colony, citizenship training could be better encouraged if women too were affected, as they would then educate their children along these lines. Female health would also improve, be it for democratic-emancipatory reasons or, not necessarily contradictory, for eugenic ones to produce 'better' offspring. The public appearance of women, including dress codes, changed as well. Female swimmers displayed arms and legs (not yet the stomach) in front of thousands of people, which previously would have caused shame. The tennis dresses of the female participants at the Seventh FECG (fig. 2.10) still look quite impractical seen from the perspective of today, but also illustrate a departure from traditional (middle- and upper-class) kimono and Spanish inspired *Baro't Saya*, often cut in a way that did not allow fast movements, or Chinese bound feet, which were even more hindering. This was all in strong contrast to the Asian Games, which saw more and more women dressed in the traditional clothes of their respective countries put into the ceremonies and entertainment programs to create authenticity after Western sports uniforms had become common. Finally, the photo featuring members of the female Chinese swimming team at the Tenth FECG illustrates that the Chinese diaspora supported the fatherland by competing in its team (fig. 2.11). Some athletes even decided to have the name of their territory of origin or residence written on their sports uniforms. For example, the characters on the swimsuit read 'Hong Kong'. (Quite interestingly in terms of representing colonies, male Korean boxers competing in the Japanese team at the same Games also were allowed to promote their country of origin and had 'Korea' written on their uniforms.[159]) In India, Sondhi had not excluded the participation of women, but no events took place during the WAG.[160] Very likely this was the result of the many problems plaguing the Games, including the very small foreign teams.

FIGURE 2.10

'Japanese female tennis players, Seventh FECG' (1925).

England, *Far Eastern*, p. 95. (Courtesy of The Olympic Studies Centre)

FIGURE 2.11

'Chinese female swimmers, Tenth FECG' (1934): Sports had a strong impact on clothing and the public appearance of women, some of whom (like Yang Xiuqiong, second from left) became well-known celebrities.

"Jinbu zhong zhi woguo youyong [Progress in Our Nation's Swimming]." *Shenbao yuekan* 3, no. 6 (1934). (Courtesy of the Harvard Yenching Library)

Taken all together, the FECG served to encourage female amateur sport and the citizenship training idea linked with it. They therefore also impacted the emancipation of women in the three East Asian countries, affected ideals of beauty and femininity, and supported a change in dress codes, which included a physical 'liberation' of women. In 1923, the already existing but informal participation of females was institutionalized. Until 1934, female participation grew in size, though it never counted toward the overall championship. It seems that the Filipino official Osías and representatives of the YWCA encouraged all of these changes, while certain male officials from Japan and China were apparently more conservative. The WAG, in contrast, despite some plans to do so, did not feature any women's events.

Assessment

Since the internationalist ideal in particular was regularly threatened by groups of Chinese and Japanese who advocated boycotting the Games, the American YMCA officials perceived their Asian colleagues as not yet ready to enforce it against the ambitions of their nationalist compatriots. This perpetuation of the 'Western civilizing mission' rhetoric of Asian inferiority nonetheless increasingly destabilized the working relationship between Americans and Asians. The Asiatization process of the continuously growing Games since the 1920s consisted of nationalization processes in Japan, China, and the Philippines, all of them happening at about the same time and influencing each other. The resulting Asiatization process was thus Asian insofar as it led—in the sense of Abraham Lincoln's statement on freedom, democracy, and 'good governance'—to Games *of* the Asians, held *for* Asians, and organized *by* Asians, without American tutelage and interference. As before, the idea of the nation was never intended to be overcome by the process. Asiatization, after all, happened in the contexts of three different nations struggling against different degrees of Western colonialism and paternalism and for sportive self-government. Hence, the FECG from 1927 onwards presented the sportive modernization processes both as 'national awakenings' and as an 'Asian awakening'.

The Asian officials—if one ignores the delegation from the Dutch East Indies in 1934 led by Dutch officials—now created Asian authenticity by personifying Asian 'kinship' instead of power asymmetries between American 'teachers' and Asian 'pupils'.[161] Furthermore, sportive pan-Asianism was rhetorically supported by Guo Taiqi, Camilo Osías, Yamamoto Tadaoki, S. K. Mukerjee, and many others by more strongly integrating Western amateur ideals into the context of Asian regional integration. To provide the ideals further authenticity, in some countries they were even integrated with cultural-religious concepts such as Bushidō, the 'spiritual East' or 'Asia as greater India', which were used to resist claims of the superiority of Western civilization. The staging at least of the later FECG, too, can be seen as a rejection of 'unequal' power relations between Asia—or at least the individual Asian countries—and the West, culminating in Japan convincing the IOC to award it the 1940 Olympic Games. In terms of symbols, appropriation processes took place by reinventing Asian cultural and religious elements along modern lines. For example, Olympic elements, whose ancient Greek religious content did not matter anymore to Westerners either, were used due to their internationalist meaning. The WAG were hereby not that different from the FECG, even though their general impact certainly was significantly more limited.

The WAG failed due to a variety of reasons, including organizing problems and took place only once. The FECG, on the other hand, ended after the unstable American- and British-dominated world order broke down during the Great Depression. The ideal of egalitarian internationalism was not entirely forsaken, but was strongly modified in its reach. Japanese and Filipino delegates after dissolving the FEAA directly founded a new organization, the Amateur Athletic Association of the Orient. The first event, planned for 1938, did not take place, nor were further FECG held in China or in the Dutch East-Indies.[162] Nevertheless, the hosting of some minor events and Japan being awarded the 1940 Olympic Games in 1936 certainly played a role in keeping the idea alive, at least until the Olympics were renounced. During the following years of the Second Sino-Japanese War further regional games took place in an attempt to communicate the message of Japanese-led egalitarian pan-Asian integration, which after the beginning of the Pacific War also included resistance against the West. [163] One therefore generally has to distinguish between the aims of the Games and how the power relations between the organizers influenced them.

When American YMCA officials still controlled the Games, they were a 'neutral' group (in the sense of not being citizens of any *Asian* country) and therefore foreign relations and questions of power between China, Japan, or the Philippines did not matter much to them. For the American YMCA, all three countries, and all those that were invited but did not participate, were equal. All were considered 'backward' and in need of Western tutelage and guidance, even if there were some differences in the respective degree of perceived 'backwardness'. After the power asymmetry between Westerners and Asians had been overcome, Asian organizers needed to find their own working relationship. Even though many were close to the YMCA or were Christians, their international ties were too weak to form a relatively homogeneous group such as the American YMCA officials. An important reason for this was that they, in contrast to the Americans, represented different Asian nations. The ties which had developed between American YMCA officials and government agencies to speed up the sportive modernization process further contributed to this issue after Asians, often politicians or government employees, took over from the Americans. Due to the political tensions in East Asia and the anti-colonial nationalism affecting nation-building processes, the Asians had many more problems than the American YMCA members with trusting each other.[164] In the discriminatory terms of the 'Western civilizing mission', the Asians attained sportive self-government before they were ready for it and before they could control their or their governments' nationalist aspirations.

When the East Asian officials struggled to set up their new working relationships, they de facto based it upon power relations between their countries. For example, the Japanese substituted the former asymmetry between Westerners and East Asians with one between Japanese and other East Asians. This did not mean that the ideal of a more egalitarian and interdependent regional order necessarily had to be given up. However, 'egalitarianism' and 'internationalism' lost their universal dimension (which in the FECG, if combined with the Open International Games, theoretically existed, even though in practice it was limited due to administrative reasons and transportation costs) and became adjusted to a region now defined by Japan. A similar thing would happen again as an outcome of the Asian Games in Indonesia in 1962, covered in the sixth chapter. Though this point will not be covered here, it is worth noting that the wartime games since 1937 had the potential to support, through demonstrations of non-Western or anti-Western egalitarian internationalism, the (quite hollow) pan-Asian discourses the Japanese military produced.

CHAPTER 3

Building Nehru's Asia through Sport: The First Asian Games, Decolonization, International Peace, Modernization, and Development (4–11 March 1951)

"You have certainly made New Delhi the Capital of Asia."[1]

—Anthony S. de Mello, main organizer of the First Asian Games, in a letter to Indian Prime Minister Jawaharlal Nehru written shortly after the end of the First Asian Games

The founding of the Asian Games Federation (AGF), bringing together East and West Asia (including South Asia), was a process directly linked with questions about the shape and image of Asia after the beginning of large-scale decolonization following the Second World War. Amateur sport again served as a means for citizenship training by encouraging internationalism, egalitarianism, and economic progress. Newly created symbols also served these national and international aims. Simultaneously, the founding process was characterized by serious debates about organizational skills, management competence, and infrastructure construction as part of showing (or not) India's development—or "level of civilization", though that term slowly lost significance after the war. The East Asians had gained and shown their competence via the Far Eastern Championship Games (FECG), while the Indians (representing the South and West Asians), had only been able to host one dubious Western Asiatic Games (WAG). The founding of the AGF therefore was directly linked with perceptions of India as a 'backward' country, especially on the part of the East Asians, and the attempt by now 'free' Indians to challenge, though in the end not to overcome, that image. Due to this image of India, it was by no means predetermined that the First Asian Games would finally take place in New Delhi in 1951.[2]

This chapter demonstrates how Indian officials founded the AGF to support their *postcolonial* foreign policy of integrating the whole Asian continent, going back to the Asian Relations Conference (1947). This includes their vision of the beginning of a new cycle of history characterized by an 'Asian rebirth' and opposition to the superpowers' power struggle. Moreover, I highlight the experience the Indian organizers gained in Asian regional cooperation and in nation-building, as well as the significant problems they faced.

India in 1951

The process of decolonization following the Second World War led to immense hope in many of the newly independent Asian nations that social needs and political problems, which during colonial times had been ignored, would now be addressed by Asian politicians. In terms of foreign policy, expectations ran high that a new, more peaceful and egalitarian world order could be created.

On 15 August 1947, India gained independence. Jawaharlal Nehru, who now served both as prime minister and as foreign minister (1947–64), had been a long-time advocate of world peace, Asian unity, and the end of colonialism and racism. Some months before independence, in March–April 1947, the Asian Relations Conference had taken place in New Delhi, attended by delegates from 28 Asian nations (including Egypt). Some of these nations were still colonies, while others were Asian republics of the USSR. The overall intention of the conference was to begin reestablishing contact between the Asian nations and to continue the creation of an Asian civilization that could be promoted as morally superior to Western civilization.[3]

Indian National Congress politicians perceived India as the obvious leader of such an Asian (and later also African, and finally global) movement. Another possible leader, China, was experiencing a civil war between Kuomintang and communist forces, while Japan was both militarily defeated and its claims to Asian leadership tainted by its oppressive rule in the territories it had occupied during the war. Nehru saw India as an emerging great power in its own right not because of its military strength, but because of its influence in Asia, its democratic form of government, and its political stability. Often using idealistic and moralistic terms, he attempted to reintegrate Asia, especially Southeast Asia, which experienced long-lasting struggles for independence, into the world community. In 1951, when the Korean War (1950–53) had escalated into a war between US-led and Chinese forces, he expressed fear of a new world war. All in all, in terms of international affairs, India between 1947 and the mid-1950s acquired the image of a major advocate of world peace and internationalism, and of an important leader of the non-aligned countries of Asia and later other regions as well.[4]

Other problems of nation-building concerned culture, religion, and questions of modernization and development. The aim of the government's transformation process was a more egalitarian society, which among other things meant overcoming discrimination against 'untouchables' as well as emancipating women. To quickly increase economic output, the Indian government's plans focused primarily on economic development instead of social welfare. The latter was to be encouraged later when the distributable sums had risen.[5]

Sport in India and the Main Organizers of the Games

In terms of sports, no major events had taken place in India since the hosting of the WAG in 1934, although the Indian hockey team had won another gold medal at the 1936 Olympic Games. The spreading of amateur sport as citizenship training had made some further progress in terms of publicity as, among other reasons, the Indian Olympic Games the Young Men's Christian Association (YMCA) had founded in 1924 had not been interrupted by the war.[6] Moreover, by 1952, the College of Physical Education the American YMCA had set up in Madras (Chennai) in 1920 had trained close to 3,000 physical educators. Amateur sport nevertheless still was no mass phenomenon. In 1952, eight institutions, all governed by graduates from Madras, trained physical educators, but the annual number of 800 graduates was still completely insufficient to staff schools and colleges.[7]

The most important Indian involved in organizing the First Asian Games was the main organizer of the WAG, Guru Dutt Sondhi, who by then was serving as the president of the Amateur Athletic Federation of India and as an International Olympic Committee (IOC) member. Another important person was Anthony S. de Mello, who would take over organizing the Games from Sondhi in 1950. Mello was a leading Anglo-Indian sports official born in Karachi and educated at the University of Cambridge. He was vice president of Sondhi's Amateur Athletic Federation of India and, more importantly, president of the influential Cricket Club of India as well as of some minor federations. Bhupinder Singh, the maharaja of Patiala, had died in 1938. His son Yadavindra Singh, an enthusiastic cricketer and the new maharaja (after independence the governor of the Patiala and East Punjab States Union), had succeeded his father as president of the Indian Olympic Association. The most important political support for the early development of amateur sport was provided by Rajkumari Amrit Kaur, the minister of health, who due to her international connections (in 1950 she became president of the World Health Organization) and long-time service in both the Young Women's Christian Association (YWCA) and the Indian National Congress served as a model for the emancipation of Indian women.[8] Prime Minister Jawaharlal Nehru also showed much interest, while Rajendra Prasad as India's president became the patron of the Games.

As will be shown below, the First Asian Games, as a tool to promote amateur sport as well as regional integration, were of special importance for independent India. Their hosting was the result of a close collaboration between social reformers and the government. In contrast to 1934, in early independent India several leading politicians provided strong moral and public support, though still no money.

Turning the Asian Relations Conference into a Sports Event: The Founding of the Asian Games Federation

This section recounts Guru Dutt Sondhi's struggle to gain national and international support for the founding of the AGF. It also illustrates the importance of the legacy of the Far Eastern Athletic Association (FEAA) and the WAG. This legacy included personal continuities and, intimately linked with them, different opinions on the regional shape of the Games. For example, the East Asians showed a remarkable lack of trust in Indian organizational competence.

In March 1945, when the victory of the allies in the Second World War was only a matter of time, Sondhi expressed his desire that India after the war should engage in hosting international sports events in hockey, cricket, water polo, and football, as well as the Second WAG. He assumed that the six member countries of the WAG (the Dutch East Indies had joined after the dissolution of the FEAA) would not disagree if the second event again took place in India, so long as the maharaja of Patiala provided the necessary funding.[9] The announcement of the Asian Relations Conference, to take place in New Delhi in March and April 1947, seems to have caused Sondhi to modify his ideas and to focus on a larger region. In early 1947, he informed the maharaja of his intention to go to the conference to promote the idea of hosting an Asian sports event, an idea for which he also received positive feedback from the IOC. At the conference, he presented his project in the 'Labour Problems and Social Services' section and approached many of the foreign delegates. His idea of 'Asiatic Games', geographically larger than 'Western Asiatic Games', was also welcomed by Nehru, who nonetheless suggested calling the Games the 'Asian Games', which Sondhi thus did in his presentation.[10] 'Asian' was a more positive term than 'Asiatic', departing from Western geographical terms that had a British-'Orientalist' touch and focused on divisions instead of unity. For example, in a minute to a document, British Prime Minister Winston Churchill, in 1953, criticized the use of the term 'Asian', which he declared to be an American expression that instead of describing the divergent communities of Asia sounded as if one was attempting to bring them all together. Churchill was then informed that the term 'Asiatic' was perceived in Asia to have a derogatory connotation and that already in 1950, the British Foreign Office had issued instructions to substitute it with 'Asian'.[11]

When Sondhi presented his idea for the Asian Games at the Asian Relations Conference, many of the discourses mentioned in connection with the WAG came up again. Sondhi's aims had not changed during the war—only the platform for promoting them in India had become larger than that in 1934. He still advocated secular 'Olympism' instead of religious approaches to encourage internationalism, egalitarianism, and economic progress. He also conceded that international competition had the potential to produce some negative outcomes, but declared that this view was based on a few incidents, which were inevitable when thousands of people met and thus would be of minor importance.[12] All in all, it was still an idealistic approach of educating and 'uplifting' humanity. International sports events were for him still an instrument of social engineering and not primarily of entertainment. His plans no doubt were further inspired by India and other Asian countries now having gained (or been promised) their independence and thus, no longer inhibited by their colonial masters, given a chance to transform their national orders and to create a more peaceful and egalitarian world order which would support their continued independence.

Sondhi afterwards approached the Indian Olympic Association and decided to host the first Games in early 1948, depending on governmental support. At about the same time, Anthony de Mello attempted to organize an Asian cricket conference. It was another, though more limited, approach to bringing the newly independent Asian countries together. According to Sondhi, these two schemes would serve as the foundation for a large-scale international sports project in Asia, which would ultimately also include some of the other events, such as hockey and soccer, which he had talked about in 1945. Despite Sondhi's plans, particularly due to a lack of funding and the fact that India did not possess even the most basic infrastructure required to host a large sports event, nothing happened until summer of 1948. In July of that year, Sondhi decided to limit himself to a track and field meeting and started to issue letters of invitation.[13] The invitations seem not to have elicited any response, since in July–August 1948, the Olympic Games were scheduled to take place in London. The Olympics, however, were attended by many Asian delegations and therefore provided the opportunity to first discuss the founding of the AGF with other sports officials (instead of politicians, as at the Asian Relations Conference) before again unilaterally declaring the intent to host an event.[14]

In London, Sondhi met some of the East Asian sports officials who had been involved in organizing the later FECG. Shortly after the beginning of the Pacific War (1941–45), Jorge B. Vargas had been ordered by President of the Commonwealth Manuel Quezon to remain in the Philippines to protect the population during the Japanese occupation. He thus served as chairman of the Executive Committee, a civil administration set up by the Japanese, and the Second Philippine Republic's (1943–45) ambassador to Japan. After Japan's surrender he spent about one year in detention until he was amnestied. Even though he did not hold important governmental offices after the war, Vargas remained an elder statesman of the Third Republic of the Philippines, independent from 1946. He also still served as the president of the Philippine Amateur Athletic Federation (PAAF) and as the Philippines' IOC member.[15]

Wang Zhengting, too, had survived the war as an important Kuomintang politician and remained an IOC member for China. China's confrontation with Japan, however, had made him, from the mid-1930s onwards, focus even more on sports for purposes of national defense in a Social Darwinist struggle, rather than a forum for international cooperation.[16] Hao Gengsheng (Hoh Gun-sun), who was to emerge as the Kuomintang's most important sports official, also attended the Games, serving as the head of the Chinese team. Before the war, Hao had been physical director of the Shanghai YMCA, had been educated at the International YMCA College in Springfield, and had assisted several times in the hosting of the FECG. After that he worked at Northeastern University in Harbin in Manchuria and later for the Chinese Ministry of Education. In 1934, he had, in the absence of Wang, led the Chinese delegation that left the meeting before Japan and the Philippines dissolved the FEAA the next day. Two years later, he had headed a study group that attended the 1936 Berlin Olympics together with the Chinese team and afterwards toured parts of Europe. His early publications demonstrate that he initially supported the YMCA's ideal of amateur sport as a 'civilizing' tool for *Christian* citizenship training at least on the national and subnational level. Like Wang, he increasingly expressed doubts regarding the Japanese and thus was less willing than the American YMCA officials to use sportive internationalism to overcome foreign policy tensions between China and Japan. Instead, he acted in accordance with official Chinese foreign policy by refusing to let Manchukuo join or compete in the FECG. Hao's thinking thus was another illustration of an appropriation process, including a secularization process, of amateur norms and values. Due to his close relations with the Chinese government, which were the result of both the American YMCA's efforts to gain support for their sportive modernization aims and of Americans slowly losing power and influence after 1923, he promoted amateur ideals in official secular ways and no longer in Christian terms. The defeat of the Kuomintang in the Chinese Civil War (1945–49) and its consequences, covered below and in the fourth chapter, further added to his perception of international sport as an instrument for national representation and self-legitimation instead of peaceful and egalitarian internationalism.[17]

In London, the East Asian sports officials had already developed plans for re-establishing the FECG, but then agreed to discuss the idea of larger games with Sondhi.[18] Sondhi still followed the regional focus given by the Asian Relations Conference and intended to bring together nations of all parts of the Asian continent. He therefore invited delegates of all Asian countries attending the Olympics to a meeting. Burma, Ceylon, China, India, Korea, and the Philippines were represented, while Afghanistan, Iran, Iraq, Lebanon, Pakistan, and Syria were not. This regional bias against the attendance of Muslim countries seems to have been the outcome of Pakistan advocating the founding of 'Muslim Games', which was certainly a counter-proposal to Sondhi's idea.[19] Sondhi also announced that he had already written to Moscow (which, however, did not compete in the Olympic Games before 1952) regarding the participation of its Asian Soviet republics in the Asian Games.[20] Despite all this, Sondhi's initial goal of hosting the first event in India was not realized during the meeting. India was only awarded an invitation event in early 1949, during which the final discussion on the founding of the AGF was to take place.

The East Asians seem to have completely outmaneuvered Sondhi, trusting neither his organizational skills nor India's sports infrastructure; they certainly also had a more East Asian regional focus. Vargas, Hao, Korean delegate K. C. Synn, and Sondhi were the most influential delegates, as demonstrated by them being elected—or considered competent—to prepare a constitution for the AGF at a follow-up meeting during the next days. At this meeting, Hao was chosen as the person responsible for turning the draft they prepared into the final constitution. According to Vargas, he, Hao, and Synn had agreed to nominate Wang as the president of the AGF when officials were to be elected. The close cooperation between them was almost a guarantee that the First Asian Games in 1950 would take place in Shanghai, not in India. Sondhi certainly anticipated this outcome, and the invitation event in India must have been a compromise between him and the East Asians.[21]

Already in late September, however, Wang raised significant doubts that the First Asian Games could be held in China, since the necessary infrastructure would still be lacking.[22] This concern can be considered a pretext for the by then increasingly problematic Kuomintang situation in the civil war after large parts of Manchuria and northern China had been lost, inflation had spiraled completely out of control, and certain reform attempts had led to a breakdown of Shanghai's economy.[23] Soon afterwards, contact with Hao broke off. However, justifying the doubts of the East Asians, the invitation event in India in February 1949 also did not materialize, though the meeting of officials took place. Since China by then could in no way organize the First Asian Games, Sondhi took over and declared that India would host them in New Delhi in February 1950. He became secretary of the AGF and the former maharaja of Patiala its president. Manila received the Second Games, to be held in 1954. However, only India, the Philippines, and Burma had sent official delegates, who then set up another committee to complete the constitution. The Iranian nominee did not attend and 'China' and 'Korea' (now formally divided) were in tumult. Afghanistan, Ceylon, the Dutch East Indies, Nepal, Pakistan, and Thailand were represented only by their diplomatic residents in New Delhi.[24] It was another demonstration of a lack of money and interest, and of doubts regarding India held by many of those countries that did not send sports officials. It nonetheless also illustrated that after Pakistan's 'Muslim Games' proposal had failed, some non-Arab, non-Mediterranean Islamic countries, which had less close ties to Egypt, showed some interest in the Asian event.[25]

In April 1949, some months after the Indians at last began thinking about constructing basic infrastructure, they decided to postpone the Games to November 1950.[26] In late 1949, the next wave of serious East Asian doubts concerning Sondhi and Indian organizational competence arose. By then, most of the Kuomintang had fled to Taiwan. After Vargas visited Hao, who in November 1949 had organized a 'national' athletic meeting in Taipei, and had contacted Wang in Hong Kong, the plan to revive the FECG in their most inclusive form came to the fore again. Considering Vargas' dealings with the Kuomintang and the close relations between the United States and the Philippines, it was obvious that communist countries like the People's Republic of China were to be excluded. Vargas declared that in case India failed in hosting the Asian Games, the PAAF would organize the next FECG in 1951 or 1952.[27]

In December 1949, Sondhi was still urging countries to respond to India's invitation. However, on 13 April 1950, three months after India had begun constructing a stadium, he finally gave up and relinquished his position as secretary of the organizing committee. According to Moin-ul-Haq, still the secretary of the Indian Olympic Association, the stadium would not have been ready in November 1950, nor had a single country responded regarding the planned event.[28] Mello took over and declared the next month that the Games would have to be postponed again, this time to March 1951.

The only reply Sondhi had received was an 'illegal' one from Japan, which he had invited in February 1950 to affiliate. Upon hearing of the invitation in March, Vargas, according to the *Manila Chronicle*, had accused Sondhi of having issued it against the agreement of the other delegates. In an official statement in April 1950, the Filipinos nonetheless were slightly more conciliatory. They declared only that they would follow the IOC's guidelines and boycott every event in which Japan participated before a peace treaty was concluded that officially ended the Second World War.[29]

The next AGF meeting took place in late July 1950, where the second postponement and the participation of Japan were to be discussed. Slightly earlier, the Philippines' foreign secretary, General Carlos P. Romulo, informed Vargas that it was considered necessary to send a leading PAAF official to the meeting despite the possibility of an escalation of the Korean War (i.e., the official might be cut off in India). If India declared at the meeting that it intended to completely give up hosting the First Asian Games, the Philippines would certainly be asked to take over.[30] This demonstrated that doubts concerning Indian organizational skills were still present and even shared by one of the most senior Filipino diplomats. The number of expected delegates finally attending also had dwindled to only those from Afghanistan, Burma, Ceylon, India, Indonesia, the Philippines, and Thailand.

At the meeting, Vargas did not press the matter despite his doubts. Sondhi's offer to also step down as secretary of the AGF was not accepted. Moreover, the delegates left India the opportunity to use the First Asian Games as a means to promote amateur sport as citizenship training among the Indian population. According to Vargas in a later interview, Sondhi asked that India be allowed to go on exactly because it "was comparatively 'backward' yet in regard to sports competition" and thus needed the event "to popularize athletics in general."[31]

The question of Japan's participation was successfully solved at the AGF meeting. Azuma Ryōtarō, a professor of pharmacology at Tokyo University, who had been a member of its student rowing team, had been allowed to attend the IOC meeting in May 1950. In 1946 he had become president of the Japan Amateur

Athletic Association (JAAA), serving until 1959, and was deeply involved in bringing the 1964 Olympic Games to Tokyo, which is discussed in more depth in the fifth chapter. In 1959, he was elected Tokyo's governor, an office he held until 1967. During the IOC meeting in May 1950, he had been co-opted as an IOC member.[32] General Douglas MacArthur, Supreme Commander of the Allied Powers in occupied Japan, who in 1927–28 had been president of the American Olympic Association and had led the US team to the Amsterdam Olympics, had personally recommended him.[33] At the meeting of the AGF in July 1950, the delegates came to the conclusion that under these circumstances, Japan's participation would be acceptable as long as it was affiliated (or would re-affiliate) with the international sports federations governing the disciplines at the First Asian Games. Vargas conceded that while Japan was still technically at war with the Philippines (and strictly speaking also with India), he would not disagree with inviting Japan to India.[34]

Despite the Filipinos' doubts, on 4 March 1951, the First Asian Games were opened in New Delhi. In terms of overcoming the image of India as a 'backward' country, which was not limited to the West but also existed in East Asia, it was both a triumph and a disaster. After a long sequence of problems, failures, two official postponements, and Sondhi's stepping down as the main organizer, the Indians demonstrated that they did possess the necessary organizational skills and the infrastructure to host a regional sports event. Mello later declared that it "was indeed a miracle that we could fix a date so near in the future as March 1951."[35] The regional shape of the Games was also not what Sondhi had planned in 1947 at the Asian Relations Conference. The vision of creating *Asian* Games—games open for *all of Asia*, not only West Asia or East Asia—certainly was realized, but only eleven nations participated and another sent observers. Many of those invited remained absent, some of them as a result of war, including the twelfth AGF member, Pakistan. The Pakistani government prohibited sending a team even though sports officials desired to do so.[36] However, if one considers the still very bellicose atmosphere in the early post-war period, such as in Indo-China, the Middle East, and Korea, the first Asian Games can hardly be called a failure. The gathering of, in the end, 11 Asian countries (here meant in the sense that it could have been even fewer), many of them newly independent, at the First Asian Games was symbolic of the vision of a more peaceful Asia. The Japanese authorities had accepted sending a delegation in early December.[37] In addition to them, Afghanistan, Burma, Ceylon, India, Indonesia, Iran, Nepal, the Philippines, Singapore, and Thailand were represented. The People's Republic of China, which the Indians had invited as the representative of the AGF member 'China' they had recognized in 1950, sent observers. Hao's Kuomintang Taiwan was not present, symptomatic of yet another conflict plaguing Asia.[38]

Taken all together, the Indian officials overcame the serious doubts of many other Asians, especially those from East Asia who had already gained a lot of experience in organizing the FECG. While not all of Asia was represented due to wars or other reasons, the AGF saw nations of both East and West Asia (including South Asia) participate, fulfilling Indian visions of Asian solidarity as expressed in the Asian Relations Conference.

Nehruvian Pan-Asianism: The Message of Asian Reunification

The aims that Asian politicians such as Jawaharlal Nehru linked to the First Asian Games were not genuinely new. However, due to the bellicose situation in Asia in the 1940s and 1950s, international peace and cooperation—as expressed by the sheer fact that the event took place at all—became as important as encouraging citizenship training.

Indian attempts at Asian integration had begun in the 1920s. In the field of sport, the WAG had been an obvious attempt to recreate ties between Asian countries during the interwar period. A variety of other, often political, organizations had also been set up by the Indians. However, their achievements had been limited due to colonial travel restrictions and, during the late 1930s, the Second Sino-Japanese War, which caused anti-Japanese demonstrations in India.[39] Following the founding of the United Nations (UN) in 1945, fears emerged that UN trusteeships would recreate the League of Nations' mandate system of de facto colonies. Jawaharlal Nehru thus envisioned the founding of a federation of Asian states in case the UN should discriminate against them. In 1946, he informed Aung San of Burma about his intention to create an Asian organization. Nehru several times denied that he intended to found an 'Asian bloc' in opposition to both the 'free world' and the 'communist bloc'. However, his promotion of Asian cooperation makes it obvious that in his view only a more united Asia would be able to remain neutral in the midst of the superpowers' power struggles.[40] As he said during his opening speech at the Asian Relations Conference, such a large number of representatives of different Asian countries being able to meet in India represented a new cycle of history, characterized by an Asian 'rebirth' and a revision of global power relations:

> This dynamic Asia from which great streams of culture flowed in all directions gradually became static and unchanging. Other countries and other continents came to the fore and with their new dynamism spread out and took possession of great parts of the world. This mighty continent became just a field for the rival imperialism of Europe, and Europe became the center of history and progress in human affairs. A change is coming over the scene now and Asia is again finding herself. We live in a tremendous age of transition and already the next stage takes shape when Asia takes her rightful place with the other continent[s].[41]

Nehru also described the hosting of the First Asian Games as an important next step in overcoming colonialism. Two weeks before the Games commenced, he commented on them in terms of Asian integration and individual national development:

> Athletic contests are good from the point of view of developing, in friendly rivalry, the youth of the nation. For us, this is specially important as we have largely neglected this aspect of national and social activity. We have to aim at the physical fitness of the entire nation and, more especially, of the youth of the nation. This fitness can only be achieved if we aim high and by organising contests. This high aim has always to be kept in view. There is another aspect, an important one, to these international gatherings of athletes. They bring together the youth of many countries and thus help, to some extent, in promoting international friendship and cooperation. In these days, when dark clouds of conflict hover over us, we must seize every opportunity to promote this understanding and cooperation between nations. (...) It must be remembered always that these games and contests are to be carried out in an atmosphere of the utmost friendliness. Each one must try his utmost, but each one, whether winner or loser, must play his part gracefully and must enter into the spirit of the game.[42]

Nehru considered the shaping of more healthy postcolonial citizens, based on supervised and controlled competition, highly important. As during the FECG and WAG, the youth were the main target, but not the only one. Through educative contests, fitness and health were to be made available to everybody, contributing to a more egalitarian society. Similar to Sondhi, he also stated that the impact of a sports event on Asian integration was limited. However, considering the many conflicts in Asia, including the Korean War which had the potential to turn into another world war ('the dark clouds of conflict'), his statement is another illustration of the relevance of the First Asian Games as a peaceful internationalist project to create a more egalitarian world order.

This interpretation of the Asian Games as a *symbol of peace* is further underlined by another speech Nehru gave at the meeting of the AGF, which took place after the Games had already commenced. This speech is the one most strongly reminiscent of moderate versions of earlier *Asia as greater India* discourses already discussed in the second chapter, focusing on ancient Indian contacts to East and Southeast Asia in particular, but without describing the Indian role as totally dominant. Moreover, a third topic was that of a *temporary superiority of the West,* very reminiscent of what he said at the Asian Relations Conference. After colonialism had ended, Asia would experience a 'renaissance' and in the long run, its subjugation by the West would shrink to a minor chapter in the history books, proving teleological claims of Western civilization being the only path to modernity and progress to be wrong:[43]

> The Asian Relations Conference held in Delhi three [sic] years ago gave me a feeling of exhilaration. On seeing athletes gathered from several Asian nations I again felt that sense of exhilaration. India's relations with her neighbours, especially in the East, go back literally to thousands of years. But in the eighteenth century came a break when the countries of the West, which had developed much more than India and other Asian nations, established colonial regimes there. Asia as a whole began to play, practically speaking, no part in world affairs. The countries of Asia, therefore, lost touch and contact with each other. (...) Now in the course of the last few years we have been regaining these contacts. Of course the major reason for that is the disappearance of colonialism from several Asian countries. (...) When I think of the present in this long perspective, it becomes less burdensome, it becomes just a page in an unending story which started long ago and which undoubtedly will go on for long years to come. (...) The countries of Asia are today thinking more and more of each other because it is natural for us to do so, being neighbours. (...) In these days, there is much conflict and tension and talk of disaster in the world; it is desirable to strengthen all such forces which tend to lessen that tension and promote goodwill and understanding.[44]

Nehru personally attending the AGF meeting, and also the opening and closing ceremonies of the Games as well as some of the events, were testaments to his interest in the First Asian Games.[45] Boria Majumdar and Nalin Mehta argue that the Games were the reason why Nehru did not give up hope after the political results of the Asian Relations Conference proved to be quite limited during the following years, and why he still personally attended the Asia-Africa Conference in Bandung in 1955.[46] I agree with this interpretation. In his speech, Nehru clearly created a discourse that put the Games in accord with independent India's project of Indian-guided Asian solidarity. At the same time, the Games were also put into a much larger historical context, which reminds one of the Indian speeches at the later FECG and the WAG about the 'awakening' of Asia. Western colonialism again was declared an unnatural, and hence only temporary, event in the millennia-long history of an interdependent Asia. Through rebuilding their ancient connections—which were not invented, but beg the question of the historic continuity of Asian countries—and slowly overcoming the power asymmetry vis-à-vis the West, Asian countries were to reclaim an important role in world affairs.

Adding a realist dimension to his reasoning, Nehru went on to remind the audience that the Asian nations should focus not on a glorious past, but on the future, and remember that in economic and military terms they could not be called strong compared to the "highly industrialized and developed Western countries". He furthermore declared that the aim was cooperation between the Asian nations, but no 'Asian Bloc' aimed against the West.[47] Many of the statements made by other Indians such as Anthony de Mello, Amrit Kaur, Yadavindra Singh,

Indian President Rajendra Prasad, and sports officials from other Asian countries followed this discourse of the Games as being a symbol of a more peaceful and interdependent Asia and a means for education.[48] Especially noteworthy are the statements of the Japanese. Azuma Ryōtarō described the First Asian Games as an opportunity to present post-war Japan to the world: "For us, the people of New Japan, this is also a memorable event to send our athletes *en masse*, representing our new nation of peace-loving democratic people, which sprang up from the ashes and debris of the last war."[49] He did not only follow the common discourse of peace, equality, and democracy, but also integrated into it an image of post-war Japan as a country that now embraced these values. This claim of a sudden change of mind on the part of millions of Japanese was certainly meant to help reintegrate Japan into Asia and the 'free world'. However, such statements did not seem to have convinced all of the AGF delegates, who were not yet ready to unofficially award the Japanese the Third Asian Games when they requested them at the AGF meeting held during the Games.[50]

All in all, many Asian politicians and sports officials declared the First Asian Games to be a symbol of peace and pan-Asian cooperation, mainly because it was one of many post-war attempts to recreate ties between the newly independent or allegedly 'reborn' Asian countries, which during colonialism had been largely interrupted.

The First Stadium in Delhi

The staging of the First Asian Games was still very much influenced by the aim of educating and not entertaining spectators. Keeping costs low and focusing on the message of amateur norms and values were aims that linked the First Asian Games to the FECG and the WAG. During many of the years to come, Sondhi regularly criticized the continuous increase of the number of disciplines at the Asian Games. What others declared to be progress was, in Sondhi's opinion, deterioration in terms of the original ideals of the Games. Countries would attempt to add disciplines to the program in which their athletes would most likely perform well. However, track and field and swimming were the only disciplines that had been put into the AGF constitution as mandatory and to be held at all Games. Sondhi also advocated some other low-cost events such as wrestling and sometimes weightlifting (though he did not really deem it healthy) or competitive gymnastics, as well as team games such as volleyball and basketball. Expensive events like yachting and horseback riding or the somewhat less expensive, but still uncommon, fencing were rejected by him and other like-minded AGF officials. These events would be a waste of money as they aimed at imitating rich Westerners. Poor Asian countries were to focus on low-cost sports which, illustrating the egalitarian ideal, everybody could—and should—participate in. It would also be non-egalitarian to have so many disciplines in the Games that hosting them would be too expensive for all but the richest AGF member countries.[51] Moreover in 1952, Sondhi, who also considered strong state nationalism challenging the internationalist ideal a problem, suggested to IOC president Avery Brundage that national flags and hymns during victory ceremonies at the Olympics should be abolished. In 1960, at an AGF meeting, he deliberated not letting athletes march in national team formation during the closing ceremony to give the events a more internationalist ending. He even advocated adding some non-competitive events, such as folk dances, to reduce the feelings of state nationalism aroused when teams of different countries competed against each other.[52]

All this is further evidence that Sondhi's opinion had not changed since the interwar period; contrast this, for example, to the Chinese. National or Asian challenges to the West via expensive disciplines or other forms of nation-branding were not the aim of the Games. Instead, it was still to spread the educative message, which included low costs, as efficiently as possible. With regards to the WAG, one therefore cannot say that his 'unspectacular' approach was simply the outcome of his failings as an organizer. There was, at least in theory, a difference between hosting low-cost Games, which the Indians had intended, and messing things up, which the East Asians feared would be the result of India's 'backwardness'. In practice, however, when it came to the staging of both the WAG and the First Asian Games, the Indian low-cost approach was strongly characterized by mismanaged affairs that spiraled out of control.

When the Second World War ended, India possessed three stadia. In the late 1930s, Mello's Cricket Club of India had built the Brabourne Stadium, named after a governor, in Bombay (Mumbai) mainly as a site for cricket matches. During the war, stadia in Patiala and in Bangalore had been constructed.[53] In November 1948, Mello had developed the idea of founding a National Sports Club of India to earn, via fees for lifelong club membership, the money to build further stadia and had approached Amrit Kaur. In February 1949, he explained the plan to Nehru and suggested that the stadium to be erected in New Delhi be called the 'Jawaharlal Nehru Stadium'. Nehru showed interest in this plan to finance the development of the sports infrastructure of India through private contributions, thus allowing the state to concentrate on economic development, and ordered Kaur to provide political support. Government funding was, however, not offered. Nehru also rejected naming the stadium after him and suggested it be called the National Stadium instead (now the Dhyan Chand National Stadium).[54] Following that, it took almost a year before Nehru laid the founding stone on 19 January 1950 on the site of the demolished Irwin Amphitheatre, where part of the WAG had taken place in 1934. By then, the First Asian Games had already been postponed once and would soon be postponed for the second time, when it became apparent that the stadium would not be ready in autumn 1950. After about one year of construction work, Nehru inaugurated it on 25 January 1951.[55] The stadium had been built by a British company, was modeled on Wembley Stadium, and accommodated about 30,000 people (fig. 3.1 and 3.2). A clubhouse for members of the National

FIGURE 3.1
'National stadium and surroundings' (1951).
First Asian Games Bulletin, pp. 12–13. (Courtesy of The Olympic Studies Centre)

FIGURE 3.2
'National stadium, panoramic view' (1951).
The Organising Committee, *Official Souvenir*, n.p. (Courtesy of the Kautz Family YMCA Archives)

Sports Club of India, as well as a swimming pool with a spectator stand for 5,000 people, was constructed in its surroundings. Most of the equipment, too, had been imported from Britain. Housing for the athletes was another quite difficult issue. Two military barracks close by were eventually used.[56]

The delays in the construction of the stadium certainly were unfortunate, but almost inevitable. Strictly speaking, they were not even delays, but a demonstration that the setting up of a basic infrastructure could not be done within weeks or months. Money, too, was a serious issue and without a 100,000

Rupee loan from the National Sports Club of India the Games might not have materialized.[57] Sondhi's time schedule (beginning with the canceled invitation event for February 1949) and, like in 1934, his financial planning were to a large degree unrealistic. The result was his eventual resignation as the main organizer in spring 1950 and Mello, with more experience in this regard, assumed control. Independent of this development, the British construction company illustrated that India still depended much on Western expertise when it came to the actual construction work. The same was true for the equipment ordered from Britain. The military barracks, however, cannot be considered anything but an emergency solution and the result of a lack of money. Compared to the WAG, the organizers at least received significant political backing from the government and not only from a few princes. This nonetheless was still a strong contrast to the East Asian governments' financial support for the later FECG, which was discussed in the second chapter. In India, the problems of lack of money and experience led to a chain of spontaneous compromises and improvised solutions, which over a period of time caused many other countries to doubt if the Indians would succeed. The final success therefore seems to have led to immense relief on the side of the organizers and increased their faith that India would always succeed in the end. Otherwise, it would be difficult to explain why Mello developed the slightly megalomaniacal idea that India would be able to host the 1960 Olympic Games.[58] Certainly more important was that India's capital now possessed a stadium, which was also useful for mass political events. For example, each 14 November, Nehru would go to the stadium to receive greetings for his birthday from the public.[59]

All in all, the Indians encountered serious problems in terms of time and money. Sondhi's schedule regarding the construction program was too optimistic and illustrated, similar to the WAG, that a visionary was not necessarily a competent organizer. The situation improved after Mello took over, but the low-cost approach, which was reminiscent of the FECG and WAG and was not challenged by other AGF officials, had an undesired touch of incompetence and Indian 'backwardness'.

The Symbols of the First Asian Games and of the Asian Games Federation

Similar to the FECG and the WAG, the Asian Games allowed the AGF, and especially the host country, to support both nation- and region-building through symbols, which created identities and represented power relations. Nehru had suggested the motto of the First Asian Games: 'Play the Game in the spirit of the Game.'[60] To find a permanent motto for the AGF all delegates would support, however, proved more difficult. During the Games, 'Ever Onward' was suggested. Some AGF delegates nonetheless rejected an English expression, since all of the participating countries would feel antipathy toward Britain. As a compromise, it was decided that 'Ever Onward' would be the motto, but would be translated into the language of the respective next host country of the Games. The translation was also to be used as a greeting during the Games.[61]

Nehru's motto was an obvious statement on the importance of amateur sports ideals for the Indian organizers. 'Ever Onward', in contrast, was a strong expression of a belief in progress, and in this context also referred to Asia growing together, modernizing, and developing through sport. The compromise regarding the language, on the other hand, highlighted the problem of having no universal Asian language. Permanently using the language of a certain Asian country would confer it a special role, which was not an option if the aim was Asian equality. English, on the other hand, was widely understood by the delegates, but was not an Asian language. The idea of equality therefore was realized by using a non-Asian language 'foreign' (at least in a certain historical sense) to all Asian countries. Simultaneously, the lack of authenticity was overcome by rotating the Asian language in the leading role. It was an obvious difference from the FECG, in which Asian languages had played only an unofficial role in the staging, as was briefly discussed in the first and second chapter.

The design of the AGF emblem (or flag) was easier. The flag of the WAG must have served as a model (fig. 2.9; p. 95), since the differences are minute. The AGF flag again depicted a red sun symbolizing Asia as the 'Continent of the Rising Sun' (fig. 3.3). The number of rings below was adjusted to 11, standing for the (wrong) number of member countries, as planned by Sondhi in 1934.[62] Their color was synchronized and the motto (in English) was added below them.

The unofficial introduction of a torch relay, beginning at the Red Fort, was another symbolic element.[63] Here, the Indians could proceed as they wanted and combined 'Asianized' Olympic elements and Indian ones. The Olympic torch

FIGURE 3.3
'Emblem used at the First Asian Games' (1951).
Mello, *1st Asian Games New Delhi 1951. Opening Ceremony*, n.p. (Courtesy of the Kautz Family YMCA Archives)

FIGURE 3.4
'Medal, Ashoka Chakra' (1951).
Nihon Taiiku Kyōkai, *Dai-1kai*, picture part. (Courtesy of the Nihon Taiiku Daigaku library)

FIGURE 3.5
'Medal, India Gate' (1951).
Nihon Taiiku Kyōkai, *Dai-1kai*, picture part. (Courtesy of the Nihon Taiiku Daigaku library)

FIGURE 3.6
'Trophy, Lion Capital of Ashoka' (1951).
The Organising Committee, *Official Souvenir*, n.p. (Courtesy of the Kautz Family YMCA Archives)

relay, introduced in 1936 (the flame in 1928), brought the Olympic fire to the host country. It stood for civilization emerging after Prometheus stole fire from the Olympic gods and gave it to humans, and was lit by the rays of the sun at the ruins of Hera's temple in Olympia, thus linking the host and the Games with the Grecian heritage.[64] During most Asian Games, the lighting procedure was similar, since here the sun was reinterpreted as representing Asia as the 'Continent of the Rising Sun'. The place of the lighting ceremony was chosen by the host country. The Red Fort gave it a national dimension. The fort had been built by Moghul Emperor Shah Jahan as his palace in his newly chosen capital. More importantly, it had been where India's flag had been hoisted to show its newly gained independence on 15 August 1947 and where Nehru addressed the people on Independence Day each year.[65] The place of the torch lighting therefore connected the First Asian Games with Indian freedom and independence, but at the same time, though to a lesser degree, also stood for decolonization in Asia in general.

Even more than the torch relay, the symbols used for medals and trophies served to establish certain traditional cultural elements as symbols of independent India's state nationalism (figs. 3.4–3.6). Due to the secular-pluralistic stance of the government, these did not heavily focus on Hinduism and the Indian National Congress. For the front and back of the medals, the India Gate and the *Ashoka Chakra* (Ashoka's Wheel) were chosen. The India Gate, modeled after the Arc de Triomphe in Paris and built to commemorate Indian soldiers killed during the First World War, was a well-known monument in Delhi. After the Second World War and India's independence, a 'Tomb of the Unknown Soldier' was added here, serving to nationalize remembrance of the Indian soldiers who had given their lives for India. The *Ashoka Chakra* had been one of the symbols of Emperor Ashoka the Great (304–232 BC), who ruled large parts of the Indian subcontinent and during his later life heavily supported Buddhism. On the Indian flag, it had taken the place of Gandhi's spinning wheel depicted on the otherwise identical *Swaraj* flag of the Indian National Congress. A trophy awarded to each team was modeled after the Lion Capital of Ashoka, another symbol of the emperor, which had been chosen as the national emblem of India.[66]

In conclusion, the symbols the AGF chose for itself represented equality between its members, with the exception of the respective host country, which was awarded a special position. In contrast, the symbols the Indian organizers used focused more on India and consisted mainly of those symbolizing its independence and its secular, pluralistic government.

The Design of the Ceremonies

As in the case of symbols, the AGF decided to adopt ceremonies that communicated both identity and power relations. Similar to the later FECG and the WAG, the AGF decided to model its official ceremonies after the Olympic Games, but modified them slightly. The Olympic ceremonies had, since the First Olympic Games in 1896, been enlarged several times to give the Games a more solemn and ritualistic form and to provide spectators the feeling of the beginning and end of a special period in 'Olympic' time.

During the opening ceremony, first the head of state, President Prasad, was welcomed by the Indian national anthem. Following that, the teams marched in alphabetical order of their country name into the stadium, except for the home team which marched in last. All of them saluted the head of state, who then declared the Games open while the AGF flag was hoisted, a salute of guns fired, and doves set free. Afterwards, the flame was lit, followed by an athlete, representing all the athletes, swearing an oath to "participate in the true spirit of sportsmanship for the honour of our country and for the glory of sport."[67] At the end, the national anthem was played again and the teams left the stadium. The AGF also prescribed opening an art exhibition during the Asian Games, which was done after the opening ceremony. In 1951, India, Iran, and Thailand contributed to it.[68] The victory ceremonies during the Games featured a traditional rostrum with three steps for the three best competitors, whose countries' national flags were hoisted and national anthems played. During the closing ceremony, the teams marched into the stadium with the host country again marching at the rear. This was followed by the flags of the AGF, the current host country and the next host country, the Philippines, being hoisted and both national anthems played. The official closing words were then spoken by the president of the AGF, former Maharaja Yadavindra Singh. Finally, the flame was extinguished, the AGF flag lowered, another salute fired, and the athletes left the stadium.[69]

In contrast to the opening ceremonies during some of the later Asian Games and more resembling those of the FECG and the WAG, the Indians added only a few additional elements. Dalip Singh, by then 53 years old, had been a member of the team sent to the Olympic Games in 1924 and was one of the most senior personifications of India's sportive modernization process. He therefore was chosen as the last runner of the torch relay, and to light the flame.[70] One also has to assume that under the specific circumstances of the First Asian Games the act of setting free doves symbolized more than its traditional meaning of peace. Their newly gained freedom can be read as mirroring the freedom of the participating Asian countries from Western imperialism. The participation of 30 female athletes from Burma, India, Indonesia, Japan, and Singapore communicated a quite similar message.[71] The female athletes illustrated and promoted the continuing liberation and emancipation of women, which was one of the aims of the Indian government's egalitarian nation-building scheme. In contrast to the FECG, which had already featured women's events but had not counted them toward the general championship, this time women could win official medals. These therefore counted for the unofficial medal rankings, invented (mainly by newspapers) after it was decided not to determine an official overall champion.

It seems to have been significantly more difficult to find music and songs for the ceremonies that could serve to create an Asian identity. Similar to the problem of the motto, they eventually chose Western songs that were foreign to all Asian countries. In the view of the organizers, they probably had a certain internationalist (but not really a pan-Asian) appeal. During the opening ceremony, *Marching through Georgia* and *Way Down upon the Swanee River* were played, while the closing ceremony featured *Last Post* to signal the end of the Games.[72]

In contrast to the FECG, no educative mass sports demonstrations were held afterwards or at any other point in time during the Games, even though Sondhi explicitly considered sports to be underdeveloped in India and hoped to promote them through the Games. It certainly is possible that the absence of demonstrations was, like during the WAG, the result of the many problems the organizers had encountered and sometimes failed to overcome. All in all, it meant that a limited symbolic staging of both a national Indian and a common Asian identity was presented during the ceremonies, while the more important educative message was only communicated through the regular sports events.

Failures to Communicate the 'Asian Renaissance'

Communicating the Indian vision of an 'Asian renaissance' and of cooperation and peace to a wider audience arguably was even more important than hosting the Games. Media connections between Asian countries also could serve integration purposes and communicate infrastructure development successes. An international news agency nonetheless criticized the Indians for having missed the chance to build up interest in the Games in large parts of Asia in advance.[73] Moreover, the many problems in planning and hosting the Games led to strong criticism in newspapers, though the ideal of peaceful Asian integration normally was appreciated.

Radio broadcasting took place. The All India Radio intended to cover the Games for two hours each day in several languages for both Indians and overseas listeners, except for the opening and closing ceremonies, which were to be covered in full. The Japan Broadcasting Company/Nippon Hōsō Kyōkai (NHK) cooperated with the All India Radio and sent two announcers to New Delhi, who in the end encountered several technical and organizational problems.[74] A film, in contrast, seems not to have been produced. The lack of an official report was another failure in terms of public relations. Finally, the Games themselves seem not to have attracted that many spectators even on the opening day. According to the *Times of India*, this was the result either of a lack of publicity or of expensive tickets.[75] Some athletes also claimed that during certain events, such as weightlifting, hardly any spectators were present.[76]

In conclusion, media attention was certainly broader than during the quite short and dubious WAG in 1934. Nonetheless, it was nothing special compared to the later FECG. The hosting of the Games also did not yet lead to aspirations of developing and improving television broadcasting. This would be an important aim during some of the later events covered in the sixth, seventh, and eighth chapters. Similar things are true for the Ninth Asian Games (New Delhi 1982), which centered very much on Prime Minister Indira Gandhi (Nehru's daughter), and led to an overhaul of the Indian television system and the introduction of color television. They thus stand in strong contrast to the First Asian Games.[77] Finally, the limited attendance in the stadium was another demonstration that public relations were, among other reasons due to a lack of experience, as much plagued by problems and flaws as the rest of the organization of the Games.

Assessment

The First Asian Games without doubt were a strong symbolic orchestration of peace between many Asian countries that were newly independent or allegedly 'reborn' (i.e., Japan). This has to be seen against the context of Asian wars for independence and civil wars following the Second World War, as well as large-scale international wars such as the Korean War. Nonetheless, the internationalist ideal, which the American YMCA had started to spread in many Asian countries, had by then undergone a geographical change. The Indians' model was the Asian Relations Conference, which had brought together delegates from all over the Asian continent. The Asian Games, too, were to incorporate the regions of West and East Asia (WAG and FECG) and thus were designed to be the Games of *all* of Asia. This geographical increase in the ideal of Asian integration was accompanied by a change, strictly speaking a decrease, in the level of practicability, realistic planning, and other organizational skills. Moreover, the enlargement strongly increased travel costs, which had been an important factor for the YMCA's initial splitting of Asia, as the largest continent, into two parts. If the focus was still on promoting mass sport, it was questionable whether an increase in the scale of the Games would make significantly more common people take up amateur sport, while the additional costs created by the increase would definitely take away resources from mass sport in the host country. The Indian organizers thus accepted Games much larger than the WAG as a necessity to implement their sportive pan-Asian vision, but attempted to keep costs low. However, the infrastructure in New Delhi was completely insufficient for an event of that scale. From the beginning, East Asian sports officials therefore had serious doubts regarding the Indian ability to host the First Asian Games, at first attempting to bring them to China and later to use the Philippines as a substitute host.

The internationalist dimension proved successful in many ways. Japanese athletes peacefully competed against athletes from several countries with which Japan was still de jure at war.[78] The Japanese even won the Games by a huge margin, illustrating their leading status in terms of sportive modernization despite the defeat in the war. The second place went to the Indian team that had been trained by Ted W. Arnold of the YMCA College of Physical Education in Madras (Chennai). It showed that certain connections to the YMCA and its sportive internationalist modernization project still existed.[79] Symbols of the AGF such as a motto and a flag also were invented to build a sports-based common Asian identity. Nonetheless, the Indians at the same time used the Games to promote the cultural elements chosen for their still very young pluralistic and secular nation-building project. The inclusion of female athletes and the strong focus on low-cost mass sport certainly also can be seen as part of this nation-building project. Moreover, they saw the Indian role in the Games as did Nehru in foreign affairs, as a special one. Boria Majumdar and Nalin Mehta described India's self-perception at the Games as the 'Big Brother of Asia',[80] guiding its 'little brothers'. Mello's statement quoted at the beginning of this chapter already hinted at the aim of India-led peaceful cooperation between Asian countries, or of 'Asia as greater India'. Another illustration is how the flag poles set up before the main entrance of the stadium had participating countries' flags hoisted at the same height, except for the Indian flag, which flew higher. The Filipinos later explicitly criticized the special position of the Indian flag as having a paternalist or even a hegemonic pan-Asian touch, not an egalitarian one.[81]

The display of progress, indicated as one of the aims of the Games by the AGF motto 'Ever Onward', was significantly less successful when it came to the 'hard facts'. The Indian referees were accused—following the tradition of the later FECG—of being insufficiently trained and of having made biased decisions. Furthermore, the Indians' limited organizational skills had not only led to problems during the preparations, but also marred the events. According to the PAAF's *The Filipino Athlete*, among other things, not a single event started on time, while seven victory ceremonies were not held since they collided with other events. *The Filipino Athlete* concluded that none of these issues had been catastrophic, but that India had simply not been ready for the Games.[82] Other sources bring up many further technical and organizational issues.[83] Finally, after no official report on the Games was published it was suspected that Mello and his assistants in the organizing committee had engaged in very dubious financial practices and tried to cover things up.[84] This allegation would begin a tradition of people involved in organizing the Asian Games being accused of corruption. As in many of the later cases, it is difficult to judge if the practices were really illegal, or legal but perceived as completely wrong from the point of view of specific cultural assumptions. Independent of this question, it certainly did not help improve the image of the host country.

All in all, the founding of the AGF and the hosting of the First Asian Games were, similar to the FECG and WAG, described as an element of national and Asian 'rebirth'. Strictly speaking, such statements had been made for more than four decades since the First FECG had been inaugurated in 1913. While East Asia had already experienced a certain politico-cultural decolonization process (not limited to sport) before the Second World War, the focus of the 'rebirth' now shifted to all of Asia after the war set a large-scale decolonization (and in Japan, a demilitarization) process into motion. Hopes of national and Asian transformations after freedom ran high, and when it came to Sondhi's and Mello's visions of rapid sportive modernization and especially infrastructure development, they even had a megalomaniacal touch.

CHAPTER 4

A 'Free Country' Belonging to the 'Free World': Philippine Independence, Dubious Democracy, and the Second Asian Games (1–9 May 1954)

> May I fervently hope that this coming athletic competitions [sic] among the best athletes from the different countries of Asia will prove to be a very effective factor in strengthening the ties of friendship and mutual understanding among them so that Asia, as a unit, could contribute to a common effort with the West and the rest of the *democracies* to insure the permanence of *democratic* institutions all over the world and the eventual establishment of a universal regime of peace, happiness and contentment among the different races. (...) All that is important is that *democracy* will triumph in all its splendor and magnificence and this coming Asian games will afford to the Asians the rare opportunity of proving to the world that they can act as one man and perform their role in the realization of a common objective the perpetuation of *democracy* as an institution so necessary to man in his pursuit of real happiness.[1]
>
> *—Carlos P. Garcia, Vice President and Secretary of Foreign Affairs of the Third Republic of the Philippines, in his message welcoming the Second Asian Games*

The Philippines had already had a long experience of hosting international sports events by 1954. However, the Second Asian Games were to be the first big international event hosted by Filipinos that did not take place under colonialism, since they had received their de jure independence from the United States in 1946. The Cold War also had a strong impact on the Games, because the islands remained a close ally of the United States. The Second Asian Games served, as the Far Eastern Championship Games (FECG) and the First Asian Games had done, as a platform for promoting Asian unity and peace. However, due to the complete absence of communist-governed countries, the organizers were able to indirectly link the event with the 'free world' and democracy. At the same time, the Games provided the possibility of focusing more strongly than the FECG on displaying a pre-American Philippine culture. Finally, the International Olympic Committee (IOC) had granted the Asian Games Federation (AGF) its patronage at the Helsinki Olympics in summer 1952.[2] This patronage had a limited impact on the Second Games, particularly regarding the staging, but would become of greater importance in Japan, Indonesia, Thailand, and Iran, covered in the following chapters.

In this chapter, I demonstrate how Filipino officials and their Asian collaborators attempted to use the Games to promote democracy and the 'free world' to other Asian countries, including a focus on their discourses and the inclusion of new AGF members. The Asian Games was turned into an event for countries that maintained a pro-Western or neutral stance in the Cold War. Simultaneously, I show that the event served to portray the Philippines as a 'free country' that rejected complete American assimilation. Moreover, I relate the organizational flaws and the ensuing public debate about them to the more general problems of Philippine democracy in the late 1940s and early 1950s, which did not help in advertising democracy to other Asian countries.

The Philippines in 1954

At the end of the Second World War, the Philippine economy was ruined. The Filipino political and economic elite therefore considered American assistance and Japanese reparations essential for rebuilding the country. However, the condition for receiving American economic assistance was accepting several unequal economic and military arrangements, meaning that although the Philippines officially became independent on 4 July 1946, they remained a de facto semi-colony of the United States. To facilitate American—Philippine cooperation, the more general problem that large parts of the Filipino elite had collaborated with the institutions the Japanese occupation forces had set up, such as the Philippine Executive Committee and later the government of the de jure independent Second Republic of the Philippines (1943–45), was afterwards relatively quickly 'forgotten' through a very broad amnesty.[3]

Another pressing issue was the deteriorating internal situation in the Philippines. External threats to the Philippines were limited, but the American Truman administration became afraid that the Philippines might, like China, experience a communist victory in a civil war. After their leader had been ousted from parliament by President Manuel Roxas, the communist forces that had been founded during the war, the Huks (*Hukbalahab*/'The Nation's Army against the Japanese') had decided to take up arms against the government.[4] American intervention prevented a possible Huk victory. In 1950, after China had been 'lost' and the battle against communism continued in other theatres like the Korean War

(1950–53) and the First Indochina War (1946–54), the geostrategic importance of the Philippines increased considerably. The archipelago was considered a very useful supply hub for the 'free world' in Asia for the 'containment' of communist expansion on the continent or, like in Korea, where the southern part had initially been almost completely conquered by the north, for attempting a 'rollback'. Even earlier, members of the Truman administration, such as Assistant Secretary of State Dean Rusk, had warned that a communist victory in a Philippine civil war would be not only a strategic setback, but also a great disaster in terms of the Cold War ideological rivalry, considering the decades-long American 'civilizing mission' in the islands. Others reasoned that advertising democracy in Asia would be more convincing if done by Asians, such as Filipinos, instead of Americans.[5] In the end, in the summer of 1950, the Central Intelligence Agency (CIA) intervened into Philippine domestic politics and assisted the new minister of national defense, Ramon Magsaysay, in his ultimately successful fight against the Huks. Since, among other reasons, Magsaysay showed a willingness to back the United States uncritically, the CIA then also encouraged and supported his successful campaign for the Philippine presidency in 1953.[6]

On the international level, a defense treaty between the United States and the Philippines was concluded in 1951 as a consequence of the Korean War. During the following years, discussions over the next step became more intense. A security system covering Southeast Asia was proposed, mainly because of the United States' new Eisenhower administration's decision to further increase American influence in Southeast Asia, particularly after French forces were defeated by the communist Vietnamese army at the battle of Dien Bien Phu (March to May 1954). About one month earlier, a South and Southeast Asian conference on this topic had been hosted in Colombo at which representatives of Burma, Ceylon, India, Pakistan, and Indonesia had met. Despite many differences between the attending delegates, it was to have an important impact on the hosting of the Asia-Africa Conference in Bandung in 1955. Another noteworthy conference in 1954 caused by the power struggle in Indochina was the Manila Conference—attended by representatives of Australia, France, New Zealand, Pakistan, the Philippines, Thailand, the United Kingdom, and the United States—which eventually led to the founding of an anti-communist alliance for Southeast Asia, SEATO (Southeast Asia Treaty Organization).[7] As a consequence, Asian countries and colonies were increasingly integrated into regional security structures due to the intensification of the Cold War.

The Organizers of the Second Asian Games

Much about the development of sport and physical education in the Philippines has already been discussed in the first and second chapters, particularly the role of the American Young Men's Christian Association (YMCA), the influence of the FECG and the Philippine Amateur Athletic Federation (PAAF), and the nationalization process through the creation of offices such as that of the Philippine national physical director. The same is true for the construction of the Rizal Memorial Sports Complex, where the Games took place. A few words on those Filipinos most involved in organizing and financing the Second Asian Games will thus suffice to underline the close ties they had to the Philippine government.[8]

President Magsaysay served, due to his office, as the patron of the Games. His personal involvement in the hosting of the Games, however, seems to have been very limited, which is not surprising since he became president only in late 1953. More important was that, as mentioned in the third chapter, Jorge Vargas had resumed the office of PAAF president after being amnestied. He was awarded the office of AGF president for the Second Asian Games.[9] Antonio de las Alas, vice president of the PAAF since 1932, became president of the organizing committee. Like Vargas, de las Alas was an American-educated Filipino, who during American colonialism had studied at Indiana University and Yale University. After his return to the Philippines, de las Alas had worked as a businessman and politician, rising to the positions of speaker of the house of representatives and secretary of public works and communication. During the Japanese occupation, he had served as secretary of finance of the Second Republic of the Philippines. After the war and his amnesty, he was involved with several companies and institutions, such as the newly created Central Bank of the Philippines.[10] The secretary of the AGF and director of the organizing committee was Regino R. Ylanan, the national physical director of the Philippines. As discussed in the second chapter, Ylanan had been trained by the American YMCA.[11] Candido C. Bartolome, the physical director of the University of the Philippines, became the secretary of the organizing committee. Bartolome, too, had been trained at the International YMCA College (the later Springfield College) before he took up his professorship.[12]

In summary, every single one of the Filipino main organizers was currently or had been either a politician or a leading civil servant. This is significant because collaboration with the government was especially important due to the dependence on it for funding the Games. The Philippine parliament eventually decided to contribute ₱300,000.[13] However, direct involvement by cabinet members, the head of state, or his relatives did not take place. This was in contrast, for instance, to the Games in Indonesia, Thailand, and Iran. Thus, the Games in the Philippines were strongly influenced by politics, but not entirely dominated by them.

Bringing the Asian Part of the 'Free World' into the Games

Between 1951 and 1954, eight new countries joined the AGF while the People's Republic of China, which had sent observers to the First Asia Games, did not join. The number of member countries therefore almost doubled, rising from 12 to 20. Even more important is that all of the new members were allies of, or colonies of allies of, the United States. Moreover, almost all were situated in South, Southeast, and East Asia. The hosting of the Second Asian Games in the Philippines thus had a considerable geographical and political-ideological impact on the regional shape of the AGF. The example of the inclusion of the Republic of China (Taiwan) serves to underline the strong influence which the Filipino organizers had on this pro-American expansion and reshaping.

When the Games opened in Manila in May 1954, Cambodia, the Republic of China (Taiwan),[14] Hong Kong, Israel, Malaya, North Borneo, South Korea, and South Vietnam competed for the first time. The same was true for Pakistan, which was an AGF founding member but had not sent a delegation in 1951. Iran and Nepal, in contrast, did not participate, while Iraq and Lebanon, which had been asked to join the AGF, had not done so.[15] In the case of Iran, Iraq, and Lebanon, all relatively pro-Western countries in the Middle East (Iran and Iraq would join the Central Treaty Organization (CENTO), a SEATO equivalent founded in 1955[16]), one can assume that travel costs was the main reason for their absence. The same is probably true for small Nepal, which had also not yet joined the Olympic Games. The return of Pakistan can easily be explained by the fact that the Games did not take place in India. It should nevertheless be remembered that Pakistan participated in the Manila Conference in autumn of 1954 and also joined CENTO. If linked to the Philippines' pro-American foreign policy, the joining of Malaya, North Borneo, and Hong Kong is also interesting, since these three territories were still under the control of Britain, another SEATO signatory. The same was true, to a certain degree, for Cambodia as well, which had gained its independence from France in 1953, but was still dependent on it and was to be protected by SEATO, though not becoming a member itself.

Most noteworthy is the participation of the Republic of China (which, like the People's Republic of China, claimed to represent 'China'), South Korea (the territory south of the military demarcation line that marked the end of the Korean War in 1953), South Vietnam (strictly speaking the Vietnamese territory Emperor Bao Dai and the French claimed to control before Vietnam split into two parts in late 1954) and Israel (the Jewish state founded in Palestine in 1948). The former three all represented the anti-communist, American-supported governments of divided countries. Israel had already asked for permission to participate in the First Asian Games, but Indian IOC member Guru Dutt Sondhi had, advised by the IOC, decided to wait until its National Olympic Committee (NOC) was recognized.[17] However, Israel was also a close American ally and the only country situated in West Asia (or the mostly Arab Middle East) to join the AGF. The inclusion of the four countries strongly influenced the regional shape of the AGF in two ways. As mentioned, it strikingly mirrored more general American and Philippine foreign policy aims. Probably even more important was that the respective rival communist governments or, in the case of Israel, several Arab countries, due to official non-recognition of their enemies, would not voluntarily join the AGF until about the Seventh Asian Games in Tehran in 1974.

American foreign policy thereby became entangled with the interpretation of the ideals of the Asian Games. Similar to the problem of the inclusion of Manchukuo in 1934, covered in the second chapter, the ideal of egalitarian internationalism now begged the question of either acting according to the international status quo (recognizing two countries or, in the case of Israel, its existence), or focusing on the status quo ante (recognizing only one country or, in the case of Israel, rejecting its existence) when permitting countries to join the AGF. For example, when it came to the question of including one or two 'Chinas', Vargas, who can be considered the most important official involved in the matter, promoted the latter solution. The IOC had already taken this route in 1953, following problems at the 1952 Helsinki Olympic Games.[18] Based on this premise of the de facto existence of two Chinas, Vargas could argue that both needed to be allowed to participate to support the ideal of egalitarian internationalism: "Speaking for the Asian governing body, Vargas said there was absolutely no political significance in the appearance of Nationalist China on the list." He also declared that "the [AGF] board's policy is to accord equal treatment to all applicants and therefore Red China will be afforded due consideration by the board if it should decide to file an application."[19] He was certainly fully aware that the People's Republic would not file an application as long as the Republic of China was a member, therefore limiting participation in the Games to the American and Philippine ally. However, this approach is reminiscent of his pro-Manchukuo decision in 1934. One therefore has to assume that he considered theoretically opening the AGF to both 'Chinas' the 'realistic' decision, since accepting mainland China's claim over Taiwan, or the Kuomintang's claim over mainland China, would defy 'reality'.[20]

According to an account by leading Kuomintang sports official Hao Gengsheng, Vargas did all he could to bring the Republic of China into the AGF after a delegation of observers from the People's Republic had attended the First Asian Games. When the first preparatory meeting of the AGF for the Second Games took place during the Helsinki Olympics in 1952, Hao had traveled to Finland to meet the IOC and the AGF and to further discuss the status of the Republic of China.[21] Vargas as the AGF president apparently privately invited Hao to attend the AGF meeting, since he could not be invited as a representative. However, before the meeting officially commenced, AGF vice president Sondhi was said to have loudly asked Vargas why Hao was present and which member country he represented. Vargas then seems to have quickly backed down before this unexpected criticism and declared that Hao did not represent a member country. Following this, Hao appears to have reminded the officials of the important role he had played during the discussions regarding the founding of the AGF at the 1948 London Olympics and stated, before leaving the building, that he had thought that some of the members were good friends of his. A clerk apparently stopped him before he found a taxi, informing him that de las Alas had proposed successfully, with unanimous acceptance, to invite him to participate as an AGF member. Hao then seems to have returned and, loudly addressing Sondhi, recalled that Chinese President Chiang Kai-shek had supported the Indian independence movement during the Second World War despite being heavily dependent on British support in his fight against the Japanese and that Mohandas Gandhi had been very thankful to Chiang. Sondhi thus should not try to take advantage of the problems of the Republic of China, which, according to Hao, had become the first victim of the spread of communism. Hao also claimed that after these remarks Sondhi became much friendlier towards him.[22]

To what extent these events were staged by Hao and the Filipinos and how much took place spontaneously remains an open question. It is also difficult to determine how Vargas and de las Alas convinced the AGF officials to invite Hao back. Based on Hao's criticism of Sondhi, one can assume that the Filipinos, too, might have used a discourse of anti-imperialist Asian solidarity, recalling the Asian struggles for independence against Western imperialism, though very likely excluding the communist contribution to it and not mentioning the difficult heritage of Japanese pan-Asianism. Possibly, they also described communism as a new form of imperialist threat to Asia's freedom, as would be done in the following years by representatives of pro-Western Asian countries at the Colombo and Bandung Conferences.[23]

After Hao had become an AGF member and the Republic of China been invited to participate in the Second Asian Games, he convinced the Kuomintang government to prepare a large delegation to underline Taipei's importance in international sport and to demonstrate its status as a 'legitimate' country. Supported by the Filipinos and IOC president Brundage, Hao eventually arranged for the Taiwanese team to be allowed to compete in all disciplines at the Second Asian Games.[24] After this problem was solved, Hao mobilized the Chinese diaspora in the Philippines to provide desperately needed funding for the team. In the end, Taipei sent the largest delegation to the Games, thereby claiming an important role in Asian sport.[25]

All in all, these events—particularly the example of the Republic of China—make clear the important role of Filipino officials such as Vargas, de las Alas, and Ylanan in molding the regional shape of the AGF. While the AGF had initially followed the geographical focus of the Asian Relations Conference, it now turned in the direction of those Asian countries that stood on the side of the US and the 'free world' in the Cold War power bloc competition. The inclusion of the anti-communist parts of divided countries de facto meant that their communist-governed rivals would not join the AGF until the situation changed again in connection with the Seventh Asian Games in Tehran in 1974. Israel's participation also had an impact on the regional shape of the AGF, since many Arab countries would not participate in the Games before they were held in Iran. Therefore, as a consequence of the Second Games, the Middle East (or West Asia) and communist ruled Asia remained heavily underrepresented for two decades.

Democracy, Peace, and the 'Free World'

The discourses around the Second Asian Games did not differ much from those articulated in connection with the First Asian Games. The focus was still on Asian unity and peace, although the absence of communist ruled countries gave them a significantly stronger pro-Western meaning than in 1951.

For example, Vargas in his messages and articles on the Second Asian Games strongly focused on Asian unity and solidarity:

> For nine days starting May 1, several hundred athletes from 18 Asian nations, from Japan in the north to Israel on the outer fringes of the massive Asian continent, will engage in friendly but hard rivalry for sports laurels. I think there is no better way to give more tangible form to the unity of this part of the world than these games. Here, there are no diplomatic barriers, no language difficulties, no difference of creeds and religions. (...) We who have worked to bring the Asian Games Federation about were thinking not only in terms of sports events and laurels, but also in terms of solidarity and our contribution to the dream of world brotherhood. While our diplomats find a place for us in the halls of [the] United Nations, we have embarked on this program to see if we, in our humble way, and through the medium of sports, can help bring this ideal closer to realization. (...) The same wind that touches our flags and our hearts will be the same wind that will bring to our brothers in far-off places our offer of friendship and hospitality, and above all, our desire to live in peace with them.[26]

Vargas' main point was without question the ideal of egalitarian internationalism that had also been characteristic of the FECG. Similar to the 'peace discourse' at the First Asian Games, it has to be understood against the background of the still bellicose situation in Asia. While the Korean War had—possibly only temporarily—ended with a ceasefire in July 1953, international attention had then shifted to the First Indochina War and, more distantly, the Cold War in divided Europe. The bellicose situation was also explicitly raised by editorials in the bulletins that the organizing committee issued, which were very likely written or at least influenced by Vargas or de las Alas.[27] Moreover, by indirectly linking the Games to the United Nations—which in June 1950, following an USSR boycott, had intervened in the Korean War on the side of South Korea, and in which the Republic of China (but not the People's Republic of China) held membership (this having been the reason for the temporary Soviet boycott)—Vargas subtly connected the sports event and peace with the 'free world'. To give this peace discourse a foundation in concrete norms and values, he also explicitly mentioned amateurism and the 'spirit of the game' in his messages and texts.[28]

De las Alas, too, touched on the point of sports events as a means for peace, understanding, and unity, and therefore for overcoming some of the gruesome outcomes of war.[29] Although this was again fairly typical rhetoric based on the ideal of egalitarian internationalism, seen in the context of the complete absence of communist governed countries, it must, like Vargas' statement on the United Nations, be understood as an implicit assertion that the communists did not support such values.

This reading was made even more obvious when President Magsaysay declared peace to be the central aim of the Games, but limited this message to those countries with which the Philippines already had friendly relations:

> Of greater consideration is the fact that through their [the foreign athletes'] presence in this country, we may be able to seize the opportunity of further strengthening the ties of friendship which already exist between them and us. This should not be difficult. For we have one thing in common: we love peace and all that it stands for. Loving peace with the same passion, we can hand in hand easily find the road to better understanding and harmony in the years to come.[30]

Participating countries such as the Republic of China, South Korea, and South Vietnam were thus integrated into this circle of peace-loving countries, while the absent communist ruled countries—the enemies in the Chinese Civil War, the Korean War, and the First Indochina War—were not. Magsaysay's pro-democracy and pro-'free world' message nevertheless was still less clear than that of Philippine Vice President and Secretary of Foreign Affairs Garcia quoted at the beginning of the chapter. Garcia, after all, declared peace and Asian unity as encouraged by the Games to be directly linked with the "permanence of democratic institutions all over the world" and he also hoped that "democracy will triumph in all its splendor and magnificence".[31] At the core, one thus can say that he considered the Games as a Philippine contribution to American Cold War foreign policy. His statement is nevertheless less focused on 'containment', such as crushing the 'Huk Rebellion', than on a 'rollback' of communism, as had been attempted by the American-led United Nations (UN) forces in Korea, or even its complete elimination.[32]

In conclusion, one can say that the discourse of 'Asian Games = peace = democracy' experienced a strong upsurge before and during the Second Asian Games as the outcome of the increased power bloc rivalry during the Cold War. It should be obvious that it is generally problematic to equate broad ideals like egalitarianism and especially internationalism only with liberal-democratic systems, as some of the later chapters on authoritarian countries will show. Instead, in most of the discourses discussed, 'democracy' was simply used to encompass, based on the perception of the Cold War as a binary conflict, *everybody* who did not belong to the 'communist bloc', which included countries considered democracies or declaring their aspirations of becoming one. The absence of communist ruled countries then served to indirectly—in some cases even directly—link 'democracy' with peace, which the Games were declared to represent.

The Official Ceremonies: A 'Free Country' Belonging to the 'Free World'

When the IOC granted its patronage in 1952, it asked the AGF to refrain from using many ceremonial elements that it thought should be limited to the Olympic Games. While the official ceremonies thus were rather short, the entertainment programs succeeding and preceding them did provide the necessary opportunity to communicate certain messages. Here, traditional Philippine cultural elements were more prominently featured than during the FECG, although internationalism was also encouraged.

When the IOC discussed awarding the AGF its patronage, it came to the conclusion that no torch relay should take place, no flame should burn in the stadium, and no white doves should be set free. Some of the most spectacular ceremonial elements introduced into the Olympic Games before the Second World War were to be, as far as possible, limited to it alone as the most important and prestigious international sports event.[33] Similar problems came up in connection with the disciplines since popular sports—such as baseball, tennis, and volleyball—that had been characteristic of the FECG were not Olympic sports, meaning that they could not be included in the Asian Games. However, like in the case of the torch relay and the flame, the Japanese organizers of the Third Asian Games would, during their preparations, successfully renegotiate the conditions and official sports disciplines with the IOC.[34]

The opening ceremony in Manila, however, proceeded as defined by the AGF and the IOC's conditions at the time. One special feature the Filipino organizers added was the singing of an official song of the Games, as it had been done at the Ninth and Tenth FECG. This song, called *Ever Onward* (after the AGF motto), was played by the constabulary band and sung by a choir of several hundred people. The choir was conducted by the composer of the song, Major Antonino Buenaventura, one of the leading Filipino composers of the time. The song was written in English and heavily focused on sportsmanship, equality, and Asian unity.[35] In the context of the event, it therefore had a strong pan-Asian internationalist meaning. Amateur norms and values served to unite the Asians, while English, though a foreign language, gave the song more international appeal than Tagalog would have, since it was also understood by many foreigners.

Following the opening ceremony, mass demonstrations by teachers, schoolchildren, and students, many of them dressed in traditional outfits—*barong Tagalog* and *baro't saya*, cut in a way that allowed fast movements—exhibited physical education practices common in the Philippines. A variety of Filipino folk dances, such as *La Jota Moncadeña*, *Bakya*, *Cariñosa*, *Mananguete*, *Tinikling*, and *Maglalatik*, were displayed (fig. 4.1). The dances brought in traditional elements of pre-American and, in some cases, also pre-Spanish Philippine culture. The same is true for some of the children's games that were performed. However, a few American elements, like dancing to jazz music, can also be found.[36]

The entertainment program demonstrates that the focus had partially shifted away from the educative demonstrations that had characterized the FECG. Teaching people physical education practices was no longer so important four decades after the First FECG had taken place. Although the performances could still motivate people to take up physical education (including dancing), entertainment and the staging of Filipino culture seems to have been more important. This goes back to the late 1920s, when academic interest in traditional Philippine folk dances began. After Jorge C. Bocobo, who as president of the University of the Philippines had encouraged the research, became secretary of public instruction, a Bureau of Education Folk Song and Dance Club was organized in 1940.[37] This club then served to encourage folk dances at public schools, demonstrating that proto-decolonization during the Philippine Commonwealth period had already led to a change in officially desired cultural elements. Most of the events at the Second Asian Games thus can be interpreted as a means to visually display the Philippines as an independent country with a genuine culture. American elements existed, but the main focus was on *pre-American* practices, thereby denying the dominance of American culture in the Philippines' postcolonial modernization process. This is not necessarily surprising, if one remembers that organizers such as Vargas and de las Alas supported American-guided Philippine anti-communist foreign policy, but also had been involved in the islands' pre-war struggle for independence and had collaborated with the Japanese, thereby arguably rejecting American dominance.

FIGURE 4.1
'Cariñosa dance at the opening ceremony's entertainment program': The Games featured American, Spanish, and pre-Spanish cultural elements to show the nation's 'unity in diversity'.

Second Asian Games Manila, Philippines: May 1–9, 1954: Official Report, p. 49. (Courtesy of The Olympic Studies Centre)

The same combination of a strong focus on the Philippines and a moderate focus on internationalism held true for the closing ceremony. The entertainment program that preceded it was not much different from the one at the opening ceremony, except that this time more Western elements were presented. Rhythmic gymnastics, modern dance studies, and American square dancing, during which the dancers wore Western clothing, were accompanied by Philippine folk dances (*Palay, Kapiil Sa Munsala, Rogelia,* and *Subli*).[38] This time, the elements associated with the United States (at least square dancing, even though it is more Western than American) thus hinted a bit more strongly at the American influence. However, with some imagination, such elements could also be interpreted as belonging to a more global modernity and the lifestyle of the 'free world', which, in the view of American politicians, was best promoted to other Asian countries through the Philippines.

At the closing ceremony, in addition to *Ever Onward,* two famous American songs, strictly speaking an American and a Hawaiian one, *God Be with You till We Meet Again* and *Aloha Oe,* were sung.[39] Although they had obvious American connotations, these songs, due to the English language and their topic—departure and an eagerness to meet again—in the context of the closing ceremony have to be understood as an expression of Asian internationalism. That Filipino marines—that is soldiers rather than AGF officials, athletes, boy scouts, or whoever—were chosen to carry away the AGF flag after it was lowered seems at first glance slightly discordant with this just mentioned Asian internationalism.[40] However, the choice might have been made to domestically and internationally promote the image of the Philippine armed forces, which had fought in Korea and, under Magsaysay's command, had defeated the Huks. In the absence of communist-governed countries, the marines—elite soldiers –could be understood by the spectators as people who defended and protected Asia, represented by the AGF flag as one of the few pan-Asian symbols at the Games, against communist aggression. At the end of the ceremony, an image reading 'Youth of Asia Ever Onward in Friendship through Sport' was displayed on the scoreboard.[41] This was a final element of the Games serving to communicate an Asian-internationalist message, visually showing what the songs audibly expressed.

In conclusion, as a result of IOC patronage the official ceremonies lacked a lot of spectacular events. More noteworthy is that, in contrast to the FECG, the entertainment programs heavily focused on elements of pre-American and sometimes pre-Spanish culture, thereby highlighting that the Philippines' modernization did not mean complete assimilation to American culture. Like in 1951, claims that Western-American civilization was the only road to modernity were thereby rejected. Some American elements were nevertheless included and were primarily used for promoting peaceful internationalism. Genuinely pan-Asian elements, in contrast, were relatively scarce. As a consequence, the Philippines appeared as a 'free country' with its own modernization process, but also belonging to the pro-American 'free world'.

The Symbols of the Games: A 'Free Country' Belonging to the 'Free World'

Similar to the official ceremonies and reminiscent of the later FECG, the symbols used in connection with the Second Asian Games focused on the Philippines and its broad cultural heritage, but also showed an appropriation process involving Olympic elements.

The medals used for the Games were prepared by a Philippine company, El Oro, with the declared aim of demonstrating that Filipinos could produce high-quality versions at least as good as those used at the Olympic Games.[42] The intention of overcoming images of the Philippines as a 'backward' country is obvious.

The front side of the victory medals showed a silhouette of an athlete, very likely a Filipino, having a laurel crown (an Olympic element) placed on his head as a symbol of victory (fig. 4.2). In the background, other athletes participating in various sports can be seen, and behind them parts of a stadium. The place, year and title of the Games, as well as 20 rings symbolizing the 20 AGF member countries, are also present. On the back was a victorious half-naked athlete sitting on a dais carried by other people and holding a palm branch as a sign of victory in his left hand while greeting an unseen audience with his right arm (a variety of Olympic elements, though the ancient Roman greeting became more problematic after the Second World War, since it had also been used in Nazi Germany and Fascist Italy). The image was thus very reminiscent of the one depicted on the reverse of summer Olympic Games victory medals awarded between 1928 and 1968.[43] However, in the background, the coliseum of the Rizal Memorial Sports Complex can be seen, placing the event in Manila.[44] All in all, Olympic elements thus dominated the victory medal. This is not surprising, since the medal's aim was to show victory in a discipline which, due to the newly gained IOC patronage and the rules linked to it, was an Olympic sport. Moreover, since victors could come from any country participating in the Games, one has

FIGURE 4.2
'Victory medal, Second Asian Games': The medal's back situates a scene regularly shown on Olympic medals in Manila.

The Secretariat, Manila Sports Service Bureau, *2nd Asian Games*, p. 148. (Courtesy of the Library of Congress)

to assume that the organizers considered Olympic elements more appropriate than national ones.

In contrast, the commemorative medal for all participants focused much more strongly on Philippine and AGF elements, since its aim was to commemorate a distinctive Asian Games event that had taken place in the Philippines, not a victory in an Olympic sport (fig. 4.3). The front of the medal is dominated by a large AGF flag, carried by a half-naked athlete (again an Olympic element) and accompanied by the title of the event. The back of this medal showed an even stronger appropriation of Olympic elements than the victory medal. The Grecian motifs, such as Goddess of Victory *Nike* (fig. 4.4), of the summer Olympic Games victory medals awarded between 1928 and 1968 had been substituted with Philippine ones.[45] *Filipinas* (the national allegory of the Philippines) is seen sitting on a chair, holding the coat of arms of the Third Republic of the Philippines (an even more obvious Philippine element) in one hand and a palm leaf (in this context meant to symbolize peace and Philippine hospitality) in the other. Next to the palm leaf is

FIGURE 4.3
'Commemorative medal, Second Asian Games': The medal's back features an Olympic setting in which *Filipinas* takes *Nike's* place, integrating the Games into a vision of the independent Philippine nation.

The Secretariat, Manila Sports Service Bureau, *2nd Asian Games*, p. 148. (Courtesy of the Library of Congress)

FIGURE 4.4
'Victory medal, 1948 Olympics': The medal shows *Nike* and an ancient stadium.

Images Service, International Olympic Committee. (Courtesy of the International Olympic Committee)

a necklace made of Sampaguita, the Philippines' national flower. Blossoms of the same flower also border the lower part of the medal, evoking the impression that they are substituting for Olympic laurel leaves. In the background, the Pasig River and the Mayon Volcano (two famous Philippine landmarks, thus further national elements) are engraved.[46] Taken all together, while the front focused on the AGF, the back of the medal was completely about the Philippines, the place where the Games were held, and elements defining Filipino state nationalism.

Finally, as prescribed by the AGF rules, an art exhibition was held at the Philippine School of Arts and Trades in Manila. Japan and the Republic of China exhibited primarily Asian images, while the Philippines combined Asian and Western styles.[47] The art exhibition was therefore another illustration of the importance attributed to the Games by the Republic of China and Japan, especially considering that no other foreign countries contributed to it. The Philippines' again displayed its different cultural heritages and hence promoted cultural unity in diversity.

All in all, similar to the ceremonies, many of the symbols and images used in connection with the Games depicted a mix of Asian, Spanish, and American elements, without showing any one of them to be predominant in Philippine state nationalism.[48] This is another discontinuity with the FECG held in a colonial context, where the focus was much less on Philippine elements in general, but on Olympic ones. These, nevertheless, were also used several times in 1954 due to their internationalist message.

Incidents, Dubious Democracy, and Heavy Criticism of the Philippine Amateur Athletic Federation

Although the Second Asian Games can be considered to be more successful than the First, they were also plagued by several flaws, some of which seem to have been the outcome of sloppiness or a lack of coordination. Others reflect some of the general problems of the Philippines at this point in time, among them favoritism and 'unconventional' interpretations of democracy, which called into question the Philippines' usefulness for advertising democracy in Asia.

Beginning around early 1953, public criticism of the PAAF and particularly the leadership of Vargas, who had been serving as its president since 1935, slowly grew louder.[49] A temporary confusion regarding the participation of 'non-Asian' athletes and Vargas' and Ylanan's seemingly contradictory statements on the topic found a negative echo in the media.[50] When the Second Asian Games began, further organizational flaws materialized. For one, during the opening ceremony only the Pakistani delegation lowered their flag before President Magsaysay. Main organizer Bartolome immediately afterwards denied that the optional gesture was important and asked journalists not to mention the incident.[51] The event can hardly be interpreted as a political statement against Magsaysay, considering that the Filipino team also did not dip its flag. Rather, one has to assume that it resulted from Bartolome or one of his assistants forgetting to remind the flag bearers of the gesture, giving spectators the impression of indecency when the Pakistanis reminded them of the gesture's existence. The impression that the slight was unintentional and the outcome of organizational flaws is further strengthened by the fact that neither Bartolome nor anyone else had assigned seats to the athletes. After the athletes marched out of the stadium and the entertainment program was to begin, they could not easily return to places reserved for them. Many athletes thus apparently watched the following events while standing, while others opted to return to their accommodations.[52] The absence or seemingly inadequate treatment of the arguably most important people at the Games again had a strong touch of accidental indecorum.

Further heavy public criticism of the organizers occurred after a group of parliamentarians boycotted the Games because they considered the free seats they were awarded, which were located in back rows, to be inappropriate for their position. A short while later, they began setting up a parliamentary committee to investigate the PAAF.[53] At about the same time, the mayor of Manila, Arsenio H. Lacson, also was displeased that he did not receive a free pass for the Games and rejected the tickets he was offered afterwards. He declared that he would not allow himself to be offended in such a way and accused the organizers of being "petrified fossils who are too old to teach our children". According to him, they were inefficient and had failed to provide Filipino athletes appropriate training opportunities for the Games. He furthermore threatened to withdraw the athletes' and delegates' police escorts.[54] After the Games, Vargas dealt with the criticism by declaring that, regarding the seats, the PAAF had acted in accordance with AGF protocol and that most of the mistakes during the first day of the Games had been made by minor personnel.[55] Furthermore, AGF vice president Sondhi, who as mentioned in the third chapter, had been criticized in connection with the First Asian Games, gave an interview before returning to India. In the interview, he called the behavior of the parliamentarians "ridiculous" and "silly", since the free tickets were no more than a courtesy. According to Sondhi, the parliamentarians should keep in mind that they had no claim to better tickets and that the ₱300,000 the parliament had contributed was not their own, but public money.[56] In a private letter to Sondhi, Vargas also described the activities of the parliamentarians and the mayor as "silly" and as "antics" most Filipinos would not understand, but that he, like Sondhi, was used to such criticism.[57]

Both Vargas and Sondhi certainly had a point. The behavior of both the mayor and the parliamentarians showed that they expected to receive certain favors due to holding political office and that they would use their political influence to retaliate if their expectations were not met. Corruption is the wrong term for describing this practice, but it can be considered wrong from the point of view of many interpretations of 'good governance'. More problematic, however, is that the enquiries by the parliament and by journalists also brought to light troublesome practices within the PAAF.

An editorialist at the *Manila Chronicle*, I. P. Soliongco, began publishing details he found on main organizer Bartolome, whom he identified as the person responsible for all the problems. Bartolome, in Soliongco's view, was perfect as a professor at the University of the Philippines "to cow gaping freshmen", but was not competent as an organizer, a job that "demands intelligence and clarity of mind", and had never been an important sportsman.[58] Some days later, after he received a letter to the editor on Bartolome, Soliongco published his new information concerning an insider relationship between Ylanan and Bartolome. Bartolome had allegedly been Ylanan's locker room attendant clerk (or student assistant) while Ylanan served as the physical director of the University of the Philippines. Later, when Ylanan had already become national physical director of the Philippines, Bartolome, who had hardly been qualified, nevertheless was said to have received the office of physical director of the University of the Philippines through Ylanan's influence when it became available upon its incumbent stepping down and a more competent candidate choosing another occupation. The physical education department of the University of the Philippines therefore was still "run by Dr. Ylanan through remote control" and when "Dr. Ylanan retires, Prof. Bartolome is groomed to take his place." These activities, if true at all, also cannot be considered corruption.[59] They have, however, a strong touch of favoritism.[60]

The parliamentary enquiry caused the PAAF further problems. Quite early, the question arose of why the Games had ended in a deficit of ₱169,000, despite the parliament's contribution of ₱300,000. Vargas then reminded the committee and the public that only a book loss had been produced, since about ₱534,000 had been spent on renovating old and damaged venues of the Rizal Memorial Sports Complex, building a new one for wrestling and boxing, and buying equipment. Had no money been invested, the Games would have taken place in "a war-torn stadium."[61]

Before the enquiry committee's report was made public, Vargas' re-election as president during the annual election of PAAF officials led to another wave of criticism (fig. 4.5). After the nomination of candidates had ended, Vargas' two 'rivals' (one of whom was de las Alas) declared that they would withdraw their candidacy. Following a demand by some PAAF delegates that new nominations take place and, apparently also uncommon, a secret vote be held, it was eventually agreed to have another round of nominations. However, all candidates except Vargas again withdrew, meaning that he was automatically elected. Criticism from newspapers followed, including accusations that Vargas was ruling the PAAF like an absolutist king and, later on, that he had broken an alleged promise to other delegates that he would step down after two months if reelected.[62]

FIGURE 4.5
'George XVI, king of the PAAF': The cartoon criticizes Jorge Vargas' 'absolutist' PAAF presidency.[63]

"George XVI." *Manila Chronicle* (30 July 1954): 4 (there are two pages numbered 4). (Courtesy of the University of the Philippines Diliman library)

It is certainly inappropriate to talk of fraudulence, such as that which characterized the elections for President of the Philippines on the national level.[64] However, the election of the president of the PAAF was somewhat tainted by Vargas' evident perception of it as little more than a performance necessary for continuing his presidency and, possibly, by a general unwillingness to resign from the office. American politicians also had accused Vargas' former superior, Manuel Quezon, of a complete unwillingness to leave office as president of the Philippine Commonwealth and using legal tricks such as changing the constitution to do so.[65]

In conclusion, the staging of the Second Asian Games encountered several organizational issues. Many of them seem to have been the outcome of carelessness or insufficient planning, but did not jeopardize the successful running of the Games at all. The subsequent reactions of some Filipino politicians who felt slighted by the organizers, but also the results of political and journalistic enquiries into the

PAAF, showed deficits in terms of certain interpretations of 'good governance'. The incidents around the Games thus reflected, on a smaller and more harmless scale, the political and social problems the Philippines were experiencing at this point in time (and which had already existed during colonialism, even being an important reason why the American YMCA had founded the FECG as a means for promoting amateur sport based citizenship training). As a consequence, they partially undermined the usefulness of the Philippines for encouraging democratic institutions in Asia.

Communicating 'Philippine Freedom' to Asia

Since the communications infrastructure in the Philippines was already comparatively well-developed, national and international attention seems to have been quite high. The official report stated that 221,680 people had been admitted to the stadia, most of them being interested in a relatively small group of disciplines such as soccer, basketball, and athletics, but not in the rest, including the official ceremonies.[66] Compared to the (smaller) FECG in 1934, this was a moderate increase of about 10 per cent. When comparing the games, one nevertheless has to remember that popular sports such as baseball were not held in 1954 as a result of IOC patronage, which otherwise would have strongly boosted the number of spectators. The proliferation of radio and television certainly also reduced the audience's willingness to watch the Games in the stadium.

International attention within other Asian countries, too, seems to have been comparatively high, since 150 foreign reporters were said to have arrived in Manila.[67] In addition to newspaper coverage, the Games were broadcasted via radio within the Philippines and to several other countries. Moreover, at least Japan sent announcers to Manila to cover the Games, as it had previously done in New Delhi in 1951 and at the Tenth FECG in 1934, as discussed in the second and third chapters. This time, however, not only the Japanese public broadcaster NHK was interested in the Games. The Second Asian Games were the first international sports event at which the opening ceremony and certain disciplines such as swimming and track and field were also covered live by Japanese commercial broadcasters.[68] Furthermore, the Second Asian Games were the first major sports event held in the Philippines that was shown on television. In addition to those people who owned television sets, others could watch the Game via the roughly 100 sets that San Miguel Brewery—which was interested in promoting and selling its beer—set up in various bars, restaurants, and kiosks.[69]

Possibly due to the strong involvement of radio and television companies, interest in producing film reels of the Games was very limited. In the end, only the United States Information Service requested permission to do so.[70] It has not been possible to find out what happened afterwards, but it is likely that one or more films or 'Cold War documentaries' were produced to promote the 'free world', as many Filipino politicians and officials had done in their discourses concerning the aim of the Games.

While much of the media attention focused on the Games' athletic results, Philippine newspapers in particular also heavily covered the organizational flaws and the political quarrels that followed. AGF vice president Sondhi explicitly stated in an interview that he considered this negative coverage totally inappropriate, since the Games had been very well organized and the problems could still be dealt with when the foreign delegations had left.[71] More generally, one has to assume that problematic relations between the organizers and Filipino journalists catalyzed the willingness to publish negative news. For instance, journalists complained about problems with the security forces. Probably more important was Bartolome—and later also Sondhi—accusing journalists of having disturbed the solemnity of the official ceremonies by running around on the field.[72]

Sondhi again certainly had a point when stating that the criticism of the main organizers could have been saved for the end of the Games, considering that their aim was to show unity and peace. However, the negative coverage is also interesting if compared to some of the later Asian Games that took place in (semi-)authoritarian countries such as Indonesia, Thailand, and Iran, where local newspapers were comparatively silent (or silenced) regarding organizational flaws. The negative coverage then highlights a considerable *freedom* of the press and a desire on the part of Philippine journalists to monitor and criticize activities in their country.

All in all, it did highlight a relatively alert awareness on the part of Filipino journalists regarding problems that plagued the Games and a willingness to address them. At least in this regard, one can thus say that the Philippines' liberal civil society might have served to promote democracy in other Asian countries.

Assessment

The Second Asian Games had a decisive impact on the regional shape of the AGF and determined it for about two decades, this impact being a result of the continued Cold War rivalry between the 'free world' and the 'communist bloc'. The staging of the Games, on the other hand, was influenced by Philippine independence, and was therefore, in several ways, a departure from the FECG that had been held during colonialism. It depicted the Philippines as not only a member of the 'free world', but also as a 'free country' not affected by colonialism anymore.

While the First Asian Games were a result of the Asian Relations Conference hosted in New Delhi in 1947, the Second Games were much more in alignment with American foreign policy during the early Cold War. This is not surprising, considering that the host country remained a close ally of the United States even after its formal independence in 1946 and had experienced its own communist uprising in the early 1950s. The countries that newly joined the AGF in the end were all close allies of the United States or colonies of American allies such as Britain. Most noteworthy in this anti-communist context is the joining of South Korea, 'Vietnam', and the Republic of China. Particularly in the case of the two 'Chinas', the Filipino organizers used an interpretation of the ideal of egalitarian internationalism similar to that used in 1934, when the question of Manchukuo's participation was discussed. The focus again was on the *status quo*, which meant allowing both parts of a divided country to participate. However, since the People's Republic of China focused on the *status quo ante* (one China), one can assume that the Filipinos were aware that in the end only the Republic of China would participate after they had used their personal contacts to make Kuomintang official Hao an AGF member. As a result, then, the Republic of China could consider itself the sole representative of 'China'.

The complete absence of members of the 'communist bloc' meant the image of Asia that the Second Asian Games communicated was that of a community of countries either pro-American or neutral in the Cold War. As a consequence, by strongly focusing on the Games as a symbol of peace, Filipino organizers and politicians such as President Magsaysay and Vice President Garcia indirectly—in some cases even directly—portrayed communist governed countries as uninterested in peace. Considering that the war in Korea and the uprising of the communist Huks in the Philippines had only calmed down in 1953, the year before the Games took place, and that the war in Indochina continued during the Games, these discourses certainly found some acceptance.[73]

The staging of the Second Asian Games was much more sophisticated than that of the First Games, highlighting the experience the Philippines had gained through the FECG. However, departures from the FECG were simultaneously demonstrated, particularly in the choice of cultural elements that were used in ceremonies and entertainment programs (the latter had not existed in 1951) and for symbols. This choice can be considered to have been directly influenced by independence and, linked with it, the intention of showing a modernization process that was not entirely based on following the model of the United States. For example, the growing academic and political interest in Philippine folk dances since the mid-1930s, many of which were used for the entertainment programs, mirrored efforts to relativize American cultural influence. As a result, many elements showing the Spanish and the pre-Spanish heritage of the Philippines were prominently featured in the staging of Philippine state nationalism. American elements were not completely absent, but in the context of the Games as an Asian event served primarily to communicate Asian internationalism. The English language, for example, was useful for partially overcoming the language barrier between Asians.[74] Some Olympic elements were also used for the same internationalist purpose. In contrast, pan-Asian elements, such as the carrying of the AGF flag by representatives of all nations at the First Games, were scarce, being more or less limited to the AGF symbols themselves.

Based on official information about the number of spectators, popular interest in the islands was high, at least when it came to certain disciplines such as basketball, soccer, and athletics. The arrival of foreign journalists and announcers in Manila also shows the interest that existed in other participating countries. Considering that interest, it is unsurprising that the PAAF intended to show Philippine progress not only through a successfully hosted event, but also by encouraging good results from Philippine athletes. One result of this latter goal, for example, was the hiring of a former American Olympic athlete as track and field coach.[75] In the end, again reminiscent of the later FECG, the Philippines managed to win second place in unofficial gold medal rankings, although the distance between them and the extremely successful Japanese was huge.[76] However, the Games were also characterized by some organizational flaws, which led to a lot of negative coverage of the PAAF and its officials. Seen from the point of view of certain interpretations of 'good governance', several of the reported activities of both the organizers and a group of Filipino politicians appear problematic. They are even somewhat reminiscent of the negative characterization of Filipinos that had been the reason for the founding of the FECG as a means for discouraging favoritism and encouraging fair play, honesty, and self-control. Despite the negative coverage and the organizational flaws, many AGF officials and other people nevertheless voiced the opinion that the Games had all in all been quite well run.[77]

CHAPTER 5

'Give Us the Olympic Games': Peaceful Internationalism, 'Reborn' Japan, Olympic-Scale Perfection, and the Third Asian Games (24 May–1 June 1958)

"It is quite evident that the coming Games are expected, both at home and abroad, to come up to the highest possible standard technically as well as organizationally. In fact, the Asian Games, which have marched 'Ever Onward' from the inauguration in New Delhi to the development in Manila, will certainly aspire[,] with a great stride, towards the[ir] perfection in Tokyo."[1]

—Azuma Ryōtarō, Japanese president of the Asian Games Federation, in his message welcoming the Third Asian Games

Like the Philippines, Japan had long experience in hosting international sports events. Tokyo had even been chosen as the site of the 1940 Olympic Games, as discussed in the second chapter, although these Games never materialized due to the Second Sino-Japanese War. After the restoration of sovereignty that came with the end of the American occupation (1945–52) following the Second World War, Japanese sports officials eagerly used the Third Asian Games to contribute to their country's more general effort to overcome the negative domestic and international legacies of the war. This process included reclaiming an important role within both Asia and the wider world.

The Third Asian Games were used to improve Japan's image particularly among the Asian countries, even though the Cold War and Japan's not entirely voluntary West-alignment meant that communist ruled countries such as China and North Korea again did not participate.[2] The message of Japan having experienced a 'rebirth' as a peaceful internationalist society and a 'country of culture' was also targeted at its own population. This message, which characterized the Third Asian Games, utilized many traditional elements of Japanese culture to counterbalance the inflow of American culture.

Simultaneously, it attempted to integrate more controversial institutions and persons such as the newly founded Self-Defense Forces or the emperor. Finally, the focus of the Japanese organizers was on convincing the International Olympic Committee (IOC), whose meeting in Tokyo during the Third Asian Games was the first to be held in a non-Western country, that Japan was competent enough to host the 1964 Olympic Games. When Tokyo was elected the next year as the site of the Olympics, Japan thus became for the second time the first non-Western country considered sufficiently modern and developed to be an Olympic host country.[3] Due to this decision by the IOC, the Third Asian Games were the first Asian Games event at which the host's nation-branding had at least one obvious impact. Through the Tokyo Olympics, Japanese sports officials and politicians then received the chance to spread their message of Japanese peaceful internationalism, of Japanese culture, and of successful economic development to an even broader audience than in 1958.

In this chapter, I show how Japanese officials used the Third Asian Games to reclaim the role of Asia's most modern and developed country and to promote that image, together with one of peaceful internationalism and being a 'country of culture', at home and abroad. Moreover, I cover the strong emphasis the Japanese organizers put on attracting the Olympic Games to Tokyo, for which they could use the experience they gained in 1958. Bringing the Olympics to their country further supported Japan's nation-branding and underlined its central position in Asia.

Japan in 1958

Following its defeat in the Second World War, Japan had been occupied by Allied—primarily American—forces and experienced demilitarization, democratization, and the partial destruction of its economic base. American anti-communism, however, motivated a change in foreign policy concerning the former enemy and its integration into the 'free world'. After Japan regained its sovereignty in 1952 during the Korean War, some of the American-instituted reforms were undone by the government, but much of the new rhetoric of peace remained.

During the occupation, the Japanese government was not abolished, but became dependent on the decisions of the Supreme Commander of the Allied Powers General Douglas MacArthur and his staff. Like earlier proponents of the 'Western civilizing mission', MacArthur considered the Japanese misguided children who needed to be taught democracy and peace. A large-scale social transformation process was thus set into motion. To support these changes, a new constitution, drafted by members of the occupational bureaucracy, was accepted by the Japanese government in 1947 with only minor changes. The emperor, who was not charged as a war criminal, remained in office, but lost his former role as sovereign and head of state. Instead, the new constitution gave him the somewhat ambiguous position of the symbol of the state and the unity of the people, the latter becoming the new sovereign. Moreover, article nine of the constitution rejected war and forbade the existence of armed forces. In accordance with these new principles, the government began to promote an image of post-war Japan that centered on the 'trinity' of peace, democracy, and culture, which did not challenge the negative images of wartime Japan, created in part by Allied propaganda, but instead proclaimed a 'new beginning'.[4]

The tensions between the 'free world' and the 'communist bloc' as a result of the Chinese Civil War (1945–49) and later the Korean War (1950–53) strongly increased Japan's role in American geostrategic thinking. Deindustrialization was stopped and the Japanese economy instead experienced a boom during the Korean War as a result of the demands of the United Nations (UN) forces fighting in Korea. Moreover, after the end of the occupation, formerly purged nationalists returned to senior positions. In 1950, article nine of the constitution was circumvented by the establishment of a police reserve of 75,000 men, which in 1954 was turned into the Japanese Self-Defense Forces, de facto the armed forces of Japan, under the command of the prime minister.[5]

Newly sovereign Japan's foreign policy was largely predetermined, since the San Francisco Peace Treaty was accompanied by an American-Japanese defense treaty that added Tokyo to the list of the United States' allies. Reintegrating Japan in the post-war international order nevertheless also included (re-) gaining membership in various international organizations. As mentioned in the third chapter, among these were the Asian Games Federation (AGF) and the IOC, but between 1951 and 1956, Japan also joined the United Nations and its sub-organizations.[6]

Reestablishing official relations with former enemies and newly independent nations was another topic of importance from 1952. Prime Minister Kishi Nobusuke (in office 1957–60), a former bureaucrat in Manchuria and minister in the wartime cabinets who had not been charged as a leading war criminal, in 1957 made two trips to Southeast Asia as well as to Australia and New Zealand.[7] As a result of the Kishi administration's activities, British diplomats in 1958 came to the conclusion that Kishi showed a strong commitment to the 'free world' but also intended to take a leading role in Asia, and they even began to perceive Japan as a re-emerging global power.[8] Establishing relations with East Asian countries, in contrast, proved significantly more problematic and resulted in the above mentioned absence of China and other communist ruled countries.

The Organizers of the Third Asian Games

The American YMCA's influence on the development of sports and physical education in Japan, the hosting of and participation in the Far Eastern Championship Games (FECG), the Japan Amateur Athletic Association's (JAAA) dependence on government funding, and the awarding to Tokyo of the 1940 Olympic Games have been covered in the first and second chapter. MacArthur's support for Japan's reintegration into the Olympic movement, the Indian willingness to invite the Japanese to the First Asian Games, and the awarding to Tokyo of the Third Asian Games in 1952 were discussed in the third chapter. After the war, sports experienced a new boom, which culminated in the 1964 Olympic Games.[9] Although the post-war JAAA was still de jure a non-governmental organization, its dependence first on decisions by the occupational bureaucracy and later its dependence on state funding to build stadia should make it obvious that relations with the government remained close. The involvement of several leading civil servants and politicians, which is reminiscent of the roles played by president of Tokyo Higher Normal School Kanō Jigorō and Upper House member Hiranuma Ryōzō during the time of the FECG, further underlined the close collaboration between the JAAA and public officials.

Azuma Ryōtarō, a professor at Tokyo University, IOC member, and president of the JAAA became the president of the AGF. As mentioned in the third chapter, he had been involved in the negotiations with the IOC concerning Japan's status in 1950. Due to his offices, he became a central figure in bringing the 1964 Olympics to Tokyo. Since he was elected as the Liberal Democratic Party candidate to be Tokyo's governor shortly before the IOC's decision in 1959, holding the office until 1967, he furthermore was involved in many of the infrastructure improvements that accompanied the Tokyo Olympics.[10] The office of secretary of the AGF was awarded to Takashima Fumio, the JAAA official who had been the secretary of the contest committee for the Ninth FECG.[11] Tsushima Juichi, a pre-war financial bureaucrat and member of the post-war Upper House for the Liberal Democratic Party, became the president of the organizing committee. In July 1957, Prime Minister Kishi appointed him director-general of the Defense Agency (now the Ministry of Defense), an office he also held during the Asian Games. Later he would be elected president of the JAAA.[12] The vice president of the organizing committee was Satō Hajime, a civil servant and the vice governor of Tokyo.[13] The secretary of the organizing committee, Tabata Masaji, had been a leading employee of the *Asahi Shinbun* newspaper and was one of the founders of the Japan Amateur Swimming Federation. Later, he served as the secretary of the organizing committee of the Tokyo Olympics and as president of Japan's National Olympic Committee (NOC) after it was formally separated from the JAAA.[14] The 'lower ranks' of the organizing committee also included prominent members such as Fujiyama Aiichirō, a businessman who in 1957 was appointed foreign minister by Prime Minister Kishi.[15] Somewhat reminiscent of the role Prince Chichibu had played at the Sixth and Ninth FECG, Crown Prince Akihito (the current emperor) became the patron of the Games.[16] This group of sports and government officials was financially supported by the National Diet's decision to pay for the construction of the Main Stadium and the Tokyo Metropolitan government's funding of smaller venues.[17]

In conclusion, similar to the Philippines in 1954, the most important officials involved in hosting the Third Asian Games had close ties to the government, which is hardly surprising due to the need for government funding. However, again similar to the Philippines and India, not all of them were government officials. This fact underlined that in contrast to the following four Asian Games events covered in the next chapters, Japan's relatively democratic political system meant that a formal separation between civil society actors and representatives of the government existed. The Third Asian Games thus were not completely dominated by a (semi-)authoritarian ruling elite, though the organizers were united by their very strong interest in large-scale nation-branding.

Peace, Amateur Ideals, and Much More: A Colorful Mix of Pan-Asian Discourses

Sportive pan-Asian discourses that described the Third Asian Games as a platform to promote peace in Asia fit very well into the Japanese post-war rhetoric of democracy, peace, and culture. Strictly speaking, the discourses did not differ much from those of the First and Second Asian Games, although in the case of the Philippines a strong touch of anti-communism, which was largely absent in the Japanese case, could be found. The most important source of inspiration was very likely Japan's constitutional rejection of war, which was useful as a contrast to Japan's image as an aggressor during the Second World War. However, several pre-war conceptions of Asia (or East Asia) were also revived, underlining their heterogeneity and sometimes their vagueness.

Producing a complex—if not entirely coherent—construct of Asia, president of the organizing committee Tsushima talked about Asian unity in cultural diversity, which possibly ended in a fusion of Asian cultures during the Games: "We intend to make every effort to creat[e] a sport festival with an atmosphere in which different languages and customs will melt into one another, by providing facilities and making arrangements to meet every requirement of the participating countries."[18] However, he later brought up amateur ideals, which he declared to be a universal means to regulate human interaction (a view which went back in part to the FECG), and also raised the topic of ancient commonality between Asian countries:

> The spirit of the amateur sports, which we never cease to love, is to pursue the common ideal of all human being[s], aiming at peace and justice irrespective of race, politics, ideologies and religions. Asian Games are the sports festival in Asia and at the same time, a festival symbolizing joy and happiness of the Asian nations, proud of their common culture, and the oldest history. I ardently hope that the youths of the Asian countries who are going to bear the responsibility on their shoulders in the future generations,

> may join in one harmonious Asia through sports and contribute toward [the] peace and prosperity of the world by their healthy physical strength and their fragrant spiritual culture.[19]

Arguably, his claim of ancient commonality ('common culture') here is nothing more than a very general repetition of former discourses, since it is not easily applicable to a region ranging—in the context of the Third Asian Games—from Israel to the Philippines, but rather begs for several sub-regions. In contrast, the claim of the 'oldest history', which goes back to earlier challenges to Western civilizational superiority, was more easily digestible. Its sheer vagueness leaves it to the reader to decide whether the focus was, for example, on India, Iran, China, or Israel. The ambiguity, if it was intentional at all, could therefore certainly be problematic, but also increased the integration potential of such claims.

Like Tsushima, Yasui Seiichirō, the governor of Tokyo during the Asian Games, fell back on a strategy of combining pan-Asian discourses of (vague) ancient commonality that were more credible in, for example, an East Asian context, with a new commonality in the form of amateur values: "I should be extremely happy if you, the peoples of Asia, bound together in blood, culture and history and above all by means of the Asian Games, will assist us in bringing the Olympic Games here in the near future and also will give us a strong support to invite the I.O.C. Session to Tokyo."[20] In this case, the claim of commonality even served as a means to encourage other Asians to support Japan's ambition of hosting the 54th session of the IOC in Tokyo during the time of the Third Asian Games and to be awarded the 1964 Olympic Games. Both events were thus declared to be not only Japanese, but also Asian projects, although Japan as the host would in consequence take the leading role in Asia.

Prime Minister Kishi, too, became involved in commenting on and promoting the Games. For example, during his trip to Southeast Asia his entourage distributed the first and second of the Games' bulletins, while Kishi himself urged representatives of the respective countries to send big teams to the Games.[21] Such promotional work certainly fit with his foreign policy aim of further reintegrating Japan into Asia and of improving relations between Japan and the Southeast Asian countries that he visited. His comments on the Games, for example those delivered the day before the opening ceremony, also took into account the broad geographical shape of the Games and focused less on ideas of ancient commonality than on the ideal of egalitarian internationalism:

> Needless to say, friendship is born of understanding. It is, however, no easy task to foster understanding among millions of peoples so widely scattered over vast areas. I am happy, therefore, that the Third Asian Games, where the athletes from more [sic] than 20 countries of the Asian region are met [sic] to demonstrate their skills in friendly rivalry, provide a splendid

> opportunity to foster mutual understanding and goodwill among the participating nations.[22]

After the opening ceremony, which impressed many spectators, Kishi furthermore integrated the Games into the discourse of a 'rising Asia' which was in the process of overcoming its power asymmetry vis-à-vis the West: The "opening ceremony provided me with a vivid account of [the] growing importance of the Asian people. I deeply felt the necessity of sports. I feel ever more the strong desire to invite the Olympics in 1964."[23] By linking this 'growing importance of the Asian people' with the Olympic Games, he nevertheless, like Yasui, showed that he considered Japan the country that was to lead and guide Asia. Arguably, his erroneous statement concerning the number of Asian countries ('more than 20') in the first quotation was another hint that the exact shape of Asia did not really matter for him as long as it centered on Japan.

Finally, Crown Prince Akihito's words at the end of the closing ceremony are noteworthy for what they reveal about the Japanese perspective. Very likely, the problematic role of the emperor during the war, in whose name Japanese troops had fought in Asia and the Pacific, made it appropriate for his son and successor to limit himself to discourses of internationalism and egalitarianism that would be acceptable to all participating Asian countries. He focused purely on amateur sports ideals and refrained from highlighting Japan's role in the Games or from addressing other (vaguely defined) forms of Asian commonality that were potentially reminiscent of wartime propaganda:

> The Third Asian Games which opened on the 24th of May has given all of us the opportunity of seeing each day the spirit of true sportsmanship and fair play. We have been able to share the fellowship and atmosphere of goodwill which is the result of wholesome and sincere efforts of the participating athletes from so many nations, combined with the teamwork of the officials and personnel associated with the Games. Today, we are about to bring the Games to a close. The setting of new records is not the ultimate purpose of sports. If every man does his best and always shows good sportsmanship, then only is the true objective attained. I have seen with my own eyes and heard with my own ears how fully the participants in the Third Asian Games have demonstrated the real meaning of sports. The Games have left on me a lasting impression of comradeship which I shall draw on in the years to come. I believe that the nations of Asia must ever strive for the enhancement of their respective cultures and for the furtherance of mutual amity, and therefore, the importance of sports in furthering these aims cannot be over-emphasized. It is my hope and trust that the Asian Games Federation will push 'Ever Onward' and that its efforts will be rewarded by a strengthening of the bonds which link the members for further successes such as we have been privileged to witness during the past week.[24]

In summary, the most important Japanese officials and politicians heavily focused on the topics of peace and commonality between Asian countries, certainly having the reintegration of their country into Asia in mind. However, while such commonality often referred to amateur sports ideals, sometimes other concepts of Asian commonality (culture, history, kinship) came up. These, nevertheless, frequently appeared inappropriate, absurd, or at least questionably applicable to the broad region covered by the Asian Games.

Asia's Most Developed Country and the Application for the 1964 Olympics

In addition to the discourses concerning peace and Asian commonality, a second string of discourses focused on Japan's organizational skills and its capability to host the Olympic Games. Evaluations of the host countries' organizing of the respective events had regularly taken place, but in the case of the Third Asian Games it turned into nation-branding that had an immediate impact on bringing the Olympic Games to Tokyo.

In October 1951, the month after the San Francisco Peace Treaty was signed, Asano Kinichi, the secretary of the JAAA, visited Tokyo's Governor Yasui and discussed with him the application to host the Third Asian Games, which was followed by an official agreement. In May 1952, the month after the peace treaty was ratified and Japan regained its sovereignty, they decided to apply for the Olympic Games as well. A formal application for the 1960 Olympics took place in summer 1952 at the Helsinki Olympic Games, but the issue was not then decided by the IOC. In May 1955, IOC president Brundage informed the Japanese that they should focus on the 1964 Games, reasoning that after the 1956 Olympics in Melbourne many IOC members (meaning those from Europe) would very likely reject Tokyo as host of the 1960 Olympics, since this would again entail expensive long-distance traveling.[25] Since Rome was chosen for the 1960 Olympics and the Japanese instead focused on 1964, the Third Asian Games became a stepping stone to being awarded these Olympic Games, particularly since the IOC held its 54th session in Tokyo during the time of the Games, allowing close observation of the organizing.[26]

AGF president Azuma's statement from September 1956, which opens this chapter, made it more than obvious that the Japanese had a large-scale demonstration of national development success in mind: the expectation "both at home and abroad" would be that the Games come up to "the highest possible standard technically as well as organizationally", therefore achieving their "perfection" in Tokyo, following the events in New Delhi and Manila.[27] In Azuma's highly teleological reasoning, Japan was therefore put above the former host countries, which were seen as having contributed to the progress of the Asian

Games but also having been, in contrast to the Japanese, unable to reach the level of 'perfection'. The claimed superior competence of the Japanese organizers, not only in comparison to other Asian countries but also to the whole world, was further hinted at by Azuma's declaration that both Japanese and other peoples expected that Japan was to reach the 'highest possible standard', indicating that with Japan hosting the Games such expectations would be perfectly reasonable.

As one might expect, Azuma was not the only Japanese engaging in such branding of Japan as a highly competent host country. Secretary of the AGF Takashima, too, shortly before the Games commenced stated that "the Japanese are doing everything to ensure that the Tokyo Games are the best international event ever held anywhere".[28] Although at first glance this claim has a slightly megalomaniacal touch, shortly after the Games had concluded the president of the organizing committee of the 1956 Melbourne Olympics Wilfrid Kent-Hughes, who attended the Asian Games, validated Takashima by indirectly conceding that the Japanese had overtrumped the last Olympic Games: "I'm rather glad the Melbourne Games came before this". He also considered the Games "magnificently organized" and came to the conclusion that the "Japanese could handle the Olympics and handle them well".[29] A statement by secretary of the organizing committee Tabata at about the same time, declaring that "Japan is fully capable of organizing the Olympic Games on the basis of the success of the Third Asian Games", made it clear that such a discourse of 'Japan is the best choice for the Olympics' was exactly what the organizers wanted to hear from foreign officials.[30] Even earlier, Erik von Frenckell, Finland's IOC member, had done them that favor when he visited Tokyo on his way to the Melbourne Olympics, saying that the city was already ready for the Olympic Games, except for the new Main Stadium that was not yet finished.[31] After the Games, Lawrence J. Johnson, a member of the United States' NOC, fell in line by stating that the Japanese had hosted an "Olympic caliber show."[32] Certainly most important was that IOC president Brundage as well was highly impressed by the Games, particularly by the opening and closing ceremonies. The latter had been the "most magnificent" he had ever seen and he had taken "notes on them and will bring them to the attention of our people."[33] Similar things were said by Willi Daume, a West German IOC member, and Indian IOC member Sondhi.[34]

With such support from important international sports officials, who particularly after the end of the Games heavily contributed to the discourse of 'Japan is the best choice for the Olympics', the Japanese organizers had achieved their aim. The seemingly megalomaniacal project of outdoing the last Olympic Games had been successful. In consequence, it was reasonable to believe that Japan would be awarded the 1964 Olympic Games after this demonstration of determination to (again) be chosen as the first non-Western country able to host the Olympics. Like Tokyo's election as site of the 1940 Olympics, it represented Japan having become an equal to the West. However, in the context of defeat in the Second World War, it also was a demonstration of Japan's successful 'rebirth' as an important power in the world—and especially in Asia—and of its having overcome the post-war era marked by misery, international weakness, and reconstruction.

It should nevertheless be mentioned that the immense Japanese focus on nation-branding had already led to a debate within the AGF in 1956. Indian and other AGF members asserted that the Asian Games were *not* the Olympic Games and that their aim was to encourage people to take up certain low-cost sports instead of letting organizational expenditures explode by adding many additional disciplines and thereby make it impossible for small Asian countries to host the Games. Such criticism was very reminiscent of what has already been mentioned in the third chapter in connection with Sondhi's aims and plans. The result then had been a compromise which allowed a moderate increase in the number of events.[35] Other elements of the staging, such as ceremonies and entertainment programs, were not brought up since these were planned by the respective hosts, but a criticism of high expenditures on them was implicit in the demand for low-costs. In the long run, the new tendency to use the staging of the Games as a large-scale demonstration of national development, sometimes driven by the desire to use the Asian Games as a stepping stone to the Olympics, was nevertheless not arrested. Rather, it became a highly important factor in addition to the much older aim of promoting Western sports among Asians.

In conclusion, not only Japanese, but also many international, sports officials in their statements concerning the Third Asian Games came to the conclusion that Japan had organized the Games in an extremely impressive way and probably had overtrumped the previous Olympic Games. While this discourse of 'Japan is the best choice for the Olympics' strongly supported the Japanese in their goal of bringing the 1964 Olympics to Tokyo, several AGF officials were quite unhappy with the results. The heavy focus on nation-branding would in their opinion lead away from the aim of low-cost events serving to promote low-cost sports that could also be hosted by member countries unable or unwilling to invest large sums of money.

Making Tokyo Ready for the Olympics: Infrastructure Development and the Asian Games

Due to the determination of the Japanese organizers, who had close ties to the government, to show that Japan was sufficiently developed to host the 1964 Olympics, the sports infrastructure in Tokyo was strongly improved. This was done particularly through the construction of new facilities, which in some cases were later further enhanced for the Olympic Games. The only problem the Japanese encountered was that of setting up a Games village since costs were already exploding. This meant that the athletes were eventually quartered in hotels, which to a certain degree supported Japan's tourism industry.

The most important building constructed was the Main Stadium, now the Kasumigaoka National Stadium, which will soon vanish for yet another new stadium for the 2020 Tokyo Olympics (fig. 5.1).[36] The cost of about 1.1 billion yen (about three million USD) was borne by the National Diet. It was erected in the Meiji Shrine Outer Gardens on the site of the older demolished stadium that had been used, for example, for the Ninth FECG in 1930. Initially, the stadium had been planned to accommodate about 70,000 people, making it the biggest stadium in Asia, although public safety officials later recommended only allowing about 55,000 people into it. The method of construction nevertheless allowed a future increase in its capacity to 100,000 people in case Japan hosted the Olympic Games. Its equipment included floodlights, loudspeakers, and an electronic scoreboard.[37]

Another prestigious building constructed in the Meiji Shrine Outer Gardens was the Metropolitan Indoor Swimming Stadium, with, as the name implies, the funding—600 million yen (about 1.7 million USD)—coming from the Tokyo metropolitan government (fig. 5.2). According to Japanese sources the stadium was as good as the one used for the Melbourne Olympic Games and provided a variety of useful features such as a water-filtering system, a chlorinating system, air-conditioning, heating, lighting, broadcasting facilities, and devices for electronic timing.[39] Finally, the metropolitan government also funded the construction of the Koishikawa Stadium for soccer matches, investing about 100 million yen (about 277,000 USD).[40] The stadium was located to the west of the Kōrakuen Garden group of sports facilities, which, like several other venues distributed over Tokyo, were used for the Games.[41]

When comparing the sports facilities of the Third Asian Games to those of the Tokyo Olympics, it becomes obvious that the latter, as one might expect, outdid the former. The facilities newly built for the Asian Games were certainly of a high quality. They nevertheless were either, as in the case of the Main Stadium, further improved or, as in the case of the Metropolitan Indoor Swimming Stadium, supplemented by another venue for the Olympics. This new venue, the Yoyogi National Gymnasium, together with its annex located close to the Meiji Shrine Outer Gardens, had been designed by star architect Tange Kenzō. Due to an impressive design that combined Japanese and modern styles, it became significantly more famous than the Indoor Swimming Stadium.[42] A main reason for the difference was without question the willingness—or unwillingness—of government institutions to contribute large amounts of funding. Already for the Third Asian Games, the costs had threatened to explode, meaning that in early 1958 a short international panic arose over whether the Games could be held after government authorities cut the budget.[43] In the end, the Games took place, but despite the still huge government contribution of about 112 million yen (about 310,000 USD)—excluding the new stadia—running the Games cost about 377 million yen (slightly more than one million USD) and ended in a deficit that needed to be covered through donations.[44] The large-scale nation-

FIGURE 5.1
'Main stadium' (1958).
Dai-3kai Ajia Kyōgi Taikai Soshiki Iinkai, *Dai-3kai*, picture part. (Courtesy of the Nihon Taiiku Daigaku library)

FIGURE 5.2
'Meiji Shrine Outer Garden sports complex' (1958) p. 38.
A. P. L. Kikaku, *Ajia*, n.p. (Courtesy of the Nihon Taiiku Daigaku library)

branding desires of the Japanese organizers were thus reflected in the high costs of the Games.

These exploding costs had a direct impact on the construction—or rather the non-construction—of a Games village. In November 1956, Tsushima still expected a village to be built, but by March 1957 it was made public that this would not be done. The reason was the estimated cost of about 150 million yen (about 417,000 USD), which was too high.[45] The organizers then reached the decision to accommodate all the male athletes in the Dai-ichi Hotel in Shinbashi district, a huge hotel built for the 1940 Olympic Games—therefore also creating a connection to these Games that never took place—and, probably more importantly, ready to house more than 1,000 guests.[46] The distance to Ginza, Tokyo's main shopping area, was less than ten minutes, while transport to the Main Stadium via busses had to cover only slightly more than four kilometers.[47] This plan nevertheless also failed since in the end more male athletes turned up than the Dai-ichi Hotel could accommodate, meaning that three additional smaller hotels and three *ryokan* (Japanese-style accommodations) were rented.[48] The women's accommodation, in contrast, was sufficiently large. It was the Prince Takeda Hotel (now Grand Prince Hotel Takanawa), the former residence of Prince Takeda Tsuneyoshi, which was located slightly further to the south in Takanawa district.[49]

Despite the high-quality hotels, the men's accommodations in particular attracted some minor criticism. Being mostly located in a downtown area with access to pubs and similar establishments, some foreign sports officials such as Philippine IOC member Jorge Vargas, captain of the Indian volleyball team C. Singh, and organizer of the Melbourne Olympics Kent-Hughes thought that this would prevent athletes from focusing on more important issues such as the competitions.[50] During the Olympic Games this issue was, to a certain degree, dealt with by setting up a village.[51] A second critical issue was traffic. The organizers had bought about 50 buses and cars from Isuzu Motors, but crossing the distance of slightly more than four kilometers from the two main hotels to the Main Stadium could easily mean getting stuck in a traffic jam, which was even worse for those vehicles that did not receive preferential treatment. The worst traffic jam apparently took place on the day the Games commenced, but on several other days it also seems to have taken up to 1.5 hours to travel from Ginza to the Main Stadium. The Japanese organizers therefore almost immediately came to the conclusion that improving the city's transport infrastructure would be necessary for the Olympic Games.[52] Such improvements were then indeed realized during Azuma's terms as Tokyo's governor beginning in 1959. They included the construction of city highways, particularly *Aoyama-dōri*, and the opening of many new subway lines, which were all important contributions to promoting Tokyo as a highly developed city that by 1964 had completely overcome the large-scale destruction suffered during the Second World War.[53]

The development of the Japanese tourism industry, which already had a comparatively long history, was another important dimension of the Third Asian Games. While Japanese tourism abroad was effectively prevented during the 1950s by Japanese authorities to save foreign exchange, not to mention the still very high costs of traveling to America or Europe for middle-class Japanese, increasing numbers of foreigners visited Japan.[54] In 1957, about 130,000 tourists arrived in the country, a number that Japanese officials planned to double by 1961. In 1964, when the Tokyo Olympics took place, this target was more than reached, since about 350,000 tourists came to Japan. Hotel construction was therefore heavily impacted by the inflow of tourists to which the Asian Games and Olympic Games contributed, and thousands of Western- and Japanese-style hotel rooms were added to the existing ones.[55] Moreover, the Japanese Travel Bureau, for example, offered foreign tourists arriving for the Asian Games trips to some of Japan's famous places.[56]

This increasing amount of foreign tourists did not only provide Japan economically useful foreign exchange, it also reflected a growing—or re-emerging—international interest in Japan. Tourism therefore was another area that illustrated Japan's overcoming of its defeat in the war and the following international isolation, here through the willingness of foreigners to visit the country. Quite obviously, these foreigners were also confronted with the above mentioned infrastructure developments—possibly one of the reasons why they went to the country in the first place—and therefore could spread at home the image of Japan experiencing a 'rebirth' as an important country in the world. The Tokyo Olympics, taking place when the Japanese post-war 'economic miracle' was unfolding further, then became an even better platform to communicate and brand that image.

All in all, the discourses of the Japanese organizers about hosting 'perfect' Games found their echo in the infrastructure construction program for the Third Asian Games. One of the results was the building of several stadia, including the Main Stadium, which was further enhanced for the Tokyo Olympics. The exploding costs of the Games nevertheless prevented the Japanese organizers from setting up a Games village, meaning that the athletes were housed in several hotels. This was one example of how Japan's tourism industry was positively affected by the Third Asian Games, while the traffic problems illustrated that further developing Tokyo's transport infrastructure was essential for the Olympic Games—but also for improving the living conditions in the city in general. Although the Olympic Games certainly had a stronger impact than the Third Asian Games on Tokyo, they were founded on the experience that had been gained in 1958. The time between the mid-1950s and mid-1960s, particularly due to the two international games, thus had an immense impact on changing Tokyo's image into that of a highly developed city with an increasingly wealthy consumer society and on overcoming the memories of the devastation the Second World War had caused.

A Semi-Olympic Torch Relay

The torch relay of 1958 was by far the most curious relay covered in this book. Various intentions of the Japanese organizers influenced the highly public-oriented event. As mentioned in the fourth chapter, the IOC as the AGF's patron had lifted its prohibition of a relay after the Second Games. The 1958 relay thus was meant to integrate both 'Olympic' and Asian elements, although the lighting ceremony thereby acquired a rather peculiar atmosphere.

The relay began some weeks before the Third Asian Games commenced, in the Rizal Memorial Coliseum in Manila, one of the buildings that had been used for the Second Asian Games. Two Filipina swimmers, Jocelyn von Giese and Haydee Coloso-Espino, clad in Grecian-looking outfits, lit two rods by focusing the rays of the sun with a thick concave lens. The rods were then used to light a torch, which was brought by a relay of Filipino runners from the Coliseum to the airport, from where two aircraft of the Japanese Self-Defense Forces brought it to Okinawa. Here, 108 runners spent four days covering the territory of the island. A ferry afterwards brought the flame to Kagoshima, which was the starting point of a relay that covered Kumamoto, Saga, Fukuoka, Yamaguchi, Hiroshima, Okayama, Kobe, Osaka, Kyoto, Otsu, Nagoya, Shizuoka, Yokohama, and finally Tokyo. While the relay, which involved a total of 13,000 runners, crossed the distance between Kumamoto and Tokyo within 26 days, an additional 4 days were spent covering Tokyo. During the opening ceremony of the Games, the last runner, Oda Mikio, carried the flame into the Main Stadium and lit the Games' flame.[57]

Certainly due to its high-publicity nature, which served to increase interest in the Games and to bring large numbers of people in touch with one of its manifestations, the Japanese organizers decided on the first large-scale relay in the history of the Asian Games, covering about 5,000 kilometers and two and a 'half' (Okinawa) countries. The Olympic torch relays since 1936 had without question been the model and this inspiration might explain why two Filipinas engaged in a seemingly Grecian ritual. The place—the Rizal Coliseum in Manila in the Philippines in Asia—certainly allowed *no* reasonable historical connection to the Olympic heritage at all, thus giving the lighting ceremony an outlandish character. One of the intentions nevertheless must have been to support Tokyo's application for the 1964 Olympics by communicating to the IOC Japan's admiration of 'Olympic' ceremonies and its willingness to accept 'Olympism' as a sports ideology. The only pan-Asian element in the lighting ceremony was the sun, which could, like in 1951, be seen as a symbol of Asia as the 'Continent of the Rising Sun', although due to the Grecian touch not even that was clear. Another Japanese intention was undoubtedly to further improve ties with the Philippines, since Manila was honored as the place where the torch was lit. As mentioned, the last Asian Games had taken place there, but there was no credible historical or mythological reason—in contrast to the Olympic lighting ceremonies in Olympia—for its selection, which was thus instead the result of voluntary cooperation between Japanese and Filipinos. Arguably, one might say that the choice of Manila was also compensation for the lack of a relay in 1954, but it was in any case still an act of Japanese–Philippine cooperation. Similar to the arrival of the 1964 torch in several Asian capitals, it was thus possible to portray the relay as an act of post-war reconciliation.[58] However, in terms of symbolizing peaceful cooperation between the two peoples, the involvement of the Self-Defense Forces, bringing in a military element potentially reminiscent of Japan's occupation of the archipelago, is more problematic and one has to assume that it was not enjoyed by all Filipinos who were attracted by the relay. One nevertheless can also argue that the Cold War situation made it necessary to make Filipinos, standing on the same side as the Japanese, aware that Japan needed soldiers to defend itself.

Even more interesting, however, is the lengthy coverage of Okinawan soil (four days). The island was still occupied by US forces and, particularly during the early years after the end of the war, expressions of a Japanese identity such as the hoisting of the *hinomaru* flag had been suppressed. In 1955, American diplomats had even warned that in the case Japan reached a compromise with the USSR concerning the Kuril Islands, the US would never return Okinawa.[59] The relay's coverage of Okinawan soil can thus be seen as a symbolic assurance that the territory was part of Japan and would eventually return to the mother country. The same idea was repeated at the Tokyo Olympics, indicating that the relay of 1958 was the inspiration.[60]

A difference with regard to the Tokyo Olympics nevertheless was the age of the Japanese runners. During the 1964 relay, all were between 16 and 20 years old, representing the post-war generation free of the 'sin' of war.[61] In the case of the Third Asian Games, taking place six years earlier, such a selection was not possible. Another difference from 1964 was that in 1958 the big cities between Kagoshima (located in the southwestern part of Kyushu) and Tokyo were visited, but the northern part of Honshu, as well as Hokkaido and Shikoku, were completely left out. In contrast, in 1964 four relay routes, each featuring an Olympic flame, were chosen, in this way covering the entirety of the Japanese archipelago (except for some small islands) and integrating all prefectures into the relay.[62] The torch relay in 1958 must therefore again have served as a model, although one that could still be improved upon. Finally, the lighters of the stadium's flames and their historical backgrounds strongly differed. Oda Mikio had been the first Japanese gold medalist at the Olympic Games, hence embodying Japan's sportive modernization process. In contrast, Sakai Yoshinori, lighter of the flame in 1964, had been born in Hiroshima shortly after the explosion of the atomic bomb, symbolizing both the end of the war and a new beginning, but also encouraging a discourse of Japan as the world's only victim of nuclear horror.[63]

In summary, the torch relay of the Third Asian Games was the first relay that, due to the amount of territory covered and the large number of runners, had a very high publicity value. The goal of impressing the IOC meant the addition of a

Grecian element to the beginning of the relay, even though this did not fit very well into the Asian context. Reconciliation with the Philippines was another important topic, while the relay also served to symbolically integrate occupied Okinawa into the Japanese territory. Moreover, the relay was, without question, a model for the Olympic relay in 1964, which was even more strongly symbolic.

Post-war Japan as a Country of Culture and Strong Supporter of 'Olympism'

Like the construction program and the torch relay, the official ceremonies and particularly the entertainment program were planned as high-publicity events. The implementation of daily entertainment routines was strongly reminiscent of the FECG, although the focus on Japanese, not only Western, physical education practices and especially songs and dances was different. This special constellation came into existence because on the one hand large amounts of funding were available since the intention was to underline Japan's readiness to host the 1964 Olympics, while on the other hand a focus on promoting sports was no longer necessary due to an already-long tradition of this in Japan. The organizers' integration of certain elements and persons associable with the war into the staging was, however, somewhat controversial.

As mentioned above, Crown Prince Akihito had been named the patron of the Third Asian Games. This was already a difference compared to the First and Second Asian Games, when the respective heads of state had assumed the office. Even more interesting is that despite Akihito's appointment as patron, it was the emperor who declared the Games open. This was a task the constitution of the AGF reserved for the head of state, as described in the third chapter.[64] The post-war Japanese constitution nevertheless did *not* definitively state that the emperor was the head of state. The situation becomes even more problematic if it is compared to the Tokyo Olympics. In 1964, the emperor again declared the Games open, but on this occasion due to his office as *patron* of the Olympic Games. As Christian Tagsold has shown, the National Diet declared him to be patron of the Olympics. It is very likely that most people did not take notice of this background, meaning that the event served to promote the belief that the emperor is Japan's head of state.[65] However, in the case of the Third Asian Games the emperor was *not* the patron of the Games. This meant either that the Japanese constitution was violated by his having acted as the head of state or, much more likely since less problematic (also compared to breaking the Olympic Charter, which was not attempted at the Tokyo Olympics), that the constitution of the AGF had been violated. Since one again has to assume that most people did not understand the legal details (or their breach), the Third Asian Games in the end also served to promote the belief that the emperor was Japan's head of state. His sitting in close proximity to the Shah of Iran, Malayan

Prime Minister Tunku Abdul Rahman, and IOC president Brundage certainly further strengthened the impression.[66]

At the same time the issue begs the question of why the emperor did not become patron of the Third Asian Games. Arguably, this was because, despite the emperor's new status in post-war Japan and his re-emerging domestic popularity, the wartime memories in Asian countries in 1958—in contrast to 1964—were not yet sufficiently overcome. Some evidence for this hypothesis is that the Philippine delegation did not lower its flag before the tribune of honor.[67] The gesture was optional, but the more delegations that did not do it, the worse an impression was given.[68] The choice of Akihito instead of the emperor as the patron may have reduced the unwillingness of the other delegations to dip their flags. Another, not mutually exclusive, explanation is that if the emperor had become the patron of the Games instead of only opening them this could have further intensified the question of his constitutional status, while in the case of the crown prince being the patron this question did not come up. The idea of solving the issue at the Tokyo Olympics through a decision of the National Diet declaring the emperor to be the patron was therefore very likely inspired by the legal problems in 1958.

Another problematic element in the staging of the Games was the involvement of uniformed Self-Defense Forces in various capacities. Official criticism from AGF members did not arise, which is hardly surprising considering that the Filipino organizers, too, had used uniformed soldiers during the official ceremonies in 1954. However, some journalists either criticized the Forces' involvement directly or gave 'common people' the chance to do so. For example, a certain Inouye Akira, a student from Hyōgo Prefecture, explained his viewpoint in the liberal *Asahi Evening News*:

> However, there was one thing that surprised me very much. That was the sight of men in military uniforms that I saw in various parts of the field. The members of the brass band and the men marching in front of the columns were all dressed in military uniforms. I was told that they were Self-Defense Corps personnel and students of the Defense University. (...) Japan's defense units are for self-defense only; the military uniform is not a symbol of peace. (...) Especially, it must be remembered that many of those participating from Asian countries cannot possibly have pleasant memories of the former Japanese Army.[69]

This comment should make it obvious that at least some Japanese considered the easily discernible involvement of armed personnel, representing war instead of peace, as contradictory to the proclaimed aim of the Third Asian Games. It is difficult to judge how widespread this aversion to the involvement of the Self-Defense Forces was, but it should be noted that mistrust of Prime Minister Kishi as a representative of the wartime elites and a promoter of the remilitarization of the country was substantial. Two years later, in 1960, the Kishi administration collapsed as a result of popular resistance to the ultimately successful renewal of the American–Japanese Security Treaty, so one has to assume that Inouye was not alone.[70] Another article printed on page one of the morning edition of the *Asahi Shinbun* on 3 June 1958 went in the same direction, asking what impression it had made on the Asian guests that Tsushima, the director-general of the Defense Agency, was also president of the Asian Games organizing committee. The involvement of uniformed forces, too, was criticized, with the author complaining that they had carried the AGF flag away during the closing ceremony so slowly that it had looked like a procession at a "funeral".[71] A former athlete from West Germany, Otto Peltzer, also made it public that he thought that there was too much militarism at the Games.[72]

The criticism apparently made no significant impression on the organizers, since the Self-Defense Forces were also heavily involved in the staging of the Tokyo Olympics.[73] As had been the case in 1964, one has to assume that the intention of the organizers of the Third Asian Games was to improve the image of the Forces. Like in the Philippines in 1954, one can argue that soldiers carrying the flag in 1958 symbolized them protecting Asia, although they were de facto limited to protecting Japan. Moreover, by letting soldiers participate in an event that focused on peace between the participating Asian countries, it was certainly also expected that Japanese—and possibly foreign—spectators considered them to be not symbols of Japanese aggression and militarism, but part of a new military force that was no threat to the participating countries and a necessity due to the Cold War. It should nevertheless be obvious that this approach could evoke a different impression in both Japanese and foreigners who were less willing to let the memory of Japanese militarism be substituted with a new image of peacefulness and 'mere' self-defense, as the newspaper articles discussed above demonstrate.

Other elements of the official ceremonies were less controversial, but are still noteworthy. Not until 1999 would *hinomaru* and *kimigayo* ('His Majesty's Reign') become Japan's national flag and anthem.[74] Despite this legal issue, the use of the flag and the song, which for leftists were symbols of militarism and imperial—not popular—sovereignty, seems not to have inspired much criticism. Although the Third Asian Games were the first big international sports event held in post-war Japan, the song and the flag had already been used at many other post-war international games and even MacArthur had encouraged their use during the later years of the occupation.[75] Moreover, in the case of several foreign officials one can see that the intention the Japanese organizers must have had in mind, namely the integration of the two former 'symbols of war'—and the emperor—into the Games' discourse of peace, was quite successfully realized. For example, Wim J. Latumeten, deputy chief of the Indonesian delegation, confessed that "[t]he singing of Kimigayo, Japan's national anthem[,] was wonderful."[76] N. M. Khan, the leader of the Pakistani delegation, declared: "I was impressed most with the presence of the Emperor and his proclamation of the opening of the Games. I really admired the perfect harmony in the singing by the mass audience of the Japanese national anthem."[77] It seems the two officials were not offended, but rather impressed, by the Japanese spectators' discipline, knowledge of the lyrics and melody of the 'national anthem', and willingness to sing it. In their view this might have illustrated a successful nation-building process that many decolonizing Asian countries had not yet undergone, and not a return to militarism. These examples are insufficient to be representative, but nevertheless provide an idea of the opinions held by some Asian foreigners. Moreover, the organizers must have gotten positive (or neutral) feedback, since at the 1964 Olympic Games *kimigayo, hinomaru,* and the emperor were again prominently featured and linked to the Games' proclaimed ideal of peace.[78]

The release of 5,000 white doves during the opening ceremony was, like at the First and Second Asian Games, an obvious symbol of peace.[79] The songs sung at the Games also focused on that aim, but the selection largely differed from that at the former Asian Games, indicating that no tradition had yet been established. The official songs of the Third Asian Games were *wakai chikara* ('Rising Youth', or, more correctly 'Youthful Power'), the song that was traditionally sung at the annual National Sports Festival of Japan that had been established in 1946, and *seinen no uta* ('Song of the Youth'), a traditional Japanese Olympic song.[80] Due to their focus on sport, both of these songs had a pan-Asian appeal, which was, however, limited by the problem that most of the foreign athletes very likely did not understand the songs' lyrics. The topic of peace was, to a certain degree, later brought up again during the closing ceremony. In addition to the two official songs, the choir also sang *God Be with You till We Meet Again* and *Auld Lang Syne.*[81] Both were Western songs, but due to the themes—saying goodbye and remembering common deeds—and the language of the lyrics they had a stronger internationalist appeal. Compared to the Second Games in 1954, the organizers had substituted *Aloha Oe,* possibly out of dislike for the 'Orientalistic' image of hula girls the song might evoke, with the well-known farewell song that was associated particularly with the boy scout movement and which thus already had a long tradition in Japan (not to mention the usage of its melody for Japanese songs).[82] Due to *Auld Lang Syne*'s internationalist message the song was later featured at many other Asian Games events.

One of the most impressive parts of the Third Asian Games was the entertainment program, which not only accompanied the opening and closing ceremonies, but also took place every single day, normally somewhere between 11:45am and 2:30pm in the Main Stadium. Their scale was gigantic, since about 45,000 participants were mobilized for a program that all in all took more than 8.5 hours over the course of the Games (fig. 5.3–5.4).[83] Already the opening day saw a wide range of songs and physical education practices that lasted for two hours and included a drum and fife band parade, a folk song—*chakkiri bushi* ('Tea-Cutting Song')—including mass performances by women from Shizuoka Prefecture, horizontal bar practices, ancient military arts such as trumpet shell sounding, a gymnastic dance, freestyle exercises during which the AGF symbol was formed,

FIGURE 5.3
'Chakkiri bushi ('Tea-cutting song')': One element of the Games' very broad entertainment program.
Dai-3kai Ajia Kyōgi Taikai Soshiki Iinkai (shikitenbu), *Ajia*, n.p. (Courtesy of the Nihon Taiiku Daigaku library)

FIGURE 5.4
'Yagi bushi ('Yagi-song')': A second element of the entertainment program that impressed many international sports officials.
Dai-3kai Ajia Kyōgi Taikai Soshiki Iinkai (shikitenbu), *Ajia*, n.p. (Courtesy of the Nihon Taiiku Daigaku library)

and a second drum and fife band parade accompanied by mass exercises by school children. During the following days, many further Japanese folk songs such as *kōjō no tsuki* ('Moon over the Ruined Castle') and *Yagi bushi* ('Yagi-Song'), with accompanying dances, were performed. Moreover, various gymnastic dances, physical exercises, and some stunts by firefighters took place, normally with three to four program entries a day.[84] The closing of the Games provided the second most extensive entertainment program. The five program entries of gymnastics, international dances, Japanese folk songs and dances, and an equestrian event lasted for 1 hour and 20 minutes.[85]

Interpreting the meaning of every single song and dance would not be the most reasonable approach, considering that the Japanese included so many of them. The overall intention of the organizers, however, certainly was to communicate the message that physical education practices—most of them Western ones—were taken seriously in the country and that many adults as well as children engaged in them, learning discipline and improving their health. This aspect would still fit into the early FECG that took place under the control of the American YMCA. However, a large number of traditional folk dances and songs (although several of them went back 'only' to the Meiji Era, 1868–1912) added the message that despite these Western-style physical education exercises Japan possessed its own cultural practices. The complete Westernization of Japan as a result of the American occupation and West-alignment was gainsaid and a possible answer given to the question of what constituted 'Japaneseness' (*nihonjinron*), a question that became even more urgent in the 1960s when rapid economic growth increasingly affected the life of urbanized Japanese in particular. The folk songs and dances thus underlined the message that the 'new' and 'reborn' Japan focused strongly on culture, thereby highlighting a major difference to the Western image of Japanese 'cultureless militarism' during the war, but also stressing a culture that was primarily Japanese and possessed ties to the pre-war era. By showing such an image of Japan, the conservative organizers wanted to recreate feelings of loyalty to the government and the Japanese nation among the Japanese spectators and participants, but simultaneously to bring about a foreign (re-)acknowledgement of Japan as a 'country of culture'. More generally, one can therefore also argue that an important aim of the organizers was to show the attending Western IOC members, including president Brundage, that Japan was willing and able to provide a large-scale entertainment program in 1964 that would, for the first time ever, integrate Japanese culture (possibly as a representative of Asian culture) into the Olympic Games, giving them a more serious reach beyond the West than ever before. As it happened, the Tokyo Olympics would indeed be the first Olympic Games to feature such a large-scale entertainment program integrating local cultural distinctiveness into the global aspirations of 'Olympism'. Due to their large size and inclusion of many folkloristic elements, the same can be said about the entertainment programs at ensuing Olympic events.[86] The Third Asian Games were therefore the testing ground for this significant change in the staging of the

Olympic Games, which meant that the entertainment programs now became an important means for host countries to engage in nation-branding and not primarily to promote sport.

The symbols used in connection with the Games also represent attempts to impress the IOC. One of the two promotional posters depicted the head of a vaguely East Asian looking athlete, crowned with an Olympic-style laurel wreath. A second one featured a vaguely West Asian looking athlete—possibly a means of integrating both West and East Asians through the two posters—running with a torch. This is reminiscent of the torch relay of the Third Asian Games, but can also be interpreted as another Olympic element. A statue portrayed in the background, Myron's *Discobolus* (discus thrower), was a reference to the ancient Olympic Games, via the modern Olympic Games.[87] Moreover, the front of the victory medals displayed the head of *Zeus*, the patron of the ancient Olympic Games (fig. 5.5). All motifs thus communicated the ideal of internationalism, but must also have been included to promote post-war Japan as a strong supporter of 'Olympism' and thus a qualified candidate for hosting the 1964 Games.

FIGURE 5.5
'Victory medal, Third Asian Games, front': The depiction of *Zeus* shows how eagerly the Japanese organizers used Olympic elements at the Games.
Photo taken by Stefan Huebner, Prince Chichibu Memorial Sports Museum.

In conclusion, several controversial elements such as the Self-Defense Forces, the emperor, the *hinomaru*, and *kimigayo* were integrated into the official ceremonies. There was some public rejection of this attempt to link the Self-Defense Forces in particular with the Asian Games' proclaimed aim of peace, but it did not escalate. Independent of this opposition, an important difference compared to the former

Asian Games was the scale of the entertainment program. Together with the other elements of the staging it highlights the strongly growing importance of the staging that began to characterize the Asian Games from 1958 (and the Olympic Games from 1964). The staging increasingly turned into a means not only for promoting Western sports. It also served as a large-scale demonstration of local culture and folklore and, linked to these, organizational skills and the availability of funding. Moreover, in 1958, Asia as a whole was relatively underrepresented in the entertainment program, unless one considered Japan as Asia's leading country and main representative, as the Japanese organizers did. Rather, the aim was to create a positive image of a reemerging post-war Japan, in combination with the intention to impress the IOC by featuring many Olympic elements.

Japan as Asia's Media Center

While large groups of people went to the stadia, Japanese media heavily covered the first big international sports event held in post-war Japan. Japanese media did not only serve to facilitate nation-branding by communicating the intended images to a very broad audience. Like at several previous events, the technological level of Japanese media and the number of Asian journalists gathering in Tokyo also emphasized the image of Japan being Asia's most developed and important country.

According to the official report of the Games, close to 2,900 journalists were in Tokyo during the time of the Third Asian Games, most of whom were Japanese.[88] Some 324 of them, however, were foreigners permanently stationed in Japan, with the largest delegations stemming from the United States, Korea, Taiwan, Britain, and France, but also with small groups from other European and 11 Asian countries.[89] Moreover, a further 94 newspaper journalists and photographers arrived from 16 participating Asian countries to report on the Games. Unlike during earlier Asian Games, these were accompanied by 26 radio announcers from 11 Asian countries (strictly speaking 12, since Singapore and Malaya here formed one group).[90] These numbers indicate that the boldly stated ambition of the Japanese organizers to host 'perfect' Games had stirred considerable interest in the other Asian countries, although the improvements to the radio infrastructure in 1958 over that in 1954 or 1951 also must have contributed to the comparatively high number of foreign announcers coming to the Games. The radio center in the Main Stadium possessed 16 studios, of which 12 were allocated to foreign broadcasters such as Voice of America (which had set up stations in Hong Kong and Taiwan) and All India Radio, while the remaining four were left to Japanese broadcasters such as the NHK and the commercial agencies.[91] These Japanese broadcasters did not limit themselves to a Japanese audience. For example, Indians not only received a daily newsreel about the Games from All India Radio, but could also get information via Radio Japan, the overseas broadcaster of the NHK.[92]

Moreover, a Japanese company produced a color film on the Third Asian Games called 'Ever Onward', which was also shown in foreign countries such as India.[93]

The Third Asian Games were the second Asian Games, following those in Manila in 1954, to be shown on television. However, one has to assume that black-and-white television, which had appeared in Japan in 1952 and been regularly broadcasted by the NHK and commercial Nippon TV since 1953, had a significantly higher impact there than in the Philippines in 1954. For example in 1960, two years after the Third Asian Games, not only did 89 per cent of the approximately 20 million Japanese households own a radio, but 54 per cent of them also had a television set.[94] In contrast to radio broadcasting, however, television broadcasting remained limited to a domestic audience.[95] Television coverage of the Games was another illustration of the advanced state of Japanese communications infrastructure as compared to many other Asian countries such as Indonesia and Thailand, covered in the sixth and seventh chapters. Television thus demonstrated Japan's return to the position of Asia's most developed country. During the Tokyo Olympics, color television and satellite communication would further contribute to that image.[96]

To sum up, considering that the Japanese organizers had 'perfect' Games in mind, it is unsurprising that Japanese media interest in the Third Asian Games seems to have been massive. Similar things can be said of the other participating countries, although these did not show the Games on television, this difference being another illustration of Japan being the most developed country in Asia, although the technical difficulties of overseas broadcasting should be remembered. Probably even more relevant and important for the Japanese organizers was the attention the IOC paid the Games by meeting in Tokyo while these were held. After all, getting permission to host the Olympic Games would eventually bring massive 'global' media attention.

Assessment

Arguably, the featuring of Olympic elements at the Third Asian Games reached a level comparable to that of the personality cults of presidents and monarchs during the succeeding Games in Indonesia, Thailand, and Iran. The hosting of the Ninth FECG had eventually inspired the successful application for the 1940 Olympics. However, as the two possible readings of the title of this chapter suggest, the Third Asian Games from the beginning were aimed at bringing the 1964 Olympics to Tokyo by fulfilling the proclaimed domestic and international expectation that the Japanese organizers were capable of organizing an 'Olympic level' event in 1958. The Japanese asked the IOC to 'give us the Olympic Games', and the world expected Japan to 'give us the Olympic Games'. The IOC was the patron of the AGF and 'Olympism' was a useful means to create internationalism, but, even bearing this in the mind, the extent to which Olympic elements were used and referenced in the ambitious rhetoric of the organizers and the cultural elements used in the staging remains striking. Very likely the most bizarre result of this emphasis was the lighting of the torch in a rather Grecian ceremony in Manila. The focus on showing Japanese organizational skills through the organization of 'perfect' Asian Games and the overtrumping of even previous Olympic Games further added to the image of readiness for the Olympics, especially since the IOC held its first meeting in a non-Western country in Tokyo during the Third Asian Games.[97]

Improving ties with other Asian countries through the Games and showing the 'reborn' Japan as a promoter of peaceful internationalism instead of an aggressor was another important topic in the discourses the Japanese organizers produced. This purpose also corresponded nicely to the overarching interest of Japanese politicians in situating Japan in decolonizing Asia. In a quite traditional way, primarily amateur sports norms and values were mentioned as a means for peaceful regional integration. Some of the Japanese organizers also added other pan-Asian topics such as blood, kinship, common culture, and history. These, however, due to the regional shape of the Asian Games that—in contrast to the FECG, now covered a region spanning from Israel to the Philippines—became increasingly vague and, to a certain degree, beg the question of how much the Japanese were really interested in the specific shape of Asia as long as it centered on Japan as the most modern and developed Asian country. In contrast, the Philippine leg of the torch relay was meant to represent friendly cooperation between Japanese and Filipinos and a campaign to encourage polite behavior regarding foreigners, most of them Asians, also fits in here.[98]

Branding the 'new' and 'reborn' Japan as a democratic 'country of culture' to create a contrast to the Western wartime image of 'cultureless militarism' was another important purpose of the Japanese organizers. This arguably corresponded to the intentions of American diplomats and area studies experts mentioned in the previous chapter to use Asian role models to show Asian countries that democratization and economic development would be attainable.[99] While Americans since about 1960 considered Japan such a role model, the Japanese organizers in 1958 did not stage an assimilation process. Instead, they featured a large-scale daily entertainment program that in addition to Western physical education practices also included many Japanese folk songs and dances. A manifest rejection of *a complete Westernization* of Japan can be considered the intention the organizers had in mind, in addition to impressing the IOC. At the same time the organizers integrated somewhat controversial persons and elements such as the emperor, the Self-Defense Forces, *hinomaru*, and *kimigayo* into Japanese state nationalism, with the intent of cutting their connection to the war. Some limited criticism from Japanese leftists nevertheless arose afterwards. Finally, the expensive building program was a visual demonstration of successful Japanese development leading to an increasingly wealthy society. It simultaneously was a means to overtrump the former Asian Games and Olympic Games, although the building program around the Tokyo Olympics would later outdo it by far.

Finally, one of the most important changes the Third Asian Games brought about was the rising importance of the staging of the Games compared to the earlier aim of educating spectators by making them take up amateur sports as citizenship training. This moving away from low-cost Games was heavily criticized by certain AGF members, such as Sondhi, but in the long run the process was not stopped. Arguably, the basic reason was the contradictory aims of officials from 'underdeveloped' countries where Western sport was still far less well-known than in Japan and very limited funding available, and Japanese officials who wanted to highlight exactly this 'developmental difference'—Azuma's statement which opens this chapter is symptomatic for that aim—and thereby show Japan as Asia's most developed country. Japan winning more than half of the gold medals further contributed to this contrast.[100] Together with the desire to show local distinctiveness, this emphasis on developmental difference meant that the Tokyo Olympics, based on the experience the organizers had gained in 1958, were the first Olympic Games to feature large-scale entertainment programs that included many folkloristic elements. However, the succeeding Asian Games, too, were affected by the Tokyo Asian Games since the (semi-)authoritarian governments of later host countries began to incorporate the respective events into their large-scale modernization and development programs.

CHAPTER 6

Turning Indonesia into the Beacon of a Non-Aligned Asia: The Sukarno Administration, the Fourth Asian Games, and the Struggle against Imperialism and Neocolonialism (24 August–4 September 1962)

"We did not conduct the Asian Games just for the heck of it. No, we conducted them on the basis of principle, on the basis of the principle of independence, on the basis of anti-imperialism, on the basis of anti-colonialism, and on the basis of anti-neo-colonialism. It was on the basis of the principle that nations should truly live in independence, free from every kind of oppression, that we held the Asian Games."[1]

—Sukarno, President of Indonesia, in a speech in 1963 after Indonesia had been banned by the International Olympic Commitee

At the first opportunity Indonesia had, that being the Third Asian Games in 1958, it successfully bid for the 1962 Asian Games, narrowly defeating Pakistan.[2] The Indonesian-hosted Games would be the first Asian Games to take place in a semi-authoritarian country and were succeeded by Games hosted in authoritarian ones. This course strongly influenced both the ideals, as well as the staging, of the Games. In terms of foreign policy, the Games were to serve as a 'sportive' successor to the Bandung Conference (1955), which had brought together many Asian and African nations that later also joined the Non-Aligned Movement.[3] In Indonesia, the ideal of egalitarian internationalism therefore was confronted with a significantly stronger anti-Western and anti-neocolonial internationalism than it had been in India, the Philippines, and Japan. In terms of domestic policy, Indonesia was more internally divided than any previous host of the Asian Games. The project of nation-building and of 'national rebirth' pursued by the Sukarno administration thus gave the Games a certain touch not of a 'national awakening' but of an 'ultranationalist rebirth'. This included mass mobilization, the generation of anti-Western nationalism and internationalism, a very strong visual-theatric dimension, and the idea of shaping physically and spiritually 'stronger' human beings in a rather socialist and nationalistic environment. As a result, the hosting of the Asian Games now became entangled with the authoritarian version of 'high modernist' thinking. As mentioned in the first chapter, Elwood Brown's activities can already be described as industrial-strength social engineering and thus had a very strong 'high modernist' touch, aspiring to a large-scale change in social norms and values. The American Young Men's Christian Association (YMCA) as a non-governmental organization was nonetheless limited by the support it received from governments, not having the manpower to bring about the changes on its own. The later Far Eastern Championship Games (FECG), the Western Asiatic Games (WAG), and the Asian Games in India, the Philippines, and Japan, certainly had a strong touch of 'high modernist' thinking. In Indonesia (1962), Thailand (1966, 1970), and in Iran (1974), however, all of James Scott's criteria were fulfilled. The lack of a civil society is of special importance here. The Fourth Asian Games thus became a showcase for the semi-authoritarian Indonesian government's large-scale modernization and development projects that were aimed at staging—and *realizing*—rapid national progress and catching up with the 'developed countries' as soon as possible. The focus thus began to shift away from the ideal of low-cost games that had primarily served in teaching Asians amateur norms and values, a direction in which the Third Asian Games had already hinted.

In this chapter, I deal with the Indonesian intention to use the Asian Games for postcolonial nation-building and for legitimizing Sukarno's rule and ideology. This includes the great importance the event possessed in communicating the image of a transforming Indonesia, which experienced a seemingly successful rapid modernization and development process. Moreover, I show the organizers' attempt to (unsuccessfully) turn the Asian Games into games of the Non-Aligned Movement, which eventually led to the founding of the Games of the New Emerging Forces to encourage anti-Western regional integration.

Indonesia in 1962

Indonesia had declared its independence from the Netherlands on 17 August 1945, during the final weeks of the Second World War. Its independence was finally recognized in 1949 after a long-lasting armed conflict, which also included Muslim and communist insurrections against the Republican government. However, in the following years, attempts at democracy and nation-building were challenged as regional, religious, racial, and ideological tensions could not properly be overcome. Java was not unanimously accepted as the center of power, nor was the problem of the large Chinese minority solved, while communists and supporters of an Islamic republic were still perceived by many as sources of potential conflict in the future. Sukarno, son of a Javanese father and a Balinese mother and one of the most important leaders of the Indonesian independence movement, had become Indonesia's president in 1945. When the many conflicts went unsolved by the parliament, he hoped to overcome internal division and to unify the nation under his leadership. Between 1957 and 1959, Sukarno began turning Indonesia into a 'guided democracy', meaning a semi-dictatorship under martial law (until 1963) with press censorship. Sukarno, who had received his education in Indonesia and thought little of Western, especially Dutch, concepts of parliamentary democracy, attempted to establish a modern society, but one partially based on traditional, pre-colonial ways of governing. In his view, nationalist, religious, and communist forces should all be integrated into a corporative society led by the president.[4]

At least some elements of the traditional Javanese concept of power, including *mandala*, can be found in the political ideas of Sukarno, who had to deal with people at least partially believing in them. For example, mass rallies demonstrated the support the regent/president had among the people. His power was even further underlined if different groups, maybe even hostile to each other, could all be brought together. Aspiring to national unity thus was an attempt to prevent the dispersal of the power of the regent or the 'state' by regaining a primordial oneness. The possession of precious or rare objects or extraordinary human beings was another traditional visual representation of having power. Moreover, the 'state' was seen as being based on a center, but having no fixed borders, with the power of the ruler shining into the distance like a beacon (or reflector lamp) until meeting the glare of a neighboring kingdom's power. Since only a fixed amount of power existed in the universe, the increase of the power of a certain ruler automatically meant a loss of power for another ruler. A growing manifestation of power in one center and the absorption of the power of other centers through their voluntary submission (war was a sign of insufficient power) would, at least in theory, finally create a world ruler. The Asian Games therefore have to be considered a means of showing Sukarno's power and of letting independent Indonesia's beacon radiate more strongly into the world, pushing back the borders of the other newly independent Asian nations, but also those of the West.[5] In more Western terms of nation-branding and personality cults, the Games were an attempt to visually demonstrate to the world, and especially to Indonesians, the achievements Sukarno's ideology and rule had brought to Indonesia.

Despite all of the Indonesian government's nation-building efforts, further insurrections took place. The PRRI-Permesta rebellion in 1958 (the last rebels surrendering in 1961) in West Sumatra and North Sulawesi against the central government could nevertheless be suppressed. The Indonesian government perceived this rebellion as especially tainted by the backing of the Central Intelligence Agency (CIA), which had supported the separatists, expecting that otherwise communists might take over in Indonesia. This was considered another sign of the still ongoing imperialistic machinations of the West. Afterwards,

Sukarno leaned even more strongly on the USSR and China for support, although relations with the United States were not totally cut off for reasons of balance. For example, development aid was accepted from both the US and the USSR.[6] In spite of all these problems, Indonesia was a very populous and resource-rich country. At least in theory it possessed the means to become an influential international actor. Indonesia's role as a leader of the (mostly) newly independent Asian and African nations had been strengthened by hosting the Asia-Africa Conference in Bandung in 1955, which strongly promoted the development of the Non-Aligned Movement.[7] Twenty-nine nations from the two continents—all of them 'non-White'—had been invited, notable exceptions being Taiwan, Israel, South Africa, and the Koreas. The first official conference of the Non-Aligned Movement, nonetheless, was not held in an Indonesian city but in Belgrade in 1961, meaning that Sukarno was in danger of losing some of his influence. Moreover, from the PRRI-Permesta rebellion onwards, he increasingly began to perceive the world's problems not as a result of the competition between the 'communist bloc' and the 'free world'. Instead, he described it as a struggle for freedom by the 'new emerging forces' against still undefeated imperialistic and neocolonialist designs (not only in a territorial sense, but also in a cultural and economic one) of the 'old established forces'.[8]

Sport in Indonesia and the Main Organizers of the Games

In contrast to the hosts of the first three Games, modern sports and sports events were still comparatively new in Indonesia. During Dutch colonial rule, the spreading of sports was very limited. The Dutch East Indies had joined the Far Eastern Athletic Association (FEAA) only in 1934. According to the Dutch leader of the delegation, track and field, swimming, basketball, and tennis had been introduced to the 'main island' Java only by 1925, while soccer had a slightly longer tradition. Moreover, Dutch athletes, as well as members of the relatively rich Chinese minority, were extremely overrepresented in the team, though all were said to have been born in the Indies.[9] Participation in the Olympic Games had not taken place until independence and an international sports event of the size of the later FECG had never been held. However, after Indonesia's independence, the government started to encourage mass sport and also held national sports weeks (PONs).[10] The Fourth Asian Games then served to further promote modern sports among Indonesians. A very important figure in this development was Raden Maladi, Indonesia's first minister of sport (1962–66). Before that, he had been minister of information (1959–62) and earlier on head of radio broadcasting service Radio Republik Indonesia. He also acted as the head of Indonesian delegations to the Asian and Olympic Games and was involved with several Indonesian and international soccer organizations such as Fédération Internationale de Football Association (FIFA), initially having been an important goalkeeper and later serving as an official. During the Fourth Asian Games, he was the vice president of the Indonesian National Olympic Committee (NOC) and the secretary of both the organizing committee (later becoming its president) and of the Asian Games Federation (AGF).[11] Other leading positions were held by Sultan Hamengku Buwono IX as president of the AGF and Prince Paku Alam VIII as president of the Indonesian NOC and president (later executive president) of the organizing committee. The position as patron of the Games was, unlike in 1958, obvious. Sukarno accepted it as Indonesia's president.[12]

The Fourth Asian Games were one of the most politically instrumentalized and state-controlled editions of the early Asian Games. During earlier events, social reformers had approached the government for assistance for their modernization plans and government officials had been involved in the hosting. In Indonesia, however, the most senior organizer was a serving minister of sport, the office obviously created in connection to the Asian Games. It shows the importance of the event for the semi-authoritarian Sukarno administration, which intended to have full control over the Games.

Modernizing Indonesia for the Sake of a Non-Aligned Asia

One of the main aims of the Indonesian government was to achieve a '(re-)birth' of their country and a furthering of national progress in various forms as a means to shed the remains of Western colonialism. Branding Indonesia as a rapidly developing country and a main representative of a new, postcolonial Asia thus was deemed highly important.

In December 1958, only a short while after Indonesia received the right to host the Fourth Asian Games, Sukarno reportedly gave the following order to clarify what enormous aims had to be realized within the next four years:

> Preparations in the most extensive way must be made at once, so that the IVth Asian Games in Djakarta will become the pride of the whole People of Indonesia and will raise the prestige of the Nation of Indonesia. The celebrations of the IVth Asian Games must be more festive than the previous Asian Games. The Asian Games Stadium must be greater and more beautiful than other stadiums. (...) In short, the IVth Asian Games must be better than the former Asian Games, in line with the Asian Games motto 'Ever Onward'.[13]

Similar remarks by Sukarno followed.[14] Basically, he intended to hold a *more spectacular event* than what Japan, *the most developed Asian nation*, had done in 1958, which had impressed many of the world's leading sports officials so greatly that it was soon afterwards awarded the 1964 Tokyo Olympic Games. Sukarno's ambitious enthusiasm was shared by his colleagues, who also talked about the value that a successfully staged Games would have for Indonesia.

One of their major themes was that in this way Indonesia would gain a leading role in Asia's postcolonial modernization and development process. The Games would visibly end the power asymmetry between Asia and the West by shattering the colonialist image of Asia as a backward region and Asians as lazy, weak, and incompetent peoples. It was to be substituted with the image of a successfully developing and modernizing continent, with Indonesia at its center. Destroying the negative image—the foundation of the former 'civilizing mission' rhetoric, but also of neocolonialist designs—would finally convince the West (and the 'eastern bloc') to accept Asia as an equal partner. Indonesian independence thus would be guaranteed in two ways: by reducing the power asymmetry vis-à-vis the West, but also by being a leading nation in Asia—not one being led. The Asian Games therefore were to be held in such a splendid way that they would become a shining example (or beacon) for the other Asian nations and even the Western nations—meaning that the Indonesians had to outdo Japan. This was a rather new dimension in the rhetoric surrounding the Games. Neither the First nor the Second Asian Games had had the intention of becoming an impressive and extremely expensive spectacle showing large-scale development progress. The Third Asian Games, on the other hand, had been meant to speak not for a recently decolonized and non-aligned Asia, but for Japan as Asia's most developed country, which already for decades was considered significantly less 'backward' than the rest of Asia. Nevertheless, due to the negative war heritage and US-alignment, the Japanese had only very limited influence in the Non-Aligned Movement, meaning that the Indonesians were much more important in this comparatively new group of countries.

Maladi, for example, expressed that "I feel the games will bring honour not only to Indonesia but to all of Asia. We do this in the interest of Asia to show other countries that Asians are capable of doing memorable things. (...) Indonesia plans to make the games meet one of the best, if not the best in the world."[15] During the meeting of the executive committee of the AGF in April 1962 Hamengku Buwono IX, too, promised his colleagues that Indonesia would fulfill its self-chosen role:

> [T]he Indonesian Nation, as has also been stated by His Excellency the Sports Minister Mr. Maladi, is not holding the IVth Asian Games for the prestige and pride of the Indonesian Nation alone, but also for the prestige of all the Asian Nations. The Indonesian Nation desires to contribute its capability to the Asian Nations in order to show the world, that Asian Nations too, after regaining their sovereignty after the second world war [sic], and having the opportunities to work according to their own ideas, can also create and organize big events.[16]

At the same meeting Paku Alam VIII seconded this: "[T]he aim of the Indonesian people to organize Asian Games IV is not only for the pride of the Indonesian people, but also for that of the other peoples in Asia."[17]

Indonesia's official yearbook of 1962, published by the foreign ministry, underlined that point: "The building of the Asian Meeting Ground in Djakarta, planned consciously as a contribution towards the transformation of a colonial center into the capital of a free and sovereign state, will long remind Indonesians of the deep purposes of the founders of the Asian Games."[18] One should note, however, that this claim reinvented the history of the Asian Games. For example, as shown in the second, third, and fifth chapters, Guru Dutt Sondhi would have disagreed with this statement. The hosting of the Games in an expensive and extravagant way—a necessary condition to challenge the West via branding Indonesia as a rapidly developing country representing postcolonial Asia—was, due to rising costs, rather inefficient in terms of encouraging people to take up amateur sport.

All the same, the Indonesian hosts also perceived the Games as a tool for 'national regeneration' and for catching up with the West in terms of bio-politics and the shaping of modern human bodies. Here Indonesia's situation was again special, since none of the former hosts of the Games had undergone and won a long-lasting revolutionary war against its colonial master. In combination with Sukarno's fears of imperialist aggression, this factor meant that physical strength, health, and fighting spirit were important topics when imagining the 'new Indonesian', who would defend Indonesia's independence. A colonial image to be overcome was that of strong, tall, and healthy Westerners (represented by the Dutch colonial masters) and small, weak, and sickly Asians (here certain Indonesian ethnicities), which apparently still many Indonesians and foreigners believed in.

The visual destruction of that image, but also the real physiological outcomes like greater strength for defending oneself, was expected to give Indonesians their self-respect and fighting spirit back. In April 1961, Sukarno told athletes in Bandung that "[t]he fifth facet of our revolution—that of sports—is a very important one and that is—we wish to become a new Indonesian man who can face the world with open eyes, upright, with a strong physique, strong mentally and spiritually".[19] Maladi, too, envisioned the potential of the 'new (hu-)man': "We feel the revolution in sports and physical culture to be a basic one. We feel the nationalism, the internationalism, the solidarity, the team spirit, the endurance, the sportsmanship, and other attributes of sports to be essential and primary in the building of our nation." However, this was not the final purpose of the 'new Indonesian':

> While we are more than proud to provide the necessary sports facilities for many countries to engage in friendly competition, nevertheless, we are aiming even higher. Our aim is to build the new Indonesian Man; the new

> Indonesian nation of men who, not only are fighting for the highest honour in every competition as all sportsmen are always striving for, but also patriots whose dedication of life is to serve their country and people. We have discovered that sport is a very important tool to build a new Indonesia, a nation of strong people, physically as well as mentally and spiritually.[20]

Finally, the already mentioned yearbook of the foreign ministry illustrates this approach to curing the colonial 'traumata' of inferiority:

> In its essence, the awakening of Asia has meant an insistence upon the human worth and dignity of the myriad peoples of Asia, who were for so long relegated to a status of inferiority and to a role of complete insignificancy in the world's affairs. Centuries of want and deprivation have taken a heavy toll amongst our people, depleting their physical energies and isolating and starving their minds. Sport and athletics are part of the answer to the problem of overcoming the ravages of a system now past. Sport and athletics can do more than build healthy physiques—they are one of the means for building that true self-respect without which a sense of the brotherhood of all humanity is impossible. These were the thoughts in the minds of the wise men who first initiated the Asian Games as a permanent institution.[21]

This was again rewriting history. Guru Dutt Sondhi and others would have agreed to most of it, but not to Maladi's overall aim of the 'dedicated patriot'. Sondhi, for instance, had received a Western education and rejected strong nationalism, so he still focused primarily on citizenship training based upon the 'civilizing' effects of amateur sports norms and values. An appropriation of muscular Christianity, through using a more secular and therefore ideologically more broadly useful version of it in the form of 'Olympism', had taken place. The athletes thus certainly were supposed to become part of an egalitarian and internationalist 'brotherhood of all humanity'. The Indonesian discourses, however, went significantly further than those made at the later FECG, the WAG, and the earlier Asian Games about 'national awakenings'. Although Maladi briefly mentioned amateur norms and values, which before had been essential to creating an internationalist and egalitarian dimension, his final aim was a different one. His 'dedicated patriot' de facto came rather close to Sondhi's negative example of the 'new-time gladiator', introduced in the second chapter. In the case of Indonesia, muscular Christianity did not undergo an appropriation process, but was largely substituted with the ambition of generating state nationalism. Moreover, the remaining *socialist* internationalism was strongly anti-Western, thus not completely egalitarian. Most important was to overcome inferiority complexes created through Western colonialism and to remain independent. This goal strongly encouraged an unfettered spirit of competition and an ambition to win by all means.[22] Moreover, the 'dedicated patriot', too, would finally become a member of the 'brotherhood of all humanity', though not due to 'naively' accepting egalitarian internationalism as long as it was considered not a means to challenge the still existent colonial power relations in international sport but a means to indirectly control Asians by making them accept the status quo. The 'dedicated patriot' thus needed to possess the determination (the 'true self-respect') to enforce the end of the power-asymmetry between Indonesia and the West, and thereby to challenge Indonesia's perceived unequal treatment wherever necessary.

In summary, the Indonesian values of international sport were nationalistic ones, like guaranteeing independence and shaping strong, patriotic bodies, or focused on anti-neocolonial and socialist (thus anti-Western) internationalism. They hence fitted well into Sukarno's ideology. However, as the following pages will show, the relation between Sukarno's vision of the Non-Aligned Movement—the 'New Emerging Forces' challenging the 'Old Established Forces'—and the Fourth Asian Games caused serious problems and made it impossible to realize all of the Indonesian aims.

Region-Building Failures I: Indonesia's Non-Aligned Asia

One of the most important issues for the Indonesians was the changing of the regional character of the Asian Games in accordance with Indonesia's non-aligned foreign policy. The aim of Asian integration therefore was not given up. However, while the Second Asian Games in Manila had brought pro-Western Asian countries into the AGF, as was shown in the fourth chapter, the focus now shifted to Indonesia's socialist and communist ruled allies in Asia and *Africa*, meaning that Asian geography did not matter all that much.

Only weeks after Indonesia's successful application in 1958 to host the Games did rumors emerge, based on demands by Indonesian newspapers, that the Indonesian organizers might try to renegotiate the scope of the participating countries according to their own political ideas.[23] Indonesia had no diplomatic relations with Taiwan, South Korea, and Israel, but recognized mainland China and North Korea, and supported the Arab nations. The latter were linked with Indonesia in terms of religion and Gamal Abdel Nasser's United Arab Republic (after Syria's secession in 1961 only Egypt) in particular was a major player in the Non-Aligned Movement. Moreover, in 1960, Iraq officially protested against the participation of Israel.[24] The importance of the Indonesian communist party and the anti-imperialist stance in Indonesia also meant that relations with the USSR and especially China were closer than those with the USA.[25] Thus, British diplomats falsely imagined, for example, in 1959 that the USSR could use its development aid-based influence in Indonesia to try to join the Games as an 'Asian' nation.[26]

One possibility of adjusting the shape of the Asian Games closer to Indonesia's idea of Asia lay in bringing more nations of the Non-Aligned Movement into them, which Indonesian organizations had already suggested only months after

Indonesia was awarded the Games.[27] The first targets were Arab countries. During the AGF meeting in April 1962 in Jakarta, Afghan delegate Sardar M. Faruq Siraj, supported by delegates from other Muslim countries such as Pakistan and Indonesia, advocated inviting the Arab nations of West Asia.[28] Pakistani delegate H. A. Soofi considered (non-Arab) Turkey an Asian nation; situated between Europe and Asia, its capital and most of its territory is in the Asian continent. According to Soofi, already about two-thirds of the nations of the Far East had joined the AGF, but those of West Asia should join as well. In the end, he suggested contacting Iraq, Saudi Arabia, and Turkey, but when summing up Hamengku Buwono IX talked of "[a]ll Arab countries".[29] The Indonesians afterwards were very generous when sending out invitations to join the AGF. As Guru Dutt Sondhi sarcastically remarked after the Games, Maladi had sent an invitation "on his own authority" to Indonesia's Non-Aligned Movement partner Egypt, "a country according to all geography books, in Africa".[30] For Sondhi, it became obvious that Maladi either had no understanding of geography or, more realistically, did not care for the geographical limit of the Games as given in the AGF constitution. However, Sondhi also seems not to have cared that Egypt had participated, for example, in the Asian Relations Conference in New Delhi in 1947. In the end, Egypt's application was refused by the delegates by a marginal ratio of 4:3.[31] Thus, regarding the Arab countries, none of which eventually joined, very likely due to the rejection of Egypt, the Indonesians failed in adjusting the Games according to their foreign policy ideas.[32]

A non-aligned geography, even if limited to Asia, also led to problems with Israel, the two Chinas, and the two Koreas. In February and March 1962, Maladi had to deny several times that China and North Korea would be invited and that Taiwan, South Korea, and Israel would not.[33] The rumors about China and North Korea ceased a short while later, since at the meeting of the AGF in April 1962 inviting them, or excluding their enemies, was not discussed. Just like in the case of Egypt, this approach to adjusting the AGF was therefore blocked for the Indonesians. Nonetheless, the possibility of illegally excluding certain nations from the Games remained open, though would have to be kept as secret as possible to limit countermeasures. During the following months, discussions began between Indonesia, China, and the Arab countries, but also within Indonesia, which finally led to the barring of Taiwan and Israel.

Several scholarly publications have focused on the role of the friendly relations Indonesia had with the Arab countries.[34] In the case of China, scholars underlined the important role of China's embassy in Indonesia as well as Premier Zhou Enlai and Foreign Minister Chen Yi, who wrote letters to Sukarno urging him not to let Taiwan participate. The Chinese portrayed Taiwan as an agent of American imperialism, instigated to sneak into the Asian Games to sabotage China's desired participation. As long as Taiwan remained an AGF member, which Indonesia had no chance at all of changing, China would not be 'able' to participate. Otherwise, the unacceptable situation of two Chinas would be realized. The Chinese thus put political pressure on Indonesia to counter this strategy of 'American imperialism' by at least barring Taiwan. A similar scholarly argument is that Indonesia needed China's and the Arabs' support in its struggle for Dutch-controlled West Papua.[35]

These points are certainly correct and provide an explanation why, for example, in the case of South Korea (and South Vietnam)[36] no problem arose, since foreign pressure was less strong. However, it should be emphasized that the Indonesian organizers and the government possessed agency and perceived Israel and Taiwan as hostile agents of Western imperialism and had no diplomatic relations with them. In 1958, shortly after the beginning of the PRRI-Permesta rebellion, even the Kuomintang's Indonesian branch had been forced to dissolve.[37] Thus, neither Taiwan nor Israel fit into Indonesia's international ideal of anti-imperialism and anti-neocolonialism, *independent* of the political and economic pressure put on the Indonesian organizers by the Chinese and Arabs. In July and August 1962, it became evident that the two countries would not be allowed to participate since they had not received valid identity cards that would serve as visa-equivalents. Government-controlled Indonesian newspapers explained the situation:

> Our country's stand is clear. Indonesia as host reserves the right to allow which country may enter and which not. Just as the London Olympic Games refused entry to Germany and Japan for being aggressors in World War Two, we refuse to receive Israel for being an aggressor against a friendly country in the Middle East (1956) [Suez Crisis: Egypt] and Taiwan for being the supplier of extensive war equipment to the PRRI-Permesta rebels in 1958.[38]

Israeli support for the PRRI-Permesta rebels and for the Dutch during their power struggle with Indonesia for control over West Papua was also reported. This conflict about a territory Indonesia intended to annex only ended some weeks before the Games commenced.[39]

Another problem for China, but indirectly also one for Indonesia, was that during the AGF meeting in April 1962, Taiwanese delegate Hao Gengsheng made clear that Taiwan would be ready to host the next Games if no other nation was interested.[40] The possibility that Taiwan might in fact be awarded them was quite high, since no other nation had yet officially applied. It would mean an increase in the inner-Asian legitimacy of Taiwan, like the 1986 Asian Games and the 1988 Olympic Games later supported South Korea,[41] and a setback in the attempt to shape the membership of the AGF closer to that of the Non-Aligned Movement. On 20 August Hao arrived again in Jakarta, this time to figure out what had happened to the identity cards for the Taiwanese athletes. Only blank sheets had arrived and he was also not able to obtain a visa to enter Indonesia. Since the Chinese were aware of his intentions and had informed the Indonesians about his plan to come to Jakarta, Hao could not get through immigration and was forced to leave. Indonesian officials later claimed that he had tried to enter the country illegally. This alleged violation of law and challenge to Indonesia's sovereignty was then presented by the Indonesian government as having caused popular outrage against Taiwan, which might endanger the successful running of the Games. Therefore, the Taiwanese team would not be allowed to participate.[42] Israel's NOC, on the other hand, never received invitation cards and all its attempts to contact the organizing committee failed. Israel finally renounced its participation on 21 August, declaring in the telegram that "the Organizing Committee in Djakarta has broken faith with the Asian nations who trusted it to act in accordance with the charter of the games".[43]

All in all, while the First Asian Games had been based on the ideal of bringing all Asian countries together, and the Second and Third Games had brought pro-Western countries such as Israel and Taiwan into the AGF, the Indonesians now attempted changing the regional shape of the Games according to their non-aligned and 'Asia-Africa solidarity'–based foreign policy. However, they experienced several setbacks: Egypt was not allowed to join, while China saw no option to apply for membership as long as Taiwan was an AGF member. The Indonesians then decided, in accordance with their foreign policy and the wishes of some of their political allies, against inviting Taiwan and Israel.[44]

Region-Building Failures II: Egalitarian Internationalism, Anti-Western Internationalism, an Angry Mob, and the Creation of the Games of the New Emerging Forces

By not inviting Taiwan and Israel, the Indonesian organizers challenged the ideal of egalitarian internationalism, at least in the sense of rejecting the legitimacy of the two pro-American countries as AGF members. Guru Dutt Sondhi, who took up the struggle against such Indonesian anti-Western internationalism, as a consequence saw himself confronted with increasing anti-imperialist pan-Asian rhetoric serving to legitimize the Indonesian activities. In the end, the clash between him and the Indonesians caused a chain of events significantly more dramatic than the American YMCA's struggle to overcome anti-colonial nationalism-driven Chinese boycotts of Japan before the 1921 and 1923 FECG, discussed in the second chapter.

The Indonesian organizers delayed official responses regarding the missing invitations of Israel and Taiwan until the foreign delegations had already arrived. On the one hand, this move guaranteed that Indonesia would not lose the Games and made boycotts almost impossible. On the other hand, however, several international sports organizations and members of the AGF perceived this as an especially perfidious violation of the ideal of egalitarian internationalism, including non-discrimination for political reasons.[45] Since the AGF decided for the time being against a boycott or a renaming of the Games, which would have taken away the official character of the Games and thus have solved the problem regarding the violation of its constitution, the Fourth Asian Games started as planned.[46]

Since Sondhi resisted the Indonesian officials' activities and campaigned for another vote, they utilized massive political and economic pressure and threats against him and India, until he finally capitulated. Sondhi then provided the Indonesians with a letter in which he withdrew his proposal to take away the official status of the Games. Nevertheless, before the decision became public, the situation exploded. An angry mob of about 20,000 demonstrators attacked the Indian embassy and later surrounded Hotel Indonesia, where Sondhi was staying. However, he was not to be found—he had taken a plane to Singapore upon being informed about the events. Simultaneously, the AGF held its meeting, a fact-finding commission was set up as a compromise and the affair ended for the time being.[47] However, on 9 February 1963, the executive board of the IOC held a meeting. The members present—Sondhi among them—decided with one dissenting vote (very likely from the Russian member) to suspend the Indonesian NOC for an unlimited time from the Olympic movement until Indonesia had redeemed itself.[48] It was this event, the very first suspension of an NOC by the IOC, that prompted Sukarno to give the anti-neocolonialist speech quoted at the beginning of this chapter.

The Indonesians as well were unhappy with the outcome of the Asian Games. Their approach to dealing with it was, however, totally different from that of Sondhi and the IOC. It was the same strategy the Japanese had used after the dissolution of the FEAA in 1934: they decided to found their own games. In contrast to the statements in some scholarly works,[49] the Games of the New Emerging Forces (GANEFO) were not the result of Indonesia's suspension by the IOC or machinations of the People's Republic of China. Nor were they an idea born in September 1962, as has also been stated.[50] The intention of fighting imperialism and neocolonialism by showing equality with the West had existed since Indonesia had been awarded the Fourth Asian Games in 1958, the year the Permesta/PRRI rebellion—supported by the CIA and pro-American countries—began. The GANEFO were the logical outcome of several unsuccessful attempts to (re-)shape the Asian Games into Games of the Non-Aligned Movement, based on Asia, but ideally also including at least parts of Africa, and the Asia-Africa Solidarity Movement. Since every step toward implementing this ideal—Egypt, China, North Korea, Taiwan, Israel—met problems, it became evident to the Indonesians that the AGF was not the proper organization within which to pursue their aims. Sondhi's resistance was simply the final trigger for the decision to found new games, while Chinese support served to solve financial and other problems. These new games did not grant formal equality to countries such as Taiwan and Israel, since the 'old established forces' also would not grant equality (in the sense of giving up neocolonialist activities) to the 'new emerging forces'.

In November, the new games received their final form, with Sukarno declaring: "I will hold another Games participated by not only by [sic] the Asian, African and Latin American but also by the socialist countries." Talks with Indonesia's most important ally in this endeavor, China, which increasingly attempted to emancipate itself from the USSR since 1958, intensified as well.[51] The new region was meant to cover all nations that fit into the scheme of an anti-imperialist and anti-neocolonial community. That Indonesia was punished by the International Amateur Athletic Federation in October 1962 and suspended by the IOC in February 1963 just radicalized the whole affair, and was seen as another act of imperialist aggression by a certain oligarchical clique dominating the IOC who were opposed to the 'new emerging forces' and their struggle for freedom. The First GANEFO was successfully held in Jakarta in November 1963 with representatives of 51 nations attending. Seen from the traditional Javanese perception of power, it turned Indonesia into the beacon standing at the center of the 'new emerging forces'—a group much larger than Asia—and shining even stronger into the world.

Nevertheless, the movement broke down comparatively quickly.[52] The Sukarno administration was overthrown in 1965/66, putting an America-friendly government in charge. This political change made the idea of a conference of the 'new emerging forces' in 1966, including setting up a permanent headquarters in Indonesia as a possible *rival* to the United Nations, impossible to realize.[53] Egypt did not host the Second GANEFO planned to take place in 1967, possibly due to conflict with other GANEFO leaders and to economic problems related to its heavy involvement in the North Yemen Civil War. China in late 1966 declared itself ready to step into the breach, but the beginning of the Cultural Revolution and Mao's attacks on his 'elitist' political opponents ended all involvement in international sport.[54]

All in all, the Indonesian government faced various defeats in its attempt to change the regional shape of the Asian Games. Sondhi's opposition, inspired by his interpretation of the ideal of egalitarian internationalism, was the final nail in the coffin.

Constructing the 'Decade of Development': Indonesian Infrastructure and Nation-Branding

The large-scale infrastructure development program that commenced in combination with the Fourth Asian Games can serve as an example of the Indonesian government's development plans. As a non-aligned country Indonesia was able to receive development aid from both the 'free world' and (mainly) the 'eastern bloc'. The construction program, like the goal of shaping more efficient Indonesians, had a strong authoritarian 'high modernist' touch and served to feed the Sukarno administration's vision of nation-building, of trumping Japan, and of overcoming the perception of Indonesia as an 'underdeveloped' country.

When Indonesia was awarded the task of hosting the Games, most of the necessary infrastructure was either insufficient or non-existent. The very narrow majority by which it had defeated Pakistan's candidature already showed that there were serious doubts on the side of some members of the AGF regarding Indonesia's ability to manage. Nevertheless, as Sukarno's and Maladi's already mentioned orders show, they were more than eager to accept the challenge and to implement their semi-authoritarian 'high modernist' plans. Both the 'free world' and the 'eastern bloc' also contributed some assistance in the form of development aid. The most important decision taken by the Indonesians was to construct, supported by a Russian loan of about 12 million USD and the help of Soviet experts, a giant two-storey main stadium for about 100,000 people (fig. 6.1). Its size, in combination with an aluminum roof and technical equipment including special booths for radio commentators, electronic scoreboards, a drainage system to deal with tropical rainfall, and floodlights, meant that it was one of the most modern and impressive facilities in the world at that point in time.[55] Smaller stadia for specific sports, including one for badminton to host the 1961 Thomas Cup, were erected in close proximity. The new Senayan Sports Complex also included an international village with accommodations for male and female athletes, as well as sports officials. Almost 50,000 people had to be 'relocated' to make room for it.[56] For special guests, tourists, and more wealthy officials, Indonesia's first modern hotel with 14 floors and more than 400 air-conditioned rooms, Hotel Indonesia, was constructed (fig. 6.2). Japanese war-time reparations of about 11 million USD were spent on the project. In front of the hotel, a special Welcome Monument was erected.[57] Using American development aid, the Jakarta Bypass, a six-lane highway linking Jakarta's harbor with inner Java, was built. Indonesia's first cloverleaf interchange connected it with the Sports Complex (fig. 6.3). Other main streets were broadened or completed as well.[58] Furthermore, a national bank building was constructed and hosted the Asian Games' art exhibition (fig. 6.4), while a new press house provided rooms for journalists. *Sarinah*, Indonesia's first modern department store with elevators and escalators, can also be seen as part of the infrastructure improvements.[59] In addition, cars and buses were bought to be dispatched to the visiting teams. Finally, various parts of Jakarta were renovated and through 'Operation Lotus', about 5,000 beggars and prostitutes were driven together and also 'relocated'—a not uncommon practice in Indonesia (and many other countries) before important public events.[60]

One can argue that the Asian Games, and the construction program to support them, strongly accelerated Jakarta's urbanization process (the urban population growing to about 3.8 million people in 1965).[61] This process was directly linked with the intentions of the Indonesian government and especially President Sukarno, who had studied civil engineering and had practiced as an architect before he became a politician.[62] Although one of the aims, as it has often been interpreted in the past, was certainly to raise the spirits of the Indonesian people and show Indonesia's equality with other nations, the whole project also has to be considered as more complex and linked with traditional Javanese perceptions of power. On

FIGURE 6.1
'The main stadium': In 1962, the stadium, featuring an aluminum roof, was one of the most advanced in the world, serving to communicate Indonesia's postcolonial development process.
Department of Foreign Affairs, *Indonesia*, p. 83. (Courtesy of the Kementerian Luar Negeri)

FIGURE 6.2
'Hotel Indonesia (from the back)': Another modern and expensive building serving Indonesian nation-branding purposes.
Department of Foreign Affairs, *Indonesia*, p. 85. (Courtesy of the Kementerian Luar Negeri)

FIGURE 6.3
'Cloverleaf interchange': Sukarno called the Jakarta By-Pass, to which the sports complex was connected, an element of postcolonial Indonesian 'nation-building'.
The Organizing Committee for the Fourth Asian Games, *Asian Games*, p. 48. (Courtesy of The Olympic Studies Centre)

FIGURE 6.4
'National bank building': The newly constructed building housed the art exhibition.
The Organizing Committee for the Fourth Asian Games, *Asian Games*, p. 55. (Courtesy of The Olympic Studies Centre)

the one hand, it was about accumulating impressive objects and buildings in a capital and in this way peacefully absorbing the power of neighbors, thus turning Jakarta into the undisputed capital of Indonesia, as Abidin Kusno suggested in his very interesting study on Indonesian architecture and urban space.[63] On the other hand, it was about turning Indonesia into a beacon attracting other Asian nations to it, as well as about demonstrating the ruler's power.

Firstly, the idea of emancipation from the West (and the 'eastern bloc') by erecting buildings comparable to or even outdoing those which could be found in Europe and North America is evident, considering the size of some of the buildings and the sheer amount of money spent on them. This idea was based on a traditional cyclical worldview according to which after the 'dark age' of Dutch colonialism a 'golden age' had begun and Indonesia would, from now on, not allow itself to be humiliated and discriminated against. Thus, to end the inferiority visually, Jakarta had to match the capitals of other countries, as Sukarno said in 1963 before the parliament:

> Projects such as the Asian Games, the National Monument, Independence Mosque, the Jakarta By-Pass, and so on, are examples of 'Nation-Building' and 'Character-Building' (...) of the whole Indonesian people striving to recover our national identity. I know and I understand very well that there are some people who are not aware of the meaning and function of those 'Nation-Building' and 'Character-Building' projects. They criticize and grumble under their breath about why such projects, which cost a lot of money, are given priority. (...) Do you remember that a great leader of a foreign country[64] told me that monuments are an absolute necessity to develop the people's spirit, as necessary as pants for somebody naked, pants and not a tie?[65]

Secondly, Abidin Kusno's interpretation of the new buildings as manifestations of Jakarta's importance, used to make the other parts of Indonesia accept it as the capital, is strongly supported by Sukarno's official decision to end the disputes regarding the capital. Since 1955, a campaign had started in parliament to move the capital to another city, maybe even to another island, prevented only by disagreement on the site of the potential new capital.[66] However, on 22 June 1962, Jakarta's 435th anniversary, Sukarno finally declared that it would remain the capital. He also explained that former governments had never seriously tried to turn Jakarta into a proper capital, since it might sooner or later be abandoned, so he considered the Asian Games and the construction program a necessity.[67] The fact that most of the new buildings were already under construction, or even finished, in June 1962 means that Sukarno's decision was, strictly speaking, only a formal one. Nevertheless, assertions that Hotel Indonesia was "a gigantic building of national pride" or Sukarno's rhetorical question "Now, who is the man who isn't proud of a stadium like this?" during the stadium's inauguration ceremony were not limited to the idea of emancipation from the West, but also served to confirm Jakarta as the capital of Indonesia.[68] If the whole nation was proud of the buildings, it was difficult not to be proud of the city in which they were standing. Or, put another way in terms of traditional Javanese conceptions of power, the power of the capital was increased while the neighbors ultimately peacefully accepted its predominance.

Thirdly, notions of national unity and independence can also be found. The aforementioned buildings were not built in one of the architectural styles of the different ethnicities of Indonesia, but represented European or North American styles. The main stadium actually reminded one of the Japanese officials of the Central Lenin Stadium (now Luzhniki Stadium) in Moscow.[69] Considering that there was, for example, only one main stadium and that the aim was to promote national unity, one might regard this as a compromise not to favor a certain ethnicity or island over the others so as to prevent the rise of further tension. Moreover, these styles had become a part of Indonesia's national heritage during the colonial era and Sukarno interpreted them as modern, not necessarily Western or communist. This is illustrated by various remarks on the important efforts of the Indonesian architects and workers. These cannot be reduced to mere justifications countering the possible impression that unskilled Indonesian workers were simply carrying out the instructions of skilled Russian architects and imitating foreign buildings. Instead, the message was that the government of *independent* Indonesia ordered the construction work and chose the styles. These styles therefore could not be declared the sole property of a certain region or power bloc Indonesians were copying, but were those of a modern world with Indonesia as a part of it and adding its own touch to them. For example, Indonesian architects had adjusted the main stadium to Indonesia's special climatic conditions, while Hotel Indonesia was described as "a piece of engineering genius on the outside and Indonesian artcreation [sic] on the inside". Moreover, Colonel Sudarman, commander of the Asian Games Construction Command, was proud that a project that normally took eight years (according to him) had been completed within only two and a half years. The president of the Construction Command, Minister of Production Suprajogi, said during the inauguration of the main stadium that "it was really a historic moment which proved the Indonesian People's capability to complete the giant buildings required by the coming Asian Games, something which was formerly left to foreigners." Finally, Sukarno underlined this at the same event by declaring that the stadium was the idea and sweat of the Indonesian nation.[70]

As Sukarno and Maladi had promised several times, the Asian Games should at the same time turn Indonesia into a symbol of a 'new' postcolonial Asia. The previously mentioned raising of the spirits of the Indonesian people and the end of tensions regarding the site of the capital were a part of achieving this goal, but national independence and unity were only necessary preconditions. Indonesian claims of leadership needed more than words, and it is therefore necessary to pay attention to the traditional idea of letting a capital with impressive monuments and spectacular events speak for itself in announcing Indonesia's power. Sukarno, for example, declared the main stadium to be the *most impressive* in the world.[71]

Even after the Games had finished, the buildings remained as symbols of Indonesian power. One can safely assume that Sukarno and Maladi would have applied for one of the next Olympic Games to be hosted in Jakarta (and perhaps for Maladi to become Indonesia's first IOC member) had the break with the IOC not taken place.[72] Although this is speculative, Indonesia would then have received an even bigger platform on which to promote itself, this time to the 'whole' world. Moreover, Indonesia would have caught up with Japan, the first Asian country to host the Olympic Games in 1964, just two years after the Fourth Asian Games. Such an assumption is somewhat justified by Sukarno's decision to use the new infrastructure to host the GANEFO in 1963, Indonesia's best global alternative to the Olympic Games. The GANEFO thus even *preceded* the Tokyo Olympics by one year, meaning that Indonesia afterwards could be declared to have been the *first* Asian country that had hosted a very large-scale international sports event.

Finally, the main stadium allowed Sukarno to give speeches to tens of thousands of people.[73] In terms of traditional Javanese perceptions of power, this mass of followers illustrated the power of the president. Furthermore, less than one and a half weeks after the Games had ended, on 17 September, the Senayan Sports Complex was renamed the Bung Karno Sports Complex (Bung Karno being Sukarno's pet name). About a month later, Kyai Haji Saifuddin Zuchri, the Minister of Religious Affairs, made a final suggestion to rename it again, this time to Bung Karno Sports Arena, dynamically abbreviated into *Gelora Bung Karno* (*gelora* being an abbreviation for *gelanggang olahraga* or 'sports arena', but at the same time meaning 'enthusiasm' or 'to have a high spirit', thus 'Spirit of Bung Karno'). This would show a more "concrete fighting spirit, placing stress on the dynamism of the Indonesian revolution", since sport would contribute to creating "a strong and capable generation".[74] That these decisions also served to illustrate the power of the president and his ideology should be obvious.

All in all, the large-scale infrastructure development program provides the most visible heritage of the Fourth Asian Games. Not only was Jakarta provided with some of the buildings also found in the capitals of 'developed' countries, but the development program also silenced disputes among Indonesian factions regarding the Indonesian capital, illustrated the achievements unified national action could lead to, and certainly also affected the international image of Indonesia. It nevertheless needs to be mentioned that, like in some earlier events, claims of corruption linked with the construction of the facilities came up.[75]

Independent Indonesia's Nation-Building during the Official Ceremonies and the Entertainment Program

The opening and the closing ceremony communicated the aims of the Indonesian government's large-scale social engineering plans targeted at creating a powerful Indonesia based on its precolonial cultures. Traditional ideas of power also were present, promoting Sukarno as a competent ruler and independent Indonesia as, in a cyclical worldview, now anticipating a 'golden age' after the 'Dutch darkness' had ended.

After the prescribed parts of the opening ceremony had been fulfilled and white doves as symbols of peace had been released, the Asian Games flame was lit. This ritual was accompanied by 17 cannon shots, with the runner entering the stadium with the torch on the eighth shot. The numbers symbolized 17 August (1945), the day Indonesia had declared its independence. The same numbers were also used in other contexts during the ceremony, for example in the ranks and files of women's army corps squads and national military academy cadets, who carried Indonesian flags and led the teams into the stadium. Since only 17 nations participated and the host's team had to march last into the stadium, the Indonesian team, too, represented the 'magic number'.[76]

To assemble the team, a national program to identify talented individuals had been held, meaning that people from various ethnicities and both genders were represented. Moreover, girls dressed in the traditional clothes of different Indonesian ethnicities awarded the medals during the Games.[77] Further, the flame lighter and the oath swearer, Effendi Saleh and Ferry Sonneville, were national sports heroes in athletics and badminton. Effendi Saleh also represented Indonesia's Asian sporting tradition, having been a track and field athlete on the Dutch East Indies' team during the Tenth FECG in 1934.[78] The organizers' hiring of foreign coaches to train Indonesian athletes brought this sporting tradition to new hights, helping the Indonesian team to win more medals and showcase the physical strength and fighting spirit of the host country. In the end, Indonesia received the second place (after Japan) in the overall ranking, something it had never achieved previously in the Asian Games, and which it would not achieve again.[79]

After the official ceremony, the main program began. First, two exhibitions of the new, modern, and disciplined Indonesian nation took place. Twelve hundred children, both boys and girls, participated in mass calisthenics (fig. 6.5). Children, representing the future of the nation, were thereby shown to be doing their best to become physically strong, disciplined, and healthy. The bio-political message was that the new generation would consist of better workers (and soldiers) who were more capable of serving the Indonesian nation. Furthermore, the display was meant to symbolize a carefree childhood, no longer threatened by colonial rule and oppression.[80] Following this first exhibition, almost 500 female senior high school students from Jakarta participated in rhythmic gymnastics and communicated

FIGURE 6.5
'Mass calisthenics by children'.
The Organizing Committee for the Fourth Asian Games, *Asian Games*, p. 130. (Courtesy of The Olympic Studies Centre)

FIGURE 6.6
'Female high school students': The event showed the students as patriots and emphasized the importance of women in nation-building.
The Organizing Committee for the Fourth Asian Games, *Asian Games*, p. 132. (Courtesy of The Olympic Studies Centre)

a similar message of modernization and discipline (fig. 6.6). Women, now being recognized as a relevant part of Indonesian society, would also strive to become more useful citizens of the new Indonesian nation. The hoops they used during the exhibition were painted red and white, the colors of the national flag of Indonesia. The fact of being an independent nation was further underlined by their shouting of "Sekali Merdeka, Tetap Merdeka" ('Once Independent, Forever Independent') at the beginning of their performance.[81]

In addition to these events, which promised a 'splendid future' for the new nation, a 'magnificent pre-colonial past' was staged, depicting traditional cultural elements via two dances. Almost 500 young men from Aceh (North Sumatra) participated in a *Seudati* dance (fig. 6.7). The dance itself, having turned into a war dance during Dutch colonialism and thus having been forbidden, was another illustration of independence. The dancers were dressed in traditional clothes and formed among other things a sun, the symbol of the AGF and thus a pan-Asian element. [82] The participation of non-Javanese ethnicities, in this case one from a region well-known as an Islamic stronghold against the central government, was considered highly important. The Indonesian news agency *Antara*, for example, remarked that by "the Atjeh participation in this Asian Games it is said that the meeting really becomes a matter of prestige for all Indonesian people[s]".[83] Not only was national unity demonstrated, but—in terms of traditional perceptions of power—the ruler's ability to make different and sometimes hostile peoples come peacefully together was underlined. The creation of an authentic Indonesian culture thus was (and certainly could) not be reserved to a single ethnicity or island.

The highlight was a *Pendet* welcome dance by about 1,000 young women, most of them from Bali, who were dressed in traditional festive costumes (fig. 6.8). Normally such a dance was performed to welcome important persons or divine beings, but here this element of traditional Balinese culture served to symbolically welcome the foreign athletes and guests.[84] Again, a demonstration of Indonesia's unity in ethnic and cultural diversity was combined with a more internationalist component. The same is probably true for the messages the dancers created via formations and different colored dresses on the field. Although it is uncertain whether or not the dance was performed as intended, it was at least planned that flowers, a fan (standing for hospitality), the Indonesian national flag, the colors of the *Pancasila* (the five principles of the state ideology which are also symbolically represented in the Indonesian coat of arms),[85] and white cotton and yellow paddy (meaning national wealth and social justice) were to be depicted.[86] Regardless, one can argue that the whole *Pancasila* was to be represented in the opening ceremony. Cotton and paddy have already been mentioned and the star formed by the *Seudati* dancers could also be seen as the star standing for belief in one god. Whether or not a chain (humanity/internationalism), a tree (national unity/nationalism) and a bull's head (democracy/sovereignty) were also to be formed remains an open question, but these principles were de facto displayed by

FIGURE 6.7
'Seudati war dance': The participation of dancers from problematic Aceh region communicated successes in integrating different ethnicities into Sukarno's Indonesia.
The Organizing Committee for the Fourth Asian Games, *Asian Games*, p. 133. (Courtesy of The Olympic Studies Centre)

FIGURE 6.8
'Pendet welcome dance': Balinese cultural elements gained a prominent place in representing Indonesia.
The Organizing Committee for the Fourth Asian Games, *Asian Games*, p. 135. (Courtesy of The Olympic Studies Centre)

different Indonesian ethnicities of both genders peacefully performing together for Indonesians and foreigners.

Similarly, the closing ceremony was adorned with some Asian as well as Indonesian elements. After the Games were declared closed and a group of boy scouts brought away the AGF flag, the flame and all other lights were extinguished and *Auld Lang Syne* was sung, with the participation of the spectators. Subsequently, about 800 Indonesian cadets standing around the field waved special torches so that the image of palm trees was created while *Rayuan Pulau Kelapa* ('Solace on Coconut Island') was chanted by 5,000 children. After the lights were turned on again, 17 Indonesian girls, dressed in the traditional clothes of different Indonesian ethnicities, brought the national flags used during the Games back to their respective teams. These were held in special trays, wood-carvings from Jepara (Central Java), which symbolized traditional Javanese art.[87] Thus, Indonesian cultural diversity was again staged, while traditional cultural elements were also present. The boy scouts were a peaceful contrast to the soldiers who had carried the AGF flag in 1954 and 1958 and during the opening ceremony in 1962. However, soldiers participated in many ways in the ceremonies, promoting the Indonesian armed forces as a guarantor of independence. Moreover, the internationalist dimension was once again emphasized by singing *Auld Lang Syne* as a farewell song remembering common deeds.

Auld Lang Syne and *Rayuan Pulau Kelapa* were not the only songs performed during the ceremonies. In addition to the national anthem, patriotic songs like *Nyiur Hijau* ('Green Coconut') and *Bangun Pemudi Pemuda* (the Indonesian youth anthem, literally 'Rise, Young Men and Women') were part of the program. The special anthem for the Fourth Asian Games called *Patriot Paripurna* ('Full-fledged Patriot'), based on a traditional Malayan form of poetry (*Syair*), was a prayer to bestow the participating young athletes with an excellent character. It had been prepared by Raden Adrianus Josephus Sudjasmin (R. A. J. Soedjasmin), who had written several patriotic songs and also served as conductor during the ceremonies.[88] The songs have to be seen as another appeal to the state nationalism of the Indonesians: foreign visitors, due to the language barrier, probably only enjoyed the melody.

In a nutshell, the ceremonies and the entertainment program of the Fourth Asian Games branded a 'new' postcolonial Indonesia. The focus was not only on unity in diversity, as shown by traditional dances, but also on independence and on shaping a more healthy, disciplined, and physically stronger generation of Indonesians.

Catching up with Japan: Television for Development

The setting up of a television system can be seen as symptomatic of the aims of the Indonesians at the time. The aim was not only to make people take up sport, but to display national development. Newspapers, radios, and public loudspeakers were certainly helpful, but were very limited in the visual dimension, arguably the most important one for Indonesian organizers. To make up for this shortcoming, a television system was established. As Raden Mas Sutarto, a well-known photographer and Indonesia's first film producer who served as chairman of the television committee, declared before the Games: "Djakarta has a population of three and a half million. No more than 200,000 will be able to see the Games daily at the actual venues. The government therefore decided to bring the Games to the rest by buying 10,000 television sets and installing them in places accessible to the greatest number of people."[89] 'To the rest' was certainly an exaggeration: it is doubtful that even a number of people equal to that of the spectators in the stadiums could be reached, although the events could certainly be re-broadcasted several times or shown in the cinema. Nevertheless, the intention is evident. After some tests on Independence Day 1962, official television broadcasting in Indonesia (Jakarta and, to a lesser degree, Bandung) began on 24 August with the opening ceremony of the Fourth Asian Games.[90] In this way, more people could be reached, while television itself contributed to the image of national development. This image very likely was further strengthened by the Japanese NHK being the *only* foreign broadcaster that was able to send a camera team.[91]

Like in the other cases, it is difficult to say what long-term impact the Games had on the lives of individual Indonesians, especially if they lived on the 'outer islands', and on people from the rest of the world. Nevertheless, one can state that more than 32,000 Indonesians were directly involved in planning and organizing them. Many more saw them in the stadium, on television, or in the cinema. Others could at least watch the torch relay covering parts of Java, were informed about the Games via newspapers, private radios or public loudspeakers, or received or sent letters with stamps depicting motifs of the Games. The *Antara* news agency claimed –reasonably—that almost one million people had asked for tickets.[92]

All in all, public and media attention in Indonesia seems to have been huge. The semi-authoritarian system's influence on the media certainly helped to facilitate communicating the Games to the public. The introduction of television for the Games is another illustration of the importance they possessed in the view of the Indonesian government as a tool to brand Indonesia as a rapidly developing country, outdoing the previous Asian Games in Tokyo.

Assessment

The Fourth Asian Games had an immense impact on the further development of the Asian Games and, to a lesser degree, the Olympic Games.

First, the hitherto very important idea of amateur sport as a means for citizenship training and egalitarian internationalism was massively challenged. The organizers of the first three Asian Games, even though Asians and not Westerners as during the early FECG, had been strongly affected by the 'Western civilizing mission'. Both Guru Dutt Sondhi and Jorge Vargas had been socialized with the idea of educating fellow Asians via amateur sports ideals. Through their collaboration with the American YMCA physical directors they had ensured that the sportive 'civilizing mission', now being carried by them, went on in their respective countries even after independence. In the case of the Japanese, anti-Western internationalism and Japanese-led pan-Asianism had modified the 'civilizing mission'. The American victory, the occupation, and MacArthur nonetheless had enforced a rapprochement with the West, even if promoting amateur sport in Japan was not that important anymore in 1958. In contrast, the Indonesian organizers aimed at shaping patriotic and competent 'new Indonesians'. Their egalitarianism excluded the West, and inferiority complexes founded in former colonialism were to be overcome. Sport therefore supported the Sukarno administration in its attempt to modernize Indonesia without Westernization of its society, and to overcome 'Orientalist' notions of dependency in order to underline independence. As one might expect, the confrontation of the two sports ideologies ended in disaster. Indonesia was banned by an IOC still convinced of its 'civilizing mission'. As a result of their non-aligned and 'Asia-Africa Solidarity' based foreign policy, the Indonesian organizers preferred countries such as Egypt and China as AGF members, but while this aim could not be realized, they were able to exclude Taiwan and Israel, two 'American puppets' whose existence they did not recognize. Due to several setbacks, including Sondhi's protests regarding the illegal exclusions, they realized that the adjustment of the regional character of the Games could not be achieved within the AGF. The GANEFO, fueled by the spirit of Asia, Africa, Latin America, and the socialist countries becoming 'truly' independent of the Western sports ideology, were the logical outcome. Teams consisting of 'progressive' people from Western countries were not generally excluded, but had to accept the GANEFO ideology.

Secondly, the Fourth Asian Games strengthened the tendency, which was already strong during the Third Games, to use them for nation-branding purposes by showing national achievements and cultural authenticity both to the population and to an international audience. In combination with the anti-Western internationalism, certain Western observers, including IOC members, thus treated the Fourth Asian Games, like the GANEFO, primarily as a pariah. They saw them as a means to mobilize the population and distract it from the domestic problems, particularly a deteriorating economic situation and internal division in Indonesia. The Games thus were not considered to be a proper 'apolitical' (meaning based on egalitarian internationalism) sports event. Clearly the Games served to gather the people behind the government and to demonstrate Sukarno's power, thus strengthening his position vis-à-vis other institutions like the army. However, more concrete nation-building and a pan-Asian message, too, were highly relevant. The cultural traditions of different Indonesian ethnicities were acknowledged and the ability of all of them to cooperate with each other for national aims under the leadership of the government was underlined. The staging primarily intended to promote Indonesia as a modern and swiftly developing nation, having the same facilities and infrastructure as the West and the 'communist bloc', but with a different political ideology. Freedom from all sorts of imperialist oppression (Sukarno calling it 'the freedom to be free', adding a fifth freedom to Franklin D. Roosevelt's 'Four Freedoms')[93] would, in a cyclical worldview, bring a 'golden age' after the 'darkness' of Dutch colonialism. However, even though national cultural elements such as symbols and songs dominated the staging, some pan-Asian elements such as King Rama of the *Ramayana*, featured with his bow on the official poster of the Games, can also be found.[94] All in all, the Asian Games, and even more so the GANEFO, were a demonstration in particular to the West that Indonesia (and Asia) was not a 'backward', colonial region anymore, and thus would not accept further imperialist or neocolonialist schemes. Hence, the Asian Games especially were characterized by an exceptionally strong state nationalism, including the idea of an '(ultra-)nationalist rebirth', and a strong anti-Western internationalism. Despite all these negative issues, sports officials, politicians, and journalists from various nations, even India, considered the event all in all to have been very impressively run.[95]

CHAPTER 7

The King, the Military, and Thai Development: Hosting the Fifth and the Sixth Asian Games Consecutively (9–20 December 1966 and 1970)

"Thailand is fortunate in having a King who is not only interested in sports, but a King who actually participates in sports. (...) There can't be anything wrong with a country that has thousands of well-disciplined and physically-trained boys and girls like those who performed yesterday."[1]

—International Olympic Committee president Avery Brundage, who attended the opening ceremony of the Sixth Asian Games

The Fourth Asian Games had taken place in Indonesia, a semi-authoritarian and non-aligned country leaning toward the communist side in the ideological struggle of the Cold War. In contrast, the Fifth and Sixth Asian Games were held in Thailand, which was one of the United States' closest allies during the Vietnam War (1955–75, with major American involvement from 1965) and was ruled by an authoritarian military regime.

The Games were thus again affected by Cold War foreign policy and by the tensions on the Southeast Asian peninsula. The Games of the New Emerging Forces (GANEFO) had spawned an Asian version of itself taking place in Cambodia, Thailand's increasingly pro-Chinese neighbor, during late 1966 only weeks before the Fifth Asian Games. As one might expect, Thai sports officials showed no intention to participate in the Chinese-sponsored First Games of the New Emerging Forces of Asia (GANEFOA).[2] Instead, they had even earlier contributed to the founding of another regional sports event. The Southeast Asian Peninsular Games (SEAP Games), whose first event was held in Bangkok in 1959, were one of several anti-communist region-building schemes in Southeast Asia of which the Association of Southeast Asian Nations (ASEAN), founded in 1967, would ultimately be the most successful. The regional shape of the Asian Games, which the Thai organizers felt themselves ready to host due to the organizational experience gained in 1959, therefore saw no important changes. Here, too, communist ruled countries still did not participate: neither at the Fifth Games, which Thailand had applied for, nor at the Sixth Games, which it agreed to hold after South Korea declared itself unable to do so.

The aims of the organizers and the staging of the Games were strongly influenced by the Thai-centered ideology of the military regime and its monarchist collaborators. The Fifth Games were the second such event characterized by an authoritarian version of 'high modernism' and formed part of a large-scale modernization and development scheme intended to increase Thailand's economic and military power. It thereby legitimized the military regime, supported the monarchy, and discouraged communist propaganda. The spread of sport as a bio-political means of shaping more efficient citizens was thus again an important aim. Another goal was the strengthening of the tourism industry, the foundations of which already existed in the form of growing numbers of American soldiers on leave from Vietnam visiting Bangkok for recreational purposes. Finally, the staging of the Games also reflects some of the other measures the military took in its attempt to create popular support and national unity, since the monarchy and elements of traditional Thai culture and Buddhist religion were featured prominently.

In this chapter, I focus on the Fifth and Sixth Games' connection to Thailand's attempts at anti-communist Asian cooperation. Furthermore, I show that due to the collaboration between the military and the monarchists, the Games contributed to the personality cult of the king as the semi-sacral figurehead of the Thai nation. I also focus on the exhibition of Thailand as a rapidly developing country that nevertheless would embrace its Buddhist cultural heritage.

Thailand (1966–70)

In 1963, one year after Bangkok was awarded the Fifth Asian Games and three years before they took place, General Thanom Kittikachorn succeeded his deceased superior, General Sarit Thanarat, as Thailand's prime minister. He was to rule until his authoritarian regime was overthrown by the pro-democratic revolution of 1973. Military rule had been rather common in Thailand after the constitutional revolution of 1932 ended monarchical 'absolutism' and Plaek Phibunsongkhram's (in the following: Phibun) pro-Japanese military regime (1938–44) had further reduced the influence of the monarchy. The democratization attempts that emerged in connection with the end of the Second World War proved to be only a very short-lived phenomenon due to a coup d'état by the military in 1947. Strongly dependent on Sarit, who was in charge of the military in Bangkok, and other military leaders, Phibun returned as prime minister, again attempting to enlarge his influence by reducing that of the monarchy's. In 1951, another coup further increased the military's control of the country, although rivalries within the regime increased in the mid-1950s. In 1957, Sarit, aided by the monarchists, deposed Phibun in yet another coup. The next year Sarit declared martial law, set up a new constitution, dissolved the parliament, arrested opponents, and began censoring the media.[3]

The Thai-centered ideology of Sarit's military regime focused heavily on educational, administrative, and—especially—private economic development. Thai society, described by American researchers as passive, lacking institutions for collective action and—due to traditional interpretations of Theravada Buddhism—overly focused on rebirths and future lives instead of the present, was to be restructured. Private economic initiative was encouraged, but also anti-communism and loyalty to nation and monarchy. In contrast to Phibun representing a generation of Thai leaders that had not been educated abroad, Sarit linked development to traditional Thai ideas such as the welfare of the people being the outcome of the religious merits of the ruler, particularly the monarch.[4] The monarchy thus experienced a revival during Sarit's regime and the influence of King Bhumibol Adulyadej, reigning since 1946, significantly increased. By the mid-1960s, the monarchy had reclaimed control over many important public functions that it had lost due to the constitutional revolution and Phibun's anti-monarchical stance. Promoting the military regime as a secular arm of the semi-sacred Buddhist monarchy was an important approach to legitimizing Sarit's rule, but also served to prevent an influx of Western interpretations of 'democracy' by encouraging traditional conceptions of social and political hierarchy.[5]

After Sarit's death in 1963, his second-in-command, Thanom, was 'promoted' to the positions of prime minister and minister of defense. Praphas Charusathien, another important general, protégé of Sarit, and father-in-law of Thanom's son, became deputy prime minister and minister of the interior. Ideological changes were limited, meaning that development planning went on with continued aid from the United States. With this help, beginning in the 1950s, annual growth rates reached about 7 per cent, while the share of the agricultural sector in the gross national product decreased from more than 50 per cent in 1951 to less than 30 per cent in 1970.[6]

The Cold War—and particularly the Vietnam War—had an important impact on Thailand's foreign policy during Sarit's and Thanom's rule. Anti-communist region building in Southeast Asia was one attempt to protect Thailand's security, but all the multilateral approaches taken up to 1967, when ASEAN was founded in Bangkok, had effectively failed due to internal rivalries or tensions with non-Southeast Asian powers.[7] The Vietnam War and the presence of large numbers of American soldiers in Bangkok, many of them being sent there for recreation purposes, also affected Thailand's internal situation. Bars, night clubs, and brothels mushroomed and up to 300,000 prostitutes served American and local customers. Beauty contests boomed as well, mirroring a combination of the military leaders' personal desires—Sarit seems to have preferred 'beauty queens' as concubines—and a general interest in beautiful women, since physical beauty was perceived as a result of merit in earlier lives and therefore good karma. An important intention behind such pageants was the strengthening of the tourism industry. In the early 1950s, this sector was not yet organized and only about 40,000 people visited Thailand each year, while by 1970 this number had risen to 600,000. Earnings grew from about 250 million baht in 1961 to 2,209 million in 1971 (and 5,600 million in 1978) as tourism became the fifth largest source of foreign exchange.[8]

Sport in Thailand and the Decision to Host Two Consecutive Asian Games

By the 1960s, Western sport already had a relatively long history in Thailand, but had had little impact on Thai society. While the Fifth Asian Games were an important development project of the Sarit and the Thanom regimes, which is illustrated by the involvement of some of their leading members, hosting the Sixth Games only four years later was a less welcome project resulting from South Korea's being unable to organize them.

When Western sport arrived in Siam in the late nineteenth century, the monarchy had been one of its most important promoters. The overall impact of physical education nevertheless was very small, most likely since the agriculturally based occupations of large parts of the population kept them physically active, meaning that they saw no need for further physical exercise. For example, the physical education school that had been set up in 1913 had produced only 57 teachers by 1934, indicating that such a qualification was not deemed particularly lucrative.[9] Moreover, the Far Eastern Athletic Association (FEAA) had several times encouraged Thailand to send a team to the Far Eastern Championship Games (FECG), but without success. The first important international sports events in which Thailand participated were the First Asian Games in 1951 and the Helsinki Olympic Games in 1952. After Sarit took power, the official attitude started to change rapidly, and international sport became linked to developmental and region-building aims. In February 1958, a decision was reached to propose at the Third Asian Games in Tokyo that a Southeast Asian sports organization be founded, the first event of which would be hosted in Bangkok the next year. Sarit declared the government's willingness to provide the necessary funding and Praphas, one of the most important organizers, was entrusted with the presidency of the organizing committee. As the name of the event already suggests, the regional shape of the First SEAP Games focused on continental Southeast Asia, therefore Thailand's close neighbors: Burma, Laos, Malaya, Singapore, South Vietnam, and Cambodia (which refrained from participating in the first event and several of those which followed).[10] Reminiscent of what happened during the Second Asian Games in the Philippines covered in the fourth chapter, the communist ruled part of a divided country, North Vietnam, did not join. It is very likely it had not been invited to do so.

The Sarit regime's next foray into international sport was, now that the Thai organizers had gained experience through the First SEAP Games, to apply for the Fifth Asian Games. Thailand was awarded them at the Fourth Asian Games in 1962. A step directly linked with the approaching Games of 1966 was the creation of the Sport Promotion Organization (later renamed the Sport Authority of Thailand) as a division of the Department of Physical Education, which had been created in 1933. Its primary task was to supervise the preparations for the Asian Games, but it was also responsible for coordinating the development of sport in rural areas (which were extremely underrepresented in national teams), organizing national and regional games within Thailand, and preparing teams for international events.[11]

An overview of the leading officials of the Sport Promotion Organization, the organizing committee of the Fifth and Sixth Asian Games, and the Asian Games Federation (AGF) will make obvious the highly important role of the military and the government in organizing and promoting sport. Praphas, who was, among other positions, already president of the organization for traditional Thai sports, accumulated more offices, becoming president of the Sport Promotion Organization in 1964, president of Thailand's National Olympic Committee (NOC) in 1965, and president of the AGF for both the Fifth and Sixth Games. His involvement in sport culminated in his 1971 election as Thailand's first International Olympic Committee (IOC) member, a capacity in which he served until 1974.[12] Kong Visudharomn, the director-general of the Department of Physical Education and treasurer of Thailand's NOC, became director of the Sport Promotion Organization and the secretary of both organizing committees. Kong was no military leader but a physical education expert who had studied at the Carnegie College of Physical Education (now part of Leeds Metropolitan University), had joined the Department of Physical Education in 1936, and had led previous Thai Olympic teams.[13] The initial president of the organizing committee for the Fifth Games had been Luang Sukhum Nayapradit, who eventually stepped down due to poor health. Sukhum, a civil servant with close ties to the monarchy, had been educated at The Gunnery and at Boston University. Later he had served, among other offices, as director-general of the Public Relations Department and as a member of the board of advisors on administration to the prime minister. In terms of sport, he had been vice president of Thailand's NOC, had been the chief delegate to several Olympic and Asian Games events and was a co-founder of the SEAP Games.[14] Air Chief Marshal Dawee Chullasapya succeeded Sukhum as president of the organizing committee for the Fifth Games and received the same office for the Sixth Games. Dawee, another important military leader, had graduated from Thailand's military academy and later studied in Great Britain and the United States, and then had risen through the military ranks to become chief of staff of the supreme command, deputy minister of defense, and minister of communication. In 1974, he succeeded Praphas as Thailand's IOC member.[15] The vice president of both organizing committees and of the Sport Promotion Organization was Police General Luang Chartrakarn Kosol, who had graduated from New York's police academy before working in the police department and eventually becoming under-secretary of state. As director of the National Lottery Bureau, another office he held, he oversaw the use of some of the lottery gains for the construction of stadia in rural areas, for which he then also became responsible.[16] Finally, Thailand's head of state, King Bhumibol, who during the Sarit and Thanom regimes regained much public influence, became the patron of both Asian Games events. Although he did not compete in either of the two Asian Games, he did take part in the 1967 SEAP Games held in Bangkok, sharing a gold medal in OK dinghy class yachting with his daughter Princess Ubolratana. This, "a King who actually participates in sports", was what IOC president Brundage referred to in the quotation which begins this chapter.[17] More precisely, according to Dawee, the goal had been to show King Bhumibol as a marvelous sportsman, similar to King Olav V of Norway, who won a gold medal in a sailing event at the 1928 Olympic Games. However, King Bhumibol had to share the gold medal with his daughter since he accidently ended up at the wrong finish line during the final race.[18]

The Thai organizers had not applied for the Sixth Asian Games, but decided to step into the breach when the South Korean organizers backed out of hosting them. Seoul had been chosen at the Fifth Games as the host city, but already in 1967 rumors spread that South Korea was facing problems. Initially, it was said that President Park Chung-hee had come to the conclusion that the Games would be too expensive and other forms of development were more pressing.[19] In 1968, the president of South Korea's NOC provided another reason, explaining that "since mid-summer of 1967, daily infiltrations into the Republic of Korea grew in intensity until January 21 this year (1968) when 31 North Korean Communist soldiers, each of them fully armed[,] reached nearly 300 meters from [sic] the Presidential Residence of Chung Hee Park of the Republic of Korea." Such daily infiltrations, which had already resulted in the complete closure of the demilitarized zone to tourists, meant that it was impossible to guarantee the security of the Games and their foreign participants.[20] As a result, *both* Japan and Thailand were asked for help, since they were considered to have the necessary competence and infrastructure to host the Games without an extended period of preparations.[21]

The Japanese declined since they were already hosting the upcoming Expo '70 in Osaka and the 1972 Olympic Winter Games in Sapporo.[22] Initially, the Thai government also rejected the pleas of the unsuccessful South Korean organizers, offering various excuses. For example, Chartrakarn noted that Thailand had already saved the SEAP Games of 1967. Thanom, in an interview with the desperate AGF subcommittee that was tasked with solving the problem, explained that hosting the 1970 Games would be financially impossible because of a "daily increase of Communist infiltrations into Thailand, which entailed increased expenditure".[23] The growing cost of the escalating Vietnam War was thus considered the main problem. This problem could, however, be more easily overcome than South Korea's security issues or Japan's prior commitment to other events. After an agreement was reached, according to which South Korea would provide a substantial sum of money and the other AGF member countries would also contribute funding, the Thai government agreed to move the Games to Bangkok. Authority over the Sixth Games was then transferred from the South Korean to the above mentioned Thai organizers.[24]

Taken all together, Western sport, and physical education in general, had already gained a certain importance in Thailand in the early twentieth century and, reminiscent of policy in other Asian countries covered in earlier chapters, had been made a part of government plans. However, the impact of these measures even in the early 1950s was still comparatively low. A large-scale take-off of sport, including the hosting of international sports events as a tool for region building and for sports development, began only during Sarit's rule with the hosting of the First SEAP Games in 1959 and the decision to apply for the Fifth Asian Games. The Thanom administration continued these plans, hosting the Fifth Games and stepping into the breach for both the SEAP Games of 1967 and the Sixth Asian Games. These moves reflected the organizational competence and infrastructure that had already been developed. The group of Thai officials chosen to organize the two Asian Games events, all of them important military leaders or civil servants with the deputy prime minister at the top, further illustrates the significance the two authoritarian military regimes awarded the Games.

The Development of Sport and Tourism

Both international sport and the spread of mass sport to rural areas experienced a boom during the Sarit and Thanom regimes. Some of the events that took place in connection with the Asian Games, but also the discourses of the organizers and the government, will show the aims that were linked with this development of sport. These include Thailand's tourism industry, social and economic modernization purposes, and national prestige. These aims were summed up in the official report on the Fifth Asian Games:

> For instance, on the economic side, the Asian Games committee received a large sum from ticket sales. On the sports side, the public[,] especially the younger generation, became more interested in sports because of the new techniques displayed during the Games. The Government also promoted and supported our sports in order to raise our own standard to approach other countries. Hosting the Fifth Asian Games made Thailand become better known to foreigners as well as promoting our own tourist trade.[25]

While the Fifth Asian Games took place 9–20 December 1966, the First International Asian Trade Fair was held in Bangkok between 17 November and 10 December. This project was supported by the Thai government and the United Nations Economic Commission for Asia and the Far East. The declared aim was to promote economic development by encouraging foreign investment and by increasing trade among Asian countries and between them and the rest of the world. After its closure, Thailand's minister of economic affairs and the foreign fair advisor (a certain R. H. C. Hammond) estimated that more than 1.5 million visitors had visited the fair.[26] Although the fair's primary aim was to encourage economic development, the close hosting of the two 'mega events' makes it obvious that Thai officials intended to use them to attract a maximum number of foreign visitors. The possibility of visiting two important events during one trip and of seeing some of Bangkok's attractions was certainly considered a good way to increase the willingness of people to travel to Thailand. The significance of this expected influx of tourists in late 1966 is further underlined by an earlier decision to bring Bangkok's sex industry under tighter control, although not to abolish it.[27] One has to assume that prostitutes were to offer their services to the tourists, particularly single men, but the image of Bangkok as a giant brothel for American soldiers, which had the potential to offend tourists coming only for the events, was not to overshadow the trade fair and the Asian Games.

The training of modern citizens, as so often before, was of great importance to the Thai officials. The most academic explanations were provided by Kong, who during a physical education congress held during the Fifth Games gave a presentation on the topic of 'Physical Education and National Development'. Quite obviously, the hosting of this congress, the founding of an Asian committee for the standardization of physical fitness tests at the same event, and the establishment of an Asian congress of sports medicine at the Sixth Asian Games were means to develop sport, here in an academic sense. Kong's presentation focused on three important points, the first concerning bio-politics and the physical efficiency of the population: "Economically, it [the development of physical education] helps man build up vitality and physical fitness which enables him to do jobs with full proficiency". His second, less clear, argument was that "it [the development of physical education] leads to political results in that it sharpens man's brain to administer and take part in political activities more actively and effectively." This was very likely hinting at amateur norms and values such as self-control, team spirit (including putting community interest above individual interest), and a belief in hard work and hard training. In addition to the ideal of economic progress, Kong's last point hinted in an almost classical way at the ideals of internationalism and egalitarianism: "Finally, socially, it [the development of physical education] provides happiness and understanding".[28]

The promotion of sport therefore has to be seen as a part of the 'high modernist' thinking of the authoritarian government, which included large-scale infrastructure construction plans not only for irrigation systems and highways in the rural areas, but also for playgrounds, for which the Sport Promotion Organization was responsible. Moreover, the official report of the Fifth Asian Games further underlines the connection between the Asian Games as a means for raising popular interest in sports, the building of sports infrastructure, and the encouragement of sports-based socially useful ideals and behavior. Similar to the Fourth Asian Games, it was a concentrated attempt to speed up a process that had been started decades ago, but which without systematic government involvement had experienced serious problems and largely been limited to urban centers.[29] The Thai endeavors were thus definitely about a "more earnest promotion of sports", as Praphas quite carefully described them in December 1966.[30] Dawee, in contrast, went further, and made clear the impact the increased focus on development had on the character of the Games, which were "an occasion of great significance for Thailand and for the national prestige".[31] Seen in a broader perspective, the Thai activities are symptomatic of a process that had a close parallel in the Indonesian activities covered in the previous chapter. Sports events had always been linked to national progress and later to development, but in 1966 a reporter of the British *Observer* was struck by the sheer amount of Asian countries that in one way or another attempted to promote themselves to the world by setting up national sports teams, strongly increasing governmental control over sport, and making it part of their development projects.[32] Another illustration of this process is the attendance of the 1970 Sixth Asian Games by Bill Toomey, an American Olympic gold medalist working for the Peace Corps' newly founded Sports Corps. At the Games, he explained the United States' willingness to send large numbers of sports experts to Asia to support the development of sport.[33] The offer must have been a reaction to a broad interest among 'Third World' countries.

It is not surprising given the great ambitions of the Thai organizers that rumors and warnings emerged that they would fail.[34] Praphas issued some warnings of his own, but these were intended only to prevent excessively high expectations regarding Thailand's rank in the medal count. He declared that he would consider a third place finish—which Thailand eventually achieved both in 1966 and 1970, while Japan won more gold medals than all other countries together—to be a very good outcome. The promotion of sport was, after all, still in its infancy.[35] As could be expected, the Fifth Asian Games did not proceed without incidents and had some deficits in terms of the quality of the infrastructure.[36] However, since no serious disasters occurred despite the warnings and rumors, a sense of enthusiasm arose.[37] For example, Thanom in his message in the official report about the Games focused on the former doubts:

> When the Olympic Committee of Thailand, under the Royal Patronage, received the honour of organizing the Fifth Asian Games at Bangkok 1966, the Government embarked upon the project with a certain amount of apprehension, because never in the history of sports in Thailand, had a sporting event of such magnitude ever been staged before. Although it is

> true that the First South East Asian Peninsular Games were inaugurated at Bangkok in 1959, there were only 6 member countries of the South East Asia Peninsular Games Federation taking part, whereas in the Fifth Asian Games, there were prospectively 18 nations.[38]

However, in this statement the doubts the government was said to have shared only served as a means to dramatize Thailand's success. The core message was that Thailand, despite limited experience, had *succeeded* in its task. Praphas, too, for some days after the Games seems to have felt very relieved. He did not develop a concrete plan, but declared that in a decade Thailand may be ready to host the Olympic Games.[39] Within days, Foreign Minister Thanat Khoman rejected this idea, explaining that Thailand needed its money for "economic development and suppressing terrorists in the borders". The secretary-general of the economic board made a similar statement.[40] This disagreement is hardly surprising, since hosting the Olympic Games would be significantly more expensive than hosting the Asian Games and the money spent on them would not be available for infrastructure projects in the rural areas, be they irrigation systems or playgrounds.

The Sixth Asian Games taken over from South Korea seem to have generated no enthusiasm comparable to the previous event among the Thai government. The most enthusiastic comments in 1970 were therefore made by IOC president Brundage, who attended parts of the Games. After he saw the opening ceremony of the Games, he made the statements quoted at the beginning of this chapter, declaring that there "can't be anything wrong with a country that has thousands of well-disciplined and physically-trained boys and girls like those who performed yesterday."[41] Brundage did not, however, focus on the authoritarian regime itself, but on the king as a sportsman and on the large-scale development of sport. In so doing, he rather simplistically declared the latter point to be the basis of the general welfare of a country. Very likely, the topic of juvenile discipline was particularly noteworthy for him due to the student activism and the riots that affected many countries beginning in the mid-1960s. This interpretation is underlined by the quite drastic rhetoric, for example, of Philippine President Ferdinand Marcos, who in 1972 declared martial law. Already in 1967, Marcos reminded the readers of the Philippine Amateur Athletic Federation's (PAAF's) *The Filipino Athlete* in rather martial terms that in ancient Sparta mothers had expected their sons leaving for war to "come home with your shield, or on it". Honor and discipline were nevertheless not only very useful for "soldiers of war, but for all the soldiers of national construction", thus metaphorically turning development in a much more extreme way than Brundage or the Thai officials into a modern form of battle. The threats Marcos saw to development were directly linked with a lack of discipline among young people, such as "wayward behavior" caused by the "laxity of the schools".[42]

Brundage, a major collector of Asian art, also voiced a comment reminiscent of what he said at the Third Asian Games in 1958, opening the introduction of this book: "Asia is less materialistic than the Western world and therefore has a great influence on the Olympic movement. Asia is the birthplace of all religions and the Olympic spirit has become the modern religion of Asia".[43] This again harkens back to Western discourses of Asia as a 'spiritual continent' covered in the second chapter. Here it was meant in the sense of Asia embracing amateurism-based 'Olympism' and of the West more and more focusing on 'materialistic' professionalism. Later on in his comments, he linked Japan's and Iran's successes in economic development with their long Olympic tradition (Japan) and a wrestling and weightlifting tradition of more than one millennium (Iran). Brundage thus again constructed a monocausal explanation for these successes, promoting amateur sports development as a very useful means for economic development. By calling Asia a 'spiritual continent', he considered this approach to be in the process of being implemented in many Asian countries. What he saw in Thailand certainly supported him in his pro-Olympic and pro-amateurism rhetoric.

Taken all together, the development of sport was an important part of the authoritarian Thai government's 'high modernist' development aims. By hosting the Fifth Asian Games in close temporal proximity to a trade fair, the tourism industry was to be strengthened. Moreover, the Games were meant to encourage sport as citizenship training, with a particularly strong focus on the ideal of economic progress. This is especially true for the Fifth Games, which caused some enthusiasm among Thai officials after many of the doubts that had come up regarding their organizational competence proved unfounded. The Sixth Games in 1970, in contrast, were less embraced by the organizers, but caused IOC president Brundage to deliberate on the connection between sports development, economic development, and national prestige that affected increasing numbers of Asian countries.

Constructing Sports Facilities and Hotels

When Bangkok was awarded the Fifth Asian Games in 1962, it already possessed a basic sports infrastructure. The Thai organizers nevertheless considered it important to add several new venues to it, the quality of which varied markedly. Most important were those prestige projects that visually demonstrated Thailand's infrastructure development. As mentioned above, strengthening the tourism industry was another development aim.

In December 1964, Sukhum, still serving as president of the organizing committee, gave an impression of what the Thai organizers had in mind: "The Asian Games will be as good as the Tokyo Olympic[s] but on a much smaller scale".[44] Japan, the most developed country in Asia, therefore again served as the *main point of reference*. The Asian Games in India, the Philippines, and Indonesia were also mentioned, but it was considered possible to outdo these, in the case of Indonesia primarily by preventing tensions rather than by having a better stadium.[45] Sukhum was therefore totally aware that the asymmetry in terms of development between Japan and Thailand could not be immediately overcome. The Games were thus an expression of Thailand's current level, which allowed the hosting of big regional events, but not yet huge global events: "But we cannot offer the same facilities and equipment. The Japanese can make everything themselves. We have to import all our equipment and everything is so expensive."[46] As a result, the total cost for the event seems to have been around 200–300 million baht (about 10–15 million USD).[47] This sum might appear relatively modest compared, for example, to what Iran would spend in 1974, covered in the next chapter. However, one should remember that the main stadium and some minor venues already existed, and the budget did not include the cost of building the athletes' village. Decorating the city also was not necessary, since this was already to be done in conjunction with King Bhumibol's birthday celebrations on 5 December.[48]

The national sports complex was located in the Pathum Wan district, directly north of Chulalongkorn University, Thailand's oldest university. Supachalasai Stadium, the main venue built in the late 1930s, initially had a capacity of 23,000 to 25,000 people (fig. 7.1).[49] Plans to raise it to 50,000 or even 60,000 were not realized due to time limitations and financial restraints, meaning that capacity was more moderately increased to 30,000 in the course of renovation work.[50]

The sports complex also featured a swimming stadium that provided seating for 10,000 people and met Olympic standards. When required, Chulalongkorn

FIGURE 7.1
'The main stadium': The stadium was renovated for the Games, but was not the most spectacular venue.
The Public Relations Committee and the Organizing Committee, *5th Asian Games Bangkok 1966 Bulletin*, No. 3, p. 22. (Courtesy of The Olympic Studies Centre)

University's swimming stadium (4,000 seats) was available as well.[51] Newly built facilities included a tennis stadium with ten courts, a field hockey stadium capable of holding 10,000 spectators, a stadium accommodating 20,000 people that was used for the soccer events and given to Chulalongkorn University, and a press center where 200 journalists could stay.[52] The stadia's quality was apparently not the best, very likely due to time constraints and climatic conditions. PAAF president de las Alas, for example, described the tennis courts as "horrible" and looking "something like asphalt which they painted".[53] Some Japanese also complained about them, primarily feeling threatened by some nearby poles that looked ready to fall over onto the courts any second.[54] Moreover, a reporter from the *Straits Times*, writing about one week before the Games commenced (meaning that the Thais still had some time to fix issues), was slightly shocked by the field hockey stadium, which he reported as having a pitch that was "uneven and sparsely grassed in patches". His description of the football stadium was even worse, observing that it "has risen out of a swamp and is surrounded by slums" and looked like "a neglected village green" from inside.[55] Two further facilities in the vicinity of the national sports complex and Chulalongkorn University were relatively small gymnasia. One of them, accommodating 6,000 spectators, already existed, while the second, seating 2,000 people, was newly constructed nearby.[56] Both, however, lacked a proper air circulation system, prompting the decision to build another, bigger indoor stadium.

The Kittikachorn Indoor Stadium (now Hua Mak Indoor Stadium) became the center of a completely new sports complex located in Hua Mak district. It was accompanied by a shooting range and a velodrome that could seat 3,000 spectators and which in size and shape resembled the cycling stadium the Japanese had built for the Olympic Games.[57] This new complex has to be seen as the place where the Thai organizers' aim of reaching the quality of the Tokyo Olympics, if on a smaller scale, was to be implemented. This is illustrated both by the buildings themselves and by the name of the indoor stadium. Naming the indoor stadium after Thanom served to symbolically link the success in developing sports infrastructure that it represented to the prime minister (fig. 7.2 and 7.3). This link is further illustrated by a governmental statement in the official report on the Games that the intention was to set up a complete "Kittikachorn Stadium Complex" by building further venues and moving the headquarters of the Sport Promotion Organization there in the future.[58] This statement is evidence that the government intended to prioritize this complex, named after the prime minister, and to eventually include the headquarters of Thailand's most important organization for the construction of sport infrastructure, over the old one.

The shape, size, and equipment of the Kittikachorn Indoor Stadium also served to communicate the message of the prime minister turning Thailand into a developed country while preventing the loss of its traditional culture in the process. The architect was Stanley Jewkes, who had also built Stadium Merdeka and Stadium Negara in Kuala Lumpur. Jewkes combined several traditional elements of Thai culture and architecture with illustrations of the possibilities of modern architecture to create a form of Thai modernist style. The stadium rose from a podium above a surrounding plain, giving the impression of a traditional flood protection technique, and materials such as gold, often found at temples, were used. In contrast, the imposing circular roof, to which the stadium owed its nickname of 'Carousel', was supported by concrete folded shells and a considerable amount of aluminum.[59] Seen from the side, the roof nevertheless is also reminiscent of the triangular gables of Thai temples, palaces, and houses. The interior of the stadium followed the same two lines. On the one hand, a national competition had served to "select artists to carry out the décor, which should be of Thai character so that the graceful stadium will perpetually stand, for the enjoyment of all its visitors, as a monument of Thai culture."[60] On the other hand, the stadium was heavily equipped with items demonstrating technological progress, such as an advanced ventilation system and an electronic scoreboard. Certainly most impressive was the fact that the stadium could also be used for concerts and other non-sport events, since it possessed an electronically operated stage, which could be lowered for sports events to give way to collapsing seats that increased the stadium's capacity to 12,000 people. All these features made Kittikachorn Indoor Stadium the most expensive building project of the Games, at a cost of about 43 million baht, an immense sum compared to the 2.5 million spent on the tennis courts or the 12 million on the hockey venue for 10,000 spectators.[61]

FIGURE 7.2
'Kittikachorn indoor stadium': The expensive and advanced stadium's name linked infrastructure development successes to the prime minister.
The Official Report of the Organizing Committee for the Fifth Asian Games Bangkok 1966, p. 40. (Courtesy of The Olympic Studies Centre)

FIGURE 7.3
'Kittikachorn indoor stadium (aerial view)'.
Public Relations Committee and the Organizing Committee, *5th Asian Games News Letter,* No. 3, p. 1. (Courtesy of The Olympic Studies Centre)

As one might expect, the stadium was highly praised and declared to represent the benevolent intentions of the government. Dawee, for example, called it a "symbol of the spirit of the Fifth Asian Games, in that it was the biggest single undertaking in connection with the staging of the big event". Moreover, he explained that "stadiums such as these were necessary for the promotion of sport and the health and well-being of the nation", thereby promising that the living conditions outside Bangkok would also be improved.[62] Thanom made similar claims when he said that the stadium was "one of the achievements of the Government to promote physical education among its people". He nevertheless indirectly hinted at the fact that not all future stadia and playgrounds would be built to the same level as this one, which he declared to be "one of the Games' showpieces", and which thus served nation-branding purposes as well.[63]

The stadia did not change much during the Sixth Asian Games. No further venues had yet been added to the Hua Mak complex, very likely due to the financial strains linked with the Vietnam War and, possibly, a lack of need. However, the stadium that had been given to Chulalongkorn University had by then been named after Praphas.[64] The deputy prime minister, too, thus was linked to the development of sports infrastructure.

The construction of the athletic village used for the Fifth Asian Games, having cost about 40 million baht (2 million USD), was not included in the organizing committee's budget. Instead, it had originally been part of a city development plan by the Department of Public Welfare to construct housing for low-income families. In Bang Kapi district, about two kilometers away from the indoor stadium and about 40 minutes by bus from the downtown area and the other sports complex, 524 units (262 twin-houses) were to accommodate four male athletes each and 190 row houses were to quarter four female athletes each. Facilities for daily life such as cafeterias, a shopping area, a practice field, and an entertainment center were set up in close proximity. A minor highlight was the administrative center, which featured three traditional Thai style roofs with triangular gables, symbolically linking authority to the Thai nation. A 'friendship garden', an idea the organizers possibly got from Indonesia in 1962, was also created.[65]

Here again, the Games were linked with development plans, specifically city development plans, but this time primarily in order to save money. Nevertheless, the entire infrastructure of the village very likely remained useful after the Games had ended and Thai families began renting or purchasing the houses. Since the village was therefore no longer available in 1970, and due to the time constraints which prevented the establishment of a new village, accommodation again became entangled with development plans. The development of the tourism industry and particularly of Western-style hotels, where the athletes were eventually quartered for the Sixth Asian Games, represented another string of development plans that had been set in motion in 1966.

Many of the Thai sources on the Games used in this chapter featured the postal address of the Tourist Organization of Thailand, founded in 1959. Until then, tourism had not been organized, only about 40,000 people visited Thailand each year and about 870 Western-style standard rooms (and an unknown number of traditional ones) were available in Bangkok. In 1970, the number of tourists reached 600,000 and the number of Western-style hotel rooms had risen by more than 7,000.[66] The increasing number of American soldiers fighting in Vietnam and being sent to Bangkok for recreation certainly provide a very important background to the growth. However, in Japan, benefiting from the Vietnam War, the economic situation during the 1960s improved by such a degree that large numbers of Japanese also began to travel overseas.[67] Of particular interest is the 1966 hotel-building frenzy, which by November 1966, before the trade fair and the Fifth Asian Games commenced, witnessed the building or expansion of 23 Western-style hotels and an increase in the number of rooms from 2,800 to 4,900 (5,600 in March 1967). In early December, the Tourist Organization of Thailand estimated that as many as 35,000 tourists and foreign athletes were currently in Bangkok. Within the next few months, hotel occupancy rates, which seem to have reached about 80 per cent during the Games and the trade fair, dropped to 40–45 per cent. Nevertheless, the American military's booking of large contingents of rooms meant that hotels apparently did not encounter serious occupancy problems after the peak in late 1966.[68] The Asian Games in 1970 then resulted in another peak and some chaos, when more than 2,000 athletes and officials needed to be quartered in first class hotels, which therefore led to other visitors' bookings getting canceled.[69]

In conclusion, the infrastructure construction programs were closely linked to several development plans that included sports infrastructure, housing to improve the living conditions of low-income families, and hotels. However, while the stadia benefitted the sports infrastructure of Bangkok and without question served national prestige purposes, they simultaneously communicated the message of a 'benevolent' government—two stadia were named after Thanom and Praphas—engaging in a larger sports development program that would affect all of Thailand. Finally, the hosting of regional 'mega events' such as trade fairs and the Asian Games contributed to the enhancement of Bangkok's international image and attracted increasing numbers of tourists, not just those interested in sex tourism.

The King Blessing the Games: The Torch Relay

The torch relay provides evidence of how the Asian Games mirrored both the increasing public influence of King Bhumibol since the Sarit regime, and the emergence of a personality cult of the semi-sacred Buddhist monarch, who served as a figurehead for national integration.

On 8 December 1966, on the lawn near the east wing of Chitralada Palace, the residence of the royal couple, King Bhumibol publically lit a golden candle by using a magnifying glass to focus the rays of the sun. After this was done, he used the candle to kindle a lamp stored in a golden palanquin, which was afterwards carried though parts of Bangkok until it reached a pavilion set up for the mayor. It was stored there until the next day, when a torch lit from it was brought by a relay of runners to the stadium to light the Games' flame. The same was done in 1970 (fig. 7.4), except that this time it was explained that the magnifying glass used was the ancient ceremonial Surayakarn Glass and that the palanquin on its way to the mayor's pavilion was accompanied by at least 500 officials and athletes.[70]

In a nutshell, the Indian organizers in 1951 had used the Red Fort as a symbol of independence, the Japanese in 1958 had made the Filipinos engage in a Grecian-looking ceremony to impress the IOC, and the Indonesians in 1962 had used an oil- or gas-fueled flame to link the Games to their country.[71] In 1966 and 1970, the lighting of the torch looked like a Buddhist ceremony in which the king symbolically bestowed his blessing on the Games. The sun, as in several previous lighting ceremonies, was a pan-Asian element representing Asia. However, in the Thai context the golden color of the items used was strongly linked with the monarchy and Buddhist temples, and the use of an ancient magnifying glass further contributed to that image. Moreover, the shape of the palanquin was strongly reminiscent of a *mondop*, the place in Buddhist temples where important items such as relics are stored, turning the Asian Games lamp kindled by the monarch into an equivalently holy item. Finally, the procession to the mayor served to give the event further publicity, thereby increasing its importance. All in all, the torch relays included some pan-Asian elements, but the main focus was on the semi-sacral Buddhist monarch.

FIGURE 7.4
'The king lighting the Games' lamp in 1970': The Games heavily promoted the king's personality cult.
Official Report of the Organizing Committee for the Sixth Asian Games Bangkok 1970, p. 37. (Courtesy of The Olympic Studies Centre)

The King and Asia: Official Ceremonies and the Entertainment Program

Even more effectively than the torch relay, the official ceremonies and entertainment programs served to communicate the government's plans for Thailand's successful large-scale modernization and development process without losing its cultural traditions. The focus was thus primarily on the monarchy and on Thailand, although the introduction of some new technical elements served to introduce a pan-Asian dimension.

In 1966, the opening day was a holiday and interest in the opening ceremony seems to have been very high. The stadium was already full three hours before it started and even the rehearsals had seen sufficient tickets sold off to fill the stadium.[72] One of the highlights, which would return in 1970, was the display by about 4,000 students from Thammasat and Chulalongkorn Universities sitting in the bleachers. Each of them was equipped with a variety of colored placards that in combination formed huge images. For example, when King Bhumibol, Queen Sirikit, the Princess Mother, and the three royal princesses arrived in the stadium, the royal anthem was played and pictures of them and of royal emblems were formed.[73] One image showed two white war elephants, hinting at King Naresuan the Great of Ayutthaya, a national hero, representative of the monarchy, and the symbol of the army; in 1593, he had defeated the Burmese at the Battle of Nong Sarai and ended their aspirations to control Siam. Between the elephants was the *Garuda* bird, Thailand's national emblem and a symbol of royal authority.[74] Both elements served to promote the personality cult of the monarchy, while the attendance of six of its members certainly attracted further attention. The students also showed images depicting the name and one or two national symbols of the country of each team that marched into the stadium.[75] In this way, a sportive pan-Asian atmosphere (which the Burmese team might have enjoyed as well) was created, based on the idea of Asian unity in diversity. Other images the students formed included, among others, the disciplines of the Games.[76] This was an obvious reminder of what was to take place during the following days and hinted at the government's plan of developing and spreading sports.

The march-in of the teams was in many ways symptomatic of the growth of the beauty 'industry' and the beauty contests that had mushroomed since the Sarit regime began. This 'beauty boom' was not necessarily a part of, but was nevertheless linked to, the sex and tourism industry. However, seen from the more traditional Thai-Buddhist perspective that the Sarit regime encouraged, beauty could also be understood as a sign of good karma and of merit achieved during a former life. Since the Thai instead of the Latin alphabet was used, this being another nationalist element, the first team that entered the stadium was South Korea. Its name plate was carried by Apasra Hongsakula, the Thai winner of the 1965 Miss Universe competition.[77] One of the world's 'officially' most beautiful women was therefore the first person in the parade of athletes. This promotion of Thailand as a country offering many beautiful women was further strengthened by the fact that all following teams, too, were led by Thai beauty queens from different competitions.[78] These women nevertheless wore the national dresses of the respective countries they led into the stadium, thereby adding an element of Asian unity in diversity. The Thai team, entering last but attracting particular attention as the host team, was another peak in the branding of 'beautiful Thailand' or 'the country of good karma'. The team was accompanied by Cheranand Savetanand, Miss Thailand 1965 and second runner-up in the 1966 Miss Universe competition, therefore arguably Thailand's second most beautiful woman after Apasra. To a certain degree, the participation of Apasra and Cheranand also served the personality cult of the monarchy. Queen Sirikit, who was often praised for her beauty, was considered to be an advisor and tutor to the two women.[79]

Another promotion of Thailand with limited international appeal was the carrying of the AGF flag by armed forces cadets.[80] Like at several earlier Asian Games events, this display can be interpreted as representing the army's defense of the 'non-communist Asia' that the regional shape of the Games represented, and which was threatened by, for example, the Vietnam War. Simultaneously, one might assume that the organizers, many of them military leaders, intended to show and promote the armed forces. The next Thai national element—with some international appeal to Buddhist countries—was the setting free of exactly 2,509 white doves;[81] these not only symbolized peace, but their number represented the current year of the Buddhist Era. The shooting into the air of parachutes bearing the national flags of the 18 participating countries, another new technique introduced in the Asian Games' ceremonies, ended the opening ceremony.[82] The flags symbolically communicated the equality of the participating Asian countries.

The following entertainment program hewed to the same general pattern that had existed since 1954, but was particularly reminiscent of the previous Games in Indonesia, from where the Thai organizers may have gotten some of their ideas. On the one hand, the results the successful spread of sport and physical education should have on society were communicated. On the other hand, a traditional dance visually rejected the idea that Thailand was giving up its particular cultural traditions, instead making them binding for the whole nation. The concrete messages of the performances nevertheless show that the whole program was strongly influenced by Thailand's individual politico-cultural context.

A group of about 1,000 cadets of the pre-military academy opened the entertainment program (fig. 7.5). Accompanied by drumbeats, they moved in formation to the center of the stadium, where they engaged in a slow precision drill, followed by a fast one. At the end, using the different colors of their sports outfits, they assembled in such a way that their bodies formed an image of four rings on a white ground.[83] The drill performances served to illustrate the results the spread of sports and physical education could have on Thai society, with the use of cadets linking the event particularly strongly to the military, which in this way was shown to be the institution most experienced in encouraging the discipline and precision of modern citizens. The event therefore also served to legitimize the ruling military regime. In contrast, the forming of the four rings can be interpreted as an internationalist element, possibly a suggestion to have four rings represent the AGF, and inspired by the IOC's five and the SEAP Games' six rings. The entertainment program was then continued by the army and police bands leaving the grandstand and forming patterns of the royal insignia and words such as 'Asian Games' and 'Ever Onward' on the stadium's ground.[84] Here again discipline, conformity, and precision were communicated, while the first images corresponded to the reclaimed public importance of the monarchy and the others possessed a pan-Asian dimension. Finally, about 1,000 female students from Suan Sunandha Teachers College (now Suan Sunandha Rajabhat University) and Suan Dusit Teachers College (now Suan Dusit Rajabhat University), dressed in traditional red and gold costumes, performed a *fawn* (a form of folk dance), the *Ram Malai* ('Flower Dance'). The female dancers, too, then formed some patterns such as the AGF symbol (fig. 7.6).[85] Similar to the *Pendet* dance of the Balinese girls in 1962, the Flower Dance is normally performed to welcome people, in this context the visitors to the commencing Asian Games. This message was even further illustrated by linking the dance to the Games through the forming of the AGF symbol. In connection with the other performances, it also showed that both men and women were expected by the government to engage in physical education and to become more disciplined and physically efficient. In this context, it should be noted that until then many school-girls and female students had refrained from engaging in sports (sometimes instead being instructed in dancing) due to a lack of facilities to clean up afterwards. Thailand's warm climate meant that they perspired more than people living in colder regions, which did not correspond to the Buddhist beauty ideal and had made a cultural integration of sport more difficult.[86] However, the modernly dressed male soldiers and the traditionally dressed female dancers simultaneously communicated that traditional gender roles were not to change much during the modernization process, at least when it came to topics such as war.[87]

The closing ceremony in 1966 did not feature an entertainment program. After the lights had been lowered, *Auld Lang Syne* was played.[88] Like the two times before, the farewell song served to create an internationalist atmosphere. When the royal couple left, the 'athletes' (probably the Thai athletes) shouted "Chaiyo" ("Cheers").[89] Their thanks thus contributed to the growing personality cult of the monarch, who, after all, the day before the Games had started, had bestowed his blessing on them through the Buddhist ceremony.

Except for some minor changes that will be covered shortly, the ceremonies and the entertainment program in 1970 followed the same pattern as in 1966 and featured the same elements.[90] The opening ceremony this time, possibly as a result of television broadcasting, only drew about 25,000 people to the stadium.[91] The Thammasat and Chulalongkorn students, in contrast, returned, this time armed with an even larger number of colored placards—allegedly several hundred—that visually accompanied the events on the ground. This included further symbols of the monarchy such as the royal barge, symbols of Bangkok such as the Golden Temple, flowers and doves as symbols of welcome and peace, and a Christmas greeting, a sign of the influence of American culture in the Buddhist country.[92] The king also got even more involved in the Games by composing a song, *Raindrop*, for them.[93] This can be interpreted as another means of giving the Games his blessing, similar to him composing songs for other events. One more new feature was that the band that was sitting in the grandstand was this time dressed in such a way that the colors of their clothes formed a huge Thai flag.[94] Like many of the other new elements in the staging of the Games, this permanent manifestation of Thai state nationalism seems to have very much impressed the Iranian organizers of the Seventh Asian Games, as will be shown in the eighth chapter. The 'Thai beauties' also returned, but with different women taking part. Apasra and Cheranand did not participate, but reigning Miss Thailand Warunee Sangsirinavin led the Thai delegation. Some other teams were accompanied by further beauty queens, Thammasat and Chulalongkorn students who had won a 'sweetheart competition'. However, some teams brought their own women to bear

FIGURE 7.5

'Male cadets engaging in a precision drill': The message of shaping efficient and fit people served to promote the very influential Thai military and needs to be seen against the background of the Vietnam War.

Bangkok World (10 December 1966): 7. (Courtesy of the Library of Congress)

FIGURE 7.6

'Female students forming the AGF symbol': Women were shown as dancers, thus referring to more traditional gender roles.

The Official Report of the Organizing Committee for the Fifth Asian Games Bangkok 1966, p. 55. (Courtesy of The Olympic Studies Centre) their countries' signs (except Nepal, which was led by a man, possibly a complete rejection of the 'beauty cult').[95] One can therefore assume that some foreign officials were no longer willing to accept Thai nation-branding so easily, but rather intended to show that their countries, too, had its own share of beautiful women. Independent of such matters, public attention during the march-in seems to have largely been on the Cambodian delegation, which wore battledress.[96] This, now, was an obvious reminder of the internal situation of the country due to the Vietnam War. In March 1970, pro-American forces led by Premier Lon Nol had overthrown Norodom Sihanouk and joined the fight against communism. The new regime also decided to participate in the Asian Games, contributing to their image of representing neutral and pro-American Asia.[97] Perhaps the most noteworthy change, possibly resulting from complaints against a 'sexist' depiction of gender roles, which were taken seriously by the slowly weakening military regime, took place in the entertainment program. This time the event started with about 800 physical education students of *both genders* engaging in gymnastic drills and marching displays.[98] The following reminder of Thai cultural traditions with an internationalist touch, however, did not change. After the mixed gender performance, about 800 female students, this time only from Suan Sunandha Teachers College, again danced and formed the AGF symbol.[99]

In summary, like the torch relays, the official ceremonies and the entertainment programs featured elements that supported a growing personality cult of the Buddhist monarchy. Other symbolic elements such as depictions of the participating countries' names, national symbols, the AGF symbol, its motto, and many flags gave the events a more pan-Asian atmosphere. Much of this was the result of the introduction of new techniques to the staging, for example colored placards, parachutes, and beauty queens leading the teams. The latter, however, were rather symptomatic of the depiction of Thai women in 1966 in two ways: as beautiful and as dancers. In 1970, this portrayal underwent certain changes. While the exclusivity of beauty was both taken over and taken away from the Thais by some foreign teams bringing their own women, the dichotomy of 'modern male soldier, traditional female dancer' was no longer featured.

The King and the Symbols of the Games

The symbols of the Games included further elements of the monarchy, thus complementing those featured at the torch relays and the ceremonies, while differences between the 1966 and 1970 events were minor.

Both the victory and commemorative medals used at the Fifth and Sixth Games had the official symbol of the respective Games engraved, based on the AGF's emblem. Although it is unclear what was on the back of the victory medals, this seemingly strong focus on a sportive pan-Asian element was challenged on the backs of the commemorative medals. Here, both times symbols of the Thai monarchy were used that again are illustrative of the highly important role of the monarchy and of turning the king into the figurehead of the Thai nation. In 1966, a part of the Grand Palace, Wat Phra Kaew (the 'Temple of the Emerald Buddha'), was chosen as the motif; in 1970 it was a war elephant together with some warriors, another nod to King Naresuan the Great (fig. 7.7).[100] The commemorative coins for the Games, due to their motifs, can be seen as equivalents to the commemorative medals, though they were not limited to 24,000 people as were the medals (very likely the athletes, the officials, and all people that had helped in the organizing), but targeted at the very broad public. For each Games, 9 million one baht coins were printed, showing the desire of the organizers to see them spread widely within the population by making them relatively affordable and available in large quantity.[101] Both in 1966 and in 1970, the front of the coins showed the symbol of the Games, while the back supported the personality cult of the monarchy by depicting the royal couple with the king in the foreground (fig. 7.8).

FIGURE 7.7
'Commemorative medal, Sixth Asian Games, back': The motif referred to King Naresuan, symbol of the army and an important element of Thai state nationalism.

Official Report of the Organizing Committee for the Sixth Asian Games Bangkok 1970, p. 68. (Courtesy of The Olympic Studies Centre)

FIGURE 7.8
'Commemorative coin, Fifth Asian Games, back': The motif again supported the personality cult of the monarchy.

Nihon Taiiku Kyōkai, *Dai-5kai*, p. 171. (Courtesy of the Nihon Taiiku Daigaku library)

The stamps produced to promote the Fifth Games provide a nice contrast to this focus on the king, depicting the disciplines and in this way representing the government's intention of using the Games to support the development of sport in Thailand. Again linked with the determination of Thailand to not lose its cultural heritage, another set showed several traditional Thai sports such as Thai boxing, *takraw*, and kite flying. Four years later, the focus moved to four of the stadia, very likely to now also show the concrete manifestations of the government's investment in sports infrastructure. However, the king kindling the Asian Games lamp and thereby blessing the Games became a second motif.[102] To sum up, the personality cult also took over here in 1970.

Bringing the King to the People: Media Development and the Vietnam War

Strong media interest in the Games paralleled the evolution of the media infrastructure in Thailand as a result of the government's development aims and American interest in spreading their perspective on the Vietnam War to Southeast Asians. At the same time, the growing importance of television broadcasting between 1966 and 1970 illustrates how another means for generating revenues to finance the Games emerged.

Domestic and foreign media attention in 1966 was high; it was estimated that close to 1,000 journalists, about 575 of them foreigners, reported on the Games.[103] Many of them were, it seems, still newspaper reporters and photographers as opposed to radio or television announcers. At the point, the telegraph was still of great importance and a breakdown of the line connecting the press center to Bangkok's general post office one day before the Games commenced caused a lot of problems.[104] Further evidence that many of the reporters must have been from newspapers is that though a radio center was available in the stadium, it contained only two microphones, allowing each country only 15 minutes of access per day.[105] Other Thai radio stations must also have covered the Games, but could not yet reach the whole country. Only in late 1966, about the time of the Games, was it made public that a very big radio station was to be constructed the next year that would make possible the high-quality reception of broadcasts in Thailand's north and northeast. The broadcaster, The Voice of Free Asia, was to be co-administered by the Thai government and the United States Information Agency and served primarily to counter communist broadcasts.[106] A television system also already existed, which Dawee used to promote the Games by giving at least one progress report, but again the station's reach was limited. Asian Television, a combination of Thai TV and Army TV, broadcasted the Games live and, apparently for the first time, used an outside recording truck to show parts of the cycling events and the marathon. People in the north, northeast and south of Thailand, however, had to wait one day until tapes of the events had arrived at the respective relay stations.[107] Apparently, the only foreign broadcaster that showed the Games was TV Malaysia (now TV1).[108]

In 1970, things had greatly changed. By then The Voice of Free Asia was operating and broadcasted the Games live in English from the national stadium, reaching many other Asian countries in addition to Thailand.[109] Moreover, a group of foreign television companies had approached the Thai organizers regarding television rights. The organizers immediately contacted the IOC, asking which fees would be reasonable.[110] This quite obviously illustrates the Thai's lack of experience in such matters, meaning that selling broadcast rights was completely new for them. They nevertheless seem to have quickly grown accustomed to it: in early December 1970, television companies from Indonesia, Iran, Israel, Japan, Hong Kong, the Philippines, Taiwan, and South Korea had already paid for the rights or were in the process of doing so. In contrast, Malaysian and Singaporean companies had simply sent cameramen without having asked for rights, the existence of whom the Singaporeans claimed to know nothing.[111] It remains unclear whether they got away without paying. Quite obviously, Thai radio and television broadcasters, which by then provided color television, also covered the events. To give the Games maximum publicity within Thailand, especially in the rural areas, Thai television companies did not have to pay for the rights.[112] This waiving of fees has to be seen as linked with the intention of further supporting the development of sport. Simultaneously, the waiver very likely also served to integrate the Games and their message of internationalism and peace into the anti-communist propaganda struggle around the protracted Vietnam War and to show the monarch to the people.

In conclusion, the two Games hosted in Thailand were strongly affected by the development of radio and television in Asia, in Thailand very much a result of the Vietnam War and of government planning. This process not only increased international attention, but the buying of television rights by foreign companies also created another source of income for the organizers, contributing to the commercialization of the Games.

Assessment

'Thailand has a king.' This was arguably one of the most prominent messages the Games communicated and it strongly reflected the revival of the Buddhist monarchy and the emerging personality cult of the king since the Sarit regime. At the same time, the large-scale sports development plans of the authoritarian government were promoted. More generally, the staging of the Asian Games gained further importance as a means to show cultural authenticity and national achievements to the local population and to an international audience. It thereby continued tendencies present since the Third Asian Games.

The basic reason was the authoritarian modernization and development plans of the Sarit and the Thanom regimes, which involved bringing about a breakthrough of sports in Thailand. In a rather classical bio-political sense, the spread of sports was considered a tool to shape more efficient and active citizens and also to improve living conditions, particularly in the rural areas. Despite this, the inclusion of male soldiers and female dancers into the program in 1966 (which was not repeated in 1970, although the beauty queens returned) showed that traditional gender roles should not change completely. In the Thai context, all this corresponded to traditional ideas of paternalistic and benevolent rulership, thereby serving to legitimize the government and to discourage communist insurgencies in the wake of the Vietnam War. The naming of the advanced indoor stadium and the new sports complex around it after the prime minister, and later of another stadium after Praphas, is characteristic of this whole process. The Fifth Asian

Games were thus a means to promote popular interest in sports, which was to be accompanied by a stadia construction program whose origins were also tied to the upcoming Games. Simultaneously, together with the Asian trade fair and against the background of growing numbers of American soldiers visiting Bangkok, the Games aided another form of development, that of the tourism industry.

Other parts of the staging such as the official ceremonies, entertainment programs, and the symbols of the Games further supported this aim of modernization and development, but in a conspicuously Thai way. This was accompanied by the introduction of several new techniques of visual communication, which represent another reason for the generally growing importance of nation-branding. These new techniques at the same time allowed the addition of more internationalist and pan-Asian messages, particularly that of Asian unity in cultural diversity. Individual Asian countries were very often depicted via their respective flags or certain cultural elements, but these were grouped together to demonstrate their belonging together. Moreover, the absence of communist ruled Asian countries since 1954 continued, meaning that they were excluded from the image of Asia that the Games created.

An important difference from the Fourth Asian Games therefore was that the organizers did not attempt to bring about dramatic changes or challenges to the regional shape of the AGF. They basically went back to the non-communist region that had existed since 1954. This has to be seen as a deliberate choice, considering that Thailand was one of the United States' closest allies in their anti-communist war in Southeast Asia. Moreover, the Games were a result of the successful hosting of the SEAP Games in 1959 and linked with various anti-communist region-building schemes in Southeast Asia, of which ASEAN, founded in Bangkok in 1967, proved the most successful. In contrast, between 1966 and 1970, the GANEFOA heritage of the Fourth Asian Games vanished due to the 'Cultural Revolution' in China and political changes in Indonesia and Cambodia.[113]

The difference in quality between the Fifth and Sixth Games is quite interesting. In 1966, after four years of preparations, the Thai organizers had to face doubts regarding their competence and the quality of some of the stadia. Moreover, they had to deal with several negative incidents during the Games.[114] The governmental sports development plans nevertheless led to some recognizable results. The most important of these in terms of international sports was that the Thai organizers, despite the lack of time and a limited budget, apparently managed to host the Sixth Games better than the previous event. The experience they had gained and the availability of the needed infrastructure meant that they, in addition to Japan—Asia's most developed country—were asked to save the Games after South Korea encountered problems. Moreover, international interest was high and feedback very positive. For example, IOC president Brundage considered the Sixth Asian Games "one of the best of recent times".[115] Stanley Rous, the president of the Fédération Internationale de Football Association (FIFA), came to a similar conclusion.[116] Also very interesting is that Willi Daume, the president of the organizing committee for the 1972 Olympic Games in Munich, in a letter to Dawee called the Asian Games one of the "greatest and important regional sports-events" and together with some assistants asked for permission to watch and study the Sixth Asian Games.[117] Some final evidence of the Thai organizer's experience and the successful development of international sport is that they—with some changes in personnel—eight years later also saved the Eighth Asian Games of 1978.

CHAPTER 8

Iran and the Indian Ocean Region Project: The Great Persian Empire, Oil Wealth, and the Seventh Asian Games (1–16 September 1974)

"The Asian Games organized by the Japanese were, as you might expect, perfect. The ancient Persian Empire could not do less well than the ancient Empire of the Rising Sun. And we succeeded."[1]

—Gholam Reza Pahlavi, brother of the last Shah of Persia, in an interview about his life

The Seventh Asian Games were another event taking place in an authoritarian country, again having a strong impact on the ideals as well as the staging of the Games. The hosting of the Asian Games for the first time in West Asia, which resulted in many Arab countries finally joining, was decisive for the regional shape of the Asian Games Federation (AGF) and power relations between West and East Asia. In terms of foreign policy, the Games this time served to support the Iranian government's great power ambitions. This included a plan to establish an Asian Union around the Indian Ocean and a desire to improve Iran's relations with China to balance against the Soviet Union. The ideal of egalitarian internationalism was therefore, like in Indonesia in 1962, partially rejected. Once again, the Games had an anti-Western and anti-neocolonial touch, even though this served only as a means of furthering Iran's aim of making the International Olympic Committee (IOC) accept China as a member of the Asian Games. Moreover, once again a 'national rebirth' was proclaimed in a non-democratic and quite militaristic setting, this time including a personality cult surrounding the shah and his family. This half-hearted anti-Westernism was, however, all in all limited and did not escalate to the same degree as in 1962 in Indonesia.

In terms of domestic policy, Iran, like Indonesia and Thailand, experienced a rapid modernization and development process. The staging of the Asian Games again was closely entangled with an authoritarian version of 'high modernism'. Iran's oil wealth meant that this time, the aim was not to catch up with the 'developed' countries, but to become one of the leading countries in the world, which included comparisons with Japan. The large-scale infrastructure development program was especially heavily affected by this desire, serving nation-branding purposes. The demonstration of national wealth, development, and power was thus once again most important for the organizers. Education through amateur norms and values almost completely vanished from the discourse, since sports consumption as entertainment and as a means of generating national pride increased in importance.

In this chapter, I deal with how the Iranians attempted to use the Asian Games to support the (unsuccessful) project of creating an Iranian-led union of Asian states against the Soviet Union. I also highlight the importance the Games possessed in portraying Iran as an emerging great power and as turning into a highly advanced nation. Moreover, I focus on the personality cult of the shah as the one presented as being responsible for the seemingly successful modernization and development process rooted in the cultural heritage of the ancient Persian Empire.

Iran in 1974

In the early 1970s, the Pahlavi dynasty, in power since 1925, was at its zenith. Since 1941, Mohammad Reza Pahlavi, the *Shāhanshāh* ('King of Kings') *Aryamehr* ('Light of the Aryans'), had been the autocratic ruler of Iran. Major problems, like the British and Soviet occupation of Iran during the Second World War and a short period of exile in 1953 had long been overcome. Democratization attempts had been successfully suppressed. The shah was head of the armed forces, could change the constitution, and appoint the government. The important positions in society, business, and administration were mainly occupied by Western-educated Iranians loyal to him. Since 1957, dissident activities were observed and suppressed via the SAVAK ('State Intelligence and Security Organization'). Radio and television were state controlled.[2]

In terms of foreign policy, Iran could rely on support from the Western world, which was particularly interested in having access to its vast reserves of oil and gas. Pressure to set up a more democratic system, though it existed, was therefore rather mild. The shah was encouraged to start the so-called 'White Revolution' (later 'Shah-People Revolution') in 1963 to modernize society and develop the economy to reduce popular opposition and prevent his rule being overthrown by a red revolution. The urbanization process also increased, so that the urban population of Iran in 1970 had risen to about 15.7 million people from 2.3 million in 1940. The reforms and new negotiations with Western oil companies resulted in annually growing revenues. Especially from 1969 onwards, large sums could be spent on further reforms and on industrialization, the latter leading to massive increases in gross national product. The process was additionally accelerated in 1973, when OPEC (Organization of the Petroleum Exporting Countries) cooperation contributed to the Oil Crisis and resulted in an explosion of Iranian income. Oil revenues grew from 34 million USD in 1954–55 to 5 billion in 1973–74 and 20 billion in 1975–76. Therefore, from 1965, the American Johnson administration no longer perceived Iran as a developing country.[3]

From the mid-1960s onwards, Iran attempted to gain more political independence. Despite the strong alignment with the West, relations with the Soviet Union had slightly improved after the conclusion of several economic agreements in 1966 and 1967. During the following years, relations with the USSR-oriented, non-aligned countries of Asia and the Middle East, particularly India, Afghanistan, and most Arab countries, slowly improved. The weakening of many Arab states during the Yom Kippur War (1973) and cooperation to affect the oil price led to closer contact between Iran and the Arabs, although relations with hostile Iraq remained difficult. Iran's previous isolation within the Middle Eastern and Persian Gulf region due to its West-leaning alignment and de facto recognition of Israel was thus reduced. This cooperation also resulted in more freedom of action regarding the US and discouraged the destabilizing activities of communists in Iran.[4]

Even more important was the British announcement in early 1968 of its intent to withdraw all its permanent troops east of Suez in 1971. This withdrawal included its forces in the Persian Gulf region defending its protectorates—Bahrain, Qatar, and what became the United Arab Emirates—against communist and other uprisings. Since the United States, stuck in Vietnam, was unable to completely take over Britain's role, the USSR began to show its interest in gaining access to the warm waters of the Indian Ocean. Rising numbers of warships and cargo ships appeared in this ocean, the Arabian Sea, and the Persian Gulf even before the actual withdrawal. According to Iranian sources, they probably transported arms to hostile Iraq. The disastrous Vietnam War and the British withdrawal thus meant that the Iranian government since the late 1960s gained growing leverage over the US concerning Persian Gulf policy and the protection of major maritime oil trade routes. The shah had ambitions that Iran would become, within one generation, the world's fifth largest conventional military power due to petrodollar-financed massive arms purchases. Therefore, in order to counter the anticipated Soviet expansion toward the Indian Ocean and the Persian Gulf, which would certainly compel the United States to also become more strongly involved, closer cooperation with the littoral states was desired. A region-building project led by Iran, declaring itself neutral, was to prevent such a destabilization and convince both superpowers to limit themselves to economic interests and to refrain from attempts to politically or militarily exploit the power vacuum following Britain's withdrawal. To further support this region building, relations with Moscow's rival Beijing were to be improved. In October 1971, the People's Republic of China had been admitted to the United Nations as the representative of 'China', replacing the Republic of China (Taiwan). Ideally, closer relations between Iran and China would result in a reduction of Chinese support for communists in the Middle East (Oman, South Yemen) and serve to balance against the USSR.[5]

From the early twentieth century onwards, beginning with the Constitutional Revolution (1906–11), Iranian reformers had faced the problem of how to modernize Iran to catch up with the West, while still giving their activities an authentic touch to reduce resistance within the population and to avoid appearing culturally inferior to the West.[6] One solution was to utilize the well-documented ancient history of Iran, which easily provided material usable in the production (or 'invention') of authenticity. Under Mohammad Reza Pahlavi, the Iranian government increasingly tried to legitimize Iran's progressing modernization as being based on its magnificent past, going back to the Great Persian or Achaemenid Empire, one of the world's first superpowers, and the rule of Cyrus the Great (reigned 559–530 BC). The government used this very positive image to describe Iran as again becoming a 'Great Civilization' in the near future. Based on the White Revolution and its allegedly ancient roots, modern Iran would finally 'regenerate' and outdo the Persian Empire of old. One instance was the celebration of the 2,500th anniversary of the monarchy in 1971. The shah's assurance to Cyrus at his grave—that Persia's founder could sleep in peace because he (stepping into Cyrus' shoes) and the Iranians were all doing their best—was symptomatic of this strategy of historical legitimization of the regime and of the personality cult of the royal family.[7]

Sport in Iran and the Main Organizers of the Games

One of the later facets of the White Revolution was modern sport. Physical education had a long tradition in Iranian culture, but focused mainly on military skills.[8] In a first modernization attempt under Reza Shah, the first ruler of the Pahlavi dynasty (1925–41), various versions of Western physical education had been made compulsory at schools. Especially schools set up by American and British reformers had begun to introduce team sports and scouting. The foundations for spreading modern sport thus had already been laid, but the overall impact, especially on the poor segments of the rural population, remained very low. Religious criticism of modern sport and sportswear also contributed to the limited impact. Despite this, sports clubs were founded by modern middle-class members of both genders, and the few Iranian social reformers followed the bio-political discourse of sport as a means to combat the results of the incipient urbanization of Iran. Health, discipline, fair play, and team spirit were valued highly by them as preventing 'degeneration' and creating a healthy and productive nation. The reformers nonetheless had no significant influence, strongly depending on the state as the promoter of change. Iran also did not participate in the Olympic Games before 1948 and only two delegates, but no team, had attended Guru Dutt

Sondhi's Western Asiatic Games (WAG) in 1934. Concerning the Asian Games, Iran had not sent representatives to any of the initial meetings in 1948 and 1949, but Iranian teams had attended the Games in 1951, 1958, 1966 and 1970. During the Sixth Games in December 1970, Iran was chosen as the host of the Seventh Asian Games.[9]

The large-scale spread of modern sport in Iran was a phenomenon of the 1960s and 1970s. From the late 1960s onwards, sport, physical education, and youth welfare attracted growing amounts of money in the Iranian five-year plans. Schools, municipal administrations, and universities began to build sporting facilities, while several sports universities were newly planned to educate sports teachers. Furthermore, foreign coaches were hired to train Iranian sports managers, athletes, and referees to provide Iran the infrastructure to host further international sports competitions. The hosting of the Seventh Asian Games was a major part of this 'sports revolution'.[10]

The most important people involved in organizing the Games were, again, very closely affiliated with the government. Personal relations between senior and junior organizers and executives also seem to have been strong.[11] These ties were another demonstration of the importance of the Asian Games for an authoritarian government, in this case centered on the shah and his loyal followers. Prince Gholam Reza Pahlavi, brother of the shah, already among other offices the president of the Iranian Olympic Committee and an IOC member, became president of the AGF. The head of the organizing committee was Lieutenant-General Ali Hojjat Kashani, a former shooting champion of the Iranian army and president of the Iranian Physical Education Organization, a post that also made him a deputy prime minister. The secretary of the organizing committee was Hassan Rassouli, who had studied at University College London and later became director-general of the Iranian Physical Education Organization. As the head of state, the shah became the patron of the Games.[12]

All in all, the Asian Games were part of the Iranian government's strategy to further promote Western sport in Iran. Earlier attempts by social reformers had taken place, but these had had a comparatively low impact. The Seventh Asian Games therefore were another strongly state-controlled event, similar to the Indonesian and Thai Games, this time serving the political aims of the shah and his government.

Building an Asian Union: Iran as the Center of the Indian Ocean Region

The Asian Games have to be seen as one of several instruments to support the Iranian government's attempt to create a superpower-free Indian Ocean region after Britain's withdrawal and to protect its maritime trade routes against Soviet intrusions. In this section, I cover the Iranian plan for an Asian union or common market, reminiscent of the unification process in Western Europe. The next section will cover the special case of China.

Inspired by the enormous increase in oil prices, which was both a political and economic success for Iran and caused serious economic problems in many other Asian countries, the shah felt powerful enough to make his first public statements concerning the region-building project in early 1974:

> The Shahanshah has proposed the establishment of an economic union or common market of Asian states, stretching from Iran to Singapore, and including 'all the northern states of the Indian Ocean.' (...) The economic union could at a later stage be expanded to include the African states lying to the south of the Indian Ocean and also the states lying to the west of Iran, he said. Iran had already started to get into Africa, the monarch stated. (...) The monarch reiterated his view that the Indian Ocean should be maintained as 'a zone of peace', safeguarded by the littoral states. If the littoral states were united, they could ask all external powers to 'refrain from getting in.' But in the meantime, it was not possible to tell only one side to 'keep out'. He said an Asian collective security pact was feasible only if it included all the Asian states, particularly China.[13]

Some months later, only days after the Asian Games had finished, the shah became more concrete and suggested the founding of such an Asian Union or common market during a round trip to Singapore, Australia, New Zealand, Indonesia, and India. In Singapore, President Benjamin H. Sheares welcomed the general idea of a free Indian Ocean and said that the Asian Games had already brought the respective countries a bit closer to each other: "The live telecast via satellite of the opening of the Asian Games, so impressively organized by your country, dispelled this sense of remoteness, especially when we could see our own contingent to these games among Iranians".[14] In Australia, the shah went further and suggested "to have a zone of peace and collaboration between the riparian states of the Indian Ocean and extended as far as Australia." After an initial economic union, a political union and a military union should follow.[15] Similar remarks about Iran offering its assistance and 'good services' to the littoral countries of the Indian Ocean were made during the later stages of the round trip and in the following months.[16] In the end, the Iranian government's plans did not prove successful before the Islamic Revolution occurred. Other countries, if they were at all interested in this Western European-looking plan whose initial stage was also reminiscent of the Association of Southeast Asian Nations (ASEAN), were well aware that the main beneficiary of such a union would be Iran. It would, due to existing asymmetries in economic power and access to cheap oil, dominate the project, possibly in combination with India.[17]

Independent of the final failure of the plan, the region the Iranian organizers wanted to participate in the Asian Games was identical with the government's vision of an extended Indian Ocean region or Asian Union, which would include at least Iran, Pakistan, India, Bangladesh (a part of Pakistan until 1971), Burma, Thailand, Malaysia, Singapore, Indonesia, Australia (including New Zealand), and China. During a later stage, the countries west of Iran, namely the different Arab states and Turkey (which had already been allied with Iran and Pakistan for many years), and some African nations should also be added.[18] The initial problem, that of bringing the Asian Games to a West Asian country, had not been that difficult to solve, since there had been no other country applying for the Seventh Asian Games. The leader of the Iranian delegation to the Sixth Asian Games and member of the Iranian Olympic Committee, R. Kashefi, was pleased that the Games would therefore for the first time ever be held in "the heart of Asia". Through this expression he was probably trying to underline the importance of the ancient Persian civilization. He also added concerning the extension of the region of host countries, which now included West Asia: "Why should we be treated different? We are also part of Asia and we do not find hostility among any Asian nation over our participation in the Games in the Far East."[19] Strictly speaking, according to Gholam Reza Pahlavi, the matter was not that easy, since to be awarded the Games did not mean that foreign teams would actually show up. It apparently cost him much energy to convince all of them to participate, although he did not specify if this was linked only with strongly increasing travel costs or also with the political problems around the inclusion of China, which will be discussed below.[20]

After Pahlavi became president of the AGF, he began trying to expand the AGF in accordance with Iran's geographical region of interest: "The forty-eight-year-old prince said he would like to see countries like Turkey and Libya, which are members of the Mediterranean Games, join the Asian Games. Australia and New Zealand, although not part of the Asian continent, may also take part in the next games."[21] However, Pahlavi was unsuccessful and none of the four countries later participated. Australia and New Zealand, in particular, seem to have been rejected due to not being Asian in a geographical and ethnic sense.[22] In contrast, the expansion to the West was successful, even though it was not valued as highly. The hosting of the Games in West Asia and the growing oil wealth of the Arab countries facilitated the matter. Prior to the opening of the Games, Bahrain, Kuwait, Saudi Arabia, and even hostile Iraq, the last being a diplomatic success for Iran, joined the AGF. Lebanon, Syria, and the United Arab Emirates were accepted during the Games. However, even if some countries were more important for Iran than others, Pahlavi intended to bring as many teams as possible to Tehran. North Korea and Mongolia followed China's lead and became members of the AGF. The number of members thus went up to 26 (29 during the Games).[23]

All in all, the region of the Seventh Asian Games was identical with that of the desired Asian Union with the exceptions of Australia and New Zealand (perceived by a significant number of AGF officials as Oceanic states not belonging to Asia), Bangladesh (still in a state of chaos), and Turkey (anyway already allied with Iran).

In the case of the Arab states, it even covered an area intended to be included (and then dominated) later.

China, 'Asian Solidarity', and the New Wave of Anti-Neocolonial Internationalism

As already shown in the last section, the Asian Games have to be seen as one of several instruments to support the Iranian government's attempt at Asian region building against the superpowers, meaning mainly the USSR. In this section, the special case of China and the new emergence of anti-neocolonial (meaning anti-Western) internationalism will be covered.

The Iranians' plan to bring China back into the Asian Games, which the latter had attended only once in 1951 through some observers, was quite similar to the Indonesians' ambitions during the Fourth Asian Games. As mentioned in the sixth chapter, these had ended in the illegal non-invitation of Taiwan and Israel. In 1974, Israel's participation was not an issue. After the Egyptian ambassador asked the Iranians in spring 1973 not to invite Israel, he was told that the 'mighty' Arabs would certainly have "wiped Israel from the map" long before 1974.[24] In a nutshell, this sarcastic response, compounded by Arab setbacks during the Yom Kippur War, meant that Israel participated as planned and that the Arab countries eventually accepted Iran's demands and took part as well. In the case of China and Taiwan, Iran nonetheless was not willing to risk a new '1962': Tehran had recognized Beijing in August 1971, months before China became a member of the United Nations. Moreover, in the same year China had decided to again become involved in international sports events as the Cultural Revolution was slowly coming to an end. Mao Zedong agreed to send a team to the Table Tennis World Cup in Japan in March 1971, leading to closer contacts not only with Japan, but also the US (the so-called 'Ping Pong Diplomacy'). Apparently in early 1972, the first secret negotiations concerning China's participation in the Asian Games began, with Pahlavi and General Hojjat telling the Chinese ambassador that the shah desired China's participation. A short while later, in September 1972, Japan and China normalized relations and in the following month, the Japanese Olympic Committee came to the conclusion that the People's Republic was the 'true' representative of China. This was not only related to China's changing status in world politics, but certainly also influenced by the desire to make the Asian Games somewhat more demanding for Japanese athletes, who had often won more gold medals than all other countries combined.[25]

With both the host of the next Asian Games and the most important sports power in Asia in favor of China's participation, official negotiations followed from January 1973 onwards.[26] The 'two Chinas problem' in international sport, however, had not made any progress since the Second Asian Games in 1954. The People's Republic was still unwilling to join the AGF as long as Taiwan, considered to be a province of China, was a member. Therefore, it was decided that the same tactic as in the United Nations would be used, namely the question of representation and credentials, to substitute the Republic of China with the People's Republic as the 'true' representative of 'China'.[27] To 'officially' expel Taiwan was impossible, since such a step would, like in 1962, be perceived as an act of discrimination against a member country for political reasons, which would be too much for many AGF members to accept. The Iranian-Japanese-Chinese approach, however, was still problematic. The AGF was not a political organization like the United Nations, which represented international power relations, but a sports organization still driven by the morally charged 'civilizing mission' of promoting egalitarian internationalism. However, such ideals did not matter that much to the Iranian organizers.

On 17–18 September 1973, the AGF held a meeting of the executive committee, during which AGF president Pahlavi decided to hold a vote on the Chinese application. Since, among other causes for concern, Iran had three votes and two members of the executive committee were absent, Malaysian delegate Dato Hamzah Haji Abu Samah disagreed that the executive committee should decide on the matter and urged a council meeting to be held. After some controversies, the executive committee nevertheless voted in favor of the People's Republic's admission, but protests from delegates forced Pahlavi to call a meeting of the AGF council to confirm the decision.[28]

Before the council came together on 15–16 November 1973, the IOC held a meeting, which Pahlavi and Rassouli attended. IOC president Lord Killanin warned the Iranian organizers that they were in the process of de facto violating the non-discrimination rule and hinted at the possibility that the IOC might withdraw its patronage.[29] Should this happen, problems with further international sports federations would be inevitable. Since the Iranians were unwilling to back down, an image of an Asia threatened by imperialistic and paternalistic Western sports organizations was created, as in 1962 and 1963, by the pro-Chinese faction. Asian solidarity, maybe even the solidarity of all 'developing' countries, would be necessary to provide them with the means to counter the (allegedly) anti-Asian stance of the IOC. According to Chinese sports functionary and later IOC member He Zhenliang, General Hojjat had assured him before the AGF Council Meeting that in the worst case, should the IOC and the international sports federations not back down, he would be willing to go as far as setting up a new series of games similar to the Games of the New Emerging Forces (GANEFO) as a further threat:

> If a confrontation occurred between the international sports federations and the Asian Games, Iran would ally with the Asian, African and Latin American countries to establish a new organization in opposition to the European-American monopoly over international sports organizations. Of course, this would be decided by the king [shah], he added. After the

> council expelled [sic] the Taiwan authorities, upon seeing the danger of the establishment of a separate new organization by Asians, Africans and Latin Americans, the international sports organizations might not dare to take this risk of prohibiting their member organizations from competing in the Asian Games.[30]

Statements of 'Asian solidarity' thus were a rhetorical extension of Iranian and Chinese foreign policy. 'Asian solidarity' would not depend on the outcome of the vote taken during the council meeting, since, if the council voted against China, Iran would, according to Hojjat, *not* host the Games.[31] Moreover, it effectively excluded the option of Taiwan (as 'Taiwan', not as the 'Republic of China') remaining a member of the AGF, which some delegates would inevitably suggest. 'Asian solidarity' was already defined in advance for communication to the other delegates in order to provide those in favor of China with a pattern of argumentation and others with a vague excuse for complying. In any case, that the council might vote against China's application proved to be an unrealistic concern, since several delegations for one reason or another changed their opinion concerning the matter before the meeting.[32] However, as one might expect, the meeting was rather turbulent. AGF president Pahlavi did not allow a vote on an amendment concerning China's membership application, which would have allowed Taiwan to remain as a separate entity within the AGF.[33]

Following that decision, which attracted much criticism, the debate began. The most important advocates of the application were Pahlavi, Rassouli, and Seyed Abul Hassan, a delegate from Iran's neighbor Pakistan. Hassan mainly attacked the IOC and the international sports federations for not properly representing Asians, and therefore having a tendency to threaten Asian and African states, as in the case of the All-Africa Games in January 1973.[34] Nevertheless, he did not want to challenge the "Superpower-Charter" of the IOC (underlining his argument that only the two power blocs were influential). Instead, he wanted to find a solution by explaining to the international sports federations the reasons for including China.[35] Pahlavi, too, promised peaceful negotiations with them, but at the same time advocated strengthening the role of Asia:

> We are here as members of the Asian Games Federation. We are all Asians. But who are they? Most of the Federations are Europeans, are Americans, one Asian is in our International Federation[s]. Who are the IOC? We are a few Asians, but most of them are Europeans, few Africans and as I pointed out we try to abide by their rules. But we as Asians have got something to say too.[36]

The boldest attacks came from Rassouli, more or less openly calling for a GANEFO-like Asian-African-Latin American struggle against Western neocolonialism and paternalism:

> But who are these bodies, who are these superlords, these great gnomes of sports sitting in Europe, these remnants of the old colonial policies of Europe dominating Asia, Africa, Latin America. Who are these self-imposed great personalities sitting and dictating to us what and how we should conduct the affairs of our own destiny. (...) We, gentlemen, are masters of our destiny, and we have to decide what our destiny is going to be as far as sports in Asia is concerned without being dictated to by International Federations nor the International Olympic Committee.[37]

It was an ironic claim that the former 'colonial masters', allegedly having shrunk to 'great gnomes', were only able to dominate sports affairs because the former colonial peoples even in 1973 still believed in an *illusion* of Western superiority. Later on, Rassouli warned the International Amateur Athletic Association, which had threatened in 1962 to ban all athletes during the Fourth Asian Games because of the non-invitation of Taiwan and Israel, that it should not try to do the same thing again. It is very likely that he was yelling by then:

> If the International Amateur Athletic Federation dare, and I say dare, tell a body such as the Asian Games Federation, who they should decide to have as a member otherwise they are going to threaten them with sanction with this and the other [sic] then we shall not take it, we shall not stand for it. We can not accept an International Federation to meddle with the internal affairs of the Asian Games Federation. (...) I put to you gentlemen, that you should not take heed of the threats, of boycotts, sanctions of the actions that the International Federations can take or will take or may take, as long as we become united, as long as we stand together not only in Asia but also in Africa and also in other countries such as in Latin America. Then we will have our voice heard not only in this room not within the periphery of the Asian Games Federation movement, but within the whole world sports movement.[38]

Finally, he claimed that as long as China did not participate, it was not possible to talk of true 'Asian Games':

> The world is watching the Asian Games Federation today to see what positive action you can take in the right direction, in upholding the opportunity to the youths of all Asians to come to participate in an atmosphere of friendship, solidarity and peace. We want the true representation of Asia in the Asian Games Federation. And the Asian Games Federation will be meaningless without the active participation of the largest country in Asia.[39]

To counter this 'Asian solidarity' rhetoric, the speakers of the pro-Taiwan faction (primarily Filipino and Taiwanese officials) started to focus on the importance of amateur sports ideals. Their opponents, they asserted, were not acting in the appropriate moral spirit, thus jeopardizing the ideal of egalitarian internationalism by turning the AGF into a power-politics plagued United Nations. There would be no way in which the de facto exclusion of Taiwan could be justified, considering that China had no control over Taiwanese sports organizations.[40] Seen from their standpoint of egalitarian internationalism, these arguments were certainly correct, but after the debate was ended by Pahlavi, the pro-China faction won the election. Since the Iranians perceived a secret ballot on such an important matter to be *inappropriate*, everybody present easily saw that more than two thirds of the delegates (38:13; 5 abstaining) voted in favor of the substitution.[41]

During the following months, the IOC and the international sports federations discussed the matter. Lord Killanin had already communicated with certain Asian sports officials like A. de O. Sales from Hong Kong, who suggested leaving the AGF alone:

> The situation in Asia is very complicated as you well know and discretion is always the better part of valour in such matters because of strong lines which divide the continent arising from differences in religion, culture, race and economic and political development. All situations must be appraised from various standpoints. I have no doubt that come what may, sport will develop strongly in Asia in due time as there can be no holding back the tide of events in rapidly changing circumstances.[42]

Strictly speaking, this was a suggestion to *end* the sportive 'Western civilizing mission' in Asia begun by Elwood Brown in 1913 through the Far Eastern Championship Games (FECG). According to this line of thinking, regional games should not attempt to serve as a platform for actively promoting egalitarian and internationalist (not to mention Christian) citizenship training aimed at improving the relations between peoples and ameliorating religious, cultural, or political differences. Instead, sport should be *adjusted* to these differences, passively following changes in circumstance. The ideal of egalitarian internationalism would inevitably be given up during that process, but the IOC was anyway already heading in that direction. Its decision during its next executive committee meeting in February 1974 came close to Sales' suggestion. Iran was not banned like Indonesia 11 years ago, even though the IOC perceived the 'Olympic' ideal to have been violated. It "agreed to continue to give patronage to the Asian Games Federation but to deplore the fact that an National Olympic Committee (NOC) had not been invited."[43] In the end, the Iranians were triumphant in hosting the first Asian Games in which the most populous Asian country actively participated without losing the IOC's patronage. As mentioned above, even the pro-Taiwan faction could eventually be convinced to attend the Games under these circumstances. China, too, welcomed the IOC's decision and within the next few months the international sports federations either accepted China as a member or at least allowed it to compete in officially recognized events. Taiwan, however, would not participate in the Asian Games again until 1990.[44]

In conclusion, the Iranians were much more successful in enforcing their aim of changing the region of the Asian Games than the Sukarno administration had been in 1962. The means, anti-neocolonial internationalism, was the same. However, by 1974 the IOC was already in the process of giving up its 'civilizing mission' and thus decided against punishing Iran and potentially provoking a GANEFO-like counter reaction. The Iranians also solved the issue in a—seen from the perspective of egalitarian internationalism, very questionable—way *before* the Games began. They thereby prevented an escalation as in the case of the angry Indonesian mob searching for Guru Dutt Sondhi.

Iranian Modernization and Development Without Western Amateur Sports Ideals

To support Iran's Asia-related foreign policy was not the only aim the Iranian organizers had with regards to the Games. Other aims were supporting the authoritarian modernization and development process, which included a certain rivalry with Japan, as well as nation-branding and promoting their state nationalism.

As mentioned in the fifth chapter and at the very beginning of this chapter, the shah and Gholam Reza Pahlavi had attended the Third Asian Games, hosted in Asia's most modern and developed country: Japan. Moreover, the 1972 Olympic Games had been held in Munich just two years before the Seventh Asian Games. These Olympics had been planned to promote a 'new' Germany and set standards at least in terms of architecture, even though they were overshadowed by the attack of Palestinian terrorists on the Israeli team.[45] The Seventh Asian Games should not only outdo the best Asian Games held until then, but even the Olympic Games, in order to illustrate Iran's seemingly unstoppable progress in becoming one of the leading powers in the world. Like in 1958, the officially declared aim, made public after Iran was awarded the Games in 1970, was to use the Asian Games to attract the Olympic Games to the host city.[46] This was one of the reasons why the Asian Games in Indonesia (which ended with the GANEFO as an alternative to the Olympic Games) were never mentioned as a role model and why the Iranians proceeded relatively carefully against the IOC. Nevertheless, the plan ultimately failed, since Iran's applications for both the 1980 and 1984 Olympic Games were not submitted or had to be withdrawn. In the case of the 1980 Games, the reason was apparently the China issue. According to Chinese sources the Iranians had made a deal with the USSR. Tehran would not run against Moscow, expecting that under these circumstances the USSR would not cause problems by contesting China's becoming a member of the AGF. Since the application for 1984 was withdrawn before the IOC executive board meeting on 19 October 1977, when the Islamic Revolution was not yet a serious issue, the reason might have been social tensions, but another explanation might be American pressure not to intervene in its 'retaliation' for the Olympics held in Moscow.[47] Therefore, in contrast to Japan, the Iranian organizers did not prove successful in their goal of attracting the Olympic Games to Tehran as a global promotional tool for their country. Hypothetically, had the Iranian monarchy not found its end in 1979, Iran might have more successfully applied for the 1988 Olympic Games, instead of South Korea becoming the second Asian country to host the Olympics and to appear as 'highly developed'.

Independent of these future plans, statements by the Iranian organizers focused mostly on popularizing sport within Iran, on Iran's ancient traditions, and on visualizing national development. Amateur values hardly came up. Gholam Reza Pahlavi hoped and wished that "the Tehran Games will prove to be the biggest and best organised so far, and that the experiences of other nations organising previous Games, will be studied carefully and taken into consideration thereby ensuring a general improvement in organisational methods and techniques."[48] He nevertheless later added that admiration for Iran's achievements should not be limited only to Iran: "I believe that the Organizing Committee has achieved a measure of success which reflects splendidly not only on the host country but all of Asia."[49] Prime Minister Amir Abbas Hoveyda also engaged in nation-branding and supporting the personality cult of the shah:

> As one of the cradles of world civilization, Iran is the inheritor of a unique treasure of man's artistic and cultural achievements. Ready access to these historic relics of our ancient past will provide a most enriching additional attraction to the sports events. I hope that our visitors will also take the opportunity of acquainting themselves with modern Iran and with some of our gigantic strides in the social and economic fields which, taken under the enlightened leadership of our August Sovereign, are rapidly transforming this ancient land into a progressive, industrialized country.[50]

At the same time, he tried to link Iranian foreign policy with the idea of peace the Games had so often been declared to represent:

> The aim of the Asian Games, as indeed the aim of any international sporting event of this magnitude, is to foster mutual understanding by personal contact, and through conciliating all mankind, promote the cause of universal peace. These are the declared aims also of the Iranian Government, and it is our firm belief that the holding of the 1974 Asian Games in this country will make a special contribution towards this goal.[51]

Quite similar remarks came from Gholam Reza Nikpay, the mayor of Tehran, who talked about goodwill between Asian peoples and infrastructure improvements in the host city. Richard Avory, a Briton married to the daughter of a high-ranking Iranian government official, who was recruited into the organizing committee, elaborated on the value of the Games for popularizing sport and providing the organizers with the experience to host further events.[52] The shah's and General Hojjat's comments focused on national progress, but also provided the spreading of sport some 'invented' authenticity. The shah talked of certain spiritual benefits linked with sport, possibly egalitarianism or economically progressive thinking, and urged his subjects to take a more active interest in it, which would hopefully lead to a 'true' renaissance of Iranian sport.[53] Hojjat perceived the Iranian year 1352 (beginning on 21 March 1973), which was proclaimed 'Sports Year', as "the first year in the continuing sports revolution in Iran".[54] Furthermore, he deliberated about ancient sports like horse riding, archery, and athletics during the time of Cyrus the Great.

Something else quite interesting is a very dubious statement regarding the value of the Seventh Asian Games for international understanding that was made in the official report about the Games: "Firstly, by bringing together Asian youth, hopefully the Games have fostered (somehow) [sic] a better understanding and have raised the standard and popularity of sport in Asia."[55] The "hopefully" and especially the "(somehow)" seem to be symptomatic of the lack of explanations the Iranian organizers had for how 'understanding' should be created. In their statements, the 'friendship and peace' discourse linked with the 'Olympic' ideal remained isolated from the discourse about amateur sports norms and values and their use as a tool for egalitarian internationalism. The Iranians substituted the latter with a discourse of bringing different people together. Their *systematic cheating* and the *misuse of power* during doping tests hardly allowed anything else.[56] Moreover, since several Arab countries had joined the AGF before the Games began, the Middle East Conflict, fueled by the Yom Kippur War, found its way into the Asian Games. The delegations from Bahrain, Kuwait, and Iraq declared that they would not compete against Israelis in contact sports and would generally refrain from all physical contact and communication with them. Following that, the delegations from Pakistan, China, and North Korea joined the boycott. The Iranian organizers officially criticized the boycotters' behavior, but prevented sanctions or even a discussion by delaying an AGF council meeting despite several appeals to hold one.[57] Officials of more Western-oriented member countries of the AGF, such as the Philippines and Japan, heavily criticized the boycott and IOC president Killanin was infuriated. In November 1975, he sent out a circular letter declaring that the IOC would under no circumstances accept boycotts of other teams.[58] Another incident was the jeering of an Israeli gold winner, which the American embassy thought might have been a hint at the overall anti-Israel feeling.[59] It is hardly surprisingly that the mere bringing together of people while breaking instead of enforcing amateur norms and values led to tensions, and thus made the value of this newly stated objective quite questionable, even for Iranians like General Hojjat. Since it is unrealistic to imagine that the Iranians were not familiar with Western amateur values, one has to assume that these simply did not matter to them. An appropriation of Western sports practices took place by linking them to ancient Iranian physical education practices. Showing similarities to Sukarno's Indonesia, the sportive 'Western civilizing mission' was, however, not appropriated and culturally integrated. Instead, its aims were substituted with those of using athletes—and the Asian Games themselves—to win glory for the nation. A confidant of the shah noted in his diary that the shah was indeed pleased that Iran placed second in the medal ranking—after Japan, which was considered impossible to beat—"since he holds that of the continent's more advanced nations, Japan should lead in the East and we in the West."[60] This is reminiscent of the statement by Gholam Reza Pahlavi opening this chapter, which focused on the comparison—or rivalry—between Japan and Iran, but indirectly also on the perceived superiority of both 'ancient empires' compared to 'lesser' nations. Quite obviously, the desire to win by all means was not mentioned in public, discretion being the most reasonable and diplomatic approach at a time when amateurism was still advocated by many.

This discretion is further highlighted by the discourses produced in countries that had been more strongly affected by Western amateur sports norms and values. Both countries in the following examples in the mid-1970s lacked the financial and other means to produce or hire world class professional athletes and thus found it easier to persist in focusing on amateurism, mass sport, and the 'civilizing' rhetoric. In the Philippines, president-turned-dictator Ferdinand Marcos in 1973 made comments on amateur sport as "citizenship building" based on "[t]he 'team' man" and "Humility in Triumph", which could almost have come from Elwood Brown.[61] In 1974, Sha'ari Tadin, Singapore's senior parliamentary secretary and leader of the delegation to the Seventh Asian Games, warned against professionalism, which had destroyed the ancient Olympic Games.[62]

All in all, the Iranian focus was on nation-branding and on the attempt to bring one of the next Olympic Games to Tehran to serve as an even better platform for showing their country to the world. Amateur sports ideals, in contrast, were of only marginal importance, even though they were—quite reasonably—not openly rejected in public. Tact aside, the goal of creating national pride and international prestige via sport was nonetheless highly important.

Building Monuments to Persian Power

To brand themselves as a wealthy, highly developed country and to challenge the doubts of some of the former organizers of the Asian Games regarding Iran's organizational skills, the Iranians decided to construct a new, modern sports complex to the northwest of Tehran. This decision fits within the trend of large-scale infrastructure development projects since the Third Asian Games and especially into the series of authoritarian 'high modernist' plans since the Fourth Asian Games. This time another spending record was achieved to illustrate national wealth, development, and catching up with—or even overtaking—the West.

The Aryamehr Sports Complex, named after the shah's title and thus serving his personality cult, was to be overshadowed by the Aryamehr Stadium, said to have been the largest earthen stadium in the world at that point in time (fig. 8.1). Close to 3 million cubic meters of earth had been dug up to create a mound—this being reminiscent of classical Iranian construction styles—into which the stadium was then integrated. It also served as a dam for the artificial lake into which the dig site was turned afterwards and which provided several hundred hectares of newly planted trees with water. The stadium thus was one expression of the Iranian ambition to become one of the leading powers in the world, possessing in addition to its special architectonic features 100,000 seats and facilities equipped with the latest technology.[63] The Omega scoreboard within it could display both Latin and Persian characters as well as graphic images, and could also play animated films.[64] For the first time in the history of the Asian Games, athletes did not compete on a cinder track but on a synthetic plastic track. Fiberglass poles replaced bamboo poles, while rubberized runways and foam pits were introduced. Photo-finish cameras and infrared technology made timing much more precise. The stadium was completed already in 1971, to be officially opened on one of the last days of celebrations for the Persian monarchy's 2,500th anniversary. Later, it was also used to celebrate the shah's birthday, again linking it with the personality cult.[65] The construction of the sports complex, which together with the stadium cost several hundred million USD, apparently led to two years of cement shortages in other parts of Iran.[66] All the stadia and sports halls met Olympic standards so that they would have been ready to accommodate the Olympic Games. It was also made public that the buildings had been erected by an Iranian company, illustrating Iranian skills and technical knowledge. One of the company's architects was Hojjat's son Reza, meaning that the Hojjat family also had a personal and financial interest in the Games and that once again, claims of corruption came up.[67]

To turn their buildings into monuments to an authentic Iranian modernity, the architects included some traditional cultural elements in their designs. Iran's rising wealth and international status was to be shown, but at the same time a certain cultural emancipation from Western architectural elements was desired to further reduce the power asymmetry. The mound used for building the Aryamehr Stadium has already been mentioned. In addition, some of the smaller buildings were built in the ancient Parsian architectural style found at the Achaemenid capitals, Persepolis and Pasargadae (fig. 8.2): "The unique architectural feature of the [sports] hall is its roof which is supported by four giant pillars."[68] Another structure displaying the same architectural feature was the swimming hall. The Asiad Village, built some distance from the sports complex in a nature reserve,

FIGURE 8.1
'Aryamehr Stadium (serving as a dam)': The extremely expensive stadium communicated Iran's infrastructure development successes, incorporated references to Persian civilization, and promoted the shah's rule.

The Organizing Committee Teheran, *Bulletin* 3, n.p. (Courtesy of The Olympic Studies Centre)

FIGURE 8.2
'Main sports hall': The massive roof on pillars connected the modern building to Persian civilization and architecture.

Official Report of the Seventh Asian Games Teheran September 1–16, 74, p. 28 (p. 30 shows the swimming hall). (Courtesy of The Olympic Studies Centre) followed the same approach. It was set up around a traditional village center that was "inspired by the traditional Persian bazaar (market place) and will reflect some of the features inherent in the bazaar concept."[69]

All in all, the giant sum of money spent on the sports complex apparently fulfilled the aim of communicating the image of Iran's growing importance as a wealthy, competent, and 'developed' country. When construction work was temporarily delayed in 1972, the shah showed his personal interest in such nation-branding (and its enforcement) by informing the minister of housing and development "that any delay to the construction work for the games will be interpreted as deliberate disobedience to my orders and will be punished accordingly."[70] As a result, the sportspersons and journalists attending the Games seem to have been more than impressed by this Iranian show of development progress. For example, René Frank, president of the International Hockey Federation, and S. S. Dhillon, secretary of Singapore's National Olympic Council, perceived the facilities to be the best ever in the history of the Asian Games. The head of the Japanese delegation, Tajima Naoto, and the president of the International Swimming Federation, Harold Henning, saw them as on par with the standard of those in Munich. Finally, IOC president Lord Killanin called them "extremely practical and well-designed. They must be the envy of most other countries in the world."[71]

The Official Ceremonies: The Royal Family and the Rebirth of an Empire

The opening ceremony and the following entertainment program strongly focused on the topic of modern Iran and its ancient heritage. Nevertheless, the organizers added some pan-Asian elements to the show. Some of the technical elements of staging such as colored placards and colored uniforms, as well as the lighting ceremony, were clearly inspired by the Thai Fifth and Sixth Asian Games.

The day before the Games commenced, Crown Prince Reza used a magnifying glass to kindle the first torch at Saadabad Palace, the royal residence.[72] The Iranian organizers thus did their best to link the ceremony with the personality cult of the royal family. The Games' flame in the stadium was lit by Ali Baghbanbashi, a veteran athlete who had won the 5,000 meter race during the First Asian Games and held several Iranian records. Below the flame, 4,000 police academy cadets were seated, equipped with colored placards. In a demonstration of (Japanese-trained) strict discipline and coordination, which was representative of the whole program, they accompanied the events on the field by depicting them via their placards. Most of the images they formed had an international and pan-Asian appeal. When the teams entered the stadium, their national flags and country names were created. Other images included peace doves (when 3,000 white doves were set free) (fig. 8.3), the word 'friendship', the motto of the Asian Games ('Ever Onward') and the Olympic rings. Like in the Thai Asian Games, the royal family

FIGURE 8.3
'Cadets with colored placards depicting doves': The staging of the Games became increasingly sophisticated.
Official Report of the Seventh Asian Games Teheran September 1–16, 74, p. 48. (Courtesy of The Olympic Studies Centre)

was also depicted and thereby linked with this sportive internationalism, serving the personality cult. To the left of the cadets was a group of 1,500 corpsmen who formed a choir that sang several songs, including the special hymn written for the Seventh Asian Games. The upper tier of the corpsmen was dressed in green, the center in white and the lower tier in red. They thus depicted a giant Iranian flag, similar to what the Thais had done in 1970 (fig. 8.4).[73] The Iranian national colors were equally pervasive during the march-in of the teams. Each team was accompanied by a young female Iranian physical education student dressed in green-white-red clothes, carrying the name plate of the team. The inspiration might have been the Thai 'sweethearts' and beauty queens who had led many national teams in 1966 and 1970, though these had worn traditional dresses of the respective nations. The Iranian women, in contrast, had the symbol of the Asian Games Federation on their shirts, in this way still adding a pan-Asian element.[74]

During the entertainment section, two aspects of classic Iranian culture and a pan-Asian element were presented. First, 400 muscular Iranian men gave a *Zurkhaneh* ('House of Strength') demonstration (fig. 8.5), a form of physical training with some military aspects going back to the pre-Islamic period. Like other traditional forms of physical education, it had undergone a slight modernization and 'reinvention' process to keep up with standards of hygiene.

FIGURE 8.4
'The Iranian flag formed by the choir': The national symbol was permanently present during the ceremony. [75]

Official Report of the Seventh Asian Games Teheran September 1–16, 74, p. 47. (Courtesy of The Olympic Studies Centre)

Initially, it had been a means of resisting foreign Arab dominance during the 'Middle Ages', later becoming entangled with Shia Islam.[76] It was an exhibition of Iran's own authentic physical culture, standing for Iranian physical strength, courage, chivalrousness, and independence. Afterwards, about 1,000 Iranian youths dressed in the traditional costumes of peoples from different Iranian regions performed folk dances (fig. 8.6). The colors of the costumes were those which people of the respective regions wore on festive occasions. Moreover, the dancers were accompanied by classical Iranian music and formed, among other things, the pattern of a Persian carpet. Similarly dressed girls had already performed a *baba karam* (a traditional dance based on a Sufi story) when the Asian Games flag had been handed over to the mayor of Tehran, and further girls wearing traditional clothes would appear later in the Games during the victory ceremonies.[77] In this way, Iran's broad cultural heritage in physical culture was represented. Simultaneously, unity in cultural diversity and the equality of people from different Iranian regions was shown, underlining efforts to create and promote state nationalism in a country with several significant minorities.

Following these performances, 800 police cadets engaged in some light calisthenics followed by a flag display, in which they marched across the field with the flags of the participating nations and the AGF (fig. 8.7).[78] Hereby was illustrated first the health, fitness, conformity, and discipline of modern Iranians, while later on, peaceful equality between all participating members of the AGF was symbolically staged, underlining the message of egalitarian internationalism. The latter idea reappeared when the following event ended the entertainment

FIGURE 8.5
'Zurkhaneh demonstration': The display communicated continuity between ancient Iranian civilization and the Iranian government's modernization process, which would reveal Western superiority to be only a temporary phenomenon.

Official Report of the Seventh Asian Games Teheran September 1–16, 74, p. 56.
(Courtesy of The Olympic Studies Centre)

FIGURE 8.6
'Iranian folk dances': The event also connected Iranian modernization to traditional cultural elements, rejecting Westernization as the only path to modernity.

Official Report of the Seventh Asian Games Teheran September 1–16, 74, p. 59.
(Courtesy of The Olympic Studies Centre)

program: like in Thailand, cardboard mortars shot parachutes into the air, carrying the flags of the participating nations and of the AGF.[79]

In addition to all this, it seems that the Iranians may have included a clear demonstration of national military power. At an unknown point in the proceedings (either during the Games or during a rehearsal), hundreds of uniformed Iranian soldiers armed with bayonet-fixed rifles apparently marched into the stadium to perform some military drills.[80] This march-in certainly communicated one of the means by which Iran was to regain the ancient position of a great power and thus was to serve in convincing Iranians that the government had the capacity to protect Iran's territory and its growing international interests. This nonetheless begs the question of how other countries felt about the message. The Iranians themselves seem to have come to the conclusion that the event had neither an internationalist dimension nor the traditional dimension possessed by the 'martial' performance of the *Zurkhaneh*-practitioners, since it was not included in the official report and other publications.

The closing ceremony was, like always, shorter than the opening and did not provide much of an entertainment section. Nevertheless, some elements of the personality cult of the shah, who had already left Iran for his Indian Ocean round-trip, were included. General Hojjat showed his reverence for the *Shahanshah Aryamehr* by chanting his title several times and the scoreboard later depicted the royal family (fig. 8.8). When the lights were afterwards turned off, a pan-Asian, strictly speaking universal prayer was said: "We pray to our creator to help Asian Nations and all nations to live in peace, friendship and amity."[81] Later on, 800 members of the imperial guard performed a torch display, again showing precision and discipline, and, as it was custom since 1958, *Auld Lang Syne* as a farewell song was sung, adding another internationalist element to the staging.[82]

The imperial guards, like the police cadets and the soldiers during the opening ceremony, but in contrast to the *Zurkhaneh*-practitioners, were dressed in Western sports clothes or uniforms. One can assume that at least one of the reasons for this contrast was to ensure that the soldiers and police cadets appeared modern instead of traditional. When it came to questions of military and policing capability, the display of traditional elements might cast doubts on their effectiveness. After all, the intention was not just to show the Iranian modernization process as having a non-Western—Iranian—origin, but also to communicate successes that would lead to parity with the West. Western civilizational supremacy thus again appeared to be only a temporary phenomenon, close to being overcome due to Iran's reemergence as a great power. Moreover, the soldiers and policemen were also all-male, in contrast to the dancers. This underlined that traditional gender roles still mattered, although a certain emancipation process was personified by the female Iranian athletes.

Taken all together, the official ceremonies and the entertainment program certainly were one of the most remarkable illustrations of nation-branding ever

FIGURE 8.7
'Flag display of the police cadets': Like the soldiers that entered the stadium, the police forces were shown as disciplined, fit, and well-organized.

Official Report of the Seventh Asian Games Teheran September 1–16, 74, p. 58. (Courtesy of The Olympic Studies Centre)

FIGURE 8.8
'The scoreboard, depicting the royal family': Another illustration of the personality cult.

Official Report of the Seventh Asian Games Teheran September 1–16, 74, p. 62. (Courtesy of The Olympic Studies Centre) seen in the Asian Games. Again, traditional Iranian cultural elements were shown together with modern Western ones, combining them to support the image of Iran as a rising country that had nonetheless not lost its authentic culture. The events were also a demonstration of Iranian organizational skills including discipline, coordination, and precision. The message of egalitarian internationalism, too, can be found therein, though several of the events had a certain militaristic touch. Finally, the ceremonies were used as another way to support the personality cult of the royal family by linking it with the impressively hosted Games.

Exhibiting the Great Persian Empire

The large sums of money available to the organizers allowed a cultural program the likes of which had never before been seen during the Asian Games. One of the reasons why Iran hosted the Games was, without question, to illustrate that its modernization process would be based on and entangled with its ancient culture. This entanglement, rejecting the claim that Western civilization was the only path toward modernity, was already shown by the architecture and by the entertainment program after the opening ceremony.

Exhibits and performances of millennia-old Persian civilization, even if not directly linked to sport or physical education, could serve to communicate the message of a 'great past'. Iranian dances, among them only recently 'rediscovered' regional dances, were performed at several places in Tehran and at the sports complex. A new theatrical interpretation of the epic of Rostam and Sohrab from Ferdowsi's *Shahnameh* (Book of Kings), recorded in several languages so that more visitors could understand it, was also shown. Exhibitions of rare Persian carpets, ancient and modern architecture, paintings, miniatures, handicrafts, and jewelry going back to the Achaemenid dynasty took place as well.[83]

Another interesting opportunity the Games provided the Iranians was that of organizing for the first time a large, multicultural program that incorporated displays of traditional elements of many participating Asian nations. This was a considerably scaled-up version of an idea, originating with the Thai organizers, to invite Asian cultural troupes to the 1966 Games.[84] In this way, quite similar to the Asian Union project, Iran could put itself into a leadership role by generously sponsoring and hosting these displays, while at the same time publicly presenting itself as respectful of and caring for the cultures of other Asian nations (or junior partners). This is illustrated by the organizers' decision to focus on performances and exhibitions containing distinctive cultural elements of other nations, while less culturally authentic elements such as electronic music (which was at best modern American or Western) were rejected. Despite this, the later complaints of some foreign artists that they were not treated well and that the organizers of the arts events did not care much for their contributions could mean that the Iranians still were primarily interested in displaying their own culture in a favorable way and perceived everything else only as a bonus to increase Iran's prestige.[85] The invitation of the Royal Chamber Orchestra of Wallonia and the Hungarian exhibition entitled 'Hungarians in the Olympic Games' further highlights that 'Asian solidarity' apparently was not the final aim.[86] Rather, the priority seems to have been to increase Iran's presence on the world stage by bringing famous groups to Tehran, even if they were not Asian. Despite all that, an impressive conglomerate of Asian artists did come to Tehran. Traditional dance and culture groups from various nations performed, among others the *Uday Shankar Dance Group* from India, the *Little Angels Children's Folk Ballet of Korea*, the *Bayanihan Philippine National Folk Dance Company*, and several groups from Nepal, Thailand, and Singapore. Indonesia contributed a batik exhibition, Hong Kong paintings, while Japanese photographer Namikawa Banri displayed photographs he had taken in several countries along the old Silk Road linking West and East Asia. In addition, the Federation of All Japan Karatedō Organizations gave some demonstrations. China sent handicrafts and a display of Chinese architecture, and also set up an exposition contrasting pre-communist and Maoist paintings.[87]

However, the Iranians' particular view of history and desire for nation-branding meant that even vague reminiscences of historical events that put Iran in a negative light were undesirable. For example, a marathon was not included in the Games' program. The unconvincing official explanation was that Asian athletes were not yet ready for such an exhausting event, despite an Asian, a Japanese team member from Korea, Sohn Kee-chung (Japanese: Son Kitei), trained by the Seoul Young Men's Christian Association (YMCA), already winning the event at the 1936 Olympic Games. The reality was that the shah did not want include a running event based on the (legendary) long-distance run of the Greek messenger Pheidippides from Marathon to Athens in 490 BC to report the *defeat* of the Persian army. According to IOC president Lord Killanin, close associates of the shah affiliated with the IOC (certainly Gholam Reza Pahlavi) informed him that in the event of the Olympic Games being hosted in Tehran the monarch would again not agree to a marathon event.[88]

In conclusion, similar to the architecture and the ceremonies, the cultural program served to brand Iranian culture locally and internationally, in this context especially other Asian countries. The Iranians also brought various Asian (and some non-Asian) culture groups to Tehran, thus presenting themselves as rich and benevolent sponsors, and Iran as the new politico-cultural center of Asia. The main focus, nonetheless, was on Iran's interpretation of its own culture and history, which served to create the image of a glorious Iranian past. As shown by the exclusion of the marathon, those events that did not fit into the narrative of the 'glorious past', but instead questioned its value as the foundation of a successful modernization process, were not welcome.

Communicating the Rebirth of the Persian Great Power

Similar to the earlier Asian Games, the development of television was closely linked with and accelerated by the hosting of the Seventh Asian Games as the biggest sports event yet held in Iran. The coverage was simultaneously symptomatic of the increasing number of sports consumers in Iran and other countries, an outcome of economic development.

More than 550 journalists attended the Games, using the newly erected high-tech press house. About 200 of them were radio and television broadcasters, coming from 22 countries.[89] A satellite antenna for the Indian Ocean region, which complemented one for the Pacific region and two for the Atlantic region, was finished to facilitate broadcasting to most parts of the world. Due to this, for the first time ever, many countries to the east of Pakistan gained access to Iranian television, both in black and white and in color. More than 12 hours of footage from the daily events of the Games were made available either live or reported later that same day.[90] The same coverage of the Games was also made available within Iran. At first, the organizers had intended to exclude Tehran from the broadcast area to prevent a scenario in which nobody would go to the stadium, which could communicate a negative image and result in claims by opponents of the regime that the stadium was not open to normal people or that they opposed the Games. Nevertheless, it was finally decided not to exclude Tehran.[91] Therefore, according to (not necessarily reliable) Iranian sources, 300 million Asians watched the opening ceremony of the Games live on television. While the number might be an exaggeration, it was a fact that the opening ceremony was broadcasted live in five countries. In Iran itself, the necessary conditions for regular sports consumption, such as an urbanized society equipped with televisions, were in place by the 1970s. As a consequence, Islamic critiques of the regime argued that sports, especially soccer, which was encouraged through the Asian Games and became extremely popular in the 1970s, were a means for the government to divert the attention of the masses away from the problems caused by Iran's modernization process. Whether this was true or not, soccer in particular became a popular spectator sport and sometimes also served to create national pride. The shah's family, which was very involved in soccer, certainly profited from it.[92]

The Iranian Ministry of Arts and Culture also prepared a movie in English about the Seventh Asian Games.[93] Moreover, lots of prospects and bulletins were published in both English and Persian, providing much information on Iranian geography and culture. They thus de facto also served as tourism advertisements to Tehran, Persepolis, and other places. Furthermore, most Iranian newspapers and news magazines published in English, thus targeted at foreigners and Western-educated Iranians, hardly mentioned negative incidents, focusing instead on the impressive staging of the Games.

In conclusion, the live broadcasting of the Games in color was definitely another illustration of Iran's successful development. The message was, moreover, not limited to Iranians. By receiving live broadcasts from Iran, spectators in other Asian countries were not only informed about the Games, but also were confronted with Iran's development process and technological progress. Iran had achieved what Japan had accomplished at the Tokyo Olympics in 1964. Moreover, as Singapore's President Sheares' quotation earlier shows, it also served to bring the Asian countries closer together by overcoming some of the distance between them, further serving regional integration. The growing focus on television nonetheless was another illustration that the ideal of educating people through encouraging them to take up amateur sport was more and more accompanied by a growing consumption of (professional) sports broadcasts.

Assessment

As many AGF members stated, the Seventh Asian Games marked a highly significant turning point in the history of the Asian Games in terms of region, sports ideals, and political instrumentalization by the host government.

The Iranian and Chinese sports officials were not the only ones who considered the Seventh Asian Games as the first 'true' Asian Games, now that the Arab countries and communist-governed countries such as China and North Korea had finally joined.[94] In terms of Cold War ideology, they overcame the former partial division of Asia into GANEFO and Asian Games. However, not all AGF members agreed that the mere geographical unity of Asia was necessarily a good thing. Geographical unity still lacked spiritual or ideological cohesion based on egalitarian internationalism as promoted through amateur norms and values. As mentioned above, the exclusion of Taiwan had not been supported by all members. Moreover, contemporary statements by Japanese officials like Shibata Katsuji, and also journalists such as Ernesto T. Bitong from *The Filipino Athlete*, illustrate the expected shift of power toward West Asia, which would not be appreciated by all East Asians. He Zhenliang from China and S. S. Dhillon from Singapore later also made quite similar statements.[95] One has to assume that the decision of the Asian Football Confederation during its meeting held at the Seventh Asian Games to follow Kuwait's suggestion not to invite Israel to tournaments anymore was already a sign for the East Asians of West Asia's rise.[96] The decision also foreshadowed Israel's exclusion from the Asian Games from 1978 onwards.

Contemporary East Asian statements certainly hinted at the problems linked with the Middle East conflict, as well as religious and ideological tensions that were now brought into the AGF. They were also critical of the exploding costs of hosting the Games with almost 30 participating teams, and at the disproportionately high influence in decision-making within the AGF exercised by the Arabs and Iran as a result of increasing oil wealth. For example, Shibata declared that serious problems would arise due to the costs. After the Games scheduled to take place in 1978 in Pakistan—which in the end took place in Thailand due to a lack of money on the part of Pakistan—indeed the question of which nation would be able to host the next ones arose. Shibata even thought about the possibility of splitting the Asian Games into 'Near and Middle Eastern Games' (including Afghanistan and the countries to its west) and 'Far Eastern Games' (which would necessarily include South Asia). Hence, for some East Asian sportspersons, the newly gained 'unity' of Asia apparently was not a triumph, but the next problem.

This situation also calls to mind the doubts of the Filipinos regarding the founding of the Asian Games, discussed in the third chapter. Bitong went even further than Shibata and stated that the escalating size of the Asian Games had already led to talks regarding the hosting of games of a manageable size between the members of ASEAN, among others. One therefore has to assume that the transformation of the Southeast Asian Peninsular Games (SEAP Games) between 1975 and 1977 into Southeast Asian Games now also including Brunei, Indonesia, and the Philippines was a concrete step to balance Southeast Asia's unquestionable marginalization in the new AGF. This general fear of marginalization was, after all, one of the reasons why Iran's Indian Ocean region project, with the Seventh Asian Games as a first step toward it, did not lead to significant results.

In terms of the sportive 'civilizing mission' of shaping 'New Asians' through amateur ideals, the Seventh Asian Games marked another end. Bitong's comment on the behavior of the cheating Iranians and the boycotters of the Israeli team might be an exaggeration, but was basically true:

> Ancient chronicles state that it took some ten centuries for the real Olympic spirit kindled in Olympia to die. From the looks of it, the essence of the Asian Games—concocted 25 years ago in New Delhi's Patiala House—has been denatured in the wake of the Tehran Asiad incidents. The spirit of competition for competition's sake has died, and we can only see more difficulties and problems for the Asian Games in the days to come.[97]

In Tehran, three different sports ideologies had finally clashed. The tensions between Western egalitarian internationalism as a means for 'civilized' interaction and the nationalistic drive to win medals by all means for prestige purposes and for supporting state nationalisms was nothing new. The American YMCA and Guru Dutt Sondhi had already perceived it as a threat. It nonetheless seems to have reached a new level at the Seventh Asian Games due to the Iranian organizers' sometimes systematic cheating. However, the inclusion of nations such as the People's Republic of China led to even more incidents and debates. Representatives of Maoist China and of some Muslim countries were publically unwilling to accept the egalitarian internationalist framework of the sportive 'civilizing mission', perceiving it as a remnant of Western colonialism and a means to make Asians internationally recognize certain countries (or 'puppet states'). What had been a boycott of the participation of Israel and Taiwan in 1962 now became a boycott of Israelis in contact sports and all social activities. The difference with regard to 1962 was, however, that by this time serious challenges to this practice, such as Sondhi had mounted against the Indonesians with the IOC's support, were no longer made. For the supporters of amateur sports ideals, the basic idea of the Games, namely to spread respect between potentially hostile social groups and peoples and to serve in building a more egalitarian and interdependent regional order, would be nullified if the acceptance of amateur ideals were not enforced. The Games would become nothing more than a mere bringing together of athletes whose behavior would be influenced by the foreign policies of their respective governments. Respect would be limited to athletes from allied or neutral countries (as in the case of China) or be overwhelmed by a focus on victory (as in the case of Iran).

However, such issues linked with decolonization and with competitions between political systems during the interwar period and especially during the Cold War were hardly limited to the AGF. Attempted or realized violations of Western amateur sports ideals by—for example, Nazi Germany (exclusion of Jewish members from the Olympic team), South Africa (apartheid), or full-time state-sponsored 'amateurs' as in the 'communist bloc'—had generated similar debates and rejection by IOC members, not to mention the problems imported from the other regional games the IOC patronized. Under Lord Killanin, however, the IOC slowly began to give up its 'civilizing mission', as A. de O. Sales, for one, had recommended regarding the Asian Games. In October 1974, the IOC finally accepted 'state amateurs', even though doing so contradicted the amateur idea that sports and money should be separated as much as possible to keep the ambition—or necessity—to win by all means under control.[98] The Iranians thus had to expect criticism for their violations of the (former) amateur or 'Olympic' spirit, but did not have to be afraid of being suspended like Indonesia in 1963. What remained was a third ideology: international sport as a business. This still promoted a certain version of economic progress, but without the amateurism-based ideals that earlier on Asians (and before them the American YMCA) had so often declared the foundation for regional integration.

In contrast, for the groups not interested in Western amateur ideals, sports events would not become useless in any way. The focus was to shift from educating and 'civilizing' masses of people (instead of producing spectators and consumers) to an even stronger usage of the Games as a tool for nation-building, nation-branding, or for illustrating national superiority. Some basic internationalism, like the attendance, or at least interest, of foreign athletes and journalists, was obviously still necessary. The 'peace' and 'friendship' discourse, which after all sounded admirable, would not vanish. It nonetheless would be isolated from the discourse about amateur sports ideals and thus would become hollow and more unconvincing. The Seventh Asian Games incorporated all of those changes and thus were a turning point in the history of the Asian Games and their predecessors.

The Iranian organizers, very close to the Iranian government, saw the Games as one of many steps on the road of turning their country into a great power. Like in Indonesia and Thailand, the Games were the outcome of extremely ambitious authoritarian 'high modernism'. With hundreds of millions of petrodollars spent on them, the Tehran Games significantly outclassed all the previous games. Hosted on an Olympic scale, they were meant to support Iran's aspiration of bringing the Olympic Games to Tehran and thus becoming the second Asian country—following Japan—to host them. Simultaneously, they served the project of Iranian-led region building. Iran could put itself symbolically into the lead within Asia by sponsoring the visits to Tehran of teams from small countries and of various Asian dance and culture groups. Finally, the Games were, like the 2,500th anniversary of the Persian monarchy, a mega event used to construct and propagate a new Iranian great power identity after the country's economic situation improved during the White Revolution and the first Oil Crisis. The lighting of the torch, images on the scoreboard and the colored placards, the name of the sports complex, and official reverence during the ceremonies put the royal family at the center of the Games. Their personality cult portrayed them as the ones responsible for bringing Iran back to 'ancient glory' and parity with the West, whose superiority was nothing but a temporary aberration of history. The facilities and technology used were the most advanced, meant to illustrate that Iran had successfully turned into one of the most modern and developed countries in the world. The cultural elements included into the staging of Iranian state nationalism were also linked with former power, wealth, and national independence, reminding the audience of a time when the West had not been dominant. Elements which referenced times of defeat, such as the marathon, were simply forbidden.

Conclusion

"Asia should be one. But such a vast Asia becoming one is difficult."[1]

—Tajima Naoto, leader of the Japanese delegation to the Seventh Asian Games (Tehran 1974)

After following this tumultuous ride, through six decades of the strenuous lives and organizational activities of many leading sports officials and politicians serving in Asia between the 1910s and 1970s, it is time to come to a conclusion. It is appropriate, since a quotation by a Westerner (specifically an American) opened the introduction, to begin the conclusion with a quotation from an Asian—as so often in those days a Japanese taking the role of Asia's main representative—and to come back to the initial problem caused by the power asymmetry between Asia and the West. Pan-Asianism, after all—and Tajima's modification of Okakura Tenshin's famous 1903 assertion that "Asia is one"[2] was certainly deliberate—had been a means to encourage cooperation between Asian countries in their struggle against Western oppression by creating discourses of Asian commonality. Tajima agreed that sportive pan-Asianism was still a desirable goal, thus indirectly conceding that the power asymmetry vis-à-vis the West still existed. However, he also conceded that while Asia, as represented by the regional shape of the 1974 Games, had become 'vast' since it now also included the Arab and some communist ruled countries, it had hardly become 'one', despite all pan-Asian claims. The Middle East Conflict and the North-South Divide made this lack of unity obvious for Tajima, who added that he had prayed for a peaceful Asia when the white doves had been released during the opening ceremony.[3] The boycotts of Israeli athletes, in particular, had challenged amateur norms and values such as equality and non-discrimination and the ideals of internationalism and egalitarianism these were based upon. Simultaneously, Iran spent many petrodollars on Games intended to brand itself as a modern and developed emergent great power, even as many other participating countries experienced extreme economic problems following the 1973 Oil Crisis and, among other consequences, had even more difficulty encouraging sports within the population than before. The division of Asia thus was not only the result of violent conflicts such as the Yom Kippur War (1973), but also of economics, as revealed by Iran's large-scale nation-branding that to a large degree had replaced the initial aim of using the Games for encouraging mass citizenship training. Below, I therefore return once again to the most important continuities and discontinuities in three key areas: a) the organizers of the Games; b) nationalism and pan-Asianism; and c) modernization, development, and nation-branding.

The Organizers of the Games

In the beginning Elwood Brown created the Far Eastern Championship Games (FECG) and the Far Eastern Athletic Association (FEAA). As part of the 'Western civilizing mission', the American branch of the Young Men's Christian Association (YMCA) had set in motion a large-scale transfer to Asia of what it considered to be white American Protestant ideals manifest in amateur sport. These ideals corresponded to the Protestant concept of masculinity that had emerged during the Progressive Era. Moreover, they included a bio-political dimension targeted at regulating and optimizing public health, which matched the aims of American businessmen and philanthropists funding the American YMCA. Even more important was amateur sport's contribution to the YMCA's more general *democratization* aims, based on *mass education* in various forms. These democratization plans intensified during the First World War and the 1920s, encouraged by a *global circulation* of American and non-American YMCA personnel leaving the US or colonial settings to spread the Social Gospel at the European battlefields and later moving on to other regions. Simultaneously, non-American YMCA trainees moved to the US to study and after graduation returned home, while YMCA-trained local leaders represented their countries as experts or politicians on an international or transnational level. This circulation of personnel was accompanied by a circulation of knowledge in transforming societies, affecting various regions such as South America, Eastern Europe, and Western Asia, but also Western Europe and North America. These topics still need much further research.

In sports, a noteworthy share of YMCA knowledge that was later applied elsewhere in the service of democratization had been gained in East Asia. To promote the 'high modernist' plan of sportive citizenship training and social transformation at first in the Philippines, Brown, the American YMCA's physical director in Manila, needed to overcome the limitations he, as a civil society actor, had to face in the American colony. Brown thus forged ties with the colonial administration, particularly the Bureau of Education and the governor-general. As a result of such 'extension work' (advisory policy), he was able not only to set up a physical education program for the new public school system that incorporated those physical education activities the YMCA perceived as supporting its ideals, but also became responsible for the national championships at the Manila Carnival. The next step in promoting the spread of amateur sport in East Asia was the establishment of the FECG. These Games became a tool to bring the YMCA into contact with important Chinese politicians such as Wu Tingfang and President Yuan Shikai—Wang Zhengting and Zhang Boling (primarily an educator) were already close collaborators—and Japanese physical educators such as Japan Amateur Athletic Association (JAAA) president and International Olympic Committee (IOC) member Kanō Jigorō, as well as the leaders of the *Kansai* regional branch of the JAAA. Later, Elwood Brown's colleague Franklin Brown also came into contact with Kanō's successor, leading Japanese lawyer Kishi Seiichi, Upper House member Hiranuma Ryōzō, and Prince Chichibu. In the Philippines, the YMCA integrated several *Nacionalista Party* politicians such as Jaime de Veyra, Manuel Quezon, and Camilo Osías into their plans.

Due to the American YMCA's lack of financial power and personnel compared to governmental institutions, such contacts with Chinese and Japanese elites were deemed useful for reproducing what had been done in the Philippines (and was continued and facilitated with the backing of Filipino elites): to influence or establish physical education programs for *public school systems*, to gain *funding* for hosting events, and to pay for the *travel fares* to them if taking place abroad. Particularly in the Philippines and in China, it was also possible to recruit locals for training as physical educators in the United States at the International YMCA College in Springfield and other colleges. After these Asians had been sufficiently assimilated, they could support the Americans and eventually take over the 'civilizing mission' of 'uplifting' the Asian masses. Moreover, contacts with the IOC also served to make members of Asian elites such as Kanō, who had initially rejected the FECG but had been outmaneuvered with the assistance of *Kansai* region officials, more willing to collaborate with the American YMCA. Elwood and Franklin Brown's approach nevertheless encountered a problem. Important colleagues in China such as John Gray rejected their plans, claiming that the problematic situation in China—warlordism and the lack of a central authority since 1916—meant that centralized national physical education programs could not be established and influenced, making the hosting of the FECG relatively futile for realizing the American YMCA's goals.

In those cases where the American YMCA's networking was successful, it laid the foundations for a *dependence* of civil society actors on their contact partners—politicians and bureaucrats—that eventually destabilized the American YMCA's position. For example, in 1921, the tensions between Japan and China made Wang Zhengting, himself an important Chinese YMCA member, willing to engage in a boycott of the Japanese, which starkly contradicted the American YMCA's internationalist ideal. Elwood Brown's intervention to convince Wang (grudgingly) to cooperate indicated that he and Franklin Brown continued to believe that their Asian 'pupils' were not yet ready to bear the sportive 'civilizing mission' on their own. As a result, anti-colonial nationalism, which had strongly grown in the 1920s in Japan, China, and the Philippines, led to an Asiatization process of the Games that was characterized by Asians taking over the important positions in contest committees from Americans (though in the Philippines a nationalization of physical education through the introduction of the administrative office of national physical director of the Philippines and the Filipinization caused by the 1916 Jones Law and Camilo Osías' influence also mattered). Many of these Asians were YMCA members or in close contact with the YMCA, but indeed proved insufficiently assimilated (if one takes the point of view of the American YMCA) to continue cooperation on an equal basis. The basic problem was that the initial organizers, all of them Americans, could deal with each other on an essentially equal basis, while their status as sports experts and their international connections placed them at an advantage with regard to their Asian collaborators. These Asians, then, had to establish new power relations, which for some years were based on the ideal of egalitarianism. Nevertheless, when the founding of Manchukuo brought up the question of its inclusion and of how to interpret the situation in terms of egalitarian internationalism, no solution was found. The result was the breakdown of the FECG and the hosting, mostly in Japan, of some international games in the late 1930s and early 1940s.[4]

In India, too, the American YMCA had been heavily involved in organizing national sports events as well as Indian participation in the Olympic Games. After Indians had taken over from Americans, the problems of civil society actors, such as Guru Dutt Sondhi, who lacked experience and were active under a colonial administration that was not forthcoming with much funding or support, became obvious. In terms of organizational arrangements, the Western Asiatic Games (WAG) in 1934 therefore provided a counter-example to the FECG that originated in an American colony. Whereas the founders of the FECG worked directly with colonial officials, Sondhi's main contacts were Indian princes, such as the maharaja of Patiala, who had significantly less influence than the colonial administration of British-India. This is, to a certain degree, an answer to the question whether or not significant differences existed if one compares sport in the American and in the British empires.

With India's independence in 1947, the situation changed slightly. Though civil society actors such as Sondhi and Anthony de Mello were now successful in gaining political backing from the government, they were still left to their own devices in terms of funding. As a consequence, the First Asian Games (New Delhi 1951) were plagued by delays and mismanagement. In contrast, in the Philippines (Manila 1954) and in Japan (Tokyo 1958) many relatively experienced sports officials who had been involved in the FECG were now involved in organizing, meaning that fewer problems than in 1951 arose in 1954 and almost none emerged in 1958. Moreover, the latter two governments provided funding for hosting the events and for building infrastructure. Relations between civil society actors on the one hand and politicians and bureaucrats on the other hand were therefore close, but the events were not totally dominated by the latter. Serious tensions between AGF officials also did not erupt. Due to the growing number of countries that joined the Asian Games Federation (AGF), the number of officials rose as well, but experienced members such as Sondhi and those East Asians who had organized the FECG were the ones who initially took care of the business of the AGF. The most important issue had been how to interpret the 'two Chinas problem' in terms of egalitarian internationalism. Due to the cooperation between Jorge Vargas, Regino Ylanan, and Hao Gengsheng, who had known each other since the FECG, the participation of both the People's Republic of China and of the Republic of China was allowed, although this de facto meant that only Taiwan joined the AGF.

Following three events in comparatively democratic countries, the last four events covered in this book took place in three (semi-)authoritarian countries (Jakarta 1962, Bangkok 1966 and 1970, Tehran 1974). The involvement of senior politicians, such as Indonesia's President Sukarno and Minister of Sport Maladi, Thailand's Deputy Prime Minister Praphas Charusathien, Iran's Prince Gholam Reza Pahlavi, and many others, was representative of the complete governmental control over the events, which became part of large-scale social engineering schemes. Moreover, heads of state such as the aforementioned President Sukarno, but also King Bhumibol Adulyadej and Shah Mohammad Reza Pahlavi, were the focus of personality cults that were significantly more intense than the attention accorded the royal family in Japan. Moreover, strong tensions erupted on two occasions between AGF officials, each time due to the 'two Chinas problem'. The first time, Sondhi almost singlehandedly challenged the Indonesian organizers who barred member countries, driven by an interpretation of egalitarian internationalism that forbade discrimination against Taiwan and Israel, which enjoyed only partial international recognition. Due to his connections in the IOC, he was able to punish the Indonesians, since the IOC, following the sportive 'civilizing mission', banned them from the Olympic movement. However, the Indonesians then used their own contacts—Chinese officials—to found their own international sports event, the Games of the New Emerging Forces (GANEFO). The Iranians' more successful handling of the 'two Chinas problem' utilized cooperation primarily with the Japanese, by then the most influential AGF officials due to Japan's leading role in Asian sport, to bring China into the AGF. At the same time, the joining of many Arab countries in West Asia introduced a group of new officials who enjoyed comparatively great influence due to financial reasons, namely oil wealth.

It is quite useful to distinguish between professional sports experts and politicians when discussing the commonalities and differences between the various elites organizing the Games. For example, the immense influence that American YMCA physical directors initially wielded was the result of the professional education they had received in the US. Most members of the first generation of Asian sports experts rose to importance through the YMCA's or Young Women's Christian Association's (YWCA's) professional network, and especially due to being sent to the US to study. While their social backgrounds initially differed, they all experienced a lot of social mobility when becoming elites by taking over a newly created field of work. Even after decolonization, a physical education or related course of study at a North American or European university seems to have been necessary to reach the highest ranks. As a consequence, one can talk about the emergence and expansion of an epistemic community, meaning a professional network with authoritative and policy-relevant expertise. Things looked a bit different for politicians and civil servants who became involved in the Games. They very often shared an anti-colonial nationalism, pan-Asian ideas, and visions of large-scale social engineering with the sports experts. Both groups were also heavily involved in rallying people behind their nationalist agendas, especially during decolonization, when newly independent states were created or older states regained control over their affairs. However, a difference from the sports experts was the politicians' and civil servants' very heterogeneous social backgrounds. Some of them can be called traditional elites, belonging to the nobility or having close ties to it or the monarchy, such as in Japan, Thailand, Iran, and, to a certain degree, India (the young Sondhi) and Indonesia (Paku Alam VIII, Hamengku Buwono IX, and Maladi, who was a lesser noble). Others, constituting a new elite created by colonialism, had gained prominence primarily (but not necessarily exclusively) because of their involvement in anti-colonial movements or due to the Western education they had received. The Republic of China and the Philippines come to mind, but examples can be found in all the host countries. These commonalities and differences within and between elites had a strong impact on the different Asianisms and nationalisms they promoted through the Games.

Pan-Asianism and Nationalism

From the beginning, the upper- and middle-class organizers of the respective Games were in favor of using them to support a conception of Asia that was based on a *regionalist* pan-movement, meaning on egalitarianism between individual Asian nations.[5] After all, egalitarianism reduced fears of being dominated by officials from a single member country as a new form of colonialism. One exception was the role of American YMCA officials, who initially controlled the Asianist project. A second exception were the *hegemonic* power struggles that took place in 1934, 1962, and 1973/74, when the Games' organizers attempted to change the regional shape of the Games according to a new vision of Asia (by including Manchukuo, excluding Taiwan and Israel, or substituting Taiwan with China). Since the initial Christian ideals were appropriated and culturally integrated by the Asian organizers since the 1920s, the *universalist* dimension of the sportive Asianist project did not vanish. Instead, the universal claim of egalitarianism was utilized to support the conception of an *anti-colonial,* meaning anti-Western, regionalism.

While the egalitarian *conception* of Asia was thus relatively undebated, the respective *contents* of Asia and Asian nationalisms differed strongly between host countries. This was the most important outcome of the heterogeneous social backgrounds of the politicians and civil servants involved in organizing the Games. The egalitarian conception meant that the cultural elements (which defined the contents) were regularly arranged in an egalitarian way: a lot of them being grouped together communicated Asian 'unity in diversity'. In contrast, cultural elements that transcended the idea of the nation, since everybody could agree on them, were quite rare. Sometimes, they came from the West and thus were foreign to all Asians, corresponding to the egalitarian conception, but also revealing some of its problems. However, more important for the elites was the choice and staging of cultural elements that supported their own nation-building projects, which I will now connect to more general research on Asian nationalisms.

Anthony Reid, in his study on the dissolution of the European colonial empires in Southeast Asia in the mid-twentieth century, differentiates between four types of Northeast and Southeast Asian nationalisms: A first type is *ethnie nationalism,* which can be described as the political assertiveness of an ethnie, which as construed by Anthony Smith is defined by a set of common cultural elements (and does not need the concept of the state). A second type is *state nationalism,* which also existed in some parts of Asia before the arrival of colonialism and relies on state-promoted culture, religion, or a monarchy as institutions that shape a common mentality. During decolonization, *state nationalism* experienced a boom: supported by mass education, state ritual, media, and revolutionary rhetoric, it integrated people into newly independent states. The third type is *anti-imperialist nationalism* (I have mostly referred to it as *anti-colonial nationalism*), deemed by Reid to be the most important one, which I agree with. *Anti-colonial nationalism* emerged as a result of the power asymmetry between colonizers and colonized, united different ethnicities, and after decolonization was often incorporated into state nationalism. A fourth type is *outrage at state humiliation,* which again focuses on states. Otherwise describing the same phenomenon as *anti-colonial nationalism* (for which reason I integrated it into *anti-colonial nationalism* to avoid awkward formulations in the text, and will continue to do so), *outrage at state humiliation* concerns countries such as China, where an embryonic state already existed before and during semi-colonialism.[6] Considered according to this consideration, the Games, since their founding by the American YMCA, served as platforms to create or promote *state nationalisms.* The most obvious evidence was the decision to have national (meaning: nation-state) teams, sometimes consisting of members of different ethnicities, instead of individual athletes or some other unit compete against each other. Simultaneously, *anti-colonial nationalism* had a strong impact on the early events during the 1910s–1930s and supported anti-colonial conceptions of Asia. Following decolonization, it decreased somewhat in importance, but elites remobilized it several times in the form of *anti-neocolonial* rhetoric.

Initially, Elwood Brown had in mind the 'civilization' of interaction within the Philippines, which addressed the negative perception of Filipinos by many Westerners. Japanese and Chinese then became the next targets. In the view of the American YMCA, Asia therefore was *one*, but due to its common 'backwardness'. This view meant that the early FECG supported a certain form of Western-controlled and dominated sportive pan-Asianism that was not genuinely Asian but stemmed from the United States. In contrast, for example, to the 'Yellow Peril' discourse, another external Asianism, this more benevolent Asianism perceived East Asians not as a threat but as a group of children needing assistance to learn 'civilized' behavior and interaction. Moreover, this 'Asia is one in its backwardness' Asianism was based on American Protestant ideals and thus has to be seen as part of a larger plan to encourage Christian internationalism and Christian egalitarianism within the US and abroad.

Conversely, creating nationalism seems not (yet) to have been part of the plan. As a consequence, both American YMCA officials and Chinese President Yuan Shikai were impressed that the FECG brought together Chinese from the north and the south, despite the strong tensions between the regions due to the Chinese Revolution (1911), its violent aftermath, and older historical reasons. The Games thus also came to be seen as having contributed to state nationalisms and the creation of modern nation-states. After all, nationalism was a foundation of inter-*nationalism*, although the latter should in turn regulate (or 'civilize') relations between nations and between individual members of these nations. The final result would be an East Asian regionalism. One example of such internationalism was the participation of Japanese athletes from the *Kansai* region, who three times in the 1910s defied boycotts of the Games by the JAAA. The JAAA boycotters rejected the idea of Japan and China being equals and were affected by foreign policy issues such as the Twenty-One Demands (1915) and the Shandong Problem (1919). These boycotts, however, ceased after the IOC recognized the FECG in 1920 and the Washington Treaty System (1921/22) stabilized the status quo in East Asia and encouraged more egalitarian conceptions of the region. During the following two events many Chinese officials would have preferred a boycott of Japan due to unsolved problems concerning Shandong province (1921) and the Kwantung Leased Territory (1923). However, the American YMCA each time was able to circumvent the boycott and to enforce its ideal of Christian internationalism, although in the case of China, this backfired and anti-colonial nationalism eventually forced John Gray out of office.

After the American YMCA had lost most of its influence in all three countries during the 1920s as a result of growing anti-colonial nationalism, and with the temporary cooling of tensions between Japan and China, pan-Asianism promoted by Asians, rather than by paternalistic Americans, emerged. As a result of the Asiatization process at the official level, kinship not only of the athletes, but now also of the *officials* was described as a pan-Asian commonality. Moreover, 'Asia awakening' and 'Asia rising' became particularly important tropes that were connected to a universal anti-colonial claim for more egalitarianism. Another important topic was the Asiatization of the amateur sports ideals, which also created commonality between Asians. The ideals lost much of their Christian background while being integrated into local cultural systems such as Bushidō, Confucianism, and Philippine Catholicism, although these systems thereby moved *closer* to the American YMCA's Christian ideals. 'Olympism' was also used as a substitute for muscular Christianity due to its more secular international message. The American YMCA therefore did not bring about any large-scale conversion of Asians to Christianity.[7] However, it did spread norms and values that were (at least temporarily) accepted by Asian elites in all three countries and promoted a Protestant humanitarianism based on the Social Gospel. One can therefore argue, as IOC president Avery Brundage did, that the norms and values, and the ideals on which they were based, were universal (or had the potential to be so), though this was not due to them being (or being recognized as) universal Christian ones spread by white American Protestants in large parts of the world. Rather, they were universal since it was possible to integrate them into many local (here: Asian) cultural contexts, which were not necessarily Christian.[8]

The pan-Asian dimension of the FECG based on claims of common ideals and kinship was not genuinely challenged in 1934. However, the question of how to deal with Manchukuo, de facto existent since 1932, in terms of egalitarian internationalism resulted in two different Asianisms. The problem was even more basic than that of how to deal with the 'imperialism of free nations',[9] as Prasenjit Duara called the phenomenon of creating de facto dependent nation-states instead of more classical colonies. Even had Manchukuo been considered a colony of Japan rather than a 'free nation', its participation (like the Philippines' participation as an American colony) would have made sense in terms of egalitarian internationalism. The Chinese officials nevertheless rejected this view. They perceived Manchuria to be a part of China that the Japanese had violently conquered in violation of the ideal of egalitarian internationalism, and felt attacked by a hegemonic Asianism (backed not only by the Japanese, but also the Filipinos). A very important reason for the Chinese stance was the already mentioned massive growth of anti-colonial nationalism in China since the May Fourth Movement (1919) and the Kuomintang's relatively successful reunification of China due to the Northern Expedition (1926–28).

The nationalist and pan-Asian sentiment created by the WAG is difficult to judge since their public impact seems to have been very limited. However, claims of cultural communality between the participating countries and the India-centered trope of 'Asia as Greater India' were in evidence. Moreover, traces of muscular Christianity were absent, since a process of appropriation of amateur sports norms and values and of 'Olympism' similar to that in East Asia had taken place in India. The conception of Asia was thus anti-colonial and egalitarian, although a touch of Indian hegemonic ambitions was present.

After the Second World War, the Asian Games were founded in an atmosphere characterized by decolonization and a new wave of pan-Asianism. The Asian Relations Conference (New Delhi 1947), bringing together countries from all over the Asian continent, was of particular importance to the founding of the Games. During the discussions concerning the founding of the AGF, no distinction was made between East and West Asia (including India) as had previously been done, though when the Indians temporarily encountered problems in organizing the First Asian Games (New Delhi 1951), Filipino and Taiwanese officials deliberated about refounding the FECG or holding the First Asian Games in the Philippines. When the Games eventually did take place in India, they were perceived by Prime Minister Jawaharlal Nehru and many other Asian politicians and sports officials as a symbol of peaceful and egalitarian pan-Asianism. After all, Asia had recently experienced, and was still experiencing, many violent conflicts, among them the Second World War, the Chinese Civil War, the Korean War, wars for independence in Indonesia and Indochina, communist uprisings, and wars between India and Pakistan, and between Israel and the Arab countries. Simultaneously, the AGF created ceremonies that were largely modeled after those of the Olympic Games, but also developed a pan-Asian symbol transcending individual state nationalisms: the sun, representing Asia as the 'Continent of the Rising Sun', accompanied by a number of rings (reminiscent of the Olympic rings) corresponding to the number of AGF member countries. Some further pan-Asian elements were integrated into the ceremonies of the Games. In terms of the new Indian state nationalism, the Indian organizers promoted primarily the cultural elements of their young, secular, and democratic republic (instead, for example, of the ruling Congress party).

In the Philippines (Manila 1954) and Japan (Tokyo 1958) the pan-Asian rhetoric of the Games as a symbol of egalitarianism and peace continued. Even though the Japanese had made some unsuccessful attempts to bring China into the Games, contrasting with the Filipinos' more successful focus on pro-American countries, the eventual absence of communist-governed countries each time excluded these from the peace and egalitarianism discourse. Considering the Cold War tensions between the 'free world' and the 'communist bloc', the involvement of soldiers in the Games underlined this non-communist or anti-communist conception of Asia. In terms of state nationalisms, the Filipino organizers intended to underline the cultural diversity of their country and to upvalue pre-American cultural elements of different ethnicities. The Japanese seem to have primarily intended to show that Japan was again a 'country of culture' and thereby wanted to increase the prestige of the monarchy and create a contrast to negative wartime images. The Japanese also used a suspicious number of Olympic elements, which certainly had an internationalist appeal, but some of them completely lacked any Asian context, leading one to assume they were primarily intended to impress the IOC and bring the 1964 Olympic Games to Tokyo.

The Fourth Asian Games (Jakarta 1962) was the first event that was characterized by both strong anti-Western (anti-neocolonial) nationalism and pan-Asianism. The Indonesian organizers were unable to successfully change the regional shape of the Games to match that of the Bandung Conference (1955) and the Non-Aligned Movement. They failed, for example, to bring Arab countries, particularly Egypt, and communist ruled countries such as China into the Games. They nevertheless were able to bar Taiwan and Israel from participating, leading to the previously noted anti-hegemonic criticism by Sondhi. The Indonesian organizers responded with anti-Western pan-Asian discourses in order to gain support from other AGF members or at least to provide them a justification for being silent. The Indonesians' rejection of an egalitarian conception of Asia that included Taiwan and Israel—for them American puppets that had assisted the Central Intelligence Agency (CIA) in supporting rebels in an uprising against the central government—then led to the founding of the GANEFO as an anti-Western sports event, heavily supported by the Chinese. The Asian Games were nevertheless also meant to serve Indonesian nation-building. The government's state nationalism, appealing to traditional ideas of power, aimed at overcoming the tensions between the different islands and the many ethnicities. It featured various cultural elements that communicated the message of Indonesian unity in cultural diversity and of different ethnicities cooperating under the guidance of President Sukarno. Maladi's talk about shaping "patriots whose dedication of life is to serve their country and people", further illustrates this focus on Indonesian nation-building. Sondhi therefore also criticized the state nationalism at the event for being too strong, turning athletes into 'new-time gladiators' and undermining the internationalist ideal.

The following two events (Bangkok 1966 and 1970) held in Thailand, the United States' closest ally during the Vietnam War, did not see any anti-Western pan-Asian rhetoric at all. The message of peaceful and egalitarian Asian cooperation the Games communicated again excluded the absent communist-governed countries. This was a contrast to the First Games of the New Emerging Forces of Asia (GANEFOA), an offspring of the GANEFO that took place shortly before the 1966 Asian Games in Thailand's pro-Chinese neighbor Cambodia. Simultaneously, new technical means introduced by the Thais intensified the egalitarian message of Asian unity in diversity, though not transcending discrete nationalism. This included the launching of national flags, which glided down on parachutes, and the utilization of large groups of people holding colored placards that formed giant images of national elements specific to the participating countries. In terms of Thailand's state nationalism, the organizers of the Games, cooperating with the monarchists, used the two events to feature elements of Thai culture that were connected to Buddhist thought and the Buddhist monarchy.

The Seventh Asian Games (Tehran 1974) can primarily be seen as a means to further the Iranian government's ambition of forging an Asian Union of the littoral states of the Indian Ocean and of improving ties with China. The aim of this conception of Asia, which gave Iran a comparatively hegemonic role, was countering the influence of the USSR following the United Kingdom's withdrawal of its permanent troops east of Suez. To bring China into the Games the Iranian organizers mobilized a limited anti-Western (anti-neocolonial) pan-Asianism against the IOC and international sports federations. These organizations were accused of continuing to be dominated by Westerners still thinking in terms of pre-decolonization power relations vis-à-vis Asians. By delivering the AGF delegates such a pattern of argumentation (or justification for collaboration), a sufficient number of votes was garnered to bring China into the AGF and to expel Taiwan in the process. The IOC, the patron of the AGF, then decided, undoubtedly remembering the problems the GANEFO had caused it, to accept the de facto expulsion of Taiwan. The Seventh Asian Games were therefore not only a turning point by virtue of being the first event taking place in West Asia, giving this region more importance in the conception of Asia. The conception of Asia also broadened due to the joining of communist ruled countries and many Arab countries (while Australia and New Zealand, as on previous occasions, were not asked to join). The boycott of Israeli delegates mentioned above nevertheless illustrated the lack of supranational Asian unity, as did the following de facto exclusion of Israel from the Games since 1978. At the same time, the organizers close to the shah staged a state nationalism that featured primarily Iranian elements that were linked to the monarchy and to ancient Persian civilization.

Quite obviously, the respective elites' shaping of state nationalisms was not limited to promoting certain elements and institutions as constituting the nation. The state nationalisms, and to a certain degree the conceptions of Asia, also addressed the elites' modernization and development projects. They therefore also communicated the images elites had of their nations' and of Asia's past and future.

Modernization, Development, and Nation-Branding

The aim of the American YMCA in founding the FECG was to modernize Asian societies through large-scale social engineering based on its ideals of Christian internationalism, Christian egalitarianism, and a 'Protestant work ethic'—or, as a YMCA article on Elwood Brown's activities called it in 1919, the "[p]hysical evangelization of the many nations of the world."[10] The basic motive was a perception that Filipinos, Chinese, and Japanese all were backward, although the degree of backwardness differed. They therefore were considered to be in need of being 'uplifted' to the standard of white American Protestant civilization, rooted in the Enlightenment and Christianity. The hosting of the Games initially served visual communication purposes, as did world exhibitions in a time when television did not yet exist, access to the cinema was very limited, and newspapers and news magazines lacked a strong visual element (compounded by the problem of illiteracy). The many exhibitions of simple games and sports that characterized the daily entertainment programs at the Games were obvious illustrations of the intention to educate masses of spectators—men and women, adults and children—and to encourage them through 'contagion' to take up amateur sport. The challenges involved in hosting such large events were also the reasons for the biennial hosting of the Games, which had initially been conceived as annual events. This focus on educating rather than entertaining masses of spectators (though some interest obviously needed to be created through elite competition to draw people to the stadia) was further underlined by the American YMCA's attempts to establish or to influence physical education curricula in the public schools of the participating countries. This focus on mass sport is also the reason why Elwood Brown, for example, was extremely skeptical about professionalism, which he (and many physical educators before and after) perceived as undermining the three ideals that constituted the goal of mass-based sportive citizenship training.[11]

Some of the perceived 'civilizational deficits' of East Asian concepts of masculinity were laziness, habitual lying, corruption, lack of egalitarianism and ability to cooperate with others, neglect of the body in favor of intellectual studies, lack of discipline, fatalism, and violent behavior. In addition, promiscuity, gambling, cock-fighting, and boozing were sometimes considered as vices to be stopped through engaging in sport as a healthy, rational, and scientific form of recreation, giving the American aims a strong bio-political touch. As O. Garfield Jones had explained, sport was to support the Philippines' transition to a democratic and capitalist society by teaching individual self-control as the precondition for being able to accept defeats without reacting violently. Fair play was to reduce corruption and favoritism, while the ability to obey duly-constituted authority should prevent 'over-individualism' and dictatorship, the latter seen as the result if the masses only accepted force. Finally, sports competitions were to create communities of shared interest independent of ethnicity or social background (in India, one might add caste) and based instead on practical efficiency, thus discouraging the setting up of teams consisting of relatives and friends and serving to change 'semi-feudal' societies founded on family and clan ties into modern democratic ones. If repeated on an international level, the creation of nation-states could also be supported, but this was to be counterbalanced by the internationalist ideal.

In a bio-political sense, American YMCA members in China identified the lack of physical education and a resulting deficit in the fitness and physical prowess of the Chinese-educated class as an important reason for the 'great divergence', as one would say today, that had emerged between China and the West. The strong focus among members of the Chinese educated class on scholarly work and their looking down on physical education was seen as the reason why China had fallen prey to the militarily better-trained European great powers and their more productive citizens. Wang Zhengting, in particular, on several occasions made rather Social Darwinist statements about China regaining its strength. Female sports were therefore also put on the agenda, particularly by American and Asian YWCA members, even though male Japanese and Chinese officials seem to have been less willing than Filipinos such as Osías to include women's events in the Games.

Growing public attention, the YMCA's initial goal for spreading amateur sport, can be demonstrated by the numbers of tickets sold at the events and by the newspaper coverage of the Games. The American YMCA also produced several films about the Games, which were used for educational purposes in those parts of China that had not yet come into contact with the Games. Moreover, during the later events, radio broadcasting became important, although the percentage of the population that could receive broadcasts differed considerably between countries. Although the focus of this study is not on providing a detailed analysis of the content of newspaper articles and radio broadcasts, one can state confidently that the development of the communication infrastructure in East Asia was useful in promoting the Games. However, journalists did not only support the organizers' educational aims, but also encouraged commercialization.

The American colonial administration supported the YMCA's activities, as Chinese and Japanese politicians would later also do. Decreasing violence and increasing productivity among Filipino subjects quite obviously benefitted the colonial power. After all, the whole adventure of annexing the Philippines had been discursively explained as a 'civilizing mission', meaning that it was desirable to advertise visible changes to the American public at home (and, in the case of the YMCA, to its donors). Moreover, the office of national physical director of the Philippines was created relatively quickly, illustrating that the colonial administration and Filipino politicians such as Osías considered physical education and sport important and wanted to have more control over it. In combination with the Filipinization process started by the Jones Law (1916), this eventually led to a Filipino being awarded the office of national physical director and Filipinos generally acquiring more influence over the modernization process.

The American YMCA (and YWCA) members very likely expected that training Asians as physical educators in amateur sport and in the corresponding ideals at the International YMCA College and other places would lead Asians to understand and accept the 'civilizational hierarchy' and thus continue the 'civilizing mission' with or without their American teachers. Asian elites considering themselves 'civilized' would then 'civilize' the 'semi-civilized' Asian masses and, after this had been accomplished, keep them 'civilized'. However, as outlined above, anti-colonial nationalism caused the American YMCA to lose influence, while the contingency plan of controlling further developments through having convinced their former Asian pupils of the path they must proceed along became a complicated matter, to say the least. Among these complications were the fact that YMCA-trained Chinese physical educators ended up on both sides of the Taiwan Strait after the Chinese Civil War (showing that they very likely had different opinions regarding the modernization of China), while Candido Bartolome was accused of incompetence, to cite one clearly negative example.[12] The politicians and civil servants the YMCA had cooperated with were yet another case. Jorge Vargas, for example, was an important promoter of sport, but was also accused of corruption and ruling the Philippine Amateur Athletic Federation (PAAF) in the manner of an absolutist king. Sondhi, too, was an important promoter of sport, but demonstrated several times that he lacked organizational skills. In the case of the Japanese, it suffices to say that General Douglas MacArthur believed that amateur sports were useful, for which reason he encouraged post-war Japan to join the AGF.

The modernization aim of spreading amateur sport and the corresponding norms and values for the purpose of mass education continued through the First Asian Games (New Delhi 1951). The organizers considered such ideas a useful means to train modern Indian citizens, the forming of whom included egalitarianism (emancipation of women and the casteless), but also economic progress and peaceful internationalism. However, this educational dimension was quite ineffectively implemented at the Games. In the case of the Philippines, the purpose of the Games began to change. Amateur sports were already quite well-known in the archipelago, meaning that the most important purpose behind hosting the Games was to communicate the message of peaceful internationalism among non-communist ruled countries. Christopher Hill's argument that it would be more effective not to spend money on an international sports event but rather to use it to send students abroad nevertheless does not yet apply,[13] since the Filipino organizers still sought to keep costs low, as they had done in the past. Developing sports infrastructure had certainly always been a consideration and had served to show willingness to support sportive modernization, but had not ended in large-scale nation-branding through infrastructure construction programs (meaning that nation-branding had been of low importance, not that it was non-existent).[14] Similar things can be said regarding the entertainment programs. Since 1954 (there was none in 1951), these communicated through the inclusion of local dances, songs, and physical education practices that sportive modernization would not mean complete Westernization. Instead, suppressed Asian civilizations would reemerge and gain parity with Western civilization, whose superiority thus would only be a temporary phenomenon—an aberration of history, some of the organizers might say.

The Third Asian Games (Tokyo 1958) were the first event at which the aim of hosting a low-cost event, be it for making masses of people familiar with amateur sport (a task no longer really necessary in Japan) or for sending a message of peaceful internationalism (or for both purposes), was given up. The reason was the intention of the Japanese organizers to use the Games for large-scale nation-branding, for which they required a large sum of money, which happened to be available. Firstly, the Games were used to show Japan as a 'country of culture' and thereby to distance it from its wartime image as a 'cultureless country'. Secondly, the Games served to show a successful post-war modernization and development process that was to reinstate Japan as Asia's most modern and developed country. Thirdly, the intention to outdo the preceding Olympic Games (Melbourne 1956) was a means to attract the 1964 Olympic Games to Japan, which then became an even better platform for nation-branding. The Third Asian Games therefore marked the beginning of the Games not only serving to spread amateur sport and the corresponding ideals, but also to aid in nation-branding. Arguably, this meant that such Asian Games were inefficient in terms of mass education due to the high costs, as AGF officials such as Sondhi, who were interested only in that purpose, noted critically. However, in those countries where amateur sport was already well known, the Games' new nation-branding purpose, together with the elite competitions they featured, meant that they continued to serve a purpose even as they moved away from their educative function.

The Asian Games events that took place in (semi-)authoritarian countries heavily focused on nation-branding by showing rapid and seemingly successful large-scale modernization and development processes. In Indonesia, Thailand, and Iran, the 'high modernist' social engineering plans of the organizers each time focused on the example set by Japan and intended to outdo it, or at least to come close to it: each group of organizers aimed at a 'great leap forward' in terms of modernization and development. The promotion of mass sport and the changing of concepts of masculinity and femininity among the population was still a major bio-political and educative topic in the three countries, which reveals that Japan was seen as much more modern and developed in this regard. Together with very large infrastructure development programs, the promotion of mass sport contributed to legitimizing the governments by showing their efforts to improve the living conditions of the people and to change the power asymmetry vis-à-vis the West, Japan, and the rest of the world. However, like in earlier cases, it was *not only* about developing or modernizing the country, as a variety of people and companies, most of them connected to the political elite, had concrete financial and personal motives. They made a lot of money, apparently not always legally, through constructing venues or organizing the events.

The Indonesian organizers in 1962 placed heavy emphasis on a 'national regeneration' after the end of colonialism, including shaping physically more efficient patriots, and on turning Jakarta, through infrastructure development, into a 'beacon' that was to metaphorically stand at the center of the various Indonesian islands and even of the Non-Aligned Movement. Moreover, although the first Asian Games event to be shown on television had been the 1954 Manila Games, the Fourth Asian Games had a strong impact on the development of the Indonesian media infrastructure, marking the beginning of television in that country. Like in Japan, developing the tourism industry was also a concern, but was at that point less important than it would become in Thailand.

During the two events in Thailand (Bangkok 1966 and 1970), modernization and development, which in their various forms were the declared aim of the Sarit and Thanom regimes, included the spreading of amateur sports to shape more efficient people. However, city development was another part of the plan, as was developing the tourism industry, which by the mid-1960s could count on Americans, particularly soldiers as a result of the Vietnam War, and on Japanese tourists as a result of growing Japanese wealth due to rapid economic growth. Branding Thailand as a country of beautiful women and of good karma contributed to the support of tourism. Simultaneously, such branding also served to show that the authoritarian large-scale transformation process should be based on Thai-Buddhist norms and values and, at least to a certain degree, should not affect traditional gender relations, though this partially changed at the event in 1970.

The Seventh Asian Games (Tehran 1974) branded Iran as a country undergoing a successful modernization and development process that in the near future would elevate the country to the level of an important great power, as the Achaemenid Empire had been an equal to the ancient Grecian West. The person primarily responsible for this national rebirth, according to the personality cult that was on display, was the shah. Hundreds of millions of petrodollars were spent on sports infrastructure construction and on other elements of the staging, such as cultural and entertainment programs, as well as security. The Iranians, however, failed to achieve one of their main aims: they did not manage to bring the Olympic Games to Tehran. This would have made Iran the second Asian country to host the Olympics, following Japan, and would have been an even better platform than the Asian Games for nation-branding and for altering power relations with the West by being judged sufficiently modern and developed to host the Olympics.

Even though one can argue that the asymmetry in power between Iran and the West thus changed less than the Iranians had hoped for, the sportive 'civilizing mission' that had characterized the Games since 1913 at last found its end.[15] The IOC accepted the exclusion of Taiwan, as it would also accept the de facto exclusion of Israel from 1978 onwards, and no intervention such as that after the Fourth Asian Games in Indonesia took place. Whether this end to the 'civilizing mission', which in a broader sense also included the growing professionalism and commercialism that affected not only the Asian Games but also many other international games including the Olympics (though, obviously, not only due to the AGF's activities), was a positive outcome or not depends on one's point of view.[16] Elwood Brown (or Pierre de Coubertin) would not have found it so. However, many businessmen, professional athletes and accompanying 'professional' fans and spectators—the very masses Elwood Brown had once hoped to 'uplift'—approved of the new ethos.[17]

Notes

Acknowledgements

1. Hübner, "Making the Weak"; Hübner, "Uplifting"; Hübner, "Muscular Christianity".

Introduction

1. First line of Rudyard Kipling's poem 'The Ballard of East and West' (1889).
2. Avery Brundage, Adresse Presidentielle, pp. 5–6. In *Avery Brundage Collection, Box 113: Japan – Third Asian Games,* TOSC.
3. I will refrain from more explicitly defining the 'West' since within the six decades that are covered in this study the term had all sorts of meanings, covering persons, organizations, and countries. In contrast, the term 'Asia' is also largely a *construct,* but one with a widely agreed upon geographical base in the form of a continent, and as one of the main topics of the study it will be further analyzed in the respective contexts this study deals with. To improve readability, I will not put the terms into quotation marks.
4. On the 'Great Divergence', *see,* for example, Kenneth Pomeranz's seminal study *The Great Divergence* (2000).
5. From now on I will use 'American' as shorthand for 'US-American'.
6. *See,* for example, Elwood Brown, My dear Frank (21 Mar. 1922), p. 2. In *International Work in Japan.* Box 16: *Correspondence and Reports. Mar. 1922,* KFYMCAA.
7. For a discussion of the term, *see* Schröder, "Mission Impossible?". On the concept of the 'civilizing mission', *see* Gong, *The Standard*; Osterhammel, "The Great Work"; Pomeranz, "Empire & 'Civilizing' Missions". For case studies *see,* for example, Conklin, *A Mission*; Barth and Osterhammel, *Zivilisierungsmissionen*; Fischer-Tiné and Mann, *Colonialism as Civilizing Mission*; Watt and Mann, *Civilizing Missions.*
8. On the 'spiritual Asia', which initially was a Western construct, *see* the second chapter. Also *see,* for example, Fischer-Tiné and Stolte, "Imagining Asia in India", pp. 76–82.
9. *See,* for example, Adas, "Contested Hegemony"; Frey, *Dekolonisierung*; Manela, *The Wilsonian* Moment; Westad, *The Global Cold War.*
10. Decolonization is not a phenomenon limited solely to the period after the Second World War, since proto-decolonization took place in Asia already during the interwar period. Since the major part of this study covers the implications of proto-decolonization and decolonization on Asian countries in the realm of sport and sports events, it should be mentioned that decolonization here is roughly defined as a "multifaceted process of the dissolution of old, colonial, structures, institutions, and ideas, and the development of new ones over an extended period of time. It can best be described as a transformative process operating in almost all spheres of life and on all levels of society." *See* Dülffer and Frey, "Introduction", p. 2.
11. I will not provide a general definition of 'modern', 'modernization process', or 'modernity' (and, to improve readability, do not put the terms into quotation marks).

All three terms, despite having varying degrees of teleological meaning aimed at achieving a certain standard, can be used, for example, by liberal democrats, socialists, communists, or fascists, though each would obviously have a different standard in mind. The epistemological benefit of general definitions of these terms in individual cases is thus quite limited. However, in a rough sense 'modernization' focuses on social organization and on affecting it through social engineering and planning. *See* Unger, "Histories of Development", p. 9. 'Modern' and 'modernity' then are terms to describe accompanying aims and outcomes.

12. 'Development' is, to a large degree, a historical term and has the teleological connotation of a superior Western (or 'communist bloc') standard. The term is nevertheless less vague than 'modernization', since it primarily focuses, at least since the twentieth century, on building infrastructure. *See* Unger, "Histories of Development", 9. To improve readability, I do not put this term into quotation marks.
13. On modernization theory *see,* for example, Berger, *The Battle,* chapter 3; Knöbl, *Die Kontingenz,* pp. 23–60.
14. *See,* for example, Conrad, *Globalgeschichte,* pp. 130–5; Sachsenmaier, Riedel, and Eisenstadt, *Reflections*; Eisenstadt, "Multiple Modernities"; Cooper, *Colonialism,* chapter 5.
15. Adas, "Contested Hegemony", pp. 31–7.
16. On 'cultural hegemony' and missionaries, *see* Tyrrell, *Reforming the World,* p. 3. On sport and imperialism, *see* Guttmann, *Games and Empires,* especially chapter 9; Pope, "Imperialism". For a differentiation between 'civilizing mission' and 'cultural imperialism', and the latter concept's weaknesses, *see* Osterhammel, "The Great Work", pp. 375–6; Dunch, "Beyond Cultural Imperialism".
17. For the definition, see Guttmann and Thompson, *Japanese Sports,* pp. 3–4. Moreover, I use 'sports' when referring to the activities and organizations, while 'sport' means the general institution.
18. Roche, *Mega-Events,* p. 1. The term 'mega event' itself will nevertheless be used only rarely in this study because many other definitions (*see,* for example, Garcia, *The Olympic Games,* pp. 15–17) make it dependent on a certain size or a certain number of participants.
19. Anthony Reid differentiates between four types of Northeast and Southeast Asian nationalisms: Reid, *Imperial Alchemy,* pp. 5–11. Reid's types will be further discussed in the conclusion.
20. Frey and Spakowski, "Einleitung", p. 8. *See also* the other articles in this special issue of *Comparativ.* Moreover, *see* Frey and Spakowski, *Asianisms*; Saaler and Koschmann, *Pan-Asianism*; Matsuura, "Japan and Pan-Asianism"; Weber, T., *Embracing "Asia"*; Acharya, "Asia Is Not One"; Duara, "Asia Redux"; and the very recent Matthiessen, *Japanese Pan-Asianism. See also* the literature in the following footnotes.
21. Aydin, *The Politics*; Duara, *Sovereignty and Authenticity*; Fischer-Tiné and Stolte, "Imagining Asia in India"; Hotta, *Pan-Asianism*; Saaler and Szpilman, *Pan-Asianism,* particularly the introduction in vol. 1. On the Asian Relations Conference and the Bandung Conference, *see* Lee, *Making a World*; Tan and Acharya, *Bandung*

Revisited; Singh, "From Delhi to Bandung"; Jones, M., "A 'Segregated' Asia?"; Miyagi, *Bandon kaigi.*

22. I use a broad definition of elites and conceptualize them as "social groups who command certain resources in a given social entity. These can be political support, economic power, or symbolic resources such as communication or knowledge." *See* Dülffer and Frey, "Introduction", p. 2.
23. In this study a discourse or a *political discourse* occurs "when political actors, in and out of government, communicate about political matters, for political purposes". This therefore includes "every citizen who deliberates and creates messages about civic affairs". See Gastil, "Undemocratic Discourse", p. 469. This definition is necessary since not only government officials, but also civil society elites with political intentions need to be considered.
24. Woodberry, "The Missionary Roots", shows some correlations between the arrival of Protestant missionaries, mass education, and democratization.
25. Further topics that cannot be covered here in detail are fans, financial issues, and security issues. Such topics might in future be published in the form of articles.
26. According to Edward Said's classic study, "Orientalism can be discussed and analyzed as the corporate institution for dealing with the Orient – dealing with it by making statements about it, authorizing views of it, describing it, by teaching it, settling it, ruling over it: in short, Orientalism as a Western style for dominating, restructuring, and having authority over the Orient." *See* Said, *Orientalism*, p. 3.
27. Hübner, "Donors".
28. For an overview of liberal, fascist, and communist visions of a 'new man', *see* Mosse, *The Image of Man.*
29. On the ideal of internationalism, *see* Iriye, *Cultural Internationalism*; Iriye, *Global Community*; Sluga, *Internationalism.* On international sports organizations, *see* Keys, *Globalizing Sport.*
30. Güldenpfennig, *Olympische Spiele*, pp. 257–67; MacAloon, *This Great Symbol.*
31. Tyrrell, *Reforming the World. See also*, Thompson, *For God.*
32. Mott, *The Evangelization.*
33. *See* especially Elias, "An Essay"; Elias, "Introduction"; Dunning, "Sport in the Civilizing Process". According to them, in Britain, where modern sport originated, the limited power of the British monarchy and a basic *consensus* within the upper classes concerning parliamentary rule, thus some degree of egalitarianism, allowed non-violent power transfers between governments (since one did not have to fear being murdered by the new party in power) and debates between parties. In the same way, team sports served to provide the enjoyment of a mock battle and an outlet for physical energy while strongly reducing the possibility of serious injury. It should be mentioned that some of Elias's and Dunning's examples of the development of sports in Britain have attracted criticism, but this criticism (and Elias's and Dunning's examples) are not relevant to this study. For a revaluation of Elias's and Dunning's work, *see also* Maguire, *Global Sport*, chapters 2–3.
34. Christesen, *Sport and Democracy*, pp. 20–7.

35. Baker, "Religion", p. 219; Cavallo, *Muscles and Morals*, chapters 4–5. In this context, *see also* the fair play typology by: Ott, "Grundelemente", especially pp. 142–5.
36. Wachter, "Sport as Mirror", pp. 92–4.
37. On American bio-politics during the late nineteenth and early twentieth century, *see*, for example, Martschukat, "The Necessity".
38. Weber, for example, described Benjamin Franklin as a representative of an ethos which saw the accumulation of wealth through living a productive life as a religious duty. Weber also viewed the ruthless struggle for personal gain as a phenomenon that had often appeared during human history, but one that was deemed unacceptable in the context of modern capitalism, which he thus considered to be different: Weber, M., "Die protestantische Ethik und der Geist des Kapitalismus. 1", pp. 12–19. For the full argument, *see also* Weber, M., "Die protestantische Ethik und der Geist des Kapitalismus. 2".
39. Becker and Woessmann, "Was Weber Wrong?".
40. Weber, M., "Die protestantische Ethik und der Geist des Kapitalismus. 1", pp. 20–3.
41. Wachter, "Sport as Mirror", p. 94. This does not mean that there is no element of 'chance' at all in a competition, but rules limit it and athletes attempt to gain control over it.
42. Osterhammel, *Die Verwandlung*, p. 946; Baker and Phongpaichit, *A History*, p. 166.
43. Arjun Appadurai created a schematic of how Indian cricket was affected by colonialism (serving to 'civilize' Indian elites), decolonization (becoming strongly nationalized with a focus on winning and professionalism) and finally was internationalized (international games and 'trade' of cricket players between clubs): Appadurai, *Modernity at Large*, chapter 5. This schematic certainly serves an illustrative purpose, though it should be remembered that one has to distinguish between the aims of elites and popular reactions.
44. *See* Sven Saalers's typology of pan-movements and the conceptions of Asia suggested by Prasenjit Duara ('imperialist' vs. 'anti-imperialist Asia') and Amitav Acharya ('regionalist', 'nationalist', 'universalist' and 'imperialist', later joined by an 'exceptionalist Asia'): Saaler, "Pan-Asianismus", p. 134; Duara, "Asia Redux"; Acharya, "Asia Is Not One".
45. In terms of regional integration, the various Games can be seen as one pillar of organized and institutionalized cooperation in fields such as culture, economy, or politics. For an overview of regional integration, *see* Frey, "Concepts of Region", pp. 24–5. On regimes of territorialization and re-territorialization, *see* Middell and Naumann, "Global History".
46. The term 'staging' in this study refers to "an underlying outline and specific plan, devised by one or more individuals and evolving through the rehearsal process (as another, slightly different feedback loop). Moreover, the concept of 'staging' includes the result of this collaboration (i.e., the planned and intended performative process of bringing forth the materiality of a performance). *See* Fischer-Lichte, "Culture as Performance", p. 3. In contrast, the performance of the events, which is the interaction between all participants (including the spectators), will not be covered here. Such an

anthropological approach is certainly interesting, but would require at least another book to explore properly.

47. In 1961 the United Nations optimistically declared the 1960s the 'decade of development'. *See* Frey, "Entwicklungspolitik", p. 298.
48. *See*, for example, Jarvie, Hwang, and Brennan, *Sport*; Brownell, *Beijing's Games*; Cha, *Beyond*; Close, Askew, and Xu, *The Beijing Olympiad*; Manzenreiter, *Sport and Body Politics*; Manzenreiter and Horne, *Football goes East*; Prince and Dayan, *Owning the Olympics*; Xu, *Olympic Dreams*; Horne and Manzenreiter, *Japan, Korea and the 2002 World Cup*. Boria Majumdar and Nalin Mehta also wrote a book about the 2010 Commonwealth Games in New Delhi: Majumdar and Mehta, *Sellotape Legacy*. Simon Creak covered sport in Laos: Creak, *Embodied Nation*. The 2020 Summer Olympics in Tokyo might serve to sustain interest. Shorter literature overviews can also be found in the respective chapters of this book that cover seven Asian countries (China, India, Indonesia, Iran, Japan, the Philippines, and Thailand).
49. For short overviews, *see* Abe, I., "Historical Significance"; Antolihao, "20 shiji"; Ozawa, "Ajia no Orinpikku", pp. 182–5; Hong, "Prologue", which more or less only summarizes Morris, *Marrow*; Liu, *Der Weg*, pp. 30–9, which is based on a very limited number of sources; Lee, Ha, and Ok, "Extraterritorial Outlet", which is a weak study on Korea lacking an analysis. For a very good organizational history of the YMCA and its physical education activities in Japan, China, and the Philippines linked with the FECG, though not touching on the YMCA's Christian ideals, *see* Takashima, "Kyokutō". On the founder of the FECG, Elwood S. Brown, *see* Hübner, "Muscular Christianity", parts of which have been used for this study. On the aims of some of the early collaborators with the YMCA, *see* Hübner, "Making the Weak", parts of which have been used for this study. On the YMCA's (and sometimes others') physical education activities in China, occasionally touching on the FECG, *see* Kolatch, *Sports*, part 1; Lu and Hong, *Sport and Nationalism*, chapter 2; Morris, *Marrow*; Risedorph, *Reformers*, chapter 7; Wu, C., *The Influence*; Xu, *Olympic Dreams*, chapters 1–3. On the FECG and China, *see* Wang, Y., *Yuandong*; Dong, "Zhongguo", which was written by an IOC member from the Peoples' Republic of China. On Japan, the Eighth FECG, and Asianism *see* Date, "Kyokutō". For a very good study of sport during the Japanese Empire, touching on the FECG, *see* Takashima, *Teikoku Nihon*. On American physical education programs abroad, but also touching on the YMCA and the FECG, *see* Gems, *The Athletic Crusade*, chapters 2–4. This study is particularly good regarding the Philippines since it is based only on English-language sources. On the Philippines, sometimes touching on the FECG, *see* Bocobo-Olivar, *History*, chapters 5–8, a semi-academic study with lists of sources but without references; Ylanan and Ylanan, *The History*, chapters 4–8, a mix of an academic study and an autobiography; Gleeck, *American Institutions*, pp. 71–81. On the breakdown of the FECG in 1934, *see* Takashima, "Manshūkoku", being the most detailed study taking sources from all three countries into consideration; Ikei, "Tōyō"; He, "Dai-10kai Kyokutō"; He, "Dai-10kai Orinpikku"; Goodman, "Athletics as Politics"; Shinno and Yasuda, "Ōshima Kenkichi".

50. There is basically no literature on these Games except for a short overview In Majumdar and Mehta, *India*, pp. 153–5.
51. Majumdar and Mehta, *India*, chapter 7, is a good overview of the First Asian Games with a strong foreign policy focus on India. Hong, *Sport, Nationalism and Orientalism*, is an edited volume lacking articles on Japan and the Philippines and with several very poor contributions such as those from Sisodia, "India", and Karnjanakit and Samahito, "Thailand"; Lutan, "Indonesia", does not provide the necessary historical background on Indonesia in 1962; Lutan and Hong, "The Politicization", is better, though I do not agree with all the conclusions on Indonesia in 1962 and 1963; Amirtash, "Iran", is a very interesting article on Iran in 1974; Hong, "Communist China", and Hong, "China, the Asian Games", provide an overview of China and the Asian Games, which is primarily important for the time since 1974. Some further articles focus on the controversial Fourth Asian Games and Indonesian foreign policy issues: Sie, "Sports and Politics"; Sie, "The Problem"; Hanna, "The Politics"; Hübner, "The Fourth". Finally, Simri, "Israel", covers Israel until its de facto exclusion from the Asian Games in 1978.
52. *See*, for example, Cha, *Beyond*, pp. 32–6; Black and Westhuizen, "The Allure"; Darnell and Black, "Introduction". The general problem of these quite interesting approaches is, however, that often sport gets mixed up with sports events and the focus is only on relatively recent events, leaving out, for example, the 'civilizing mission' and the amateur ideal.
53. Scott, *Seeing Like*, especially chapter 3.
54. On this issue *see* Black, "Dreaming Big", p. 471.
55. Scott's study attracted some heavy criticism for relying on simplified case studies and having a narrow focus on extreme events caused by lack of knowledge of local conditions without acknowledging that even the possession of local knowledge is no guarantee for successful social improvement. *See*, for example, Cooper, *Colonialism*, pp. 140–2. The hosting of the various Games certainly did not lead to humanitarian disasters comparable to collectivization in Josef Stalin's USSR, so Scott's case studies and their criticism are not the point here.
56. Scott, *Seeing Like*, p. 97.
57. Ibid., pp. 88–9, 91.
58. Currently, the best overview on ethno-symbolism is Smith, A., *Ethno-Symbolism*.
59. A working definition for 'nation' is "a named and self-defining human community whose members cultivate shared memories, symbols, myths, traditions and values, inhabit and are attached to historic territories or 'homelands', create and disseminate a distinctive public culture, and observe shared customs and standardised laws". *See* Smith, A., *Ethno-Symbolism*, p. 29.
60. This is largely based on Gienow-Hecht, "Nation Branding".
61. Suzuki, "Ajia Taikai", p. 188; *III Asian Games. Official Programme*, pp. 12–13; Minutes of the Special Conference F.E.A.A., Apr. 9, 1934, Morning Session. In *H-FC03-EXORI/002*, TOSC.

62. The overview of the overall victors of the Games shows that initially the host country won each event, being able to enter the most athletes into the Games. From 1921 it nonetheless becomes obvious that the Chinese team experienced increased problems due to China's internal problems, while the Japanese team, rising to Olympic standards, since 1927 had become so strong that it won all Games. Finally, in 1934 it was decided to abolish the overall championship, adjusting the Far Eastern Championship Games to the Olympic system that rejected such a focus on nations over individual athletes. In the case of the Western Asiatic Games no overall champion was decided, but Indian athletes won most of the events.

Chapter 1

1. Meeting of the War Historical Bureau of the Young Men's Christian Association, p. 22. In *Armed Services: World War I. Box 23: Elwood Brown Interview. Athletics in the Far East. Early Work in France. 1920,* KFYMCAA.
2. For a general overview on sport (both traditional and modern) and Christianity, *see* Baker, "Religion"; Hoffman, *Good Game.* For further literature on muscular Christianity, *see* Collins and Parker, "Faith", especially pp. 205–9 (fn. 5, 9, 14, 30, 44), and the following footnotes here in this text.
3. Putney, *Muscular Christianity,* chapters 1–3 (and chapter 6 on women). On the Progressive Era, social reform, and its spreading to other countries, see Rodgers, *Atlantic Crossings.*
4. Putney, *Muscular Christianity,* chapter 2 (especially pp. 56–7, 70), and chapter 3 (especially pp. 92–4, 98).
5. *See,* for example, Baker, *Playing,* with focus on the YMCA in chapter 3; Higgs, *God,* with focus on the YMCA in chapter 10; Johnson, *The History;* Ladd and Mathisen, *Muscular Christianity,* especially chapters 1–3, with a strong focus on the YMCA in chapter 2; Latourette, *World Service;* Hopkins, *History,* chapter 10; Tournès, "La foundation", on changes in American philanthropy. The connection between Mott and the Rockefeller family needs further research.
6. British poet Rudyard Kipling published the poem of this title in early 1899 during the American debate concerning annexation in order to support the pro-imperialist faction.
7. Recently, several books have been published on the debate about war and annexation, and on the early American images of Filipinos: Halili, *Iconography;* Harris, *God's Arbiters;* Hoganson, *Fighting;* Kramer, *The Blood;* Preston, *Sword,* chapter 12.
8. Kramer, *The Blood,* especially pp. 191–9, 209–11, 308, 312–14.
9. Golay, *Face,* p. 157; Goodman, "The Problem", p. 173; Yu Jose, "Philippine", p. 49.
10. Chin, *Modernity,* pp. 26–30, 143, 147–9; Spence, *Chinas Weg,* pp. 347–8.
11. Karl, *Staging;* Dabringhaus, *Geschichte,* pp. 46–8; Spence, *Chinas Weg,* pp. 342–6, 351–3, 358–60; Manela, *The Wilsonian Moment,* chapters 5, 9.

12. Chin, *Modernity*, pp. 30–3; Ikura, "Japan". On the 'yellow peril' in the United States, *see also* the relevant parts in Mehnert, *Deutschland*; Iikura, *Ierō periru*; Spence, *Chinas Weg*, pp. 263–7.
13. Aydin, *The Politics*, chapter 4; Chin, *Modernity*, pp. 33–6, 63–70. On Japanese elites, *see* Matsusaka, *The Making*, p. 354; Yu Jose, *Japan Views*, pp. 22–3. On Japanese 'mimetic' colonialism, engaging in a 'civilizing mission' both at home and in its colonies, *see* Heé, *Imperiales Wissen*.
14. For a very short biographical article, *see* Buchanan, "Elwood S. Brown". For an overview of Brown's lifework as a 'civilizer' and civil society engineer including the time after he left the Philippines, *see* Hübner, "Muscular Christianity".
15. Elwood S. Brown, We have a little daughter (...). In *Biographical Records, Box 23: Brown, Elwood S. 1913–1924 (B)*, KFYMCAA; Memorandum Concerning Mr. Elwood Stanly [sic] Brown, Appointed to Become Physical Director at Manila; 1. Name: Brown, Elwood Stanley. Both in *Biographical Records, Box 23: Brown, Elwood Stanley. Biographical Data (C)*, KFYMCAA.
16. Before Brown left the United States, Robertson visited him in autumn 1909 and discussed with him the possibility of holding a sports contest between the 'Oriental' peoples. *See* Takashima, "Kyokutō", p. 475; Wu, C., *The Influence*, p. 130. As the following pages will show, this was not yet a decisive event, but the general idea certainly remained at the back of Brown's mind.
17. *See,* for example, Takashima, "Kyokutō", pp. 466–8; Beran, "Americans". On the YMCA's and others' later physical education activities in the Philippines, occasionally touching the FECG, *see* Bocobo-Olivar, *History*, chapters 5-8; Gleeck, *American Institutions*, pp. 71–81; Gems, *The Athletic Crusade*, chapter 4; Ylanan and Ylanan, *The History*, chapters 7–8. On basketball in the Philippines *see* Antolihao, *Playing.*
18. Meeting of the War Historical Bureau of the Young Men's Christian Association, pp. 2–5. In *Armed Services: World War I. Box 23: Elwood Brown Interview. Athletics in the Far East. Early Work in France. 1920*, KFYMCAA.
19. On certain success stories and 'Orientalist' topoi regularly featured in American YMCA publications and lantern slide presentations that addressed donors, *see* Hübner, "Donors". The private correspondence between YMCA officials is a more reliable source.
20. Brown, E., "Physical Work", pp. 258–9; Meeting of the War Historical Bureau of the Young Men's Christian Association, pp. 6–8. In *Armed Services: World War I. Box 23: Elwood Brown Interview. Athletics in the Far East. Early Work in France. 1920*, KFYMCAA; "The Work of the Physical Director." *The Outlook* 103, 14 (1913): 748. The given number was lower than the total number of school children due to illnesses, absences, etc. *See also* Crone, "Physical Training", pp. 984, 986–8.
21. Elwood Brown, Significance of Physical Education in South America Today, p. 3. In *Biographical Records, Box 23: Brown, Elwood S. 1913–24 (B)*, KFYMCAA.

22. Meeting of the War Historical Bureau of the Young Men's Christian Association, pp. 9–10. In *Armed Services: World War I. Box 23: Elwood Brown Interview. Athletics in the Far East. Early Work in France. 1920,* KFYMCAA; William Tutherly, The World at Play. A Program of Practical Athletics for the Millions, part I, chapters 1, 6. In *H-FC03-EXORI/003,* TOSC.
23. Elwood Brown, Annual Report for the Year Ending Sept. 30, 1917, pp. 10–11. In *Philippines. Box 5: Administrative Reports. 1917–19,* KFYMCAA.
24. The Carnival, an instrument of American colonial policy, provided a broad entertainment program and often took place together with industrial fairs and the annual meetings of societies, therefore drawing many people from the more remote areas to Manila, showing them the modernization and development efforts of the colonial administration. *See* Forbes, *The Philippine Islands,* p. 187; Takashima, "Kyokutō", pp. 476–7. On similar connections between expos and the early Olympic Games, *see* Roche, *Mega-Events,* pp. 87–94.
25. Meeting of the War Historical Bureau of the Young Men's Christian Association, p. 10. In *Armed Services: World War I. Box 23: Elwood Brown Interview. Athletics in the Far East. Early Work in France. 1920,* KFYMCAA.
26. Ibid., pp. 8 (quotation) and 10.
27. William Tutherly, The World at Play. A Program of Practical Athletics for the Millions, part I, chapter 1. In *H-FC03-EXORI/003,* TOSC.
28. Meeting of the War Historical Bureau of the Young Men's Christian Association, p. 11. In *Armed Services: World War I. Box 23: Elwood Brown Interview. Athletics in the Far East. Early Work in France. 1920,* KFYMCAA.
29. An early description of the mentioned anxiety, as well as IOC president Pierre de Coubertin's partial criticism of it (which included the positive role of sport as a 'civilizing instrument'), can be found in Coubertin, *Essais,* pp. 235–41. In the case of the US-colonial empire, the small number of colonial subjects compared to the huge population of the United States could hardly evoke such an anxiety.
30. Elwood Brown, Annual Report for the Year Ending Sept. 30, 1911, p. 9 [there are two pages numbered 9]. In *Philippines. Box 5: Administrative Reports. 1910–12,* KFYMCAA.
31. "Athletics in Asia." *The Outlook* 103, 14 (1913): 747–8, here: 747; Brown, E., "Physical Work", p. 262; Groves, My dear Mr. Mott (15 Feb. 1912). In *Philippines. Box 1: Correspondence and Reports. 1912,* KFYMCAA; Suzuki, "Kyokutō", p. 117.
32. Meeting of the War Historical Bureau of the Young Men's Christian Association, p. 12. In *Armed Services: World War I. Box 23: Elwood Brown Interview. Athletics in the Far East. Early Work in France. 1920,* KFYMCAA. On the preparations in China *see* Kolatch, *Sports,* pp. 53–5. On the YMCA's (and sometimes others') physical education activities in China, *see also* Gems, *The Athletic Crusade,* chapter 2 (due to the sources covering primarily the American perspective); Lu and Hong, *Sport and Nationalism,* chapter 2; Morris, *Marrow*; Risedorph, *Reformers,* chapter 7; Wu, C., *The Influence*;

Xu, *Olympic Dreams*, chapters 1–3. On the YMCA's educational activities in China more generally, *see* Garrett, *Social Reformers*; Keller, *Making Model Citizens*; Reilly, "Wu Yaozong", p. 268, fn. 8 (for a literary overview).

33. Meeting of the War Historical Bureau of the Young Men's Christian Association, p. 12. In *Armed Services: World War I. Box 23: Elwood Brown Interview. Athletics in the Far East. Early Work in France. 1920*, KFYMCAA. On physical education programs in schools, Kanō becoming an IOC member, and the founding of the JAAA, *see* Niehaus, *Leben*, pp. 29–61, 130–4. On the (limited) spreading of 'Olympism' and muscular Christianity (including its mixing with Bushidō), *see* Abe and Mangan, "Sportmanship"; Abe and Mangan, "The British Impact"; Abe, I., "Muscular Christianity"; Blackwood, "Bushidō"; Guttmann and Thompson, *Japanese Sports*, chapter 3; Kiku, "The Japanese"; Wada, "First Contact"; Gems, *The Athletic Crusade*, chapter 3 (due to the sources covering primarily the American perspective); Funaba and Ikeda, "Britain"; Ceuster, "Wholesome Education".
34. Suzuki, "Kyokutō", pp. 117–21. This text was directly or indirectly used as the source of most publications written by Japanese authors about Kanō and the Games (including Abe, I., "Historical Significance", pp. 69, 71–3; Imamura, *Nihon taiikushi*, pp. 504, 537–8; Kanō Sensei Denki Hensankai, *Kanō*, pp. 607–9). The reasons given for Kanō's lack of interest were: He and other IOC members thought that the designation 'Olympic' should be reserved for the Olympic Games; since Japan already participated in the Olympic Games, there would be no reason to set up another, only regional organization; feelings of superiority because of Japan's role in the Olympic movement, in contrast to (other) Asian countries like China and the Philippines; rules made by Americans; big financial difficulties; suspicions regarding the role of a Christian organization like the YMCA; the inclusion of team sports, like volleyball and basketball. The last point is particularly important and will be discussed later.
35. "Olympiad of Far East is Described." *Manila Times* (1 Oct. 1912): 8; William Tutherly, The World at Play. A Program of Practical Athletics for the Millions, part I, Exhibit 2. In *H-FC03-EXORI/003*, TOSC.
36. Brown, E. "Physical Work", p. 263.
37. William Tutherly, The World at Play. A Program of Practical Athletics for the Millions, part I, chapter 1 (quotation). In *H-FC03-EXORI/003*, TOSC.
38. Suzuki, "Kyokutō", p. 117.
39. "Far Eastern Olympiad." *Singapore Free Press and Mercantile Advertiser* (9 Oct. 1912): 12.
40. "Far Eastern Athletic Meeting." *Straits Times* (27 July 1914): 10. See also *Preliminary Announcement. Far Eastern Championship Games*, pp. 4–5.
41. *Preliminary Announcement. Far Eastern Championship Games*, p. 1.
42. On the Japanese delegations, *see* Suzuki, "Kyokutō", pp. 117–24. On Kanō's doubts, *see* Kanō, "Jūdō", pp. 404–5.
43. Brown, Jo., "Elwood S. Brown", pp. 249–50.

44. Meeting of the War Historical Bureau of the Young Men's Christian Association, p. 21 (quotations). In *Armed Services: World War I. Box 23: Elwood Brown Interview. Athletics in the Far East. Early Work in France. 1920,* KFYMCAA.
45. "The Prince a Spectator." *Philippines Free Press-Olympic Supplement* (24 May 1919): 36; Brown, F., *The Sixth Championship Games,* p. 2.
46. William Tutherly, The World at Play. A Program of Practical Athletics for the Millions, part I, chapter 3 (quotation) and Exhibit 1 (Constitution of the FEAA). In *H-FC03-EXORI/003,* TOSC. The underline is given in the original text. See also Meeting of the War Historical Bureau of the Young Men's Christian Association, p. 21. In *Armed Services: World War I. Box 23: Elwood Brown Interview. Athletics in the Far East. Early Work in France. 1920,* KFYMCAA.
47. Meeting of the War Historical Bureau of the Young Men's Christian Association, p. 14 (quotation). In *Armed Services: World War I. Box 23: Elwood Brown Interview. Athletics in the Far East. Early Work in France. 1920,* KFYMCAA. *See also* Annual Report of Franklin H. Brown for the Year Ending Sept. 30, 1915, p. 3. In *International Work in Japan. Box 4: Annual and Quarterly Reports. 1915. B-F,* KFYMCAA; Brown, E., "Far Eastern", p. 167; William Tutherly, The World at Play. A Program of Practical Athletics for the Millions, part I, chapters 1, 3, 9. In *H-FC03-EXORI/003,* TOSC. The Second FECG were at first planned to take place in Shanghai in Oct. 1914. *See* Tener, Dear Colton (15 May 1914). In *Philippines. Box 1: Correspondence and Reports. 1914,* KFYMCAA.
48. Meeting of the War Historical Bureau of the Young Men's Christian Association, pp. 14–17. In *Armed Services: World War I. Box 23: Elwood Brown Interview. Athletics in the Far East. Early Work in France. 1920,* KFYMCAA. *See also* Crone, "Physical Training", p. 987.
49. The quotation can be found in both: Elwood Brown, "Teaching the World to Play." *The Outlook* 129, 17 (1921): 689–93, here: 690; William Tutherly, The World at Play. A Program of Practical Athletics for the Millions, part I, chapter 3. In *H-FC03-EXORI/003,* TOSC.
50. Gems, *The Athletic Crusade,* pp. 38–9.
51. On the Open International Games held in 1915, *see Preliminary Announcement. Far Eastern Championship Games,* pp. 10, 12, 16–17.
52. William Tutherly, The World at Play. A Program of Practical Athletics for the Millions, part I, chapters 3 (quotation), 7. In *H-FC03-EXORI/003,* TOSC. *See also* Suzuki, "Kyokutō", p. 117.
53. Franklin Brown, My dear Count Baillet Latour (12 Aug. 1926), p. 1 (quotation). In *H-FC03-EXORI/001,* TOSC. *See also* Coubertin, *Olympism,* pp. 703–4. On Coubertin's plans since 1912 to host the African Games *see* Liu, *Der Weg,* pp. 23–30.
54. Crone, "Physical Training", pp. 985–6 (quotation: 985).
55. On the article *see* Coubertin, *Olympism,* pp. 695–7. On the IOC meeting in 1920, *see* Procès-verbaux des séances du Comité International Olympique à Anvers (Hôtel de Ville), Août 1920, pp. 8–9, and Du Lundi 23 Août 1920 (procès-verbal

dactylographié, 3 pages), pp. 1–2. Both in *Comité International Olympique—Session 1894–2008*, TOSC.

56. Elwood Brown, To: E. C. Jenkins (17 Jan. 1920), p. 3. In *Biographical Records, Box 23: Brown, Elwood S. 1913–24 (B)*, KFYMCAA. On Brown, the YMCA, and these regional games *see* Hübner, "Muscular Christianity". Africa was not included since IOC president Coubertin already planned since 1912 to host African Games: Liu, *Der Weg*, pp. 23–30.
57. Fisher, "Editorial Comment", p. 803. For more specific information on the different types of defects and on rejection rates, *see* Davenport and Love, "Defects".
58. William Tutherly, The World at Play. A Program of Practical Athletics for the Millions, part I, chapters 7, 9. In *H-FC03-EXORI/003*, TOSC.
59. Crone, "Physical Training", pp. 988–9.
60. Elwood Brown, Annual Report for the Year Ending Sept. 30, 1915, p. 9. In *Philippines. Box 1: Correspondence and Reports. 1915*, KFYMCAA.
61. Elwood Brown, Teaching the World to Play, p. 9 (both quotations). In *Biographical Records, Box 23: Brown, Elwood S. 1913–24 (B)*, KFYMCAA. That document is a draft. For the published article with minor changes, *see* Elwood Brown, "Teaching the World to Play." *The Outlook* 129, 17 (1921): 689–93, here: 692.
62. Elwood Brown, To: E. C. Jenkins (17 Jan. 1920), p. 2. In *Biographical Records, Box 23: Brown, Elwood S. 1913–1924 (B)*, KFYMCAA. *See also* J. M. Groves, Annual Report, Oct. 1, 1910–Sept. 30, 1911, p. 6. In *Philippines. Box 5: Administrative Reports. 1910–12*, KFYMCAA. On health and American colonialism in the Philippines, *see* Anderson, Warw., *Colonial Pathologies.*
63. Elwood Brown, Annual Report for the Year Ending Sept. 30, 1911, p. 7 (quotation). In *Philippines. Box 5: Administrative Reports. 1910–1912*, KFYMCAA; The Vargas-Saulo Interviews. A Series of Fourteen Tape-Recorded Interviews with MR. JORGE B. VARGAS and son EDDIE, from 19 April to May 24, 1977. Conducted, transcribed and edited by Alfredo B. Saulo, p. 139. In *The Vargas-Saulo Interviews*, JBVM. *See also* Brent's letter to Coubertin: Brent, Dear Sir (30 Sept. 1914). In *D.RM01.PHILI/012*, TOSC. *See also* Crone, "Physical Training", p. 989. In Japan, YMCA general secretary J. M. Davis said that sport would keep people away from visiting prostitutes and drinking: Annual Report Letter of J. M. Davis (...) for the Year Ending Sept. 30, 1919, p. 3. In *International Work in Japan. Box 6: Annual and Quarterly Reports. 1919 A-D*, KFYMCAA.
64. "First Far Eastern Olympic Is Officially Opened by Governor." *Cablenews American* (1 Feb. 1913): 1. For the closing speech, *see* "P. I. Victors in First Orient Olympiad." *Manila Times* (10 Feb. 1913): 9. To interpret the words Forbes used is problematic, since we do not know exactly what he said. For a slightly different wording of the opening remarks, *see* "Governor General Opens Olympiad." *Manila Times* (1 Feb. 1913): 5. On his letter to Sloane, *see* Forbes, Dear Sir (27 Feb. 1913). In *fMS Am 1366, Vol. 16*, HHL.
65. Jones, O., *The Unhappy*; "Says Taft Is Partisan." *New York Times* (30 Nov. 1915; Special to the *New York Times*): 1.

66. On his dissertation, *see* http://dpg.lib.berkeley.edu/webdb/seasia/search?degree=&page=3&itemno= [accessed: 22 May 2012]. On his later career, *see* https://www.utfoundation.org/foundation/home/pdfs/endowmentreport2009.pdf (p. 4) [accessed: 20 Feb. 2015].
67. Jones, O., "Athletics", p. 592.
68. Ibid., p. 586. One can assume that Jones had begun to show interest in the new president's (and former history and political science professor's) views or had learned about them during his own studies. On Wilson's views, *see* Wilson, "Character", especially p. 582.
69. Ibid., p. 588.
70. Ross, *Francisco I. Madero*, pp. 328–9.
71. Jones, O., "Athletics", pp. 588–9 (quotation: 589). The quotation, which Jones also used and discussed, was from a certain Professor Macy (certainly historian Jesse Macy). Jones' interpretation of the English Civil War can thus be described as relatively typical for the nineteenth and early twentieth century.
72. Ibid., pp. 589–90.
73. Ibid., p. 590.
74. Ibid.
75. Ibid., p. 586.
76. Ibid., pp. 586, 590–1 (quotation: 590). *See also* Wilson, "Character", p. 582.
77. Jones, O., "Athletics", p. 591.
78. For a more detailed analysis of newspaper cartoons on the FECG, *see* Hübner, "Images".
79. William Tutherly, The World at Play. A Program of Practical Athletics for the Millions, Exhibit 2. In *H-FC03-EXORI/003*, TOSC.
80. Wu, T., *America*, pp. 24, 90 (quotation).
81. Ibid., 90.
82. Ibid.
83. Ibid.
84. Elwood Brown, To: E. C. Jenkins (17 Jan. 1920), p. 3 (quotations). In *Biographical Records, Box 23: Brown, Elwood S. 1913–24 (B)*, KFYMCAA. *See also* William Tutherly, The World at Play. A Program of Practical Athletics for the Millions, part I, chapter 3. In *H-FC03-EXORI/003*, TOSC; "Eastern Champions." *Association Men* 40, 8 (1915): 414–15.
85. For a short analysis, *see* Pomerantz-Zhang, *Wu Tingfang*, pp. 126–8.
86. Wang, C., *Ō Seitei*, pp. 4–5, 18.
87. Ibid., pp. 18–19.
88. Wang, Z., "Guan di 2 ci", pp. 11–14.
89. Mao in 1917, during the height of the First World War, perceived modern physical education as valuable and rejected the traditional Chinese focus on developing only the mind. Mastery of both the mind and of the body would be possible, since Confucius, Jesus, Buddha Shakyamuni, and Mohammed all would have done so. Basically, it was a means to build up Chinese military strength, as Germany had

evidently done so successfully via fencing (Mao did not mention gymnastics) and Japan via Bushidō based martial arts: Mao, "A Study".

90. On further support from Chinese politicians, *see* Elwood Brown, Annual Report for the Year Ending Sept. 30, 1915, p. 7. In *Philippines. Box 1: Correspondence and Reports. 1915*, KFYMCAA. *See also* Luo, *Aoyun*, pp. 91–3; Morris, *Marrow*, pp. 25–6; "A Happy Union—Athletics Unite North and South China." *Philippines Free Press* (24 May 1919): 23 (Olympic Special).
91. "More Athletes Arrived Yesterday." *Cablenews American* (1 Feb. 1913): 5; "Olympic Trophies Were Awarded by G.G." *Manila Times* (17 May 1919): 5; "The Man Who Headed China's Big Delegation of Athletes." *Philippines Free Press* (24 May 1919): 20 (Olympic Special); Morris, *Marrow*, pp. 68–9, 77–8, 252, fn. 15; William Tutherly, The World at Play. A Program of Practical Athletics for the Millions, Exhibit 2. In *H-FC03-EXORI/003*, TOSC; "Chinese Come for Olympiad." *Manila Times* (30 Jan. 1913): 1.
92. Macario Bernardo, General Paper no. 97. The Far Eastern Olympic Games as a Social Factor in the Orient. Manila 1915, pp. 3 (first quotation) and 4 (second quotation). In *BEY26/4 Philippine Ethnography General Paper no. 97 2/5*, NLotP. Bernardo had received his B.A. at the University of the Philippines in 1915 and went on to study law as a graduate student: The University of the Philippines, *Catalogue*, pp. 360, 408.
93. The Vargas-Saulo Interviews. A Series of Fourteen Tape-Recorded Interviews with MR. JORGE B. VARGAS and son EDDIE, from April 19 to May 24, 1977. Conducted, transcribed and edited by Alfredo B. Saulo, p. 138. In *The Vargas-Saulo Interviews*, JBVM.
94. Quezon served as president of the PAAF between 1917 and 1935, when he became president of the Philippine Commonwealth. He also served as president of the FEAA between 1917–19, 1923–25, and 1930–34, but very often asked other Filipino politicians to act on his behalf. *See* Brown, F., *Official Report of the Ninth*, pp. 5–6; Saulo, *Let George*, pp. 225–6; Ylanan, *Philippine Amateur*, pp. 14–18.
95. Bananal, *Camilo Osias*, pp. 12–14; Ylanan, *Philippine Amateur*, pp. 16–18; "Olympic Team Leaves Manila on Shanghai Trip Last Night." *Manila Daily Bulletin* (20 May 1921): 3; Brown, F., "The Sixth Far Eastern", p. 376; *Philippine Amateur Athletic Federation. Annual Report of the Secretary Treasurer*, p. 5; *Far Eastern Athletic Association. Official Program*, p. 9.
96. Ylanan and Ylanan, *The History*, pp. 39–41; England, *Far Eastern*, p. 19.
97. "Olympic Team Leaves Manila on Shanghai Trip Last Night." *Manila Daily Bulletin* (20 May 1921): 3; Ylanan and Ylanan, *The History*, pp. 39–41; Brown, F., *The Sixth*, pp. xv and 29.
98. The Governor-General awarded the prizes and gave speeches. *See*, for example, "Yeater Awards Olympic Prizes." *Manila Daily Bulletin* (19 May 1919): 3; *Tenth Far Eastern Championship Games. Rizal Memorial Field*, pp. 4–7.
99. Bushidō was partially 'reinvented' and made popular in the West by Christian internationalist Nitobe Inazō to challenge claims of Japanese cultural inferiority by explaining that Japan possessed an ethic equivalent to Western medieval chivalry.

See, especially Nitobe, *Bushido*. In terms of sports (especially baseball), Japanese Christian socialist Abe Isoo and others used Bushidō as a substitute for the Christian interpretation of sportsmanship to give the idea more authenticity and to justify its spreading in Japan. *See* Blackwood, "Bushidō", pp. 228–31; Benesch, *Inventing*, pp. 164–7. Kanō's interpretation nevertheless was not identical with Nitobe's and Abe's, since the origin (martial arts practices) was different and his focus initially less on internationalism. On Bushidō and muscular Christianity, *see also* Abe, I., "Muscular Christianity", pp. 30–2. On Kanō, *see also* Niehaus, *Leben*, pp. 145–64, 198–205. More generally on martial arts in Meiji Japan, *see* Gainty, *Martial Arts*.

100. Meeting of the War Historical Bureau of the Young Men's Christian Association, pp. 18–19 (quotation: p. 18). In *Armed Services: World War I. Box 23: Elwood Brown Interview. Athletics in the Far East. Early Work in France. 1920*, KFYMCAA. For further negative remarks by Brown concerning Japanese martial arts in contrast to 'civilized' sports, *see* Gems, *The Athletic Crusade*, p. 38. *See also* Kanō, "Jūdō", pp. 405, 407–8. Kanō wrote this text in 1917 after the Third FECG, but since a slight aversion against team sports can still be found in it, the same had to be even truer for the time before 1917.
101. Niehaus, *Leben*, pp. 130–2, 135; Noguchi, "Sports", p. 449. Kanō did not attend any pre-First World War IOC meetings except for the one in 1912. See the respective protocols in *Comité International Olympique—Session 1894–2008*, TOSC.
102. Annual Report of Franklin H. Brown for the Year Ending Sept. 30, 1915, pp. 4–5. In *International Work in Japan. Box 4: Annual and Quarterly Reports. 1915. S-V.* [sic], KFYMCAA; Norudō, *Gendai*; Nordau, *Entartung*.
103. Meeting of the War Historical Bureau of the Young Men's Christian Association, pp. 18–19. In *Armed Services: World War I. Box 23: Elwood Brown Interview. Athletics in the Far East. Early Work in France. 1920*, KFYMCAA; Elwood Brown, Annual Report for the Year Ending Sept. 30, 1915, p. 8. In *Philippines. Box 1: Correspondence and Reports. 1915*, KFYMCAA (here Brown names JAAA members Takeda Chiyosaburō and Kishi Seiichi as strong supporters of Western sport); Elwood S. Brown, Annual Report for the Year Ending Sept. 30, 1917, p. 7. In *Philippines. Box 5: Administrative Reports. 1917–19*, KFYMCAA; Elwood Brown, "Teaching the World to Play." *The Outlook* 129, 17 (1921): 689–93, here: 692; William Tutherly, The World at Play. A Program of Practical Athletics for the Millions, part I, chapters 3, 8. In *H-FC03-EXORI/003*, TOSC. On the negotiations between Kanō and the Browns on the disciplines, *see* Suzuki, "Kyokutō", pp. 121–2.
104. Elwood Brown, My dear Frank (22 Mar. 1922) (quotation). In *International Work in Japan: Box 16: Correspondence and Reports. April–June 1922* [sic], KFYMCAA. *See also* Franklin Brown, Some Recollections (continued) (11 Feb. 1953), p. 4. In *Biographical Records. Box 23: Brown, Franklin H. 1932–73 (B)*, KFYMCAA.
105. Meeting of the War Historical Bureau of the Young Men's Christian Association, p. 19. In *Armed Services: World War I. Box 23: Elwood Brown Interview. Athletics in the Far East. Early Work in France. 1920*, KFYMCAA; Elwood S. Brown, Annual Report for the Year Ending Sept. 30, 1917, p. 7. In *Philippines.*

Box 5: Administrative Reports. 1917–1919, KFYMCAA; Franklin Brown, Some Recollections (continued) (11 Feb. 1953), p. 4. In *Biographical Records. Box 23: Brown, Franklin H. 1932–73 (B),* KFYMCAA. Kanō, "Jūdō", is a wonderful illustration of the appropriation process and of Kanō trying to bring modern competitive sport and Bushidō-based judo together. On Kanō's change of mind, *see also* Niehaus, "Crossing Borders", especially pp. 27–9. The impact of the Third FECG in 1917, the preparations for them since 1915, and the recognition of the FEAA by the IOC in 1920 nonetheless are not covered there. On the sportification of judo, *see* Sato, "The Sportification".

106. Elwood Brown, Dear Sir (16 Sept. 1916). In *YOUNG MEN'S CHRIS[T]IAN ASSOCIATIONS. 1909–27,* TOSC.
107. Elwood Brown, Annual Report for the Year Ending Sept. 30, 1917, p. 7. In *Philippines, Box 5: Administrative Reports. 1917–19,* KFYMCAA. On Franklin Brown's initial problems *see* Annual Report of Franklin H. Brown for the Year Ending Sept. 30, 1916, p. 10. In *International Work in Japan, Box 5: Annual and Quarterly Reports. 1916. A-F,* KFYMCAA.
108. Franklin Brown, Dear Count Latour [sic] (18 Dec. 1930), pp. 2–4. In *H-FC03-EXORI/001,* TOSC.
109. Brent, *The Splendor.*
110. Elwood Brown, Annual Report for the Year Ending Sept. 30, 1917, pp. 7–8 (quotation: 8). In *Philippines. Box 5: Administrative Reports. 1917–19,* KFYMCAA. See also: Annual Report of Franklin H. Brown for the Year Ending Sept. 30, 1916, pp. 10–11. In *International Work in Japan. Box 5: Annual and Quarterly Reports. 1916. A-F,* KFYMCAA; Homer J. Grafton, Annual Report for the Year 1916–17, p. 5, and Annual Report of W. S. Ryan, Jan. 20, 1917 to Sept. 30, 1917, p. 4. Both in *International Work in Japan. Box 5: Annual and Quarterly Reports. 1917. 2.: G-W,* KFYMCAA; William Tutherly, The World at Play. A Program of Practical Athletics for the Millions, part I, chapter 7. In *H-FC03-EXORI/003,* TOSC.
111. "An Ambassador of Trade and Athletics." *Philippines Free Press* (24 May 1919): 22 (Olympic Special); Suzuki, "Kyokutō", pp. 122–3; Nihon Seinen Kurabu, *Dai-4kai,* pp. 1–2 (here it says that newspapers from the *Kansai* region supported the team).
112. Brown, E., "Far Eastern", p. 165 (here Brown says that the number of children was close to one thousand); "First Far Eastern Olympiad Is Officially Opened by Governor." *Cablenews American* (1 Feb. 1913): 1.
113. On this idea of sportive nation-building, *see* Hobsbawm, *Nations,* p. 143.
114. L. C. Wilson, Annual Report for the Year Ending Sept. 30, 1917, p. 3. In *International Work in Japan. Box 5: Annual and Quarterly Reports. 1917. 2.: G-W.,* KFYMCAA; The Contest Committee of the Far Eastern Athletic Association, *Report,* pp. 49–52.
115. Takashima Kō brought up this topic. I found no sources mentioning competitions on a Sunday.
116. On the First FECG, *see* "More Athletes Arrived Yesterday." *Cablenews American* (1 Feb. 1913): 5. *See also* Morris, "Native Songs"; Chen, Liang, and Du, *Zhongguo,* p. 30; Dong, "Zhongguo", p. 85.

117. Kolatch, *Sports*, p. 56; Morris, *Marrow*, p. 29; Hoh [Hao], *Physical Education*, pp. 110–11; John Crocker, National Physical Director Young Men's Christian Association, China, Annual Report for the Year Ending Sept. 30, 1915, p. 1. In *International Work in China. Box 5: Annual and Quarterly Reports (C). 1915*, KFYMCAA; Elwood Brown, "The Far Eastern Championship Games." *Foreign Mail* 22, 5 (1915): 14–19, here: 15; *Preliminary Announcement. Far Eastern Championship Games*, pp. 13–15, 18 (map of the Recreation Ground).
118. Morris, *Marrow*, p. 29.
119. Jansen, *The Making*, pp. 500–1.
120. Brown, F., *The Sixth*, p. xii (quotation). *See also* Suzuki, "Kyokutō", pp. 121–2; Franklin Brown, Annual Report for Year Ending Sept. 30, 1917, pp. 10–11. In *International Work in Japan. Box 5: Annual and Quarterly Reports. 1917. 1.: A-F*, KFYMCAA; Brown, F., "The Third", pp. 387–8; F. E. Wilber, "The Far Eastern Championship Games." *Foreign Mail* 24, 4 (1917): 19–22, here: 21.
121. Gilbert, Ext. from cable (22548–8) (25 Nov. 1912). In *Record Group 350: Records of the Bureau of Insular Affairs, 1868–1945. Series: General Classified Files, 1898–1913. Box 947: #26063*, NARAII.
122. *Preliminary Announcement. Far Eastern Championship Games*, p. 7; William Tutherly, The World at Play. A Program of Practical Athletics for the Millions, part I, chapter 5. In *H-FC03-EXORI/003*, TOSC; "Aguinaldo Cup." *Philippines Herald* (12 May 1934): 25 (F. E. Games Supplement).
123. Meeting of the War Historical Bureau of the Young Men's Christian Association, p. 17. In *Armed Services: World War I. Box 23: Elwood Brown Interview. Athletics in the Far East. Early Work in France. 1920*, KFYMCAA.
124. On the Second National Meeting at the Temple of Heaven in May 1914, *see* Hoh [Hao], *Physical Education*, p. 95; Kolatch, *Sports*, p. 13. On Yuan Shikai, *see* Spence, *Chinas Weg*, p. 351.
125. Sloane, Dear Pierre (8 June 1915). In *PT-PDC-CORR. Sloane à Coubertin 1897–1924*, TOSC; Brown, F., *The Sixth*, p. 165.
126. Brown, F., *The Sixth*, p. 165.
127. Ibid., pp. 165, 175 (pictures).
128. On the same page a medal used for the Open International Games is depicted, showing a similar motif. On the First Games, *see* http://www.olympic.cn/museum/collection/2014–11–28/2347890.html [accessed 22 Oct. 2015].

Chapter 2

1. Annual Administration Report to New York of Dr. J. H. Gray, Shanghai, China, for the Year 1923, p. 6. In *International Work in China, Box 12: Annual and Quarterly Reports (G-M). 1923*, KFYMCAA.
2. 'Asia awakened' and 'Asia oppressed' are two quite common pan-Asian topoi, which many actors in the 1920s, but also later, recurred to. On their relevance, for example,

in connection to a conference of the Asiatic Labour Congress in Colombo in 1934, *see* Stolte, "Bringing Asia", p. 273. On 'China Awakening', *see* Wagner, "China".

3. Matsusaka, *The Making*, pp. 227–41; Zöllner, *Geschichte Japans*, pp. 344–6, 349–50; Jansen, *The Making*, pp. 519–22 and chapter 16.
4. Jansen, *The Making*, pp. 507–11, chapter 16; Huffman, *Japan*, pp. 91–6.
5. Matsusaka, *The Making*, pp. 258, 265–6, 271; Jansen, *The Making*, p. 521; Spence, *Chinas Weg*, pp. 358–60; Zöllner, *Geschichte Japans*, p. 345.
6. Matsusaka, *The Making*, pp. 272, 313, 327, 342–3; Jansen, *The Making*, pp. 522–6; Zöllner, *Geschichte Japans*, pp. 350–2.
7. Spence, *Chinas Weg*, pp. 360–6, 413, 442–3, 446, 463–6; Reilly, "Wu Yaozong", p. 269.
8. Matsusaka, *The Making*, pp. 355, 379–80, 385; Zöllner, *Geschichte Japans*, pp. 354–7; Jansen, *The Making*, p. 596.
9. Golay, *Face*, chapters 8–10; Yu Jose, "Philippine", p. 71.
10. Adas, "Contested Hegemony", pp. 31–7, 49–53; Fischer-Tiné and Stolte, "Imagining Asia in India", pp. 76–88.
11. Metcalf and Metcalf, *A Concise History*, chapter 6; Wolpert, *A New History*, chapter 21; Adas, "Contested Hegemony", pp. 54–5; Manela, *The Wilsonian Moment*, chapters 4, 8.
12. Kanō stepping down did not mean that he became inactive, especially since he still was Japan's IOC member. *See* Kanō Sensei Denki Hensankai, *Kanō*, p. 609. On Kishi, *see* England, *Far Eastern*, p. 16; Franklin Brown, The Prince of Wales Cup, pp. 2–2 (there are two pages numbered 2). In *International Work in Japan, Box 16: Correspondence and Reports. July-Aug. 1922*, KFYMCAA.
13. Elwood Brown, To: Dr. D. W. Lyon (3 Apr. 1922), p. 3 (quotation). In *International Work in China, Box 38: Correspondence and Reports. April 1921* [sic], KFYMCAA. See also: Elwood Brown, My dear Frank (22 Mar. 1922). In *International Work in Japan, Box 16: Correspondence and Reports. April–June 1922* [sic], KFYMCAA.
14. Gray, Dear Elwood (26 Oct. 1921). In *International Work in China, Box 39: Correspondence and Reports. Sept.–Oct. 1921*, KFYMCAA; Gray, Dear Mr. Wu (22 Aug. 1952), pp. 3–4, 6. In *Biographical Files, Box 73: Gray, John Henry. Biographical Data (C)*, KFYMCAA. Elwood Brown thought that Gray would sabotage his doings due to enviousness: Elwood Brown, To: Dr. D. W. Lyon (3 Apr. 1922). In *International Work in China, Box 38: Correspondence and Reports. April 1921* [sic], KFYMCAA.
15. Franklin Brown, Dear Elwood (29 Jan. 1922), p. 12. In *International Work in Japan, Box 16: Correspondence and Reports. Jan.–Feb. 1922*, KFYMCAA.
16. Ibid., pp. 2–3; Elwood Brown, My dear Brownie (29 Mar. 1922), pp. 2–3. In *International Work in Japan, Box 16: Correspondence and Reports. April–June 1922* [sic], KFYMCAA.
17. Franklin Brown, Dear Elwood (29 Jan. 1922), p. 3 (quotation). In *International Work in Japan, Box 16: Correspondence and Reports. Jan–Feb. 1922*, KFYMCAA. *See also* The Contest Committee of the Far Eastern Athletic Association, *Report*, p. 43.
18. Date, "Kyokutō", p. 219; Suzuki, "Kyokutō", p. 127.

19. Osaka was as a compromise between the *Kantō* region and *Kansai* region branch of the JAAA to end their difference, which had erupted as a result of Kanō's boycott of the Fourth Games in 1919.
20. Brown, F., *The Sixth*, p. 29. The Japanese government, taking the boycotts seriously, also gathered information on them. *See* the relevant items in *Kyokutō 'Orinpikku' Kyōgi Taikai kankei ikken. 7. Dai-6kai (Ōsaka)* [Documents relating to Far East Olympics Competitive Meets/7. 6th Games (Osaka)], TDA.
21. Annual Administration Report to New York of Dr. J. H. Gray, Shanghai, China, for the Year 1923, p. 6. In *International Work in China, Box 12: Annual and Quarterly Reports (G-M). 1923*, KFYMCAA. *See also* Morris, *Marrow*, pp. 77–8; Gray, Dear Mr. Wu (22 Aug. 1952), p. 5. In *Biographical Files, Box 73: Gray, John Henry. Biographical Data (C)*, KFYMCAA.
22. Brown, F., *The Sixth*, p. 39.
23. Ibid., pp. 39, 151.
24. On sports during the Taishō and early Shōwa era, *see*, for example, Guttmann and Thompson, *Japanese Sports*, chapter 6. After 1931/32, the military aspect in physical education again gained more influence: Collins, *The 1940 Tokyo Games*, p. 12; Takashima, "Manshūkoku", pp. 143–4.
25. The sports boom in Weimar Germany promoted stronger gender equality and individualism and thereby stood in contrast to norms and values of the Second German Empire: Jensen, *Body*. On the transfer of British sports to Germany, *see* Eisenberg, *English Sports*, chapters 3–7. On the German military's growing acceptance of sport during the course of the war, which already saw an erosion of social borders, *see* Tauber, *Vom Schützengraben*.
26. Physical Activities of the YMCA, 1929. In *YMCA Lantern Slides, Box 31: Lantern Slide Lecture Guides, 1900–29*, KFYMCAA.
27. "Bujiu Yuandong yundonghui shibai zhi banfa [A Way to Remedy the Failure in the FECG]." *Shenbao* (8 June 1923): 13. On Shen *see* The China Weekly Review, *Who's Who*, p. 342.
28. http://kotobank.jp/word/%E5%B9%B3%E6%B2%BC%E4%BA%AE%E4%B8%89 [accessed: 18 Aug. 2012]. On Hiranuma and the Yokohama YMCA, *see* Franklin Brown, Dear Buckley (25 Feb. 1953). In *International Work in Japan, Box 39: Physical Education Dept. Correspondence and Recollections (F. H. Brown). 1953–64 (1930 also)*, KFYMCAA.
29. On the full Chinese organizing team, *see* Sung [Shen], *Far Eastern*, pp. iv-vi, viii, 3–13, 16.
30. Ibid., pp. 37–9. On the main organizer Shen, being thankful to the American YMCA for its activities, but considering national independence as illustrated through sportive self-government very important, *see* Shen, "Zhonghua", p. 177.
31. Saaler and Szpilman, *Pan-Asianism*, vol. 1 and 2, particularly vol. 2, chapter 5.
32. "Dr. Wu Says China Is not a Republic." *Manila Times* (15 May 1925): 1.
33. Strictly speaking, Chiang Kai-shek organized a boycott of Japanese goods in Shanghai in May 1927, but had no intention of completely interrupting negotiations with the

Japanese and of thus jeopardizing his military success. The Japanese certainly also appreciated Chiang's killing his communist allies in Shanghai in April 1927. To find a compromise regarding northern and northeastern China, as it happened in 1928, was difficult, but possible: Jansen, *The Making*, pp. 523–5; Spence, *Chinas Weg*, pp. 431–2, 441–5.

34. "Japan's Nine Wins as Olympics Open." *Japan Advertiser* (28 Aug. 1927): 8.
35. On Yamamoto and the YMCA, *see* Franklin Brown, Dear Buckley (10 Jan. 1953), p. 2. In *International Work in Japan, Box 39: Physical Education Dept. Correspondence and Recollections (F. H. Brown). 1953–64 (1930 also)*, KFYMCAA. On Yamamoto, *see also* Yamamoto Tadaoki hakushi denki kankōkai, *Yamamoto*.
36. Dainihon Taiiku Kyōkai, *Dai-8kai*, pp. 44–6.
37. Ibid., pp. 1–2 (Kishi being glad that amateur sports ideals were kept up), 4 (instruction from the Ministry of Education to behave well), 6–9 (Hiranuma), 290, 292 (further warnings); Hiranuma, *Supōtsu*, pp. 144–5 (the text of his speech). *See also* Date, "Kyokutō", p. 212.
38. As one might expect, some journalists disagreed and published negative stories particularly about the Filipinos: Morris, *Marrow*, pp. 98, 267 fn. 89.
39. Dainihon Taiiku Kyōkai, *Dai-9kai*, p. 13 (quotation). *See also* Brown, F., *Official Report of the Ninth*, pp. 42–3, 48–9.
40. Jansen, *The Making*, p. 535.
41. On Vargas, *see* Jorge B. Vargas—Biographical Notes (May 1, 1937), p. 1–2. In *Manuel Luiz Quezon Papers, Roll 53: Jorge B. Vargas, 1914–1940*, BHL; Saulo, *Let George*.
42. The Vargas-Saulo Interviews. A Series of Fourteen Tape-Recorded Interviews with MR. JORGE B. VARGAS and son EDDIE, from April 19 to May 24, 1977. Conducted, transcribed and edited by Alfredo B. Saulo, pp. 84, 87, 138–41. In *The Vargas-Saulo Interviews*, JBVM; Saulo, *Let George*, chapter 19.
43. *See also* his official writings: Vargas, "Athletic Progress", pp. 388 (first quotation), 399 (second quotation).
44. On Vargas religious views and his affinity to Baptism, *see* The Vargas-Saulo Interviews. A Series of Fourteen Tape-Recorded Interviews with MR. JORGE B. VARGAS and son EDDIE, from April 19 to May 24, 1977. Conducted, transcribed and edited by Alfredo B. Saulo, p. 60. In *The Vargas-Saulo Interviews*, JBVM.
45. Ibid., p. 139.
46. On favoritism, gambling, cheating, and sportsmanship, *see* Ibid., pp. 142, 252–3; Vargas, Dear President Quezon (28 Apr. 1930), and Quezon, Secretary Vargas (10 June 1930). Both in *Manuel Luiz Quezon Papers, Roll 53: Jorge B. Vargas, 1914–1940*, BHL. Vargas being accused of corruption during the Tenth FECG and of ruling the PAAF like an absolutist king after the Second Asian Games (discussed below and in the fourth chapter), casts a shadow over him.
47. Brown, F., *Official Report of the Ninth*, pp. 45–6.
48. For the plan in 1927 *see* Supplementary Olympic Bulletin Issued to all Indian Olympic Constituents with Particular Reference to the Special Selection Meeting to be Conducted at Lahore on the 3rd and 4th Feb. 1928. In *D.RM01.INDE/003*, TOSC.

49. "Far Eastern Olympic Games." *Straits Times* (23 Apr. 1930): 13; Brown, F., *Official Report of the Ninth*, pp. 12, 30, 46; Mukerjie, Sharajit Kumar. In *Alumni Relations Office Records, Alumni Biographical Information Books, Class of 1926*, SCASC.
50. Brown, F., *Official Report of the Ninth*, p. 46.
51. "Indian Olympic Team." *The Japan Weekly Chronicle* (15 May 1930): 524.
52. Fischer-Tiné and Stolte, "Imagining Asia in India", pp. 76–88.
53. On Bose, *see* Nakajima, *Bose.* On him and the Ninth FECG, *see* Tomita, "Dai-9kai". On the 'flag incident', *see* Evan A. Hunter, Dear Sir [Berdez] (15 July 1930); Kishi, Dear Sir [Berdez] (8 Sept. 1930); Sondhi, Dear Mr. Hunter (11 Aug. 1930), and Report of the Manager of the Indian Team to the Far Eastern Games on the Flag Controversy. All In *H-FC03-EXORI/006*, TOSC.
54. Minutes of the Meeting of the Assembly of the Far Eastern Athletic Association. Held in the Meiji Memorial Art Museum Tokyo, Japan, 29–30 May 1930, p. 11. In *H-FC03-EXORI/002*, TOSC.
55. *See*, for example, Sondhi, My dear President [Baillet-Latour] (1 May 1935). In *D.RM01.INDE/003*, TOSC. On the financial difficulties of the Indian delegations to the Olympic Games in the late 1920s and 1930s, *see* Majumdar and Mehta, *India*, pp. 30, 57, 63–5, 69, 96.
56. Conference des Jeux d'Extrême-Orient. In *H-FC03-EXORI/003*, TOSC.
57. For an overview of all organizers, *see* Brown, F., *Official Report of the Ninth*, pp. 25–8.
58. Franklin Brown, Dear Count Latour [sic] (18 Dec. 1930), p. 3. In *H-FC03-EXORI/001*, TOSC.
59. *See*, for example, Takashima, "Manshūkoku"; Ikei, "Tōyō"; He, "Dai-10kai Kyokutō"; He, "Dai-10kai Orinpikku"; Shinno and Yasuda, "Ōshima Kenkichi"; Goodman, "Athletics as Politics"; Antolihao, "20 shiji", pp. 228–9; Abe, I., "Historical Significance", pp. 78–85; Zhou, "Yuandong"; Yu, "Zhong Ri", pp. 48–9; Kolatch, *Sports*, pp. 65–6; Morris, *Marrow*, pp. 162–6; Hong, "Prologue", pp. xxi-xxii. *See also* Dainihon Taiiku Kyōkai, *Dai-10kai*, pp. 289–311; Dainihon Taiiku Kyōkai, *Manshūkoku*; Dainihon Taiiku Kyōkai, *Dainihon Taiiku*, vol. 1, pp. 556–605; Nihon Rikujō Kyōgi Renmei, *Manira enseiki*, pp. 270–7.
60. "Army Men Demand Japan Leave Games." *Japan Advertiser* (25 Apr. 1934): 1–2. On the Japanese debate, *see*, for example, the articles published in 1934 in *Bungei shunjū*, *Chūō kōron*, *Kaizō*, *Orimupikku*, *Shinseinen*, and *Undōkai*.
61. Okabe in 1929 informed Amos Alonzo Stagg, one of his teachers at the University of Chicago, that he intended to teach the Japanese and Chinese in Manchuria fair play and sportsmanship, since Chinese and Japanese politicians would be unable to improve relations: Okabe, Dear Mr. Stagg (6 Feb. 1929). In *Amos Alonzo Stagg Papers: Box 2*, RL. For a balanced interpretation of Okabe's activities, *see* Takashima, "Sensō".
62. Okabe, Dear Prof. Stagg (25 Feb. 1918); Okabe, Dear Mr. Stagg (27 May 1918); Okabe, Dear Mr. + Mrs. Stagg (16 Mar. 1921); "Jujitsu Teacher Quits because Experts Are to Meet Americans"; Okabe, Mr. + Mrs. Stagg (17 Aug. 1925), pp. 2–4. All in *Amos Alonzo Stagg Papers: Box 2*, RL.

63. Okabe Heita, "Taikyō no yowagoshi [The Weak Attitude of the Japanese Amateur Athletic Association]." *Bungei shunjū* 12, 5 (1934): 216–18, here: 218.
64. Jansen, *The Making*, pp. 600–5, 609–13.
65. Hiranuma, *Supōtsu*, p. 184; Tabata, *Supōtsu*, p. 23; Abe, K., *Mizu*, p. 36; "Athletes Attacked by Mob as Olympic Trouble Boils Over." *Japan Advertiser* (27 Apr. 1934): 1–2; "Olympic Athletes Again Assaulted." *Japan Advertiser* (29 Apr. 1934): 3.
66. Hiranuma, *Supōtsu*, pp. 185–7; "Team Embarks under Guard." *The Japan Weekly Chronicle* (3 May 1934): 598.
67. "Claim Question Should Not Have Been Raised." In *Yamamoto Tadaoki shiryō/3: Supōtsu no shinkō/Kyokutō Senshuken Kyōgi Taikai* [Material on Yamamoto Tadaoki/3: Promotion of Sports/Far Eastern Championship Games], *226*, WUA. *See also* the relatively neutral overview of the issue "In Memorandum: Controversy resulting from the Far Eastern Games Held in Manila" (12 July 1934). In *Record Group 350: Records of the Bureau of Insular Affairs, 1868–1945. Series: General Classified Files, 1914–45. Box 343: #1887*, NARAII.
68. After being questioned by Baillet-Latour, Wang informed him that Indochina had been a Chinese vassal and that its annexation had been accepted, but that Manchuria was perceived by the Chinese government and the League of Nations as a part of China: Wang, My dear Count de Baillet Latour (23 Oct. 1934); Baillet Latour, My dear Colleague [Wang] (29 Aug. 1934). Both in *H-FC03-EXORI/007*, TOSC. The League of Nations had also recommended against allowing Manchukuo to participate in international competitions due to Japan's act of aggression, but its recommendation was not binding: Takashima, "Manshūkoku", p. 139.
69. The Vargas-Saulo Interviews. A Series of Fourteen Tape-Recorded Interviews with MR. JORGE B. VARGAS and son EDDIE, from April 19 to May 24, 1977. Conducted, transcribed and edited by Alfredo B. Saulo, pp. 142–3, 233–4. In *The Vargas-Saulo Interviews*, JBVM; Saulo, *Let George*, p. 231.
70. "In the Name of Sports." *Philippines Herald* (26 May 1934), in *Record Group 350: Records of the Bureau of Insular Affairs, 1868–1945. Series: General Classified Files, 1914–1945. Box 343: #1887*, NARAII.
71. Minutes of the Meeting of the Congress of the Far Eastern Athletic Association Held at the Philippine Columbian Club House, May 20th, 1934, 10:35 a.m., especially pp. 5–17; Abstract of the Proceedings of the Special Meeting of the F.E.A.A. Held in the Philippine Columbian Club House, May 21st, 1934 at 11:20 a.m. Both in *H-FC03-EXORI/002*, TOSC. The question was whether or not the Dutch East Indies and French Indochina were proper members and if a quorum to change the constitution, which would need a two-thirds majority (either two of three or, being a second interpretation, three of five members), was raised. Grant Goodman assumes that Hiranuma and Quezon had made a deal regarding the Games in advance: The Japanese would attend them and prevent their cancelation and the Filipinos would support their aims. Vargas would have agreed to take the blame for Quezon: Goodman, "Athletics as Politics", p. 63. This is not completely unconvincing, but based on the documents I think that the Filipinos at best agreed to assist in allowing Manchukuo to participate in the

FECG (being their compromise offer), but not to make it a member or to antagonize the Chinese. Only during the night and especially the following morning did they change their stance, though Vargas then might have agreed to take the blame for Quezon, who anyway did not attend the meetings. Apparently, the Japanese delegates also announced that they would be forced to commit ritual suicide (*seppuku*) in the case that Manchukuo was not admitted, thus in an uncommon way appealing to Filipino compassion. Finally, Hiranuma (one of the 'bad cops') previously seems to have threatened the Filipinos at a meeting of the Pan-Pacific Union with a naval invasion and the Japanese consul, who earlier had argued for dissolving the FEAA and was well-known for his 'tough talk', also attended the meeting. *See* Takashima, "Manshūkoku", pp. 158, 174–6; "Sports Letter Box." *Manila Daily Bulletin* (23 May 1934): 3. I nevertheless do not think that the Filipinos took these absurd utterances seriously, considering that the United States would protect the archipelago for at least another decade. *See also* the very interesting article, "Stupidity—Nothing More or Less", *Philippine Magazine* 31, 6 (1934): 237–8.

72. Abe, K., *Mizu*, p. 36.
73. Hiranuma later said that Vargas had supported them despite the strong opposition of overseas Chinese: Hiranuma, *Supōtsu*, p. 188.
74. "Stupidity—Nothing More or Less", *Philippine Magazine* 31, 6 (1934): 237–8.
75. Abstract of the Proceedings of the Special Meeting of the F.E.A.A. Held in the Philippine Columbian Club House, May 21st, 1934 at 11:20 a.m. In *H-FC03-EXORI/002*, TOSC. On the negotiations concerning the Amateur Athletic Association of the Orient, *see* Amateur Athletic Association of the Orient. Minutes of the First Congress. Tokyo, Japan - December 14, 1934. In *H-FC03-EXORI/001*, TOSC; Dainihon Taiiku Kyōkai, *Dainihon Taiiku*, vol. 2, pp. 61–5.
76. On the JAAA delegates and Japanese nationalistic organizations, *see* Takashima, "Manshūkoku", p. 172. Japanese Prime Minister Saitō Makoto also had declared that Japan would do its best to bring Manchukuo into the Games: "Far East Politics and Sport." *Singapore Free Press and Mercantile Advertiser* (23 Mar. 1934): 15.
77. Comité International Olympique, séance du vendredi 31 juillet 1936, matin, pp. 1–2. In *Comité International Olympique—Session 1894–2008*, TOSC.
78. On muscular Christianity and missionaries in India, *see* Fischer-Tiné, "Fitness for Modernity?"; Alter, "Indian Clubs"; Alter, "Yoga"; Holt, *Sport*, pp. 212–13; Mangan, "Christ". On the 'civilizing mission' and racial stereotypes, *see* Dimeo, "Colonial Bodies"; Dimeo, "Sporting". For a more general overview on sport in India, *see* Valiotis, "South Asia".
79. Literature on the WAG is scarce. For a short overview, *see* Majumdar and Mehta, *India*, pp. 153–5.
80. Name: Gray, John Henry M.D. In *Biographical Records, Box 73: Gray, John Henry. Biographical Data (C)*, KFYMCAA; Elwood Brown, My dear Frank (21 Mar. 1922), pp. 1–3. In *International Work in Japan. Box 16: Correspondence and Reports. Mar. 1922*, KFYMCAA; Noehren, "The Olympic Games Meeting at Delhi." *The Young Men of India* 35, 3 (Mar. 1924): 160–8, here: 161, 167; "Olympic Games at Delhi." *Times of*

India (27 Oct. 1923): 14; "Olympic Ideals. Dr. Noehren's Appeal to Indians." *Times of India* (7 Oct. 1925): 12; "A Waste of Time. Indian Olympics." *Times of India* (10 Sept. 1928): 15; David, *The YMCA*, pp. 172–4.

81. On Sondhi, *see* "The Punjab Olympic Committee." *Times of India* (20 Jan. 1926): 6; "First Indian Principle of Lahore College." *Times of India* (30 Mar. 1936): 15; "Mr. G. D. Sondhi." *Times of India* (3 Nov. 1939): 10; M.G.D. SONDHI. (Inde.). In *MBR. SONDHI, Guru Dutt*, TOSC.
82. Guru Dutt Sondhi, "Voice of India. Athletic Development of Asia." *Olympic Review* 82 (May 1963): 45–8 (quotations: 47). To gain an impression of Sondhi's aims as an educator and modernizer at least since the 1930s, *see also* Guru Dutt Sondhi, "Wanted. A Department of Urban Recreation". Reprinted from 'Sports Annual', Dec. 1936. In *MBR. SONDHI, Guru Dutt*, TOSC; Sondhi, *A Plan*.
83. Gray, My dear Count Latour [sic] (28 Dec. 1928), pp. 1–2 (quotation: 2). In *D. RM01. INDE/003*, TOSC; Tata, Dear Count Baillet Lataur [sic] (21 Feb. 1927), p. 2. In *PT-BAILL-CORR. Correspondance de H. de Baillet-Latour (Président). 1925–1927*, TOSC. See also: Tata, Dear Count Baillet Latour (15 Jan. 1928), p. 1, and Tata, Dear Monsieur de Baillet Latour (21 May 1929), pp. 1–5. Both in *PT-BAILL-CORR. Correspondance de Baillet-Latour (Président). 1928–1930*, TOSC. *See also* Majumdar and Mehta, *India*, pp. 28–30 and chapter 2.
84. Arguably, another reason why India would not attend the FECG anymore was its bad performance. The three athletes had not scored a single point: Brown, F., *Official Report of the Ninth*, p. 50. It was another illustration of India's relative 'backwardness' in terms of sport compared to East Asia.
85. *First Western Asiatic Games. New Delhi 1934. Official Report*, p. 15; "India to Send Team to Olympic Games in Spring." *Times of India* (21 Oct. 1931), p. 10. On hockey, *see* Majumdar and Mehta, *India*, chapter 3.
86. "International Athletics. Scheme for Eastern Olympiad." *Times of India* (8 Feb. 1933): 13; "Asiatic Olympic Championships." *Times of India* (7 Apr. 1933): 3; *First Western Asiatic Games. New Delhi 1934. Official Report*, pp. 17–20, 28–30, 91. On p. 35 it is also mentioned that the authorities in Bombay (Mumbai) and Madras (Chennai) had been unwilling to provide the foreign athletes passing through the cities with an official reception. This might be an illustration of the colonial administration at best half-heartedly supporting the event, which might (similar to the canceled African Games) increase anti-colonial nationalism and pan-Asianism.
87. *First Western Asiatic Games. New Delhi 1934. Official Report*, pp. 13–14.
88. This claim was also mentioned in the official program: *Programme. First Western Asiatic Games and VI Indian Olympic Games*, p. 1. Some British authors in the nineteenth century had developed theories that significant parts of ancient Greek civilization came from India. *See*, for example, Pococke, *India*. On the 'out of India-theory' of Hindu nationalists already mentioned above, *see* Fischer-Tiné and Stolte, "Imagining Asia in India", pp. 82–8.
89. *First Western Asiatic Games. New Delhi 1934. Official Report*, p. 91; "Western Asiatic Games. Palestine to be Venue." *Times of India* (5 July 1937): 12; "Photo Standalone."

Times of India (17 Feb. 1938): 4; "Palestine Unable to Stage Games. Mr. Sondhi's Statement." *Times of India* (13 May 1938): 17; "Western Asiatic Games. Offer by Lahore." *Times of India* (25 May 1938): 15; "National Swimming Body for India." *Times of India* (26 Oct. 1938): 15.

90. The Contest Committee of the Far Eastern Athletic Association, *Report*, p. 20.

91. I would like to thank Takashima Kō for sharing some of his sources with me. The sources I used for the tablet are: Dainihon Taiiku Kyōkai, *Dainihon Taiiku*, vol. 1, pp. 761–7 (on Japan, except 1915, 1919, 1921, and 1934); "Japanese Stars Due 8 P.M. today for Orient Meet." *Manila Daily Bulletin* (7 May 1934): 3–4, here: 4 (on the Dutch East Indies); Brown, F., *Official Report of the Ninth*, p. 46 (on India); "Yuandong geguo yundongyuan", pp. 2–4 (on 1915); "Far Eastern Olympic Games." *North China Herald* (22 Feb. 1913): 540 (on China in 1913); Brown, E., "Physical Work", p. 263 (on the Philippines in 1913); "Di 4 ci Yuandong yundonghui jishi [Record of the Fourth Far Eastern Championship Gamnes]." *Dongfang zazhi* 16, 10 (1919): 59–67, here: 60 (on 1919); "Di 5 ci Yuandong yundonghui jishi [Record of the Fifth Far Eastern Championship Games]." *Dongfang zazhi* 18, 11 (1921): 13–24, here: 14 (on 1921); Dainihon Taiiku Kyōkai, *Dai-8kai*, pp. 304–5 (on China and the Philippines in 1927); "Chinese Team Off for Japan." *North China Daily News* (16 May 1930): 18 (on China in 1930); "520 Will Compete in Olympics Here." *Japan Advertiser* (7 May 1930): 8 (on the Philippines in 1930; the size of the Chinese and Japanese team changed after the article was published); Dainihon Taiiku Kyōkai, *Dai-10kai*, pp. 116–18 (on Japan in 1934); "Chinese Given Huge Welcome upon Arrival." *Manila Bulletin* (9 May 1934): 1, 3, 7 (on China in 1934); *Tenth Far Eastern Championship Games. Rizal Memorial Field*, pp. 35, 37, 85, 113, 127, 141, 155, 169, 177, 179 (on the Philippines in 1934); Dainihon Taiiku Kyōkai, *Dai-7kai*, p. 9 (on China and the Philippines in 1917, 1923 and 1925). Much of the data provided in Huang, "Table 1", pp. 116–17, does not make sense.

92. The Indian swimmers in Patialia were not included in the poorly numbered list of competitors in the official program. According to the list of victors in the *Times of India*, there were at least five Indian swimmers who competed in the WAG. The only swimmer from Palestine was included in the list of competitors in the official program. However, it is not clear if those swimmers from Palestine who arrived too late for official competition were included. Compare: *Programme. First Western Asiatic Games and VI Indian Olympic Games*, p. 28E; "India's Victory over Palestine." *Times of India* (28 Feb. 1934): 5; "Western Asiatic Games. Swimming Events." *Times of India* (27 Feb. 1934): 14.

93. Frederick O. England, "US Soldiers Gave Games to Filipinos." *China Press* (5 June 1921): 3 (Games Special); England, *Far Eastern*, p. ix.

94. Kolatch, *Sports*, p. 54; "Baseball Supplants the Cockpit." *Association Men* 38, 10 (1913): 515; L. C. Wilson, Secretary National Committee Young Men's Christian Association, China, Annual Report for the Year Ending Sept. 30, 1915, p. 3. In *International Work in China, Box 15: China YMCA Foreign Secretaries' Report Letters 1900–28. Incomplete*, KFYMCAA; Franklin Brown, Annual Report for Year Ending Sept. 30, 1917, pp.

9–10. In *International Work in Japan. Box 5: Annual and Quarterly Reports. 1917. 1.: A-F.,* KFYMCAA; The Contest Committee of the Far Eastern Athletic Association, *Report,* p. 12; Brown, F., *The Sixth,* p. xi; England, *Far Eastern,* p. ix; "Filipino Athletes Victorious." *Philippines Herald* (24 May 1925): 1–2, here: 2; "Big Attendance in F. E. Games." *Philippines Herald* (24 May 1925): 4; Dainihon Taiiku Kyōkai, *Dai-9kai,* p. 306; "Far Eastern Olympic Games Championship Won by Japan; 450,000 See Eight-Day Meet." *New York Times* (1 June 1930): S4; "Friendship *Not* Competition." *Graphic* (10 May 1934): 14; "Olympic Games Net ₱107,000." *Manila Daily Bulletin* (22 May 1934): 3, 5.

95. "India's Victory over Palestine." *Times of India* (28 Feb. 1934): 5.
96. This is based on the assumption that ticket prices in New Delhi and in Patiala were about the same (0.1 Rupee). In Patiala about 400 Rupees and in New Delhi about 1,000 Rupees were earned: *First Western Asiatic Games. New Delhi 1934. Official Report,* p. 86.
97. The events in East Asia are not that different, for example, from those in the United States. The 1920s there also saw a growing consumption of sports events, *see* Dyreson, "The Emergence".
98. *See* the lantern slide collections in *Lantern Slide Lecture Guides, 1900–1929,* KFYMCAA.
99. For example, in Japan 90 per cent of the adult population had attended at least six years of school by 1930. The number of copies the *Ōsaka Mainichi Shinbun* sold went up from 260,000 in 1912 to 670,000 in 1921 and 1,500,000 in 1930, *see* Jansen, *The Making,* p. 570. On English language newspapers in East Asia, *see* O'Connor, *The English-Language*; Lent, "The Philippines".
100. Examples are the *Manila Times, The Philippines Herald,* the *Cablenews American,* the *Philippines Free Press, The Tribune,* and the *Manila Daily Bulletin.*
101. Examples are the *New York Times* and the *Washington Post.*
102. Examples are *China Press,* the *North China Daily News* and the *North China Herald.* A very good example for Chinese newspapers is the Shanghai-based *Shenbao.*
103. On the support of Japanese newspapers (and transportation companies, which brought people to the stadia) for the spread and popularization of baseball *see,* for example, Nishihara, "Tōkyō".
104. "Corps of Foreign Newspapermen here to Cover Eastern Games." *Philippines Herald* (12 May 1934): 27 (F. E. Games Supplement). For example, the *Nippon Denpō Tsūshinsha,* the *Shinbun Rengōsha,* the Osaka and Tokyo *Asahi Shinbun,* the *Hōchi Shinbun,* the *Jiji Shinpō,* the *Yomiuri Shinbun,* and the *Yamato Shinbun* sent reporters. Other (English language) newspapers that showed great interest in the Games at least since the Third FECG in Tokyo are the *Japan Advertiser* and the *Japan Weekly Chronicle.* Many Japanese journals, including sports journals closely affiliated with the JAAA, also covered the FECG and especially the controversy about the 1934 Games. Examples are *Bungei shunjū, Chūō kōron, Kaizō, Orimupikku, Shinseinen,* and *Undōkai.*
105. "PAAF to Install Wire Apparatus." *Manila Daily Bulletin* (4 Apr. 1934): 3.

106. For an overview, *see* the articles used below on the WAG. The *Times of India* also had already since the early 1920s covered the Olympic Games and the Indian Olympic Games.
107. Charles A. Siler, "A Week of Physical Education in Tientsin." *Foreign Mail* 23, 2 (1916): 6–7, here: 6.
108. "Katsudōshashin no miyage [Film Souvenir]." *Asahi Shinbun* (26 Feb. 1913, Tokyo Morning Edition): 5; Brown, F., "The Third", p. 392; Franklin Brown, Dear Elwood (29 Jan. 1922), p. 5. In *International Work in Japan, Box 16: Correspondence and Reports. Jan–Feb. 1922*, KFYMCAA; Morris, *Marrow*, p. 89; "Results of Games Will Be Broadcasted." *Manila Times* (5 Apr. 1925): 4.
109. Information which company was to broadcast the Games is contradictory. *See* "Games' Results to Be Radioed." *Manila Daily Bulletin* (15 May 1925): 4; "Results of Far Eastern Games to Be Broadcasted." *Manila Times* (13 Apr. 1925): 1; "Results of Games Will Be Broadcasted." *Manila Times* (5 Apr. 1925): 4; "Games Results Broadcast." *Philippines Herald* (19 May 1925): 3.
110. "Three Japanese Announcers Will Cover Olympics." *Philippines Herald* (9 May 1934): 10. On the number of households *see* Gordon, "Consumption", p. 5.
111. "Olympic Stars to Broadcast." *Manila Daily Bulletin* (26 Apr. 1934): 3–4; "Along the Olympic Front." *Manila Daily Bulletin* (10 May 1934): 3–4, here: 3; "Mammoth Radio Set-Up Will Bring Results of Orient Classic over KZRM." *Manila Daily Bulletin* (5 May 1934): 3, 5.
112. "Shanghai Will Snatch Olympic News over KZRM." *Philippines Herald* (9 May 1934): 10.
113. "Along the Olympic Front." *Manila Daily Bulletin* (10 May 1934): 3–4, here: 4; "Three Japanese Announcers Will Cover Olympics." *Philippines Herald* (9 May 1934): 10. On the Los Angeles Olympics (and Japanese sports broadcasting in general), *see also* Hashimoto, *Nihon*, p. 60 (the data on the Tenth FECG provided there is not entirely correct).
114. On the Japanese consumer society since the 1920s, *see* Gordon, "Consumption".
115. *First Western Asiatic Games. New Delhi 1934. Official Report*, p. 39.
116. The Contest Committee of the Far Eastern Athletic Association, *Report*, p. 10; "Chinese Girl Athletes." *The Playground* 15, 6 (1921): 360; Morris, *Marrow*, p. 89.
117. The Contest Committee of the Far Eastern Athletic Association, *Report*, p. 10; Morris, *Marrow*, pp. 290–91, fn. 75.
118. The description says: "The Girl Guides made a hit with their Bayonet drill at the games." Hao Gengsheng, who was involved in organizing the Games, also used the picture in his book on physical education in China, but only called it a demonstration of skill with wands, not explicitly describing them as substitutes for rifles with bayonets. *See* Hoh [Hao], *Physical Education*, p. 31.
119. Information Bulletin (22 Dec. 1922). In *H-FC03-EXORI/004*, TOSC; Brown, F., *The Sixth*, pp. 19, 21. For a summary of critical news on the stadium, *see* "The Osaka Olympic Games." *The Japan Weekly Chronicle* (31 May 1923): 768–72.
120. Brown, F., *The Sixth*, pp. 29, 31.

121. Ibid., pp. 33–35, 37, 138.
122. England, *Far Eastern*, p. 9; Ylanan and Ylanan, *The History*, pp. 69–70; Rufino G. Hechanova, "The Rizal Memorial Field—Site of the Second Asian Games." In *Sports 1953–1954*, JBVM. Some fund-raising had taken place already in 1921 after Governor-General Leonard Wood had created the Playground and Recreation Commission, whose secretary was Frederick England. Another, more important fund-raising attempt took place in August and September 1924.
123. Date, "Kyokutō", pp. 207–8, 223.
124. The Contest Committee of the Far Eastern Athletic Association, *Report*, p. 23; Gray, Report of the Physical Work of the National Committee of the YMCA of China for the Triennial Convention at Tsinan, Shantung, 4–10 Aug. 1926, pp. 4–5. In *International Work in China. Box 13: Annual and Quarterly Reports. 1926*, KFYMCAA.
125. Sung [Shen], *Far Eastern*, pp. xi, 15. *See also* "Olympic Games Chit Chat." *Philippines Free Press* (30 May 1925): 8, 41 (here Shen claimed that they had received no funding at all from the Beijing government, which is not true).
126. Sung [Shen], *Far Eastern*, p. 99; Dainihon Taiiku Kyōkai, *Dai-8kai*, pp. 49–50, 303 (providing a map of the venue).
127. Collins, *The 1940 Tokyo Games*, p. 112. For photos of the venues, *see* Dainihon Taiiku Kyōkai, *Dai-9kai*, pp. 284–93.
128. The picture also shows the five flags of the four participating countries (the Philippines used the Star Spangled Banner and what is now used as the National Flag of the Philippines) and three loudspeakers on top of the construction.
129. Collins, *The 1940 Tokyo Games*, pp. 25–6, 43, fn. 9. Collins here leaves the Ninth FECG out. The closeness between the Games ending on 31 May and Yamamoto being contacted by Nagata in June cannot be a mere coincidence.
130. Ibid., especially pp. 27, 42, 74–6, 162–4, and chapter 5 (on the debates). On the Olympic Games which were never held *see* Abel, *The International Minimum*, chapter 4; Tagsold, *Die Inszenierung*, chapter 3. Like Collins' study (see note 129), these two publications also do not cover the 1930 Games. In their application the Japanese obviously discussed the importance of the FECG for the spreading of sport in Japan: Japan and the XIIth Olympiad, p. 4. In *VIL-1940S-CAND*, TOSC.
131. Brown, F., *Official Report of the Ninth*, pp. 212–14; Dainihon Taiiku Kyōkai, *Dai-9kai*, pp. 209–11, 218, 220. On Bukh, *see* Bonde, *Gymnastics*, especially pp. 116–3.
132. Brown, F., *Official Report of the Ninth*, pp. 8–9, 47. The Tenth Games also featured a song: *Tenth Far Eastern Championship Games. Rizal Memorial Field*, pp. 191–2.
133. Vargas and Quezon had introduced sweepstakes to finance the construction of the sports complex. The PAAF, of which Vargas was a vice president, then awarded the right to hold the sweepstakes to a partnership consisting of Vargas and two other people. This highly dubious combination of offices and responsibilities attracted criticism, finally forcing Vargas to leave the partnership, which seems to have made a gross profit of about 330,000 Philippine Pesos (165,000 USD): "How Games Were

Mismanaged." *Philippines Free Press* (26 May 1934): 5, 40. On Vargas and the end of the FEAA, *see above.*

134. *Philippine Amateur Athletic Federation. Annual Report of the Secretary Treasurer*, pp. 74–7; "Rizal Stadia to Seat 35,562 for Olympic Games." *Manila Daily Bulletin* (12 Apr. 1934): 3–4; "PAAF to Install Wire Apparatus." *Manila Daily Bulletin* (4 Apr. 1934): 3; "Gigantic Stadium nearly ready for Far East Olympics." *Singapore Free Press and Mercantile Advertiser* (17 Mar. 1934): 15; Rufino G. Hechanova, "The Rizal Memorial Field—Site of the Second Asian Games." In *Sports 1953–1954*, JBVM.
135. See for example JAAA vice president Hiranuma's comments on the venues: Hiranuma, *Supōtsu*, pp. 189–90. For some further criticism *see* "How Games Were Mismanaged." *Philippines Free Press* (26 May 1934): 5, 40.
136. Morris, *Marrow*, p. 149; "Nanking Athletic Plant Costing $2,000,000 to House Chinese National Meet in October", *New York Times* (29 Mar. 1931), S3. On the building program in Nanjing and the main stadium, which combined Western and Chinese architectural elements to illustrate a Chinese modernity, *see* Rowe and Kuan, *Architectural Encounters*, pp. 73–4, 78. On Chiang Kai-shek's general support of sport, *see* Shen, "Zhonghua".
137. *First Western Asiatic Games. New Delhi 1934. Official Report*, pp. 26, 32–3; "A Stadium for Athletics. An Urgent Necessity for India." *Times of India* (17 Oct. 1931): 17; Basu and Majumder, *The Asiad Stadia*, p. 20.
138. The Organizing Committee of the Games of New Delhi, India, *1st Western*, p. 9; *First Western Asiatic Games. New Delhi 1934. Official Report*, pp. 44–6; "Western Asiatic Games. Swimming Events." *Times of India* (27 Feb. 1934): 14; "India's Victory over Palestine." *Times of India* (28 Feb. 1934): 5; "Seven Indian Sports Records Established at Delhi." *Times of India* (5 Mar. 1934): 13.
139. *First Western Asiatic Games. New Delhi 1934. Official Report*, pp. 26, 40–2, 44, 47–54, 74–5, 80–1. The constitution of the WAG declared that the ceremonies should be as close to those of the patron, the Olympic Games, as possible: Constitution of the Western Asiatic Games Federation, Article IX. In *H-FC03-ASIOU/001*, TOSC.
140. Sondhi had (wrongly) expected the Games would cost about 6,000 Rupees, but initial donations had only produced about 2,000 and gate fees 1,467 Rupees. The final deficit was about 4,000 Rupees and was covered through further calls for money and especially by a contribution by the Maharaja of Patiala: *First Western Asiatic Games. New Delhi 1934. Official Report*, pp. 82–9.
141. Brown, F., *The Sixth*, pp. 166–8, 177 (picture). Silver cups were donated by Minister of Home Affairs Mizuno Rentarō, Minister of Education Kamada Eikichi, Minister of Foreign Affairs Count Uchida Yasuya, president of the South Manchurian Railway Company Kawamura Takeji, and others.
142. Brown, F., *The Sixth*, pp. 165, 181–2 (pictures).
143. Ibid., 166, 177 (picture).
144. Hiranuma, *Supōtsu*, pp. 146–8.
145. On Sun and Chiang, *see* Wells, *The Political Thought*, pp. 105–9, 125. On the Taiping Rebellion, *see* Spence, *God's Chinese Son.*

146. Images of medals or actual medals can be found in *Yamamoto Tadaoki shiryō/3: Supōtsu no shinkō/Kyokutō Senshuken Kyōgi Taikai* [Material on Yamamoto Tadaoki/3: Promotion of Sports/Far Eastern Championship Games], *217* and *218*, WUA; Brown, F., *The Sixth*, p. 17; Exhibition at the PCMSM.
147. Kishi, Dear Baron [Godefroy de Blonay] (7 July 1931), pp.1–2 (quotation: 1). In *MBR. KISHI, Sei[i]chi*, TOSC.
148. Available at http://prewar-sculptors.blogspot.jp/2012/10/blog-post_27.html [accessed: 18 May 2015]. Hint by Takashima Kō.
149. *Programme. First Western Asiatic Games and VI Indian Olympic Games*, p. 8; *First Western Asiatic Games. New Delhi 1934. Official Report*, pp. 37–8; Baillet-Latour, My dear Colleague [Sondhi] (26 June 1934). In *H-FC03-ASIOU/001*, TOSC.
150. Raita, "The Movement", p. 121.
151. Brown, F., *The Sixth*, pp. xi-xii; England, *Far Eastern*, p. 96. Female Japanese athletes having participated in the Sixth Games also encouraged women to take up sport through articles in women's journals: Kajikawa, "Kyokutō"; Tamura, "Kyokutō". On sportswomen in Japan in the 1920s and 1930s, *see*, for example, Kietlinski, *Japanese Women*; Frost, *Seeing Stars*, chapter 3. On China, *see*, for example, Yu, *Yundongchang*; Gao, *Sporting Gender*. There seems to be no monograph on the Philippines.
152. England, *Far Eastern*, p. 96; Brown, F., *Official Report of the Ninth*, p. 23.
153. On Zhang, *see* Gao, *Sporting Gender*, chapter 1.
154. On China, the 'sick man of East Asia', and sports, *see* Takashima, "Tōa Byōfu".
155. Huilan Zhang, "Di 8 jie Yuandong yundonghui zhi nüzi tiyu guan [The Notion of Women's Physical Education in the Eighth FECG]." *Shenbao* (19 Aug. 1927): 17 (Supplement). For some basic information on the female division of the National Amateur Athletic Federation of America, *see* Epstein, "Sameness"; Theriot, "Towards".
156. Brown, F., *Official Report of the Ninth*, p. 46.
157. Ibid., p. 23; "Closing Banquet of Olympic Games Attended by over 600 who Took Part in Contests." *China Press* (3 Sept. 1927): 7–8, here: 8.
158. Jansen, *The Making*, pp. 553–5; Molony, "Crossing Boundaries", pp. 93–104 (also covering the YWCA in Japan); Roces, "Rethinking", especially pp. 35–6; Edwards, "Chinese Feminism", pp. 54, 56–63.
159. "Five Japanese Boxers for Tenth Olympics." *Philippines Free Press* (12 May 1934): 25. Other parts of the Japanese colonial empire, like Taiwan, also provided athletes for the Japanese team; *see* Morris, *Colonial Project*, p. 16.
160. The Organizing Committee of the Games of New Delhi, India, *1st Western*, p. 6.
161. On the delegation from the Dutch East Indies, *see* "Japanese Stars Due 8 P.M. today for Orient Meet." *Manila Daily Bulletin* (7 May 1934): 3–4, here: 4.
162. In 1935 the secretary of the Sumatra Athletiek Bond asked the IOC if there would be a chance to award the 1938 FECG to Java. *See* Paul L. Driessen, Monsieur le Secrétaire du C.I.O. [Berdez] (12 Sept. 1935). In *H-FC03-EXORI/001*, TOSC. Nothing happened afterwards, which is not surprising, considering that already in 1933 Kishi had rejected the idea of Games hosted in the Dutch East Indies. In early 1937 the Chinese

gave up their plan to host the 1938 FECG, declaring their willingness to dissolve the FEAA: Takashima, "Manshūkoku", pp. 177–8.

163. Research on the wartime games is even sparser than that on the FECG. The Amateur Athletic Association of the Orient did not produce noteworthy results, but in 1939 a sports event between Japan, Manchukuo, and (occupied) 'China' took place: Takashima, *Teikoku Nihon,* chapter I, 2. The same year the International Amateur Athletic Federation also provisionally accepted Manchukuo as a member: Wang, My dear Chairman [Baillet-Latour] (6 Dec. 1939). In *MBR. WANG, Chengting T.*, TOSC. In June 1940 the East Asian Games (*Tōa Taikai*) were held as a substitute for the abandoned Olympic Games during the 2,600th Anniversary of the Imperial Era. Japan, China (Wang Jingwei Regime), Hawaii, Inner Mongolia (Mengjiang), Manchukuo, the Philippines, and a group of foreign residents participated in these games. On them, *see* Collins, "Sporting", pp. 2456–68 (also providing pictures); Ozawa, "Ajia no Orinpikku"; Dainihon Taiiku Kyōkai, *Dainihon Taiiku,* vol. 2, pp. 156–203; Takashima, *Teikoku Nihon,* chapter I, 3. In Aug. 1942 a second version of the East Asian Games was opened in Xinjing (Changchun) in Manchukuo (winter games followed in early 1943) to celebrate the tenth anniversary of the territory. This time Japan, China (Wang Jingwei Regime), and Manchukuo participated, while Inner Mongolia (Mengjiang) was integrated into the Chinese team: Irie, "Kindai Nihon", pp. 417–19; Takashima, *Teikoku Nihon,* chapter I, 4. The Greater East Asia Conference (5–6 Nov. 1943) was also accompanied by a meeting of scholarship holders from occupied countries participating not in sports but in calisthenics and other physical education practices: Asis, *From Bataan,* pp. 74–6; Takashima, *Teikoku Nihon,* pp. 229–30. That and the general context, including the presence of most of the conference participants and observers, gave the event a quite militaristic, anti-Western, and pan-Asian touch.

164. I mentioned above the problems between John Gray and Elwood and Franklin Brown. These certainly existed, but as described could always be solved.

Chapter 3

1. Mello, *Portrait,* p. 291.
2. For example Boria Majumdar and Nalin Mehta in their otherwise very interesting study leave the tensions between the Indians and the East Asians out, possibly due to a lack of sources: Majumdar and Mehta, *India,* chapter 7.
3. Abraham, "From Bandung", pp. 200–1; Brown, Ju., *Nehru,* pp. 185, 244–5; Guha, *India,* pp. 162–3.
4. Brown, Ju., *Nehru,* pp. 245–6, 255–7, 267, 270. For a contemporary Congress perspective, *see also* Gautam, "India's Foreign Policy", especially pp. 107–8, 110–11.
5. Brown, Ju., *Nehru,* pp. 186–9, 190–202, 229–30, 236–7, 240; Metcalf and Metcalf, *A Concise History,* pp. 229–30.
6. Literature on sport in early independent India is scarce and mostly covers the First Asian Games and the Olympic victories in hockey. Majumdar and Mehta, *India,*

deal with these topics in chapters 5 and 7. Sisodia, "India", provides a quite poor overview of the First (and Eighth) Asian Games. For a less academic, more personal and somewhat self-praising overview of the early years, *see* the respective parts of Mello, *Portrait.*

7. C. C. Abraham, "Physical Education in a Democracy." *Association Men* (India) 4, 1–2 (1952): 6–7.
8. On the organizers, *see* Mello, *Portrait*, pp. 274–5; Majumdar and Mehta, *India*, p. 162; *First Asian Games Bulletin*, p. 10; "Lt-Gen Yadavindra Singh." *The Times* (19 June 1974): 18; "Move to Form Asian Games Federation." *Times of India* (23 July 1947): 6. On Mello's, Nehru's, and Kaur's later activities concerning sport see also: Mellow, *Reaching*, p. 60.
9. "Scope for India in Post-War Sport Arena." *Times of India* (14 Mar. 1945): 8. As the author of the newspaper article mentioned, at least some of Sondhi's plans were rather unrealistic.
10. Sondhi, My dear Mr. Edstrom [sic] (27 Mar. 1947). In *H-FC02-ASIAN/007*, TOSC; Mello, *Portrait*, p. 299; "Background of the Organization of the Asian Games Federation." *The Filipino Athlete* (May 1951): 12–14, here: 12; Asian Relations Organization, *Asian Relations*, p. 288; Sondhi, *Asian Relations Conference*, p. 3.
11. Jones, M., "A 'Segregated' Asia?", pp. 843–44.
12. Sondhi, *Asian Relations Conference*, pp. 1–3.
13. "India Should Sponsor the Asian Games." *Times of India* (16 Nov. 1947): 13. *See also* "Move to Form Asian Games Federation." *Times of India* (23 July 1947): 6; "Background of the Organization of the Asian Games Federation." *The Filipino Athlete* (May 1951): 12–14, here: 12 (leaving out the very important problem of insufficient funding).
14. "Background of the Organization of the Asian Games Federation." *The Filipino Athlete* (May 1951): 12–14, here: 12.
15. On Vargas' wartime activities, *see* Saulo, *Let George*, chapters 13–17.
16. See his proposal to the Fifth National Congress of the Kuomintang in 1935 as given in Xu, *Olympic Dreams*, p. 65. On his and his colleagues activities concerning the 1948 Olympics, which included mismanagement and the problem of initially having insufficient money to bring the team back to China, *see* Morris, *Cultivating*, pp. 592–8; Xu, *Olympic Dreams*, p. 48. After the communists' victory in the civil war Wang did not move with the Kuomintang to Taiwan, but went to Hong Kong, *see* Brownell, "Sport and Politics", p. 255.
17. L. C. Wilson, Annual Report for the Year Ending Sept. 30, 1917, p. 3. In *International Work in Japan. Box 5: Annual and Quarterly Reports. 1917. 2.: G-W*, KFYMCAA; Xu, *Olympic Dreams*, p. 45. See also Hao's book on physical education in China, which is full of the YMCA's 'civilizing' and citizenship training ideas: Hoh [Hao], *Physical Education.* His memoirs written shortly before his death show a strong bitterness against the Chinese communists and the Japanese. *See* the respective parts in Hao, *Hao.* On his life in general, including during wartime, *see* Ye, *Hao.* On the offices he accumulated during the war *see* Morris, *Cultivating*, p. 530.

18. IOC president Edström's questions at the IOC meeting in London indicate that the East Asians at first had intended to revive the FECG: Session du Comite International Olympique, Londres 1948, pp. 18–19. In *Comité International Olympique - Session 1894–2008*, TOSC.
19. "The Pan-Islamic Games." *The Filipino Athlete* (Aug. 1948): 13. The Games seem not to have taken place, but the countries invited were Afghanistan, Egypt, Iran, Iraq, Lebanon, Pakistan, Syria, and Turkey.
20. "Mr. Sondhi to Try for Asian Olympiad." *The Indian Express* (25 July 1948): 7.
21. On the plan, *see* Vargas' personal notes written on: Constitution of the Asian Amateur Athletic Federation. In *Sports 1948*, JBVM. On Hao and his plan regarding Shanghai, *see* Hao, *Hao*, p. 38. In May 1948 it still had been possible to host the Seventh National Games in Shanghai: Morris, *Cultivating*, pp. 584–92. *See also* "Background of the Organization of the Asian Games Federation." *The Filipino Athlete* (May 1951): 12–14, here: 12–13.
22. "Indian Team Praised." *Times of India* (20 Sept. 1948): 8.
23. Spence, *Chinas Weg*, pp. 594–9.
24. "Background of the Organization of the Asian Games Federation." *The Filipino Athlete* (May 1951): 12–14, here: 13–14; "Asian Games." *Times of India* (13 Feb. 1949): 5.
25. The Mediterranean Games, in which some Asian countries such as Lebanon and Syria as well as (in terms of Asian geography more problematically) Turkey participated, were in the process of being set up. The first event took place in Egypt in 1951. *See* "Les Jeux méditerranéens à Alexandrie." *Bulletin du Comité International Olympique* (Mar. 1951): 18. Moreover, Abdul Rahman Hassan Azzam, the first secretary general of the Arab League, in 1947 had suggested the establishment of a sports organization. However, his idea remained dormant until April 1953: Rolim Silva and Gerber, "The Arab Games", pp. 6–7, 12.
26. "Delhi Sports Stadium Will Be Ready for Asian Games." *Times of India* (6 May 1949): 8; Mello, *Portrait*, p. 306.
27. On Hao, *see* Hao, *Hao*, p. 56; "Asian Games Will Decide Far East Meet Revival." *Manila Times* (3 Nov. 1949): 8; "PAAF Approves Plan to Revive Far Eastern Olympic Games." *Manila Times* (12 Nov. 1949): 6.
28. Mello, *Portrait*, p. 307; "First Asian Games." *Times of India* (8 Dec. 1949): 11; "The Asian Games Postponed." *Times of India* (25 May 1950): 3.
29. Sondhi, Dear Sir [Asano] (1 Feb. 1950), and Africa, Dear Mr. Neufeld (24 Apr. 1950). Both in *Record Group 331: Allied Operational and Occupation Headquarters, World War II, 1907–1966, Series: Topical File, 1945–1951, Box 5724: Asian Games Federation, 1945–1951* [sic], NARAII; "May Withdraw from New Delhi Asian Olympics." *Manila Chronicle* (3 Mar. 1950): 11.
30. Romulo, My dear Mr. Vargas (13 July 1950). In *SG-Philippine Amateur Athletic Association*, JBVM.
31. The Vargas-Saulo Interviews. A Series of Fourteen Tape-Recorded Interviews with MR. JORGE B. VARGAS and son EDDIE, from April 19 to May 24, 1977. Conducted,

transcribed and edited by Alfredo B. Saulo, pp. 145 (quotation), 151. In *The Vargas-Saulo Interviews*, JBVM. *See also* Minutes of the 2nd Meeting of the Council of Asian Games Federation Held on 31st July, 1950, at 11.30 a.m., at Patiala House, New Delhi, pp. 1–2. In *H-FC02-ASIAN/006*, TOSC.

32. On Azuma, *see* Masaji Tabata (...), p. 2. In *D. RM01. JAPON/003*, TOSC.
33. Procès-verbal de la Session de Copenhague, 15, 16, 17 mai 1950 (Hôtel d'Angleterre), pp. 2–4, 9–10, and Annexe no. 5 bis (texte anglais). In *Comité International Olympique - Session 1894–2008*, TOSC. On MacArthur's Olympic activities *see* Lucas, "USOC"; MacArthur, *Reminiscences*, pp. 86–7.
34. Minutes of the 2nd Meeting of the Council of Asian Games Federation Held on 31st July, 1950, at 11.30 a.m., at Patiala House, New Delhi, p. 2. In *H-FC02-ASIAN/006*, TOSC. Sondhi informed the Japanese in August about the AGF's decision: Sondhi, Dear Sir [Azuma] (14 Aug. 1950). In *Record Group 331: Allied Operational and Occupation Headquarters, World War II, 1907–1966, Series: Topical File, 1945–51, Box 5724: Asian Games Federation, 1945–1951* [sic], NARAII. About the same time the IOC came to the conclusion that its recognition and Japan re-affiliating with the relevant international sports federation would de jure allow it to participate in the 1952 Olympic Games: Réunion de la Commission Exécutive à Lausanne. Séance du 28 août 1950, 9 H. 30 min., p. 4. In *Comité International Olympique - Commission exécutive 1921–1979*, TOSC.
35. Mello, *Portrait*, p. 306.
36. Harold Milks, "Asian Games Open Today." *Straits Times* (4 Mar. 1951): 19.
37. *See* the short resolution in *Ajia Kyōgi Taikai e Nihon daihyōdan haken ni kan suru ketsugi* [Decision on Sending a Japanese delegation to the Asian Games], NAoJ.
38. King Tribhuvan of Nepal, gaining control of his country only in Feb. 1951 after many years as nominal head of state, had made a special request to have Nepal admitted shortly before the Games started: "Stage Set for First Asian Games." *Times of India* (4 Mar. 1951): 9.
39. Framke, "International Events"; Stolte, "Bringing Asia"; Stolte, "The Asiatic Hour"; Singh, "From Delhi to Bandung".
40. Stolte, "The Asiatic Hour", pp. 59–60.
41. Nehru, *Selected Works*, vol. 2, p. 504.
42. Nehru, *Selected Works*, vol. 15: 2, pp. 105–6. *See also* "Asian Games Welcomed by Pandit Nehru." *Times of India* (22 Feb. 1951): 9.
43. Nehru's speech is relatively close to the statement of S. K. Mukerjee in connection to the Ninth FECG covered in the second chapter. On Nehru and the 'Asia as greater India' discourse, *see also* Fischer-Tiné and Stolte, "Imagining Asia in India", p. 87.
44. Nehru, *Selected Works*, vol. 16: 1, pp. 619–20. *See also* "Nehru Opens Congress of Asian Games Federation." *The Overseas Hindustan Times* (8 Mar. 1951): 4; "Regaining Lost Touch and Contact with Neighbours." *The Indian Express* (4 Mar. 1951): 6.
45. "Japan Finishes First, India Second as Asian Games End in New Delhi." *New York Times* (12 Mar. 1951): 38; "Picture." *The Overseas Hindustan Times* (15 Mar. 1951): 3 (showing Nehru awarding some medals).

46. Majumdar and Mehta, *India*, pp. 167–8.
47. Nehru, *Selected Works*, vol. 16:1, p. 620. *See also* "Nehru Opens Congress of Asian Games Federation." *The Overseas Hindustan Times* (8 Mar. 1951): 4.
48. On Anthony de Mello, *see* Mello, *Portrait*, p. 291; "Asian Games—Programme Based on World Olympiad." *The Hindu* (1 Mar. 1951): 8; The Organising Committee, *Official Souvenir*, n.p. On Amrit Kaur, see *First Asian Games Bulletin*, p. 7; The Organising Committee, *Official Souvenir*, n.p. On Yadavindra Singh, *see* The Organising Committee, *Official Souvenir*, n.p.; "Rajpramuk of Pepsu's Message." *The Indian Express* (5 Mar. 1951): 5. On Rajendra Prasad, *see* The Organising Committee, *Official Souvenir*, n.p. On the foreign delegations, *see* The Organising Committee, *Official Souvenir*, n.p. On the Chinese observers' activities, *see* "Wo zhu Yindu dashi juxing jiuhui [Our Ambassador in India Held a Reception]." *Renmin ribao* (21 Mar. 1951): 1.
49. The Organising Committee, *Official Souvenir*, n.p. Accentuation given in the original text. *See also* "Japanese Team in India." *New York Times* (27 Feb. 1951): 43; Oda, "Ajia", p. 157.
50. On the Japanese request to host the Games of 1958, *see* Nihon Taiiku Kyōkai, *Dai-1kai*, p. 16. Japan nonetheless was awarded the 1958 Games at the next AGF meeting at the Helsinki Olympic Games in 1952, in which Japan finally had been allowed by the IOC to participate: "The Asian Games Federation Second Conference at Helsinki." *The Filipino Athlete* (Oct. 1952): 7, 9, here: 7. By then Japan had also signed and ratified the San Francisco Peace Treaty.
51. Sondhi, Remarks on the Circular Letter Issued by Mr. Avery Brundage, the New President of the International Olympic Committee [1952], pp. 1–3, and Sondhi, Dear President [Brundage] (23 Oct. 1960). Both in *MBR. SONDHI, Guru Dutt*, TOSC; Guru Dutt Sondhi, "Voice of India. Athletic Development of Asia." *Olympic Review* 82 (May 1963): 45–8; *Minutes of the Sixth Congress of the Asian Games Federation Held in Rome, Italy, 23rd and 26th Aug. 1960*, pp. 13–16 (here the delegates from Pakistan, Hong Kong, Taiwan, and South Korea agree with Sondhi against Indonesia on not including yachting and fencing).
52. *Minutes of the Meeting of the Executive Committee of the Asian Games Federation Held in Rome, Italy, 22nd Aug. 1960*, p. 17 (here Sondhi is informed that such a closing ceremony had been tested at the 1958 British Empire and Commonwealth Games, but would have led to a lack of discipline of the athletes; the Olympic Games nonetheless featured such a ceremony from 1956); Sondhi, Remarks on the Circular Letter Issued by Mr. Avery Brundage, the New President of the International Olympic Committee, p. 3. In MBR. *SONDHI, Guru Dutt*, TOSC. The idea of giving up national anthems and flags could not be established in the Olympic Games. *See also* Sondhi, "The Asian and the Olympic Games." *The Hindu* (24 May 1958): 10 (Supplement); Gajek, *Imagepolitik*, p. 291.
53. Jal D. Pardivala, The Sport in India, p. 18. In *D. RM01. INDE/013*, TOSC.
54. Mello, *Portrait*, pp. 275–8. On the plans for other stadia in Bombay (Mumbai), Madras (Chennai), Calcutta (Kolkata), and Ahmedabad, *see* "Plans for the National Stadium Finalised." *Times of India* (23 Mar. 1950): 11. On the failure of large parts of the plan, *see* Mello, *Portrait*, p. 278.

55. *First Asian Games Bulletin*, p. 13; Mello, *Portrait*, p. 278; "Plans for the National Stadium Finalised." *Times of India* (23 Mar. 1950): 11.
56. Mello, *Portrait*, pp. 278–9, 307–8; "Delhi Diary." *Times of India* (28 Jan. 1951): 6; *First Asian Games Bulletin*, p. 13.
57. Mello, *Portrait*, pp. 281, 308.
58. "Delhi Diary." *Times of India* (28 Jan. 1951): 6. Later on, Mello would argue for the 1964 Olympic Games: Mello, *Portrait*, pp. 339–40.
59. Mello, *Portrait*, p. 283.
60. Mello, *1st Asian Games New Delhi 1951. Closing Ceremony*, n.p.
61. Nihon Taiiku Kyōkai, *Dai-1kai*, pp. 16–17.
62. Either Nepal was left out, since it had joined late, or Pakistan, since it had not sent a delegation.
63. "First Asian Games Declared Open in Colourful Setting." *Times of India* (5 Mar. 1951): 1.
64. Gold and Revill, "The Cultural Olympiads", pp. 83–4; "Das Olympische Feuer und der Fackellauf [The Olympic Fire and the Torch Relay]." Available at http://www.olympic.org/Documents/Reports/FR/fr_report_656.pdf [accessed: 27 Aug. 2013].
65. The symbolic meaning must have been widely understood. Oda Mikio, the first Japanese Olympic gold medalist, explicitly mentioned the Red Fort as the place where the Indian flag had been hoisted in 1947 in his article on the approaching First Asian Games: Oda, "Ajia", p. 159.
66. Available at http://knowindia.gov.in/knowindia/culture_heritage.php?id=44 [accessed 5 Apr. 2014]; and http://india.gov.in/india-glance/national-symbols [accessed 5 Apr. 2014].
67. Asian Games Federation, *Asian Games Rules*, p. 9.
68. "First Asian Games Declared Open in Colourful Setting." *Times of India* (5 Mar. 1951): 1.
69. For the articles in the AGF constitution on the ceremonies and the art exhibition, *see* Asian Games Federation, *Asian Games Rules*, pp. 8–11. On the development of the Olympic ceremonies and the Olympic art exhibition, *see* Gold and Revill, "The Cultural Olympiads", pp. 83–106.
70. "First Asian Games Open in New Delhi." *The Overseas Hindustan Times* (8 Mar. 1951): 12.
71. Ibid.; "Stage Set for First Asian Games." *Times of India* (4 Mar. 1951): 9; Harold Milks, "Over 500 Athletes of 10 Nations Vie for Honors." *Manila Times* (4 Mar. 1951): 9. It was the first time that an Indian team attending a large international sports event included some female (track and field) athletes. The second event would be the 1952 Summer Olympic Games: Jal D. Pardivala, "Our Women Athletes." *The Hindu* (24 May 1958): 5, 11, here: 5 (Supplement).
72. "First Asian Games Declared Open in Colourful Setting." *Times of India* (5 Mar. 1951): 1; Puri, *The Asian Games*, p. 12.
73. "Current Topics." *Times of India* (6 Mar. 1951): 4. The fact that American newspapers eventually published some articles on the Games was, showing some pride, mentioned

in the *Times of India*: "First Asian Games Earned Prominence in US Press." *Times of India* (13 Mar. 1951): 8.

74. The Organising Committee, *Official Souvenir*, n.p.; Hashimoto, *Nihon*, p. 202.
75. "Delhi Diary." *Times of India* (11 Mar. 1951): 6.
76. *See*, for example, Interviewee: DE CASTRO, Harold, 002968, Reel/Disc no. 4. In *Oral History Centre*, NAoS.
77. Majumdar and Mehta, *India*, chapter 8.
78. The *Time* magazine claimed, however, that the Japanese and some other athletes stayed away from the observers the People's Republic of China had sent. This does not sound unrealistic: "India: First Asiad." *Time* (19 Mar. 1951): 36.
79. "First Asian Games Formally Opened." *New York Times* (5 Mar. 1951): 25. On the YMCA in independent India *see* David, *The YMCA*, chapters 8–9. The large number of Indian athletes (the 'home factor') certainly contributed to it gaining the unofficial second place. On the number of victories of each country *see* Nihon Taiiku Kyōkai, *Dai-1kai*, p. 174.
80. Majumdar and Mehta, *India*, title of chapter 7.
81. "Lessons at the Asian Games in New Delhi." *The Filipino Athlete* (May 1951): 16, 21, here: 16. For a photo, *see* Zhu et al., *Yayunhui*, p. 2.
82. "Lessons at the Asian Games in New Delhi." *The Filipino Athlete* (May 1951): 16, 21. *See also* "Franco, Other Winners among 'Forgotten People'." *Manila Times* (13 Mar. 1951): 5; Interviewee: KEE Soon Bee, 001808, Reel/Disc no. 6 and Interviewee: MITCHELL, Keith; Mitchell, Barry; Wolters, Wiebe, A1999/000839 and 002133, Reel/Disc no. 5. All in *Oral History Centre*, NAoS.
83. "Mahmud Namdjou Sets up New Figures for Weight-Lifting." *Times of India* (6 Mar. 1951): 1, 5; "Stage Set for First Asian Games." *Times of India* (4 Mar. 1951): 9; W. E. Trevor, "Officials Forgot the Runners." *Straits Times* (9 Mar. 1951): 1, 12, here: 1; Interviewee: MITCHELL, Keith; Mitchell, Barry; Wolters, Wiebe, A1999/000839 and 002133, Reel/Disc no. 5. In *Oral History Centre*, NAoS.
84. Leon, "Our Committees are Being Packed with Personalities Who are Not Familiar with the Intricacies of Sports." *Times of India* (17 June 1951): 9; Leon, "Unmitigated Nonsense Is Uttered in what Purports to Be the Interests of Indian Sports." *Times of India* (6 May 1951): 9; Leon, "Somnolence of Indian Olympic Association May Jeopardise Our Participation in Games at Helsinki." *Times of India* (9 Dec. 1951): 11. The organizers later were also accused of having taken away cars, bikes, typewriters, and other things as a remuneration, which would have led to a deficit of about 60,000 Rupees: P. Misra et al., Dear Sir [Brundage] (10 Apr. 1956), p. 3. In *Avery Brundage Collection, Box 133: India*, TOSC. *See also* Leon, "Sport News and Views of the Day." *Times of India* (4 Nov. 1953): 10.

Chapter 4

1. Organizing Committee Second Asian Games, *Asian Games Bulletin*, no. 8, p. 4. Italics are my own.
2. "The Asian Games Federation Second Conference at Helsinki." *The Filipino Athlete* (Oct. 1952): 7, 9, here: 7.
3. Brands, *Bound*, pp. 209, 214–19, 222–3, 228, 231–4; Doronila, *The State*, pp. 45–9; Shalom, *The United States*, pp. 33–67.
4. Brands, *Bound*, pp. 213–14, 227–8, 234–6; Shalom, *The United States*, pp. 68–71.
5. Brands, *Bound*, p. 229; Shalom, *The United States*, pp. 71–3.
6. Brands, *Bound*, pp. 236–45, 250–5; Doronila, *The State*, p. 74; Shalom, *The United States*, pp. 76–93.
7. Brands, *Bound*, pp. 248–50, 256–9; Ohno, *War*, pp. 45, 53; "India: Discord in Colombo." *Time* (10 May 1954): 26–7. On the First Indochina War and American foreign policy, *see also*, for example, Bradley, *Vietnam*, chapter 2; Frey, *Geschichte*, chapters 3–7.
8. For a broad overview of the people involved in managing the Games, see *Second Asian Games Manila, Philippines: May 1–9, 1954: Official Report*, p. 16.
9. Ibid., 5.
10. Ylanan, Dear Sir [Baillet Latour] (14 June 1935). In *PT-BAILL-CORR. Correspondance de Baillet-Latour (Président). 1935–38*, TOSC; Antonio de las Alas. In *D. RM01. PHILI/006*, TOSC; Vargas, "The Second", p. 86.
11. *Second Asian Games Manila, Philippines: May 1–9, 1954: Official Report*, pp. 5, 16; The Secretariat, Manila Sports Service Bureau, *2nd Asian Games*, p. 45.
12. Vargas, "The Second", 86. On Bartolome, *see also* Ylanan and Ylanan, *The History*, pp. 46–7.
13. Vargas, "The Second", 86.
14. From now until the conclusion both terms will be used to describe the same political entity.
15. *Second Asian Games Manila, Philippines: May 1–9, 1954: Official Report*, pp. 4–5; Puri, *The Asian Games*, pp. 13–14; Organizing Committee Second Asian Games, *Asian Games Bulletin*, no. 1, p. 17; *Official Report of the Organizing Committee for the Sixth Asian Games Bangkok 1970*, pp. 3–7.
16. On CENTO, which until 1959 was called the 'Baghdad Pact', *see* Jalal, "Towards".
17. Mayer, Dear Mr. Sondhi (6 Feb. 1949 [incorrectly given as: 1959]). In *H-FC02-ASIAN/007*, TOSC.
18. Hong, "Communist China", p. 77. On the 'Two Chinas Problem' and the IOC, *see* Xu, *Olympic Dreams*, chapter 4; Pei, *A Question*.
19. Francisco Garay, "AGF Body Explains Sino View." *The Evening News* (8 Aug. 1952), In *Sports 1952–53*, JBVM.
20. The Vargas-Saulo Interviews. A Series of Fourteen Tape-Recorded Interviews with MR. JORGE B. VARGAS and son EDDIE, from April 19 to May 24, 1977. Conducted, transcribed and edited by Alfredo B. Saulo, pp. 142–3, 233–4. In *The Vargas-Saulo*

Interviews, JBVM. AGF vice president and Indian member of the IOC Sondhi also in 1952 had come to the conclusion that both China and 'Taiwan' or 'Formosa' (not a 'Republic of China') needed to be recognized, not because of political or legal considerations, but due to the 'real' situation: Sondhi, Remarks on the Circular Letter Issued by Mr. Avery Brundage, the New President of the International Olympic Committee, p. 4. In *MBR. SONDHI, Guru Dutt*, TOSC.

21. On Hao's prominent role in Taiwan's discussions with the IOC between 1952 and 1970, *see* Brownell, "Sport and Politics", p. 257. For the People's Republic's official portrayal of events in 1952, accusing Hao of trying to steal the name of China and spreading negative rumors, *see* "Zhongguo tiyu daibiaotuan guanyu canjia di 15 jie guoji Aolinpike yundonghui de baogao [The Chinese Sports Delegation Made a Report concerning the Participation in the 15th International Olympic Games]." *Renmin ribao* (25 Aug. 1952): 3.
22. Hao, *Hao*, pp. 57–63.
23. Abraham, "From Bandung", pp. 204–8; "India: Discord in Colombo." *Time* (10 May 1954): 26–7.
24. Hao, *Hao*, pp. 65–9. *See also*, for example, Brundage contacting the International Swimming Federation regarding the Republic of China's membership: Brundage, Dear Mr. Sallfors (23 Feb. 1954). In *H-FC02-ASIAN/008*, TOSC. *See also* "Asian Games Federation Cannot Bolt I.O.C.; Regional Body not a Member." *Manila Bulletin* (3 Nov. 1953), in *Sports 1953–1954*, JBVM; "Second Asian Games to Remain under IOC." *Manila Times* (9 Dec. 1953), in *Sports 1953–1954*, JBVM.
25. Hao, *Hao*, pp. 68–71. The four largest delegations came from Taiwan (211 athletes), Japan (208 athletes), the Philippines (172 athletes), and Indonesia (97 athletes): Nihon Taiiku Kyōkai, *Dai-2kai*, p. 142.
26. The Secretariat, Manila Sports Service Bureau, *2nd Asian Games*, p. 7.
27. Organizing Committee Second Asian Games, *Asian Games Bulletin*, no. 4, p. 2, and no. 6, p. 3.
28. Vargas, "The Second", p. 85. *See also* Organizing Committee Second Asian Games, *Asian Games Bulletin*, no. 8, p. 5; "Second Asian Games End; Int'l Amity Stressed during Rites." *Manila Chronicle* (10 May 1954), In *3rd Asian Games, Ramon Teodoro Vargas, Aug. 1950-May 1958*, JBVM. For another anonymous editorials fitting these aspects *see* Organizing Committee Second Asian Games, *Asian Games Bulletin*, no. 5, p. 3.
29. The Secretariat, Manila Sports Service Bureau, *2nd Asian Games*, p. 9; De las Alas, "Significance of 2nd Asian Games." *Manila Bulletin* (9 Apr. 1954): 9, 11; Organizing Committee Second Asian Games, *Asian Games Bulletin*, no. 8, p. 5. For an anonymous editorial fitting these aspects *see* Organizing Committee Second Asian Games, *Asian Games Bulletin*, no. 4, p. 2.
30. Organizing Committee Second Asian Games, *Asian Games Bulletin*, no. 8, p. 3. *See also* The Secretariat, Manila Sports Service Bureau, *2nd Asian Games*, p. 3. For further similar statements, *see* "See World Amity in Asian Games." *Manila Bulletin*

(1 May 1954): 2; Organizing Committee Second Asian Games, *Asian Games Bulletin,* no. 6, p. 5.

31. Organizing Committee Second Asian Games, *Asian Games Bulletin,* no. 8, p. 4.
32. An example of a more successful 'rollback' had happened in Aug. 1953 when American and British secret services overthrew Iranian Prime Minister Mohammad Mossadegh's government, replacing it with an autocratic system under the more cooperative Iranian Shah Mohammad Reza Pahlavi: Saikal, "Iranian", p. 442.
33. 47th Session—Helsinki 1952, pp. 26–29. In *Comité International Olympique—Session 1894–2008,* TOSC; "2nd Asian Games End; Tokyo Site of Next Meet." *Manila Times* (10 May 1954): 1, 9, here: 9; "Asian Officials Meet Today." *Manila Bulletin* (5 May 1954): 19.
34. The Secretariat, Manila Sports Service Bureau, *2nd Asian Games,* p. 147; Suzuki, "Ajia Taikai", p. 189. *See also* Minutes of the 52nd Session of the I.O.C. in Melbourne, 19–20–21 Nov. and 4 Dec. 1956, p. 8, and 49ème Session du Comité International Olympique, Athenes, 12–12–13–14–15 Mai 1954, Hôtel Grande-Bretagne, p. 18. Both in *Comité International Olympique - Session 1894–2008,* TOSC.
35. *2nd Asian Games Official Program,* p. 12; *Second Asian Games Manila, Philippines: May 1–9, 1954: Official Report,* p. 50; Organizing Committee Second Asian Games, *Asian Games Bulletin,* no. 4, p. 14; The Secretariat, Manila Sports Service Bureau, *2nd Asian Games,* p. 35. The lyrics of the song were written by Colonel C. B. Rigor.
36. *2nd Asian Games Official Program,* p. 13; *Second Asian Games Manila, Philippines: May 1–9, 1954: Official Report,* p. 49.
37. Ylanan and Ylanan, *The History,* p. 49; Bocobo-Olivar, *History,* chapter 10.
38. *2nd Asian Games Official Program,* p. 97.
39. "200 Girls Sing 'Till We Meet Again'." *Straits Times* (10 May 1954): 12; *Second Asian Games Manila, Philippines: May 1–9, 1954: Official Report,* p. 105.
40. *Second Asian Games Manila, Philippines: May 1–9, 1954: Official Report,* pp. 105–6; "Photo." *Manila Bulletin* (10 May 1954): 1.
41. *Second Asian Games Manila, Philippines: May 1–9, 1954: Official Report,* p. 108.
42. The Secretariat, Manila Sports Service Bureau, *2nd Asian Games,* p. 150.
43. On the medals, *see* http://www.olympic.org/london-1948-summer-olympics [accessed 1 June 2013].
44. The Secretariat, Manila Sports Service Bureau, *2nd Asian Games,* p. 148.
45. On the medals *see,* for example, http://www.olympic.org/london-1948-summer-olympics [accessed 1 June 2013].
46. The Secretariat, Manila Sports Service Bureau, *2nd Asian Games,* p. 148.
47. Organizing Committee Second Asian Games, *Asian Games Bulletin,* no. 3, p. 11; *Second Asian Games Manila, Philippines: May 1–9, 1954: Official Report,* p. 103. For some of the exhibition objects *see* Nihon Taiiku Kyōkai, *Dai-2kai,* pp. 119–21.
48. Spanish architecture was featured prominently on the delegates' medals: The Secretariat, Manila Sports Service Bureau, *2nd Asian Games,* p. 149.

49. "Editorial: In Justice to Mr. Vargas." *The Filipino Athlete* (Feb. 1953): 11, 17, here: 17. *See also* Saulo, *Let George*, p. 226.
50. Based on Olympic precedents, the eventually agreed upon conditions for being sufficiently 'Asian' in terms of nationality to participate in the Games was a minimum residence time of five years and being a civilian: "Vargas Answers H'kong Charges." *Manila Chronicle* (25 Sept. 1953), in *Sports 1953–1954*, JBVM.
51. "2nd Asian Games Opening Highlights." *Manila Times* (2 May 1954): 9; Ernesto T. Bitong, "Asian Athletes and the Games." *The Evening News* (3 May 1954): 2, 19, here: 2.
52. Ernesto T. Bitong, "Asian Athletes and the Games." *The Evening News* (3 May 1954): 2, 19, here: 2. The official report of the organizers shows that only about 12,000 people had been admitted, meaning that the stadium featuring 30,000 seats cannot have been fully occupied if the official numbers are not completely wrong (although this is not impossible). One therefore has to assume that 'courageous' athletes could find empty seats if they really desired so, although the lack of coordination certainly meant that most of them were confused and refrained from walking around to do so.
53. "The PAAF and the Asian Games." *The Evening News* (5 May 1954): 8; "Govt. Probe into the Organisation of Games." *Times of India* (5 May 1954): 10; "Disown Part in Asiad Seats Mess." *Manila Bulletin* (6 May 1954): 5.
54. "Mayor Raps PAAF for 'Inefficiency'." *Manila Chronicle* (10 May 1954), in *3rd Asian Games, Ramon Teodoro Vargas, Aug. 1950–May 1958*, JBVM. *See also* "Govt. Probe into the Organisation of Games." *Times of India* (5 May 1954): 10.
55. Vargas, "The Second", p. 88.
56. "Sondhi Assails Critics of Games." *Manila Bulletin* (12 May 1954): 9.
57. Vargas, Dear Mr. and Mrs. Sondhi (27 May 1954). In *SS-Second Asian Games*, JBVM.
58. I. P. Soliongco, "Seriously Speaking." *Manila Chronicle* (2 May 1954), In *3rd Asian Games, Ramon Teodoro Vargas, Aug. 1950–May 1958*, JBVM.
59. I. P. Soliongco, "Seriously Speaking." *Manila Chronicle* (5 May 1954), In *3rd Asian Games, Ramon Teodoro Vargas, Aug. 1950-May 1958*, JBVM. The author of the letter to the editor was a certain Amador Bayani. In the letter he claimed that, after an apparently more competent candidate had rejected the position, Bartolome was sent "post-haste to Springfield College and after nine months of study, came home to become U. P. Physical Director". Bartolome's CV shows that he received his B.P.E. in 1929. The same year he also received his M.P.E. in absentia after attending some summer schools (possibly what Bayani meant) and became acting U.P. physical director. *See* Curriculum Vitae of Candido C. Bartolome. In *Bartolome, Candido C.*, SCASC.
60. It should also be noted, although this might be a coincidence, that the office of national physical director of the Philippines was abolished in 1961 after Ylanan retired, the PAAF reformed by the government, and Bartolome remained a professor at the University of the Philippines: Ylanan and Ylanan, *The History*, p. 41 (here it reads that the office was abolished in 1951, which is a typo), 46; Antonio de las Alas, "An Evaluation of Philippine Sports." *The Filipino Athlete* (May-June 1967): 4–6, 26–9, here: 27.

61. Memorandum on the Report of the Congressional Committee Assigned to Investigate the Philippine Amateur Athletic Federation (PAAF) Pursuant to House Regulation no. 40, p. 10. In *SG-Philippine Amateur Athletic Federation*, JBVM. For a summary of the report, *see* "House Probers Discover Anomalies in PAAF; Propose Drastic Overhaul." *Manila Chronicle* (4 Jan. 1955), In *Sports / Clippings 1954–1958*, JBVM. On the finances, *see also*, *Second Asian Games Manila, Philippines: May 1–9, 1954: Official Report*, p. 40; Vargas, "The Second", p. 87.
62. *Philippine Amateur Athletic Federation. Minutes of the Thirty Seventh*, pp. 19–21. *See also* "Vargas Re-Elected PAAF President; Announces Early Retirement." *Manila Chronicle* (31 July 1954): 7; "Jorge Vargas Must Go." *Manila Chronicle* (5 Jan. 1955): 4.
63. The cartoon depicts Jorge ('George') Vargas as absolutist monarch Louis XIV of France, instead of 'L'état c'est moi' (I am the state) declaring 'L'PAAF est moi' (I am the PAAF). A baseball bat and ball replaced the sceptre and globus cruciger as symbols of authority. Courtiers, representing most of the PAAF delegates, declare that Vargas would be indispensable, hinting at his already sixteen year-long rule (which, strictly speaking, is incorrect, since Vargas became PAAF president in 1935). An athlete with a black eye, representing the organizational flaws of the Second Asian Games, is depicted in the background being completely ignored by Vargas and the courtiers. Also ignored is a Sherlock Holmes like person, standing for the parliamentary investigation into Vargas 'rule'. Arguably, by calling him 'George XVI', the cartoonist might not have hinted at sixteen years of presidency (which are anyway wrong), but at Louis XVI of France, one of Louis XIV's successors. His rule eventually found a deadly end during the French Revolution, the possible claim therefore being that Vargas 'rule' sooner or later would also end in a complete disaster for him and the PAAF (maybe through the investigation). Strictly speaking it did not, since in 1955 de las Alas became (or 'inherited') the PAAF presidency when Vargas refrained from running again, although he remained an IOC member. *See* "Vargas Announced PAAF Retirement." *Manila Chronicle* (8 June 1955), in *Sports / Clippings 1954–1958*, JBVM.
64. Brands, *Bound*, pp. 227, 235–6, 253–4; Shalom, *The United States*, pp. 70, 92.
65. Brands, *Bound*, pp. 213–14.
66. The report also shows that half of the admissions were for soccer matches alone and one quarter for basketball. According to the numbers, the opening ceremony taking place in a stadium providing 30,000 seats was attended by about 12,000 people, while the closing ceremony seems to have drawn only 4,000 people to the venue: *Second Asian Games Manila, Philippines: May 1–9, 1954: Official Report*, pp. 38–9. Vargas after the event initially had talked of an overall number of 300,000 spectators: Vargas, "The Second", p. 85.
67. Vargas, "The Second", p. 88. Vargas claims that the biggest groups came from Japan (38), the Republic of China (30), India (20), and Indonesia (19).
68. Hashimoto, *Nihon*, p. 239.
69. Vargas, "The Second", p. 88; *Second Asian Games Manila, Philippines: May 1–9, 1954: Official Report*, p. 25; "San Miguel to Broadcast Games." *Manila Bulletin* (1 May 1954): 11.

70. *Second Asian Games Manila, Philippines: May 1–9, 1954: Official Report*, p. 25.
71. "Sondhi Assails Critics of Games." *Manila Bulletin* (12 May 1954): 9.
72. Antonio Escoda, "Guards at Asian Games So Efficient Even Scibes' Passes of Little Help." *Manila Bulletin* (4 May 1954): 2; Ernesto T. Bitong, "Asian Athletes and the Games." *The Evening News* (3 May 1954): 2, 19; "Sondhi Assails Critics of Games." *Manila Bulletin* (12 May 1954): 9.
73. Like the wars, some of the major conferences held at about the time of the Games expressed a lot of disunity. A Philippine newspaper therefore came to the conclusion that the Second Asian Games, compared to the Geneva Conference, at which the end of the First Indochina War was negotiated, and the Colombo Conference at which the Indochina War was hotly debated, had shown a much more cordial atmosphere. *See* "The Athlete's Way." *The Evening News* (3 May 1954): 8.
74. The use of English certainly was the best solution in terms of affecting as many people as possible, but certainly not a perfect one. For example, an athlete from Singapore later stated that the Koreans, Iranians, and Pakistanis he met during training could not speak English: Interviewee: DE CASTRO, Harold, 002968, Reel/Disc No: 4. In *Oral History Centre*, NAoS.
75. Organizing Committee Second Asian Games, *Asian Games Bulletin*, no. 7, p. 12. The case on the one hand shows a continuity of the strong influence that Americans had on Philippine sports during colonialism and that they were still valued highly as more experienced advisors. On the other hand, one has to assume that the Filipino officials had a certain eagerness to improve their country's chance of winning medals and thereby to show the Philippines' own progress in relation to the other participating Asian countries.
76. Nihon Taiiku Kyōkai, *Dai-2kai*, p. 142.
77. "Departing Athletes and Officials Praise Management of Asian Games." *Manila Bulletin* (13 May 1954): 13; Granville Ramage, Sir [Eden] (26 May 1954). In *366/54 (Second Asian Games Held in Manila—1954.) Microfilm Number: PRO 10, Government Files*, NAoS; "Sondhi Assails Critics of Games." *Manila Bulletin* (12 May 1954): 9.

Chapter 5

1. The Organizing Committee for the IIIrd Asian Games, *3rd Asian Games Bulletin*, no. 1, p. 2. The bulletin was published in Sept. 1956.
2. "China Not to Participate in 1958 Asian Games." *Survey of China Mainland Press* (19 Mar. 1958): 38–9; "North Korea and Asian Games." *Times of India* (23 Mar. 1958): 13.
3. On the Tokyo Olympic Games *see*, for example, Abel, *The International Minimum*, chapter 5; Droubie, "Phoenix"; Low, "Japan"; Smith, M., "Between East". Christian Tagsold is the only one who shortly focuses on the Third Asian Games as a means to convince the IOC to award Tokyo the Olympic Games of 1964: Tagsold, *Die Inszenierung*, p. 63.

4. Jansen, *The Making*, pp. 666–714; Zöllner, *Geschichte Japans*, pp. 385, 387, 390–1; Ohno, *War*, p. 8. On Allied propaganda, see Dower, *War*, especially part 2.
5. Jansen, *The Making*, p. 701; Zöllner, *Geschichte Japans*, pp. 394, 396, 400.
6. Zöllner, *Geschichte Japans*, pp. 398, 401. The United Nations' sub-organizations included UNESCO, the International Labour Organization, and the International Court of Justice. Japan also joined the International Monetary Fund. In 1958, Japan became a non-permanent member of the United Nations' Security Council: Oba, "Japan's Entry", p. 99; Tomaru, "Japan", p. 66.
7. Jansen, *The Making*, p. 673; Zöllner, *Geschichte Japans*, pp. 397, 401; Tomaru, "Japan", p. 65; Olson, *Japan*, pp. 22, 25–6, 38, 42; Ohno, *War*, pp. 103, 118; Miyagi, "Post-War", pp. 5–6.
8. Tomaru, "Japan", pp. 64, 67–8.
9. On sport in Japan after the Second World War *see* Guttmann and Thompson, *Japanese Sports*, chapters 7–8; Blackwood, "Bushidō", pp. 235–7.
10. Masaji Tabata (...), p. 2. In *D. RM01.JAPON/003*, TOSC; The Organizing Committee for III Asian Games, *Official Report*, p. 5.
11. The Organizing Committee for III Asian Games, *Official Report*, p. 5; Brown, F., *Official Report of the Ninth*, p. 25.
12 Available at http://kotobank.jp/word/%E6%B4%A5%E5%B3%B6%E5%AF%BF%E4%B8%80 [accessed: 2 Sept. 2013]; The Organizing Committee for III Asian Games, *Official Report*, p. 7; The Organizing Committee for the IIIrd Asian Games, *3rd Asian Games Bulletin*, no. 3, p. 3.
13. Available at http://kotobank.jp/word/%E4%BD%90%E8%97%A4%E5%9F%BA [accessed: 2 Sept. 2013]; The Organizing Committee for III Asian Games, *Official Report*, p. 7.
14. Available at http://kotobank.jp/word/%E7%94%B0%E7%95%91%E6%94%BF%E6%B2%BB [accessed: 2 Sept. 2013]; Masaji Tabata (...), p. 1. In *D. RM01.JAPON/003*, TOSC; Tabata, *Supōtsu*; The Organizing Committee for III Asian Games, *Official Report*, p. 7.
15. The Organizing Committee for the IIIrd Asian Games, *3rd Asian Games Bulletin*, no. 3, p. 3. For the other members of the organizing committee, *see* The Organizing Committee for III Asian Games, *Official Report*, pp. 7–10.
16. The Organizing Committee for III Asian Games, *Official Report*, picture part.
17. The Organizing Committee, *Progress Report on Preparation*, p. 3.
18. The Organizing Committee for the IIIrd Asian Games, *3rd Asian Games Bulletin*, no. 1, p. 3.
19. "Tsushima's Address." In *3rd Asian Games, Jorge B. Vargas Jr., May–July 1958*, JBVM.
20. The Organizing Committee for the IIIrd Asian Games, *3rd Asian Games Bulletin*, no. 1, p. 4.
21. The Organizing Committee for the IIIrd Asian Games, *3rd Asian Games Bulletin*, no. 3, p. 3.
22. "No Title." *The Hindu* (24 May 1958): 3 (Asian Games Supplement).
23. "Short Quotes Here... There." In *3rd Asian Games, Jorge B. Vargas Jr., May–July 1958*, JBVM. For some further comments by Kishi that focused on amateur sports norms

and values as a foundation for Asian regional integration *see* "Competing Nations Salute the Games." *Straits Times* (16 May 1958): 15.

24. "Crown Prince Hails Asian Games Spirit." *Japan Times* (2 June 1958): 1. The quotation provides the full text of his speech.
25. The Organizing Committee for III Asian Games, *Official Report*, p. 1; Seiichiro Yasui, Governor of Tokyo Metropolis, Statement for the Invitation of the 54th IOC Congress to Tokyo. In *Avery Brundage Collection, Box 113: Japan—Third Asian Games,* TOSC; Guttmann and Thompson, *Japanese Sports*, pp. 195–6.
26. As one might expect, in their application for 1964 the Japanese did not list only the Third Asian Games and the FECG as examples of their experience in hosting big international sports events, but also provided some of the statements of IOC members and others regarding the very high quality of the Third Asian Games. *See* Réponses au Questionnaire au Sujet des Jeux Olympiques de 1964 (Provisoire), p. 4. In *VIL-1964S-CAND: Candidatures de Bogota, Bruxelles,* TOSC; Réponses au Questionnaire au Sujet des Jeux Olympiques de 1964, p. 3. In *VIL-1964S-CAND: Candidature de Tokyo pour les Jeux été en 1964,* TOSC. Moreover, the JAAA declared the Third Asian Games to be Asia's 'Olympic Games', thus a smaller version (or testing ground) for the bigger global event: Nihon Taiiku Kyōkai, *Ajia no Orinpikku.*
27. The Organizing Committee for the IIIrd Asian Games, *3rd Asian Games Bulletin*, no. 1, p. 2.
28. Norman Siebel, "Comfort is Keynote at Games 'Village'." *Straits Times* (19 Mar. 1958): 16.
29. Shinobu Higashi, "Country ready for Olympics—Brundage." *Manila Times* (3 June 1958): 8. It should be mentioned that the Melbourne Games had received some bad publicity due to delays in constructing the stadia, meaning that some IOC members had thought about relocating them, *see* Gajek, *Imagepolitik*, p. 107.
30. "Japan Capable of Organizing Olympics: Tabata." *The Mainichi* (3 June 1958), in *Avery Brundage Collection, Box 113: Japan—Third Asian Games,* TOSC.
31. The Organizing Committee for the IIIrd Asian Games, *3rd Asian Games Bulletin*, no. 2, p. 11.
32. Shinobu Higashi, "Country ready for Olympics—Brundage." *Manila Times* (3 June 1958): 8.
33. "70,000 Attend Closing of Third Asian Games." *Japan Times* (2 June 1954): 1 (first quotation); "Brundage Reports of Japan Readiness." *Japan Times* (2 June 1958), in *Avery Brundage Collection, Box 113: Japan—Third Asian Games,* TOSC (second quotation). *See also* "Third Asian Games Big Success, Says Brundage." *The Mainichi* (2 June 1958), in *Avery Brundage Collection, Box 113: Japan—Third Asian Games,* TOSC.
34. "Taikai o owatte [Games Are Closed]." *Asahi Shinbun* (2 June 1958, Tokyo Morning Edition): 5.
35. "For Betterment of Asia: Sondhi." In *3rd Asian Games, Jorge B. Vargas Jr., May–July 1958,* JBVM; The Organizing Committee for the IIIrd Asian Games, *3rd Asian Games Bulletin*, no. 2, pp. 3–4.

36. Reminiscent of the discourses concerning Japan's capability to host the 1964 Olympics, the application for the 2020 Olympics describes the anticipated new Main Stadium as "one of the most advanced stadiums in the world". Available at http://tokyo2020.jp/en/plan/applicant/dl/TOKYO2020_02_enfr.pdf [accessed 10 Sept. 2013].
37. The Organizing Committee for the IIIrd Asian Games, *3rd Asian Games Bulletin*, no. 1, p. 14; The Organizing Committee for the IIIrd Asian Games, *3rd Asian Games Bulletin*, no. 2, p. 11; "Jap Govt to Build Stadium." *Straits Times* (15 Dec. 1956): 16; Hessell Tiltman, "A Candidate for 1964 Olympics." *Guardian* (12 June 1958): 7; "Japan Gets ready." *Straits Times* (5 Mar. 1958): 14 (here the final cost of about 1.1 billion yen is mentioned by Tsushima).
38. The picture depicts the newly built main stadium (back left), the Metropolitan Gymnasium (front left-center) and the newly built Metropolitan Indoor Swimming Stadium (right).
39. The Organizing Committee for the IIIrd Asian Games, *3rd Asian Games Bulletin*, no. 2, p. 11; "Preparing the 3rd Asian Games." *Tokyo Municipal News* 7, 4 (1957): 2; "Japan Gets ready." *Straits Times* (5 Mar. 1958): 14 (here the final cost of about 600 million yen is mentioned by Tsushima).
40. The Organizing Committee for the IIIrd Asian Games, *3rd Asian Games Bulletin*, no. 3, p. 6; "Preparing the 3rd Asian Games." *Tokyo Municipal News* 7, 4 (1957): 2.
41. The Main Stadium, the Metropolitan Gymnasium, the Metropolitan Indoor Swimming Stadium, and the National Tennis Courts were located at the Meiji Shrine Outer Gardens. The Kōrakuen Velodrome, the Kōrakuen Ice Palace, the *Kōdōkan* and the Koishikawa Stadium were located around Kōrakuen garden. Moreover, the Komazawa Volleyball Grounds, the Palace Courts, Waseda University's Memorial Hall, Toyama High School's gymnasium, and several shooting ranges were used: The Organizing Committee for III Asian Games, *Official Report*, p. 47.
42. On Tange and the Tokyo Olympics, *see* Coaldrake, *Architecture*, pp. 256–66. It should be mentioned that the Japanese had intended from the beginning to build another, much bigger swimming stadium for the Olympics, meaning that the Indoor Swimming Stadium was never planned to be the main venue: Réponses au Questionnaire au Sujet des Jeux Olympiques de 1964 (Provisoire), p. 15. In *VIL-1964S-CAND: Candidatures de Bogota, Bruxelles*, TOSC.
43. "Japan May Cancel the Asian Games." *Times of India* (12 Jan. 1958): 12; "Asian Games Will Not Be Cancelled." *Times of India* (28 Jan. 1958): 10.
44. The Organizing Committee for III Asian Games, *Official Report*, p. 33; "Japan Loses on the Games." *Straits Times* (10 July 1958): 16.
45. The Organizing Committee for the IIIrd Asian Games, *3rd Asian Games Bulletin*, no. 2, p. 5; "Japs Abandon Games Village Plan." *Straits Times* (25 Mar. 1957): 12. Japanese officials thought about the possibility of turning the village facilities into regular houses after the Games, but determining that buildings such as the dining hall would then become useless.

46. The Organizing Committee for the IIIrd Asian Games, *3rd Asian Games Bulletin*, no. 6, p. 5; "All Eyes on Tokyo." *The Hindu* (24 May 1958): 4 (Asian Games Supplement).
47. Norman Siebel, "Comfort is Keynote at Games 'Village'." *Straits Times* (19 Mar. 1958): 16; The Organizing Committee for the IIIrd Asian Games, *3rd Asian Games Bulletin*, no. 3, p. 4.
48. The Organizing Committee for III Asian Games, *Official Report*, pp. 36–8.
49. Norman Siebel, "Comfort is Keynote at Games 'Village'." *Straits Times* (19 Mar. 1958): 16; The Organizing Committee for the IIIrd Asian Games, *3rd Asian Games Bulletin*, no. 3, p. 2; "All Eyes on Tokyo." *The Hindu* (24 May 1958): 4 (Asian Games Supplement).
50. "Vargas Praises Tokyo Facilities." In *3rd Asian Games, Jorge B. Vargas Jr., May–July 1958*, JBVM (Vargas); "Visitors Give Views on Asian Games Setup." *Asahi Evening News* (30 May 1958), in *Avery Brundage Collection, Box 113: Japan—Third Asian Games*, TOSC (Singh); "Country ready for Olympics—Brundage." *Manila Times* (3 June 1958): 8 (Kent-Hughes).
51. The village was located at the 'Washington Heights', the site where most barracks of the US army had been built during the occupation. After long negotiations the site was returned to Japanese control, meaning that the barracks could then be used to accommodate the athletes, *see* Tagsold, "Modernity", pp. 293–4.
52. "Sidelights of Games." In *3rd Asian Games, Jorge B. Vargas Jr., May–July 1958*, JBVM; Virgilio Pantaleon, "Asian Games Notes." *Manila Chronicle* (26 May 1958): 13; Virgilio Pantaleon, "Asian Games Notes." *Manila Chronicle* (22 May 1958): 6; "Japan Gets Ready." *Straits Times* (5 Mar. 1958): 14.
53. Shimizu, "Rebuilding", pp. 42–3; Tagsold, *Die Inszenierung*, pp. 108–19; Abel, "Japan's Sporting Diplomacy", p. 214. Other highly important transport infrastructure improvements, which did not directly affect travel within Tokyo, were the construction of the *Shinkansen* (bullet train) line connecting Tokyo and Osaka and the monorail connecting Haneda airport and downtown Tokyo.
54. Carlile, "Economic Development", pp. 11–12.
55. Ibid., p. 12; Robert Trumbull, "Japan's Five Year Plan: More Hotels." *New York Times* (2 Mar. 1958): XX35 [sic].
56. "Package Tours Arranged for Visitors to Games." In *3rd Asian Games, Jorge B. Vargas Jr., May–July 1958*, JBVM.
57. "Photo." *Manila Times* (23 Apr. 1958): 8; Mario Roxas, "Asiad 'Flame' on Way to Tokyo Site." *Philippines Herald* (23 Apr. 1958), in *3rd Asian Games, Ramon Teodoro Vargas, Aug. 1950–May 1958*, JBVM; Thangarajah, *Asia*, p. 44; The Organizing Committee for III Asian Games, *Official Report*, p. 39.
58. On the Asian part of the 1964 torch relay, *see* Tagsold, *Die Inszenierung*, p. 132.
59. Hasegawa, "Introduction", p. 7.
60. The 1964 Olympic Games torch relay also covered Okinawa, thereby claiming it as Japanese territory. *See* Shimizu, "Rebuilding", pp. 48–51; Tagsold, *Die Inszenierung*, pp. 132–3.

61. Droubie, "Phoenix", p. 2315.
62. On the four routes, *see* Tagsold, *Die Inszenierung*, pp. 132, 135.
63. On Sakai *see* Ibid., pp. 133–4.
64. "Third Asian Games Opened by Emperor in Gala Ceremony." *Japan Times* (25 May 1958): 1.
65. Tagsold, "The Tokyo Olympics", pp. 64–5; Tagsold, *Die Inszenierung*, p. 77.
66. "Photo." *Manila Times* (26 May 1958): 12.
67. Virgilio Pantaleon, "Asian Games Notes." *Manila Chronicle* (25 May 1958): 14; "Highlights of the Opening Ceremonies." *Manila Times* (25 May 1958): 16–17.
68. Statements declaring who received the salutes from the delegations entering the stadium—the emperor or the crown prince—are contradictory: "Athletes Make their Bow." *Straits Times* (26 May 1958): 1; "Third Asian Games Inaugurated by Emperor Hirohito." *Times of India* (25 May 1958): 13; Virgilio Pantaleon, "Asian Games Notes." *Manila Chronicle* (25 May 1958): 14. One in any case has to assume that no clear distinction could be made due to the distance between flag bearer and tribune of honor, so the question of dipping the flag or not needed to be decided in advance.
69. "Japanese Viewpoint." *Asahi Evening News* (4 June 1958), in *3rd Asian Games, Jorge B. Vargas Jr., May–July 1958*, JBVM.
70. After the treaty had been signed, socialist Diet members tried to prevent its ratification by blocking the entrance to the lower house, moving the government to assign policemen to forcibly clear the entrance. The opposition then boycotted the vote, so the ratification took place and the treaty was eventually renewed. The tensions between opposition and government nevertheless led to large-scale rioting by leftist groups, which prevented a visit to Japan by US President Dwight D. Eisenhower: Jansen, *The Making*, pp. 707–8.
71. "Tensei jingo [Vox populi, vox dei]." *Asahi Shinbun* (3 June 1958, Tokyo Morning Edition): 1.
72. Mok Sin Pin, "Peltzer: Tokyo Games Badly Run." *Straits Times* (11 July 1958): 16.
73. Droubie, "Phoenix", pp. 2313–14; Tagsold, *Die Inszenierung*, pp. 75, 83–5; Skabelund, "Public Service".
74. Saaler, *Politics*, p. 88. More controversial was that it was also made mandatory to use the national anthem and flag during school ceremonies.
75. Smith, M., *Representing*, pp. 205–11.
76. "Short Quotes Here... There." In *3rd Asian Games, Jorge B. Vargas Jr., May–July 1958*, JBVM.
77. Ibid.
78. On the use of the three former 'symbols of war' at the Tokyo Olympics, *see* Tagsold, *Die Inszenierung*, pp. 76–82.
79. The Organizing Committee for III Asian Games, *Official Report*, p. 41.
80. The Organizing Committee for III Asian Games, *Official Report*, pp. 41, 43–4; *III Asian Games. Official Programme. Tokyo 1958*, p. 199; "Orinpikku no uta [Olympic Songs]." *Yomiuri Shinbun* (25 June 1956, Morning Edition): 4.

81. The Organizing Committee for III Asian Games, *Official Report*, pp. 41, 45; A Brief Report on the IIIrd Asian Games, p. 5, attached to: Tabata, Dear Mr. Mayer (27 Aug. 1958). In *H-FC02-ASIAN/009*, TOSC.
82. Although having taken place in a different context, *Auld Lang Syne* had also been played in the NHK when Supreme Commander of the Allied Powers MacArthur left Japan: Dower, *Embracing*, p. 549.
83. *III Asian Games. Official Programme. Tokyo 1958*, p. 26.
84. The program lists 21 entries: Ibid. For a very detailed overview, *see* Dai-3kai Ajia Kyōgi Taikai Soshiki Iinkai, *Dai-3kai*, pp. 324–9. For further pictures of the events, *see* Dai-3kai Ajia Kyōgi Taikai Soshiki Iinkai (shikitenbu), *Ajia*, n.p.
85. *III Asian Games. Official Programme. Tokyo 1958*, p. 26.
86. Gold and Revill, "The Cultural Olympiads", pp. 83–4.
87. Dai-3kai Ajia Kyōgi Taikai Soshiki Iinkai, *Dai-3kai*, picture part.
88. The Organizing Committee for III Asian Games, *Official Report*, p. 20.
89. Ibid., p. 22.
90. Ibid., pp. 21, 24.
91. Ibid., p. 24. *See also* "Games Broadcast." *Times of India* (22 May 1958): 10; "Good News for Basketball Fans!" *Manila Chronicle* (25 May 1958): 14.
92. "Advertisement." *Times of India* (23 May 1958): 7; "Games Broadcast." *Times of India* (22 May 1958): 10.
93. "Film of Tokyo Games Offers Excellent Fare." *Times of India* (30 Sept. 1958): 10; The Organizing Committee for III Asian Games, *Official Report*, p. 21.
94. Gordon, "Consumption", p. 17; Zöllner, *Geschichte Japans*, p. 407.
95. The Organizing Committee, *Progress Report on Preparation*, p. 15; Hashimoto, *Nihon*, p. 241.
96. On the Tokyo Olympics, *see* Tagsold, *Die Inszenierung*, pp. 105–106.
97. At least one AGF member, India's Moin-ul-Haq, thought that the desire of East German sports officials to send a two man delegation to Tokyo to study the Games was another illustration of how "important" the Asian Games had become internationally: Moin-ul-Haq, Dear Dr. Azuma (9 Apr. 1958). In *DR510/183 (Sofia 1957)*, BArch.
98. On the campaign, which discouraged insulting language, violent behavior, discrimination against foreigners, and leaving waste near hotels and sports venues, *see* Ajia Kyōgi Taikai kaisai ni tomonai raihō suru gaikokujin no ōtai ni tsuite [Concerning the Treatment of the Foreigners that Will Arrive due to the Hosting of the Asian Games]. In *Ajia Kyōgi Taikai kaisai ni tomonai raihō suru gaikokujin no ōtai ni tsuite* [Concerning the Treatment of the Foreigners that Will Arrive due to the Hosting of the Asian Games], NAoJ.
99. Smith, M., *Representing*, p. 123.
100. Nihon Taiiku Kyōkai, *Ajia no Orinpikku*, n.p. (last page).

Chapter 6

1. Sukarno said this during a speech called 'Sports Cannot Be Separated from Politics'. It was made on 13 Feb. 1963, about one week after the IOC had suspended Indonesia from the Olympic movement, *see* Modelski, *The New*, pp. 88–9 (quotation: 88).
2. Department of Information, *The Fourth*, p. 6. The final result was 22:20.
3. As one might expect, the Indonesians used the Bandung Conference to underline their pan-Asian spirit in their application for the Games, *see* Committee for Publication of the Indonesian Olympic Committee, *Indonesia*, p. 9 (being the first page of the actual application). On the Bandung Conference, *see* Lee, *Making a World*; Tan and Acharya, *Bandung Revisited*; Singh, "From Delhi to Bandung"; Jones, M., "A 'Segregated' Asia?"
4. Cribb and Brown, *Modern Indonesia*, chapters 2–6; Frey, *Dekolonisierung*, pp. 177–87; Vickers, *A History*, chapters 4–6.
5. Anderson, B., *Language*, chapter 1.
6. Cribb and Brown, *Modern Indonesia*, chapters 5–6; Frey, *Dekolonisierung*, pp. 229–34; Vickers, *A History*, chapter 5.
7. I will use the term 'non-alignment' to describe Indonesia's foreign policy. However, strictly speaking the Bandung Conference and the Non-Aligned Movement Conferences differed in participants, intellectual content, and the interest the superpowers had in influencing the outcome: Abraham, "From Bandung", p. 197.
8. Brunnell, "Guided Democracy", pp. 56–8; Cribb and Brown, *Modern Indonesia*, chapter 6. For Sukarno's speeches regarding the 'New Emerging Forces' *see also* Modelski, *The New*, especially pp. 2–31.
9. "Japanese Stars Due 8 P.M. today for Orient Meet." *Manila Daily Bulletin* (7 May 1934): 3–4; "Growth of Javanese Athletics Discussed by Delegation Head." *Philippines Herald* (10 May 1934): 1, 16.
10. On the usage of sport in colonial and independent Indonesia see especially: Adams, "Pancasila"; Harsuki, *Olahraga*; Sie, "The Problem"; Sie, "Historical Development"; Brown, C., "Playing the Game"; Brown, C., "Sport"; Colombijn, "The Politics"; Kusuda, "Koroniaru". For the Games of the New Emerging Forces held in Indonesia in 1963, *see below*.
11. On Maladi *see* "Indonesia's First Minister of Sport." *The Asia Magazine* (19 Aug. 1962): 6 (Special Issue: The Fourth Asian Games); Kitley, *Television*, pp. 23–5, 369–70.
12. The Organizing - Committee 4th Asian Games (1960), *Bulletin*, no. 1, pp. 10–12; The Organizing Committee for the Fourth Asian Games, *Asian Games*, pp. 11, 15, 301–3 (and 304–9 on other people involved in organizing the Games).
13. The Organizing Committee for the Fourth Asian Games, *Asian Games*, p. 10.
14. Organizing Committee Asian Games IV 1962, Djakarta (1962), *Bulletin*, no. 5, p. 3. For an earlier short speech of Sukarno made only days after Jakarta received the right to host the Games, *see* Sie, "Sports and Politics", p. 281.

15. *Asian Games 4. Djakarta 1962. 24 Aug.–4 Sept.*, p. 7. These statements were also made public in other countries like India: "Asian Games Will Start on Schedule." *Times of India* (22 Apr. 1962): 13.
16. *Minutes of the Meeting of the Executive Committee of the Asian Games Federation held in Djakarta, Indonesia 21st–22nd April 1962*, p. 6.
17. The Organizing Committee for the IVth Asian Games, *Asian Games*, p. 1. See also *Minutes of the Meeting of the Executive Committee of the Asian Games Federation held in Djakarta, Indonesia 21st–22nd April 1962*, p. 27.
18. Department of Foreign Affairs, *Indonesia*, p. 84.
19. *Asian Games 4. Djakarta 1962. 24 Aug.–4 Sept.*, p. 5.
20. Maladi, "Forward", p. 6.
21. Department of Foreign Affairs, *Indonesia*, pp. 79, 84.
22. On Indonesian maneuvers to win medals, *see* Hanna, "The Politics", pp. 198–9; Nihon Taiiku Kyōkai, *Dai-4kai*, pp. 35, 300–1; Thangarajah, *Asia*, p. 53; "The Asian Games Was a Farce—Dailey." *Straits Times* (9 Sept. 1962): 18.
23. *See*, for example, "No Games Bar on Formosa." *Straits Times* (5 Aug. 1958): 13; "Three Nations Might Be Kept out of Asiad." *Times of India* (26 June 1958): 10; "Vargas Doubts Indonesia Will Bar China." *China News* (26 June 1958): 4.
24. Iraqi Embassy have [sic] protested against Israeli participation in 1962 Asian Games. In *FO 371/152198 (Preparations for South East Asia Peninsular Games, 1961 and Asian Games, 1962)*, TNA.
25. Sie, "Sports and Politics", p. 283.
26. Asian Games to be Held in Djakarta in 1962. In *FO 371/144156 (Preparations for Asian Games in Indonesia in 1962)*, TNA.
27. "Afro-Asian Games Move." *Straits Times* (10 Feb. 1959): 13.
28. *Minutes of the Meeting of the Executive Committee of the Asian Games Federation held in Djakarta, Indonesia 21st–22nd April 1962*, p. 20.
29. Ibid., pp. 21–2 (quotation: 22).
30. Sondhi, Report of the Asian Games as Held in Djakarta - Indonesia, Aug. 1962, p. 8. In *H-FC02-ASIAN/011*, TOSC. Cultural contacts between Egypt and Indonesia had already been strengthened by Egypt inviting Indonesia to the First Arab Games (Alexandria 1953): Rolim Silva and Gerber, "The Arab Games", p. 12.
31. Sondhi, Report of the Asian Games as Held in Djakarta - Indonesia, Aug. 1962, p. 9. In *H-FC02-ASIAN/011*, TOSC. *See also* "Sondhi against Taking Part at Jakarta." *Times of India* (8 Aug. 1962): 10.
32. Only Brunei and Sarawak joined the AGF in 1962: *Minutes of the Meeting of the Executive Committee of the Asian Games Federation held in Djakarta, Indonesia 21st–22nd April 1962*, pp. 15–16.
33. "Invitations for Asian Games to be Issued this Month." *Antara* (15 Jan. 1962, N): 1; Norman Siebel, "Stadium Is Rated Best in World." *Straits Times* (10 Feb. 1962): 17.
34. *See*, for example, Adams, "Pancasila", pp. 302–3; Sie, "Sports and Politics", p. 283. Lutan, "Indonesia", pp. 12, 19, does not even deliver an explanation why Israel was excluded.

35. *See,* for example, Adams, “Pancasila”, pp. 302–3; Liang, *He Zhenliang,* p. 82; Lutan and Hong, “The Politicization”, pp. 22, 26; Sie, “Sports and Politics”, pp. 283. *See also* the articles in Chinese newspapers and news magazines, for example, Wei-Ming Wen [Weiming Wen], “US ‘Two Chinas’ Scheme in World Politics”, *Peking Review* 31 (1962): 14–15.
36. The *Indonesian Observer,* which can be considered as reporting the government’s point of view, complained during the Games that the stance of certain members of the AGF prevented the participation of not only China and North Korea, but also North Vietnam. This accusation has to be seen in the light of North Vietnamese unwillingness to join as long as its rival was recognized as a member. *See* “Sports and Politics.” *Indonesian Observer* (29 Aug. 1962): 2.
37. Ricklefs, *A Modern History,* p. 301.
38. “Sports and Politics.” *Indonesian Observer* (29 Aug. 1962): 2. *See also* Miyamoto, “Ma ga sashita”, p. 208, describing the anti-Taiwanese atmosphere in Indonesia he experienced as a Games correspondent of the Japanese *Asahi Shinbun.*
39. “Taiwan and Israel’s Reported Participation in A.G. Attacked.” *Antara* (14 July 1962, LOS): 5. *See also* “Disapproval with Taiwan & Israel.” *Antara* (29 July 1962, LOS): 7. *See also* Katō, “Ajia Taikai”, p. 654, on the perception of Taiwan as an enemy during the West Papua struggle.
40. *Minutes of the Meeting of the Executive Committee of the Asian Games Federation held in Djakarta, Indonesia 21st–22nd April 1962,* pp. 17, 19. Hao officially offered it at least twice.
41. On this topic *see,* for example, Cha, *Beyond,* pp. 54–61.
42. “Indonesia Bar Taiwan’s Team into Indonesia in Order to Smooth Games.” *Antara* (24 Aug. 1962, BUS): 8. *See also* Liang, *He Zhenliang,* p. 83, mentioning spies reporting Hao’s plans; Xu, *Olympic Dreams,* pp. 51–2. Hao’s biography states that Hao arrived in Indonesia together with several other AGF members, but since he had no visa could not leave the airport. After he was informed that his life would be in danger and still received no visa he finally left again: Ye, *Hao,* pp. 113–14. One can assume that the Indonesian organizers simply did not want to have him in the country and were happy to have a (dubious) excuse for disinviting Taiwan.
43. Israel Olympic Committee, *Djakarta,* p. 14. *See also* Alperovich, *Israel,* pp. 272–5.
44. It should be noted that the participation of Malaya never caused any problems. In August 1962, the president of the Malayan NOC, Tun Abdul Razak, among other offices deputy prime minister, even sent “warmest greetings and good wishes” to the AGF and “our fraternal Indonesian hosts”. *See* Federation of Malaya Olympic Council, *Federation,* p. 7. The *Konfrontasi,* Indonesia’s struggle against Malaysia as a ‘neocolonialist’ construct of Britain, had not yet begun.
45. Hübner, “The Fourth”, pp. 1299–301. The Indonesians took the Cold War problems in international sport into account. Due to the Cold War situation, certain countries such as East Germany and Israel were often not invited to international games or contests, which prompted boycotts from allies of the victim of discrimination and criticism from international sports organizations. For example, in the case of Israel

problems had arisen regarding its invitation to the 1959 Mediterranean Games in Beirut: Stanton, "Pioneer", pp. 2121–2.

46. *Minutes of the 7th Congress of the Asian Games Federation Held in Djakarta on the 23rd and [24th] August 1962.*
47. On the meeting *see Minutes of the Meeting of the Council Members of the Asian Games Federation Held in Djakarta, Indonesia 28th August 1962.* For a detailed overview, *see* Hübner, "The Fourth", pp. 1302–5. On the angry mob, *see* Hanna, "The Politics", pp. 199–200; Hiro, "Munen", p. 197; "Indo taishikan osou [Indian Embassy Attacked]." *Asahi Shinbun* (3 Sept. 1962, Tokyo Evening Edition): 1; "Jakarta Riot." *Straits Times* (4 Sept. 1962): 1. It should be added that attacks on embassies were not that uncommon in early independent Indonesia. On the other events, *see* Sondhi, Report of the Asian Games as Held in Djakarta—Indonesia, Aug. 1962, pp. 36–9. In *H-FC02-ASIAN/011*, TOSC.
48. Minutes of the Conference of the Executive Board of the International Olympic Committee. Lausanne, Mon Repos—9 Feb 1963, pp. 1–2. In *Comité International Olympique - Commission exécutive 1921–1979*, TOSC.
49. Older works with this assessment are: Kanin, *A Political History*, p. 85; Kolatch, *Sports*, pp. 189–90.
50. *See*, for example, Lutan and Hong, "The Politicization", p. 28. Lutan and Hong nevertheless rightly state that Sukarno's ideology was very important for the founding of the GANEFO.
51. "Mankind is One." *Antara* (11 Nov. 1962, LOS): 1, 9, here: 1. See also: "A-A-A Games." *Indonesian Observer* (12 Sept. 1962): 2; Liang, *He Zhenliang*, p. 84; "Proposal to Set up AA or AAA Games Federation to Rid Sports from Western Influence & Control." *Antara* (7 Oct. 1962, LOS): 1, 9; "Subandrio on IAAF Decision on Asian Games IV." *Antara* (27 Sept. 1962, @): 2.
52. One cannot say that the GANEFO were unsuccessful, since they forced the IOC to turn a blind eye on African countries not inviting South Africa (due to apartheid in its sport system) to the First All-Africa Games in 1965: Gitersos, "The Sporting". On the GANEFO, *see also* Connolly, "The Politics"; Hong, "Sport, Militarism and Diplomacy"; Lutan and Hong, "The Politicization"; Field, "Re-Entering"; Pauker, "Ganefo I"; Shuman, *The Politics*, chapter 5; Sie, "Sports and Politics"; Sie, "The Problem"; Kolatch, *Sports*, pp. 189–201; Parks, *Red Sport*, pp. 179–87.
53. Seymour Topping, "Sukarno Shapes a Grandiose Jakarta to Embody his Vision." *New York Times* (26 Aug. 1965): 2 (Special).
54. Kolatch, *Sports*, p. 199; Connolly, "The Politics", p. 1319–20. Connolly here also expresses, based on Chinese documents, some doubts regarding Egyptian explanations that it lacked the necessary funding for the Games, but does not cover its military involvements. Egyptian sources might thus provide a definite answer.
55. *Asian Games 4. Djakarta 1962. 24 Aug.–4 Sept.*, p. 13; The Organizing Committee for the IVth Asian Games, *Asian Games*, p. 3; "President Sukarno Inaugurates Main Stadium." *Antara* (22 July 1962, LOS): 1, 6, 7: here: 7. On the negotiations with the Russians, *see* Sie, "Sports and Politics", p. 282.

56. *Asian Games 4. Djakarta 1962. 24 Aug.–4 Sept.*, p. 15; The Organizing Committee for the IVth Asian Games, *Asian Games*, pp. 4–10; "Report on Plans and Preparations for the IVth Asian Games", p. 411. The 'relocation', which certainly was not welcomed by all people concerned, was enforced through martial law and served to 'free' the land of the illegal settlements erected there as a result of the lack of housing in the rapidly growing Jakarta. *See* Abeyasekere, *Jakarta*, p. 198.
57. *Asian Games 4. Djakarta 1962. 24 Aug.–4 Sept.*, p. 20; The Organizing Committee 4th Asian Games (1960), *Bulletin*, no. 1, p. 15; Hanna, "The Politics", p. 194.
58. *Asian Games 4. Djakarta 1962. 24 Aug.–4 Sept.*, pp. 17, 20; The Organizing Committee for the IVth Asian Games, *Asian Games*, p. 13; Sie, "Sports and Politics", p. 282.
59. Lutan, "Indonesia", p. 17; The Organizing Committee for the Fourth Asian Games, *Asian Games*, pp. 54–5.
60. Hanna, "The Politics", pp. 194–5; "Pre-Games Clean-up of Jakarta." *Straits Echo and Times of Malaya* (9 Aug. 1962): 8; The Organizing Committee for the Fourth Asian Games, *Asian Games*, pp. 84–5. The 'relocation' of beggars and prostitutes followed the same development schemes as in the case of the almost 50,000 illegal squatters: Abeyasekere, *Jakarta*, p. 198.
61. Abeyasekere, *Jakarta*, p. 171.
62. Ibid., p. 168.
63. Kusno, *Behind*, pp. 51–2, 60–6. An overview of older interpretations can also be found there.
64. Sukarno most likely referred either to Anastas Mikoyan, who in 1962 had visited the stadium Russian experts had helped to construct, or to Nikita Khrushchev, who had visited the construction site in 1960. *See* "President Sukarno Inaugurates Main Stadium." *Antara* (22 July 1962, LOS): 1, 6, 7; here: 6–7.
65. Leclerc, "Mirrors", pp. 51–2, from Sukarno, *Deklarasi Ekonomi*, pp. 150–1. The (English) terms 'nation-building' and 'character-building' were used in the original text of Sukarno's speech.
66. Abeyasekere, *Jakarta*, p. 182.
67. Department of Foreign Affairs, *Indonesia*, p. 131.
68. "Asian Games Atmosphere Prevails in the Capital." *Antara* (6 July 1962, VOS): 4–5, here: 4 (first quotation); "President Opens Senajan Stadium." *Indonesian Observer* (23 July 1962): 1 (second quotation).
69. Nihon Taiiku Kyōkai, *Dai-4kai*, p. 74.
70. *Asian Games 4. Djakarta 1962. 24 Aug.–4 Sept.*, p. 13 (on the main stadium); The Organizing Committee for the Fourth Asian Games, *Asian Games*, p. 53 (on Hotel Indonesia); "Construction. Medals." *Indonesian Observer* (24 Aug. 1962): 1 (on Sudarman); "President Sukarno Inaugurates Main Stadium." *Antara* (22 July 1962, LOS): 1, 6, 7; here: 7 (on Suprajogi); "President Opens Senajan Stadium." *Indonesian Observer* (23 July 1962): 1 (on Sukarno).
71. "President Sukarno Inaugurates Main Stadium." *Antara* (22 July 1962, LOS): 1, 6, 7; here: 1; The Organizing Committee for the Fourth Asian Games, *Asian Games*, p. 89.

72. Hints can be found for instance in newspaper articles on Maladi or suggestions by sports functionaries: "Indonesia's First Minister of Sport." *The Asia Magazine* (19 Aug. 1962): 6; "Mr. Sondhi Is Not a True Asian, Says M.S. Osman." *Indonesian Observer* (31 Aug. 1962): 1; "Jakarta Will Stage Games in Grand Style." *Straits Times* (10 Feb. 1962): 17.
73. Abeyasekere, *Jakarta*, p. 207.
74. "'Bung Karno Sport Arena' Recommended for 'Bung Karno Sport Center'." *Antara* (16 Oct. 1962, AS): 5. *See also* "'Bung Karno' Sports Centre." *Indonesian Observer* (6 Sept. 1962): 1. On the later development of Senayan City, *see* Kusno, *The Appearances*, pp. 84–7.
75. "Corruption in Indonesia." *The Guardian* (28 June 1962): 9; "Asian Games Press House Corruption Case Opens." *Straits Times* (14 July 1962): 2.
76. "2,200 Athletes from 22 [sic] Countries To Compete." *Indonesian Observer* (24 Aug. 1962): 1; "Magic Number." *Indonesian Observer* (25 Aug. 1962): 1; Organizing Committee Asian Games IV 1962, Djakarta (1962), *Bulletin*, no. 5, pp. 13–14; The Organizing Committee for the Fourth Asian Games, *Asian Games*, pp. 113, 125.
77. Lutan, "Indonesia", p. 18; The Organizing Committee for the Fourth Asian Games, *Asian Games*, pp. 59, 98–9.
78. "Japanese Stars Due 8 P.M. today for Orient Meet." *Manila Daily Bulletin* (7 May 1934): 3–4; Organizing Committee Asian Games IV 1962, Djakarta (1962), *Bulletin*, no. 5, p. 14; Department of Information, *The Fourth*, p. 5.
79. Lutan, "Indonesia", p. 18; The Organizing Committee for the Fourth Asian Games, *Asian Games*, p. 59; The Organizing Committee for the Fourth Asian Games, *Asian Games*, p. 312.
80. "Mass Demonstration at Asian Games Opening Ceremony." *Antara* (12 Aug. 1962, LOS): 4; The Organizing Committee, *Opening Ceremony. Asian Games IV*, p. 7; The Organizing Committee for the Fourth Asian Games, *Asian Games*, pp. 130–1.
81. "Mass Demonstration at Asian Games Opening Ceremony." *Antara* (12 Aug. 1962, LOS): 4; The Organizing Committee, *Opening Ceremony. Asian Games IV*, p. 7 (quotation); The Organizing Committee for the Fourth Asian Games, *Asian Games*, p. 132. Sukarno's Indonesia was not a society promoting total equality, but the women's organization (*Gerwani*) affiliated with the Communist Party was quite strong, having had about 1.5 million female members before being crushed by Suharto in 1965/66: Blackburn, "Feminism", p. 26.
82. The Organizing Committee for the Fourth Asian Games, *Asian Games*, 133; "Mass Demonstration at Asian Games Opening Ceremony." *Antara* (12 Aug. 1962, LOS): 4; The Organizing Committee, *Opening Ceremony. Asian Games IV*, p. 7.
83. "Mass Demonstration at Asian Games Opening Ceremony." *Antara* (12 Aug. 1962, LOS): 4.
84. Ibid.; The Organizing Committee, *Opening Ceremony. Asian Games IV*, p. 7; The Organizing Committee for the Fourth Asian Games, *Asian Games*, pp. 134–5.
85. On the Indonesian state ideology, *see* Vickers, *A History*, pp. 118–41.

86. "Mass Demonstration at Asian Games Opening Ceremony." *Antara* (12 Aug. 1962, LOS): 4.
87. Organizing Committee Asian Games IV 1962, Djakarta (1962), *Bulletin*, no. 5, pp. 28–9; "'The Flag' Comes Down at Senayan." *Indonesian Observer* (5 Sept. 1962): 1, 3; The Organizing Committee for the Fourth Asian Games, *Asian Games*, p. 296.
88. Band Music; Poster. In *Arch GV 722.5 .A7 (Asian Games)*, LA84; Organizing Committee Asian Games IV 1962, Djakarta (1962), *Bulletin*, no. 5, pp. 28–9; "'The Flag' Comes Down at Senayan." *Indonesian Observer* (5 Sept. 1962): 1, 3. The anthem therefore was not 'A Struggle Full of Fairness', written by Ramadhan K. H., as given by Lutan, "Indonesia", pp. 17–18, and Harsuki, *Olahraga*, p. 374.
89. "17 Million Dollars to Stage the Fourth Asian Games." *The Asia Magazine* (19 Aug. 1962): 8–10, here: 9. Sutarto here names universities, schools, halls, recreation centers, and other public places as the locations where the television sets were to be installed. *See also* "Television for the Asian Games." *Antara* (2 Feb. 1962, LUNIK): 3. It is therefore rather doubtful that the 10,000 television sets had all been donated to public servants, as Philip Kitley says (*see* Kitley, *Television*, p. 32), who also mentions a different manufacturer, although it is certainly possible that some of them were.
90. Kitley, *Television*, pp. 22, 31.
91. See the pictures in The Organizing Committee for the Fourth Asian Games, *Asian Games*, p. 136.
92. "Rp. 135.5 Million Proceeds of Sales of IVth Asian Games Tickets." *Antara* (7 Sept. 1962, AS): 3–4; The Organizing Committee for the Fourth Asian Games, *Asian Games*, p. 311.
93. "Mankind is One." *Antara* (11 Nov. 1962, LOS): 1, 9.
94. The Organizing Committee for the Fourth Asian Games, *Asian Games*, p. 12.
95. To name only a few: "Asian Games Is One of the Best Run Games—Larsson." *Indonesian Observer* (4 Sept. 1962): 4 (Karl A. Larsson, president of the technical committee of the International Shooting Union); Indian Olympic Association, *Annual Report 1962*, p. 3 (Pankaj Gupta, secretary of the Indian Olympic Association); "Kawashima kokumushō, kikoku shite kataru [Minister Kawashima Comes Home and Talks]." *Asahi Shinbun* (Tokyo Morning Edition, 3 Sept. 1962): 1 (Kawashima Shōjirō, Japanese minister for the 1964 Tokyo Olympic Games).

Chapter 7

1. *Official Report of the Organizing Committee for the Sixth Asian Games Bangkok 1970*, p. 105.
2. As Charles Little has noted, literature on the GANEFOA is scarce: Little, "South-East Asia", pp. 594, 598, fn. 44. *See also*, for example, Liang, *He Zhenliang*, pp. 89–90; Ross and Collins, *Building Cambodia*, particularly pp. 11, 28–9, 163, 207–29.

3. Grabowsky, *Kleine Geschichte*, pp. 152–64, 168–72; Baker and Phongpaichit, *A History*, pp. 142–3, 145, 148; Fessen and Kubitscheck, *Geschichte Thailands*, p. 131; Wyatt, *Thailand*, pp. 269–70; Handley, *The King*, pp. 137–8.
4. Grabowsky, *Kleine Geschichte*, pp. 170, 173–4; Baker and Phongpaichit, *A History*, pp. 144, 148, 150, 163, 166; Schmidt-Braul, "Bücher", pp. 333–4; Terwiel, *Thailand's Political History*, pp. 282–3; Wyatt, *Thailand*, pp. 269, 271–3.
5. Grabowsky, *Kleine Geschichte*, pp. 172–3; Baker and Phongpaichit, *A History*, p. 170; Fessen and Kubitscheck, *Geschichte Thailands*, pp. 131–2; Wyatt, *Thailand*, p. 271. Paul Handley in his biography of King Bhumibol asked the question of whether it was really the case that Sarit used the king to legitimize his rule, as has often has been stated (see much of the literature in this and the preceding footnotes) or if it was the monarchists who used Sarit to reclaim the former power of the monarchy: Handley, *The King*, chapters 8–10, particularly pp. 154–6. Certainly both perspectives contain some truth and are not mutually exclusive, and the question itself will not be addressed here, but the emergence of a personality cult-like public focus on the king will become obvious throughout the chapter.
6. Grabowsky, *Kleine Geschichte*, pp. 173–4, 176; Baker and Phongpaichit, *A History*, pp. 149, 170; Fessen and Kubitscheck, *Geschichte Thailands*, p. 132; Wyatt, *Thailand*, pp. 276, 287–92.
7. Acharya, *Constructing*, pp. 54–5, 58, 230. On the Vietnam War, which has produced overwhelming amounts of literature, *see*, for example, Frey, *Geschichte*; Bradley, *Vietnam*.
8. Baker and Phongpaichit, *A History*, pp. 149, 170–1; Handley, *The King*, pp. 156, 171; Wyatt, *Thailand*, p. 283.
9. Tapsuwan, *The Role*, pp. 82–86, 139–40; Anderson, Wan., "Sport", pp. 134, 138; Indrapana, *Sport*, pp. 105–14, 199–200, 220–31, 233–5.
10. Anderson, Wan., "Sport", p. 142; Indrapana, *Sport*, pp. 236, 238–9, 243–5; Tapsuwan, *The Role*, p. 84.
11. Indrapana, *Sport*, pp. 216–18. The importance of the Sport Promotion Organization is illustrated, for example, by the involvement of high government officials such as a minister from the prime minister's office, the secretary-generals of the ministries of defense, interior, and education, and the director-general of the Department of Physical Education: Anderson, Wan, "Sport", p. 139. The problem of the under-representation of rural areas is highlighted by the fact that the large majority of the Thai athletes for the Fifth Asian Games came from Bangkok: "Some Sober Reflections on the Asian Games." *Bangkok Post* (17 Apr. 1966): 18; Manoj Vudha, "Royalty... Asian Games." *Bangkok World* (20 Dec. 1966): 4.
12. *The Official Report of the Organizing Committee for the Fifth Asian Games Bangkok 1966*, p. 2; *Official Report of the Organizing Committee for the Sixth Asian Games Bangkok 1970*, p. 2; Chaloke, Dear Mr. Brundage (19 Dec. 1968), p. 2. In *Avery Brundage Collection, Box 197: VI Asian Games*, TOSC; "Thailand and Olympism." *Olympic Review* 161 (Mar. 1981): 175–80, here: 175, 180; Indrapana, *Sport*, pp. 207, 235.

13. *The Official Report of the Organizing Committee for the Fifth Asian Games Bangkok 1966,* p. 9; *Official Report of the Organizing Committee for the Sixth Asian Games Bangkok 1970,* p. 19; Curriculum Vitae—Mr. Kong Visudarom. In *D. RM01. THAIL (Burex),* TOSC; Memorandum. To: A.G.F. President, Key Young Chang, p. 1 (attached to: Sales, Dear President Brundage (11 July 1968)). In *Avery Brundage Collection, Box 197: VI Asian Games,* TOSC.
14. Public Relations Committee and the Organizing Committee, *5th Asian Games News Letter,* no. 2, p. 3; Name: Luang Sukhum Nayapradit. In *D. RM01. THAIL (Burex),* TOSC.
15. *The Official Report of the Organizing Committee for the Fifth Asian Games Bangkok 1966,* p. 9; *Official Report of the Organizing Committee for the Sixth Asian Games Bangkok 1970,* p. 19; "Thailand and Olympism." *Olympic Review* 161 (Mar. 1981): 175–80, here: 175, 180; "Dawee to Meet with SEATO Advisers here." *Bangkok Post* (4 Dec. 1966): 1; Tudor Wijayasinha, "Asian Games Burst into its Brightest ever Life." *Bangkok World* (9 Dec. 1970): 9; Public Relations Committee and the Organizing Committee, *5th Asian Games News Letter,* no. 2, p. 3.
16. *The Official Report of the Organizing Committee for the Fifth Asian Games Bangkok 1966,* p. 9; *Official Report of the Organizing Committee for the Sixth Asian Games Bangkok 1970,* p. 19; Public Relations Committee and the Organizing Committee, *5th Asian Games News Letter,* no. 1, p. 3; Curriculum Vitae—Police General Luang Chartrakarn. In *D. RM01. THAIL (Burex),* TOSC.
17. *The Official Report of the Organizing Committee for the Fifth Asian Games Bangkok 1966,* picture page; *Official Report of the Organizing Committee for the Sixth Asian Games Bangkok 1970,* picture page; "King's Victory Marks Asian Games." *New York Times* (23 Dec. 1967; Special): S17.
18. "Dawee Aging not Fading." *The Nation* (14 Aug. 1994): D4.
19. "Korea to Step Down as Hosts for 1970." *Straits Times* (25 Nov. 1967): 22.
20. *Transactions. Special Council Congress, Asian Games Federation, April 29–May 4, 1968,* p. 14.
21. Ibid., pp. 15, 30.
22. Tudor Wijayasinha, "The Sixth Asian Games ... A Rags to Riches Story." *Bangkok World* (29 Nov. 1970): 15; "AGF to Meet on How to Keep A-Games Alive." *Straits Times* (19 Dec. 1967): 23.
23. *Official Report of the Organizing Committee for the Sixth Asian Games Bangkok 1970,* pp. 8–12 (quotation: p. 11); *Transactions. Asian Games Federation Sub-Committee Meeting,* pp. 13–14.
24. Karnjanakit and Samahito, "Thailand", pp. 41–2. In total, Thailand received 412,000 USD from AGF member countries. The most important contributions came from South Korea (250,000 USD), the failed initial host of the Games, and Japan (75,000 USD), the economically strongest member country.
25. *The Official Report of the Organizing Committee for the Fifth Asian Games Bangkok 1966,* p. 58.

26. "Thanom Lauds Fair at Closure." *Bangkok Post* (11 Dec. 1966): 3; A. A. Razak, "First Asian Trade Fair Ends Today, Profitably." *Bangkok Post* (10 Dec. 1966): 17; The Public Relations Committee and the Organizing Committee, *5th Asian Games Bangkok 1966 Bulletin*, no. 3, pp. 26–7; Public Relations Committee and the Organizing Committee, *5th Asian Games News Letter*, no. 1, pp. 1, 4.
27. Jack Foisle, "'More Fun, Less Sin', Is Bangkok's Purpose." *Washington Post* (27 Nov. 1966): M9.
28. Don Kumjing, "Delegates Meet to Promote Sport." *Bangkok Post* (9 Dec. 1970): 12. On the congresses, see *Official Report of the Organizing Committee for the Sixth Asian Games Bangkok 1970*, pp. 107–10.
29. *The Official Report of the Organizing Committee for the Fifth Asian Games Bangkok 1966*, p. 39. On the importance Praphas gave the construction of a sports infrastructure in rural areas, *see* "Thailand Aspires to Stage Olympics-Prap[h]as." *Bangkok Post* (25 Nov. 1966): 11.
30. Manoj Vudha, "Sports ... Corruption." *Bangkok World* (16 Dec. 1966): 4.
31. Public Relations Committee and the Organizing Committee, *5th Asian Games News Letter*, no. 2, p. 3.
32. "Japanese Know their Rice." *Observer* (11 Dec. 1966): 19.
33. "US Plans Sport Help for Asians." *Washington Post* (7 Dec. 1970): 69. On the Peace Corps' sports development program for example in the Philippines, beginning in 1971, *see* Ylanan and Ylanan, *The History*, chapter 10.
34. "Games Village ready for the Visitors." *Straits Times* (15 Nov. 1966): 18.
35. "Preparations for Games Completed Says Gen. Prap[h]as." *Bangkok Post* (8 Dec. 1966): 11. On the medal rankings *see* Puri, *The Asian Games*, pp. 38, 45.
36. Quite interestingly in terms of Cold War propaganda, the negative incidents were the only item reported by the Chinese *Renmin ribao*, which otherwise ignored the Fifth Asian Games and strongly covered the GANEFOA in Cambodia: "Choutai baichu de di 5 jie 'Yayunhui' [The Ridiculous Fifth 'Asian Games']." In *Renmin ribao* (28 Dec. 1966): 4. The article also includes some insults of the Republic of China.
37. Anton Perera, "The Fifth Asiad, the Games with a Question Mark." *Bangkok Post* (10 Dec. 1966): 10; "India Set for Asiad after all." *Bangkok Post* (4 Dec. 1966): 11.
38. *The Official Report of the Organizing Committee for the Fifth Asian Games Bangkok 1966*, pp. 13–14.
39. "Praphas Hails AG Job." *Bangkok Post* (22 Dec. 1966): 11. *See also* "Thailand Aspires to Stage Olympics—Prap[h]as." *Bangkok Post* (25 Nov. 1966): 11.
40. Tee Mahapaurya, "No Olympics here." *Bangkok Post* (27 Dec. 1966): 3.
41. *Official Report of the Organizing Committee for the Sixth Asian Games Bangkok 1970*, p. 105.
42. Ferdinand Marcos, "Sports and National Discipline." *The Filipino Athlete* (Mar.–Apr. 1967): 4–5 (quotations: 4).
43. "Brundage Blasts 'Amateur' Alpine Skiers." *Bangkok Post* (11 Dec. 1970): 9. On Brundage and East Asia, *see* Guttmann, *The Games Must Go on*, chapter 12.
44. "As Good as at Tokyo Is Thai Target." *Straits Times* (15 Dec. 1964): 22.

45. Ibid.
46. Ibid.
47. Indrapana, *Sport*, p. 247; "Praphas Hails AG Job." *Bangkok Post* (22 Dec. 1966): 11.
48. "As Good as at Tokyo Is Thai Target." *Straits Times* (15 Dec. 1964): 22.
49. Navy captain Luang Supachalasai had been a leading figure in the constitutional revolution of 1932 and had become director-general of the Department of Physical Education in 1933: Indrapana, *Sport*, pp. 104–5, 199.
50. Public Relations Committee and the Organizing Committee, *5th Asian Games News Letter*, no. 1, pp. 1, 4; Public Relations Committee and the Organizing Committee, *5th Asian Games News Letter*, no. 4, pp. 2–3; Norman Siebel, "Thais Battle Feverishly to Meet the Deadline." *Straits Times* (29 Nov. 1966): 18.
51. Public Relations Committee and the Organizing Committee, *5th Asian Games News Letter*, no. 2, p. 2, and no. 5, pp. 2–3. For a picture of the swimming stadium, see *Official Report of the Organizing Committee for the Sixth Asian Games Bangkok 1970*, p. 64.
52. Public Relations Committee and the Organizing Committee, *5th Asian Games News Letter*, no. 1, p. 2, and no. 5, pp. 2–3. For a picture of the press house *see* Tudor Wijayasinha, "Excellent Facilities, Housing for Asian Games Newsmen." *Bangkok World* (22 Nov. 1966): 7.
53. "Press Blamed for Mona's Decision." *Bangkok Post* (9 Dec. 1966): 10.
54. "30,000 Fans See Asian Games Open." *New York Times* (10 Dec. 1966): 53.
55. Norman Siebel, "Thais Battle Feverishly to Meet the Deadline." *Straits Times* (29 Nov. 1966): 18. *See also* Norman Siebel, "Thailand's Readiness Will Prove the Critics Wrong." *Bangkok Post* (29 Nov. 1966): 10.
56. *The Official Report of the Organizing Committee for the Fifth Asian Games Bangkok 1966*, pp. 38–9.
57. Public Relations Committee and the Organizing Committee, *5th Asian Games News Letter*, no. 4, p. 2; *The Official Report of the Organizing Committee for the Fifth Asian Games Bangkok 1966*, p. 41. The velodrome cost about five million baht.
58. *The Official Report of the Organizing Committee for the Fifth Asian Games Bangkok 1966*, p. 41.
59. "As Good as at Tokyo Is Thai Target." *Straits Times* (15 Dec. 1964): 22; "Kittikachorn Stadium Unique Sports and Cultural Centre." *Bangkok Post* (30 Nov. 1966): 11; *The Official Report of the Organizing Committee for the Fifth Asian Games Bangkok 1966*, p. 40.
60. Public Relations Committee and the Organizing Committee, *5th Asian Games News Letter*, no. 3, p. 2.
61. "Kittikachorn Stadium Unique Sports and Cultural Centre." *Bangkok Post* (30 Nov. 1966): 11; Public Relations Committee and the Organizing Committee, *5th Asian Games News Letter*, no. 3, p. 2. On the cost of the hockey and the tennis stadium *see* Public Relations Committee and the Organizing Committee, *5th Asian Games News Letter*, no. 4, pp. 2–3.

62. Anton Perera, "Prime Minister Opens Hua Mark Sports Complex." *Bangkok Post* (29 Nov. 1966): 11.
63. Ibid. Some South Korean sports officials were apparently very impressed, calling the stadium "the best in the Far East". *See* Public Relations Committee and the Organizing Committee, *5th Asian Games News Letter,* no. 7, p. 3.
64. The Organizing Committee for the Sixth Asian Games Bangkok 1970, *Opening Ceremony,* p. 15.
65. Public Relations Committee and the Organizing Committee, *5th Asian Games News Letter,* no. 1, p. 2, and no. 4, p. 3; "Int. Village Formally Opens Today." *Bangkok Post* (8 Dec. 1966): 9; *The Official Report of the Organizing Committee for the Fifth Asian Games Bangkok 1966,* pp. 44–5. For a picture of the village, *see* Public Relations Committee and the Organizing Committee, *5th Asian Games News Letter,* no. 2, p. 4. On the 'friendship garden' in 1962 *see* Ronnie Muntu, "Friendship Park." *Indonesian Observer* (4 Sept. 1962): 2; "Parties & Entertainment for A.G. Members." *Antara* (26 Aug. 1962, AS): 10.
66. Baker and Phongpaichit, *A History,* p. 149.
67. Official Japanese numbers indicate that in 1960 about 128,000 people (about 15 per cent claiming to be tourists) traveled to foreign countries, going up to 500,000 (about 51 per cent claiming to be tourists) in 1969 and 2.3 million in 1974 (about 80 per cent claiming to be tourists). Thailand was an important destination, the number of Japanese visitors (not only tourists) growing from about 15,000 in 1964 to 132,000 in 1974. *See* Carlile, "Economic Development", pp. 12, 16.
68. "Asian Games Warning for Motorists." *Bangkok Post* (9 Dec. 1966): 3; Peter Braestrup, "A Spree Is Over for Bangkok Hotels." *New York Times* (19 Mar. 1967; Special): F14.
69. *Official Report of the Organizing Committee for the Sixth Asian Games Bangkok 1970,* pp. 13, 39–40, 48–61. It should be noted that the official report provided a picture of every single hotel that was used, certainly also serving promotional purposes and possibly being part of a deal that had been made with the hotels.
70. Ibid., pp. 36–8; Anton Perera, "A Red Letter Day for Thailand." *Bangkok Post* (9 Nov. 1966): 11; "His Majesty to Kindle Asian Olympiad's Eternal Flame'." *Bangkok World* (25 Nov. 1970): 6; "HM Ignites 6th Asiad Flame." *Bangkok Post* (9 Dec. 1970): 12.
71. On the Indonesian torch relay, *see* The Organizing Committee, *Opening Ceremony. Asian Games IV,* p. 9; The Organizing Committee for the Fourth Asian Games, *Asian Games,* pp. 102–3.
72. Thangarajah, *Asia,* p. 62; "Final Games Ceremonies Rehearsal Dec. 4." *Bangkok Post* (1 Dec. 1966): 9; "Asian Games Warning for Motorists." *Bangkok Post* (9 Dec. 1966): 3. Constitution Day (10 Dec.) fell on a Saturday, so the holiday was moved to the Friday the Games commenced.
73. "Photo." *Bangkok Post* (10 Dec. 1966): 11; "King Declares 5th Asian Games Open." *Bangkok World* (10 Dec. 1966): 1–2; "Schedule for Games Opening Ceremony Set." *Bangkok Post* (3 Dec. 1966): 11; Ye, *Hao,* p. 124.

74. *The Official Report of the Organizing Committee for the Fifth Asian Games Bangkok 1966*, picture part.
75. "Photos." *Bangkok World* (10 Dec. 1966): 7.
76. "Photo." *Bangkok World* (10 Dec. 1966): 7.
77. "Photo." *Bangkok Post* (2 Dec. 1966): 28; "Asian Games Close in Impressive Ceremonies." *Bangkok World* (21 Dec. 1966): 1–2, here: 2.
78. "HM Opens 5th Asian Games." *Bangkok Post* (10 Dec. 1966): 1, 12, here: 1; *The Official Report of the Organizing Committee for the Fifth Asian Games Bangkok 1966*, pp. 327–28, 332, 335, 339, 342, 346, 350, 353, 355, 362, 369, 374–5, 377, 382, 385, 393.
79. "Home Team." *Bangkok World* (10 Dec. 1966): 5; "Photo." *Bangkok Post* (10 Dec. 1966): 11.
80. "Schedule for Games Opening Ceremony Set." *Bangkok Post* (3 Dec. 1966): 11.
81. Thangarajah, *Asia*, p. 62.
82. "HM Opens 5th Asian Games." *Bangkok Post* (10 Dec. 1966): 1, 12, here: 12.
83. "King Declares 5th Asian Games Open." *Bangkok World* (10 Dec. 1966): 1–2, here: 2.
84. Ibid.
85. Public Relations Committee and the Organizing Committee, *5th Asian Games News Letter*, no. 3, p. 4; "Schedule for Games Opening Ceremony Set." *Bangkok Post* (3 Dec. 1966): 11; "Grand Finale." *Bangkok World* (10 Dec. 1966): 1.
86. Tapsuwan, *The Role*, p. 159.
87. Thai women had gained voting rights in 1932 as a result of the constitutional revolution and increasing numbers of them began working, but this did not mean complete emancipation. After the Thanom regime ended in 1973, the following short-lived democratization period resulted in another struggle for women's rights: Falk, "Feminism", pp. 111–14.
88. "Asian Games Ends with Big Ceremony." *Bangkok Post* (21 Dec. 1966): 1.
89. "Asian Games Close in Impressive Ceremonies." *Bangkok World* (21 Dec. 1966): 1–2, here: 2.
90. Compare for example: *Official Report of the Organizing Committee for the Sixth Asian Games Bangkok 1970*, pp. 75–104; Tudor Wijayasinha, "Asian Games Over." *Bangkok World* (21 Dec. 1970): 8.
91. Anton Perera, "Flying Start to Games." *Bangkok Post* (10 Dec. 1970): 1; "25,000 Give Asian Games Rousing Start." *Straits Times* (10 Dec. 1970): 1.
92. "Colour Spectacle Will Open Asiad." *Bangkok Post* (25 Nov. 1970): 12; *Official Report of the Organizing Committee for the Sixth Asian Games Bangkok 1970*, p. 76; "Majesty and Grandeur Open Asiad." *Bangkok World* (10 Dec. 1970): 9; "Photo." *Bangkok Post* (10 Dec. 1970): 1.
93. Tudor Wijayasinha, "Asian Games Over." *Bangkok World* (21 Dec. 1970): 8. On the king as a composer, *see also* Handley, *The King*, pp. 123, 160.
94. "Majesty and Grandeur Open Asiad." *Bangkok World* (10 Dec. 1970): 9.
95. "Lovely Varunee (Miss Thailand) to Carry Thai Standard." *Bangkok World* (29 Nov. 1970): 15; *Official Report of the Organizing Committee for the Sixth Asian Games*

Bangkok 1970, pp. 77–96; "The Honored Chulalongkorn, Thammasat Students." *Bangkok World* (29 Nov. 1970): 15.

96. *Official Report of the Organizing Committee for the Sixth Asian Games Bangkok 1970*, p. 78.
97. Ibid., p. 28.
98. Ibid., p. 101.
99. "The Games Are On!" *Bangkok Post* (10 Dec. 1970): 12; Anton Perera, "Flying Start to Games." *Bangkok Post* (10 Dec. 1970): 1.
100. For pictures of the medals *see The Official Report of the Organizing Committee for the Fifth Asian Games Bangkok 1966*, p. 63; Nihon Taiiku Kyōkai, *Dai-5kai*, p. 282; *Official Report of the Organizing Committee for the Sixth Asian Games Bangkok 1970*, pp. 67–68. It is certainly possible that the victory medals depicted the same images as the commemorative medals on their back.
101. "Asian Games Coin Minted." *Bangkok Post* (29 Nov. 1966): 3; "9 Million One Baht Coins to Be Produced." *Bangkok World* (29 Nov. 1970): 15.
102. For pictures of the stamps, *see* Zhu et al., *Yayunhui*, pp. 20–3, 25. The stadia pictured were the swimming stadium, the indoor stadium, the main stadium, and the velodrome.
103. "Games Record by Press." *Straits Times* (15 Dec. 1970): 30. Quite obviously, some of the foreign reporters might have been in Thailand anyway due to the Vietnam War.
104. "Wire Service Breakdown Nags Foreign Journalists." *Bangkok Post* (8 Dec. 1966): 11.
105. Public Relations Committee and the Organizing Committee, *5th Asian Games News Letter*, no. 7, p. 1.
106. "'Voice of Free Asia' to Operate from Thailand." *Bangkok Post* (17 Dec. 1966): 1.
107. "Live TV to Cover Games." *Bangkok Post* (8 Dec. 1966): 3; The Public Relations Committee and the Organizing Committee, *5th Asian Games Bangkok 1966 Bulletin*, no. 3, p. 12.
108. "Games on TV Malaysia." *Straits Times* (9 Dec. 1966): 23. Broadcasting started on 10 December and lasted until 21 December. Due to the delay by one day it seems possible that the Malayans also received some of the tapes or sent a group of cameramen and produced their own.
109. *See*, for example, "Closing Live by 'Free Asia' Radio." *Bangkok Post* (20 Dec. 1970): 12.
110. Chaloke, Dear Madame Berlioux (7 May 1970). In *D. RM01. THAIL (CORR). Correspondance. 1950–87*, TOSC.
111. "Asian Games Live on TV." *Bangkok Post* (1 Dec. 1970): 4; Manoon Atibead, "Avery Brundage to Attend Asiad." *Bangkok World* (25 Nov. 1970): 7; "All Set for the Royal Opening." *Straits Times* (9 Dec. 1970): 31.
112. "Colour Spectacle Will Open Asiad." *Bangkok Post* (25 Nov. 1970): 12; Manoon Atibead, "Avery Brundage to Attend Asiad." *Bangkok World* (25 Nov. 1970): 7.
113. On the end of the GANEFO movement *see*, for example, Kolatch, *Sports*, p. 199; Connolly, "The Politics", pp. 1319–20.
114. *See*, for example, "'Bangkok Belly' Strikes Again." *Bangkok Post* (10 Dec. 1970): 12; "Football Tempers Erupt, Police Save Match." *Bangkok Post* (11 Dec. 1970): 12; "Asian

Games Marred by Riots, Death, Disorganization Charges." *New York Times* (23 Dec. 1966; Special): 35; "Cagers Fight Way to Final." *Bangkok Post* (18 Dec. 1966): 1.

115. Prasert Manomayangkul, "Praise for the King." *Bangkok Post* (11 Dec. 1970): 9.
116. Anton Perera, "Staging 'Most Impresses' Sir Stanley." In *Bangkok Post* (20 Dec. 1970): 11.
117. Daume, Dear Mr. President [Dawee] (5 Nov. 1970), p. 2. In *Avery Brundage Collection, Box 197: Regional Games, VI Asian Games,* TOSC. Daume's enquiry is illustrative of the transfers of organizational experience and techniques between global and regional events, which are often very difficult to reconstruct.

Chapter 8

1. Ansari and Germain, *Mon père,* p. 235. Gholam Reza Pahlavi, already in exile for more than 20 years, mentioned this in an interview after he was asked for what Iran had used its growing oil revenues in the 1970s.
2. Abrahamian, *A History,* p. 128; Keddie, *Modern Iran,* pp. 134–5, 140–2.
3. Abrahamian, *A History,* pp. 124, 131–4; Afkhami, *The Life,* pp. 324, 327; Ansari, *Modern Iran,* pp. 148, 157, 167, 182; Saikal, "Iranian", pp. 445, 449–50; Keddie, *Modern Iran,* pp. 133–4, 139, 145–6, 162–3; Mirsepassi, *Intellectual Discourse,* p. 75; Ramazani, *Iran's Foreign Policy,* pp. 380–5.
4. Afkhami, *The Life,* p. 340; Saikal, "Iranian", pp. 442–3, 445, 447–9, 454; "Iraqi Jets Bomb Border Village." *Kayhan International* (14 Sept. 1974): 3; Ramazani, *Iran's Foreign Policy,* pp. 404, 416–18, 425, 436–7; Tahir-Kheli, "Iran", p. 485.
5 Abrahamian, *A History,* pp. 124–5, 131; Afkhami, *The Life,* p. 351; Alvandi, "Nixon"; Ansari, *Modern Iran,* pp. 176–177; Saikal, "Iranian", pp. 450–5; Ramazani, *Iran's Foreign Policy,* pp. 408–11, 413, 425, 427–33; Tahir-Kheli, "Iran", pp. 479, 487.
6. *See,* for example Mirsepassi, *Intellectual Discourse,* chapter 2.
7. Afkhami, *The Life,* pp. 404–14; Ansari, *Modern Iran,* pp. 169–75; Keddie, *Modern Iran,* p. 167; Schayegh, "Sport", pp. 364–5.
8. Nazari-Kangarloo, *The History,* pp. 43–60.
9. Chehabi, "The Juggernaut", pp. 278–81; Nazari-Kangarloo, *The History,* pp. 145, 206–16; Schayegh, "Sport", pp. 344, 347–51, 359–63.
10. *See,* for example, Amirtash, "Iran", p. 53; "Aryamehr Sports Centre." *Iran Tribune* 6, 85 (1971): 42–4, here: 42; Nazari-Kangarloo, *The History,* pp. 149, 156, 164–5, 167; "Sporting Facilities Expanding." *Kayhan International* (16 Nov. 1974): 8; The Organizing Committee Teheran, *Bulletin 1,* n.p.; *Tehran 1974. Seventh Asian Games. Souvenir Programme,* p. 28.
11. David Hunn, "Tehran Talk." *Observer* (18 May 1975): 21.
12. On Gholam Reza Pahlavi, *see* Ansari and Germain, *Mon père,* pp. 182–3; Nazari-Kangarloo, *The History,* pp. 142–3. On Ali Hojjat Kashani, *see* Anna Francis, "Shooting Champ General Hojjat." *The Tehran Journal* (1 Sept. 1974): Asian Games Special Page 5; *Tehran 1974. Seventh Asian Games. Souvenir Programme,* p. 27;

The Organizing Committee Teheran, *Bulletin 1,* n.p. On Hassan Rassouli, *see* The Organizing Committee Teheran, *Bulletin* 1, n.p. See also *Tehran 1974. Seventh Asian Games. Souvenir Programme,* p. 27.

13. "Shahanshah Proposes Asia Common Market." *Kayhan International* (6 Apr. 1974): 1. The shah had made these statements in an interview with a weekly Indian newspaper. On the idea, *see also* Tahir-Kheli, "Iran", p. 482.
14. "Dawn of New Era: Sheares." *Straits Times* (20 Sept. 1974): 1, 32 (quotation: 1). *See also* the speech of Iran's Premier Amir Abbas Hoveyda at a reception for people involved in the Asian Games: "Asian Union Would Be Biggest Ever—Hoveyda." *Kayhan International* (28 Sept. 1974): 2. *See also* "Ambitious Plan for the Indian Ocean Littoral." *Kayhan International* (5 Oct. 1974): 4.
15. "Fruits of an Asian Union." *Kayhan International* (5 Oct. 1974): 4–6 (quotation: 4).
16. For example on India, *see* "An Era of Asian Prosperity." *Kayhan International* (12 Oct. 1974): 4–6; "Shah: Peace through Closer Cooperation." *Straits Times* (5 Oct. 1974): 4. *See also* "The Shah: Thoughts of a Royal Decision Maker." *Time (Magazin)* (4 Nov. 1974): 22; "Shah Says Iran's Peace Role Extends to Indian Ocean." *Kayhan International* (9 Nov. 1974): 1.
17. Halliday, "The Arc", pp. 382–3.
18. "Shahanshah Proposes Asia Common Market." *Kayhan International* (6 Apr. 1974): 1; "Dawn of New Era: Sheares." *Straits Times* (20 Sept. 1974): 1, 32; "Ambitious Plan for the Indian Ocean Littoral." *Kayhan International* (5 Oct. 1974): 4.
19. "Most Spectacular Games Bid by Iran." *Straits Times* (16 Dec. 1970): 29; *Official Report of the Organizing Committee for the Sixth Asian Games Bangkok 1970,* pp. 15–16.
20. Ansari and Germain, *Mon père,* p. 234.
21. "Preparing for 1974." *Iran Tribune* 6, 76 (1971): 14–15, here: 14.
22. "A Welcome Awaits Australia, NZ to Asian Games." *Straits Times* (16 Dec. 1970): 29; "Arab-Israeli Conflict Won't Affect Teheran." *Straits Times* (17 Dec. 1970): 30. *See also* Amirtash, "Iran", pp. 55–6.
23. Ansari and Germain, *Mon père,* p. 234; *Official Report of the Seventh Asian Games Teheran Sept. 1–16, 74,* pp. 13, 184; The Organizing Committee Teheran, *Bulletin* 6, n.p. To increase the number of teams coming to Tehran, Iran sponsored some of the poor countries. *See* Amirtash, "Iran", p. 50. Saudi Arabia was the only country not sending a team, meaning that all in all 25 teams participated.
24. Alam, *The Shah,* p. 285.
25. Brownell, "Sport and Politics", p. 264; Cao and Brownell, "The People's Republic", p. 73; Nihon Taiiku Kyōkai and Nihon Orinpikku Iinkai, *Dai-7kai,* p. 61; Liang, *He Zhenliang,* pp. 100, 207.
26. On the negotiations, which I do not cover in detail, *see,* for example, Amirtash, "Iran", pp. 54–5; Liang, *He Zhenliang,* pp. 99–115; Nihon Taiiku Kyōkai and Nihon Orinpikku Iinkai, *Dai-7kai,* p. 61; *Official Report of the Seventh Asian Games Teheran Sept. 1–16, 74,* p. 176; The Organizing Committee Teheran, *Bulletin* 3, n.p.

27. Chung Sung [Zhong Song], Dear Mr. President [Pahlavi] (7 Aug. 1973). In *H-FC02-ASIAN/002*, TOSC. On the 'two Chinas problem' and the IOC, *see* Brownell, "Sport and Politics"; Pei, *A Question*; Xu, *Olympic Dreams*, pp. 75–116.
28. "Future of Games in State of Uncertainty." *Straits Times* (20 Sept. 1973): 23; Short Summary of what Happened in the A.G.F. Executive Committee Meeting in the Morning of Sept. 18, 1973 in Bangkok. In *H-FC02-ASIAN/002*, TOSC; The Organizing Committee Teheran, *Bulletin 5*, n.p.; Liang, *He Zhenliang*, p. 105.
29. 74th Session of the International Olympic Committee. 5th, 6th & 7th Oct. 1973—Varna, pp. 30–1. In *Comité International Olympique—Session 1894–2008*, TOSC; Meeting of the I.O.C. Executive Board. Varna, 29th-30th Sept. and 2nd Oct. 1973, pp. 5–6. In *Comité International Olympique—Commission exécutive 1921–1979*, TOSC.
30. Liang, *He Zhenliang*, pp. 110–11. It is improbable that the quotation contains the exact wording of General Hojjat, but the general content fits together with some of Pahlavi's and Rassouli's statements. The fact that He Zhenliang talks about 'expelling the Taiwanese authorities' also illustrates that the idea of 'substitution' had been nothing but a legal trick.
31. Hushang Nemazee, "Hojjat: No Games without China." *Kayhan International* (26 Jan. 1974): 2; Liang, *He Zhenliang*, pp. 110–11; "The Travails of the Games." *Iran Tribune* 9, 113 (1974): 7.
32. On the political reflections of the pro-China faction *see* Liang, *He Zhenliang*, p. 112. The Taiwanese accused China of putting serious political pressure on several countries such as Malaysia to make their delegations vote in favour of China: Ping-yih Niu [Bingyi Niu], Dear Madam [Berlioux] (20 Nov. 1973), pp. 2–3. In *H-FC02-ASIAN/002*, TOSC.
33. Draft Amendment to the Decision Made by the Executive Committee on Sept. 18, 1973, and Transcription of the Tape Recording of the AGF Special Council Meeting, Teheran, Nov. 15 and 16, 1973, especially pp. 20–5. Both in *H-FC02-ASIAN/002*, TOSC.
34. Host country Nigeria had deliberately not invited South Africa for a political reason, namely its apartheid-policy. On South Africa and the Olympic Games, *see* Hill, *Olympic Politics*, chap. 10.
35. Transcription of the Tape Recording of the AGF Special Council Meeting, Teheran, Nov. 15 and 16, 1973, pp. 28–9, 38 (quotation: 28–29). In *H-FC02-ASIAN/002*, TOSC.
36. Ibid., p. 34.
37. Ibid., pp. 57–8.
38. Ibid., p. 59.
39. Ibid.
40. Ibid., pp. 7 (quotation), 9, 66.
41. Ibid., p. 65. Pro-China: Afghanistan, Bahrain, Burma, Ceylon, Hong Kong, India, Iran, Japan, Kuwait, Malaysia, Nepal, Pakistan, Singapore. Pro-Taiwan: Cambodia, Indonesia, Philippines, South Vietnam. Abstaining: Israel, South Korea. Not attending: Laos, Thailand. Taiwan was only allowed to attend as an observer. *See* John

Hennessy, "'Political' Replacement of Taiwan by Mainland China." *The Times* (17 Nov. 1973): 19.

42. Sales, Dear President Killanin (29 Oct. 1973), p. 4. In *H-FC02-ASIAN/001*, TOSC.
43. Minutes of the Executive Board Meeting. Château de Vidy, 9th Feb., 1974, pp. 36–40 (quotation: 40). In *Comité International Olympique—Commission exécutive 1921–1979*, TOSC. In their official publications the Iranians left the second part out: The Organizing Committee Teheran, *Bulletin 6*, n.p.
44. On the *Xinghua* news item about the IOC meeting, *see* 020911-decision of all-China sports federation on participation in seventh Asian games. In *H-FC02-ASIAN/014*, TOSC. On similar Chinese discourses *see* Bai and Gu, "Di 7 jie", p. 2; Tse-yu Chang [Zeyu Zhang], "Ever Onward. Sidelights of the 7th Asian Games." *Peking Review* 37 (1974): 18–20, here: 20. On the quarrels between Iran, China, and the international sports federations see the documents in *H-FC02-ASIAN/014*, TOSC; *D.RM01. TAIPE/004*, TOSC; *H-FC02-ASIAN/002*, TOSC.
45. On the Munich Olympic Games, *see* Schiller and Young, *The 1972 Munich*, especially chapters 4 (on architecture and the ceremonies) and 7 (on the terrorist attack). In addition to their delegation, the Iranians sent ten experts to study the hosting of the Games: The Organizing Committee Teheran, *Bulletin 2*, n.p.
46. "Most Spectacular Games Bid by Iran." *Straits Times* (16 Dec. 1970): 29. *See also* Amirtash, "Iran", p. 59; Chehabi, "The Juggernaut", p. 287.
47. On 1980, *see* "Iran Drops out of Bidding for '80 Olympics." *Washington Post* (6 Oct. 1973): C3; Liang, *He Zhenliang*, p. 111; "Teheran Drop Plan." *The Times* (6 Oct. 1973): 16. On 1984, *see* Minutes of the Meeting of the I.O.C. Executive Board. Lausanne, 19th and 20th Oct. 1977, p. 6. In *Comité International Olympique - Commission exécutive 1921–1979*, TOSC; "Killanin Says Iran Could Host Olympic Games." *Japan Times* (4 Sept. 1974): 9; *Official Report of the Seventh Asian Games Teheran Sept. 1–16, 74*, pp. 17–18; "Tehran's Bid for the 1984 Olympic Games." *Olympic Review* 95–6 (Sept.-Oct. 1975): 425.
48. The Organizing Committee Teheran, *Bulletin 1*, n.p.
49. *Tehran 1974. Seventh Asian Games. Souvenir Programme*, n.p.
50. The Organizing Committee Teheran, *Bulletin 1*, n.p.
51. Ibid.
52. On Nikpay, *see* Ibid. On Avory, *see* Steve Crawford, "Already Looking Ahead." *The Tehran Journal* (10 Sept. 1974): Asian Games Special Page 1.
53. The Organizing Committee Teheran, *Bulletin 2*, n.p.
54. Ibid.
55. *Official Report of the Seventh Asian Games Teheran Sept. 1–16, 74*, p. 17.
56. *See* especially the Japanese criticism: Nihon Taiiku Kyōkai and Nihon Orinpikku Iinkai, *Dai-7kai*, pp. 24, 27, 29, 44–5. *See also* AMEMBASSY TEHRAN to SECSTATE WASHDC 8167 et al. (12 Sept. 1974; 1974TEHRAN07708). In *Telegrams, 1/1/1974–12/31/1974* (Film Number: D740255–0239), RG 59, NARAII; "China Make Brilliant Start in Athletics Events." *The Times* (10 Sept. 1974): 12; "Sensational Win by Tan." *Times of India* (13 Sept. 1974): 10; Thangarajah,

Asia, pp. 84–5; "When Fighting Ended Boxing." *Kayhan International* (14 Sept. 1974): 2.

57. "Games Competition Ends with 75 Golds for Japan." *Japan Times* (17 Sept. 1974): 8; Katayun Mihan, "Off-Form Israel Pulls in Cage Gold." *The Tehran Journal* (16 Sept. 1974): Asian Games Special Page 1; "Politics and Sports Don't, and Should Not, Mix." *The Tehran Journal* (15 Sept. 1974): 4; Nihon Taiiku Kyōkai and Nihon Orinpikku Iinkai, *Dai-7kai*, p. 32. *See also* Amirtash, "Iran", p. 55; "Blackout." *The Guardian* (12 Sept. 1974): 4. On the heavy criticism by Israeli sports officials of the events in Tehran and other games, *see* The Olympic Committee of Israel and the Sports Federations of Israel, *Playing Politics*.
58. 75th Session of the International Olympic Committee. Vienna, 21–24 Oct. 1974, pp. 28, 60–1, and Agenda for the 77th Session of the International Olympic Committee. Innsbruck, 2–3 Feb. 1976, pp. 31–2. Both in *Comité International Olympique - Session 1894–2008*, TOSC; Killanin, Dear Colleague [Pahlavi] (17 Sept. 1974), and Pahlavi, Dear Mr. President [Killanin] (27 Jan. 1975). Both in *H-FC02-ASIAN/014*, TOSC; "China Kept Waiting for Membership." *The Times* (22 July 1975): 8. *See also* Ambrosio Padilla, "The Threat to Olympic Solidarity." *The Filipino Athlete* (Sept.–Oct. 1974): 6; Nihon Taiiku Kyōkai and Nihon Orinpikku Iinkai, *Dai-7kai*, p. 32 (Prince Takeda).
59. AMEMBASSY TEHRAN to SECSTATE WASHDC 8167 et al. (12 Sept. 1974; 1974TEHRAN07708). In *Telegrams, 1/1/1974–12/31/1974* (Film Number: D740255–0239), RG 59, NARAII.
60. Alam, *The Shah*, p. 389.
61. Ferdinand E. Marcos, "Sports for Physical Fitness & Brotherhood." *The Filipino Athlete* (May-June 1973): 4.
62. Talk on 'Olympism and our Participation in the Asian Games' by Haji Sha'ari Tadin, Senior Parliamentary Secretary (Culture) and also Leader of the Republic's Sports Contingent to the Seventh Asian Games, Teheran, at a Luncheon Meeting of the Rotary Club on Wednesday, 21 Aug. 74, at 12.45 PM at the Mandarin Hotel, p. 3. In *PressR19740821, Microfilm Number: NA 1258, Ministry of Culture*, NAoS.
63. Nazari-Kangarloo, *The History*, pp. 160–1; The Organizing Committee Teheran, Bulletin 1, n.p.
64. *Tehran 1974. Seventh Asian Games. Souvenir Programme*, pp. 68, 70; The Organizing Committee Teheran, *Bulletin 4*, n.p. On the many ways in which the Iranians used the scoreboard, *see also* Tse-yu Chang [Zeyu Zhang], "Ever Onward. Sidelights of the 7th Asian Games." *Peking Review* 37 (1974): 18–20, here: 19.
65. Thangarajah, *Asia*, p. 83; "Seventh Asian Games: The Most Elaborate ever." *Iran Tribune* 9,119 (1974): 14–18, here: 15–16; The Organizing Committee Teheran, *Bulletin 1*, n.p., and *Bulletin 4*, n.p.
66. "The Shah Tours $375m Games Complex." *Straits Times* (22 Aug. 1974): 24. It nevertheless seems impossible to determine the definite sum of money spent on the Games. See also: Amirtash, "Iran", p. 54.
67. Ansari and Germain, *Mon père*, p. 235; The Organizing Committee Teheran, *Bulletin 1*, n.p. Even though it was an Iranian company, its staff was not entirely Iranian.

See also Hushang Nemazee, "I Am No Thief, Says Sports Chief Hojjat." *Kayhan International* (23 Nov. 1974): 8.

68. "The Big Games." *Iran Tribune* 9, 117 (1974): 12–13, here: 12. See also *Official Report of the Seventh Asian Games Teheran Sept. 1–16, 74*, p. 22; The Organizing Committee Teheran, *Bulletin 1*, n.p., and *Bulletin 6*, n.p.; Hushang Nemazee, "I Am no Thief, Says Sports Chief Hojjat." *Kayhan International* (23 Nov. 1974): 8.
69. The Organizing Committee Teheran, *Bulletin 2*, n.p.
70. Alam, *The Shah*, p. 256.
71. On Frank, *see* The Organizing Committee Teheran, *Bulletin 3*, n.p. On Dhillon *see* Hushang Nemazee, "China Gives Games its Greatest Glory." *Kayhan International* (16 Mar. 1974): 8. He also confirmed this during an interview: Interview with S. S. Dhillon, Former Secretary-General of the Singapore National Olympic Council (13 Dec. 2011), SNOC. On Tajima, *see* Nihon Taiiku Kyōkai and Nihon Orinpikku Iinkai, *Dai-7kai*, p. 24. On Henning, *see* Steve Crawford, "Already Looking Ahead." *The Tehran Journal* (10 Sept. 1974): Asian Games Special Page 1. On Lord Killanin *see* "IOC Head Killanin Says Iran Could Hold Olympics." *The Tehran Journal* (4 Sept. 1974): 1 (quotation). *See also* "Killanin Says Iran Could Host Olympic Games." *Japan Times* (4 Sept. 1974): 9.
72. "Crown Prince Sets Games Torch Alight." *Kayhan International* (7 Sept. 1974): 2.
73. "16 Days in Tehran." *The Filipino Athlete* 29 (Sept.-Oct. 1974): 4–5, here: 4; Nihon Taiiku Kyōkai and Nihon Orinpikku Iinkai, *Dai-7kai*, p. 46; *Official Report of the Seventh Asian Games Teheran Sept. 1–16, 74*, pp. 45, 48, 50–1; "The Curtain Rises at Aryamehr." *Kayhan International* (7 Sept. 1974): 1–2, here: 1; "Photos." *The Tehran Journal* (2 Sept. 1974): Asian Games Special Page 3; "Seventh Asian Games. A Technological Marvel." *Iran Tribune* 9, 118 (1974): 14–17, here: 16.
74. Katayoun Mihan, "Monarch Opens 7th Asian Games." *The Tehran Journal* (2 Sept. 1974): 1; Nihon Taiiku Kyōkai and Nihon Orinpikku Iinkai, *Dai-7kai*, p. 46.
75. Gholam Reza Pahlavi is shown addressing the audience and Ali Hojjat Kashani waiting behind him.
76. Jamal M. Kashani, "The Ethics of the Sacred Pit." *Iran Tribune* 9, 115 (1974): 8–9; "The Curtain Rises at Aryamehr." *Kayhan International* (7 Sept. 1974): 1–2, here: 2; The Organizing Committee Teheran, *Bulletin 1*, n.p.
77. Mehdi Akhavan, "Mass Music Program for Asian Games." *The Tehran Journal* (14 Aug. 1974): 3; *Official Report of the Seventh Asian Games Teheran Sept. 1–16, 74*, p. 123; "Seventh Asian Games: The Most Elaborate ever." *Iran Tribune* 9, 119 (1974): 14–18, here: 18; "The Curtain Rises at Aryamehr." *Kayhan International* (7 Sept. 1974): 1–2.
78. Katayoun Mihan, "Monarch Opens 7th Asian Games." *The Tehran Journal* (2 Sept. 1974): 1; *Official Report of the Seventh Asian Games Teheran Sept. 1–16, 74*, p. 58.
79. "The Curtain Rises at Aryamehr." *Kayhan International* (7 Sept. 1974): 1–2, here: 2.
80. A short movie shows the march-in of a group of uniformed and armed Iranian soldiers apparently during the opening ceremony: "Iran, Asian Games of 1974 in Tehran". Available at https://www.youtube.com/watch?v=CuvSrOuWvbM [accessed 2 Aug. 2012]. Based only on this short sequence it is not possible to definitely say if it

was an official part of the Games (which I nevertheless assume) or if only a rehearsal is shown or if different events were cut together.

81. "More than 70,000 Attending Closing Ceremony." *Straits Times* (17 Sept. 1974): 27. *See also* Nihon Taiiku Kyōkai and Nihon Orinpikku Iinkai, *Dai-7kai*, pp. 27, 47 (on the almost religious personality cult of the royal family); *Official Report of the Seventh Asian Games Teheran Sept. 1–16, 74*, p. 62.
82. Hushang Nemazee, "Grand Finale to Seventh Asian Games." *Kayhan International* (21 Sept. 1974): 8; "Pageant Closes Asian Games." *The Tehran Journal* (17 Sept. 1974): 1; *Tehran 1974. Seventh Asian Games. Souvenir Programme*, p. 64.
83. "Culture at the Site." *The Tehran Journal* (10 Sept. 1974): Asian Games Special Page 1; "Iranian Music and Dance." *The Tehran Journal* (5 Sept. 1974): Asian Games Special Page 2; Jamshid Foroughi, "Look Out for the Lion and Snake Dancers too." *The Tehran Journal* (1 Sept. 1974): Asian Games Special Page 1; "Seventh Asian Games." *Iran Tribune* 9, 120 (1974): 14–19, here: 17; *Tehran 1974. Seventh Asian Games. Souvenir Programme*, p. 93.
84. Nayapradit, Proposed Point to A.G.F. Council for 5th Asian Games. In *Avery Brundage Collection, Box 197: V Asian Games*, TOSC; *The Official Report of the Organizing Committee for the Fifth Asian Games Bangkok 1966*, p. 42.
85. Gail Hughes, "Some Harsh Words Backstage." *The Tehran Journal* (16 Sept. 1974): Asian Games Special Page 4; Steve Crawford, "On Organizing a Cultural Program." *The Tehran Journal* (5 Sept. 1974): Asian Games Special Page 3.
86. "Prince Gholam Reza Hosts Dinner for IOC Executive." *The Tehran Journal* (1 Sept. 1974): 6; "Seventh Asian Games." *Iran Tribune* 9, 120 (1974): 14–19, here: 17.
87. AMEMBASSY TEHRAN to SECSTATE WASHDC 8158 (12 Sept. 1974; 1974TEHRAN07695). In *Electronic Telegrams, 1/1/1974-12/31/1974* (Film Number: D740254–1072), RG 59, NA II; "Art of the People: Art with a Purpose." *The Tehran Journal* (8 Sept. 1974): Asian Games Special Page 4; Gail Hughes, "Some Harsh Words Backstage." *The Tehran Journal* (16 Sept. 1974): Asian Games Special Page 4; Jamshid Foroughi, "Look out for the Lion and Snake Dancers too." *The Tehran Journal* (1 Sept. 1974): Asian Games Special Page 1; Katayun Mihan, "A Silk Road for the 7th Games." *The Tehran Journal* (5 Sept. 1974): Asian Games Special Page 1; "Seventh Asian Games. Take a Cultural Break." *The Tehran Journal* (5 Sept. 1974): Asian Games Special Page 3; *Tehran 1974. Seventh Asian Games. Souvenir Programme*, p. 93; "Seventh Asian Games." *Iran Tribune* 9, 120 (1974): 14–19, here: 17; "Seventh Asian Games: The Most Elaborate ever." *Iran Tribune* 9, 119 (1974): 14–18, here: 18.
88. Alan McGregor, "IOC Open Way for China's Eventual Return." *The Times* (11 Feb. 1974): 9; John Rodda, "No Challenge to Miss Hartman." *The Guardian* (20 Feb. 1974): 26; Killanin, *My Olympic Years*, p. 226.
89. *Official Report of the Seventh Asian Games Teheran Sept. 1–16, 74*, p. 126; "Seventh Asian Games." *Iran Tribune* 9, 120 (1974): 14–19, here: 15; "Seventh Asian Games: The Most Elaborate Ever." *Iran Tribune* 9,119 (1974): 14–18, here: 17; The Organizing Committee Teheran, *Bulletin 1*, n.p.

90. Amirtash, "Iran", p. 52; "Seventh Asian Games: The Most Elaborate Ever." *Iran Tribune* 9, 119 (1974): 14–18, here: 15; *Tehran 1974. Seventh Asian Games. Souvenir Programme*, pp. 89–90; The Organizing Committee Teheran, *Bulletin* 6, n.p.
91. "Switch-off Gets a Switch-on." *Kayhan International* (24 Aug. 1974): 8. Regime opponents had criticized that the 2,500 years' celebration would not have been open to ordinary Iranians: Ansari, *Modern Iran*, p. 174. Similar accusations that only government and armed forces members would be allowed in the station during the opening ceremony of the Seventh Asian Games came up, but according to the Japanese report they were not true. Instead, the stadium would have been packed by people: Nihon Taiiku Kyōkai and Nihon Orinpikku Iinkai, *Dai-7kai*, p. 46.
92. Chehabi, "A Political History", p. 388.
93. Ernest Frida, "Teheran all Keyed Up for Today's Opening." *Straits Times* (1 Sept. 1974): 24; *Official Report of the Seventh Asian Games Teheran Sept. 1–16, 74*, p. 183.
94. See for example on the Japanese: Nihon Taiiku Kyōkai and Nihon Orinpikku Iinkai, *Dai-7kai*, pp. 24, 33, 45.
95. Ernie T. Bitong, "What's the Pitch?" *The Filipino Athlete* (Sept.—Oct. 1974): 31; Nihon Taiiku Kyōkai and Nihon Orinpikku Iinkai, *Dai-7kai*, pp. 31 (on the Near and Middle East), 33. In his memoirs, He Zhenliang mentions tensions between East and West Asia due to the Middle East Conflict and the disproportionately high influence for example of Kuwait, a country rather unimportant in world sports, as well as talks about splitting the Asian Games into games for West and East Asia. S. S. Dhillon made quite similar comments regarding a strong divide between East and West Asia due to the Middle East Conflict and other problems in an interview: Liang, *He Zhenliang*, pp. 207–39; Interview with S. S. Dhillon, Former Secretary-General of the Singapore National Olympic Council (13 Dec. 2011), SNOC.
96. On Israel's exclusion *see* Alperovich, *Israel*, pp. 285–93; Simri, "Israel", p. 90.
97. Ernie T. Bitong, "What's the Pitch?" *The Filipino Athlete* (Sept.–Oct. 1974): 31.
98. In 1981, the IOC finally accepted two professional sports (tennis and table tennis) for the 1988 Olympic Games. On the change of the eligibility rules between the early 1970s and 1981 *see*, for example, John Samuel, "'Eligibles' Replaces Amateurs." *The Guardian* (22 Oct. 1974): 25; Bertling, "The Loss", p. 53.

Conclusion

1. Nihon Taiiku Kyōkai and Nihon Orinpikku Iinkai, *Dai-7kai*, p. 24.
2. Okakura, *The Ideals of the East*, p. 1. Okakura saw closeness between ancient Indian and Chinese civilization due to a common "love for the Ultimate and Universal, which is the common thought-inheritance of every Asiatic race, enabling them to produce all the great religions of the world".
3. Nihon Taiiku Kyōkai and Nihon Orinpikku Iinkai, *Dai-7kai*, p. 24.
4. Although the question cannot be covered here, it would nevertheless be interesting to find out to which degree cooperation of other Asians with Japanese sports officials

was voluntarily undertaken, since, for example, these other Asians also did not take the Kuomintang seriously as the representative of China.

5. I here come back to the studies on pan-movements and conceptions of Asia I addressed in the introduction: Saaler, "Pan-Asianismus", p. 134; Duara, "Asia Redux"; Acharya, "Asia Is Not One".
6. Reid, *Imperial Alchemy*, pp. 5–11.
7. As mentioned in the second chapter in connection to Jorge Vargas, one has to remember that many Filipinos were already Christians (Catholics), meaning that the change in terms of norms and values is more interesting than the actual act of conversion to a Protestant denomination. In China, a large part of the Kuomintang elite were Christians, begging the question of what would have happened had the communists not won the Chinese Civil War, though the question of whether or not a boom of Christianity similar to that in South Korea would have taken place there obviously cannot be answered. Finally, in Japan, the impact of conversion was most limited, but differences in the interpretation of Bushidō (one having a strongly Christian touch) are interesting to notice.
8. I am aware that significant parts of the globe are not covered in this study, but it should be noticed that I do not even claim that the ideals were unchallenged in Asian countries.
9. Duara, "The Imperialism".
10. "Leaders in Physical Training", p. 330.
11. These were primarily egalitarianism and internationalism, but also economic progress, since sport should not be a business but serve to help in leading a productive life. Quite obviously, if economic progress is interpreted in a different way, professionalism could support it.
12. It is certainly an interesting question how successful the International YMCA College was in terms of training Asian physical educators, but this question cannot be answered here.
13. Hill, *Olympic Politics*, p. 35.
14. The Kuomintang had had such intentions in Nanjing, but the Eleventh FECG never took place there, as mentioned in the second chapter.
15. A trajectory of Olympic participation describes the following steps: Participate, win medals, get national sports accepted, host games, influence Olympic philosophy: Kelly, "Beijing", pp. 9–10. In a modified form that focuses on the Asian Games, whose patron organization the IOC was, and on 'Olympism', one can say that the last step had been reached around 1974.
16. The Olympic Games turned professional between 1971 and 1988: Bertling, "The Loss", pp. 52–3.
17. My own more paternalistic judgment as an academic would be that education (and academic research) is more valuable than entertainment—after all, this study's main purpose is education, while entertainment is only a secondary concern, albeit one which has hopefully not been entirely neglected.

Bibliography

Archival Material and Interviews

BArch / Bundesarchiv, Berlin-Lichterfelde, Germany

DR510/183 (Sofia 1957).

BHL / Bentley Historical Library, University of Michigan, Ann Arbor, United States

Manuel Luiz Quezon Papers:

Roll 50: W. W. Marquardt, 1918–22; Roll 53: Jorge B. Vargas, 1914–40.

HHL / Harvard Houghton Library, Harvard University, Cambridge, MA, USA

fMS Am 1366: Forbes, W. Cameron, 1870–1959; Letter-file; Pressed and carbon copies of TS. and MS. correspondence (outgoing); 1904–46. 86 Volumes, and 12 trays of file cards in two wooden cabinets: Volume 16.

JBVM / Jorge B. Vargas Museum and Filipiniana Research Center, University of the Philippines Diliman, Manila, The Philippines

3rd Asian Games, Jorge B. Vargas Jr., May–July 1958.

3rd Asian Games, Ramon Teodoro Vargas, Aug. 1950–May 1958.

SG-Philippine Amateur Athletic Federation.

SS-Second Asian Games.

Sports 1948.

Sports 1952–53.

Sports 1953–54.

Sports / Clippings 1954–58.

The Vargas-Saulo Interviews. A Series of Fourteen Tape-Recorded Interviews with MR. JORGE B. VARGAS and son EDDIE, from April 19 to May 24, 1977. Conducted, transcribed and edited by Alfredo B. Saulo.

KFYMCAA / Kautz Family YMCA Archives, University of Minnesota, Minneapolis, USA

Armed Services: World War I

Box 23: Elwood Brown Interview. Athletics in the Far East. Early Work in France. 1920; Interview with Elwood Brown. A.E.F. Games. Inter-Allied Games. 1920.

Biographical Records

Box 23: Brown, Elwood S. 1913–24 (B); Brown, Elwood Stanley. Biographical Data (C); Brown, Franklin H. 1932–73 (B); Brown, Franklin Hartwell. Biographical Data (C).

Box 25: Buck, Harry Crowe (C).
Box 42: Crocker, John Howard. 1930–66 (B).
Box 73: Gray, John Henry. Biographical Data (C).
Box 139: McCloy, Dr. Charles H. 1928–68 (B).
Box 154: Noehren, Dr. Arthur (C).
Box 181: Ryan, Winfield Scott. Biographical Data (C).
Box 198: Swan, Alfred H. (B); Swan, Alfred Hjalmar. Biographical Data (C).

International Work in China

Box 4: Annual and Quarterly Reports (Robertson). 1913; Annual and Quarterly Reports (S). 1913; Annual and Quarterly Reports (A–C). 1914.
Box 5: Annual and Quarterly Reports (C). 1915.
Box 6: Annual and Quarterly Reports (Ma–Mi). 1915; Annual and Quarterly Reports (S). 1915.
Box 12: Annual and Quarterly Reports (A–H). 1921; Annual and Quarterly Reports (G–M). 1923.
Box 13: Annual and Quarterly Reports (E–K). 1925; Annual and Quarterly Reports (L–P). 1925; Annual and Quarterly Reports.1926.
Box 15: China YMCA Foreign Secretaries' Report Letters 1900–28. Incomplete.
Box 31: Correspondence and Reports. Mar 1914.
Box 38: Correspondence and Reports. Apr 1921; Correspondence and Reports. July–Aug. 1921.
Box 39: Correspondence and Reports. Sept–Oct. 1921; Correspondence and Reports. Apr–June 1922; Correspondence and Reports. July–Aug. 1922.
Box 40: Correspondence and Reports. June 1923.
Box 41: Correspondence and Reports. Nov. 1923.

International Work in Japan

Box 4: Annual and Quarterly Reports. 1915. B–F; Annual and Quarterly Reports. 1915. S–V.
Box 5: Annual and Quarterly Reports. 1916. A–F; Annual and Quarterly Reports. 1917. 1: A–F; Annual and Quarterly Reports. 1917. 2: G–W; Annual and Quarterly Reports. 1918. 1: A–F.
Box 6: Annual and Quarterly Reports. 1919 A–D; Annual and Quarterly Reports. 1919 G–R; Annual and Quarterly Reports. 1921; Annual and Quarterly Reports. 1922.
Box 15: Correspondence and Reports. Aug–Dec. 1913; Correspondence and Reports. 1915; Correspondence and Reports. Jan–May 1916.
Box 16: Correspondence and Reports. Jan–Feb. 1922; Correspondence and Reports. Mar 1922; Correspondence and Reports. Apr–June 1922; Correspondence and Reports. July–Aug. 1922.
Box 17: Correspondence and Reports. Jan–Aug. 23, 1923.
Box 18: Correspondence and Reports. Jan–Feb. 1930.

Box 19: Correspondence and Reports. July–Dec. 1932.

Box 39: Physical Education Dept. Correspondence and Recollections (F. H. Brown). 1953–64 (1930 also).

International Work in the Philippines

Box 1: Correspondence and Reports. 1912; Correspondence and Reports. 1914; Correspondence and Reports. 1915; Correspondence and Reports. 1917.

Box 2: Correspondence and Reports. Jan–May 1922; Correspondence and Reports. 1925.

Box 5: Administrative Reports. 1910–12; Administrative Reports. 1914–16; Administrative Reports. 1917–19.

Physical Education Program Records

Box 37: National Amateur Athletic Federation: Miscellaneous, 1920–22.

YMCA Lantern Slides

Box 31: Lantern Slide Lecture Guides, 1900–29.

LA84 / L.A. '84 Foundation Library, Los Angeles, USA

Arch GV 722.5 .A7 (Asian Games): Band Music; Poster.

NA / Nationaal Archief, Den Haag, Lower Countries

Ministerie van Buitenlandse Zaken, 1955–64: B815.1 Sport en spel

Inv. Nr. 13740 (Rapportage over de Aziatische spelen in Djakarta en in het bijzonder de uitsluiting van Israël en India, 1962).

Inv. Nr. 13741 (Rapportage over de Games of the New Emerging Forces (GANEFO) en in het bijzonder de Nederlandse deelname, 1963–64).

NAJ / National Archives of Japan (Kokuritsu Kōbunshokan), Tokyo, Japan

Ajia Kyōgi Taikai e Nihon daihyōdan haken ni kan suru ketsugi [Decision on sending a Japanese delegation to the Asian Games]. Call No. Main Building 2A-010–03, 03424100.

Ajia Kyōgi Taikai kaisai ni tomonai raihō suru gaikokujin no ōtai ni tsuite [Concerning the treatment of the foreigners that will arrive due to the hosting of the Asian Games]. Call No. Main Building 3D-002–00, 00102100.

NAS / National Archives of Singapore, Singapore

Government Files

366/54 (Second Asian Games Held in Manila – 1954.) Microfilm Number: PRO 10.

Ministry of Culture

PressR19740821 (Talk on 'Olympism and our Participation in the Asian Games' by Haji Sha'ari Tadin, Senior Parliamentary Secretary (Culture) and also Leader of the

Republic's Sports Contingent to the Seventh Asian Games, Teheran, at a Luncheon Meeting of the Rotary Club on Wednesday, 21 Aug. 74, at 12.45 PM at the Mandarin Hotel), Microfilm Number: NA 1258.

Oral History Centre

Interviewee: DE CASTRO, Harold; 002968, Reel/Disc No: 4.
Interviewee: KEE Sun Bee; 001808, Reel/Disc No: 6.
Interviewee: KUNALAN, C.; 002572, Reel/Disc No: 7.
Interviewee: MITCHELL, Keith; Mitchell, Barry; Wolters, Wiebe, A1999/000839 and 002133, Reel/Disc No: 5.
Interviewee: TAN Eng Liang (Dr); 001951, Reel/Disc No: 8.

NARAII / National Archives and Record Administration II, College Park, MD, USA

Record Group 59: General Records of the Department of State, 1763–2002.
Series: Central Foreign Policy Files, created, 7/1/1973–12/31/1976, documenting the period 7/1/1973? –12/31/1976.
Electronic Telegrams, 1/1/1974–12/31/1974 [on microfilm].
Electronic Telegrams, 1/1/1975–12/31/1975 [on microfilm].

Record Group 331: Allied Operational and Occupation Headquarters, World War II, 1907–66.
Series: Topical File, 1945–51.
Box 5724: Asian Games Federation, 1945–51 [sic].

Record Group 350: Records of the Bureau of Insular Affairs, 1868–1945.
Series: General Classified Files, 1898–1913.
Box 947: #26063
Series: General Classified Files, 1914–45.
Box 343: #1887

NLotP / National Library of the Philippines, Manila, Philippines

BEY26/4 Philippine Ethnography General Paper No. 97 2/5, p. 1–4.

PCMSM / Prince Chichibu Memorial Sports Museum (Chichibunomiya Kinen Supōtsu Hakubutsukan), Tokyo, Japan

Photos of Exhibited Items (taken by Stefan Huebner).

RL / Regenstein Library, University of Chicago, Chicago, USA:

Amos Alonzo Stagg Papers: Box 2.

SNOC / Singapore National Olympic Council, Singapore

Interview with S. S. Dhillon, Former Secretary-General of the Singapore National Olympic Council (13 Dec. 2011).

SCASC / Springfield College Archives and Special Collections, Springfield, MA, USA

Alumni Relations Office Records (Files)

Bartolome, Candido C. (File)

TDA / The Diplomatic Archives of the Ministry of Foreign Affairs of Japan (Gaimushō Gaikōshiryōkan), Tokyo, Japan

Kyokutō 'Orimupikku' Kyōgi Taikai kankei ikken 7. Dai-6kai (Ōsaka) [Documents relating to the Far Eastern 'Olympic' Games / 7. 6th Event (Osaka)]. Reference Code: B04012509300.

TOSC / The Olympic Studies Centre (Historical Archives), Lausanne, Switzerland

Avery Brundage Collection

Comité International Olympique – Commission exécutive 1921–79.

Comité International Olympique – Session 1894–2008.

D.RM01.INDE/003. Correspondance 1924–59.

D.RM01.INDE/013. Rapports. 1951–61.

D.RM01.INDOC/001. Demande de reconnaissance: correspondance. 1932–33.

D.RM01.INDON/002. Correspondance. 1953–87.

D.RM01.INDON/004. Publications 1962–76.

D.RM01.INDON/006. Demande de reconnaissance: Correspondance et reconnaissance. 1963–64.

D.RM01.IRAN/002. Correspondance. 1948–79.

D.RM01.JAPON/003. Correspondance. 1970–75.

D.RM01.MANDC/001. Demande de reconnaissance: correspondance et statuts. 1932.

D.RM01.PHILI/006. Correspondance. 1934–79.

D.RM01.PHILI/012. Demande de reconnaissance: correspondance. 1914–29.

D.RM01.TAIPE/004 – D.RM01.CHNRP / 004. Participation des 2 Chine aux JO et aux 7s Jeux Asiatiques. Correspondance. 1952–74.

D.RM01.THAIL(Burex). Bureau Executif: correspondance et biographies. 1965–84.

D.RM01.THAIL(CORR). Correspondance. 1950–87.

D.RM01.THAIL(RECON). Demande de reconnaissance: correspondance et reconnaissance. 1905–50.

H-FC02-ASIAN/001. Jeux asiatiques et Fédération des Jeux asiatiques: Correspondance. 1953–82.

H-FC02-ASIAN/002. Situation de la Chine et Chinese Taipei (Taiwan) aux Jeux asiatiques: Correspondance, transcription des discussions à la réunion spéciale du Conseil de l'AGF à Téhéran les 15–16 nov. 1973, rapport de Niu Ping-yik, projet d'amendement à la décision prise par le Comité Exécutif de l'AGF à Bangkok le 18 sept. 1973 et résumé de cette réunion, déclaration de P. Chang, memo et article de presse. 1973–74.

H-FC02-ASIAN/006. Jeux Asiatiques et Fédération des Jeux asiatiques (AGF), réunions du Conseil de l'AGF à New Delhi le 31 juil. 1950 et les 26–27 nov. 1981, du Comité Exécutif de l'AGF à Bangkok le 5 juin 1978: procès-verbaux et rapport. Analyse des sports pratiqués pendant les 5es, 6es et 7es Jeux. 1950–81.

H-FC02-ASIAN/007. 1ers Jeux asiatiques à New Delhi en 1951: Correspondance et bulletin. 1947–51.

H-FC02-ASIAN/008. 2es Jeux asiatiques à Manille (Philippines) en 1954: Correspondance et résultats. 1953–54.

H-FC02-ASIAN/009. 3es Jeux asiatiques à Tokyo (Japon) en 1958: Correspondance, rapport, bulletin et invitation officielle. 1956–58.

H-FC02-ASIAN/011. 4es Jeux asiatiques à Djakarta (Indonésie) en 1962: Correspondance, rapports et candidature de l'Indonésie. 1962.

H-FC02-ASIAN/012. 5es Jeux asiatiques à Bangkok (Thaïlande) en 1966: Correspondance. 1963–66.

H-FC02-ASIAN/014. 7es Jeux asiatiques à Teheran (Iran) en 1974: Correspondance, articles de presse et rapports de la visite de A. Taka[c] au Comité d'organisation et au CNO d'Iran. 1972–75.

H-FC03-ASIOU/001. Fédération des Jeux de l'Asie de l'ouest: Correspondance et constitution. 1933–36.

H-FC03-EXORI/001. Jeux d'Extrême Orient et la 'Far Eastern Athletic Association (FEAA)': Correspondance. 1925–35.

H-FC03-EXORI/002. Jeux d'Extrême Orient et réunions de la 'Far Eastern Athletic Association (FEAA)': Procès-verbaux. 1930–34.

H-FC03-EXORI/003. Jeux d'Extrême Orient et la 'Far Eastern Athletic Association (FEAA)': Constitution, conférence en marge de la session du CIO en 1924, documents sur la FEAA et règles de volleyball adoptées par l'Association. 1920–30.

H-FC03-EXORI/004. 5es et 6es Jeux d'Extrême Orient à Shanghai (Chine) en 1921 et à Osaka (Japon) en 1923: Correspondance. 1921–24.

H-FC03-EXORI/005. 7es et 8es Jeux d'Extrême Orient à Manille (Philippines) en 1925 et à Shanghai (Chine) en 1927: Correspondance et programme. 1927–29 [sic].

H-FC03-EXORI/006. 9es Jeux d'Extrême Orient à Tokyo (Japon) en 1930: Correspondance et programme. 1929–32.

H-FC03-EXORI/007. 10es Jeux d'Extrême Orient à Manille (Philippines) en 1934: Correspondance. 1933–36.

MBR. KANO, Jigoro. Ecrits + correspondance. 1909–35.

MBR. KISHI, Sei[i]chi. Correspondance 1925–33.

MBR. SONDHI, Guru Dutt. Correspondance 1929–67.

MBR. WANG, Chengting T. Biographie et correspondance. 1924–57.

PT-BAILL-CORR. Correspondance de Henri de Baillet-Latour (membre). 1915–25.

PT-BAILL-CORR. Correspondance de H. de Baillet-Latour (Président). 1925–27.

PT-BAILL-CORR. Correspondance de Baillet-Latour (Président). 1928–30.

PT-BAILL-CORR. Correspondance de Baillet-Latour (Président). 1931–34.

PT-EDSTR-CORR. Correspondance de S. Edström (Président). 1948.

PT-KILLA-CORR. KILLANIN, Michael Morris. CORRESPONDANCE. 1974.

PT-PDC-CORR. COUBERTIN, Pierre de. CORRESPONDANCE. Sloane à Coubertin 1897–1924.

VIL-1940S-CAND: Candidatures des villes de Budapest, Canada, Chicago, Helsinki, Londres, Rome, Tokyo pour les JO été en 1940: correspondance, publications, rapports, articles et votes.

VIL-1964S-CAND: Candidatures de Bogota, Bruxelles, Lausanne, Vienne et Tokyo pour les Jeux été en 1964: correspondance et publications.

VIL-1964S-CAND: Candidature de Tokyo pour les Jeux été en 1964: réponses au questionnaire, 1958.

YOUNG MEN'S CHRIS[T]IAN ASSOCIATIONS. 1909–27.

TNA / The National Archives, Kew, United Kingdom

FO 371/144156 (Preparations for Asian Games in Indonesia in 1962)

FO 371/1522198 (Preparations for South East Asia Peninsular Games, 1961 and Asian Games, 1962).

WUA / Waseda University Archives (Waseda Daigaku Daigakushi Shiryō Sentā), Tokyo, Japan

Yamamoto Tadaoki shiryō [Material on Yamamoto Tadaoki] / 3: Supōtsu no shinkō [3. Promotion of Sports] / Kyokutō Senshuken Kyōgi Taikai [Far Eastern Championship Games]

217: Medaru (Dai-8kai Kyokutō Senshuken Taikai, 1927nen 8gatsu [Medal (8th Far Eastern Championship Games, Aug. 1927)].

218: Kyōshō (Dai-9kai Kyokutō Senshuken Kyōgi Taikai, Shōwa 5nen 5gatsu) [Breast Badge (9th Far Eastern Championship Games, May 1930)].

226: Shinbunkiji kirinukichō (Kyokutō Manshū sanka mondai 1 [Newspaper Article Scrapbook (Question regarding Manchukuo's Participation the the Far Eastern Championship Games, 1)].

Newspapers and News Magazines

Antara. Jakarta.

Asahi Evening News. Tokyo.

Asahi Shinbun. Osaka / Tokyo.

Association Men. Chicago.

Association Men (India). Kolkata (Calcutta).
Bangkok Post. Bangkok.
Bangkok World. Bangkok.
Bulletin du Comité International Olympique (also: *Bulletin officiel du Comité International Olympique*) / *Official Bulletin of the International Olympic Committee* / *Olympic Review.* Lausanne.
Bungei shunjū. Tokyo.
Cablenews American. Manila.
China News. Taipei.
China Press. Shanghai.
China's Young Men (English Edition). Shanghai.
Chūō kōron. Tokyo.
Dongfang zazhi. Shanghai.
Foreign Mail. New York.
Graphic. Manila.
Hōchi Shinbun (now: *Supōtsu Hōchi*). Tokyo.
Indonesian Observer. Jakarta.
Iran Tribune. Tehran.
Japan Times. Tokyo.
Jiji Shinpō. Tokyo.
Kaizō. Tokyo.
Kayhan International. Tehran.
Mainichi Shinbun. Osaka / Tokyo.
Manila Chronicle. Manila.
Manila Daily Bulletin. Manila.
Manila Times. Manila.
New York Times. New York.
Newsweek. New York.
North China Daily News. Shanghai
North China Herald. Shanghai.
Official Bulletin of the International Olympic Committee: see *Bulletin du Comité International Olympique.*
Olympic Review: see *Bulletin du Comité International Olympique.*
Orimupikku. Tokyo.
Ōsaka Mainichi Shinbun: see *Mainichi Shinbun.*
Outdoor World and Recreation. New York.
Peking Review. Beijing.
Philippine Magazine. Manila.
Philippines Free Press. Manila.
Renmin ribao. Beijing.
Shenbao. Shanghai. (There are two different databases of *Shenbao* – this one was used): http://www.egreenapple.com/english/contents/136/372.html
Shenbao yuekan. Shanghai.

Shinseinen. Tokyo.
Singapore Free Press and Mercantile Advertiser. Singapore.
Sports. Singapore.
Straits Echo and Times of Malaya. Penang.
Straits Times. Singapore.
Survey of China Mainland Press. Hong Kong.
The Asia Magazine. Hong Kong [et al.].
The Evening News. Manila.
The Filipino Athlete. Manila.
The Guardian (until 1959: *The Manchester Guardian*). Manchester (since 1964: London).
The Hindu. Chennai (Madras).
The Indonesian Herald. Jakarta.
The Japan Advertiser. Tokyo.
The Japan Weekly Chronicle. Kobe.
The Mainichi. Tokyo.
The Nation. Bangkok.
The Observer. London.
The Overseas Hindustan Times. New Delhi.
The Outlook: An Illustrated Weekly Journal of Current Life. New York.
The Philippines Herald. Manila.
The Pioneer / The Kaitakusha. Tokyo.
The Playground. New York.
The Tehran Journal. Tehran.
The Times. London.
The Tribune. Manila.
Times of India. Mumbai (Bombay).
Time (Magazin). New York.
Washington Post. Washington.
The Young Men of India. Kolkata (Calcutta).
Tokyo Municipal News. Tokyo.
Undōkai. Tokyo.
Yamato Shinbun. Tokyo.
Yomiuri Shinbun. Tokyo.

Literature

2nd Asian Games Official Program. Manila[?]: n.p., 1954.

III Asian Games. Official Programme. Tokyo 1958. May 24–June 1. Tokyo: n.p., 1958.

A. P. L. Kikaku. (ed.), *Ajia Kyōgi Taikai ekijibijon shutsujō kinen* [Commemoration of the Participation in the Exhibitions at the Third Asian Games]. Tokyo: Nihon Taiiku Shidōsha Renmei, 1958.

Abe, Ikuo and James A. Mangan. "The British Impact on Boys' Sports and Games in Japan: An Introductory Survey." *International Journal of the History of Sport* 14, 2 (1997): 187–99.

———. "Sportmanship' – English Inspiration and Japanese Response: F. W. Strange and Chiyosaburo Takeda." In James A. Mangan and Fan Hong (eds.), *Sport in Asian Society. Past and Present*. London: Frank Cass, 2003, pp. 99–128.

Abe, Ikuo. "Historical Significance of the Far Eastern Championship Games: An International Political Arena." In Andreas Niehaus and Max Seinsch (eds.), *Olympic Japan. Ideals and Realities of (Inter)Nationalism*. Würzburg: Ergon, 2007, pp. 67–87.

———. "Muscular Christianity in Japan: The Growth of a Hybrid." In John J. MacAloon (ed.), *Muscular Christianity in Colonial and Post-Colonial Worlds*. London: Routledge, 2008, pp. 14–38.

Abe, Kitarō. *Mizu to tomo ni 70nen* [70 Years with the Water]. Tokyo: Mizu to tomo ni 70nen kankōkai, 1975.

Abel, Jessamyn R. "Japan's Sporting Diplomacy: The 1964 Tokyo Olympiad." *International History Review* 34, 2 (2012): 203–20.

———. *The International Minimum. Creativity and Contradiction in Japan's Global Entanglement, 1933–1964*. Honolulu: University of Hawaii Press, 2015.

Abeyasekere, Susan. *Jakarta. A History*. Revised ed. Singapore: Oxford University Press, 1990.

Abraham, Itty. "From Bandung to NAM: Non-Alignment and Indian Foreign Policy, 1947–65." *Commonwealth & Comparative Politics* 46, 2 (2008): 195–219.

Abrahamian, Ervand. *A History of Modern Iran*. Cambridge: Cambridge University Press, 2008.

Acharya, Amitav. *Constructing a Security Community in Southeast Asia. ASEAN and the Problem of Regional Order*. 2nd ed. London: Routledge, 2009.

———. "Asia Is Not One." *Journal of Asian Studies* 69, 4 (2010): 1001–13.

Adams, Iain. "Pancasila: Sport and the Building of Indonesia – Ambitions and Obstacles." In James A. Mangan and Fan Hong (ed.), *Sport in Asian Society. Past and Present*. London: Frank Cass, 2003, pp. 295–318.

Adas, Michael. "Contested Hegemony: The Great War and the Afro-Asian Assault on the Civilizing Mission Ideology." *Journal of World History* 15, 1 (2004): 31–63.

Afkhami, Gholam R. *The Life and Times of the Shah*. Berkeley: University of California Press, 2009.

Alam, Asadollah. *The Shah and I. The Confidential Diary of Iran's Royal Court, 1969–1977*. Introduced and Edited by Alinaghi Alikhani. London: Tauris, 1991.

Alperovich, Amichai. *Israel in der Olympischen Bewegung* [Israel in the Olympic Movement]. Unpublished Dissertation, Deutsche Sporthochschule Köln, Cologne, 2008.

Alter, Joseph S. "Indian Clubs and Colonialism. Hindu Masculinity and Muscular Christianity." *Comparative Studies in Society and History* 46, 3 (2004): 497–534.

———. "Yoga at the Fin de Siècle. Muscular Christianity with a 'Hindu' Twist." In John J. MacAloon (ed.), *Muscular Christianity in Colonial and Post-Colonial Worlds*. London: Routledge, 2008, pp. 59–76.

Alvandi, Roham. "Nixon, Kissinger, and the Shah: The Origins of Iranian Primacy in the Persian Gulf." *Diplomatic History* 36, 2 (2012): 337–72.

Amirtash, Ali-Mohammad. "Iran and the Asian Games: The Largest Sports Event in the Middle East." In Fan Hong (ed.), *Sport, Nationalism and Orientalism: The Asian Games*. London: Routledge, 2007, pp. 46–63.

Anderson, Benedict R. *Language and Power. Exploring Political Cultures in Indonesia*. Ithaca: Cornell University Press, 1990.

Anderson, Wanni W. "Sport in Thailand." In Eric A. Wagner (ed.), *Sport in Asia and Africa: A Comparative Handbook*. New York: Greenwood, 1989, pp. 121–46.

Anderson, Warwick. *Colonial Pathologies. American Tropical Medicine, Race, and Hygiene in the Philippines*. Durham: Duke University Press, 2006.

Ansari, Iman and Patrick Germain. *Mon père, mon frère, les Shahs d'Iran. Entretiens avec Son Altesse Impériale le prince Gholam-Reza Pahlavi* [My Father, My Brother: The Shahs of Iran. Conversations with His Imperial Highness Prince Gholam-Reza Pahlavi]. Nantes: Normant, 2004.

Ansari, Ali M. *Modern Iran since 1921. The Pahlavis and After*. London: Pearson Education, 2003.

Antolihao, Lou. "20 shiji chu Yatai diqu Yuandong yundonghui yu 'Yazhou yishi' de fazhan. The Far Eastern Games and the Formation of Asian Identity in the Asia-Pacific during the Early Twentieth Century." In *Yazhou chuanmei yanjiu* (2007): 214–30.

———. *Playing with the Big Boys. Basketball, American Imperialism, and Subaltern Discourse in the Philippines*. Lincoln: University of Nebraska Press, 2015.

Appadurai, Arjun. *Modernity at Large. Cultural Dimensions of Globalization*. Minneapolis: University of Minnesota Press, 1996.

Asian Games 4. Djakarta 1962. 24 August–4 September. Jakarta[?]: n.p., 1962.

Asian Games Federation. (ed.), *Asian Games Rules*. New Delhi[?]: n.p., 1950.

Asian Relations Organization. (ed.), *Asian Relations. Being Report of the Proceedings and Documentation of the First Asian Relations Conference New Delhi, March–April, 1947*. New Delhi: Asian Relations Organization, 1948.

Asis, Leocadio de. *From Bataan to Tokyo. Diary of a Filipino Student in Wartime Japan 1943–1944*. Edited by Grant Goodman. Lawrence: Center for East Asian Studies, University of Kansas, 1979.

Aydin, Cemil. *The Politics of Anti-Westernism in Asia. Visions of World Order in Pan-Islamic and Pan-Asian Thought*. New York: Columbia University Press, 2007.

Bai, Lei and Shiquan Gu. "Di 7 jie Yayunhui Yilangren bufu zhongwang [The Iranians Fulfilled the Expectations of the Masses at the Seventh Asian Games]." *Tiyu wenshi* 42, 2 (1990): 2–3.

Baker, Chris and Pasuk Phongpaichit. *A History of Thailand*. 2nd ed. Cambridge: Cambridge University Press, 2009.

Baker, William J. *Playing with God: Religion and Modern Sport*. Cambridge, MA: Harvard University Press, 2007.

———. "Religion." In Steven W. Pope and John Nauright (eds.), *Routledge Companion to Sports History*. London: Routledge, 2010, pp. 216–28.

Bananal, Eduardo. *Camilo Osias. Educator and Statesman*. Quezon City: Manlapaz, 1974.

Barth, Boris and Jürgen Osterhammel (eds.). *Zivilisierungsmissionen. Imperiale Weltverbesserung seit dem 18. Jahrhundert* [Civilizing Missions. Imperial World Improvement since the 18th Century]. Konstanz: UVK, 2005.

Basu, Subrata and Sumit D. Majumder. *The Asiad Stadia*. New Delhi: National Book Trust, 1988.

Becker, Sascha O. and Ludger Woessmann. "Was Weber Wrong? A Human Capital Theory of Protestant Economic History." *Quarterly Journal of Economics* 124, 2 (2009): 531–96.

Benesch, Oleg. *Inventing the Way of the Samurai. Nationalism, Internationalism, and Bushidō in Modern Japan*. Oxford: Oxford University Press, 2014.

Beran, Janice A. "Americans in the Philippines: Imperialism or Progress through Sport?" *International Journal of the History of Sport* 6, 1 (1989): 62–87.

Berger, Mark T. *The Battle for Asia: From Decolonization to Globalization*. London: RoutledgeCurzon, 2004.

Bertling, Christoph. "The Loss of Profit? The Rise of Professionalism in the Olympic Movement and the Consequences for National Sport Systems." *Journal of Olympic History* 15, 2 (2007): 50–9.

Black, David R and Janis van der Westhuizen. "The Allure of Global Games for 'Semi-Peripheral' Polities and Spaces: A Research Agenda." *Third World Quarterly* 25, 7 (2004): 1195–214.

Black, David. "Dreaming Big: The Pursuit of 'Second Order' Games as a Strategic Response to Globalization." *Sport in Society* 11, 4 (2008): 467–80.

Blackburn, Susan. "Feminism and the World's Largest Islamic Nation." In Mina Roces and Louise Edwards (eds.), *Women's Movements in Asia. Feminism and Transnational Activism*. London: Routledge, 2010, pp. 21–33.

Blackwood, Thomas. "Bushidō Baseball? Three 'Fathers' and the Invention of a Tradition." *Social Science Japan Journal* 11, 2 (2008): 223–40.

Bocobo-Olivar, Celia. *History of Physical Education in the Philippines*. Quezon City: University of the Philippines Press, 1972.

Bonde, Hans. *Gymnastics and Politics. Hans Bukh and Male Aesthetics*. Copenhagen: University of Copenhagen Press, 2006.

Bradley, Mark P. *Vietnam at War*. Oxford: Oxford University Press, 2009.

Brands, Henry W. *Bound to Empire. The United States and the Philippines*. Oxford: Oxford University Press, 1992.

Brent, Charles H. *The Splendor of the Human Body. A Reparation and an Appeal*. New York: Longmans, Green, and Co., 1904.

Brown, Colin. "Playing the Game: Ethnicity and Politics in Indonesian Badminton." *Indonesia* 81 (2006): 71–93.

———. "Sport, Modernity and Nation Building. The Indonesian National Games of 1951 and 1953." *Bijdragen tot de Taal-, Land- en Volkenkunde* 164, 4 (2008): 431–49.

Brown, Elwood S. "Far Eastern Olympic Games." In Athletic League of the Young Men's Christian Association of North America (ed.), *Y.M.C.A. Athletic League. Official Handbook 1913*. New York: American Sports Publishing, 1913, pp. 165–7.

——. "Physical Work in the Philippines." *Physical Training* 11, 8 (1914): 256–64.

Brown, Franklin H. (ed.), "The Third Far Eastern Championship Games. Tokyo, May 8th–12th, 1917." *Physical Training* 14, 9 (1917): 386–93.

——. (ed.), *The Sixth Championship Games of the Far Eastern Athletic Association Held in Osaka, May 21–26, 1923 under the Patronage of His Imperial Highness Prince Chichibu and by the Sanction of the International Olympic Committee. Official Report*. Kobe: Japan Chronicle Press, 1923a. (Cover page: The Sixth Far Eastern Championship Games. Osaka 1923. Official Report.)

——. "The Sixth Far Eastern Championship Games." *Physical Training* 20,10 (1923b): 375–7.

——. (ed.), *Official Report of the Ninth Championship Games of the Far Eastern Athletic Association Held in Tokyo, Japan, May 24–31, 1930 under the High Patronage of H. I. H. Prince Chichibu*. Yokohama: Hori Printing Company, 1930[?]. (Cover page: The Ninth Far Eastern Championship Games. Tokyo 1930. Official Report.)

Brown, John, Jr. "Elwood S. Brown. A Tribute to a Friend." *Physical Training* 21, 7 (1924): 247–51.

Brown, Judith M. *Nehru. A Political Life*. New Haven: Yale University Press, 2003.

Brownell, Susan. "'Sport and Politics Don't Mix.' China's Relationship with the IOC during the Cold War." In Stephen Wagg and David L. Andrews (eds.), *East Plays West. Sport and the Cold War*. London: Routledge, 2007, pp. 253–71.

——. *Beijing's Games: What the Olympics Mean to China*. Lanham: Rowman & Littlefield, 2008.

Brunnell, Frederick P. "Guided Democracy Foreign Policy, 1960–1965." *Indonesia* 2 (1966): 37–76.

Buchanan, Ian. "Elwood S. Brown. Missionary Extraordinary." *Journal of Olympic History* 6, 3 (1998): 12–3.

Cao, Xiangjun and Susan Brownell. "The People's Republic of China." In Laurence Chalip, Arthur Johnson, and Lisa Stachura (eds.), *National Sport Policies: An International Handbook*. Westport: Greenwood Press, 1996, pp. 67–88.

Carlile, Lonny E. "Economic Development and the Evolution of Japanese Overseas Tourism, 1964–1994." *Tourism Recreation Research* 21, 1 (1996): 11–18.

Cavallo, Dominick. *Muscles and Morals: Organized Playgrounds and Urban Reform, 1880–1920*. Philadelphia: University of Pennsylvania Press, 1981.

Ceuster, Koen de. "Wholesome Education and Sound Leisure: The YMCA Sports Programme in Colonial Korea." *European Journal of East Asian Studies* 2, 1 (2003): 53–88.

Cha, Victor D. *Beyond the Final Score. The Politics of Sport in Asia*. New York: Columbia University Press, 2009.

Chehabi, Houchang E. "A Political History of Football in Iran." *Iranian Studies* 35, 4 (2002): 371–402.

———. "The Juggernaut of Globalization: Sport and Modernization in Iran." In James A. Mangan and Fan Hong (eds.), *Sport in Asian Society. Past and Present.* London: Frank Cass, 2003, pp. 275–94.

Chen, Xianming, Youde Liang, and Kehe Du, *Zhongguo bangqiu yundongshi* [History of Baseball in China]. Wuhan: Xinhua faxing, 1990.

Chin, Carol C. *Modernity and National Identity in the United States and East Asia, 1895–1919.* Kent: Kent State University Press, 2010.

Christesen, Paul. *Sport and Democracy in the Ancient and Modern Worlds.* Cambridge: Cambridge University Press, 2012.

Close, Paul, David Askew, and Xin Xu. *The Beijing Olympiad. The Political Economy of a Sporting Mega-Event.* London: Routledge, 2007.

Coaldrake, William H. *Architecture and Authority in Japan.* London: Routledge, 1996.

Collins, Mike and Andrew Parker. "Faith and Sport Revival in Britain. Muscular Christianity and Beyond." *Stadion* 35 (2011): 193–210.

Collins, Sandra. *The 1940 Tokyo Games: The Missing Olympics. Japan, the Asian Olympics and the Olympic Movement.* London: Routledge, 2007.

———. "Sporting Japanese-ness in an Americanised Japan." *International Journal of the History of Sport* 28, 17 (2011): 2448–73.

Colombijn, Freek. "The Politics of Indonesian Football." *Archipel* 59 (2000): 171–200.

Committee for Publication of the Indonesian Olympic Committee (ed.), *Indonesia & the Asian Games.* Jakarta[?]: Indonesian Olympic Committee[?], 1958[?].

Conklin, Alice L. *A Mission to Civilize. The Republican Idea of Empire in France and West Africa, 1895–1930.* Stanford: Stanford University Press, 1997.

Connolly, Chris A. "The Politics of the Games of the New Emerging Forces (GANEFO)." *International Journal of the History of Sport* 29, 9 (2012): 1311–24.

Conrad, Sebastian. *Globalgeschichte. Eine Einführung* [Global History. An Introduction]. Munich: Beck, 2013.

Cooper, Frederick. *Colonialism in Question: Theory, Knowledge, History.* Berkeley: University of California Press, 2005.

Coubertin, Pierre de. *Essais de psychologie sportive* [Essays on Sport Psychology]. Lausanne: Payot & Cie, 1913.

———. *Olympism: Selected Writings.* Edited by Norbert Müller. Lausanne: IOC, 2000.

Creak, Simon. *Embodied Nation. Sport, Masculinity, and the Making of Modern Laos.* Honolulu: University of Hawai'i Press, 2015.

Cribb, Robert and Colin Brown. *Modern Indonesia. A History since 1945.* London: Longman, 1995.

Crone, Frank L. "Physical Training in the Philippine Public Schools." In National Education Association of the United States (ed.), *Journal of Proceedings and Addresses.* Ann Arbor: National Education Association, 1915, pp. 984–9.

Dabringhaus, Sabine. *Geschichte Chinas im 20. Jahrhundert* [History of China during the 20th Century]. Munich: Beck, 2009.

Dai-3kai Ajia Kyōgi Taikai Soshiki Iinkai. (ed.), *Dai-3kai Ajia Kyōgi Taikai hōkokusho* [Report on the Third Asian Games]. Tokyo: Dai-3kai Ajia Kyōgi Taikai Soshiki Iinkai, 1959.

Dai-3kai Ajia Kyōgi Taikai Soshiki Iinkai (shikitenbu)—(ed.), *Ajia Kyōgi Taikai: shikiten. ekijibijon arubamu* [Asian Games: Ceremonies – Exhibitions Album]. Tokyo: Dai-3kai Ajia Kyōgi Taikai Soshiki Iinkai (shikitenbu), 1958.

Dainihon Taiiku Kyōkai. (ed.), *Dai-7kai Kyokutō Senshuken Kyōgi Taikai hōkokusho* [Report on the Seventh Far Eastern Championship Games]. Tokyo: Dainihon Taiiku Kyōkai, 1925.

———. (ed.), *Dai-8kai Kyokutō Senshuken Kyōgi Taikai hōkokusho* [Report on the Eighth Far Eastern Championship Games]. Tokyo: Dainihon Taiiku Kyōkai, 1928.

———. (ed.), *Dai-9kai Kyokutō Senshuken Kyōgi Taikai hōkokusho* [Report on the Ninth Far Eastern Championship Games]. Tokyo: Dainihon Taiiku Kyōkai, 1930[?].

———. (ed.), *Dai-10kai Kyokutō Senshuken Kyōgi Taikai hōkokusho* [Report on the Tenth Far Eastern Championship Games]. Tokyo: Dainihon Taiiku Kyōkai, 1934a[?].

———. (ed.), *Manshūkoku no Kyokutō Taikai sanka mondai. 3gatsu 3ka made no keika* [The Problem of Manchukuo's Participation in the Far Eastern Championship Games]. Tokyo: Dainihon Taiiku Kyōkai, 1934b.

———. (ed.), *Dainihon Taiiku Kyōkaishi* [History of the Great-Japan Amateur Athletic Association]. 3 Vols. Reprint of 1936/1937. Tokyo: Daiichi Shobō, 1983.

Darnell, Simon C. and David R. Black. "Introduction. Mainstreaming Sport into International Development Studies." *Third World Quarterly* 32, 3 (2011): 367–78.

Date, Yoshimi. "Kyokutō Senshuken Taikai no sekai – Ajia shugi teki na supōtsukan no risō to genjitsu [The World of the Far Eastern Championship Games – Ideal and Reality of an Asianist Perspective on Sports]." In Hajime Hirai (ed.), *Supōtsu de yomu Ajia* [Asia Read through Sports]. Tokyo: Sekai Shisōsha, 2000, pp. 205–24.

Davenport, C. B. and Albert G. Love. "Defects Found in Drafted Men." *Scientific Monthly* 10, 1 (1920), 5–25.

David, Mohan D., *The YMCA and the Making of Modern India. A Centenary History.* New Delhi: National Council of YMCAs of India, 1992.

Department of Foreign Affairs. (ed.), *Indonesia, 1962.* Jakarta: Departemen Luar Negeri, 1962.

Department of Information (ed.), *The Fourth Asian Games.* Jakarta: Department of Information, 1962[?].

Dimeo, Paul, "Colonial Bodies, Colonial Sport: 'Martial' Punjabis, 'Effeminate' Bengalis and the Development of Indian Football." *International Journal of the History of Sport* 19, 1 (2002): 72–90.

———. "Sporting and the 'Civilizing Mission' in India." In Harald Fischer-Tiné and Michael Mann (eds.), *Colonialism as Civilizing Mission. Cultural Ideology in British India.* London: Anthem Press, 2004, pp. 165–78.

Dong, Shouyi. "Zhongguo yu Yuandong yundonghui [China and the Far Eastern Championship Games]." In *Zhongguo tiyushi cankao ziliao* 2 (1957): 81–92.

Doronila, Amando. *The State, Economic Transformation, and Political Change in the Philippines, 1946–1972*. Oxford: Oxford University Press, 1992.

Droubie, Paul. "Phoenix Arisen: Japan as Peaceful Internationalist at the 1964 Tokyo Summer Olympics." *International Journal of the History of Sport* 28, 16 (2011): 2309–22.

Duara, Prasenjit. *Sovereignty and Authenticity: Manchukuo and the East Asian Modern*. Lanham: Rowman & Littlefield, 2003.

———. "The Imperialism of 'Free Nations'. Japan, Manchukuo, and the History of the Present." In Ann Laura Stoler, Carole McGranahan, and Peter Perdue (eds.), *Imperial Formations*. Santa Fe: School of American Research Press, 2007, pp. 211–40.

———. "Asia Redux: Conceptualising a Region for Our Time." *Journal of Asian Studies* 69, 4 (2010): 963–83.

Dülffer, Jost and Marc Frey. "Introduction." In Jost Dülffer and Marc Frey (eds.), *Elites and Decolonization in the Twentieth Century*. Basingstoke: Palgrave Macmillan, 2011, pp. 1–10.

Dunch, Ryan. "Beyond Cultural Imperialism: Cultural Theory, Christian Missions, and Global Modernity." *History and Theory* 41 (2002): 301–25.

Dunning, Eric G. "Sport in the Civilizing Process: Aspects of the Development of Modern Sport." In Eric G. Dunning, Joseph Maguire, and Robert E. Pearton (eds.), *The Sports Process. A Comparative and Developmental Approach*. Champaign: Human Kinetics Publishers, 1993, pp. 39–70.

Dower, John W. *War without Mercy. Race and Power in the Pacific War*. 7th ed. New York: Pantheon Books, 1993.

———. *Embracing Defeat. Japan in the Wake of World War II*. London: W. W. Norton, 1999.

Dyreson, Mark. "The Emergence of Consumer Culture and the Transformation of Physical Culture: American Sport in the 1920s." *Journal of Sport History* 16, 3 (1989): 261–81.

Edwards, Louise. "Chinese Feminism in a Transnational Frame. Between Internationalism and Xenophobia." In Mina Roces and Louise Edwards (eds.), *Women's Movements in Asia. Feminism and Transnational Activism*. London: Routledge, 2010, pp. 53–74.

Eisenberg, Christiane. *"English Sports" und deutsche Bürger. Eine Gesellschaftsgeschichte 1800–1939* ["English Sports" and German Citizens. A Social History, 1800–1939]. Paderborn: Schöningh, 1999.

Eisenstadt, Shmul N. "Multiple Modernities." *Daedalus* 129, 1 (2000): 1–29.

Elias, Norbert. "An Essay on Sport and Violence." In Norbert Elias and Eric Dunning (eds.), *Quest for Excitement. Sport and Leisure in the Civilizing Process*. Oxford: Blackwell, 1993a, pp. 150–74.

———. "Introduction." In Norbert Elias and Eric Dunning (eds.), *Quest for Excitement. Sport and Leisure in the Civilizing Process*. Oxford: Blackwell, 1993b, pp. 19–62.

England, Frederick O. (ed.), *Far Eastern Athletic Association. Official Report. From May 31, 1923 to May 31, 1925*. Manila: Sugar News Press, 1925[?]. (Front Cover: The Seventh Far Eastern Championship Games. Manila 1925. Official Report.)

Epstein, Karen V. "Sameness or Difference? Class, Gender, Sport, the WDNAAF and the NCAA/NAAF." *International Journal of the History of Sport* 9, 2 (1992): 280–87.

Falk, Monica L. "Feminism, Buddhism, and Transnational Women's Movements in Thailand." In Mina Roces and Louise Edwards (eds.), *Women's Movements in Asia. Feminism and Transnational Activism.* London: Routledge, 2010, pp. 110–23.

Far Eastern Athletic Association. Official Program. Seventh Far Eastern Championship Games. Manila P. I. May 16 to 23, 1925. Manila[?]: n.p., 1925. (Cover Title: The Seventh Far Eastern Championship Games. Manila P.I. 16–23 May, 1925).

Federation of Malaya Olympic Council. (ed.), *Federation of Malaya. IV Asian Games. Djakarta 24–8 ~ 4–9–62.* Kuala Lumpur: Khee Meng Press, 1962.

Fessen, Helmut and Hans-Dieter Kubitscheck. *Geschichte Thailands* [History of Thailand]. Münster: Lit, 1994.

Field, Russell, "Re-Entering the Sporting World. China's Sponsorship of the 1963 Games of the New Emerging Forces GANEFO." *International Journal of the History of Sport* 31, 15 (2014): 1852–67.

First Asian Games Bulletin. Vol. 1, No. 1. Delhi: Harbans Art Press, 1950.

First Western Asiatic Games. New Delhi 1934. Official Report. Lahore: Ripon Printing Press, 1934.

Fischer-Lichte, Erika. "Culture as Performance." *Modern Austrian Literature* 42, 3 (2009): 1–10.

Fischer-Tiné, Harald and Michael Mann (eds.). *Colonialism as Civilizing Mission. Cultural Ideology in British India.* London: Anthem Press, 2004.

Fischer-Tiné, Harald and Carolien Stolte. "Imagining Asia in India: Nationalism and Internationalim (ca. 1905–1940)." *Comparative Studies in Society and History* 54,1 (2012): 65–92.

Fischer-Tiné, Harald. "Fitness for Modernity? – The American Y.M.C.A. and Physical Education Schemes in Late-Colonial South Asia (circa 1890–1940)." Unpublished article manuscript, ETH Zürich, 2015.

Fisher, George W. "Editorial Comment: The Need for Universal Physical Education." *Physical Training* (April 1919): 803–5.

Forbes, W. Cameron. *The Philippine Islands.* Vol. 2. Boston: Houghton Mifflin, 1928.

Framke, Maria. "International Events, National Policy. The 1930s in India as a Formative Period for Non-Alignment." In Nataša Mišković, Harald Fischer-Tiné, and Nada Boškovska (eds.), *The Non-Aligned Movement and the Cold War. Delhi – Bandung – Belgrade.* London: Routledge, 2014, pp. 37–56.

Frey, Marc and Nicola Spakowski (eds.), *Asianisms. Regionalist Interactions and Asian Integration.* Singapore: NUS Press, 2015.

Frey, Marc and Nicola Spakowski. "Einleitung: Asianismen seit dem 19. Jahrhundert. 'Asien' als Gegenstand nationaler und transnationaler Diskurse und Praktiken [Introduction: Asianisms since the 19th Century. 'Asia' in National and Transnational Discourses and Practices]." *Comparativ* 18, 6 (2008): 7–15.

Frey, Marc. *Geschichte des Vietnamkriegs: Die Tragödie in Asian und das Ende des amerikanischen Traums* [History of the Vietnam War. The Tragedy in Asia and the End of the American Dream]. 7th ed. Munich: Beck, 2004.

———. "Concepts of Region in International History." In Lothar Hönnighausen et al. (eds.), *Regionalism in the Age of Globalism.* Vol. 1: *Concepts of Regionalism.* Madison: Center for the Study of Upper Midwestern Cultures, University of Wisconsin, 2005, pp. 15–26.

———. *Dekolonisierung in Südostasien. Die Vereinigten Staaten und die Auflösung der europäischen Kolonialreiche* [Decolonization in Southeast Asia. The United States and the Dissolution of the European Colonial Empires]. Munich: Oldenbourg, 2006.

———. "Entwicklungspolitik [Development Policy]." In Jost Dülffer and Wilfried Loth (eds.), *Dimensionen Internationaler Geschichte* [Dimensions of International History]. Munich: Oldenbourg, 2012, pp. 293–312.

Frost, Dennis J. *Seeing Stars: Sports Celebrity, Identity, and Body Culture in Modern Japan.* Cambridge, MA: Harvard University Press, 2010.

Funaba, Daishi and Keiko Ikeda. "Britain and the Development of Modern Japanese Sport: From Sporting Amateurism to Fascism during the Period of Japanese Imperialism." *Pan-Asian Journal of Sports & Physical Education* 3, 1 (2011): 9–16.

Gainty, Denis. *Martial Arts and the Body Politic in Meiji Japan.* London: Routledge, 2013.

Gajek, Eva M. *Imagepolitik im Olympischen Wettstreit. Die Spiele von Rom 1960 und München 1972* [Image Politics in the Olympic Competition. The Games in Rome 1960 and Munich 1972]. Göttingen: Wallstein, 2013.

Gao, Yunxiang. *Sporting Gender: Women Athletes and Celebrity-Making during China's National Crisis, 1931–45.* Vancouver: UBC Press, 2013.

Garcia, Beatriz. *The Olympic Games and Cultural Policy.* London: Routledge, 2012.

Garrett, Shirley S. *Social Reformers in Urban China. The Chinese Y.M.C.A., 1895–1926.* Cambridge, MA: Harvard University Press, 1970.

Gastil, John. "Undemocratic Discourse: A Review of Theory and Research on Political Discourse." *Discourse & Society* 3, 4 (1992): 469–500.

Gautam, Mohanlal. "India's Foreign Policy: The Congress View." *India Quarterly* 7 (1951): 105–12.

Gems, Gerald R. *The Athletic Crusade. Sport and American Cultural Imperialism.* Lincoln: University of Nebraska Press, 2006.

Gienow-Hecht, Jessica. "Nation Branding." In Frank Costigliola and Michael Hogan (eds.), *Explaining the History of American Foreign Relations.* 3rd ed. New York: Cambridge University Press, 2016 (in print).

Gitersos, Terry V. "The Sporting Scramble for Africa: GANEFO, the IOC and the 1965 African Games." *Sport in Society* 14, 5 (2011): 645–59.

Gleeck, Lewis E., Jr. *American Institutions in the Philippines (1898–1941).* Manila: Historical Conservation Society, 1976.

Golay, Frank H. *Face of Empire. United States-Philippine Relations, 1898–1946.* Madison: Center for Southeast Asian Studies, University of Wiscounsin-Madison, 1998.

Gold, Margaret M. and George Revill. "The Cultural Olympiads. Reviving the Panegyris." In John R. Gold and Margaret M. Gold (eds.), *Olympic Cities. City Agendas, Planning of the World Games, 1896–2016.* 2nd ed. London: Routledge, 2011, pp. 80–107.

Gong, Gerrit W. *The Standard of "Civilization" in International Society.* Oxford: Clarendon Press, 1984.

Goodman, Grant K. "The Problem of Philippine Independence and Japan: The First Three Decades of American Colonial Rule." *Southeast Asia* 1, 3 (1971): 165–90.

———. "Athletics as Politics: Japan, the Philippines and the Far Eastern Olympics of 1934." *Pilipinas* 20 (1993): 55–66.

Gordon, Andrew. "Consumption, Leisure, and the Middle Class in Transwar Japan." *Social Science Japan Journal* 10, 1 (2007): 1–21.

Grabowsky, Volker. *Kleine Geschichte Thailands* [Short History of Thailand]. Munich: Beck, 2010.

Gregory, Thomas. "Modern Athletics in the Far East." *The World's Work* 36, 2 (1918): 197–206.

Guha, Ramachandra. *India after Gandhi. The Story of the World's Largest Democracy.* New York: Ecco, 2007.

Güldenpfennig, Sven. *Olympische Spiele als Weltkulturerbe. Zur Neubegründung der Olympischen Idee* [Olympic Games as World Cultural Heritage. The Recreation of the Olympic Idea]. Sankt Augustin: Academia-Verlag, 2004.

Guttmann, Allen and Lee Thompson. *Japanese Sports. A History.* Honululu: University of Hawai'i Press, 2001.

Guttmann, Allen. *The Games Must Go on. Avery Brundage and the Olympic Movement.* New York: Columbia University Press, 1984.

———. *Games and Empires. Modern Sports and Cultural Imperialism.* New York: Columbia University Press, 1994.

Halili, Servando D., Jr. *Iconography of the New Empire. Race and Gender Images and the American Colonization of the Philippines.* Quezon City: University of the Philippines Press, 2006.

Halliday, Fred. "The Arc of Revolutions: Iran, Afghanistan, South Yemen, Ethiopia." *Race & Class* 20 (1979): 373–90.

Handley, Paul M. *The King Never Smiles. A Biography of Thailand's Bhumibol Adulyadej.* New Haven: Yale University Press, 2006.

Hao, Gensheng: *see also* Hoh, Gun-Sun

Hao, Gengsheng. *Hao Gengsheng huiyilu* [Hao Gengsheng's Memoirs]. Taipei: Zhuanjiwenxue chubanshe, 1969.

Hanna, Willard A. "The Politics of Sport. Indonesia as the Host to the 'Fourth Asian Games'." *Southeast Asia Series* 10, 19 (1962): 193–203.

Harris, Susan K. *God's Arbiters: Americans and the Philippines, 1898–1902.* Oxford: Oxford University Press, 2011.

Harsuki, H. et al. *Olahraga Indonesia dalam Perspektif Sejarah. Periode 1945–1965* [Indonesian Sport in Historical Perspective. Period 1945–1965]. Jakarta: Departemen Pendidikan Nasional, 2004.

Hasegawa, Tsuyoshi. "Introduction: East Asia – The Second Significant Front of the Cold War." In Tsuyoshi Hasegawa (ed.), *The Cold War in East Asia 1945–1991.* Washington: Woodrow Wilson Center, 2011, pp. 1–34.

Hashimoto, Kazuo. *Nihon Supōtsu Hōsōshi* [History of Japanese Sports Broadcasting]. Tokyo: Taishūkan Shoten, 1992.

He, Wenjie. "Dai-10kai Kyokutō Senshuken Taikai Manshūkoku sanka ni tai suru Chūgoku no hannō – 'Shenbao' kiji no bunseki o tooshite. On the Chinese Reaction against the Participation of Manchurian Athletes in the Xth Far Eastern Games – through the Analysis of the Reports in the Newspaper 'Shenbao'." *Taiikushi kenkyū* 16 (1999): 37–48.

——. "Dai-10kai Orinpikku Taikai Manshūkoku senshu haken mondai ni tai suru Nihon to Chūgoku no taiō – Nihon Gaimushō gaikō to Chūgoku shinbun 'Shenbao' no bunseki o tooshite. The Response of Japan and China to the Manchurian Delegation to the Xth Olympiad – through the Analysis of the Documents in the Diplomatic Record Office of Japan Ministry of Foreign Affairs and the Reports in the Newspaper 'Shenbao'." *Taiikushi kenkyū* 17 (2000): 61–71.

Heé, Nadin. *Imperiales Wissen und koloniale Gewalt. Japans Herrschaft in Taiwan 1895–1945* [Imperial Knowledge and Colonial Violence. Japan's Rule over Taiwan 1895–1945]. Frankfurt: Campus, 2012.

Higgs, Robert J. *God in the Stadium. Sports and Religion in America.* Lexington: University Press of Kentucky, 1995.

Hill, Christopher R. *Olympic Politics.* 2nd ed. Manchester: Manchester University Press, 1996.

Hiranuma, Ryōzō. *Supōtsu seikatsu rokujūnen / Seika o kakagete: Supōtsu shichō – Hiranuma Ryōzō-den* [Sixty Years of Sportive Life / Holding up the Holy Fire: The Life of Sports Mayor Hiranuma Ryōzō]. Ed. by Kō Matsumoto. Tokyo: Ōzorasha, 1994.

Hiro, Kentarō. "Munen no taijin, Jakaruta jiken [The Deeply Regretted Resignation: the Jakarta Incident]." In Bēsubōru Magajin-sha (ed.), *Ningen Tabata Masaji: Orinpikku to tomo ni 50nen* [The Man Tabata Masaji: 50 Years with the Olympics]. Tokyo: Bēsubōru Magajin-sha, 1985, pp. 187–202.

Hobsbawm, Eric J. *Nations and Nationalism since 1780: Programme, Myth, Reality.* Cambridge: Cambridge University Press, 1992.

Hoffman, Shirl J. *Good Game. Christianity and the Culture of Sport.* Waco: Baylor University Press, 2010.

Hoganson, Kristin L. *Fighting for American Manhood: How Gender Politics Provoked the Spanish-American and Philippine-American Wars.* New Haven: Yale University Press, 1998.

Hoh, Gun-Sun: *see also* Hao, Gensheng

Hoh, Gun-Sun [Pinyin: Hao, Gengsheng]. *Physical Education in China. Zhongguo tiyu gailun.* Shanghai: Commercial Press, 1926.

Holt, Richard. *Sport and the British. A Modern History.* Oxford: Clarendon Press, 1989.

Hong, Fan. "Communist China and the Asian Games 1951–1990: The Thirty-nine Year Struggle to Victory." In Fan Hong (eds.), *Sport, Nationalism and Orientalism: The Asian Games.* London: Routledge, 2007a, pp. 75–88.

——. "Prologue: The Origin of the Asian Games: Power and Politics." In Fan Hong (ed.), *Sport, Nationalism and Orientalism: The Asian Games*. London: Routledge, 2007b, pp. xiii–xxiv.

——. (ed.), *Sport, Nationalism and Orientalism: The Asian Games*. London: Routledge, 2007c.

——. "China, the Asian Games and Asian Politics (1974–2006)." *International Journal of the History of Sports* 29,1 (2012a): 98–112.

——. "Sport, Militarism and Diplomacy: Training Bodies for China (1960–1966)." *International Journal of the History of Sports* 29,1 (2012b): 30–52.

Horne, John and Wolfram Manzenreiter (eds.). *Japan, Korea and the 2002 World Cup*. London: Routledge, 2002.

Hopkins, C. Howard. *History of the Y.M.C.A. in North America*. New York: Association Press, 1951.

Hotta, Eri. *Pan-Asianism and Japan's War 1931–1945*. New York: Palgrave Macmillan, 2007.

Huang, Xiong. "Table 1: The Far Eastern Championship Games 1913–1934." In Fan Hong (ed.), *Sport, Nationalism and Orientalism: The Asian Games*. London: Routledge, 2007, pp. 116–17.

Hübner, Stefan. "The Fourth Asian Games (Jakarta 1962) in a Transnational Perspective: Japanese and Indian Reactions to Indonesia's Political Instrumentalization of the Games." *International Journal of the History of Sport* 29, 9 (2012): 1295–310.

——. "'Making the Weak and Degenerated Races of East Asia Ready for Self-Government': American and East Asian Views of Sport and Body in Early Twentieth-Century East Asia." In Walter Demel and Rotem Kowner (eds.), *Race and Racism in Modern East Asia*. Vol. 2: *Interactions, Nationalism, Gender and Lineage*. Leiden: Brill, 2015a, pp. 196–217.

——. "Muscular Christianity and the 'Western Civilizing Mission': Elwood S. Brown, the YMCA and the Idea of the Far Eastern Championship Games." *Diplomatic History* 39,3 (2015b): 532–57.

——. "Uniting the East via Western Amateur Sports Values: Asian Integration, the Olympic Ideal and the Far Eastern Championship Games." In Marc Frey and Nicola Spakowski (eds.), *Asianisms: Regionalist Interactions and Asian Integration*. Singapore: NUS Press, 2015c, pp. 75–98.

——. "Donors and the Global Sportive 'Civilizing Mission': Asian Athletics, American Philanthropy, and YMCA Media (1910s-1920s)." *Itinerario* 40, 1 (2016a): 29–54.

——. "Images of the Sportive 'Civilizing Mission': The Far Eastern Championship Games (1913–1934) and Visions of Modernization in English-Language Philippine Newspapers." *Journal of World History* (2016b), in print.

Huffman, James L. *Japan in World History*. Oxford: Oxford University Press, 2010.

Iikura, Akira. *Ierō periru no shinwa. Teikoku Nihon to "kōka" no gyakusetsu* [The Myth of the Yellow Peril. Imperial Japan and the Paradox of the Yellow Peril]. Tokyo: Sairyūsha, 2004.

———. "Japan under Paternalism: The Changing Image of Japan during the Russo-Japanese War." In John W. M. Chapman and Chiharu Inaba (eds.), *Rethinking the Russo-Japanese War, 1904–05*. Vol. 2: *The Nichinan Papers*. Folkestone: Global Oriental, 2007, pp. 257–73.

Ikei, Masaru. "Tōyō 'Orinpikku' 'Manshūkoku' sanka mondai [The Problem of 'Manchukuo's' Participation in the 'Far Eastern Olympic Games']." In Katsunori Nakamura (ed.), *Kindai Nihon seiji no shosō. Jidai ni yoru tenkai to kōsatsu* [Different Aspects of Modern Japanese Politics. Enquiries into the Developments Caused by this Period]. Tokyo: Keiō Tsūshin, 1989, pp. 29–52.

Imamura, Yoshio. *Nihon taiikushi* [History of Sports in Japan]. Tokyo: Fumaidō Shuppan, 1970.

Indian Olympic Association. (ed.) *Annual Report 1962. With the Compliments of the Hony. Secretary.* Calcutta: n.p., 1963.

Indrapana, Nat. *Sport and Physical Education in Thailand 1932–1966.* Unpublished Dissertation, University of Alberta, Edmonton, 1973.

Irie, Katsumi. "Kindai Nihon ni okeru shokuminchi taiiku seisaku no kenkyū (dai-6pō): Daitōa Kyōgi Taikai no kaisai to Gimanshūkoku no hōkai. A Study on the Colonial Policy of Physical Education by the Pre-War Japanese Authorities (Part 6): Opening the 10th Anniversary Athletic Meeting of East Asia and the Collapse of Puppet Manchukuo." *Tottori Daigaku kyōiku gakubu kenkyū hōkoku. Kyōiku kagaku* 28, 2 (1996): 415–23.

Iriye, Akira. *Cultural Internationalism and World Order.* Baltimore: Johns Hopkins University Press, 1997.

———. *Global Community. The Role of International Organizations in the Making of the Contemporary World.* Berkeley: University of California Press, 2002.

Israel Olympic Committee. (ed.). *Djakarta. A Lesson and a Warning. Une leçon et un avertissement.* Tel Aviv[?]: n.p., 1962.

Jalal, Ayesha. "Towards the Baghdad Pact: South Asia and Middle East Defense in the Cold War, 1947–1955." *International History Review* 11, 3 (1989): 409–33.

Jansen, Marius B. *The Making of Modern Japan.* First Paperback ed. Cambridge, MA: Harvard University Press, 2002.

Jarvie, Grant, Dong-Jhy Hwang, and Mel Brennan, *Sport, Revolution and the Beijing Olympics.* Oxford: Berg, 2008.

Jensen, Erik N. *Body by Weimar: Athletes, Gender, and German Modernity.* Oxford: Oxford University Press, 2010.

Johnson, Elmer L. *The History of YMCA Physical Education.* Chicago: Association Press, 1979.

Jones, Matthew. "A 'Segregated' Asia? Race, the Bandung Conference, and Pan-Asianist Fears in American Thought and Policy, 1954–1955." *Diplomatic History* 29, 5 (2005): 841–68.

Jones, O. Garfield. "Athletics Helping the Filipino." *Outing* 64, 5 (1914): 585–92.

———. *The Unhappy Conditions in the Philippine Islands.* Oakland: Oakland Tribune, 1915.

Kajikawa, Hisako. "Kyokutō Orinpikku Taikai ni sanka shite – Kimochi no ii kokusai kyōgi [I Participated in the Far Eastern Olympic Games – An International Competition with a Good Atmosphere]." *Fujin kōron* 8,7 (1923): 62.

Kanin, David B. *A Political History of the Olympic Games.* Boulder: Westview Press, 1981.

Kanō, Jigorō. "Jūdō yori mitaru Kyokutō Senshuken Kyōgi Taikai [The Far Eastern Championship Games, Seen from Judo]." In Jigorō Kanō, *Kanō Jigorō chosakushū* [Kanō Jigorō-Collection]. Vol. 2: *Jūdō-hen* [Volume about Judo]. Edited by Minoru Tsuruta[?]. Reprint. Tokyo: Gogatsu Shobō, 1992, pp. 404–8.

Kanō Sensei Denki Hensankai. (ed.), *Kanō Jigorō.* Tokyo: Kōdōkan, 1964.

Karl, Rebecca. *Staging the World. Chinese Nationalism at the Turn of the Twentieth Century.* Durham: Duke University Press, 2002.

Karnjanakit, Sombat and Supitr Samahito. "Thailand and the Asian Games: Coping with Crisis." In Fan Hong (ed.), *Sport, Nationalism and Orientalism: The Asian Games.* London: Routledge, 2007, pp. 37–45.

Katō, Hiroo. "Ajia Taikai – sono kigen, genjō, kadai [The Asian Games – Their Origin, their Present Situation, and their Task]." *Taiiku no Kagaku* 32, 9 (1982): 653–6.

Keddie, Nikki R. *Modern Iran. Roots and Results of Revolution.* Updated ed. New Haven: Yale University Press, 2006.

Keller, Charles A. *Making Model Citizens: The Chinese YMCA, Social Activism, and Internationalism in Republican China, 1919–1937.* Unpublished Dissertation, University of Kansas, Lawrence, 1996.

Kelly, William W. "Beijing 2008 and the Limits of Exceptionalism." In William W. Kelly and Susan Brownell (eds.), *The Olympics in East Asia. Nationalism, Regionalism, and Globalism on the Center Stage of World Sports.* New Haven: Council on East Asian Studies, Yale University, 2011, pp. 5–18.

Keys, Barbara J. *Globalizing Sport. National Rivalry and International Community in the 1930s.* Cambridge, MA: Harvard University Press, 2006.

Kietlinski, Robin. *Japanese Women and Sport: Beyond Baseball and Sumo.* London: Bloomsbury Academic, 2011.

Kiku, Koichi. "The Japanese Baseball Spirit and Professional Ideology." In Joseph Maguire and Masayoshi Nakayama (eds.), *Japan, Sport and Society. Tradition and Change in a Globalizing World.* London: Routledge, 2006, pp. 35–54.

Killanin, Michael Morris. *My Olympic Years.* London: Secker & Warburg, 1983.

Kitley, Philip. *Television, Nation, and Culture in Indonesia.* Athens: Ohio University Center for International Studies, 2000.

Knöbl, Wolfgang. *Die Kontingenz der Moderne. Wege in Europa, Asien und Amerika* [The Contingency of Modernity. Paths in Europe, Asia, and America]. Frankfurt: Campus, 2007.

Kolatch, Jonathan. *Sports, Politics and Ideology in China.* New York: David Publishers, 1972.

Kramer, Paul A. *The Blood of Government. Race, Empire, the United States & the Philippines.* Chapel Hill: University of North Carolina Press, 2006.

Kusno, Abidin. *Behind the Postcolonial. Architecture, Urban Space and Political Cultures in Indonesia.* London: Routledge, 2000.

———. *The Appearances of Memory. Mnemonic Practices of Architecture and Urban Form in Indonesia.* Durham: Duke University Press, 2010.

Kusuda, Kenta. "Koroniaru kara kyōzō e. Chihō kara mita Indoneshia – futtobōru-shi josetsu. From Colonial to Reflecion [sic]. A Local History of Indonesian Football." *Ajia – Afurika chiiki kenkyū* 6, 1 (2006): 44–76.

Ladd, Tony and James A. Mathisen. *Muscular Christianity: Evangelical Protestants and the Development of American Sport.* Grand Rapids: Baker Books, 1999.

Latourette, Kenneth S. *World Service. A History of the Foreign Work and World Service of the Young Men's Christian Associations of the United States and Canada.* New York: Association Press, 1957.

"Leaders in Physical Training, No. 45, Elwood S. Brown." *Physical Training* 17, 7 (1919): 328–30.

Leclerc, Jaques. "Mirrors and the Lighthouse. A Search for Meaning in the Monuments and Great Works of Sukarno's Jakarta, 1960–1966." In Peter J. M. Nas (ed.), *Urban Symbolism.* Leiden: Brill, 1993, pp. 38–58.

Lee, Karam, Jung-Hee Ha, and Gwang Ok. "Extraterritorial Outlet of Korean Nationalism in the Far Eastern Championship Games, 1913–1934." *International Journal of the History of Sport* 32, 3 (2015): 455–65.

Lee, Christopher J. (ed.), *Making a World after Empire. The Bandung Moment and its Political Afterlifes.* Athens: Ohio University Press, 2010.

Lent, John A. "The Philippines." In John A. Lent (ed.), *The Asian Newspapers' Reluctant Revolution.* Ames: Iowa State University Press, 1971, pp. 191–209.

Liang, Lijuan. *He Zhenliang and China's Olympic Dream.* Beijing: Foreign Language Press, 2007.

Little, Charles. "South-East Asia." In Steven W. Pope and John Nauright (eds.), *Routledge Companion to Sports History.* London: Routledge, 2010, pp. 587–98.

Liu, Xiaofei. *Der Weg der Dritten Welt in die Olympische Bewegung* [The Third World's Path into the Olympic Movement]. Sankt Augustin: Academia Verlag, 1998.

Low, Morris. "Japan, Modernity and the Tokyo Olympics." *Humanities Research* 2 (1999): 33–51.

Lu, Zhouxiang and Fan Hong (eds.). *Sport and Nationalism in China.* London: Routledge, 2014.

Luo, Shiming. *Aoyun laidao Zhongguo* [The Olympic Games Come to China]. Beijing: Qinghua daxue, 2005.

Lucas, John A. "USOC President Douglas MacArthur and His Olympic Moment, 1927–1928." *OLYMPIKA* 3 (1994): 111–15.

Lutan, Rusli and Fan Hong. "The Politicization of Sport: GANEFO – A Case Study." In Fan Hong (ed.), *Sport, Nationalism and Orientalism: The Asian Games.* London: Routledge, 2007, pp. 22–36.

Lutan, Rusli. "Indonesia and the Asian Games: Sport, Nationalism and the 'New Order'." In Fan Hong (ed.), *Sport, Nationalism and Orientalism: The Asian Games*. London: Routledge, 2007, pp. 11–21.

MacAloon, John J. *This Great Symbol. Pierre de Coubertin and the Origins of the Modern Olympic Games*. Chicago: University of Chicago Press, 1981.

MacArthur, Douglas. *Reminiscences*. New York: McGraw-Hill, 1964.

Maguire, Joseph. *Global Sport. Identities, Societies, Civilizations*. Reprint. Cambridge: Polity Press, 2001.

Majumdar, Boria and Nalin Mehta. *India and the Olympics*. London: Routledge, 2009.

——. *Sellotape Legacy. Delhi and the Commonwealth Games*. New Delhi: HarperCollins, 2010.

Maladi. "Forward." In Tom Rosandich (ed.), *Track and Field Journal*. Jakarta: The Organizing Committee for the IVth Asian Games, 1962, pp. 6–7.

Manela, Erez. *The Wilsonian Moment: Self-Determination and the International Origins of Anticolonial Nationalism*. Oxford: Oxford University Press, 2007.

Mangan, James A. "Christ and the Imperial Games Fields: Evangelical Athletes of the Empire." *British Journal of Sports History* 1 (1984): 184–201.

Manzenreiter, Wolfram and John Horne. (eds.), *Football goes East. Business, Culture and the People's Game in China, Japan and South Korea*. London: Routledge, 2004.

Manzenreiter, Wolfram. *Sport and Body Politics in Japan*. London: Routledge, 2014.

Mao, Zedong. "A Study of Physical Education." http://www.marxists.org/reference/archive/mao/selected-works/volume-6/mswv6_01.htm [accessed: 9 December 2009] (Originally published as: Mao, Zedong, "Tiyu zhi yanjiu [A Study of Physical Education]." *Xin qingnian* 4 (1917): 5–12)

Martschukat, Jürgen. "'The Necessity for Better Bodies to Perpetuate Our Institutions, Insure a Higher Development of the Individual, and Advance the Conditions of the Race.' Physical Culture and the Formation of the Self in the Late Nineteenth and Early Twentieth Century USA." *Journal of Historical Sociology* 24, 4 (2011): 472–93.

Matsusaka, Yoshihisa T. *The Making of Japanese Manchuria, 1904–1932*. Cambridge, MA: Harvard University Asia Center, 2001.

Matsuura, Masataka. "Japan and Pan-Asianism." In Antony Best (ed.), *The International History of East Asia, 1900–1968. Trade, Ideology and the Quest for Order*. London: Routledge, 2010, pp. 81–98.

Matthiessen, Sven. *Japanese Pan-Asianism and the Philippines from the Late Nineteenth Century to the End of World War II*. Leiden: Brill, 2015.

Mehnert, Ute. *Deutschland, Amerika, und die Gelbe Gefahr: Zur Karriere eines Schlagworts in der Großen Politik 1905–1917* [Germany, the US, and the Yellow Peril. The Career of a Keyword in High Politics, 1905–1917]. Stuttgart: Steiner, 1995.

Mello, Antony S. de. (ed.), *1st Asian Games New Delhi 1951. Closing Ceremony. National Stadium Sunday, 11th March at 5–45 P.M. Official Program*. New Delhi: Services Press, 1951a.

——. (ed.), *1st Asian Games New Delhi 1951. Opening Ceremony. National Stadium Sunday, 4th March at 4 P.M. Official Program*. New Delhi: Services Press, 1951b.

———. *Portrait of Indian Sport*. London: Macmillan, 1959.

Mellow, Melville de. *Reaching for Excellence. The Glory and Decay of Sport in India*. New Delhi: Kalyani Publishers, 1979.

Metcalf, Barbara D. and Thomas R. Metcalf. *A Concise History of India*. Cambridge: Cambridge University Press, 2002.

Middell, Matthias and Katja Naumann. "Global History and the Spatial Turn: From the Impact of Area Studies to the Study of Critical Junctures of Globalization." *Journal of Global History* 5, 1 (2010): 149–70.

Minutes of the 7th Congress of the Asian Games Federation Held in Djakarta on the 23rd and [24th] August 1962. Jakarta[?]: n.p., 1962[?]. (Front Cover: 7th Congress A.G.F. 23 Aug. 1962. 24 Aug. 1962.)

Minutes of the Meeting of the Council Members of the Asian Games Federation Held in Djakarta, Indonesia 28th August 1962. Draft. Jakarta[?]: n.p., 1962[?].

Minutes of the Meeting of the Executive Committee of the Asian Games Federation Held in Djakarta, Indonesia 21st – 22nd April 1962. Draft. Jakarta[?]: n.p., 1962[?].

Minutes of the Meeting of the Executive Committee of the Asian Games Federation Held in Rome, Italy, 22nd August 1960. Jakarta: Pertjetakan Negara, 1960[?].

Minutes of the Sixth Congress of the Asian Games Federation Held in Rome, Italy, 23rd and 26th August 1960. Draft. Jakarta: Pertjetakan Negara, 1960[?].

Mirsepassi, Ali. *Intellectual Discourse and the Politics of Modernization. Negotiating Modernity in Iran*. Cambridge: Cambridge University Press, 2000.

Miyagi, Taizō. *Bandon kaigi to Nihon no Ajia fukki: Amerika to Ajia no hazama de* [The Bandung Conference and Japan's Return to Asia: About the Gorge between America and Asia]. Tokyo: Sōshisha, 2001.

———. "Post-War Japan and Asianism." *Asia-Pacific Review* 13, 2 (2006): 1–16.

Miyamoto, Yoshitada. "Ma ga sashita Tabata hatsuken [Tabata's Evil-Possessed Speech]". In Bēsubōru Magajin-sha (ed.), *Ningen Tabata Masaji: Orinpikku to tomo ni 50nen* [The Man Tabata Masaji. 50 Year with the Olympics]. Tokyo: Bēsubōru Magajin-sha, 1985, pp. 203–9.

Modelski, George. (ed.), *The New Emerging Forces. Documents on the Ideology of Indonesian Foreign Policy*. Canberra: Department of International Relations, Australian National University, 1963.

Molony, Barbara. "Crossing Boundaries. Transnational Feminism in Twentieth-Century Japan." In Mina Roces and Louise Edwards (eds.), *Women's Movements in Asia. Feminism and Transnational Activism*. London: Routledge, 2010, pp. 90–109.

Morris, Andrew D. *Cultivating the National Body: A History of Physical Culture in Republican China*. Unpublished Dissertation, University of California, San Diego, 1998.

———. "Native Songs and Dances: Southeast Asia in a Greater Chinese Sporting Community, 1920–48." *Journal of Southeast Asian Studies* 31, 1 (2000): 48–69.

———. *Marrow of the Nation. A History of Sport and Physical Culture in Republican China*. Berkeley: University of California Press, 2004.

——. *Colonial Project, National Game. A History of Baseball in Taiwan.* Berkeley: University of California Press, 2011.

Mosse, George L. *The Image of Man. The Creation of Modern Masculinity.* Oxford: Oxford University Press, 1996.

Mott, John R. *The Evangelization of the World in this Generation.* New York: Student Volunteer Movement for Foreign Missions, 1900.

Nakajima, Takeshi. *Bose of Nakamuraya: An Indian Revolutionary in Japan.* New Delhi: Promilla, 2009.

Nazari-Kangarloo, Hassan-Ali. *The History and Development of Physical Education and Sports in Iran.* Unpublished Dissertation, George Washington University, Washington, 1976.

Nehru, Jawaharlal. *Selected Works of Jawaharlal Nehru.* Second Series. Vols. 2, 15:2, 16:1. Edited by S. Gopal. New Delhi: Jawaharlal Nehru Memorial Fund, 1984–94.

Niehaus, Andreas. "Crossing Borders: Kanō Jigorō's Sport Philosophy and the Olympic Idea." *Iphigeneia: Nihon Taiiku Daigaku Daigakuin Taiiku Kagaku Kenkyūka Supōtsu Bunka - Shakai Kagakukei Kiyō* 4 (2003): 21–41.

——. *Leben und Werk Kanō Jigorōs (1860–1938). Ein Forschungsbericht zur Leibeserziehung und zum Sport in Japan* [Life and Work of Kanō Jigorō (1860–1938): A Research Report on Physical Education and Sports in Japan]. 2nd ed. Würzburg: Ergon, 2010.

Nihon Rikujō Kyōgi Renmei. (ed.), *Manira enseiki* [Report on the Manila-Expedition]. Tokyo: Nihon Rikujō Kyōgi Renmei Henshū Iinkai, 1934.

Nihon Seinen Kurabu. (ed.), *Dai-4kai Kyokutō Kyōgi Taikai senshu haken hōkokusho* [Report on the Delegation Sent to the Fourth Far Eastern Championship Games]. Osaka: Ōsaka Asahi Shinbun, 1919.

Nihon Taiiku Kyōkai and Nihon Orinpikku Iinkai. (eds.), *Dai-7kai Ajia Kyōgi Taikai hōkokusho* [Report on the Seventh Asian Games]. Tokyo: Nihon Taiiku Kyōkai and Nihon Orinpikku Iinkai, 1974.

Nihon Taiiku Kyōkai. (ed.), *Dai-1kai Ajia Kyōgi Taikai hōkokusho* [Report on the First Asian Games]. Tokyo: Nihon Taiiku Kyōkai, 1951.

——. (ed.), *Dai-2kai Ajia Kyōgi Taikai hōkokusho, 1954nen, Manira.* [Report on the Second Asian Games, 1954, Manila]. Tokyo: Nihon Taiiku Kyōkai, 1955.

——. (ed.), *Ajia no Orinpikku: Dai-3kai Ajia Kyōgi Taikai kinen* [Asia's Olympic Games: Commemoration of the Third Asian Games]. Tokyo: Nihon Taiiku Kyōkai, 1958.

——. (ed.), *Dai-4kai Ajia Kyōgi Taikai hōkokusho* [Report on the Fourth Asian Games]. Tokyo: Nihon Taiiku Kyōkai, 1966.

——. (ed.), *Dai-5kai Ajia Kyōgi Taikai hōkokusho* [Report on the Fifth Asian Games]. Tokyo: Nihon Taiiku Kyōkai, 1967.

Nishihara, Shigeki. "Tōkyō Ōsaka ryōtoshi no shinbunsha ni yoru yakyū (supōtsu) ibento no tenkai katei - 1910–1925nen o chūshin ni [The Process of the Development of Baseball- (Sports-)Events Held by Newspaper Companies from Tokyo and Osaka, 1910–1925]." *Ritsumeikan sangyō shakai ronshū* 40, 3 (2004): 115–34.

Nitobe, Inazo. *Bushido. The Soul of Japan*. Philadelphia: Leeds & Biddle, 1900.

Noguchi, Genzaburo. "Sports in Japan." In Inazo Nitobe et al. (ed.), *Western Influences in Modern Japan. A Series of Papers on Cultural Relations*. Chicago: University of Chicago Press, 1931, pp. 447–68.

Nordau, Max S. *Entartung* [Degeneration]. Berlin: Duncker, 1892.

Norudō [Nordau, Max S.]. *Gendai no daraku* [Modern Degeneration]. Translated by Moichi Nakajima. Tokyo: Dainihon Bunmei Kyōkai, 1914.

Oba, Mie. "Japan's Entry into ECAFE." In Makoto Iokibe et al. (eds.), *Japanese Diplomacy in the 1950s. From Isolation to Integration*. London: Routledge, 2008, pp. 98–113.

O'Connor, Peter. *The English-Language Press Networks of East Asia, 1918–1945*. Folkestone: Global Oriental, 2010.

Oda, Mikio. "Ajia Orinpikku Taikai – Supōtsu ni musubu Ajia minzoku [The Asian Games – Uniting the Asian Peoples through Sports]." *Kaizō* 32,4 (1951): 157–9.

Official Report of the Organizing Committee for the Sixth Asian Games Bangkok 1970. Bangkok: Sivaphorn, 1971[?].

Official Report of the Seventh Asian Games Teheran September 1–16, 74. Teheran: Editeam, 1975[?].

Ohno [Ōno], Takushi. *War Reparations and Peace Settlement. Philippines-Japan Relations 1945–1956*. Manila: Solidaridad Publishing House, 1986.

Okakura, Kakasu [sic] (correct name: Okakura, Kakuzō; also known as Okakura, Tenshin). *The Ideals of the East. With Special Reference to the Art of Japan*. London: John Murray, 1903.

Olson, Lawrence. *Japan in Postwar Asia*. London: Pall Mall Press, 1970.

Organizing Committee Asian Games IV 1962. Djakarta. (ed.), *IV Asian Games Bulletin. No. 5*. Jakarta: State Printing Office[?],1962.

Organizing Committee Second Asian Games. (ed.), *Asian Games Bulletin*. No. 1–8. Manila: n.p., 1953–4.

Osterhammel, Jürgen. *Die Verwandlung der Welt. Eine Geschichte des 19. Jahrhunderts* [The Transformation of the World. A Global History of the 19th Century]. Munich: Beck, 2009.

———. "'The Great Work of Uplifting Mankind.' Zivilisierungsmission und Moderne ['The Great Work of Uplifting Mankind': Civilizing Mission and Modernity]." In Boris Barth and Jürgen Osterhammel (eds.), *Zivilisierungsmissionen. Imperiale Weltverbesserung seit dem 18. Jahrhundert* [Civilizing Missions. Imperial World Improvement since the 18th Century]. Konstanz: UVK, 2005, pp. 363–425.

Ott, Konrad. "Grundelemente der Gerechtigkeit im Sport [Basic Elements of Justice in Sport]." In Claudia Pawlenka (ed.), *Sportethik. Regeln – Fairneß – Doping* [Sports Ethics. Rules – Fairness – Doping]. Paderborn: Mentis, 2004, pp. 133–47.

Ozawa, Takato. "Ajia no Orinpikku – Tōa Kyōgi Taikai. Kigen 2600nen no saiten [Asia's Olympic Games – the East Asian Games. The Festival at the 2,600th Anniversary of the Imperial Era]." In Yasuhiro Sakaue and Hiroyuki Takaoka (eds.), *Maboroshi no Tōkyō Orinpikku to sono jidai. Senjiki no supōtsu, toshi, shintai* [The Illusion of the Tokyo Olympic Games and their Times. Sport, City, and Body during the War Period]. Tokyo: Seikyūsha, 2009, pp. 172–97.

Parks, Jenifer. *Red Sport, Red Tape: The Olympic Games, the Soviet Sports Bureaucracy, and the Cold War, 1952–1980.* Unpublished Dissertation, University of North Carolina, Chapel Hill, 2009.

Pauker, Ewa T. "Ganefo I: Sports and Politics in Djakarta." *Asian Survey* 5, 4 (1965): 171–85.

Pei, Dongguang. *"A Question of Names": The Two Chinas Issue and the People's Republic of China in the Modern Olympic Movement.* Unpublished Master Thesis, University of Western Ontario, London, ON, 1995.

Philippine Amateur Athletic Federation. Annual Report of the Secretary Treasurer and the National Physical Director. From March 18, 1927 to July 20, 1928. Manila: n.p., 1928[?].

Philippine Amateur Athletic Federation. Minutes of the Thirty Seventh Annual General Meeting of the P.A.A.F. Board of Governors. Held at the Rizal Memorial Coliseum, Manila, July 30, 1954 - 10a.m. Manila: n.p., 1954[?].

Pococke, Edward. *India in Greece; or, Truth in Mythology: Containing the Sources of the Hellenic Race, Colonisation of Egypt and Palestine, the Wars of the Grand Lama, and the Bud'histic Propaganda in Greece.* London: J. J. Griffin, 1852.

Pomerantz-Zhang, Linda. *Wu Tingfang (1842–1922). Reform and Modernization in Modern Chinese History.* Hong Kong: Hong Kong University Press, 1992.

Pomeranz, Kenneth. *The Great Divergence: China, Europe, and the Making of the Modern World Economy.* Princeton: Princeton University Press, 2000.

——. "Empire & 'Civilizing' Missions, Past and Present." *Daedalus* 134, 2 (2005): 34–45.

Pope, Steven W. "Imperialism." In Steven W. Pope and John Nauright (eds.), *Routledge Companion to Sports History.* London: Routledge, 2010, pp. 229–47.

Preliminary Announcement. Far Eastern Championship Games. Shanghai, May 1915. Shanghai: n.p., 1915.

Preston, Andrew. *Sword of the Spirit, Shield of Faith. Religion in American War and Diplomacy.* New York: Alfred A. Knopf, 2012.

Prince, Monroe E. and Daniel Dayan. (ed.), *Owning the Olympics. Narratives of the New China.* Ann Arbor: University of Michigan Press, 2008.

Programme. First Western Asiatic Games and VI Indian Olympic Games, February 27–March 3, Irwin Amphitheatre, New Delhi. Lahore: Mufid-i-'am Press, 1934.

Puri, Narottam. *The Asian Games.* New Delhi: National Book Trust, 1982.

Putney, Clifford. *Muscular Christianity. Manhood and Sports in Protestant America, 1880–1920.* Cambridge, MA: Harvard University Press, 2001.

Raita, Kyoko. "The Movement for the Promotion of Competitive Women's Sport in Japan, 1924–35." *International Journal of the History of Sport* 16,3 (1999): 120–134.

Ramazani, Rouhollah K. *Iran's Foreign Policy 1941–1973. A Study of Foreign Policy in Modernizing Nations.* Charlottesville: University Press of Virginia, 1975.

Reid, Anthony. *Imperial Alchemy. Nationalism and Political Identity in Southeast Asia.* Cambridge: Cambridge University Press, 2010.

Reilly, Thomas. "Wu Yaozong and the YMCA: From Social Reform to Social Revolution, 1927–1937." *Journal of American-East Asian Relations* 19 (2012): 263–87.

"Report on Plans and Preparations for the IVth Asian Games." In Tom Rosandich (ed.), *Track and Field Journal.* Jakarta: The Organizing Committee for the IVth Asian Games, 1962, pp. 395–413.

Ricklefs, Merle C. *A Modern History of Indonesia since c. 1200.* 4th ed. Basingstoke: Palgrave Macmillan, 2008.

Risedorph, Kimberly A. *Reformers, Athletes and Students: The YMCA in China, 1895–1935.* Unpublished Dissertation, Washington University, St. Louis, 1994.

Roces, Mina. "Rethinking 'the Filipino Women'. A Century of Women's Activism in the Philippines." In Mina Roces and Louise Edwards (eds.), *Women's Movements in Asia. Feminism and Transnational Activism.* London: Routledge, 2010, pp. 34–52.

Roche, Maurice. *Mega-Events and Modernity: Olympics and Expos in the Growth of Global Culture.* London: Routledge, 2000.

Rodgers, Daniel T. *Atlantic Crossings. Social Politics in a Progressive Age.* Cambridge, MA: Harvard University Press, 1998.

Rolim Silva, Luis H. and Hans-Dieter Gerber. "The Arab Games: Establishment and Role (1953–1965)." *Journal of Olympic History* 19, 3 (2011): 4–19.

Ross, Helen G. and Darryl Collins. *Building Cambodia: "New Khmer Architecture" 1953–1970.* Bangkok: Key Pub., 2006.

Ross, Stanley R. *Francisco I. Madero. Apostle of Mexican Democracy.* Reprint. New York: Columbia University Press, 1970.

Rowe, Peter G. and Seng Kuan. *Architectural Encounters with Essence and Form in Modern China.* Cambridge, MA: MIT Press, 2002.

Saaler, Sven and Christopher W. A. Szpilman. (eds.), *Pan-Asianism. A Documentary History.* 2 Vols. Lanham: Rowman & Littlefield, 2011.

Saaler, Sven and Victor J. Koschmann. (eds.), *Pan-Asianism in Modern Japanese History. Colonialism, Regionalism and Borders.* London: Routledge, 2007.

Saaler, Sven. "Pan-Asianismus im Japan der Meiji- und der Taisho-Zeit. Wurzeln, Entstehung und Anwendung einer Ideologie [Pan-Asianism in Japan during the Meiji and Taishō Period: Roots, Emergence, and Application of an Ideology]." In Iwo Amelung et al. (eds.), *Selbstbehauptungsdiskurse in Asien: China – Japan – Korea* [Discourses of Self-Assertion in Asia: China – Japan – Korea]. Munich: Iudicium, 2003, pp. 127–58.

———. *Politics, Memory and Public Opinion. The History Textbook Controversy and Japanese Society.* Munich: Iudicium, 2005.

Sachsenmaier, Dominic, Jens Riedel, and Shmuel Eisenstadt (eds.), *Reflections on Multiple Modernities. European, Chinese and Other Interpretations.* Leiden: Brill, 2002.

Said, Edward W. *Orientalism.* New York: Vintage Books, 1979.

Saikal, Amin. "Iranian Foreign Policy, 1921–1979." In Peter Avery, Gavin Hambly, and Charles Melville (eds.), *The Cambridge History of Iran*. Vol. 7: *From Nadir Shah to the Islamic Republic*. Cambridge: Cambridge University Press, 1991, pp. 426–56.

Sato, Shohei. "The Sportification of Judo: Global Convergence and Evolution." *Journal of Global History* 8, 2 (2013): 299–317.

Saulo, Alfredo B. *"Let George do it!" A Biography of Jorge B. Vargas*. Manila: University of the Philippines Press, 1992.

Schayegh, Cyrus. "Sport, Health, and the Iranian Middle Class in the 1920s and 1930s." *Iranian Studies* 35, 4 (2002): 341–69.

Schiller, Kay and Christopher Young. *The 1972 Munich Olympics and the Making of Modern Germany*. Berkeley: University of California Press, 2010.

Schmidt-Braul, Ingo-Eric. "Bücher und Massenmedien [Books and Mass Media]." In Jürgen Hohnholz and Karl-Heiz Bechtold (eds.), *Thailand. Geographie-Geschichte-Kultur-Religion-Staat-Gesellschaft-Politik-Wirtschaft* [Thailand. Geography-History-Culture-Religion-State-Society-Politics-Economy]. Stuttgart: Thienemann, 1984, pp. 316–37.

Schröder, Wolfgang M. "'Mission Impossible?' Begriff, Modelle und Begründungen der 'Zivilisierungsmission' aus philosophischer Sicht ['Mission Impossible?' Term, Models, and Justifications of the 'Civilizing Mission' from a Philosophical Point of View]." In Boris Barth and Jürgen Osterhammel (eds.), *Zivilisierungsmissionen. Imperiale Weltverbesserung seit dem 18. Jahrhundert* [Civilizing Missions. Imperial World Improvement since the 18th Century]. Konstanz: UVK, 2005, pp. 13–32.

Scott, James C. *Seeing Like a State. How Certain Conditions to Improve the Human Condition Have Failed*. New Haven: Yale University Press, 1998.

Second Asian Games Manila, Philippines: May 1–9, 1954: Official Report. Manila: n.p., 1954.

Shalom, Stephen R. *The United States and the Philippines. A Study of Neocolonialism*. Philadelphia: Institute for the Study of Human Issues, 1981.

Shen, Siliang: *see also* Sung, Wm. Z. L.

——. "Zhonghua quanguo tiyu xiejinhui lüeshi [A Brief History of the Chinese National Sport Association]." *Tiyu jikan* 1, 2 (1935): 177–8.

Shimizu, Satoshi. "Rebuilding the Japanese Nation at the 1964 Tokyo Olympics: The Torch Relay in Okinawa and Tokyo." In William W. Kelly and Susan Brownell (eds.), *The Olympics in East Asia. Nationalism, Regionalism, and Globalism on the Center Stage of World Sports*. New Haven: Council on East Asian Studies, Yale University, 2011, pp. 39–59.

Shinno, Mamoru and Tadanori Yasuda. "Ōshima Kenkichi to Manshūkoku no dai-10kai Kyokutō Taikai sanka mondai. Kenkichi Oshima and the 10th Far Eastern Championship Games." *Shintai undō bunka ronkō* 8 (2009): 511–36.

Shuman, Amanda. *The Politics of Socialist Athletics in the People's Republic of China, 1949–1966*. Unpublished Dissertation, University of California, Santa Cruz, 2014.

Sie, Swanpo. "Historical Development of Physical Education and Sports in Indonesia." In Uriel Simri (ed.), *Proceedings of the Pre-Olympic Seminar on the History of Physical Education and Sport in Asia*. Netanya: Wingate Institute for Physical Education and Sport, 1972, pp. 143–67.

———. "Sports and Politics: The Case of the Asian Games and the GANEFO." In Benjamin Lowe, David B. Kanin, and Andrew Strenk (eds.), *Sport and International Relations.* Champaign: Stipes Pub., 1978a, pp. 279–96.

———. "The Problem of Sport and Nation Building in South East Asia." In Benjamin Lowe, David B. Kanin, and Andrew Strenk (eds.), *Sport and International Relations.* Champaign: Stipes Pub., 1978b, 551–61.

Simri, Uriel. "Israel and the Asian Games." In Uriel Simri and Sarah Lieberman (eds.), *Sport and Politics: Proceedings of the 26th ICHPER World Congress 1983, Wingate Institute, Israel.* Vol 2. Jerusalem: E. Gill Pub. House, 1984, pp. 87–93.

Sisodia, Mithlesh K. S. "India and the Asian Games: From Infancy to Maturity." In Fan Hong (ed.), *Sport, Nationalism and Orientalism: The Asian Games.* London: Routledge, 2007, pp. 1–10.

Singh, Sinderpal. "From Delhi to Bandung: Nehru, 'Indian-ness' and 'Pan-Asian-ness'." *South Asia* 34, 1 (2011): 51–64.

Skabelund, Aaron. "Public Service / Public Relations: The Mobilization of the Self-Defense Force for the Tokyo Olympic Games." In William M. Tsutsui and Michael Baskett (eds.), *The East Asian Olympiads, 1934–2008. Building Bodies and Nations in Japan, Korea, and China.* Leiden: Global Oriental, 2011, pp. 63–76.

Sluga, Glenda. *Internationalism in the Age of Nationalism.* Philadelphia: University of Philadelphia Press, 2013.

Smith, Anthony D. *Ethno-Symbolism and Nationalism: A Cultural Approach.* London: Routledge, 2009.

Smith, Martyn D. "Between East and West: The Cold War, Japan and the 1964 Tokyo Olympics." *Comparativ* 23, 3 (2013): 100–16.

———. *Representing Nation in Postwar Japan: Cold War, Consumption and the Mass Media: 1952–1972.* Unpublished Dissertation, SOAS, London, 2014.

Sondhi, Guru Dutt. *Asian Relations Conference, March–April 1947. Organisation of an Asian Games Federation. Group C: Economic Development & Social Services. Topic VI: Labour Problems & Social Services.* New Delhi: Indian Council of World Affairs, 1947.

———. *A Plan for Youth Welfare.* New Delhi: Ministry of Education, 1956.

Spence, Jonathan D. *God's Chinese Son. The Taiping Heavenly Kingdom of Hong Xiuquan.* London: HarperCollins, 1996.

———. *Chinas Weg in die Moderne* [The Search for Modern China]. 2nd ed. Munich: Deutscher Taschenbuch-Verlag, 2001.

Stanton, Andrea L. "'Pioneer of Olympism in the Middle East.' Gabriel Gemayel and Lebanese Sport." *International Journal of the History of Sport* 29, 15 (2012): 2115–30.

Stolte, Carolien. "Bringing Asia to the World: Indian Unionism and the Long Road towards the Asiatic Labour Congress, 1919–37." *Journal of Global History* 7, 2 (2012): 257–78.

———. "'The Asiatic Hour.' New Perspectives on the Asian Relations Conference, New Delhi, 1947." In Nataša Mišković, Harald Fischer-Tiné, and Nada Boškovska (eds.), *The Non-Aligned Movement and the Cold War. Delhi – Bandung – Belgrade.* London: Routledge, 2014, pp. 57–75.

Sukarno. *Deklarasi Ekonomi. Diutjapkan oleh Presiden Sukarno di Istana Negara, Djakarta, tanggal 28 Maret 1963, djam 20.00* [Deklarasi Ekonomi. Speech of President Sukarno at the State Palace, Jakarta, 28 March, 1963, 8 p.m.]. Jakarta: Jajasan Prapantja, 1963. [Alternative title: *Ambeg parama-arta*; Cover page: Deklarasi ekonomi dan 'Ambeg parama-arta'! (Berwatak pandai mendahulukan urusan jang penting)]

Sung, Wm. Z. L.: *see also* Shen, Siliang

Sung, Wm. Z. L. [Pinyin: Shen, Siliang] (ed.), *Far Eastern Athletic Association. Official Report. From May 31, 1925 to September 30, 1927.* Shangai: The Oriental Press, 1927. (Cover Page: The Eighth Far Eastern Championship Games. Shanghai 1927. Official Report.)

Suzuki, Yoshinori. "Kyokutō Senshuken Kyōgi Taikai shōshi [Short History of the Far Eastern Championship Games]." *Orimupikku* 12, 4 (1934): 116–27.

——. "Ajia Taikai e no hansei to kitai [Reflections and Expectations regarding the Asian Games]." *Taiiku no Kagaku* 4, 5 (1954): 188–90, 194.

Tabata, Masaji. *Supōtsu to tomo ni hanseiki* [Half a Century together with Sports]. Shizuoka: Shizuoka-ken Taiiku Kyōkai, 1978.

Tagsold, Christian. *Die Inszenierung der kulturellen Identität in Japan. Das Beispiel der Olympischen Spiele Tōkyō 1964* [The Staging of Cultural Identity in Japan. The Example of the Tokyo Olympic Games, 1964]. Munich: Iudicium, 2002.

——. "Modernity, Space, and National Representation at the Tokyo Olympics 1964." *Urban History* 37, 2 (2010): 289–300.

——. "The Tokyo Olympics: Politics and Aftermath." In William W. Kelly and Susan Brownell (eds.), *The Olympics in East Asia. Nationalism, Regionalism, and Globalism on the Center Stage of World Sports.* New Haven: Council on East Asian Studies, Yale University, 2011, pp. 61–73.

Tahir-Kheli, Shirin. "Iran and Pakistan: Cooperation in an Area of Conflict." *Asian Survey* 17, 5 (1977): 474–90.

Takashima, Kō. "Kyokutō Senshuken Kyōgi Taikai to YMCA [The Far Eastern Championship Games and the YMCA]." In Susumu Fuma (ed.), *Chūgoku Higashiajia gaikō kōryūshi no kenkyū* [Research on the History of Chinese Diplomacy and Cultural Exchange in East Asia]. Kyoto: Kyōto Daigaku Gakujutsu Shuppankai, 2007, pp. 461–505.

——. "'Manshūkoku' no tanjō to kyokutō supōtsukai no saihen [The Founding of 'Manchukuo' and the Reorganization of the Far Eastern Sports World]." *Kyōto Daigaku bungakubu kenkyū kiyō* 47 (2008): 131–81.

——. "Sensō – kokka – supōtsu. Okabe Heita no 'tenkō' o tooshite [War – Nation – Sport. Okabe Heita's 'Conversion']." *Shirin* 93, 1 (2010): 98–130.

——. *Teikoku Nihon to supōtsu* [The Empire of Japan and Sport]. Tokyo: Hanawa Shobō, 2012.

——. "'Tōa Byōfu' to supōtsu – koroniaru masukyuriniti no shiten kara [The 'Sick Man of East Asia' and Sports – from the Perspective of Colonial Masculinity]." In Yoshihiro Ishikawa and Naoki Hazama (eds.), *Kindai Higashi Ajia ni okeru honyaku gainen no tenkai* [The Development of Translated Concepts in Modern East Asia]. Kyoto: Kyōto Daigaku Jinbun Kagaku Kenkyūjo, 2013, pp. 309–42.

Tamura, Fumiko. "Kyokutō Orinpikku Taikai ni sanka shite – Minasama ni tai suru kansha [I Participated in the Far Eastern Championship Games – Thank you to Everybody]." *Fujin Kōron* 8,7 (1923): 63.

Tan, See Seng and Amitav Acharya (eds.), *Bandung Revisited: The Legacy of the 1955 Asian-African Conference for International Order.* Singapore: NUS Press, 2008.

Tapsuwan, Sakchye. *The Role and Function of Physical Education and Sport in the Nation Building of Thailand.* Unpublished Dissertation, Oregon State University, Corvallis, 1984.

Tauber, Peter. *Vom Schützengraben auf den grünen Rasen. Der Erste Weltkrieg und die Entwicklung des Sports in Deutschland* [From the Trench to the Green Lawn. The First World War and the Development of Sport in Germany]. Münster: Lit, 2008.

Tehran 1974. Seventh Asian Games. Souvenir Programme. Tehran: Offset Press, 1974.

Tenth Far Eastern Championship Games. Rizal Memorial Field. Manila P. I. May 12–19, 1934. Manila[?]: n.p., 1934. (Cover: Official Program. Xth Far Eastern Championship Games. Manila P.I. 12–19 May 1934.)

Terwiel, Barend J. *Thailand's Political History.* Bangkok: River Books, 2005.

[Thangarajah, Edward.] (ed.), *Asia on the March. History of the Asian Games.* Bangkok: St. Joseph's Publ., 1995[?].

The China Weekly Review. (ed.), *Who's Who in China. Containing the Pictures and Biographies of China's Best Known Political, Financial, Business and Professional Leaders.* 4th ed. Shanghai: The China Weekly Review, 1931.

The Contest Committee of the Far Eastern Athletic Association. (ed.), *Report of the Fifth Far Eastern Championship Games Held May 30th–June 4th 1921 at Hongkew Park, Shanghai, China.* Shanghai[?]: n.p., 1921[?].

The Official Report of the Organizing Committee for the Fifth Asian Games Bangkok 1966. Bangkok: n.p., 1967[?].

The Olympic Committee of Israel and the Sports Federations of Israel (eds.), *Playing Politics with Sport.* Tel Aviv[?]: n.p., 1975[?].

The Organising Committee. (ed.), *Official Souvenir of the 1st Asian Games New Delhi -1951.* Bombay: Indian Market Press, 1951. (Cover: First Asian Games New Delhi 1951. Official Souvenir.)

The Organizing Committee. (ed.), *Opening Ceremony. Asian Games IV Djakarta 1962.* Jakarta[?]: n.p., 1962.

The Organizing Committee. (ed.), *Progress Report on Preparation for the III Asian Games Toyko 1958.* Tokyo: Toppan Printing, 1957.

The Organizing Committee 4th Asian Games. (ed.), *IV. Asian Games. Bulletin. No. 1.* Jakarta: State Printing Office, 1960[?].

The Organizing Committee for III Asian Games. (ed.), *Official Report of III Asian Games.* Tokyo: n.p., 1958.

The Organizing Committee for the IIIrd Asian Games. (ed.), *3rd Asian Games Bulletin.* No. 1–6. Tokyo: n.p., 1957–8.

The Organizing Committee for the IVth Asian Games. (ed.), *Asian Games. Djakarta 1962. 24 August 4 September.* Tokyo: Indonesian Embassy in Tokyo, 1962.

The Organizing Committee for the Fourth Asian Games. (ed.), *Asian Games Report 4. Djakarta 1962.* Vol. 1: *Photographic Report.* Jakarta[?]: n.p., 1963[?].

The Organizing Committee for the Sixth Asian Games Bangkok 1970. (ed.), *Opening Ceremony. Official Programme.* Bangkok: Siva Phorn Partnership, 1970.

The Organizing Committee of the Games of New Delhi, India. (ed.), *1st Western Asiatic Games, New Delhi, 1934. General Regulations and Programme.* Lahore[?]: n.p., 1934. (Front Cover: First Western Asiatic Games – General Regulations and Information 1934.)

The Organizing Committee Teheran. (ed.), *Teheran 1974. Seventh Asian Games. Bulletin.* No. 1–6. Tehran[?]: n.p., 1972–4.

The Public Relations Committee and the Organizing Committee. (ed.), *5th Asian Games Bangkok 1966 Bulletin.* No. 2–4. Bangkok: Bamrumg Nukoulkit Press, 1965–6.

The Public Relations Committee and the Organizing Committee. (ed.), *5th Asian Games News Letter.* No. 1–7. Bangkok: Bamrumg Nukoulkit Press, 1965–6.

The Secretariat, Manila Sports Service Bureau. (ed.), *2nd Asian Games. Manila, Philippines, May 1 to 9 1954. Commemorative Publication.* Manila: Collegiate Press, 1954.

The University of the Philippines. (ed.), *Catalogue 1916–1917. Announcements 1917–1918.* Manila: Bureau of Printing, 1917. (Alternative Title: The University of the Philippines Bulletin No. 7)

Theriot, Nancy. "Towards a New Sporting Ideal: The Women's Division of the National Amateur Athletic Federation." *Frontiers* 3, 1 (1978): 1–7.

Thompson, Michael G. *For God and Globe. Christian Internationalism in the United States between the Great War and the Cold War.* Ithaca: Cornell University Press, 2015.

Tomaru, Junko. "Japan in British Regional Policy towards South-East Asia, 1945–1960." In Makoto Iokibe et al. (eds.), *Japanese Diplomacy in the 1950s. From Isolation to Integration.* London: Routledge, 2008, pp. 98–113.

Tomita, Kōsuke. "Dai-9kai Kyokutō Senshuken Kyōgi Taikai ni okeru Eiryō Indo senshudan daihyō hata mondai. Shinbun hōdō o tagakari toshite. Flag Incident in the Ninth Far Eastern Championship Games [sic]. An Analysis Based on Newspapers." *Supōtsushi kenkyū* 27 (2014): 43–59.

Tournès, Ludovic. "La fondation Rockefeller et la naissance de l'universalisme philanthropique américain [The Rockefeller Foundation and the Birth of American Philanthropic Universalism]." *Critique Internationale* 35 (2007): 173–97.

Transactions. Asian Games Federation Sub-Committee Meeting, Executive Committee Meeting, Ordinal Council Meeting. During 67th Session IOC and XIX Olympiade, Mexico City 1968. No. 5. Seoul[?]: n.p., 1968[?].

Transactions. Special Council Congress, Asian Games Federation, April 29 – May 4, 1968. Seoul[?], n.p., 1968[?].

Tyrrell, Ian. *Reforming the World. The Creation of America's Moral Empire.* Princeton: Princeton University Press, 2010.

Unger, Corinna R. "Histories of Development and Modernization: Findings, Reflections, Future Research." *H-Soz-u-Kult* 09 Dec. 2010, http://hsozkult.geschichte.hu-berlin.de/forum /2010–12–001 [accessed: 10 Dec. 2010].

Valiotis, Chris. "South Asia." In Steven W. Pope and John Nauright (eds.), *Routledge Companion to Sports History.* London: Routledge, 2010, pp. 571–86.

Vargas, Jorge B. "Athletic Progress in the Philippines." In Zoilo M. Galang (ed.), *Encyclopedia of the Philippines. The Library of Philippine Literature, Art and Science.* Vol. 10: *General Information and Index.* Manila: Philippine Education Co., 1936, pp. 386–409.

———. "The Second Asian Games." In The Fookien Times (ed.), *The Fookien Times Year Book 1954.* Manila: The Fookien Times, 1954, pp. 85–8.

Vickers, Adrian. *A History of Modern Indonesia.* Cambridge: Cambridge University Press, 2005.

Wachter, Frans de, "Sport as Mirror on Modernity." *Journal of Social Philosophy* 32, 1 (2001): 90–8.

Wada, Kōichi. "First Contact. Olympic Ideas and Ideals in Japan until 1909." In Andreas Niehaus and Max Seinsch (eds.), *Olympic Japan. Ideals and Realities of (Inter) Nationalism.* Würzburg: Ergon, 2007, pp. 17–32.

Wagner, Rudolf. "China 'Asleep' and 'Awakening'. A Study in Conceptualizing Asymmetry and Coping with It." *Transcultural Studies* 1 (2011): 4–139.

Wang, Chengting [Pinyin: Zhengting] *T. Ō Seitei* [Wang Zhengting] *kaikoroku. Looking Back and Looking Forward* [Wang Zhengting's Memoirs]. Edited by Ryūji Hattori. Tokyo: Chūō Daigaku Shuppanbu, 2008.

Wang, Yan. *Yuandong yundonghui yu jindai Dongya shehui de fazhan* [The Far Eastern Championship Games and the Development of the Modern East Asian Society], Unpublished Dissertation, Suzhou daxue, Suzhou, 2014.

Wang, Zhengting. "Guan di 2 ci Yuandong yundonghui zhi ganyan [Observations of the Second Far Eastern Championship Games]." *Jinbu* 8, 3 (1915): 11–4.

Watt, Carey and Michael Mann. (eds.), *Civilizing Missions in Colonial and Postcolonial South Asia. From Improvement to Development.* London: Anthem Press, 2011.

Weber, Max. "Die protestantische Ethik und der Geist des Kapitalismus. 1. Das Problem [The Protestant Ethic and the Spirit of Capitalism. 1. The Problem]." *Archiv für Sozialwissenschaft und Sozialpolitik* 20 (1905a): 1–54.

———. "Die protestantische Ethik und der Geist des Kapitalismus. 2. Die Berufsidee des asketischen Protestantismus [The Protestant Ethic and the Spirit of Capitalism. 2. The Practical Ethics of the Ascetic Branches of Protestantism]." *Archiv für Sozialwissenschaft und Sozialpolitik* 21 (1905b): 1–110.

Weber, Torsten. *Embracing "Asia". Japanese Asianism Discourse in a Transnational Setting, 1912–1933.* Unpublished Dissertation, Universität Heidelberg, Heidelberg, 2011.

Wells, Audrey. *The Political Thought of Sun Yatsen: Development and Impact.* Basingstoke: Palgrave, 2001.

Westad, Odd Arne. *The Global Cold War. Third World Interventions and the Making of Our Times.* Cambridge: Cambridge University Press, 2007.

Wilson, Woodrow. "Character of Democracy in the United States." *The Atlantic Monthly* 64, 385 (Nov. 1889): 577–88.

Woodberry, Robert D. "The Missionary Roots of Liberal Democracy." *American Political Science Review* 106,2 (2012): 244–74.

Wolpert, Stanley. *A New History of India.* 4th ed. Oxford: Oxford University Press, 1993.

Wu, Chih-Kang. *The Influence of the YMCA in the Development of Physical Education in China.* Unpublished Dissertation, University of Michigan, Ann Arbor, 1956.

Wu, Tingfang. *America through the Spectacles of an Oriental Diplomat.* New York: Frederick A. Stokes Co., 1914.

Wyatt, David K. *Thailand. A Short History.* 2nd ed. New Haven: Yale University Press, 2003.

Xu, Guoqi. *Olympic Dreams. China and Sports, 1895–2008.* Cambridge, MA: Harvard University Press, 2008.

Yamamoto Tadaoki hakushi denki kankōkai. (ed.), *Yamamoto Tadaoki-den* [The Life of Yamamoto Tadaoki]. Tokyo: Yamamoto Tadaoki hakushi denki kankōkai, 1953.

Ye, Longyan. *Hao Gengsheng zhuan* [The Life of Hao Gengsheng]. Nantou: Taiwan sheng wenxian weiyuanhui, 1993.

Ylanan, Regino R. and Carmen W. Ylanan. *The History and Development of Physical Education and Sports in the Philippines.* 2nd ed. Quezon City: University of the Philippines Press, 1974.

Ylanan, Regino R. (ed.), *Philippine Amateur Athletic Federation. Official Rule and Handbook. 1934–1935.* Manila[?]: n.p., 1935. (Cover Page: PAAF Rule and Handbook 1934–35.)

Yu, Chien-ming. *Yundongchang neiwai: jindai Huadong diqu de nüzi tiyu (1895–1937)* [On and off the Playing Fields: A Modern History of Physical Education for Girls in Eastern China (1895–1937)]. Taipei: Zhongyang yanjiuyuan jindaishi yanjiusuo, 2009.

Yu, Ri. "Zhong Ri Yuanyun juezhushi [History of the Competition between Japan and China in the Far Eastern Championship Games]." *Tiyu wenshi* 42, 2 (1990): 44–50.

Yu Jose, Lydia. N. *Japan Views the Philippines, 1900–1944.* Manila: Ateneo de Manila University Press, 1992.

———. "Philippine, American, and Japanese Relations as Seen through the Issue of Neutralization, 1900 to 1939." In Setsuho Ikehata and Lydia N. Yu Jose (eds.), *Philippines-Japan Relations.* Manila: Ateneo de Manila University Press, 2003, pp. 47–80.

"Yuandong geguo yundongyuan [Overview of Athletes Participating in the Far Eastern Championship Games]." *Jinbu* 8, 3 (1915): 2–4.

Zhou, Dingchang. "Yuandong yundonghui Zhong Ri Fei changhui jingguo [The Course of the Chinese-Japanese-Philippine Far Eastern Championship Games Conference]." *Qinfen tiyu yuebao* 1, 8 (1934): 13–15.

Zhu, Zuwei et al. (ed.), *Yayunhui youpiao quanji. A Complete Collection of Asian Games Stamps.* Beijing: Beijing Yanshan chubanshe, 1990.

Zöllner, Reinhard. *Geschichte Japans. Von 1800 bis zur Gegenwart* [History of Japan. From 1800 to the Present]. Paderborn: Schöningh, 2006.

Index

Noble and other titles have been excluded (except in case of members of monarchies).

Abe Isoo, 291n99
Abe Kitarō, 72
Achaemenid Empire (Great Persian Empire; *see also* Iran), 15, 230, 233, 246, 254, 277
Afghanistan, 76–7, 79, 90, 107–10, 232, 258, 310n19, 343n41
African Games (Alexandria 1929; aborted) (*see also* All-Africa Games), 29, 75, 288n53, 289n56, 301n86
Aguinaldo, Emilio, 19, 48
Akihito (crown prince and emperor of Japan), 150, 153, 163–4, 325n68
All-Africa Games, 239, 330n52
All India Radio, 122, 170
Amateur Athletic Association of the Orient, 70, 72, 100, 300n75, 308n163
Antara, 196, 199
Arab Games, 310n25, 328n30
Aristotle, 32, 34
Asahi Evening News, 164
Asahi Shinbun, 91, 150, 165, 303n104, 329n38
Asano Kinichi, 154
Ashoka the Great, 120
Asia-Africa Conference (Bandung 1955), 5, 113, 127, 131, 174, 177, 271, 279n21, 327n3
Asian Games
    1978 (Bangkok), 229, 257, 272, 277
    1982 (New Delhi), 122
    1986 (Seoul), 184
    1990 (Beijing), 242
Asian Relations Conference (1947), 5, 102–3, 105–7, 110–3, 122, 131, 144, 183, 270, 279n21
Asianism (*see* pan-Asianism)
Associated Press, 81
Association of Southeast Asian Nations (ASEAN), 202, 204, 228, 235, 258
Aung San, 111
Australia, 127, 149, 235–6, 272
Avory, Richard, 244
Azuma Ryōtarō, 109, 114, 147, 150, 154–5, 159, 173

Baghbanbashi, Ali, 248
Bahrain, 232, 236, 244, 343n41
Baillet-Latour, Henri de, 29, 72, 299n68
Bandung, 5, 113, 127, 131, 174, 177, 180, 199, 271, 279n21, 327n3
Bandung Conference (*see* Asia-Africa Conference)
Bangkok, 14, 27, 202–5, 207–12, 216–8, 222, 226, 228, 265, 271, 276, 334n11
Bangladesh, 236
Bao Dai (emperor of Vietnam), 129
Barger, Vera V., 83, 96
Bartolome, Candido C., 128, 139–41, 144, 275
Beijing, 10, 28, 48, 57, 65, 86, 92, 232, 237, 305n125
Bernardo, Macario, 40, 291n92
Bhumibol Adulyadej (Rama IX, king of Thailand), 14, 203–4, 207, 213, 218–9, 222, 224–7, 265, 334n5, 339n93
Bhupinder Singh (maharaja of Patiala), 75, 90, 104, 264, 306n140
Bitong, Ernesto T., 257–8
body as temple theology, 19, 44
Bose, Rash Behari, 69, 298n53
Brent, Charles H., 19, 24, 31, 44, 289n63
Britain (including England and United Kingdom), 18–9, 29, 32–4, 37, 59, 74–5, 77, 116–7, 127, 129, 145, 170, 206, 232, 234, 280n33, 329n44

Brown, Elwood S., 22, 25, 29, 37, 41–5, 48, 52–3, 55, 60, 63, 67, 69, 74, 80, 95, 97, 175, 241, 245, 262–3, 268, 272–3, 277, 285n14, 285n16, 289n56, 292n100, 292n103, 293n112, 295n14, 308n164
Brown, Franklin H., 29, 42–3, 47, 52–3, 55, 60–1, 63, 66, 69, 80–1, 85, 88, 263, 292n102, 293n107, 308n164
Brundage, Avery, 1–3, 115, 131, 154–5, 164, 168, 202, 207, 211–2, 228, 269, 316n24
Buck, Harry C., 74
Buddhism, 8, 14, 59, 66, 93–4, 120, 203–4, 218–22, 224–5, 227, 271, 277, 290n89
Buenaventura, Antonino, 134
Bukh, Niels, 88, 305n131
Burma (Myanmar), 76, 107–11, 121, 127, 205, 236, 343n41
Bushidō, 42–4, 53, 66, 99, 269, 287n33, 291n89, 291–2n99, 293n105, 349n7

Cambodia, 129, 202, 205, 224, 228, 271, 336n36, 343n41
Caulfield James, Joseph, 27
Central News Agency (Zhongyang Tongxunshe), 81
Ceylon (Sri Lanka), 76, 79, 90, 107–10, 127, 343n41
character building, 19, 191, 331n65
Charusathien, Praphas, 204–7, 210–1, 216, 218, 227, 265, 336n29
Chen Yi, 183
Chiang Kai-shek (Jiang Jieshi), 57, 89, 92–3, 131, 296–7n33, 306n136
Chichibu (prince of Japan), 46, 62, 66, 71, 150, 263
China (Chinese Empire until 1912, Republic of China until 1949, People's Republic of China since 1949), 13, 15, 103, 106–10, 123, 126–33, 145, 147, 149, 152, 177, 182–7, 200, 228, 230, 232–3, 235–44, 255, 257–9, 263–75, 282n48–9, 283n53, 284n62, 286–7n32, 287n34, 297n33, 304n118, 307n151, 307n154, 308n163, 309n16–7, 314n78, 316n20–1, 329n36, 343n32, 343n41, 344n44, 349n4, 349n7
China Press, 84
Chinese Civil War (1945–49), 103, 107–8, 122, 126, 133, 149, 270, 274, 309n16, 349n7
Chinese Revolution (1911), 20, 38, 268
Christian egalitarianism, 6, 7, 13, 17, 30, 95, 268, 272
Christian internationalism, 6, 7, 10, 13, 17, 26, 30, 59, 95, 268, 272, 291n99
Chullasapya, Dawee, 206–7, 210, 216, 226, 229
Churchill, Winston, 105
citizenship training, 2, 9, 18, 24, 33, 44, 53, 58, 64, 67, 75, 77, 83–4, 96–7, 99, 102, 104, 107, 109, 111, 143, 173, 181, 199, 212, 241, 245, 262, 273, 309n17
Coloso-Espino, Haydee, 161
'communist bloc' (*see also* 'Eastern bloc'), 111, 133, 144–5, 149, 177, 201, 259, 270, 279n12
Confucianism, 8, 38, 269, 290n89
Coubertin, Pierre de, 43, 91, 277, 286n29
Crocker, John H., 25, 37
Crone, Frank R., 23–4, 26, 29, 31, 45
Cyrus the Great (founder of the Achaemenid Empire), 233, 244

Daume, Willi, 155, 228, 341n117
Davis, J. M., 289n63
De las Alas, Antonio, 128, 130–2, 135, 141, 214
development policy and results (*see* the respective subchapters)
Dhillon, S. S., xi, 248, 257, 346n71, 348n95
Dutch East Indies (*see* Indonesia)

East Asian Games (Tōa Taikai, 1940 and 1942–43), 100, 308n163
'eastern bloc' (*see also* 'communist bloc'), 179, 187–8, 191
economic progress (ideal) (*see* 'Protestant work ethic')
Edström, Sigfrid, 310n18
egalitarianism (ideal) (*see* Christian egalitarianism)
Egypt, 29, 103, 108, 182–7, 200, 237, 271, 310n19, 310n25, 328n30, 330n54
Eisenhower, Dwight D., 127, 325n70
England (*see* Britain)
England, Frederick O., 41, 96, 305n122

Ferdowsi, 254
Filipinas (Philippine national allegory), 35, 138
Filipino Athlete (news magazine), 124, 211, 257
film (media), 78, 80–3, 122, 143, 171, 199, 246, 274
First World War, 3, 11, 21, 28, 30, 41–2, 56–8, 62, 69, 74, 119, 262, 290n89, 292n101
Forbes, W. Cameron, 23–4, 26, 32, 45, 48, 53, 289n64
France, 29, 75, 127, 129, 170, 319n63
Frank, René, 248
Franklin, Benjamin, 281n38
'free world', 111, 114, 126–8, 131–4, 136–7, 143–4, 148–9, 177, 187–8, 270
Frenckell, Erik von, 155
Fujiyama Aiichirō, 150

Games of the New Emerging Forces (GANEFO), 186–7, 193, 200–2, 238–9, 242, 257, 265, 271–2, 330n50, 330n52, 340n113
Games of the New Emerging Forces of Asia (GANEFOA), 202, 228, 333n2, 336n36
Gandhi, Indira, 122
Gandhi, Mohandas K. ("Mahatma"), 59, 120, 131
Garcia, Carlos P., 125, 133, 145
Germany, 21, 44, 57, 62, 88, 137, 155, 165, 184, 242, 259, 290n89, 296n25, 326n97, 329n45
Giese, Jocelyn von, 161
Gray, John H., 55, 60–3, 74–5, 78, 81, 86, 263, 268, 295n14, 308n164
Great Depression, 7, 58, 61, 78, 89, 100
'Great Divergence', 1, 273, 278n4
Great Persian Empire (*see* Achaemenid Empire)
Guo Taiqi (Quo Tai-chi), 64–5, 86, 99
Gupta, Pankaj, 333n95

Hamaguchi Osachi, 66–7
Hamengku Buwono IX, 178–9, 183, 266
Hamzah Abu Samah, 238
Hao Gengsheng (Hoh Gun-sun), 106–8, 110, 130–1, 145, 184, 265, 304n118, 309n17, 310n21, 310n27, 316n21, 329n40, 329n42
Harrison, Francis B., 32, 40
Hashim, Noor Mohamed, 27
Hassan, Seyed Abul, 239
Hawaii, 46, 136, 308n163
He Zhenliang, 238, 257, 343n30, 348n95
Hejaz, 76
Henning, Harold, 248, 346n71
'high modernism' (including its authoritarian version), 11–2, 17, 43, 83, 91, 175, 187–8, 203, 209, 212, 246, 260, 262, 276
Hinduism, 8, 59, 74, 77, 119, 301n88
Hiranuma Ryōzō, 63, 66, 71, 92, 150, 263, 296n28, 297n37, 299–300n71, 300n73, 306n135
Hojjat Kashani, Ali, 234, 237–9, 244–6, 252, 341n12, 343n30, 346n75

Hong Kong, 25, 27, 29, 37, 46, 78, 97, 108, 129, 170, 226, 241, 255, 309n16, 312n51, 343n41
Hongsakula, Apasra, 220, 222
Hoveyda, Amir Abbas, 243, 342n14

Ikegami Shirō, 62, 91
India, 4, 14–5, 28, 30–1, 127, 129, 131, 140, 150–2, 155–6, 159, 170–1, 174–5, 186, 201, 212, 218, 232, 235–6, 255, 264, 266, 269–70, 273, 275, 281n43, 282n48, 283n51, 284n62, 298n55, 300n78, 301n84, 301n88, 302n92, 308n2, 308n6, 311n43, 313n65, 313n71, 314n79, 316n20, 319n67, 328n15, 343n41, 348n2
Indian National Congress, 58–9, 69, 103–4, 119–20, 270, 308n4
Indian Olympic Games, 74, 104, 304n106
Indian Olympic Association, 74–5, 77, 104, 106, 109, 333n95
Indochina (*see also* Cambodia, Laos, and Vietnam), 72, 76, 110, 127, 145, 270, 299n68, 299n71
Indochina War, First (1946–54), 127, 132–3, 315n7, 320n73
Indonesia (including Dutch East Indies), 5, 11, 14, 28, 46, 69, 78–9, 89, 99–101, 105, 108–10, 121, 126–8, 144, 165, 171, 177, 194, 202, 210, 212, 217–8, 221, 226, 228, 230, 234–7, 241–2, 245, 255, 258–9, 265–6, 270–1, 276–7, 282n48, 283n51, 299n71, 302n91, 307n161–2, 312n51, 316n25, 319n67, 327n1, 327n3, 327n7, 327n10, 328n22, 328n30, 329n38, 329n42, 329n45, 330n47, 332n81, 332n85, 338n71, 343n41
International Olympic Committee (IOC), 1, 2, 6, 13, 26, 29–30, 32, 38, 42–4, 50, 62, 67, 72–6, 88, 91, 93–4, 100, 104–6, 109–10, 115, 126, 129–31, 134, 136–7, 143, 148–50, 152, 154–5, 159, 161–2, 164, 168–72, 186–7, 193, 200, 206–7, 211–2, 218, 226, 228, 230, 234, 238–9, 241–4, 248, 255, 259, 263, 265, 268–70, 272, 277, 286n29, 287n33–4, 289n56, 292n101, 293n105, 295n12, 307n162, 310n18, 311n34, 312n50, 320n3, 322n26, 322n29, 327n1, 330n52, 348n98, 349n15
International YMCA College, 19, 41, 68, 107, 128, 263, 274, 318n59, 349n12
internationalism (ideal) (*see* Christian internationalism)
Iran (and Persia), 11, 14–5, 76, 107, 110, 120, 126, 128–9, 131, 144, 152, 163, 171, 175, 212–3, 226, 230, 261, 266, 272, 276–7, 282n48, 310n19, 341n1, 342n23, 343n41, 344n44
Iranian Physical Education Organization, 234
Iraq, 76, 107, 129, 182–3, 232, 236, 244, 310n19
Islamic Revolution (1979), 235, 243
Israel, 14, 129–32, 152, 172, 177, 182–6, 200, 226, 232, 237, 240, 242, 244, 257–8, 261, 265–6, 270–2, 277, 283n51, 328n34, 329n45, 343n41, 345n57, 348n96

Jakarta (including Djakarta), 14, 178, 184–5, 187-8, 191–4, 199, 265, 271, 276, 327n14
Japan, 5, 10, 14–5, 103, 106–7, 109, 110, 114, 122–4, 126, 132, 139, 143, 174–5, 178–9, 184–5, 187, 193–4, 198, 200, 207, 210, 212–3, 217, 226, 228, 231, 237, 242–5, 257, 260, 263–6, 268–70, 275–7, 287n34, 291–2n99, 300n76, 303n99, 308n163, 311n34, 312n50, 316n25, 319n67, 321n6, 325n70, 335n24, 343n41, 349n7
Japan Athletic Youth Club (*Nihon Seinen Undō Kurabu*), 44

Japanese emperor (*see* Meiji Tennō, Shōwa Tennō, Taishō Tennō)
Java (*see also* Indonesia), 28, 175–7, 187–8, 192–3, 198–9, 307n162
Jesus Christ, 18–9, 290n89
Jewkes, Stanley, 214
Johnson, Lawrence J., 155
Johnson, Lyndon B., 232
Jones, Ossie Garfield, 32–5, 37, 39, 97, 273, 290n68, 290n71
judo, 26, 41, 43, 71, 293n105

Kamada Eikichi, 62, 306n141
Kanō Jigorō, 26–7, 41–5, 50, 53, 59, 62, 66, 71, 150, 263, 287n33–4, 287n42, 292n99–101, 292n103, 293n105, 295n12, 296n19
Kashefi, R., 236
Kaur, Amrit, 104, 113, 115, 309n8, 312n48
Kawamura Takeji, 306n141
Kawashima Shōjirō, 333n95
Kent-Hughes, Wilfrid, 155, 159, 324n50
Khoman, Thanat, 211
Khrushchev, Nikita, 331n64
King of Thailand (*see* Bhumibol Adulyadej)
Kipling, Rudyard, 278n1, 284n6
Kishi Nobusuke, 149–50, 152–3, 164, 321n23
Kishi Seiichi, 50, 59, 63, 66–7, 69, 71, 93, 263, 292n103, 295n12, 297n37, 307n162
Kittikachorn, Thanom, 203–5, 207–8, 210, 214–6, 218, 227, 277, 339n87
Korea, 22, 82, 97, 107–8, 110, 127, 133, 136, 145, 149, 255, 282n49
  North Korea, 147, 177, 182–3, 186, 236, 244, 257, 329n36
  South Korea, 10, 129, 132–3, 145, 170, 177, 182–4, 203, 205, 207–8, 211, 220, 226, 228, 243, 312n51, 320n74, 335n25, 338n63, 343n41, 349n7
Korean War (1950–53), 103, 109, 112, 122, 126–7, 129, 132–3, 136, 145, 148–9, 270
Kosol, Chartrakarn, 207
Kuomintang, 21, 38, 57–8, 64–7, 70–1, 73, 86, 89, 92, 96, 103, 106–8, 110, 130–1, 145, 184, 269, 309n16, 349n4, 349n7, 349n14
Kuwait, 236, 244, 257, 343n41, 348n95

Lacson, Arsenio H., 140
Laos, 205, 282n48, 343n41
Larsson, Karl A., 333n95
League of Nations, 30, 57, 111, 299n68
Lebanon, 107, 129, 236, 310n19, 310n25
Li Yuanhong, 39, 48–9
Libya, 236
Lincoln, Abraham, 57, 99
Lon Nol, 224
Lord Killanin (Michael Morris), 238, 241, 244, 248, 255, 259, 346n71

MacArthur, Douglas, 110, 148, 150, 165, 200, 275, 311n33, 326n82
Madero, Francisco I., 33
Magsaysay, Ramon, 127–8, 133, 136, 139, 145
Maladi, 177, 179–81, 183, 188, 192–3, 265–6, 271, 327n11, 332n72
Malaya, 27, 76, 129, 163, 170, 198, 205, 329n44
Malaysia, 227, 236, 238, 329n44, 343n32, 343n41
Manchukuo, 14, 58, 71–3, 78, 82, 89, 107, 130, 145, 264, 266, 269, 299n68, 299–300n71, 300n76, 308n163
Manchuria (*see also* Manchukuo), 56–8, 70–1, 73, 85, 107–8, 149, 269, 298n61, 299n68
Manila, 13–15, 17, 22-7, 35, 40–1, 48, 52, 81–2, 83, 96, 108, 129, 134, 137, 143, 146–7, 154, 161–2, 171–2, 182, 262–4, 270, 276, 286n24

Manila Carnival, 24–5, 36
Mao Zedong, 39, 237, 290–1n89
Marcos, Ferdinand, 211, 245
Marquardt, Walter W., 41
May Fourth Movement, 21, 44, 57, 84, 269
McKenzie, R. Tait, 50
Mediterranean Games, 236, 310n25, 330n45
Meiji Tennō (emperor of Japan), 87
Mello, Anthony S. de, 102, 104, 106, 109–10, 113, 115, 117, 123–4, 264, 309n8, 313n58
Mexico, 32, 34
Mikoyan, Anastas, 331n64
Mizuno Rentarō, 306n141
Moin-ul-Haq, Seyd Mohd., 77, 109, 326n97
Mongolia, 236
Moscow, 107, 192, 232, 242–3
Mossadegh, Mohammad, 317n32
Motono Ichirō, 46
Mott, John R., 7, 19, 44, 52, 284n5
Mukerjee (sometimes Mukerjie), Sharajit Kumar, 68–9, 74, 76, 99, 311n43
muscular Christianity, 18–9, 22, 52, 54, 63, 75, 77, 95, 181, 269, 284n2, 300n78 (*see also* Christian egalitarianism, Christian internationalism, 'Protestant work ethic')
'Muslim Games', 107–8
Myron of Eleutherae, 169

Nacionalista Party (Philippines), 40–1, 48, 58, 65, 263
Nagata Hidejirō, 88, 305n129
Namikawa Banri, 255
Nanjing, 21, 26, 81, 89, 92–3, 96, 306n136, 349n14
Naresuan the Great (king of Ayutthaya), 220, 225
Nasser, Gamal Abdel, 182
nation-branding, 10, 12–4, 83, 85, 89, 93, 115, 148, 151, 154, 156, 169–70, 176, 187, 189, 200, 216, 224, 228, 231, 242–3, 245, 248, 252, 262, 272, 275–7
National Sports Club of India, 115, 117
nationalism
    anti-colonial/anti-imperialist, 2, 5, 13–4, 29, 56–7, 57–9, 62–3, 65, 72, 76, 100, 185, 264, 266–8, 274, 301n86
    state, 9, 115, 119, 139, 145, 172, 181, 198, 201, 225, 242, 250, 258, 260, 267–8, 270–2
Nayapradit, Sukhum, 206, 212–3
Nehru, Jawaharlal, 14, 58–9, 69, 102–5, 111–3, 115, 117–9, 123, 270, 309n8, 311n43, 311n45
Nepal, 76, 108, 110, 129, 224, 255, 311n38, 313n62, 343n41
New Delhi, 5, 14–5, 74, 76, 80, 90, 102–3, 105, 108, 110, 115, 122–3, 143–4, 147, 154, 183, 264, 270, 275, 282n48, 303n96
New York Times, 80, 303n101
New Zealand, 127, 149, 235–6, 272
newspapers (media), 19, 26, 37, 73, 78, 80–4, 91, 96, 121–2, 141, 143–4, 150, 165, 170, 182, 184, 198–9, 226, 256, 272, 274, 290n78, 293n111, 303n99, 303n102–4, 309n9, 313n73, 320n73, 329n35, 332n72, 342n13
NHK (Nippon Hōsō Kyōkai/Japan Broadcasting Company), 82, 122, 143, 170–1, 199, 326n82
Nike (goddess), 52, 138
Nikpay, Gholam Reza, 244
Nippon TV, 171
Nitobe Inazō, 291–2n99
Noehren, Arthur G., 74–5
Non-Aligned Movement, 174–5, 177, 179, 182–4, 186, 271, 276, 327n7
Nordau, Max, 42
Norodom Sihanouk (king of Cambodia), 224
North Borneo, 129

North Vietnam (*see* Vietnam)
Northern Expedition (1926–28), 57, 64–6, 86, 269

Oda Mikio, 161–2, 313n65
Oil Crisis (1973), 15, 232, 260–1
Okabe Heita, 71, 73, 298n61
Okakura Tenshin, 261, 348n2
Okinawa, 161–3, 324n60
Ōkuma Shigenobu, 47
Olav V (king of Norway), 207
Olympic Council of Asia, 5
Olympic Games
- 1896 (Athens), 120
- 1912 (Stockholm), 26, 45, 42
- 1920 (Antwerp), 30
- 1924 (Paris), 121
- 1928 (Amsterdam), 110, 137–8, 207
- 1932 (Los Angeles), 46, 76, 82, 137–8
- 1936 (Berlin), 104, 107, 137–8, 255
- 1940 (Tokyo; abandoned), 73, 88, 91, 100, 147, 150, 159, 171–3, 308n163
- 1948 (London), 106, 130, 137–8, 184, 309n16
- 1952 (Helsinki), 107, 126, 130, 137–8,154, 205, 311n34, 312n50
- 1956 (Melbourne), 137–8, 154–7, 159, 172, 276, 312n52
- 1960 (Rome), 117, 137–8, 154
- 1964 (Tokyo), 14, 43, 110, 137–8, 148, 150, 152–7, 159–6, 168, 170–3, 178, 193, 214, 257, 271, 276
- 1972 (Munich), 229, 242, 248
- 1980 (Moscow), 242
- 1984 (Los Angeles), 242–3
- 1988 (Seoul), 184, 243, 348n98
- 2008 (Beijing), 10
- 2020 (Tokyo), 157, 282n48

'Olympism', 42–3, 75, 77, 91, 95, 105, 161, 163, 168–9, 171, 181, 212, 269, 287n33, 349n15
Open International Games, 28, 79, 101, 288n51, 294n128
Osaka, 15, 42–3, 47, 50, 61–2, 78, 80, 84–6, 91, 96, 161, 207, 296n19, 303n104, 324n53
Ōsaka Mainichi Shinbun, 26, 81, 91, 96, 303n99
Osías, Camilo, 40–1, 65, 67, 69, 72, 85–6, 89, 96–7, 99, 263–4, 274
Osmeña, Sergio, 48

Pacific War (1941–45), 5, 71, 100, 106
Pahlavi, Gholam Reza (prince of Iran), 230, 234, 236–9, 241–3, 245, 255, 265, 341n1, 341n12, 343n30, 346n75
Pahlavi, Mohammad Reza (shah of Iran), 163, 230–5, 237–8, 242–8, 252, 255–6, 265, 272, 277, 317n32, 342n13
Pahlavi, Reza (crown prince of Iran), 248
Pakistan, 107–8, 110, 127, 129, 139–40, 165, 174, 183, 188, 236, 239, 244, 256–7, 270, 310n19, 312n51, 313n62, 320n74, 343n41
Paku Alam VIII, 178, 180, 266
Palestine, 76–7, 79, 90, 129, 302n92
Pan-asianism
- anti-colonial pan-movement (conception), 9, 267, 281n44
- 'Asia as greater India', 58–9, 68, 77, 99, 112, 123, 269, 301n88, 311n43
- 'Asia awakening', 38, 44, 56, 99, 113, 181, 269, 294n2
- 'Asia is one' (Okakura Tenshin), 261
- 'Asia oppressed', 56, 65, 174, 201, 261, 294n2
- 'Asian bloc', 111, 113
- Asian Union (*see* Pan-Asianism, Indian Ocean region project)
- commonalities (including amateur ideals) and kinship, 5, 14, 63–4, 66, 68, 70, 99, 151–4, 172, 261, 265–6, 269

Greater East Asia Conference (5–6 Nov. 1943), 308n163
Greater East Asia Co-Prosperity Sphere, 5
hegemonic pan-movement (conception), 9, 123, 266, 269–72, 281n44
imperialist pan-movement (conception), 9, 281n44
Indian Ocean region project (*see* chapter 8), 258
Nehruvian pan-Asianism (*see* chapter 3), 111–13
Non-aligned Asia (*see* chapter 6; also chapter 3 on Nehruvian ideas), 178–9, 182–5
non-communist Asia (*see* chapter 4; also chapters 5 and 7), 220, 228, 270
'rebirth' of Asia, 103, 111, 124
regionalist pan-movement (conception), 9, 266, 281n44
'spiritual Asia', 1, 3, 58, 70, 75–7, 99, 103, 152, 212, 278n8
'unity in backwardness', 2, 3, 12–3, 100, 179, 268, 272
'unity in diversity', 12, 139, 151, 220, 228, 267, 271
universalism, 3, 4, 6, 14, 52, 101, 118, 125, 151, 243, 252, 266, 269
universalist pan-movement (conception), 9, 266–7, 269, 281n44
'yellow peril', 22, 268

Pancasila, 196
Paris Peace Conference (1919), 3, 5, 21, 36, 38, 44, 56–7, 59, 64
Park Chung-hee, 207
Patiala (city and state), 15, 74–6, 79–80, 90, 104–5, 108, 115, 264, 303n96, 306n140
Peace Corps, 210
Persia (*see* Iran; see also Achaemenid Empire)
Phibunsongkhram, 203–4
philanthropy (and donations), 7, 12, 19, 23, 47–8, 50, 61, 80, 86, 90–2, 157, 262, 284n5, 306n140
Philippine Amateur Athletic Federation (PAAF), 24–5, 27–8, 41, 67, 106, 109, 124, 128, 139–43, 146, 211, 214, 275, 291n94, 297n46, 305n133, 318n60, 319n63
Philippine-American War (1899–1902), 19
Philippines, 11, 13–5, 106–10, 120, 123, 147, 151–2, 161, 163, 165, 171–2, 174–5, 205, 212, 226, 244–5, 258, 262–4, 266, 268–70, 273–5, 282n48–9, 283n51, 285n14, 285n17, 305n128, 308n163, 316n25, 318n60, 320n75
Prasad, Rajendra, 104, 114, 120, 312n48
professionalism, 8, 18, 24, 26, 29, 45, 53, 212, 245, 257, 273, 277, 281n43, 348n98, 349n11, 329n16
'Protestant work ethic', 6, 8, 13, 17, 30, 53, 95, 272
PRRI-Permesta rebellion (1958–61), 176–7, 184, 186

Qatar, 232
Quezon, Manuel L., 40, 50, 89, 106, 142, 263, 291n94, 299–300n71, 305n133

radio (media), 78, 80–3, 122, 143, 170–1, 177, 198–9, 226–7, 231, 256, 274, 304n109
Rahman, Abdul, 164
Rama (King Rama of the Ramayana), 201
Rassouli, Hassan; 234, 238–40, 342n12, 343n30
Razak, Abdul, 329n44
regional games (YMCA-IOC cooperation), 18, 30, 60, 62, 75, 289n56

Republic of China (until 1949 *see* China; after 1949 see Taiwan)
Rizal, José (including places and stadia named after him), 45, 85–6, 89, 128, 137, 141, 161
Robertson, Charles H. 22, 285n16
Rockefeller Foundation, 86
Rockefeller (family), 284n5
Romulo, Carlos P., 109
Roosevelt, Franklin D., 201
Rous, Stanley, 228
Roxas, Antonio R., 48, 51
Roxas, Manuel, 126
Royal Bangkok Sports Club, 27
Rusk, Dean, 127
Russia (*see also* Soviet Union), 5, 21–2, 26, 57
Russo-Japanese War (1904–5), 41, 57

Sakai Yoshinori, 162, 325n63
Saleh, M. Effendi, 194
Sales, A. de O., 241, 259
Sangsirinavin, Warunee, 22
Satō Hajime, 150
Saudi Arabia, 183, 236, 342n23
Savetanand, Cheranand, 220, 222
Second Sino-Japanese War (1937–45), 71, 88–9, 100, 111, 147
Self-Defense Forces (Japan), 148–9, 161–2, 164–5, 169, 172
self-government, 20, 32, 34, 39–41, 43, 55, 58–9, 61–2, 66, 86, 89, 99, 101, 296n30
Sha'ari Tadin, 245
Shanghai, 15, 27–9, 37, 43, 46, 48, 59–60, 63, 78–83, 85–6, 96, 107–8, 288n47, 296–7n33, 303n102, 310n21
Sheares, Benjamin H., 235, 257
Shen Siliang (William Z. L. Sung), 63, 86, 296n27, 296n30, 305n125
Shenbao, 303n102
Shibata Katsuji, 257–8
Shōwa Tennō (emperor of Japan), 46, 148, 150, 153, 163–6, 169, 172, 325n68
Siam (*see* Thailand)
Singapore, 25, 27, 76, 110, 121, 170, 186, 205, 227, 235–6, 245, 248, 255, 257, 320n74, 343n41
Singh, Dalip, 121
Sirikit (queen of Thailand), 219–20
Sloane, William M., 32, 50, 289n64
Sohn Kee-chung (Japanese, Son Kitei), 255
Soliongco, I. P., 141
Sondhi, Guru Dutt, 74–7, 80, 90, 94–5, 97, 104–10, 112, 114–15, 117–18, 121, 124, 129–31, 140, 144, 155–6, 173, 180–1, 183, 185–7, 200, 234, 242, 258–9, 264–6, 271, 275–6, 301n81, 301n82, 306n140, 309n9, 311n34, 312n51–2, 316n20
Sonneville, Ferry, 194
Soong May-ling, 57
South Vietnam (*see* Vietnam)
Southeast Asian Peninsular Games (SEAP Games), 202, 205–8, 221, 228, 258
Soviet Union (*see also* Russia; Moscow), 4–5, 15, 22, 103, 107, 132, 162, 177, 182, 186–8, 192, 231–4, 237, 242, 272, 283n55, 330n55, 331n64
Spain, 19–20, 22, 32–3, 86, 97, 135, 139, 145, 317n48
Spanish-American War (1898), 19
Sport Authority of Thailand (*see* Sport Promotion Organization)
Sport Promotion Organization (Sport Authority of Thailand), 206–7, 210, 214, 334n11
Springfield College (*see* International YMCA College)
Straits Settlements (*see also* Singapore), 27, 46, 76
Straits Times, 214
Student Volunteer Movement, 7

Sudarman, 192
Sudjasmin, Raden Adrianus Josephus (R. A. J. Soedjasmin), 198
Suez Crisis (1956), 184
Suharto, 332n81
Sukarno, 14, 174–8, 180, 182–3, 186–8, 190–4, 197, 200–1, 242, 245, 265, 271, 327n1, 331n64, 332n81
Sumitomo Kichizaemon, 91
Sun Yat-sen, 21, 57, 65, 89, 92
Suprajogi, 192
Sutarto, 199
Synn, K. C., 108
Syria, 76, 107, 182, 236, 310n19, 310n25

Tabata Masaji, 150, 155
Tagore, Rabindranath, 58, 68, 76
Taishō Tennō (emperor of Japan), 91–3, 95
Taiwan (including Republic of China since 1949), 14, 22, 72, 82, 108, 110, 129–33, 139, 145, 170, 177, 182–6, 200, 226, 233, 237–42, 257–8, 265–6, 270–2, 274, 277, 307n159, 309n16, 312n51, 316n20–1, 316n24–5, 319n67, 329n38, 329n39, 329n42, 336n36, 343n30, 343n32, 343n41
Tajima Naoto, 248, 261, 346n71
Takamatsu (prince of Japan), 46
Takashima Fumio, 150, 155
Takeda Chiyosaburō, 292n103
Takeda Tsuneyoshi, 159, 345n58
Tanaka Ryūzō, 66
Tange Kenzō, 157, 323n42
Tata, Dorab, 74–5
Tehran, 13–4, 129, 131, 236–7, 242–5, 250, 254–6, 258, 260–1, 265, 271, 277, 342n23, 345n57
television (media), 122, 143, 171, 198–9, 222, 226–7, 231, 256–7, 272, 276, 333n89
Teus, Juan, 48
Thailand (including Siam), 11, 14, 27–8, 76, 108–10, 120, 126–8, 144, 171, 175, 202–14, 217–22, 225–8, 230, 236, 252, 255, 257, 259, 265–6, 271, 276–7, 282n48, 335n24, 338n67, 340n103, 343n41
Thanarat, Sarit, 203–8, 218, 220, 227, 277, 334n5
Times of India (newspaper), 81, 122, 302n92, 304n106
Tokyo, 1, 14–5, 26, 28, 42–3, 45–7, 50, 52–3, 58, 61, 66, 69, 73–4. 78–80, 85, 87–8, 93, 96, 110, 147–50, 152, 154–63, 165, 168, 170–3, 178, 193, 199, 205, 212, 214, 257, 264, 270–1, 275, 282n48, 324n53
Toomey, Bill, 210
tourism, 156, 160, 203, 205, 208, 212, 217–8, 220, 228, 256, 276–7
Tribhuvan (king of Nepal), 311n38
Truman, Harry S., 126–7
Tsushima Juichi, 150–2, 159, 165, 323n37, 323n39
Turkey, 76, 183, 236, 310n19, 310n25
Tutherly, William, 24, 26, 28, 45
Twenty-One Demands (1915), 37, 47, 57, 268

Ubolratana (princess of Thailand), 207, 219
Uchida Yasuya, 306n141
Uncle Sam (US national allegory), 19, 35–6
United Arab Emirates, 232, 236
United Kingdom (*see* Britain)
United Nations, 111, 132–3, 149, 187, 209, 232, 237–8, 241, 282n47, 321n6
United States Information Agency, 226
USA, 6–7, 11, 13–4, 56, 63–4, 66–72, 77, 80–3, 86–7, 97, 99–100, 103, 105, 109, 147–9, 155, 160, 162, 165, 168, 170, 172, 177, 179, 183–5, 187, 191–2, 200, 202–4, 206–10, 222, 224, 226, 228, 232–3, 237–8, 243–4, 254, 261–6, 268–74, 278n5, 284n6, 285n16,

286n24, 286n29, 300n71, 303n97, 317n32, 324n51, 325n70 (*see also* Young Men's Christian Association, Young Women's Christian Association, Philippines; see also the US presidents and governor generals in this index)
USSR (*see* Soviet Union)

Vajiravudh (Rama VI) (king of Thailand), 27
Vargas, Jorge B., 67, 72–3, 89, 106, 108–10, 128, 130–3, 135, 139–42, 159, 200, 265, 275, 297n44, 297n46, 299–300n71, 300n73, 305–6n133, 309n15, 319n63, 319n66–7, 349n7
Veyra, Jaime de, 40, 67, 263
Vietnam, 129, 133, 145, 184, 203, 20–6, 217, 232, 329n36, 343n41
Vietnam War (1955–75), 202, 204, 208, 216–7, 220, 223–4, 226–7, 232, 271, 277, 334n7, 340n103
Vivekananda, Swami, 58, 68, 76
Visudharomn, Kong, 206, 209
Voice of America (broadcaster), 170
Voice of Free Asia (broadcaster), 226

Wang Zhengting (Chengting Thomas Wang), 38–40, 60, 84, 106–8, 263, 273, 299n68, 309n16
Washington Post, 303n101
Weber, Max, 8, 281n38
White, Frank R., 23
Wilson, Woodrow, 3, 20, 32–4, 40, 56, 58, 290n68
Wood, Leonard, 305n122
Worcester, Dean C., 20–1
World Student Christian Federation, 7
Wu Chaoshu, 65
Wu Tingfang, 37–40, 263

Yadavindra Singh, (maharaja of Patiala), 104–5, 108, 113, 120, 312n48
Yamamoto Tadaoki, 65, 88, 99, 297n35, 305n129
Yang Xiuqiong, 98
Yangco, Teodoro R., 48
Yasui Seiichirō, 152–4
Ylanan, Regino R., 41, 63, 89, 128, 131, 139, 141, 265, 318n60
YMCA College of Physical Education (Chennai), 74, 123
Yom Kippur War (1973), 232, 237, 244, 262
Young Men's Christian Association (YMCA), 1, 2, 6–8, 11–3, 104, 107, 122–3, 127–8, 143, 168, 175, 200, 255, 258–9, 262–9, 272–5, 282n49, 285n19, 287n34, 289n56, 289n63, 296n30, 297n35, 314n79, 349n12
Young Women's Christian Association (YWCA), 7, 57, 83, 85, 96–7, 99, 104, 266, 274
Yuan Shikai, 21, 28–30, 37–9, 48–50, 54, 92, 96, 263, 268, 294n124
Yugala (prince of Siam), 28

Zeus (god), 169
Zhang Boling, 39–40, 263
Zhang Huilan (Chang Hwei Lan), 96–7, 307n153
Zhou Enlai, 183
Zuchri, K. H. Saifuddin, 193